KT-573-707

# Audio Culture

## READINGS IN MODERN MUSIC

**Edited by Christoph Cox
and Daniel Warner**

BLOOMSBURY
NEW YORK · LONDON · NEW DELHI · SYDNEY

**Bloomsbury Academic**

An imprint of Bloomsbury Publishing Inc

| | |
|---|---|
| 1385 Broadway | 50 Bedford Square |
| New York | London |
| NY 10018 | WC1B 3DP |
| USA | UK |

**www.bloomsbury.com**

**Bloomsbury is a registered trade mark of Bloomsbury Publishing Plc**

First published in 2004 by the Continuum International Publishing Group Inc
Reprinted 2011
Reprinted by Bloomsbury Academic 2013 (twice)

© Christoph Cox, Daniel Warner, and the contributors, 2004

All rights reserved. No part of this publication may be reproduced or transmitted in
any form or by any means, electronic or mechanical, including photocopying, recording,
or any information storage or retrieval system, without prior permission in writing from
the publishers.

No responsibility for loss caused to any individual or organization acting on or refraining
from action as a result of the material in this publication can be accepted by Bloomsbury
or the author.

**Library of Congress Cataloging-in-Publication Data**
Audio culture: readings in modern music/edited by
Christoph Cox and Daniel Warner.
p. cm.
Includes discography (p. ), bibliographical references (p. ), and index.
ISBN 0-8264-1614-4 (hardcover: alk. paper)—
ISBN 0-8264-1615-2 (pbk.: alk. paper)
1. Music—20th century—History and criticism. 2. Music—21st century—
History and criticism. I. Cox, Christoph, 1965– II. Warner,
Daniel, 1954–
ML197.A85 2004
780.904—dc22 2004009124

ISBN: 978-0-8264-1615-5

Printed and bound in the United States of America

ST HELENS
COLLEGE

780.904

COX

127524

Sept 2015

LIBRARY

# Contents

## Part Two: PRACTICES

# Acknowledgments

Several years in the making, this book was helped along by a large network of people. Big thanks to Continuum's David Barker for his enthusiastic support of the project and his extraordinary patience. Gabriella Page-Fort superbly copyedited the manuscript and made helpful suggestions and wise decisions. Rob Young, editor of *The Wire* (the world's finest music magazine), connected us with Continuum and supported the project in a number of ways. Thanks also to *The Wire*'s Tony Herrington, Chris Bohn, and Anne Hilde Neset, for whom it has been a pleasure and an education to write over the past decade. Andrew Kesin gave the project a push at a crucial moment. Aaron Berman, Dean of Faculty at Hampshire College, supported our work on the book with a series of Faculty Development Grants for which we are very grateful. A grant from Hampshire's European Studies Program, directed by Jim Miller, helped to make possible the translation of Pierre Schaeffer's "Acousmatics." Several of our students put in hours of work to help prepare the manuscript: Matt Krefting, Matthew Latkiewicz, Daniel Lopatin, Julie Beth Napolin, Aaron Rosenblum, Charlotte Schwennsen, and John Shaw. Amherst College Music librarians Ann Maggs and Jane Beebe generously granted us access to that library's fine collections. Thanks, too, to a number of friends and colleagues who helped us to locate materials and track down authors and artists: Robert Walser, David Rothenberg, Marta Ulvaeus, Stephen Vitiello, Andrew Deutsch, Jon Abbey, Jonas Leddington, Oren Ambarchi, Eddie Prévost, Keith Rowe, Jason Tors, and Eyal Hareuveni. Discographical advice was generously offered by Michael Ehlers, Alan Licht, Thurston Moore, Philip Sherburne, and Matt Krefting. Brian Eno's assistant, Catherine Dempsey, put in hours of work comparing and correcting manuscripts. John Zorn offered helpful criticisms and generously took the time to talk with us about his work. We thank Daniel W. Smith for his superb translation of Pierre Schaeffer's text, and Philip Sherburne for the fine essay he wrote for this volume.

Our warmest and deepest thanks go to Molly Whalen for her patience, support, and enthusiasm even during countless hours of single-parenting, and to Mary Russo for her love, advice, and encouragement. Finally, we express our sincere gratitude to the writers, composers, and musicians who generously allowed us to reprint their work for much less compensation than they deserve.

# Sources and Permissions

Every reasonable effort has been made to locate the owners of rights to previously published works and the translations printed here. We gratefully acknowledge permission to reprint the following material:

## Chapter

1   From Jacques Attali, *Noise: The Political Economy of Music*, trans. Brian Massumi (Minneapolis: University of Minnesota Press, 1985). Used by permission of the University of Minnesota Press.
2   From Luigi Russolo, *The Art of Noises*, trans. Barclay Brown (New York: Pendragon, 1986). Used by permission of Pendragon Press.
3   From *Give My Regards to Eighth Street: Collected Writings of Morton Feldman*, ed. B.H. Friedman (Cambridge, MA: Exact Change, 2000). Used by permission of Exact Change Press.
4   From *Contemporary Composers on Contemporary Music*, Expanded Edition, ed. Elliott Schwartz and Barney Childs (New York: Da Capo, 1998). Used by permission of Chou-Wen Chung for the Estate of Edgard Varèse.
5   From *Essential Cowell: Selected Writings on Music*, ed. Dick Higgins (Kingston, NY: McPherson & Company, 2002). Used by permission of McPherson & Company and the David and Sylvia Teitelbaum Fund, Inc.
6   From *Silence: Lectures and Writings by John Cage* (Hanover, NH: University Press of New England/Wesleyan University Press, 1961). Used by permission of Wesleyan University Press.
7   From R. Murray Schafer, *The Music of the Environment* (Vienna: Universal Edition, 1973). Used by permission of the author.
8   From *Harper's Magazine* (April 1999). Used by permission of the author.
9   From *Discourse* 10, no. 1 (Fall–Winter 1987–1988): 55–76. Used by permission of the authors.
10  From Simon Reynolds, *Blissed Out: The Raptures of Rock* (London: Serpent's Tail, 1990). Used by permission of the author and Serpent's Tail Press.
11  From " 'The Beauty of Noise': An Interview with Masami Akita of Merzbow," conducted by Chad Hensley, *Seconds* 42 (1997). Used by permission of the author.
12  From Marshall McLuhan and Bruce R. Powers, *The Global Village* (New York: Oxford, 1989) © 1992 by Corinne McLuhan and Bruce R. Powers. Used by permission of Oxford University Press, Inc.
13  From Theodor Adorno and Hanns Eisler, *Composing for the Films* (New York: Oxford University Press, 1947). Used by permission of Continuum Press.
14  From Pierre Schaeffer, *Traité des objets musicaux* (Paris: Éditions du Seuil, 1966). Translated for this volume by Daniel W. Smith. Used by permission of Jacqueline Schaeffer and Éditions du Seuil.
15  From Francisco López, "Blind Listening," in *The Book of Music and Nature*, ed. David Rothenberg and Marta Ulvaeus (Middletown, CT: Wesleyan University Press, 2001). Used by permission of the author and David Rothenberg. Modified in consultation with the original version of the article, which appeared as liner notes to *La Selva*, V2-Archief V228.
16  From *Keeping Score: Music, Disciplinarity, Culture*, ed. David Schwarz et al., (Charlottesville, VA: University of Virginia Press, 1997). Used by permission of the author.
17  From Brian Eno, *A Year With Swollen Appendices* (London: Faber & Faber, 1996). Used by permission of the author.
18  From Iain Chambers, *Migrancy, Culture, Identity* (London: Routledge, 1994). Used by permission of the author and Routledge/Taylor & Francis.

19   From Pauline Oliveros, *Software for People: Collected Writings 1963–80* (Baltimore: Smith Publications, 1984). Used by permission of the author.

20   From *Perspectives of New Music* 10, no. 2 (Spring–Summer 1972). Used by permission of the author.

21   From *The Glenn Gould Reader*, ed. Tim Page (New York: Alfred A. Knopf, 1984). Used by permission of Malcolm Lester for the Glenn Gould Estate.

22   This article first appeared, in two parts, in *Down Beat* 50, no. 7 (July 1983) and 50, no. 8 (August 1983), edited by Howard Mandel. Used by permission of the author.

23   From *The Whole Earth Review* (Winter 1987). Used by permission of the author.

24   From *Musicworks* 60 (Fall 1994). Slightly modified and used by permission of the author.

25   From Kodwo Eshun, *More Brilliant Than the Sun: Adventures in Sonic Fiction* (London: Quartet, 1998). Used by permission of the author.

26   From Umberto Eco, *The Open Work*, trans. Anna Cancogni (Cambridge, MA: Harvard University Press, 1989). Used by permission of the author.

27   From *Silence: Lectures and Writings by John Cage* (Hanover, NH: University Press of New England/Wesleyan University Press, 1961). Used by permission of Wesleyan University Press.

28   From *Pulse!* (October 1999), slightly modified. Used by permission of the author.

29   From *Current Musicology* 67/68 (2002). Used by permission of Micah Silver for The Earle Brown Music Foundation.

30   The first portion of this chapter appeared as liner notes to John Zorn, *Cobra* (Tzadik TZ 7335), used by permission of the author. The interview that follows was conducted for this volume by Christoph Cox.

31   From Anthony Braxton, *Catalog of Works* (Synthesis Music, 1989). Used by permission of the author.

32   From Michael Nyman, *Experimental Music: Cage and Beyond* (Cambridge: Cambridge University Press, 1999). Used by permission of the author and Cambridge University Press.

33   From John Cage, *Themes & Variations* (Barrytown, NY: Station Hill Press, 1982). Used by permission of Barrytown/Station Hill Press.

34   From *Studio International* (Nov./Dec. 1976). Used by permission of the author.

35   From *Scratch Music*, ed. Cornelius Cardew (London: Latimer New Dimensions, 1972). Used by permission of Horace Cardew for the Estate of Cornelius Cardew.

36   From David Toop, "The Generation Game," *The Wire* 207 (May 2001). Used by permission of the author.

37   From the liner notes to Ornette Coleman, *Change of the Century* (Atlantic SD 1327).

38   From Derek Bailey, *Improvisation: Its Nature and Practice in Music* (New York: Da Capo, 1992). Used by permission of the author.

39   From *Current Musicology* 67/68 (2002). Used by permission of the author.

40   From *Black Music Research Journal* 16 (1996). Slightly modified and used by permission of the author.

41   From Susan McClary, "Rap, Minimalism, and Structures of Time in Late-Twentieth Century Culture," the Norman and Jane Geske Lecture (Lincoln: University of Nebraska Press, 1999). Used by permission of the author.

42   From Kyle Gann, "Minimal Music, Maximal Impact," *NewMusicBox* 31, vol. 3, no. 7 (November 2001). Used by permission of the author and *NewMusicBox*, the web magazine from the American Music Center.

43   From Steve Reich, *Writings on Music, 1965–2000*, ed. Paul Hillier (Oxford: Oxford University Press, 2002) © 2002 by Steve Reich. Used by permission of Oxford University Press, Inc.

44   From Wim Mertens, *American Minimal Music*, trans. J. Hautekier (London: Kahn & Averill, 1983) © Usura 1980. Used by permission of the author.

45   From liner notes to Tony Conrad, *Early Minimalism, Vol. 1* (Table of the Elements TOE-CD-33). Used by permission of the author.

46   Commissioned for this volume.

47   From "Production–Reproduction" and "New Form in Music: Potentialities of the Phonograph," in *Moholy-Nagy*, ed. Krisztina Passuth (London: Thames and Hudson, 1985). Used by permission of Hattula Moholy-Nagy.

48 From William S. Burroughs, *The Ticket that Exploded* (New York: Grove Press, 1968). Used by permission of Grove/Atlantic, Inc.
49 From an untitled discussion between Christian Marclay and Yasunao Tone in *Music* 1 (1997). Used by permission of the authors.
50 From the liner notes to DJ Spooky, *Songs of a Dead Dreamer* (Asphodel ASP0961). Used by permission of the author.
51 From David Toop, *Ocean of Sound: Aether Talk, Ambient Sound and Imaginary Worlds* (London: Serpent's Tail, 1995). Used by permission of the author and Serpent's Tail.
52 From *The Village Voice* (August 29, 1995). Used by permission of the author.
53 From the liner notes to *Columbia-Princeton Electronic Music Center* (Columbia MS 6566 LP). Used by permission of the author.
54 "Electronic and Instrumental Music" was delivered as a lecture in October 1958 and published in German in *Die Reihe* 5 (Vienna: Universal Edition, 1959). Newly translated here by Jerome Kohl in collaboration with Suzanne Stephens and John McGuire, the essay will appear in Karlheinz Stockhausen, *Texts on Music,* Vol. I, forthcoming from the Stockhausen Foundation for Music. The essay is reprinted with the kind permission of the author.
55 From *The Wire* 141 (November 1995). Used by permission of Richard Witts, Lizzie Jackson for Soundbite Productions Limited, and Tony Herrington for *The Wire*.
56 From *Leonardo Music Journal* 12 (2002). Used by permission of the author.
57 From *Computer Music Journal* 24, no. 4 (Winter 2000). Used by permission of the author.

# Introduction:
# Music and the New Audio Culture

Over the past half-century, a new audio culture has emerged, a culture of musicians, composers, sound artists, scholars, and listeners attentive to sonic substance, the act of listening, and the creative possibilities of sound recording, playback, and transmission. This culture of the ear has become particularly prominent in the past decade, as evidenced by a constellation of events. The academy has witnessed an explosion of interest in auditory history and anthropology led by social scientists who have turned their attention to sound as a marker of temporal and cultural difference.[1] In the art world, sound art has suddenly become a viable field, finding venues at prominent museums and galleries across the globe.[2] And, in music, once-marginal sonic and auditory explorers—Luigi Russolo, John Cage, Pierre Schaeffer, Pauline Oliveros, R. Murray Schafer, and others—have come to be acknowledged as ancestors and influences by an extraordinary number and range of musicians working across the boundaries of jazz, classical, rock, and dance music.

What accounts for this auditory turn in contemporary culture? Technological innovations have certainly played a decisive role. "Sound recording, audio tracking of movies and video, online MP3's, all have re-sounded our ways of thinking," notes historian Richard Cullen Rath, recapitulating a view advocated by media theorist Marshall McLuhan in the 1960s.[3] McLuhan argued that the emergence of electronic media was causing a shift in the sensorium, deposing the visual from its millennia-old hegemony and giving way to an immersive experience exemplified by the auditory.[4] In an illuminating history of musical technology, musician and theorist Chris Cutler offers a related view. He argues that sound recording has deposed the culture of the eye exemplified by the highly literate and score-governed field of European art music, and has "throw[n] the life of music production back onto the ear." As with the orally transmitted folk music that was eclipsed by the European classical tradition, "the first matter is again Sound. Recording *is* memory of sound."[5]

Invented in the mid-1930s, but commercially unavailable until a decade and a half later, the tape recorder revolutionized music. Early experimenters such as Cage and Schaeffer noted that this device opened music to "the entire field of sound,"[6] rather than merely the restricted body of sounds produced by traditional musical instruments. Indeed, trained as a radio engineer instead of a composer, Schaeffer came to represent the new breed of musician: an amateur explorer working directly ("concretely," as he put it) with sound material rather than going through the detours of musical notation, conductors, and performers. And just as

Schaeffer prefigured today's music producer, who manipulates sound with inexpensive hardware and software on his or her home computer, he also prefigured the age of the remix. For recorded sound obscures the difference between the original and the copy, and is available for endless improvisatory manipulations and transformations. Finally, the tape recorder (and allied technologies such as the phonograph and the radio) made possible a new mode of listening, what Schaeffer termed "acousmatic listening": listening to sounds in the absence of their original sources and visual contexts, a listening that thus gives access to sound-as-such.

A second technological revolution has contributed to the rise to prominence of audio culture within the past decade: the advent of digital media. Compact discs, the Internet, MP3, Napster, the CD burner—all of these digital technologies have led to the creation of a vast virtual archive of sound and music available on a massive scale. The pristine clarity of digital sound fosters an attention to sonic matter and detail; and its replicability and microscopic malleability allows even a novice to become a sound artist or remixer. Finally, cyberspace enables the formation and flourishing of new audio communities, networks, and resources.

Exploiting these technologies and networks, the emergent audio culture has achieved a new kind of sonic literacy, history, and memory. If the traditional conception of history as a continuous, linear unfolding can be thought of as *analog*, this new sonic sensibility might be called a *digital* one. It flattens the distinction between "high art" and "mass culture," and treats music history as a repository from which to draw random-access sonic alliances and affinities that ignore established genre categories. For example, on the track "Djed," by the post-rock quintet Tortoise, a sample from Edgard Varèse's *Ionisation* is conjoined with Jamaican dub, motoric Krautrock, and minimalist mallet music reminiscent of Steve Reich or Philip Glass. Sonic Youth links punk rock to the work of experimental music founders Pauline Oliveros, Christian Wolff, and Takehisa Kosugi. Derek Bailey puts free improvisation into conversation with drum 'n' bass. DJ Spooky performs with composer Iannis Xenakis and free jazz giants William Parker and Matthew Shipp. Techno producers sample, emulate, and remix the music of minimalist masters. *Musique concrète* pioneer Luc Ferrari collaborates with free improviser Noël Akchoté, electronica producer Scanner, and turntablists DJ Olive and Erik M . . . [7] The combinations are myriad and the cross-fertilizations ongoing.

Indeed, across the field of modern music, one discovers a host of shared practices and theoretical concerns. For example, John Cage's critique of the composer's authority is also explicitly an issue in House and Techno, where producers take on a protean array of aliases and make their mark by mixing and remixing the music of others. The boundary between "music" and "noise" is challenged as much by Pauline Oliveros' environmental sound compositions as by Japanese noise composer Masami Akita's aural sado-masochism. Issues around technology and aesthetic originality pervade the contemporary musical spectrum, from the early collages of James Tenney to the work of composer/improviser John Oswald, rock renegades Negativland, and HipHop turntablists DJ Q-Bert and the X-Ecutioners.

*Audio Culture* attempts to map the musical terrain of this new sonic landscape. Rather than offering a *history* of contemporary music, the book traces the *genealogies* of contemporary musical practices and theoretical concerns, drawing lines of connection between recent musical forms and earlier moments of audio experimentation. It aims to foreground the various rewirings of musical composition and performance that have taken place in the past few decades and to provide a critical and theoretical language for this new audio culture. As such, the book poses, and seeks to answer, questions such as: What new modes of production, circulation, reception, and discourse are mobilized by vanguard musical production today? How do musical practices within the new audio culture complicate the definition of "music" and its distinction from "silence," "noise," and "sound"? In what ways do they challenge traditional conceptions of authorship, textuality, and ownership? How are musical strategies such as indeterminacy, minimalism, free improvisation, turntablism, and electronic experimentation employed by artists from different backgrounds?

The texts included here are drawn from a heterogeneous array of sources. Statements by composers, improvisers, and producers are printed alongside essays by theorists and critics who provide lines of connection and historical contexts. Excerpts from books sit beside magazine articles, liner notes, and interviews that first appeared on the World Wide Web. This heterogeneity reflects the fact that the new audio culture is a *discourse*, a loose collection of terms, concepts, and statements gathered from across the cultural field. This discourse not only challenges aesthetic distinctions between "high art" and "popular culture." In the age of the Internet, it also flattens traditional hierarchies between "high" and "low" venues for publishing. Most of the texts were written within the past half-century, though the book also includes several older texts that have been reanimated by the new audio culture.

The group of texts in Part One explores some key ontological and epistemological issues that have shaped music and sound over the past few decades. These texts investigate the shifting definition of "music" and examine the various modes of listening necessitated by the contemporary soundscape. Several texts discuss changes in the production and reception of sound that have resulted from newer technologies such as the Walkman, the sampler, and the laptop computer, and from reappropriations of older technologies such as magnetic tape and the phonograph. The incursion of music into everyday life and the spaces of everyday living raises political issues concerning the ways in which sound constructs us as human subjects and locates us in particular social and cultural contexts; hence, several texts in Part One suggest strategies for navigating the current sonic landscape.

Part Two more closely examines a spectrum of musical practices that are currently providing resources for musicians from different generations and backgrounds. Practices such as open-form composition, free improvisation, and experimentalism are taken here not as fixed historical entities but as ongoing musical strategies that are continually being adopted and reshaped for new contexts. Hence, each section attempts to give a sense of the particular practice as a general strategy, to trace some of its genealogical strands, and to examine some of its current inhabitations.

Throughout the book, we have tried to foreground the ways in which these theoretical concerns and practices, though to some degree distinct, significantly overlap or flow into one another. All the issues in Part One are interlinked: musical ontology is shaped by musical technologies and by modes of listening and aural attention. The practices explored in Part Two similarly overlap. At its limit, open-form composition becomes experimental music; Reich's early tape works and Alvin Lucier's *Music on a Long Thin Wire* propel experimental music into the minimalist domain; and minimalist methodologies drive a great deal of contemporary electronica. Turntablists such as Christian Marclay, Otomo Yoshihide, and Marina Rosenfeld, merge DJ Culture with free improvisation, which is also currently practiced by electronica producers such as Spring Heel Jack, Marcus Schmickler, and Christian Fennesz. And, indeed, all contemporary music is, in some sense, electronic music; hence, texts on electronic music are not only confined to the final section but are spread out over the entire book. Moreover, most of the authors and musicians presented in the book are linked to one another via myriad networks of influence or collaboration. Several of these—John Cage, Pierre Schaeffer, and Brian Eno, for example—form key nodal points to which most of the developments in contemporary music can be linked. Hence, their names are ubiquitous and constantly cross-referenced here.

It will have been noticed that what we are calling "contemporary music" or "modern music" has a peculiar character. Though it cuts across classical music, jazz, rock, reggae, and dance music, it is resolutely avant-gardist in character and all but ignores the more mainstream inhabitations of these genres. In our view, it is the vanguard fringe within each of these generic categories that is fully and richly challenging prevailing assumptions about the nature of music and sound, *and* challenging these genre categories themselves. These vanguard practices destabilize the obvious, and push our aesthetic and conceptual sensibilities to their limits. They force us to confront the unheard core of all music: the sonic and auditory as such; and, hence, they provide the musical currency of the new audio culture.

## NOTES

1. Prominent examples include: Richard Cullen Rath, *How Early America Sounded* (Ithaca: Cornell University Press, 2003); Jonathan Sterne, *The Audible Past: Cultural Origins of Sound Reproduction* (Durham, NC: Duke University Press, 2003); John M. Picker, *Victorian Soundscapes* (Oxford: Oxford University Press, 2003); Emily Thompson, *The Soundscape of America: Architectural Acoustics and the Culture of Listening in America, 1900–1933* (Cambridge, MA: MIT Press, 2002); Mark M. Smith, *Listening to Nineteenth-Century America* (Chapel Hill, NC: University of North Carolina Press, 2001); Leigh Eric Schmidt, *Hearing Things: Religion, Illusion and the American Enlightenment* (Cambridge, MA: Harvard University Press, 2000); James H. Johnson, *Listening in Paris: A Cultural History* (Berkeley: University of California Press, 1995); Alain Corbin, *Village Bells: Sound and Meaning in the 19th-Century French Countryside*, trans. Martin Thom (New York: Columbia University Press, 1998); and David Howes, ed., *The Varieties of Sensory Experience: A Sourcebook in the Anthropology of the Senses* (Toronto: University of Toronto Press, 1991).

2. A recent sampling includes: *Treble*, SculptureCenter, New York City, May–July 2004; *Sounding Spaces: Nine Sound Installations*, NTT InterCommunication Center, Tokyo, July–September 2003; *Sonic Process: A New Geography of Sounds*, Centre Pompidou, October, 2002–January 2003; *S.O.S.: Scenes of Sounds*, Tang Museum of Art, October 2000–January 2001; *Volume: Bed of Sound*, P.S. 1, New York City, July–September 2000; and *Sonic Boom*, Hayward Gallery, London, April–June 2000.

3. Richard Cullen Rath, interviewed by Emily Eakin in "History You Can See, Hear, Smell, Touch, and Taste," *New York Times* (December 20, 2003).

4. This view is presented most fully in Marshall McLuhan and Bruce R. Powers, *The Global Village: Transformations in World Life and Media in the 21st Century* (Oxford: Oxford University Press, 1989), particularly the chapter "Visual and Acoustic Space" (chap. 12,

below). See also Walter J. Ong, "The Shifting Sensorium," in *The Varieties of Sensory Experience*.

5. See Chris Cutler, "Necessity and Choice in Musical Forms," *File Under Popular: Theoretical and Critical Writings on Music* (New York: Autonomedia, 1993), 33. For a related account, see Mark Poster, "Authors Analogue and Digital," *What's the Matter with the Internet?* (Minneapolis: University of Minnesota Press, 2001).

6. John Cage, "Future of Music: Credo," chap. 6 below.

7. Tortoise, *Millions Now Living Will Never Die*, Thrill Jockey THRILL 025; Sonic Youth, *Goodbye 20ᵗʰ Century*, SYR 4; Derek Bailey, *Guitar, Drums 'n' Bass*, Avant AVAN 060; Iannis Xenakis, *Kraanerg*, Paul D. Miller and the ST-X Ensemble, Charles Zacharie Bornstein, Asphodel ASP 0975; Various Artists, *Reich Remixed*, Nonesuch 79552-2; The Orb, "Little Fluffy Clouds," *The Orb's Adventures Beyond the Ultraworld*, Big Life BLR 98; Noël Akchoté/Roland Auzet/Luc Ferrari, *Impro-Micro-Acoustique*, Blue Chopsticks BC 12 CD; and performances with DJ Olive, Scanner, and Erik M in 2003.

# Part One
# THEORIES

The concept of noise was a by-product of the Industrial Revolution. Throughout the jerry-built and already shabby proletarian living quarters and workplaces of Europe in the 1840s and 1850s, there was a constant din of construction and pounding, of the shrieking of metal sheets being cut and the endless thump of press machinery, of ear-splitting blasts from huge steam whistles, sirens, and electric bells that beckoned and dismissed shifts of first-generation urbanized laborers from their unending and repetitive days. The normal sounds of rural life—the bleating of domesticated animals, the chirping of birds and insects, the ping of hand-held tools shaping wood and stone—whether pleasant or not, were all recognizable. Here, however, the cacophony of sounds in the nineteenth-century street, factory shop, and mine—seemingly random and meaningless—could not be easily isolated or identified. They became novel and potentially dangerous intrusions on the overworked human mind.

—Mel Gordon[1]

The twentieth century is, among other things, the Age of Noise. Physical noise, mental noise, and noise of desire—we hold history's record for them. And no wonder; for all the resources of our almost miraculous technology have been thrown into the current assault against silence. That most popular and influential of all recent inventions, the radio, is nothing but a conduit through which pre-fabricated din can flow into our homes. And this din goes far deeper, of course, than the ear-drums. It penetrates the mind, filling it with a babel of distractions—news items, mutually irrelevant bits of information, blasts of corybantic or sentimental music, continually repeated doses of drama that bring no catharsis, but merely create a craving for daily or even hourly emotional enemas. And where, as in most countries, the broadcasting stations support themselves by selling time to advertisers, the noise is carried from the ears, through the realms of phantasy, knowledge and feeling to the ego's central core of wish and desire. Spoken or printed, broadcast over the ether or on wood-pulp, all advertising copy has but one purpose—to prevent the will from ever achieving silence.

—Aldous Huxley[2]

Look at it this way: there are many here among us for whom the life force is best represented by the livid twitching of one tortured nerve, or even a full-scale anxiety attack. I do not subscribe to this point of view 100%, but I understand it, have lived it. Thus the shriek, the caterwaul, the chainsaw gnarlgnashing, the yowl and the whizz that decapitates may be reheard by the adventurous or emotionally damaged as mellifluous bursts of unarguable affirmation.

—Lester Bangs[3]

[P]ost-Renaissance music differs from nearly all other musics, which love to use noise—sounds, that is, of no precise pitch or definite harmonic structure—as well as those pitches which lie between our twelve divisions of the octave, and which our music considers to be "out of tune" [. . .] Post-Renaissance musicians could not tolerate these acoustically illogical and unclear sounds, sounds which were not susceptible to total control.

—Christopher Small[4]

Edgard Varèse described himself as an "organizer of sound." That concept is probably more valid today than in any previous era.

—John Zorn[5]

There is no such thing as an empty space or an empty time. There is always something to see, something to hear. In fact, try as we may to make a silence, we cannot. For certain engineering purposes, it is desirable to have as silent a situation as possible. Such a room is called an anechoic chamber [. . .] a room without echoes. I entered one at Harvard University several years ago and heard two sounds, one high and one low. When I described them to the engineer in charge, he informed me that the high one was my nervous system in operation, the low one my blood in circulation. Until I die there will be sounds. And they will continue following my death.

—John Cage[6]

Noise may have lost its power to offend. Silence hasn't.

—Dan Warburton[7]

The fear of silence is nothing new. Silence surrounds the dark world of death. Sometimes the silence of the vast universe hovers over us, enveloping us. There is the intense silence of birth, the quiet silence of one's return to the earth. Hasn't art been the human creature's rebellion against silence? Poetry and music were born when man first uttered sound, resisting the silence.

—Toru Takemitsu[8]

A noise is a resonance that interferes with the audition of a message in the process of emission. A resonance is a set of simultaneous, pure sounds of determined frequency and differing intensity. Noise, then, does not exist in itself, but only in relation to the system within which it is inscribed: emitter, transmitter, receiver. Information theory uses the concept of noise (or rather metonymy) in a more general way: noise is the term for a signal that interferes with the reception of a message by a receiver, even if the interfering signal itself has a meaning for that receiver. Long before it was given this theoretical expression, noise had always been experienced as destruction, disorder, dirt, pollution, and aggression against the code-structuring messages. In all cultures, it is associated with the idea of the weapon, blasphemy, plague. In its biological reality, noise is a source of pain [. . . .] Diminished intellectual capacity, accelerated respiration and heartbeat, hypertension, sound in the environment. A weapon of death. It became that with the advent of industrial technology. But just as death is nothing more than an excess of life, noise has always been perceived as a source of exaltation, a kind of therapeutic drug capable of curing tarantula bites or, according to Boissier de Sauvages (in his *Nosologica methodica*), "fourteen forms of melancholy."

—Jacques Attali[9]

There is no difference between noise and music in my work. I have no idea what you term "music" and "noise." It's different depending on each person. If noise means uncomfortable sound, then pop music is noise to me.

—Masami Akita (a.k.a. Merzbow)[10]

# I: Music and Its Others: Noise, Sound, Silence

## Introduction

What is music? A century ago, the question was fairly easy to answer. But, over the course of the twentieth century, it became increasingly difficult to distinguish music from its others: noise, silence, and non-musical sound.

The reasons for this are many. Already at the turn of the nineteenth century, the music of Debussy, Schoenberg, and Stravinsky challenged tonality on a number of fronts. Not long after, Cowell, Varèse, and Cage began to explore non-pitched sounds. Ethnomusicological research into the nature of music outside of Europe began to suggest a need to expand the concept of music beyond the narrow and specialized domain it demarcated in the West.

The tape recorder played a crucial role in blurring the lines of distinction between music and its others. Tape composition allowed the composer to bypass musical notation, instruments, and performers in one step. Further, it gave composers access to what John Cage called "the entire field of sound," making conventional distinctions between "musical" and "non-musical" sounds increasingly irrelevant.[1] In 1948, Pierre Schaeffer broadcast over French radio a "Concert of Noises," a set of pieces composed entirely from recordings of train whistles, spinning tops, pots and pans, canal boats, percussion instruments, and the occasional piano. Schaeffer called his new music "*musique concrète,*" in contrast with traditional "*musique abstraite,*" which passed through the detours of notation, instrumentation, and performance. Trained as a radio-engineer rather than a musician, Schaeffer's method of composition bore a closer resemblance to cinematic montage than it did to traditional musical composition. The major European avant-garde composers (Stockhausen, Boulez, etc.) flocked to his Paris studio; but, ultimately, the impact of Schaeffer's work was felt most strongly outside classical music, for example, in the early tape experiments of Les Paul, the studio manipulations of Beatles producer George Martin, the *concrète* pranks of Frank Zappa, the live tape-loop systems of Terry Riley and the sampling and turntablism of HipHop DJs from Grandmaster Flash to Q-Bert.

In his 1913 manifesto, Russolo wrote that the traditional orchestra was no longer capable of capturing the imagination of a culture immersed in noise, and that the age of noise demanded new musical instruments he called "noise instruments" (*intonarumori*). Composer Edgard Varèse dismissed the conventional distinction between "music" and "noise," preferring to define music as "organized sound." In his writings of the 1930s, he described his own music as the "collision of sound-masses," blocks of sound "moving at different speeds and at different angles." Varèse's use of sirens in the groundbreaking percussion piece *Ionisation* (1929–31) gestured back to Russolo and forward to the development of electronic instruments that could provide the "parabolic and hyperbolic trajectories of sound" of which he dreamt. Two decades later, in the early 1950s, the European avant-garde became captivated by the extraordinary powers of these electronic instruments, which extended the domain of music far beyond that of traditional instrumental sonorities.

In the decades that followed, commercial synthesizers tamed these unruly powers and made tidy electronic instruments available to the general public. By the 1970s, such instruments had become the norm in rock and dance music. Aiming to revive and celebrate the powers of noise, British and European "industrial" bands merged punk rock attitudes, performance art sensibilities, and a Russolian fascination with mechanical noise to forge a retro-futurist music made with found objects: chains, tire irons, oil drums, and other industrial debris. "Industrial music" and the "noise bands" that followed highlighted certain cultural and political features of noise: noise as disturbance, distraction, and threat.

Noise has also functioned as a vehicle for ecstasy and transcendence, shaping the musical aesthetic of drone-based minimalists La Monte Young and Tony Conrad as well as the free jazz players from Albert Ayler and John Coltrane through David S. Ware and Sabir Mateen. And punk, HipHop, and Heavy Metal have revalued the notion of noise, transforming it into a marker of power, resistance, and pleasure.

The rise of interest in "noise" in contemporary music has gone hand in hand with a new interest in its conceptual opposite: silence. With his Zen embrace of contradiction, John Cage attempted to erase the distinction between silence and music, while simultaneously noting that perfect silence is never more than a conceptual ideal, an aural vanishing point. In the face of rising noise levels in urban and rural environments, composer and acoustic ecologist R. Murray Schafer called for "the recovery of positive silence" and a subtle attention to the endangered non-musical sounds of our environment. Microphones and headphones brought the vanishing point of silence within aural reach, forever transforming the relationship of silence to sound, giving them equal ontological status.

What is music? According to Jacques Attali, it is the constant effort to codify and stratify noise and silence, which, for their part, always threaten it from without. From Russolo through DJ Culture, experimental musical practices have inhabited that borderland where noise and silence become music and vice versa.

### NOTES

1. John Cage, "Future of Music: Credo," chap. 6, below.

# 1

# Noise and Politics

## JACQUES ATTALI

During the 1980s, economic theorist Jacques Attali (1943–   ) was Special Counselor to French President François Mitterand. He subsequently headed the European Bank for Reconstruction and Development and is currently contributing editor to *Foreign Policy* magazine. With the publication of *Noise* in 1977, Attali quickly became one of Europe's leading philosophers of music. For Attali, music, like economics and politics, is fundamentally a matter of organizing dissonance and subversion—in a word, "noise." Yet Attali argues that, an all-but-immaterial force, music moves faster than economics and politics and, hence, prefigures new social relations.

[. . .] Listening to music is listening to all noise, realizing that its appropriation and control is a reflection of power, that it is essentially political. More than colors and forms, it is sounds and their arrangements that fashion societies. With noise is born disorder and its opposite: the world. With music is born power and its opposite: subversion. In noise can be read the codes of life, the relations among men. Clamor, Melody, Dissonance, Harmony; when it is fashioned by man with specific tools, when it invades man's time, when it becomes sound, noise is the source of purpose and power, of the dream—Music. It is at the heart of the progressive rationalization of aesthetics, and it is a refuge for residual irrationality; it is a means of power and a form of entertainment.

Everywhere codes analyze, mark, restrain, train, repress, and channel the primitive sounds of language, of the body, of tools, of objects, of the relations to self and others.

All music, any organization of sounds is then a tool for the creation or consolidation of a community, of a totality. It is what links a power center to its subjects, and thus, more generally, it is an attribute of power in all of its forms. Therefore, any theory of power today must include a theory of the localization of noise and its endowment with form. Among birds a tool for marking territorial boundaries, noise is inscribed from the start within the panoply of power. Equivalent to the articulation of a space, it indicates the limits of a territory and the way to make oneself heard within it, how to survive by drawing one's sustenance from it.[1] And since noise is the source of power, power has always listened to it with fascination. In an extraordinary and little known text, Leibniz describes in minute detail the ideal political organization, the "Palace of Marvels," a harmonious machine within which all of the sciences of time and every tool of power are deployed.

> These buildings will be constructed in such a way that the master of the house will be able to hear and see everything that is said and done without himself being perceived, by means of mirrors and pipes, which will be a most important thing for the State, and a kind of political confessional.[2]

Eavesdropping, censorship, recording, and surveillance are weapons of power. The technology of listening in on, ordering, transmitting, and recording noise is at the heart of this apparatus. The symbolism of the Frozen Words,[3] of the Tables of the Law, of recorded noise and eavesdropping—these are the dreams of political scientists and the fantasies of men in power: to listen, to memorize—this is the ability to interpret and control history, to manipulate the culture of a people, to channel its violence and hopes. Who among us is free of the feeling that this process, taken to an extreme, is turning the modern State into a gigantic, monopolizing noise emitter, and at the same time, a generalized eavesdropping device. Eavesdropping on what? In order to silence whom?

The answer, clear and implacable, is given by the theorists of totalitarianism. They have all explained, indistinctly, that it is necessary to ban subversive noise because it betokens demands for cultural autonomy, support for differences or marginality: a concern for maintaining tonalism, the primacy of melody, a distrust of new languages, codes, or instruments, a refusal of the abnormal—these characteristics are common to all regimes of that nature [. . . .]

The economic and political dynamics of the industrialized societies living under parliamentary democracy also lead power to invest art, and to invest in art, without necessarily theorizing its control, as is done under dictatorship. Everywhere we look, the monopolization of the broadcast of messages, the control of noise, and the institutionalization of the silence of others assure the durability of power. Here, this channelization takes on a new, less violent, and more subtle form: laws of the political economy take the place of censorship laws. Music and the musician essentially become either objects of consumption like everything else, recuperators of subversion, or meaningless noise.

Musical distribution techniques are today contributing to the establishment of a system of eavesdropping and social surveillance. Muzak, the American corporation that sells standardized music, presents itself as the "security system of the 1970s" because it permits use of musical distribution channels for the circulation of orders. The monologue of standardized, stereotyped music accompanies and hems in a daily life in which in reality no one has the right to speak any more. Except those among the exploited who can still use their music to shout their suffering, their dreams of the absolute and freedom. What is called music today is all too often only a disguise for the monologue of power. However, and this is the supreme irony of it all, never before have musicians tried so hard to communicate with their audience, and never before has that communication been so deceiving. Music now seems hardly more than a somewhat clumsy excuse for the self-glorification of musicians and the growth of a new industrial sector. Still, it is an activity that is essential for knowledge and social relations.

## NOTES

1. "Whether we inquire into the origin of the arts or observe the first criers, we find that everything in its principle is related to the means of subsistence." Jean-Jacques Rousseau, *Essai sur l'inégalité*.

2. Gottfried Wilhelm Leibniz, "Drôle de pensée touchant une nouvelle sorte de représentation," ed. Yves Belaval, *La Nouvelle Revue Francaise* 70 (1958): 754–68. Quoted in Michel Serres, "Don Juan ou le Palais des Merveilles," *Les Eludes Philosophiques* 3 (1966): 389.

3. [A reference to Rabelais, *Gargantua and Pantagruel,* b. 4, chap. 54.—trans.]

# 2

## *The Art of Noises: Futurist Manifesto*

### LUIGI RUSSOLO

Luigi Russolo (1885–1947) was a prominent painter in the Italian Futurist movement. Yet he is best known for *The Art of Noises*, among the most important and influential texts in 20th century musical aesthetics. Written in 1913 as a letter to his friend, the Futurist composer Francesco Balilla Pratella, this manifesto sketches Russolo's radical alternative to the classical musical tradition. Drawing inspiration from the urban and industrial soundscape, Russolo argues that traditional orchestral instruments and composition are no longer capable of capturing the spirit of modern life, with its energy, speed, and noise. A year after composing this letter, Russolo introduced his *intonarumori* ("noise instruments") in a series of concerts held in London.

None of Russolo's music remains; and the *intonarumori* were destroyed in a fire during World War II. Yet, since the War, Russolo's manifesto has become increasingly important, inspiring a host of musicians and composers, among them *musique concrète* pioneers Pierre Schaeffer and Pierre Henri, 1980s dance-pop outfit The Art of Noise, "industrial" bands such as Einstürzende Neubauten and Test Dept., turntablist DJ Spooky, and sound artist Francisco López.

[. . . .] Ancient life was all silence. In the 19th Century, with the invention of machines, Noise was born. Today, Noise is triumphant and reigns sovereign over the sensibility of men. Through many centuries life unfolded silently, or at least quietly. The loudest of noises that interrupted this silence was neither intense, nor prolonged, nor varied. After all, if we overlook the exceptional movements of the earth's crust, hurricanes, storms, avalanches, and waterfalls, nature is silent.

In this scarcity of *noises,* the first *sounds* that men were able to draw from a pierced reed or a taut string were stupefying, something new and wonderful. Among primitive peoples, *sound* was attributed to the gods. It was considered sacred and reserved for priests, who used it to enrich their rites with mystery. Thus was born the idea of sound as something in itself, as different from and independent of life. And from it resulted music, a fantastic world superimposed on the real one, an inviolable and sacred world. The Greeks greatly restricted the field of music. Their musical theory, mathematically systematized by Pythagoras, admitted only a few consonant intervals. Thus, they knew nothing of harmony, which was impossible.

The Middle Ages, with the developments and modifications of the Greek tetrachord system, with Gregorian chant and popular songs, enriched the musical art. But they continued to regard sound *in its unfolding in time,* a narrow concept that lasted several centuries, and which we find again in the very complicated polyphony of the Flemish contrapuntalists. The chord did not exist. The development of the various parts was not subordinated to the chord that these parts produced in their totality. The conception of these parts, finally, was horizontal not vertical. The desire, the search, and the taste for the simultaneous union of different sounds, that is, for the chord (the complete sound) was manifested gradually, moving from the consonant triad to the consistent and complicated dissonances that characterize contemporary music. From the beginning, musical art sought out and obtained purity and sweetness of sound. Afterwards, it brought together different sounds, still preoccupying itself with caressing the ear with suave harmonies. As it grows ever more complicated today, musical art seeks out combinations more dissonant, stranger, and harsher for the ear. Thus, it comes ever closer to the *noise-sound.*

*This evolution of music is comparable to the multiplication of machines,* which everywhere collaborate with man. Not only in the noisy atmosphere of the great cities, but even in the country, which until yesterday was normally silent. Today, the machine has created such a variety and contention of noises that pure sound in its slightness and monotony no longer provokes emotion.

In order to excite and stir our sensibility, music has been developing toward the most complicated polyphony and toward the greatest variety of instrumental timbres and colors. It has searched out the most complex successions of dissonant chords, which have prepared in a vague way for the creation of MUSICAL NOISE. The ear of the Eighteenth Century man would not have been able to withstand the inharmonious intensity of certain chords produced by our orchestra (with three times as many performers as that of the orchestra of his time). But our ear takes pleasure in it, since it is already educated to modern life, so prodigal in different noises. Nevertheless, our ear is not satisfied and calls for ever greater acoustical emotions.

Musical sound is too limited in its variety of timbres. The most complicated orchestras can be reduced to four or five classes of instruments different in timbres of sound: bowed instruments, metal winds, wood winds, and percussion. Thus, modern music flounders within this tiny circle, vainly striving to create new varieties of timbre.

*We must break out of this limited circle of sounds and conquer the infinite variety of noise-sounds.*

Everyone will recognize that each sound carries with it a tangle of sensations, already well-known and exhausted, which predispose the listener to boredom, in spite of the efforts of all musical innovators. We futurists have all deeply loved and enjoyed the harmonies of the great masters. Beethoven and Wagner have stirred our nerves and hearts for many years. Now we have had enough of them, *and we delight much more in combining in our thoughts the noises of trams, of automobile engines, of carriages and brawling crowds, than in hearing again the "Eroica" or the "Pastorale."*

We cannot see the enormous apparatus of forces that the modern orchestra represents without feeling the most profound disillusionment before its paltry acoustical results. Do you know of a more ridiculous sight than that of twenty men striving to redouble the mewling of a violin? Naturally, that statement will make the musicomaniacs scream—and perhaps revive the sleepy atmosphere of the concert halls. Let us go together, like futurists, into one of these hospitals for anemic sounds. There—the first beat brings to your ear the weariness of something heard before, and makes you anticipate the boredom of the beat that follows. So let us drink in, from beat to beat, these few qualities of obvious tedium, always waiting for that extraordinary sensation that never comes. Meanwhile, there is in progress a repugnant medley of monotonous impressions and of the cretinous religious emotion of the Buddha-like listeners, drunk with repeating for the thousandth time their more or less acquired and snobbish ecstasy. Away! Let us leave, since we cannot for long restrain ourselves from the desire to create finally a new musical reality by generously handing out some resounding slaps and stamping with both feet on violins, pianos, contrabasses, and organs. Let us go!

It cannot be objected that noise is only loud and disagreeable to the ear. It seems to me useless to enumerate all the subtle and delicate noises that produce pleasing sensations.

To be convinced of the surprising variety of noises, one need only think of the rumbling of thunder, the whistling of the wind, the roaring of a waterfall, the gurgling of a brook the rustling of leaves, the trotting of a horse into the distance, the rattling jolt of a cart on the road, and of the full, solemn, and white breath of a city at night. Think of all the noises made by wild and domestic animals, and of all those that a man can make, without either speaking or singing.

Let us cross a large modern capital with our ears more sensitive than our eyes. We will delight in distinguishing the eddying of water, of air or gas in metal pipes, the muttering of motors that breathe and pulse with an indisputable animality, the throbbing of valves, the bustle of pistons, the shrieks of mechanical saws, the starting of trams on the tracks, the cracking of whips, the flapping of awnings and flags. We will amuse ourselves by orchestrating together in our imagination the din of rolling shop shutters, the varied hubbub of train stations, iron works, thread mills, printing presses, electrical plants, and subways [. . . .]

*We want to give pitches to these diverse noises, regulating them harmonically and rhythmically.* Giving pitch to noises does not mean depriving them of all irregular movements and vibrations of time and intensity but rather assigning a degree or pitch to the strongest and most prominent of these vibrations. Noise differs from sound, in fact, only to the extent that the vibrations that produce it are confused and irregular. *Every noise has a pitch, some even a chord, which predominates among the whole of its irregular vibrations.* Now, from this predominant characteristic pitch derives the practical possibility of assigning pitches to the noise as a whole. That is, there may be imparted to a given noise not only a single pitch but even a variety of pitches without sacrificing its character, by which I mean the timbre that distinguishes it. Thus, some noises obtained through a rotary motion can offer an entire chromatic scale ascending or descending, if the speed of the motion is increased or decreased.

Every manifestation of life is accompanied by noise. Noise is thus familiar to our ear and has the power of immediately recalling life itself. Sound, estranged from life, always musical, something in itself, an occasional not a necessary element, has become for our ear what for the eye is a too familiar sight. Noise instead, arriving confused and irregular from the irregular confusion of life, is never revealed to us entirely and always holds innumerable surprises. We are certain, then, that by selecting, coordinating, and controlling all the noises, we will enrich mankind with a new and unsuspected pleasure of the senses. Although the characteristic of noise is that of reminding us brutally of life, the *Art of Noises should not limit itself to an imitative reproduction.* It will achieve its greatest emotional power in acoustical enjoyment itself, which the inspiration of the artist will know how to draw from the combining of noises.

Here are the 6 *families of noises* of the futurist orchestra that we will soon realize mechanically:

1. Roars, Thunderings, Explosions, Hissing roars, Bangs, Booms
2. Whistling, Hissing, Puffing
3. Whispers, Murmurs, Mumbling, Muttering, Gurgling
4. Screeching, Creaking, Rustling, Humming, Crackling, Rubbing
5. Noises obtained by beating on metals, woods, skins, stones, pottery, etc.
6. Voices of animals and people, Shouts, Screams, Shrieks, Wails, Hoots, Howls, Death rattles, Sobs

In this list we have included the most characteristic of the fundamental noises. The others are only associations and combinations of these.

*The rhythmic motions of a noise are infinite. There always exists, as with a pitch, a predominant rhythm*, but around this there can be heard numerous other, secondary rhythms.

**Conclusions**

1. Futurist composers should continue to enlarge and enrich the field of sound. This responds to a need of our sensibility. In fact, we notice in the talented composers of today a tendency toward the most complicated dissonances. Moving ever farther from pure sound, they have almost attained the *noise-sound*. This need and this tendency can be satisfied only *with the addition and the substitution of noises for sounds*.

2. Futurist musicians should substitute for the limited variety of timbres that the orchestra possesses today the infinite variety of timbres in noises, reproduced with appropriate mechanisms.

3. The sensibility of musicians, being freed from traditional and facile rhythms, must find in noise the means of expanding and renewing itself, given that every noise offers a union of the most diverse rhythms, in addition to that which predominates.

4. Every noise having in its irregular vibrations *a predominant general pitch*, a sufficiently extended variety of tones, semitones, and quartertones is easily

attained in the construction of the instruments that imitate it. This variety of pitches will not deprive a single noise of the characteristics of its timbre but will only increase its tessitura or extension.

5. The practical difficulties involved in the construction of these instruments are not serious. Once the mechanical principle that produces a noise has been found, its pitch can be changed through the application of the same general laws of acoustics. It can be achieved, for example, through the decreasing or increasing of speed, if the instrument has a rotary motion. If the instrument does not have a rotary motion, it can be achieved through differences of size or tension in the sounding parts.

6. It will not be through a succession of noises imitative of life but through a fantastic association of the different timbres and rhythms that the new orchestra will obtain the most complex and novel emotions of sound. Thus, every instrument will have to offer the possibility of changing pitches and will need a more or less extended range.

7. The variety of noises is infinite. If today, having perhaps a thousand different machines, we are able to distinguish a thousand different noises, tomorrow, with the multiplication of new machines, we will be able to distinguish ten, twenty, or *thirty thousand different noises, not simply by imitation but by combining according to our fancy.*

8. Therefore, we invite talented and audacious young musicians to observe all noises attentively, to understand the different rhythms that compose them, their principal pitch, and those which are secondary. Then, comparing the various timbres of noises to the timbres of sounds, they will be convinced that the first are much more numerous than the second. This will give them not only the understanding of but also the passion and the taste for noises. Our multiplied sensibility, having been conquered by futurist eyes, will finally have some futurist ears. Thus, the motors and machines of our industrial cities can one day be given pitches, so that every workshop will become an intoxicating orchestra of noises [. . . .]

# 3

## *Sound, Noise, Varèse, Boulez*

### MORTON FELDMAN

Composer Morton Feldman (1926–1987) began his career in the 1950s as a member of the "New York School" of artists and composers. Indeed, Feldman's music emulated the canvases of Abstract Expressionist painters such as Mark Rothko, Franz Kline, and Philip Guston, who were among his close friends. Against the great modern systematizers, Pierre Boulez and Karlheinz Stockhausen, Feldman championed an intuitive musical abstraction that he felt was exemplified by the music of Edgard Varèse. During his own lifetime, Feldman worked in the shadow of his mentor, John Cage. But, over the past decade, Feldman's work has become increasingly influential within and beyond the boundaries of contemporary classical music. Here, Feldman offers an eloquent description of the power and fascination of noise.

[. . . .] If one hears what one composes—by that I mean not just paper music—how can one not be seduced by the sensuality of the musical sound? It is unfortunate that when this sensuality is pursued we find that the world of music is not round, and that there do exist demonic vastnesses when this world leaves off.

Noise is something else. It does not travel on these distant seas of experience. It bores like granite into granite. It is physical, very exciting, and when organized it can have the impact and grandeur of Beethoven.

The struggle is between this sensuousness which is elegance and the newer, easier to arrive at, excitement.

You have no idea how academic music is, even the most sublime. What is calculated is for me academic. Chance is the most academic procedure yet arrived at, for it defines itself as a technique immediately. And, believe me, the throw of the dice may be exciting to the player, but never to the croupier.

Is noise actually so easy to arrive at? Noise is a word of which the aural image is all too evasive. On the one hand sound is comprehensible in that it evokes a sentiment, though the sentiment itself may be incomprehensible and far-reaching. But it is noise that we really understand. It is only noise which we secretly want, because the greatest truth usually lies behind the greatest resistance.

Sound is all our dreams of music. Noise is music's dreams of us. And those moments when one loses control, and sound like crystals forms its own planes, and with a thrust, there is no sound, no tone, no sentiment, nothing left but the significance of our first breath—such is the music of Varèse. He alone has given us this elegance, this physical reality, this impression that the music is writing about mankind rather than being composed.

# 4

## The Liberation of Sound

### EDGARD VARÈSE

Born in France, Edgard Varèse (1883–1965) emigrated to the United States in 1915. Like Russolo, he called for a new concept of music and new musical instruments. Yet, where Russolo was inspired by the concrete noises of everyday life, Varèse's new musical vision was sparked by metaphors drawn from chemistry, astronomy, cartography, and geology. Describing himself as "a worker in rhythms, frequencies, and intensities," Varèse redefined music as "organized sound," side-stepping the conventional distinction between "music" and "noise."

Varèse's music focuses on the matter of sound—on timbre, texture, and musical space, elements that would become increasingly important in later electronic and Ambient music. Indeed, in the 1950s, Varèse composed two early masterpieces of electronic music: *Déserts* (1950–54), realized in Pierre Schaeffer's Paris studio, and *Poème Électronique* (1957–58), part of a "spectacle of sound and light" installed in the Phillips Pavilion designed by Le Corbusier for the World's Fair in Brussels. Varèse's description of music as "the movement of sound-masses, of shifting planes" and "beams of sound" aptly describes not only his own music but a good deal of modern experimental music as well, from Musica Elettronica Viva's live electronic music to Merzbow's noise composition and contemporary Powerbook music. The following text is excerpted from a series of lectures given by Varèse from 1936 to 1962 and compiled by his student Chou Wen-Chung.

**New Instruments and New Music (1936)**

[. . . .] When new instruments will allow me to write music as I conceive it, the movement of sound-masses, of shifting planes, will be clearly perceived in my work, taking the place of the linear counterpoint. When these sound-masses collide, the phenomena of penetration or repulsion will seem to occur. Certain transmutations taking place on certain planes will seem to be projected onto other planes, moving at different speeds and at different angles. There will no longer be the old conception of melody or interplay of melodies. The entire work will be a melodic totality. The entire work will flow as a river flows.

We have actually three dimensions in music: horizontal, vertical, and dynamic swelling or decreasing. I shall add a fourth, sound projection—that feeling that sound is leaving us with no hope of being reflected back, a feeling akin to that aroused by beams of light sent forth by a powerful searchlight—for the ear as for the eye, that sense of projection, of a journey into space.

Today with the technical means that exist and are easily adaptable, the differentiation of the various masses and different planes as well as these beams of sound, could be made discernible to the listener by means of certain acoustical arrangements. Moreover, such an acoustical arrangement would permit the delimitation of what I call "zones of intensities." These zones would be differentiated by various timbres or colors and different loudnesses. Through such a physical process these zones would appear of different colors and of different magnitude, in different perspectives for our perception. The role of color or timbre would be completely changed from being incidental, anecdotal, sensual or picturesque; it would become an agent of delineation, like the different colors on a map separating different areas, and an integral part of form. These zones would be felt as isolated, and the hitherto unobtainable non-blending (or at least the sensation of non-blending) would become possible.

In the moving masses you would be conscious of their transmutations when they pass over different layers, when they penetrate certain opacities, or are dilated in certain rarefactions. Moreover, the new musical apparatus I envisage, able to emit sounds of any number of frequencies, will extend the limits of the lowest and highest registers, hence new organizations of the vertical resultants: chords, their arrangements, their spacings—that is, their oxygenation. Not only will the harmonic possibilities of the overtones be revealed in all their splendor, but the use of certain interferences created by the partials will represent an appreciable contribution. The never-before-thought-of use of the inferior resultants and of the differential and additional sounds may also be expected. An entirely new magic of sound!

I am sure that the time will come when the composer, after he has graphically realized his score, will see this score automatically put on a machine that will faithfully transmit the musical content to the listener. As frequencies and new rhythms will have to be indicated on the score, our actual notation will be inadequate. The new notation will probably be seismographic. And here it is curious to note that at the beginning of two eras, the Mediaeval primitive and our own primitive era (for we are at a new primitive stage in music today), we are faced with an identical problem: the problem of finding graphic symbols for the transposition of the composer's thought into sound. At a distance of more than a thousand years we have this analogy: our still primitive electrical instruments find it necessary to abandon staff notation and to use a kind of seismographic writing much like the early ideographic writing originally used for the voice before the development of staff notation. Formerly the curves of the musical line indicated the melodic fluctuations of the voice; today the machine-instrument requires precise design indications [. . . .]

## Music as an Art-Science (1939)

Personally, for my conceptions, I need an entirely new medium of expression: a sound-*producing* machine (not a sound-*reproducing* one). Today it is possible to build such a machine with only a certain amount of added research.

If you are curious to know what such a machine could do that the orchestra with its man-powered instruments cannot do, I shall try briefly to tell you: whatever I write, whatever my message, it will reach the listener unadulterated by "interpretation." It will work something like this: after a composer has set down his score on paper by means of a new graphic notation, he will then, with the collaboration of a sound engineer, transfer the score directly to this electric machine. After that, anyone will be able to press a button to release the music exactly as the composer wrote it—exactly like opening a book.

And here are the advantages I anticipate from such a machine: liberation from the arbitrary, paralyzing tempered system; the possibility of obtaining any number of cycles or, if still desired, subdivisions of the octave, and consequently the formation of any desired scale; unsuspected range in low and high registers; new harmonic splendors obtainable from the use of sub-harmonic combinations now impossible; the possibility of obtaining any differentiation of timbre, of sound-combinations; new dynamics far beyond the present human-powered orchestra; a sense of sound-projection in space by means of the emission of sound in any part or in many parts of the hall, as may be required by the score; cross-rhythms unrelated to each other, treated simultaneously, or, to use the old word, "contrapuntally," since the machine would be able to beat any number of desired notes, any subdivision of them, omission or fraction of them—all these in a given unit of measure or time that is humanly impossible to attain [. . . .]

## Rhythm, Form, and Content (1959)

My fight for the liberation of sound and for my right to make music with any sound and all sounds has sometimes been construed as a desire to disparage and even to discard the great music of the past. But that is where my roots are. No matter how original, how different a composer may seem, he has only grafted a little bit of himself on the old plant. But this he should be allowed to do without being accused of wanting to kill the plant. He only wants to produce a new flower. It does not matter if at first it seems to some people more like a cactus than a rose [. . . .]

Because for so many years I crusaded for new instruments[1] with what may have seemed fanatical zeal, I have been accused of desiring nothing less than the destruction of all musical instruments and even of all performers. This is, to say the least, an exaggeration. Our new liberating medium—the electronic—is not meant to replace the old musical instruments, which composers, including myself, will continue to use. Electronics is an additive, not a destructive, factor in the art and science of music. It is because new instruments have been constantly added to the old ones that Western music has such a rich and varied patrimony [. . . .]

## The Electronic Medium (1962)

First of all, I should like you to consider what I believe is the best definition of music, because it is all-inclusive: "the corporealization of the intelligence that is in sound," as proposed by Hoëne Wronsky.[2] If you think about it you will realize that, unlike most dictionary definitions, which make use of such subjective terms as beauty, feelings, etc., it covers all music, Eastern or Western, past or present, including the music of our new electronic medium. Although this new music is being gradually accepted, there are still people who, while admitting that it is "interesting," say: "but is it music?" It is a question I am only too familiar with. Until quite recently I used to hear it so often in regard to my own works that, as far back as the twenties, I decided to call my music "organized sound" and myself, not a musician, but "a worker in rhythms, frequencies, and intensities." Indeed, to stubbornly conditioned ears, anything new in music has always been called noise. But after all, what is music but organized noises? And a composer, like all artists, is an organizer of disparate elements. Subjectively, *noise* is any sound one doesn't like.

Our new medium has brought to composers almost endless possibilities of expression, and opened up for them the whole mysterious world of sound. For instance, I have always felt the need of a kind of continuous flowing curve that instruments could not give me. That is why I used sirens in several of my works. Today such effects are easily obtainable by electronic means. In this connection, it is curious to note that it is this lack of flow that seems to disturb Eastern musicians in our Western music. To their ears, it does not glide, sounds jerky, composed of edges of intervals and holes and, as an Indian pupil of mine expressed it, "jumping like a bird from branch to branch." To them, apparently, our Western music seems to sound much as it sounds to us when a record is played backward. But playing a Hindu record of a melodic vocalization backward, I found that I had the same smooth flow as when played normally, scarcely altered at all.

The electronic medium is also adding an unbelievable variety of new timbres to our musical store, but most important of all, it has freed music from the tempered system, which has prevented music from keeping pace with the other arts and with science. Composers are now able, as never before, to satisfy the dictates of that inner ear of the imagination. They are also lucky so far in not being hampered by esthetic codification—at least not yet! But I am afraid it will not be long before some musical mortician begins embalming electronic music in rules.

We should also remember that no machine is a wizard, as we are beginning to think, and we must not expect our electronic devices to compose for us. Good music and bad music will be composed by electronic means, just as good and bad music have been composed for instruments. The computing machine is a marvelous invention and seems almost superhuman. But in reality it is as limited as the mind of the individual who feeds it material. Like the computer, the machines we use for making music can only give back what we put into them. But, considering the fact that our electronic devices were never meant for making music, but for the sole purpose of measuring and analyzing sound, it is remarkable that what has already been achieved is musically valid. These devices are still somewhat unwieldy and time-consuming, and not entirely satisfactory as an art-medium. But this new art is still in its infancy, and I hope and firmly believe, now that composers and physicists are at last working together and music is again linked with science as it was in the Middle Ages, that new and more musically efficient devices will be invented.

# NOTES

1. As early as 1916, Varèse was quoted in the *New York Morning Telegraph* as saying: "Our musical alphabet must be enriched. We also need new instruments very badly. . . . In my own works I have always felt the need of new mediums of expression . . . which can lend themselves to every expression of thought and can keep up with thought." And in the *Christian Science Monitor*, in 1922: "The composer and the electrician will have to labor together to get it."

2. Hoëne Wronsky (1778–1853), also known as Joseph Marie Wronsky, was a Polish philosopher and mathematician, known for his system of *Messianism*. Camille Durutte (1803–1881), in his *Technie Harmonique* (1876), a treatise on "musical mathematics," quoted extensively from the writings of Wronsky.

# 5

## *The Joys of Noise*

### HENRY COWELL

John Cage called Henry Cowell (1897–1965) "the open sesame for new music in America." Through his New Musical Edition, Cowell championed experimental music, publishing Varèse's *Ionisation* and other scores. Cowell's own theoretical text, *New Musical Resources,* laid out his compositional innovations, most significantly extended piano techniques such as the use of "tone clusters" and the practice of striking or plucking the piano strings. This impulse to treat conventional instruments in unconventional ways directly influenced Cage's "prepared piano" and, more generally, the unorthodox performance practices of free jazz, avant-rock, and turntablism.

Cowell was probably the earliest 20th century composer to study African and Asian musics (a path later followed by Lou Harrison and Steve Reich, among others); and his own musical practice draws on those resources, extending the boundaries of compositional practice in the areas of rhythm and timbre.

Russolo offered a largely historical argument in favor of noise, embodying the Futurist idea that speed, power, and noise will progressively overtake music and art traditionally conceived. Cowell's argument in the following piece, first published in 1929, is more conceptual. It presents a deconstruction of the binary opposition between music and noise, arguing that the latter is always already contained in the former.

Music and noise, according to a time-honored axiom, are opposites. If a reviewer writes "It is not music, but noise," he feels that all necessary comment has been made.

Within recent times it has been discovered that the geometrical axioms of Euclid could not be taken for granted, and the explorations outside them have given us non-Euclidian geometry and Einstein's physically demonstrable theories.

Might not a closer scrutiny of musical axioms break down some of the hard-and-fast notions still current in musical theory, and build up a non-Bachian counterpoint, a non-Beethovenian harmony, or even a non-Debussian atmosphere, and a non-Schoenbergian atonality? [. . . .]

In almost any reliable book on harmony, you will find the axiom that the primary elements of music are melody, harmony and rhythm. If noise were admitted at all, and I doubt if it ever has been, it would unquestionably be classified as part of rhythm. This, however, is a faulty idea of rhythm. Rhythm is a conception, not a physical reality. It is true that, to be realized in music, rhythm must be marked by some sort of sound, but this sound is not itself the rhythm. Rhythmical considerations are the duration of sounds, the amount of stress applied to sounds, the rate of speed as indicated by the movement of sounds, periodicity of sound patterns, and so on.

Sound and rhythm thus are the primary musical elements, sound comprising all that can be heard, and rhythm the formulating impulse behind the sound. Before sound can be divided into melody and harmony, another and more primary division must take place: a division into tone—or sound produced by periodic vibration—and noise—or sound produced by non-periodic vibration. Tone may then be divided into melody and harmony; noise remains a much-used but almost unknown element, little developed from its most primitive usages, perhaps owing to its ill-repute [. . . .]

We are less interested [. . .] in primitive and oriental uses of percussion than in our own employment of it, and its power of moving. Noise-making instruments are used with telling effect in our greatest symphonies, and were it not for the punctuation of cymbal and bass drum, the climaxes in our operas would be like jelly-fish.

In the search for music based on pure tone, we may turn hopefully to vocal works, only to find that they too are riddled by noises; for it is only while singing a vowel that a singer makes anything like a "pure" tone—the pronunciation of most consonants produces irregular vibrations, hence noise.

But most shocking of all is the discovery that there is a noise element in the very tone itself of all our musical instruments. Consider the sound of a violin. Part of the vibrations producing the sound are periodic, as can be shown by a harmonic analyzer. But others are not—they do not constantly re-form the same pattern, and consequently must be considered noise. In varying proportions all other instruments yield similar combinations. A truly pure tone can be made only in an acoustical laboratory, and even there it is doubtful whether, by the time the tone has reached our ear, it has not been corrupted by resonances picked up on the way.

As musical sound grows louder, the noise in it is accentuated and the tone element reduced. Thus a loud sound is literally noisier than a soft one; yet music does not touch our emotional depths if it does not rise to a dynamic climax. Under the best circumstances, the emotions are aroused by musical noise and lulled musical tone.

Since the "disease" of noise permeates all music, the only hopeful course is to consider that the noise-germ, like the bacteria of cheese, is a good microbe, which may provide previously hidden delights to the listener, instead of producing musical oblivion.

Although existing in all music, the noise-element has been to music as sex to humanity, essential to its existence, but impolite to mention, something to be cloaked by ignorance and silence. Hence the use of noise in music has been largely unconscious and undiscussed. Perhaps this is why it has not been developed, like the more talked-of elements, such as harmony and melody. The use of noise in most music today is little beyond the primitive; in fact, it is behind most native music, where the banality of the thumps often heard in our concerts would not be tolerated.

Men like Varèse, in his *Hyperprism* or *Arcana* or Bartôk, in his *Piano Concerto*, where he uses percussion noises canonically, render a service by opening a wide field for investigation—although they arrive at nothing conclusive. If we had scales of percussion-sounds, with each "key" determined by some underlying quality, such as drum-sound, cymbal-sound, and so on, we could produce music through the conscious use of the melodic steps that would then be at the disposal of the composer. Perhaps this is one of the things music is coming to, and a new chemistry of sound will be the result.

# 6

# *The Future of Music: Credo*

## JOHN CAGE

No figure has had a more profound influence on contemporary musical thought and practice than John Cage (1912–1992; see also chaps. 27 and 33). A student of Schoenberg and Cowell, Cage pioneered a host of techniques and practices that have become central to contemporary music making. In his early percussion ensembles, he included tin cans and other found objects alongside standard orchestral instruments. His *Imaginary Landscape No. 1* (1939) was among the very first compositions to employ turntables; and he was an early proponent of live electronics, composing pieces for radios, phonograph cartridges, computers, and other electronic devices. In 1940, Cage began composing for "prepared piano," which called for the insertion of screws, bolts, cardboard, weather stripping, and other objects into the piano's strings to highlight the instrument's percussive character and to extend its sonorous possibilities. In the early 1950s, he pioneered the use of "chance" or "indeterminate" techniques in composition. Cage's most famous piece *4'33"* (1952) calls for performers and audience members alike to experience four minutes and 33 seconds of "silence," or non-intentional sound.

In the following piece, written in 1937, Cage joins Russolo and Varèse in imagining a musical future in which "noise" will be a crucial resource. "Whereas in the past," Cage writes, "the point of disagreement has been between dissonance and consonance, it will be, in the immediate future, between noise and so-called musical sounds." The future of music—from *musique concrète* and the classical avant-garde to free jazz, industrial music, HipHop and beyond—would certainly bear out Cage's prediction.

I BELIEVE THAT THE USE OF NOISE

Wherever we are, what we hear is mostly noise. When we ignore it, it disturbs us. When we listen to it, we find it fascinating. The sound of a truck at fifty miles per hour. Static between the stations. Rain. We want to capture and control these sounds, to use them not as sound effects but as musical instruments. Every film studio has a library of "sound effects" recorded on film. With a film phonograph it is now possible to control the amplitude and frequency of any one of these sounds and to give to it rhythms within or beyond the reach of the imagination. Given four film phonographs, we can compose and perform a quartet for explosive motor, wind, heartbeat, and landslide.

## TO MAKE MUSIC

If this word "music" is sacred and reserved for eighteenth- and nineteenth-century instruments, we can substitute a more meaningful term: organization of sound.

WILL CONTINUE AND INCREASE UNTIL WE REACH A MUSIC PRODUCED THROUGH THE AID OF ELECTRICAL INSTRUMENTS

Most inventors of electrical musical instruments have attempted to imitate eighteenth- and nineteenth- century instruments, just as early automobile designers copied the carriage. The Novachord and the Solovox are examples of this desire to imitate the past rather than construct the future. When Theremin provided an instrument with genuinely new possibilities, Thereministes did their utmost to make the instrument sound like some old instrument, giving it a sickeningly sweet vibrato, and performing upon it, with difficulty, masterpieces from the past. Although the instrument is capable of a wide variety of sound qualities, obtained by the turning of a dial, Thereministes act as censors, giving the public those sounds they think the public will like. We are shielded from new sound experiences.

The special function of electrical instruments will be to provide complete control of the overtone structure of tones (as opposed to noises) and to make these tones available in any frequency, amplitude, and duration.

WHICH WILL MAKE AVAILABLE FOR MUSICAL PURPOSES ANY AND ALL SOUNDS THAT CAN BE HEARD. PHOTOELECTRIC, FILM, AND MECHANICAL MEDIUMS FOR THE SYNTHETIC PRODUCTION OF MUSIC

It is now possible for composers to make music directly, without the assistance of intermediary performers. Any design repeated often enough on a sound track is audible. Two hundred and eighty circles per second on a sound track will produce one sound, whereas a portrait of Beethoven repeated fifty times per second on a sound track will have not only a different pitch but a different sound quality.

WILL BE EXPLORED. WHEREAS, IN THE PAST, THE POINT OF DISAGREEMENT HAS BEEN BETWEEN DISSONANCE AND CONSONANCE, IT WILL BE, IN THE IMMEDIATE FUTURE, BETWEEN NOISE AND SO-CALLED MUSICAL SOUNDS.

THE
PRESENT METHODS OF WRITING MUSIC, PRINCIPALLY THOSE WHICH
EMPLOY HARMONY AND ITS REFERENCE TO PARTICULAR STEPS IN THE
FIELD OF SOUND, WILL BE INADEQUATE FOR THE COMPOSER, WHO WILL
BE FACED WITH THE ENTIRE FIELD OF SOUND.

The composer (organizer of sound) will be faced not only with the entire field of
sound but also with the entire field of time. The "frame" or fraction of a second,
following established film technique, will probably be the basic unit in the measurement of time. No rhythm will be beyond the composer's reach.

NEW METHODS WILL BE
DISCOVERED, BEARING A DEFINITE RELATION TO SCHOENBERG'S TWELVE-
TONE SYSTEM

Schoenberg's method assigns to each material, in a group of
equal materials, its function with respect to the group. (Harmony assigned to each
material, in a group of unequal materials, its function with respect to the fundamental or most important material in the group.) Schoenberg's method is analogous to
a society in which the emphasis is on the group and the integration of the individual
in the group.

AND PRESENT METHODS OF WRITING PERCUSSION MUSIC

Percussion music is a contemporary transition from keyboard-influenced music to
the all-sound music of the future. Any sound is acceptable to the composer of percussion music; he explores the academically forbidden "non-musical" field of
sound insofar as is manually possible.
    Methods of writing percussion music have as their goal the rhythmic structure
of a composition. As soon as these methods are crystallized into one or several
widely accepted methods, the means will exist for group improvisations of unwritten but culturally important music. This has already taken place in Oriental cultures
and in hot jazz.

AND ANY OTHER METHODS WHICH ARE FREE FROM THE
CONCEPT OF A FUNDAMENTAL TONE.

THE PRINCIPLE OF
FORM WILL BE OUR ONLY CONSTANT CONNECTION WITH THE PAST.
ALTHOUGH THE GREAT FORM OF THE FUTURE WILL NOT BE AS IT WAS
IN THE PAST, AT ONE TIME THE FUGUE AND AT ANOTHER THE SONATA,
IT WILL BE RELATED TO THESE AS THEY ARE TO EACH OTHER:

Before this
happens, centers of experimental music must be established. In these centers,
the new materials, oscillators, turntables, generators, means for amplifying small

sounds, film phonographs, etc., available for use. Composers at work using twentieth-century means for making music. Performances of results. Organization of sound for extra-musical purposes (theatre, dance, radio, film).

THROUGH THE PRINCI-PLE OF ORGANIZATION OR MAN'S COMMON ABILITY TO THINK.

# 7

# The Music of the Environment

## R. MURRAY SCHAFER

Canadian composer and theorist R. Murray Schafer (1933– ) came to prominence in the early 1970s with a series of writings on environmental sound
and noise pollution. In 1977, Schafer published *The Tuning of the World*,
which presented his most thorough and cogent argument for what he termed
"acoustic ecology." Inspired by the Pythagorean (and, later, Cagean) idea
that the cosmos itself is a musical composition, the book looked back on
the history of modern literature, music, and audio theory (Russolo, Cage,
Schaeffer, etc.) and offered prescriptions for a new kind of listening to the
world "soundscape," a term Schafer coined. Schafer also founded the World
Soundscape Project, which drew attention to the sonic environment through
location recordings and environmental advocacy. The "acoustic ecology"
movement is still thriving today, notably represented by The World Forum
for Acoustic Ecology and the work of environmental sound artists such as
Hildegard Westerkamp, David Dunn, Douglas Quinn, and Chris Watson. The
following piece is drawn from Schafer's *The Music of the Environment*, a
1973 pamphlet that presents, in distilled form, the argument Schafer elabo-
rated in *The Tuning of the World*.

The soundscape of the world is changing. Modern man is beginning to inhabit a
world with an acoustical environment radically different from any he has hitherto
known. These new sounds, which differ in quality and intensity from those of the
past, have already alerted researchers to the dangers of the imperialistic spread
of more and larger sounds into every corner of man's life. In various parts of the
world important research is being undertaken in many independent areas of sonic
studies: acoustics, psychoacoustics, otology, audiology, noise abatement practices and procedures, communications and sound recording engineering (electro-
acoustics and electronic music), aural pattern perception and the structural analysis of speech and music. These researches are related; each is dealing with
aspects of the world soundscape, the vast musical composition which is unfolding
around us ceaselessly. In one way or another researchers engaged on these vari-

ous themes are asking the same questions: what is the relationship between man and the sounds of his environment and what happens when these sounds change? Is the soundscape of the world an indeterminate composition over which we have no control or are *we* its composers and performers, responsible for giving it form and beauty? These researches have been given an additional impetus lately since noise pollution has now emerged as a world problem. It would seem that the world soundscape has reached an apex of vulgarity in our time and many experts have predicted universal deafness as the ultimate consequence unless the problem can be brought quickly under control. Noise pollution results when man does not listen carefully. Noises are the sounds we have learned to ignore. Noise pollution today is being resisted by noise abatement. This is a negative approach. We must seek a way to make environmental acoustics a *positive* study program. Which sounds do we want to preserve, encourage, multiply? When we know this, the boring or destructive sounds will be conspicuous enough and we will know why we must eliminate them. Only a total appreciation of the acoustic environment can give us the resources for improving the orchestration of the world. Ear cleaning in the schools to eliminate audiometry in factories. Clairaudience, not ear muffs.

The following thoughts are crosshatchings on this theme designed to suggest how a new subject of acoustic design might develop, knitting together scientific discipline and artistic imagination.

**The Musician is an Architect of Sounds**

Throughout this essay I am going to treat the world soundscape as a macrocosmic musical composition. This is perhaps an unusual idea but I am going to nudge it forward relentlessly. The definition of music has undergone radical change in recent years. In one of the more contemporary definitions John Cage has declared: "Music is sounds, sounds heard around us whether we're in or out of concert halls (cf. Thoreau)."[1] The reference is to Thoreau's *Walden* where the author experiences in the sounds and sights of nature an inexhaustible entertainment.

There are two basic ideas of what music is or ought to be. These may be seen clearly in two Greek myths dealing with the origin of music. Pindar's twelfth Pythian Ode tells how the art of aulos playing was invented by Athena on hearing the heart-rending cries of Medusa's sisters after Perseus had killed the Gorgon. In a Homeric hymn to Hermes an alternative origin is proposed. The lyre is said to have been invented by Hermes when he surmised that the shell of the turtle, if used as a body of resonance, could produce sound.

In the first of these myths music arises as subjective emotion; in the second it arises with the discovery of sonic properties in the materials of the universe. These are the cornerstones on which all subsequent theories of music are founded. In the former myth, music is conceived as subjective emotion breaking forth from the human breast; in the latter it is external sound possessing secret unitary properties. This is the *anahata* of the Indian theorists and the music of the spheres of Pythagoras. It suggests that the universe is held together by the harmonies of some precise acoustic design, serene and mathematical. For many decades, however, it is the other view of music that has dominated Western musical thought.

This is the musical expression of the romanticist. Its tempo fluctuations, dynamic shadings and tonal colourings are the means by which the subjective and irrational art of the virtuoso artist is created.

The research I am about to describe represents a reaffirmation of music as a search for the harmonizing influence of sounds in the world about us. In Robert Fludd's *Utriusque Cosmi Historia* there is an illustration entitled "The Tuning of the World" in which the earth forms the body of an instrument across which strings are stretched and are tuned by a divine hand. We must try once again to find the secret of that tuning [. . . .]

## Clairaudience

We will not argue for the priority of the ear. Modern man, who seems to be in the process of deafening himself apparently regards this as a trivial mechanism. In the West the ear has given way to the eye as the most important gatherer of environmental information. One of the most evident testaments of this change is the way in which we have come to imagine God. It was not until the Renaissance that God became portraiture. Previously He had been conceived as sound or vibration. In the Middle East the message of Mohammed is still heard through the recitation of his Koran. *Sama* is the Sufi word for audition or listening. The followers of Jalal al-Din Rumi worked themselves into the *sama* state by whirling in mystical dances. Their dancing is thought by some scholars to have represented the solar system, recalling also the deep-rooted mystical belief in the music of the spheres, which the attuned soul could at times hear. In the Zoroastrian religion the priest Srosh (representing the genius of hearing) stands between man and the pantheon of the gods transmitting the divine messages to humanity.

When man was fearful of the dangers of an unexplored environment, the whole body was an ear. In the virgin forests of North America, where vision was restricted to a few feet, hearing was the most important sense. *The Leatherstocking Tales* of Fenimore Cooper are full of beautiful and terrifying surprises.

> . . . for, though the quiet deep of solitude reigned in that vast and nearly boundless forest, nature was speaking with her thousand tongues, in the eloquent language of night in the wilderness. The air sighed through ten thousand trees, the water rippled, at places, even roared along the shores and now and then was heard the creaking of a branch, or a trunk as it rubbed against some object similar to itself, under the vibrations of a nicely balanced body . . . When he desired his companions, however, to cease talking, in the manner just mentioned, his vigilant ear had caught the peculiar sound that is made by the parting of a dried branch of a tree, and which, if his senses did not deceive him, came from the western shore. All who are accustomed to that particular sound will understand how readily the ear receives it, and how easy it is to distinguish the tread which breaks the branch from every other noise of the forest . . . "Can the accursed Iroquois have crossed the river, already, with their arms and without a boat?"[2]

## The Rural Soundscape

When men lived mostly in isolation or in small communities their ears operated with seismographic delicacy. In the rural soundscape sounds are generally uncrowded, surrounded by pools of stillness. For the farmer, the pioneer or the woodsman the minutest sounds have significance. The shepherd, for instance, can determine from sheep bells the precise state of his flock.

> Just before dawn he was assisted in waking by the abnormal reverberation of familiar music. . . . In the solemn calm of the awakening morn that note was heard by Gabriel beating with unusual violence and rapidity. This exceptional ringing may be caused in two ways—by the rapid feeding of the sheep bearing the bell, as when the flock breaks into new pasture, which gives it an intermittent rapidity, or by the sheep starting off in a run, when the sound has a regular palpitation.[3]

The sounds of the environment signalled in many ways.

> He was disturbed in his meditation by a grating noise from the coach-house. It was the vane on the roof turning round, and this change in the wind was the signal for a disastrous rain.[4]

Even when sounds had no special messages, poets among men knew how to make larger interpretations of them. Goethe, his ear pressed to the grass:

> When I hear the humming of the little world among the stalks, and am near the countless indescribable forms of the worms and insects, then I feel the presence of the Almighty, Who created us in His own image. . . .[5]

When Phillip Grove travelled the Manitoba prairies in his buggy in 1916, often by night or in dense marsh fog, he travelled by ear as much as eye.

> I had become all ear. Even though my buggy was silent and though the road was coated with a thin film of soft clay-mud, I could distinctly hear from the muffled thud of the horses' hoofs on the ground that they were running over a grade. . . . I listened intently for the horses' thump. Yes, there was that hoofbeat again—I was on the last grade that led to the angling road across the corner of the marsh. . . .[6]

## The Hi-Fi and the Lo-Fi Soundscape

A hi-fi system is one possessing a favourable signal to noise ratio. The hi-fi soundscape is one in which discrete sounds can be heard clearly because of the low ambient noise level. The country is generally more hi-fi than the city; night more than day; ancient times more than modern. In a hi-fi soundscape even the slightest disturbance can communicate interesting or vital information. The human ear is alert, like that of an animal.

> . . . footfalls followed a round drive in the rear of the hotel, taking their tone in turn from the dust road, the crushed-stone walk, the cement steps and then reversing the process in going away.[7]

In a lo-fi soundscape individual acoustic signals are obscured in an overdense population of sounds. The pellucid sound—a footstep in the snow, a train whistle in the distance or a church bell across the valley—is masked by broad-band noise. Perspective is lost. On a downtown street corner there is no distance; there is only presence. Everything is close-miked. There is cross-talk on all the channels, and in order for the most ordinary sounds to be heard they have to be monstrously amplified. In the ultimate lo-fi soundscape the signal to noise ratio is 1 to 1 and it is no longer possible to know what, if anything, is to be listened to.

## Muscle Sounds [. . .]: The Industrial Revolution

The industrial revolution began to produce the lo-fi soundscape. Let us briefly chronicle its development. When industry first intruded into town life it was immediately conspicuous by the aberration of its novel noises. Stendhal, writing in 1830, noticed how it upset the rhythms of French provincial towns.

> No sooner has one entered the town than one is startled by the din of a noisy machine of terrifying aspect. A score of weighty hammers, falling with a clang which makes the pavement tremble, are raised aloft by a wheel which the water of the torrent sets in motion. Each of these hammers turns out, daily, I cannot say how many thousands of nails. A bevy of fresh, pretty girls subject to the blows of these enormous hammers, the little scraps of iron which are rapidly transformed into nails.[8]

By the early twentieth century such sounds had become more acceptable to the urban ear, "blending" with the natural rhythms of antiquity. As Thomas Mann described it,

> We are encompassed with a roaring like that of the sea; for we live almost directly on the swift-flowing river that foams over shallow ledges at no great distance from the popular avenue . . . Upstream, in the direction of the city, construction troops are building a pontoon bridge. Shouts of command and the thump of heavy boots on the planks sound across the river; also, from the further bank, the noise of industrial activity, for there is a locomotive foundry a little way downstream. Its premises have been lately enlarged to meet increased demands, and light streams all night long from its lofty windows. Beautiful glittering new engines roll to and fro on trial runs; a steam whistle emits wailing head-tones from time to time; muffled thunderings of unspecified origin shatter the air, smoke pours out of the many chimneys to be caught up by the wind and borne away over the wooded country beyond the river, for it seldom or never blows over to our side. Thus in our half-suburban, half-rural seclusion the voice of nature mingles with that of man, and over all lies the bright-eyed freshness of the new day.[9]

Ultimately the throb of the machine began to intoxicate man everywhere with its incessant vibrations.

> As they worked in the fields, from beyond the now familiar embankment came the rhythmic run of the winding engines, startling at first, but afterwards a narcotic to the brain.[10]

Before long, the noises of modern industrial life swung the balance against those of nature. This significant flashpoint occurred about the time of the First World War, the first mechanized war of history. In 1913 the futurist Luigi Russolo proclaimed the event in his manifesto *The Art of Noises* [. . . .][11]

Russolo invented an orchestra of noise makers, consisting of buzzers, howlers and other gadgets calculated to advance his philosophy. The "pastorale" and the "nocturne" give way before machine-music like Honegger's *Pacific 231* (1924), an imitation of a locomotive, Antheil's *Ballet mécanique* (1926), which employed a number of airplane propellers, Prokofiev's *Pas d'acier* (Dance of Steel), Mossolov's *Iron Foundry* and Carlos Chávez's *HP* (Horse-power) all dating from 1928. This blurring of the edges between music and environmental sounds is the most striking feature of twentieth-century music. Finally in the practices of *musique concrète* it became possible to insert any sound from the environment into a composition via tape; while in electronic music the hard-edge sound of the tone generator may be indistinguishable from the police siren or the electric tooth-brush [. . . .]

## Schizophonia

The Greek prefix *schizo* means split, separated. Schizophonia refers to the split between an original sound and its electroacoustical transmission or reproduction. It is another twentieth-century development.

Originally all sounds were originals. They occurred at one time and in one place only. Sounds were then indissolubly tied to the mechanisms which produced them. The human voice travelled only as far as one could shout. Every sound was uncounterfeitable, unique. Sounds bore resemblances to one another, such as the phonemes which go to make up the repetition of a word, but they were not identical. Tests have shown that it is physically impossible for nature's most rational and calculating being to reproduce a single phoneme in his own name twice in exactly the same manner.

Since the invention of electroacoustical equipment for the transmission and storage of sound, any sound, no matter how tiny, can be blown up and shot around the world, or packaged on tape or record for the generations of the future. We have split the sound from the maker of the sound. Sounds have been torn from their natural sockets and given an amplified and independent existence. Vocal sound, for instance, is no longer tied to a hole in the head but is free to issue from anywhere in the landscape. In the same instant it may issue from millions of holes in millions of public and private places around the world.

The twentieth century has given us the ability to dislocate sounds in time as well as in space. A record collection may contain items from widely diverse cultures and historical periods in what would seem, to a person from any century but our own, an unnatural and surrealistic juxtaposition.

Most recently, the quadraphonic sound system has made possible a 360 degree soundscape of moving and stationary sound events which allows any sound environment to be simulated in time and space. This provides for the complete portability of acoustic space. Any sonic environment can now become any other sonic environment. When I originally coined schizophonia in *The New Soundscape* I said it was intended to be a nervous word. Related to schizophrenia, I intended it to convey the same sense of aberration and drama. The benefits of

electroacoustic transmission and reproduction of sound are well-enough celebrated, but they should not obscure the fact that at precisely the time hi-fi was
being engineered, the world soundscape was slipping into a lo-fi condition. Indeed
the overkill of hi-fi gadgetry contributes generously to the lo-fi problem.

A character in one of Borges' stories dreads mirrors because they multiply
men. The same might be said of radios. As the cry broadcasts distress, the loudspeaker communicates anxiety. "We should not have conquered Germany without
. . . the loudspeaker," wrote Hitler in 1938.[12] In the USA, Americans were listening
to 268,000,000 radios by 1969. Modern life has been ventriloquized.

### Towards the Integrity of Inner Space

The desire to dislocate sounds in time and space has been evident for some time
in the history of Western music, so that the recent technological developments are
merely the consequences of aspirations that have been building for some centuries. The introduction of dynamics, echo effects, the splitting of resources, the separation of soloist from the ensemble, are all attempts to create virtual spaces which
are larger or different from natural room acoustics; just as the simultaneous breaking forward to find new musical resources and the turning back to recover the past
represents a desire to transcend the present.

If I speak of music it is because I believe music to be a barometer giving clues
to our whole attitude towards making and hearing sound. Certainly in the growth
of the orchestra we have a clue to the present day imperialistic spread of sounds
of all kinds. And there is little difference between Beethoven's attempts to *épater
le bourgeois* with sforzando effects and that of the modern teen-ager with his
motorcycle. The one is an embryo of the other.

The concert hall made concentrated listening possible, just as the art gallery
encouraged, focused and selected viewing. Music designed for outdoor performance—such as most folk music—does not demand great attention to detail, but
brings into play what we might call "peripheral hearing," similar to the way the eye
drifts over an interesting landscape. Today the transistor is reviving interest in the
outdoor concert while headphone listening is isolating the listener in a private
acoustic space.

Messages on earphones are always private property. "Head space" is a popular expression with the young, referring to the geography of the mind, which can
be reached by no telescope. Drugs and music are the means of invoking entry. In
the headspace of earphone listening, the sounds not only circulate around the listener, they literally seem to emanate from points in the cranium itself, as if the
archetypes of the unconscious were in conversation. There is a clear resemblance
here to the functioning of Nada Yoga in which interiorized sound (vibration)
removes the individual from this world and elevates him towards higher spheres of
existence. When the yogi recites his mantra he *feels* the sound surge through his
body. His nose rattles. He vibrates with its dark, narcotic powers. Similarly when
sound is conducted directly through the skull of the headphone listener, he is no
longer regarding events on the acoustic horizon; no longer is he surrounded by a
sphere of moving elements. He is the sphere. He is universe. While most twentieth-century developments in sound production tend to fragment the listening expe-

rience and break up concentration, headphone listening directs the listener towards a new integrity with himself [. . . .]

**Acoustic Design [. . .] : Quiet Groves and Times**

The huge noises of our civilization are the result of imperialistic ambitions. Territorial expansion has always been one of our aims. Just as we refuse to leave a space of our environment uncultivated, unmastered, so too we have refused to leave an acoustic space quiet and unpunctured by sound. The moon probes are undoubtedly a great achievement, but they may likewise be interpreted as an expression of that same imperialism that made Western man a world colonial power.

The amplifier was also invented by an imperialist; for it responds to the instinct to dominate others with one's own sound. But in a crowded and restless world, imperialism loops back on itself; its proponents become its victims as the locus of the battlefield shifts. For the first time in history, Constantin Doxiadis reminds us, man is less safe in the heart of his city than outside the city gates.

Just as man requires time for sleep to refresh and renew his life energies, so too he requires quiet periods for mental and spiritual recomposure. At one time stillness was a precious article in an unwritten code of human rights. Man held reservoirs of stillness in his life to facilitate this restoration of the spiritual metabolism. Even in the hearts of cities there were the dark, still vaults of churches and libraries, or the privacy of drawing-room and bedroom. Outside the throb of cities the countryside was accessible with its lulling whir of natural sounds. There were still times too. The holy days were quiet before they became holidays. In Christendom Sunday was the quietest day before it became Fun-day. The importance of these quiet groves far transcended the particular purposes to which they were put. We see this now that they are being destroyed. The city park is situated next to the parkway, the library is next to a construction or demolition site, the church is next to a heliport.

Acoustic design will want to pay special attention to the repatriation of quiet groves and times. Genclik Park in Ankara is merely one of many in the cities of the world today that has been wired throughout for background music, though the volume at which it is played is louder than most. This practice betrays an important principle of acoustic design: always to let nature sing for itself.

A park or a garden is a place where nature is cultivated. It is a humanized treatment of landscape. It may contain human artifacts (a bench, a swing) but they must harmonize with the natural inheritance (trees, water)—otherwise we no longer have a park but a highway or a slum. If synthetic sounds are introduced, if we venture to produce what I would call "the soniferous garden," care must be taken to ensure that they are sympathetic vibrations of the garden's original notes. The wind chimes of the Japanese, or the once-popular aeolian or wind harp, are reinforcements of natural sounds in the same way as the trellis reinforces the presence of the rose. The object in creating a soniferous garden would be to work up from natural sounds, materials, formations [. . . . ]

**The Recovery of Positive Silence**

In October 1969 the General Assembly of the International Music Council of UNESCO passed a most interesting resolution.

We denounce unanimously the intolerable infringement of individual freedom and of the right of everyone to silence, because of the abusive use, in private and public places, of recorded or broadcast music. We ask the Executive Committee of the International Music Council to initiate a study from all angles—medical, scientific and juridical—without overlooking its artistic and educational aspects, and with a view to proposing to UNESCO, and to the proper authorities everywhere, measures calculated to put an end to this abuse.

For the first time in history an organization involved primarily in the *production* of sounds suddenly turned its attention to their *reduction*. In the present article I have been suggesting that a saturation point has been reached with regard to all sounds. It remains to discuss how best to accomplish their reduction. I have suggested that the least effective way would be by the introduction of more noise abatement bylaws, sound-proof walls or ear plugs. An uncomprehending public with a developed appetite for noise would scarcely accept these means, unless they were necessary for public health—though in many instances this can now be demonstrated to be the case.

My approach [. . .] has been to treat the world soundscape as a huge macro-cosmic composition which deserves to be listened to as attentively as a Mozart symphony.[13] Only when we have truly learned how to listen can we make effective judgements about the world soundscape. I am especially anxious that musicians should take the initiative in this field, because musicians are the architects of sounds; they are concerned with making balances and arrangements of interest-ing sounds to produce desired aesthetic effects.

Silence is the most potentialized feature of Western music. Because it is being lost, the composer today is more concerned with silence; he composes with it. Anton Webern moved composition to the brink of silence. The ecstasy of his music is enhanced by his sublime use of rests. By this means he produces hi-fi works in which diminutive but stunning musical gestures inhabit containers of stillness.

Simultaneous with Webern's rediscovery of the value of silence in music, his compatriot Freud discovered its value for psychoanalysis. "The analyst is not afraid of silence. As Saussure remarked, the unconscious monologue of the patient on the one side and the almost absolute silence of the psychiatrist on the other was never made a methodological principle before Freud."[14]

In the West, silence has for many centuries been unfashionable. It will be recalled that when Galileo's telescope first suggested the infinity of space, the phi-losopher Pascal was deeply afraid of the prospect of an infinite and eternal silence. "*Le silence éternal de ces espaces infinis m'effraye* [The eternal silence of these infinite spaces frightens me]."[15]

When silence is conceived as the rejection of the human personality, the ulti-mate silence is death. Then man likes to surround himself with sounds in order to nourish his fantasy of perpetual life. In Western society silence is negative, an embarrassment, a vacuum. Silence for Western man equals communication hang-up. If one does not speak, the other will speak. This has not always been so, nor is it so for all peoples today. I have seen Arabs sitting quietly in a circle saying nothing for long stretches of time. Even the conversation of farmers is much more leisurely than that of citydwellers.

In the West we may assume that silence as a condition of life and a workable concept disappeared sometime towards the end of the thirteenth century, with the death of Meister Eckhart, Ruysbroeck, Angela de Foligno and the anonymous English author of *The Cloud of Unknowing*. This is the era of the last great Christian mystics and contemplation as a habit and skill began to disappear about that time.

I am about to suggest that the soundscape will not again become ecological and harmonious until silence is recovered as a positive and felicitous state in itself. We need to regain that state in order that fewer sounds could intrude on it with pristine brilliance. The Indian mystic Kirpal Singh expresses this eloquently:

> The essence of sound is felt in both motion and silence, it passes from exis-
> tent to nonexistent. When there is no sound, it is said that there is no hearing,
> but that does not mean that hearing has lost its preparedness. Indeed, when
> there is no sound, hearing is most alert, and when there is sound the hearing
> nature is least developed.[16]

It is this same idea that Rilke expresses in his *Duineser Elegien* when he speaks of "*die unterbrochene Nachricht der Stille*" ["the endless report that grows out of silence"]. Silence is indeed news for those possessing clairaudience.

Among our students we have declared days of moratorium on speech. In our classes we have also been trying to employ some yogic or relaxing exercises as a preparation to the listening and creating experience. Little by little the muscles and the mind relax and the whole body becomes an ear. This may take some time but at the conclusion, students have told me, they have heard music as never before.

It is in exercises such as these that I have come to believe our ultimate hope lies in improving the acoustic design of the world. Still the noise in the mind: that is the first task—then everything else will follow in time.

## NOTES

1. R. Murray Schafer, *The New Soundscape*, Universal Edition, London and Vienna, 1971, p. 1.
2. J. Fenimore Cooper, *The Pathfinder*, New York, 1961, pp. 113–114.
3. Thomas Hardy, *Far from the Madding Crowd*, London, 1902, p. 43.
4. ibid, p. 254.
5. Johann Wolfgang von Goethe, *Die Leiden des jungen Werther*, Leipzig, 1774, p. 9.
6. F. Phillip Grove, *Over Prairie Trails*, Toronto, 1922, p. 34.
7. F. Scott Fitzgerald, *Tender is the Night*, New York, 1962, p. 40.
8. Stendhal, *The Red and the Black*, New York, 1926, p. 10.
9. Thomas Mann, "A Man and His Dog," *Stories of Three Decades*, New York, 1936, pp. 440–441.
10. D. H. Lawrence, *The Rainbow*, New York, 1915, p. 7.
11. [See chap. 2, above. —Eds.]
12. Adolf Hitler, "*Ohne Kraftwagen, ohne Flugzeug und ohne Lautsprecher hätten wir Deutschland nicht erobert*," *Manual of the German Radio*, 1938–39.

13. These ideas are expounded more fully in my booklets, *Ear Cleaning*, *The New Soundscape*, and *When Words Sing*, Universal Edition, London and Vienna, 1970–71.

14. Theodor Reik, *Listening With the Third Ear*, New York, 1949, pp. 122–23.

15. Pascal, *Pensées*, Ch. M. des Granges, ed., Granier Frères, 1964, p. 131.

16. Kirpal Singh, *Naam or Word*, Ruhani Satsang, Delhi, India, 1970, p. 59.

# 8

# *Listening for Silence:*
# *Notes on the Aural Life*

## MARK SLOUKA

Mark Slouka (1958– ) is the author of *War of the Worlds: Cyberspace and the High-Tech Assault on Reality* (1995), a critical examination of the Internet and its political promises. He has also written *God's Fool* (2002), a novel about the 19th century Siamese twins Chang and Eng, and a collection of stories titled *Lost Lake* (1998). The following piece, first published in *Harper's Magazine*, draws on Debussy, Melville, Cage, and others to offer a compelling meditation on silence—and the loss of silence—in contemporary life. The essay extends and updates R. Murray Schafer's groundbreaking examination of silence, noise, and the modern soundscape; and it helps to explicate the fascination with silence that runs throughout modern music, from Cage and Feldman to Radu Malfatti and the "onkyo" improvisation scene in Japan.

Music, Claude Debussy once famously remarked, is the stuff between the notes, an observation that resonates, pardon the pun, from the flawless spacing of a Billie Holiday tune to the deletions—whether generous or cruel—in our daily lives. Essentially neuter, neither balm nor curse, silence, like light or love, requires a medium to give it meaning, takes on the color of its host, adapts easily to our fears and needs. Quite apart from whether we seek or shun it, silence orchestrates the music of our days.

I'm well aware, of course, that one man's music is another man's noise, that the primary differences between a cork-lined room and solitary confinement are the lock on the door and the sensibility of the inmate. I wish not to define silence but to inquire about its absence, and I ask the question not to restate the obvious— that silence, in its way, is fundamental to life, the emotional equivalent of carbon— but because everywhere I turn I see a culture willing to deny that essential truth. In my idle moments I picture a god from my son's book of myths (with an Olympian straw and sucked-in cheeks) drawing the silence out of the land, and if the conceit is fanciful, the effect, sadly, is not: as silence disappears, the world draws tighter, borders collapse, the public and the private bleed and intermix. Victim to the centripetal pull, the imagination crackles with the static of outside frequencies, while somewhere in the soul—listen!—a cell phone is chirping. Answer it quickly, before someone else does.

At the close of the millennium, a new Tower of Babel, monolingual (despite the superficial mixture of tongues), homogeneous (because almost invariably pitched in the vernacular of the marketplace), casts its shadow over the land. Ubiquitous, damn-near inescapable, it is rearranging the way we live, forcing crucial adjustments in our behavior, straining our capacity for adaptation. If it continues to grow, as I believe it will, future generations may one day distinguish our age not for its discovery of Elsewhere, as E. B. White called the world beyond the television screen, but for its colonization of silence.

Ensnared in webs of sound, those of us living in the industrialized West today must pick our way through a discordant, infinite-channeled auditory landscape. Like a radio stuck on permanent scan, the culture lashes us with skittering bits and bytes, each dragging its piece of historical or emotional context: a commercial overheard in traffic, a falsely urgent weather report, a burst of canned laughter, half a refrain. The pager interrupts lectures, sermons, second acts, and funerals. Everywhere a new song begins before the last one ends, as though to guard us against even the potential of silence. Each place we turn, a new world—synthetic, fragmented, often as not jacked into the increasingly complex grid that makes up the global communications network—encroaches on the old world of direct experience, of authentic, unadorned events with their particular, unadorned sounds.

Although a great deal has been said about our increasingly visual age, the changes to our aural landscape have gone relatively unremarked. The image has grown so voracious that any child asked to sum up the century will instantly visualize Einstein's hair and Hitler's mustache, mushroom clouds and moon landing; this despite the fact that each of these visual moments has its aural correlative, from the blast over Hiroshima to the high-pitched staccato ravings of the Führer, to Neil Armstrong's static-ridden "giant leap for mankind."

But make no mistake: sound will have its dominion. The aural universe, though subtler than the one that imprints itself on our retina, is more invasive, less easily blocked. It mocks our sanctuaries as light never can. If my neighbor decides to wash his car in front of my study window, as he does often, I can block out the uninspiring sight of his pimpled posterior by drawing the shades; to block out his stereo, I must kill noise with noise. We hear in our sleep. There is no aural equivalent for the eyelid. In our day, when the phone can ring, quite literally, anywhere on the planet, this is not necessarily good news.

I have nothing against my aural canal. I adore music (though I make it badly). I have nothing against a good party, the roar of the crowd. But I make a distinction between nourishment and gluttony: the first is a necessity, even a pleasure; the second, a symptom. Of what? In a word, fear. One of the unanticipated side effects of connectedness. Perhaps because it's never enough, or because, having immersed ourselves in the age of mediation (as Bill Gates refers to it), accustomed ourselves to its ways and means, we sense our dependency. Or because, finally, like isolated apartment dwellers running the TV for company, we sense a deeper isolation beneath the babble of voices, the poverty of our communications. So, adaptable to a fault, we embrace this brave new cacophony, attuned, like apprentice ornithologists, to the distinguishing calls of a mechanical phylum. Capable of differentiating between the cheeps and chimes of the cell phones, portable phones, baby monitors, pagers, scanners, personal digital assistants, laptop computers, car alarms, and so on that fill our lives, we've grown adept, at the same time, at blocking them out with sounds of our own, at forcing a privacy where none exists.

At the supermarket, a middle-aged man in a well-cut suit is calling someone a bitch on the phone. Unable to get to the ricotta cheese, I wait, vaguely uncomfortable, feeling as though I'm eavesdropping. At the gym, the beeps of computerized treadmills clash with the phones at the front desk, the announcements of upcoming discounts, the disco version of Gordon Lightfoot's "If You Could Read My Mind." A number of individuals in Walkman earphones, unaware that they've begun to sing, bellow and moan like the deaf.

"I love a wide margin to my life," Thoreau remarked, quaintly, referring to the space—the silence—requisite for contemplation, or, more quaintly, the forming of a self. A century and a half later, aural text covers the psychic page, spills over; the margin is gone. Walking to work, we pass over rumbling pipes and humming cables, beneath airplane flight corridors and satellite broadcasts, through radio and television transmissions whose sounds, reconstituted from binary code, mix and mingle, overlap and clash, and everywhere drifts the aural refuse of our age.

Thus may the stuff between the discordant notes of our lives require—and I'm not unaware of the irony here—a few words in its defense. Begin anywhere. The cottage in which I spend my summers is silent yet full of sound: the rainy hush of wind in the oaks, the scrabble of a hickory nut rolling down the roof, the slurp of the dog in the next room, interminably licking himself . . . I've never known perfect silence. I hope to avoid making its acquaintance for some time to come, yet I court it daily.

My ambivalence toward silence is natural enough: the grave, the scythe, the frozen clock, all the piled symbols of death, reinforce an essential truth, a primal fear: beneath the sloping hood, death is voiceless. Silence spits us out and engulfs us again, one and all, and all the noisemakers on Bourbon Street, all the clattering figurines in Cuernavaca can't undo the unpleasant fact that *el día*, properly understood, always ends in *la muerte*, that quiet, like a pair of great parentheses around a dependent clause, closes off our days. Sorry.

But if it's true that all symphonies end in silence, it's equally true that they begin there as well. Silence, after all, both buries and births us, and just as life without the counterweight of mortality would mean nothing, so silence alone, by offering itself as the eternal Other, makes our music possible. The image of Beethoven composing against the growing void, like all clichés, illuminates a common truth: fear forces our hand, inspires us, makes visible the things we love.

But wait. Does this mean that all is well? That the pendulum swings, the chorus turns in stately strophe and antistrophe, the buds of May routinely answer winter's dark aphelion? Not quite. We are right to be afraid of silence, to resist that sucking vacuum—however much we depend on it—to claw and scratch against oblivion. The battle is in deadly earnest. And therein lies the joke. Resistance is one thing, victory another.

Left partially deaf by a childhood inflammation of the mastoid bones, Thomas Edison throughout his life embraced the world of silence, reveled in its space, allowed it to empower him; as much as any man, perhaps, he recognized silence as the territory of inspiration and cultivated its gifts. Deafness, his biographers agree, acted like an auditory veil, separating him from the world's distractions, allowing him to attend to what he called his business: thinking.

I mention these facts, however, not for the small and obvious irony that a man so indebted to silence should do more than any other to fill the world with noise—but to set the context for a scene I find strangely compelling. In June 1911, hard at work on what would eventually become the disk phonograph, Edison hired a pianist to play for him (as loudly as possible) the world's entire repertoire of waltzes. And there, in the salon at Glenmont, either out of frustration at not being able to hear the music to his satisfaction or, as I'd like to believe, out of sudden desperate love for the thing he'd missed (as charged as any of love's first fumblings), the sixty-four-year-old Edison got on his hands and knees and bit into the piano's wood, the better to hear its vibrations. Will Edison's fate be our own? Afloat in the river of sound loosed upon the world by Edison's inventions, having drunk from it until our ears ring, we now risk a similar thirst.

Tacked to the wall above my desk, staring out from a page torn from the back of *The New York Times Magazine*, are the faces of seventeen men and women whose portraits were taken by KGB photographers more than half a century ago, then filed, along with hundreds of thousands like them, in the top-secret dossiers of Stalin's secret police. Over the years, I've come to know the faces in these photographs nearly as well as I know those of the living. I study them often—the woman at the left whose graying hair has begun to loosen, the beautiful young man at the right, the fading lieutenant at the bottom corner whose cheeks, I suspect, had the same roughness and warmth as my father's—because each and every one of them, within hours of having his or her picture taken, was driven to a forest south of Moscow and executed; because all, or nearly all, knew their fate at the time their pictures were taken; and because, finally, having inherited a good dose of Slavic morbidity (and sentimentalism), I couldn't bear to compound the silence of all of those lives unlived by returning them—mothers and fathers, sons and lovers—to the oblivion of yet another archive, the purgatory of microfiche. On my wall, in some small measure, they are not forgotten; they have a voice.

Today, as the panopticon reveals to us, as never before, the agony of our species, the lesson is repeated daily. We read it in the skulls of Srebrenica, growing out of the soil, in the open mouths of the dead from Guatemala to the Thai-Cambodian border, whose characteristic posture—head back, neck arched—seems almost a universal language: the harvest of dictatorship, properly understood, is not death, but silence. Mr. Pinochet's "los desaparecidos" (like Slobodan Milosevic's, or Heinrich Himmler's), are really "los callados" (the silenced), the snuffing of their voices only the last, most brutal expression of a system dependent on silence as a tool of repression. The enforced quiet of censorship and propaganda, of burning pages and jammed frequencies, is different from the gun to the temple only in degree, not in kind.

mark slouka • 43

And yet who could deny that silence, though both the means and end of totalitarian repression, is also its natural enemy? That silence, the habitat of the imagination, not only allows us to grow the spore of identity but, multiplied a millionfold, creates the rich loam in which a genuine democracy thrives. In the silence of our own minds, in the quiet margins of the text, we are made different from one another as well as able to understand others' differences from us.

In the famous John Cage composition *4' 33"*, the pianist walks on stage, bows, flips the tail of his tuxedo, and seats himself at the piano. Taking a stopwatch out of his vest pocket, he presses the start button then stares at the keys for precisely four minutes and thirty-three seconds. When the time is up, he closes the piano and leaves the stage.

Nearly half a century after it was first performed, *4' 33"* rightly strikes us as hackneyed and worn, a postmodern cliché intent on blurring a line (between art and non-art, order and disorder, formal structure and random influence) that has long since been erased. As simple theater, however, it still has power. Cage's portrait of the artist frozen before his medium, intensely aware of his allotted time, unable to draw a shape out of the universe of possibilities, carries a certain allegorical charge, because we recognize in its symbolism—so apparently childlike, so starkly Manichaean—a lesson worthy of Euripedes: art, whatever its medium, attempts to force a wedge beneath the closed lid of the world, and fails; the artist, in his or her minutes and seconds, attempts to say—to paint, to carve; in sum, to communicate—what ultimately cannot be communicated. In the end, the wedge breaks; the lid stays shut. The artist looks at his watch and leaves the stage, his "success" measurable only by the relative depth of his failure. Too bad. There are worse things.

But if silence is the enemy of art, it is also its motivation and medium: the greatest works not only draw on silence for inspiration but use it, flirt with it, turn it, for a time, against itself. To succeed at all, in other words, art must partake of its opposite, suggest its own dissolution. Examples are legion: once attuned to the music of absence, the eloquence of omission or restraint, one hears it everywhere—in the sudden vertiginous stop of an Elizabeth Bishop poem; in the space between souls in an Edward Hopper painting; in Satchmo's mastery of the wide margins when singing "I'm Just a Lucky So and So." In the final paragraph of Frank O'Connor's small masterpiece "Guests of the Nation," an Irish soldier recalls looking over patch of bog containing the graves of two British soldiers he's just been forced to execute, and observes, simply, "And anything that happened to me afterwards, I never felt the same about again." Such a black hole of a line, dense with rejected possibilities, merciless in its willingness to sacrifice everything for a quick stab at truth.

"Silence," wrote Melville, only five years before withdrawing from writing more or less for good, "is the only Voice of our God." The assertion, like its subject, cuts both ways, negating and affirming, implying both absence and presence, offering us a choice; it's a line that the Society of American Atheists could put on its letterhead and the Society of Friends could silently endorse while waiting to be moved by the spirit to speak. What makes the line particularly notable, however, is that it appears in *Pierre, or, the Ambiguities*, a novel that, perhaps more than any other in American literature, calls attention to its own silences, its fragility. Offering us a hero who is both American Christ and Holy Fool, martyr and murderer, writer and subject, Melville propels him toward his death with such abandon, with such a feel for what Thomas Mann would one day call "the voluptuousness of doom," that even his language gets caught in the vortex: in one particularly eerie passage we watch the same sentence, repeated four times, pruned of adverbs, conjunctions, dependent clauses, until it very nearly disappears before our eyes.

There's nothing safe about this brinksmanship, nothing of the deconstructionists' empty posturings. "He can neither believe," Hawthorne wrote, "nor be comfortable in his unbelief." Melville had simply allowed his doubts to bleed into his art. As they will. Having "pretty much made up his mind to be annihilated," he quite naturally took his writing with him.

Reading *Pierre* is an uncomfortable business, akin to watching an artist painstakingly put the finishing touches on his own epitaph. One naturally hopes for a slightly more redemptive vision, a vision that shifts the stress from the inevitability of doom and the triumph of silence to the creative energy these release to the living. Within Melville's own work, we don't have far to look. In *Moby Dick*, the book he wrote just before *Pierre*, Melville also engineered an apocalypse yet managed to remain far enough away to avoid its pull, to save something, to offer us a metaphor that captures perfectly the tensions essential to our work and our lives. Something survives the *Pequod*'s sinking; though silence may reign over the waters, the vortex eventually slows. The coffin bursts to the surface. And on that coffin are the hieroglyphics of our art.

If one of the characteristics of capitalism is that it tends to shut down options, narrow the margins, then perhaps what we are seeing these days is one of the side effects of the so-called free market: most of the noises we hear are the noises of buying and selling. Even the communication between individuals has been harnessed to the technologies that make them possible: to be deprived of the fax machine, the cell phone, the TV, the pager, etc., is to be relegated to silence. Communication, having been narrowed into whatever can be squeezed into binary code, has been redefined by the marketplace into a commodity itself.

Yet capitalism, we know, always tries to feed the hungers it creates, to confect its own antidotes—so long as the price is right. As the vast silences of the republic are paved over by designer outlets and shopping malls, a kind of island ecosystem remains, self-conscious in its fragility, barely viable. The proof is detectable in any upscale travel magazine: there you will find exclusive spas advertising the promise of silence—no pagers, no cell phones, just the sounds of lake water lapping—as though silence were a rare Chardonnay or an exclusive bit of scenery, which, of course, is precisely what it now is.

That silence, like solitude, is now a commodity should not surprise us. Money buys space, and space buys silence; decibels and dollars are inversely proportional. Lacking money, I've lived with noise—with the sounds of fucking and feuding in the airshaft, MTV and Maury Povitch coming through the walls, in apartments with ceilings so thin I could hear the click of a clothes hanger placed on a rod or the lusty stream of an upstairs neighbor urinating after a long night out. I've accepted this, if not gracefully at least with a measure of resignation. The great advantage that money confers, I now realize, is not silence per se but the *option* of silence, the privilege of choosing one's own music, of shutting out the seventeen-year-old whose boombox nightly rattles my panes.

But if the ability to engineer one's own silence has been one of the age-old prerogatives of wealth, it's also true that the rapidly changing aural landscape of the late twentieth century has raised the status (and value) of silence enormously. As the world of the made, to recall e. e. cummings, replaces the world of the born, as the small sounds of fields at dusk or babies crying in the next apartment are erased by the noise of traffic and Oprah, as even our few remaining bits of wilderness are pressed thin and flat beneath satellite transmissions, Forest Service bulldozers, and airplane flight corridors, we grow sentimental for what little has escaped us and automatically reach for our wallets. Like a telltale lesion that appears only on those who are desperately ill, value—even outrageous value— often blossoms on things just before they leave us, and if the analogy is an ugly one, it is also appropriate; the sudden spasm of love for the thing we're killing, after all, is as obscene as it is human. As we continue to pave the world with sound, we will continue to crave what little silence escapes us, an emptiness made audible by its disappearance.

# 9

# Rough Music, Futurism, and Postpunk Industrial Noise Bands

## MARY RUSSO AND DANIEL WARNER

Mary Russo (1944– ) teaches comparative literature and critical theory at Hampshire College and is the author of *The Female Grotesque: Risk, Excess, and Modernity.* Composer and theorist Daniel Warner (1954– ) teaches music and sound art at Hampshire College. His electronic compositions have appeared on the Neuma and Open Space labels; his multimedia installations have been exhibited in the U.S. and Europe; and his writing has been published in *Perspectives of New Music* and *DisCourse.* In this article, Russo and Warner chart the social history of noise from the charivari in early modern Europe to postpunk industrial music. Drawing on the work of Russolo, Attali, Claude Lévi-Strauss, and Michel Serres, they show that "noise" is a complex and ambiguous social category that is constantly being renegotiated.

A number of boys attended with shovels, playing the rough music. (1770)

—*O.E.D.* ("Rough Music")

Poor Nixon . . . had been more than once rough-musicked by his neighbours. (1847)

—*O.E.D.* ("Rough Music")

Rough music is the name given in England for the practice of noisy, masked demonstrations which were usually held at the residence of some wrongdoer in the community. From the very rich historical materials on carnival and the carnivalesque in early modern Europe, including the historical work of scholars such as E. P. Thompson and Natalie Davis, one gathers that these demonstrations involved the banging of sauce pans, frying pans, kettles, the rattling of bones and cleavers, bell-ringing, hooting, blowing bull's horns, and generally "playing" any other possible utensils gathered from the kitchen and barnyard in the interest of creating a tremendous and, to the object of these serenades which lasted for days, very embarrassing din.[1]

Participants in these "music groups," which lasted well into the nineteenth century, were most often young men—bachelors or *célibataires*—temporarily granted a power of rule over the everyday affairs of the community.[2] Although it appears, especially in England, that other members of the community sanctioned the demonstrations and were occasionally present, "it was the young men who took the initiative."[3] Pretexts for rough music varied, but they most often involved issues of sexuality, reproduction, and domestic hierarchy. In early modern France, as Natalie Davis notes, charivari or rough music was typically directed at socially problematic couples: young couples who had failed to produce children, partners in second marriages with gross disparity in age, and, on occasion, couples of disparate size. Henpecked or complacent husbands who permitted their wives to dominate them either physically or morally (as in repeated or tolerated adulteries) were a favorite target for the boys in the band [. . . .]

**Noise**

> Noise comes out of the black box. Noise and shivarees . . . I am afraid of the grating noise, of stridulation, of the shivaree.
>
> —Michel Serres[4]

> It is impossible to object that noise is always loud and disagreeable to the ear.
>
> —Luigi Russolo, *The Art of Noises* (1913)[5]

A general theory of noise can be derived from information theory. In the classical textbook definition, noise is "any undesirable signal in the transmission of a message."[6]

> . . . shocks, crackling, and atmospherics are noises in a radio transmission. A white or black spot on a television screen, a gray fog, some dashes not belonging to the transmitted message, a colored spot of ink on a newspaper, a tear in a page of a book, a colored spot on a picture are "noises" in visual messages. A rumor without foundation is a "noise" in a sociological message.[7]

[Jacques] Attali and also Dick Hebdige, whose important work on punk music as subculture is otherwise more specific, simply expand the range of this definition to cover virtually any cultural channel.[8] Thus, music, modes of speech, modes of dress, certain discourses, indeed anything could be noisy in a particular context: "there is no absolute structural difference between noise and signal. The only difference which can be logically established between them is based exclusively on the concept of intent on the part of the transmitter. *A noise is a signal the sender does not want to transmit.*"[9] And what if the sender wants to transmit a deliberately noisy signal, acoustical or otherwise? Expanding the limits of an intentional model, information theory moves to a definition based on cultural reception, one that is both well-formed scientifically and inadvertently useful for our purposes: "*A noise is a sound we do not want to hear. It is a signal we do not want to receive, one we try to eliminate.*"[10] If this larger sense of "cultural noise" is uninteresting to information theorists, it nonetheless grounds the entire scientific discourse of information theory.

Attali, attempting to theorize *through* music, uses the concept of noise most often as general, cultural noise. For example, he suggests that "the transition from the Greek and medieval scales to the tempered and modern scales can be interpreted as aggression against the dominant code by noise destined to become a new dominant code."[11] In attempting to theorize *about* music and cultural production, however, it is necessary to examine more closely the intersections in Western music between cultural "noise" and what we shall call *virtual acoustical noise*.

In direct contrast to information theory, Western musical discourse has as its foundation the notion of a structural difference between noise and signal. Western music's "noise" is virtual acoustical noise (the non-periodic vibrations of ambient or concrete sounds) and its "signals" are the tones (periodic vibrations of strings, air, vocal chords, etc.) of the tempered scale. This structural distinction with its clear bias toward the discrete, measurable pitch, and clean, clear production value (i.e., an absolute minimum of breath sounds, string "noise," etc.), along with its pretense of highly developed pitch systems (e.g., tonality, dodecaphony, and other serial techniques), is often the strategy with which Western music holds at arms length its "others"—jazz, world musics, rock, and folk musics.

This oppositional structural distinction breaks down quickly, however, under psychoacoustic scrutiny. Psychoacoustics is a discourse which has only recently begun to find its way into musical activities, primarily in computer music synthesis and timbral theory (sound "color"). Nonetheless, noise is, and always has been, inscribed in all sound and music. In fact, noise plays a primary role in the perception of virtually every musical sound. Noise components at the beginning of musical instrument tones (usually no longer than a few milliseconds in duration), referred to as *attack transients*, very often provide the primary perceptual cues for aural identification. Without these noise components it is virtually impossible for a listener to differentiate between, for instance, a clarinet and piano tone sounding at the same frequency, because their pitched or "steady-state" portions (comprising most of all instrumental tone's duration) happen to be timbrally similar. In fact, no acoustic instrument or concrete sound is actually a "pure tone." It is possible to electronically produce pure pitch (sine wave) or pure noise (white noise). But aside from these two esoteric exceptions, the entire sound world is one in which periodic and non-periodic vibrations intermingle in an endless variety of ways.

So, to a large extent, a culture's musical conventions are a set of aural negotiations between signal and noise. In the most current scientific definition of virtual noise, noise is a constitutive element of signal (in music, a discrete, quantified pitch). It props up the notion of signal. That any opposition between noise and signal is scientifically untenable deepens, but never completely buries, the ideological resonance of information theory's concept of noise: Western music and musical discourse must admit together the asymmetrical propositions: 1) that noise is present in every musical signal and, 2) that noise is a signal we do not want to hear. The advantage of this inelegant definition is that together it exposes the covert claims of Western music as both universal and exclusive. This is a noisy definition—ideology is made of such noise.

The lesser known proposition that noise and signal are untenable distinctions was proclaimed dramatically in 1913 by Luigi Russolo in *The Art of Noises* and embodied in his fantastic noise-intoning machine. Although the "scientific" claims of his project and the genealogy of modernism which appropriated it are somewhat speciously constructed, Russolo's non-oppositional model of noise and signal represented a radical intervention into Western music.

## Futurist Music

> Ancient life was all silence. In the nineteenth century, with the invention of machines, Noise was born.
>
> —Luigi Russolo

Luigi Russolo, one of the early and most enthusiastic young followers of Marinetti, was a signatory of many of the most audacious and interesting futurist manifestos. Russolo seems to have endorsed all the major principles of Marinetti's futurist program: radical and innovative interventions into the art forms; the glorification of the machine and the virile qualities of speed, volume, and power associated with it; the spectacularity of war; and the eternal exuberance of youth and cultural revolution. The old, the traditional, and the feminine were relegated to the "silence of the ancient world"; modernity in Futurist terms was noisy. The futurist project included not only the much-quoted manifestos (many of which were declaimed from theater stages), but their enactment in and intrusion into various political scenarios, transforming and aestheticizing the tumultuous activities of modern life [. . . .][12]

To bring art to life and life to art involved the futurist in a reform of the institution of art and music making and a rereading of experience as sonic performance. In both the *Manifesto of Futurist Music* written in 1911 by Balilla Pratella, a respected and relatively conservative composer, and in Russolo's *The Art of Noises,* written two years later, the displacement of musical contexts and institutions was demanded. Pratella had in many ways set the stage for "noise music." His *Manifesto of Futurist Music* railed against the institutions of music, urging young musicians to "desert schools, conservatories and musical academies" ("hotbeds of impotence"), to pursue "free study," to avoid musical competitions, and to destroy the "prejudice for 'well-made' music."[13] Russolo's theory and practice of composition advanced much further than his predecessor, as one of the first twentieth century artists to build upon his own unprofessionalism, suggesting that the cultural codes of creativity and the very status of "artist" and "musician" had to be demystified if radical innovation in art forms was to become a possibility. In *The Art of Noises* which he addresses to Balilla Pratella, he evokes his amateur status as if it were an impeccable credential: "unconcerned by my apparent incompetence and convinced that daring possesses every right and can open every door, I have been able to imagine the great renewal of music by means of the Art of Noises" [. . . .]

It would seem, though, that Russolo's ideas were not strong enough to stem the tide of musical modernism which still carried with it very traditional notions of composition and performance practice. For Pratella, much like Varèse and later composers of *musique concrète*, the musical implication of Russolo's work was that manufactured noise would fit into known "musical" contexts: "Their *timbre* does not unite itself with the other *sonorous elements* like heterogeneous material, but unites itself as a new *sonorous, emotive,* and essentially *musical element*."[14] No sooner did Russolo invent the noise machine than Pratella and other composers strove to purge it of its heterogeneity.

## Noise and Modernist Music

> A composer who hears sounds will try to find a notation for sounds. One who has ideas will find one that expresses his ideas, leaving their interpretation free, in confidence that his ideas have been accurately and concisely notated.
>
> —Cornelius Cardew[15]

It is worth noting that the futurist manifestos of music prefigure, in an important way, much of the ideas and compositional activity of the experimental music of the 1960s in the music of Cornelius Cardew, John Cage, and others. *Ideas* are the key to this prefiguration, for it was not until then that the musical score began to lose its status as a virtual text which merely stored traditional "musical thought." With the advent of performance pieces, process music, and electronic systems, the score becomes discursive, much in the same way that Pratella's and Russolo's manifestos and machines, not simply their music, *are* the musical discourse.[16] Nonetheless, the most radical futurist musical ideas have been elided by musicology which has placed emphasis on later "legitimate" composers whose work is said to be influenced by the work of Russolo and Pratella [. . . .]

Clearly, much of the experimental music of the sixties, particularly the music of Cage, called many of these Western musical conventions into contention, due in part to the work of the futurists. For the purposes of this study it is worthwhile noting that in much of the work of Cage and other experimental composers two qualities are evident: 1) noise and signal are treated as noncanonical and can stand in for each other through a kind of Duchampian "aesthetic indifference," and 2) traditional modes of musical expertise and presentation persist (some notable exceptions are the work of The Scratch Orchestra, AMM, Musica Elettronica Viva, and the work of J. K. Randall and Benjamin Boretz).

Varèse's notions of musical timbre were remarkable in that pitched and non-pitched (i.e., noise) elements gradually do gain parity in his music. This feature is probably the most important intersection between the futurists and Varèse. Although his music, too, calls many musical conventions into question, Varèse's use of noise is contained by rather traditional notions of musical contexts (as one would expect given his historical positioning), particularly on the inter-note level. That is to say that their attack and decay patterns are molded into relatively traditional musical time-shapes modeled after those produced by acoustic instruments ("poeticized" as his biographer would have it). This suggests, not so much a non-canonical treatment of noise, but an attempt to "clean up" noise, to make it musically respectable.

## Noisy Boys: Postpunk Industrial Music

Hearing is our heroic opening to trouble and diffusion.

—Michel Serres[17]

Listen with pain. Hear with pain. Ears are wounds.

—"Schmerzen Hören," Einstürzende Neubauten[18]

Punk rock, usually associated with the appearance of the Sex Pistols on the London music scene in 1976, was fast, loud, and transgressive. Coming as it did during a rather prosaic phase of pop music, punk had the mark of authenticity—it was noisy, literally and figuratively. Malcolm McLaren, manager of the Sex Pistols, claimed that punk was a radical working class music, a line echoed in the British rock press.[19] In fact, much punk music and culture emanated from working class districts and neighborhoods in England and from the "Rust Belt" in the United States. It was never exclusively so, and to the limited extent it contained an incipient class politics, "working class" was increasingly in that period the "unworking class," the "disoccupied," the marginal left-overs of late capitalism. Punk music sounds rough, harsh, and angry; visually it signals nothing so much as overproduction—a world of junk. Noise and junk. The dilemma of interpreting punk as emblematic of a structural shift in late capitalism revolves around the alternatives of seeing it as a playful, imaginative, and subversive response to a glutted and implosive political economy, or its in expression of pain, loss, and ambiguity [. . . .]

What began as a spectacular assault on "musical" technique during the heyday of punk rock becomes a clearly defined do-it-yourself rhetoric in new wave music: "This is a chord. This is another. This is a third. *Now form a band.*"[20] This do-it-yourself aspect extends both to a kind of virtuosic amateurism among the musicians, and to the modes of music production itself.

It may be the case that this return to earlier production modes is merely nostalgic, a new kind of musical populism, because this activity is primarily centered on the record making process itself (recording, pressing, packaging, distribution, etc.). But while most punk and new wave music moves, even if obliquely, to become a rock and roll commodity, there are a few interesting moments when the musical object itself may be changed, recursions when alternative production values have become inscribed in the creative process itself.[21]

The work of Einstürzende Neubauten (Collapsing New Buildings), one of the so-called industrial bands, is indicative of how these alternative values can generate new modes of music making and new social textualizations of music. Like "rough musicians," these noise artists are said to visit scrapyards in the cities in which they perform to collect sound-making objects. Thus, each performance is characterized by different sounds of industrial refuse (automobile springs, huge pieces of sheet metal, empty oil drums, etc.), all of which is amplified and then played as if they were percussion instruments. The occasional use of traditional electric instruments and texts does give this group the appearance, at least, of a rock band.

Much industrial music incorporates found musical objects, automatic, mechanical, and electronic systems for generating music. The processes by which this material is assembled are communal. The sound making is characterized by non-competent competence.[22] Industrial music builds upon the failure of punk to withstand the commercial pressures of the pop music industry. Jon Savage writes that punk's style had become "a pose, window-dressing for packaging and consumption through the usual commercial channels" and suggests that what was needed was "an even more comprehensive investigation of capitalism's decay."[23] Incorporating the shock tactics of punk and the do-it-yourself rhetoric of new wave music, industrial music is an even noisier resistance to mainstream pop culture. When one encounters musical formations "playing", as guerrilla musicians, on air conditioning ducts, freeway underpasses (Einstürzende Neubauten), utilizing complex tape-loops and transforming metal refuse into meditative gamelan-like sound worlds (23 Skidoo), or making direct political statements layered over bits and pieces of industrial sounds in a dance beat (Test Department), it suggests that, momentarily at least, new social textualizations of music are possible in pop music, an industry which has been moving increasingly towards over-produced, empty musical surfaces.

[. . . .] In *The Raw and the Cooked,* Claude Lévi-Strauss meditates on noise as a dangerous negotiation of structural polarities.[24] Two kinds of stories from Bororo, Apinaye, and Timbira myth recount the ordeal of failed heroes. In one myth, the hero is sent to steal three sound-making objects: two rattles and a string of bells. He *makes* noise and is punished. In the other myth, the hero is instructed to respond to only certain noises. He *hears* too many noises and, crossing the acoustic threshold, he too is punished. For Lévi-Strauss, noise is a question of life and death, "a function of man's inability to define himself, unambiguously, in relation to silence and noise."[25]

Noise, as we have described it, is a differential. There is no absolute state of noise, nor is there foreseeably (*pace* Habermas) a noise-free state of music, of communication and information, of life. Noise is not that which escapes or is prior, but is the mark of entry. Noise is ambiguity: it is not meaningless or without social contents and hierarchies (the band). Noise is cruel. Noise is not, as information theorists would have it, a signal that *we* do not want to hear. It is it signal that *someone* does not want to hear. Noise is pain. Schmerzen Hören.

## NOTES

1. E. P. Thompson, "Rough Music; Le charivari anglais," *Annales* 20 (1972): 295–312; Natalie Davis, "The Reasons of Misrule," *Society and Culture in Early Modern France* (Stanford: Stanford UP, 1975), 97–124.

2. Natalie Davis traces these groups of unmarried men or "youth-abbeys"—as they sometimes called themselves—from the twelfth century throughout France and sees in their activities a rigor and organization which parodied ruling structures. Like Mikhail Bahktin and Victor Turner she sees in these and other festive or carnivalesque activities the possibility of social transformation. For an excellent treatment of the carnivalesque as transgression, see Peter Stallybrass and Allon White, *The Politics and Poetics of Transgression* (Ithaca: Cornell UP, 1986).

3. Davis, 106.

4. Michel Serres, "Noises," *The Parasite,* trans. Lawrence R. Schehr (Baltimore: The Johns Hopkins UP, 1982), 123, 125.

5. Luigi Russolo, "The Art of Noises" [for all quotations from Russolo, see chap. 2, above—Eds.].

6. Abraham Moles, *Information Theory and Esthetic Perception,* trans. Joel E. Cohen (Urbana: U. of Illinois Press, 1968), 78.

7. Moles, 78.

8. See Dick Hebdige, *Subculture: The Meaning of Style* (London: Methuen, 1979).

9. Moles, 78–79.

10. Moles, 79.

11. Jacques Attali, *Noise: The Political Economy of Music,* trans. Brian Massumi (Minneapolis: U. of Minnesota Press, 1985), 34.

12. For a general introduction to futurism, see Angelo Bozzolla and Caroline Tisdall, *Futurism* (New York: Oxford UP, 1978), Michael Kirby, *Futurist Performance* (New York: Dutton, 1971), and Pontus Hulten, ed., *Futurism & Futurisms* (New York: Abbeville Press, 1986).

13. U. Apollonio, *Futurist Manifestos* (London: Thames-Hudson, 1973), 33–37.

14. Franceso Pratella, "The *Intonarumori* in the Orchestra," in *Futurist Performance,* ed. Michael Kirby (New York: Dutton, 1971), 193.

15. Quoted in Michael Nyman, *Experimental Music* (New York: Schirmer Books, 1974), 3.

16. Duchamp's work is similar in this regard. His "Green Box" of 1934 is not a curatorial "catalog" for the "Large Glass" but a kind of parallel discourse to the object itself.

17. Serres, 126.

18. Einstürzende Neubauten, "Schmerzen Hören," *Strategies Against Architecture,* Homestead Records HMS 063, 1983. [Reissued on CD as *Strategies Against Architecture, Vol. 1,* Mute CDSTUMM14].

19. See John Street, *Rebel Rock* (New York: Basil Blackwell, 1986), 84–88, for an analysis of the promotion of punk by record companies and the rock press in Britain.

20. Text from a punk rock magazine quoted in Iain Chambers, *Urban Rhythms: Pop Music and Popular Culture* (New York: St. Martin's Press, 1985), 177.

21. See Roland Barthes, "The Grain of the Voice," *Image-Music-Text,* trans. Stephen Heath (New York: Hill and Wang, 1977), 179–89.

22. For suggestions about new musical consumption, see Attali, 140–48.

23. Jon Savage, introduction, *Industrial Culture Handbook,* ed. V. Vale and Andrea Juno (San Francisco: Re/Search Publications, 1983), 4.

24. Claude Lévi-Strauss, *The Raw and the Cooked,* trans. John and Doreen Weightman (New York: Harper and Row, 1969), 147–49.

25. Lévi-Strauss, 149.

# 10

## *Noise*

### SIMON REYNOLDS

Simon Reynolds (1963– ; see also chap. 52) is among the most insightful and wide-ranging of contemporary pop music critics and theorists. A contributing writer at *SPIN*, his articles have appeared in *The Wire, Artforum*, the *Village Voice, Rolling Stone, The New York Times*, and other magazines. He is the author of two books, *Blissed Out: The Raptures of Rock* (1990) and *Generation Ecstasy: Into the World of Techno and Rave Culture* (1998), and co-author of another, *The Sex Revolts: Gender, Rebellion, and Rock 'n' Roll* (1995). The following excerpt from *Blissed Out* examines the discourse of "noise" in rock. It exposes and criticizes the latent presuppositions of rock's affirmations of noise; and it proposes an alternative conception of noise that Reynolds would later find exemplified by Techno and rave culture.

[. . . .] Such a satisfying idea—noise annoys—at once simple-to-grasp kernel and yet capable of inflation into the most grandiose theories of subversion. But . . . who is there to be annoyed, and in what ways? What is noise anyway?

### Noise/Horror

If music is like a language, if it communicates some kind of emotional or spiritual message, then noise is best defined as interference, something which blocks transmission, jams the code, prevents sense being made. The subliminal message of most music is that the universe is essentially benign, that if there is sadness or tragedy, this is resolved at the level of some higher harmony. Noise troubles this worldview. This is why noise groups invariably deal with subject matter that is anti-humanist—extremes of abjection, obsession, trauma, atrocity, possession—all of which undermine humanism's confidence that through individual consciousness and will, we can become the subjects of our lives, and work together for the general progress of the commonwealth.

This dark, unmanageable matter of horror and sickness is a kind of cultural noise, causing a blockage and destabilization of the codes by which we make sense of the world, make life habitable.

Noise then, occurs when language breaks down. Noise is a wordless state in which the very constitution of our selves is in jeopardy. The pleasure of noise lies in the fact that the obliteration of meaning and identity is ecstasy (literally, being out-of-oneself).

Historically, what has happened is that the rock vanguard has shifted its focus from eroticism to the psychedelic powers of horror. When sex was a scarce, invisible, unattainable quantity, to sing about it was publicly transgressive and personally mindblowing (because unthinkable). But after the permission of the seventies, when sex was banalized by becoming available, it could no longer be the instigator of desperation (it's that state of mind that is indispensable to rock, not physical fun). The site, the cue, for jouissance, shifted to the unspeakable [. . . .]

## Stop Making Sense

The problem is that, to speak of noise, to give it attributes, to claim things for it, is immediately to shackle it with meaning again, to make it part of culture. If noise is where language ceases, then to describe it is to imprison it again with adjectives. To confer the status of value upon excess and extremism is to bring these things back within the pale of decency. So the rhetoricians of noise actually destroy the power they strive to celebrate; they are the very start of the process by which subversion is turned into contribution, which is absorbed as a renewal for the system. As rhetoric enfolds a group or initiative, so fibres of meaning interpenetrate every strand of sound, ensuring that the experience reaches us already placed in a general scheme of significance [. . . .] We are constantly made conscious. However sick, vile and depraved the material may be, nothing can prevent an aura of moral and spiritual superiority from entwining the latest noise/horror collision, like a halo.

Here are some examples of noise overdetermined by meaning.

*Noise as reality effect*:

There is a widely held view that beauty and harmony are a lie, presenting a bourgeois vision of nature and society as fundamentally balanced and ordered. And that we have an obligation to listen to noise because it shows us the grim truth of reality [. . . .]

*Noise as anti-pop gesture*:

With the death of the parochial, the media now constitutes our new environment. Pop looms as the largest thing in our lives, but as something we've lost control of. Rock'n'roll was originally a revolt against straitlaced stuffy mores (encountered in the family, at school, in the small town); but now it's "brainwashing media images and fantasies," the very institution of pop itself, that we define ourselves against [. . . .] Oblivion is forestalled because we are constantly made conscious that this is a reaction *against*. [Yet] anti-pop doesn't challenge its listeners, as it purports to, it flatters them.

## The Subversive Fallacy

Both the above viewpoints represent noise as subversive. There seems to be a need to maintain the belief that "straights," grown-ups would be shocked, damaged, altered, if they were around to hear the music. But the blindingly obvious fact is that no one is around to be disturbed. The fiction that "the enemy" occupies the same space as our noisemaking seems integral to the pleasure people derive from noise, the significance they confer [. . . .]

But the whole discourse of noise-as-threat is bankrupt, positively inimical to the remnants of power that still cling to noise. Forget subversion. The point is self-subversion, overthrowing the power structure in your own head. The enemy is the mind's tendency to systematize, sew up experience, place a distance between itself and immediacy [. . . .]

The goal is OBLIVION (a.k.a. jouissance, the sublime, the ineffable) [. . . .]

## Out-Of-Your-Head-Is-The-Place-To-Be

[. . . .] Noise is about fascination, the antithesis of meaning. If music is a language, communicating moods and feelings, then noise is like an eruption within the material out of which language is shaped. We are arrested, fascinated, by a convulsion of sound to which we are unable to assign a meaning. We are mesmerized by the materiality of music. This is why noise and horror go hand in hand—because madness and violence are senseless and arbitrary (violence is the refusal to argue), and the only response is wordless—to scream.

## A Dead End

The problem is that, as with any drug or intoxicant, tolerance builds up rapidly. The result is an exponential curve of increased dosages of noise/horror, an upward spiral that will one day, sooner than later, culminate in SEIZURE. As the barriers in the head get broken down, the noise buff becomes a kind of hip vegetable, by a process that paradoxically combines both brutalization and weakening. To be shocked (i.e. get your hit) requires that the individual be immersed to some degree in a culture or value system. But noise hipsters have uprooted themselves so successfully from their parent culture, they can cope with absurd levels of outrage/dissonance, and therefore require extreme after extreme in order to feel stimulated/mindblown. Burnout approaches.

The noise/horror aesthetic has driven itself into a dead(ening) end. A sublime, monumental dead end, that has produced some brilliant sado-masochist poetry from band and critic alike. But a dead end nonetheless. Here are some clues to THE WAY OUT.

## Inconsistency

Too often, noise has meant a level plane of abraded texture, which can merely add up to a different kind of blandness, a sense-dulling consistency. There needs to be more dips, swerves, lapses, use of space and architecture. HipHop is something the noise bands can learn from. The current HipHop aesthetic [. . .] is based around the forcing-into-friction of antagonistic ambiences and idioms, sampled from random points in pop history. The effect is psychedelic, dispersing consciousness as effectively as any pure din.

## Textural Luxury

The guitar is still privileged as the source of noise. There needs to be renewed awareness of the capacity of the synthesizer and sampling to produce filthy noxious tones. There needs to be a realization of how far rock noise trails behind the avant garde and new jazz. People have to attend to the possibilities for the human voice opened up by Diamanda Galas and Tim Buckley; listen again to Faust, Can, Hendrix, Sun Ra, Cabaret Voltaire, Suicide . . .

## The Voice

All this depends still on the assumption that noise is a state with defined boundaries. But if noise is the point at which language buckles and culture fails, then you could argue that noise occurs in moments, tiny breakages and stresses dispersed all over the surface of music, all kinds of music. Maybe we should listen out for the noise in the voices of Kristin Hersh, Tim Buckley, Prince, Michael Jackson—the way they chew and twist language not for any decipherable, expressive reason [. . .], but for the gratuitous voluptuousness of utterance itself. In their voices, you can hear a surplus of form over content, of genotext over phenotext, semiotic over symbolic, Barthes's "grain" (the resistance of the body to the voice) over technique. Of "telling" over "story" [. . . .]

## Dirtdish v. Unearth

There seem to be two choices in noise right now, two routes to oblivion. One is the noise/horror interface, in which violent imagery and musical dissonance are applied concussively, inducing a shell-shocked state of catatonia [. . . .] The alternative? [. . . .] Noise/horror undoes the self by confronting it with the other that dwells within it, the monstrous potential latent in us all, waiting to be catalysed by an extreme predicament; what I've called the new psychedelia undoes the self by letting it drift off and disappear into the otherwordly.

Noise/horror strikes me as a limited form of self-destruction, that can only yield diminishing returns. Compare its claustrophobic confines and concealed machismo with the open spaces and fragility of the new psychedelia [. . . .]

## Frost in Music

Both "strategies" are alike in one thing—they demand from the listener an immobility—one stunned, the other spellbound. Unlike the soulboys or decent songwriters, resistance does not take the form of becoming a subject, but through becoming an object. Refusing (at least in the domain of leisure) to deploy power over the self; to escape, for a few blissful moments, the network of meaning and concern.

# 11

# The Beauty of Noise: An Interview With Masami Akita of Merzbow

Merzbow is the recording name of sound artist Masami Akita (1956– ), the most well known of the Japanese noise artists that also includes Boredoms, Ruins, Fushitsusha, Masonna, and Melt Banana. The name Merzbow is taken from the *magnum opus* of German Dadaist Kurt Schwitters, who called his architectural installation the *Merzbau*. Inspired, on the one hand, by Dadaism, Surrealism, and Futurism, and, on the other hand, by the Japanese strain of sado-masochism exemplified by the writer Yukio Mishima, Merzbow has been continually fascinated by noise as both sonic detritus and vehicle for spiritual ecstasy. An astonishingly prolific artist, the Australian label Extreme recently released a 50-CD retrospective of Merzbow's vast output over his 20-year career. The following interview was conducted by Chad Hensley for *Seconds* Magazine.

**What first attracted you to Noise?**

I was influenced by aggressive blues rock guitar sounds like Jimi Hendrix, Lou Reed, Robert Fripp and fuzz organ sounds such as Mike Ratledge of Soft Machine. But the most structured Noise influence would have to be free jazz such as Albert Ayler, Cecil Taylor, and Frank Wright. I saw the Cecil Taylor Unit in 1973 and it was very influential. I was a drummer for a free-form rock band in the late '70s and I became very interested in the pulse beat of the drums within free jazz. I thought it was more aggressive than rock drums. I also became interested in electronic kinds of sounds. I started listening to more electro-acoustic music like Pierre Henry, Stockhausen, François Bayle, Gordon Mumma and Xenakis. Then I found the forum for mixing these influences into pure electronic noise. I was trying to create an extreme form of free music. In the beginning, I had a very conceptual mind set. I tried to quit using any instruments which related to, or were played by, the human body. It was then that I found tape. I tried to just be the operator of the tape machine—I'm glad that tape is a very anonymous media. My early live performances were very dis-human and dis-communicative. I was using a slide projector in a dark room at that point. I was concentrating on studio works until 1989 then I assembled some basic equipment before I started doing live Noise performances. Equipment included an audio mixer, contact mic, delay, distortion, ring modulator and bowed metal instruments. Basically, my main sound was created by mixer feedback. It was not until after 1990, on my first American tour, that I started performing live Noise Music for presentation to audiences. The first US tour was a turning point for finding a certain pleasure in using the body in the performance. Right now I'm using mixer feedback with filters, ring, DOD Buzz Box, DOD Meat Box, and a Korg multi-distortion unit. I am using more physically rooted Noise Music not as conceptually anti-instrument and anti-body as before. If music was sex, Merzbow would be pornography.

**In America, pornography is often viewed as vulgar and offensive—especially to women. Are you implying that Merzbow is for men?**

No. I mean that pornography is the unconsciousness of sex. So, Noise is the unconsciousness of music. It's completely misunderstood if Merzbow is music for men. Merzbow is not male or female. Merzbow is erotic like a car crash can be related to genital intercourse. The sound of Merzbow is like Orgone energy—the color of shiny silver.

**How did you get involved with tape trading through the mail in the early '80s?**

When I started Merzbow the idea was to make cheap cassettes which could also be fetish objects. I recorded them very cheaply and then packaged them with pornography. I got very involved with the mail art network which included home tapers like Maurizio Bianchi, Jupitter Larsen of Haters, and Trax of Italy. Just as Dadaist Kurt Schwitters made art from objects picked up off the street, I made sound from the scum that surrounds my life. I was very inspired by the Surrealist idea "Everything is Erotic, Everywhere Erotic." So, for me Noise is the most erotic form of sound. The word "noise" has been used in Western Europe since Luigi Russolo's *The Art of Noises*. However, industrial music used "noise" as a kind of technique. Western Noise is often too conceptual and academic. Japanese Noise relishes the ecstacy of sound itself.

**You have been quoted as saying, "There are no special images of ideology behind Merzbow"—unlike the early industrialists such as Throbbing Gristle, SPK, and Whitehouse that used shocking imagery. Yet you have repeatedly used pornography. Isn't pornography a shocking image that creates a certain ideology, whether intended or not?**

I have two directions in the use of pornography. In my early cassettes and mail art projects I used lots of pornography. I made many collages using pornography as it was a very important item in my mail art/mail music. I thought my cheap Noise cassettes were of the same value as cheap mail order pornography. These activities were called "Pornoise." In this direction, I would say that I used pornography for its anti-social, cut-up value in information theory. I soon started to release Merzbow vinyl which was very different from the cassettes of this same time period. I think my vinyl works concentrated more on sound itself because I think vinyl is a more static medium. So, Merzbow went in two separate directions in the '80s—a cassette direction and a vinyl direction. In the '90s, these directions were mixed for one Merzbow [. . . .]

**What kind of reaction did you get when you started performing in Japan?**

In Japan, the Noise audience looks very normal. I think most of them are middle-class salary men. Recently, we have more young, underground music types coming to a show. In the early days, the reaction was nothing. People thought that the music was just too difficult and loud. Recently, more people know how to comprehend my music. Many people have said they could get into a trance from the music. This is a better way of understanding Merzbow [. . . .]

**How has growing up in Japan effected your Noise creation?**

Sometimes, I would like to kill the much too noisy Japanese by my own Noise. The effects of Japanese culture are too much noise everywhere. I want to make silence by my Noise. Maybe, that is a fascist way of using sound.

You know, there's a need to create furniture music, that is to say, music that would be a part of the surrounding noises and that would take them into account. I see it as melodious, as masking the clatter of knives and forks without drowning it completely, without imposing itself. It would fill up the awkward silences that occasionally descend on guests. It would spare them the usual banalities. Moreover, it would neutralize the street noises that indiscreetly force themselves into the picture.

—Erik Satie[1]

Careful listening is more important than making sounds happen.

—Alvin Lucier[2]

In the flow of Japanese music [. . .] short fragmented connections of sounds are complete in themselves. Those different sound events are related by silences that aim at creating a harmony of events. Those pauses are left to the performer's discretion. In this way there is a dynamic change in the sounds as they are constantly reborn in new relationships. Here the role of the performer is not to produce sound but to listen to it, to strive constantly to discover sound in silence. Listening is as real as making sound; the two are inseparable.

—Toru Takemitsu[3]

It could be said that the moment one recognizes a certain sound in terms of meaning, one stops hearing the sound as sound; that the emphasis shifts from sound per se to a certain fixed meaning. The aim of [. . .] "absentminded" listening training [is] the opposite [. . .]: to obstruct or control the functioning of the sound classification recognition software in our brains, in an attempt to stop ourselves from discovering meaning through sound or finding something predetermined in the sound setting.

—Otomo Yoshihide[4]

[. . . . M]odern listening no longer quite resembles [. . .] *listening to indices* and *listening to signs* [. . . . W]hat is listened to here and there (chiefly in the field of art, whose function is often utopian) is not the advent of a signified, object of a recognition or of a deciphering, but the very dispersion, the *shimmering* of signifiers [. . .] this phenomenon of shimmering is called *signifying [significance]*, as distinct from signification: "listening" to a piece of classical music, the listener is called upon to "decipher" this piece, i.e., to recognize (by his culture, his application, his sensibility) its construction, quite as coded (predetermined) as that of a palace at a certain period; but "listening" to a composition (taking the word here in its etymological sense) by John Cage, it is each sound one after the next that I listen to, not in its syntagmatic extension, but in its raw and as though vertical *signifying:* by deconstructing itself, listening is externalized, it compels the subject to renounce his "inwardness."

—Roland Barthes[5]

Almost all the music which mercilessly surrounds us today has the same underlying structure: neverending gabbiness. What's the difference between MTV music and most of the classical avant-garde? They use different material, but they're both intensively talkative. We're surrounded by noises and sensory overstimulation wherever we go. For me, the true avant garde is the critical analysis or issue-taking with our cultural surroundings. What's needed is not faster, higher, stronger, louder—I want to know about the lull in the storm.

—Radu Malfatti[6]

Classical music works around a body of "refined" sounds—sounds that are separated from the sounds of the world, pure and musical. There is a sharp distinction between "music" and "noise," just as there is a distinction between the musician and the audience. I like blurring those distinctions—I like to work with all the complex sounds on the way out to the horizon, to pure noise, like the hum of London. If you sit in Hyde Park just far enough away from the traffic so that you don't perceive any of its details, you just hear the average of the whole thing. And it's such a beautiful sound. For me that's as good as going to a concert hall at night.

—Brian Eno[7]

If we had a keen vision and feeling of all ordinary human life, it would be like hearing the grass grow and the squirrel's heart beat, and we should die of that roar which lies on the other side of silence. As it is, the quickest of us walk about well wadded with stupidity.

—George Eliot[8]

When I look back at the last couple of years and at what's going on in [improvised] music, listening has become more and more important; silence became a major part of it. Maybe it's a question of my age, so that listening also in life is more important than when I was twenty years old. But I wish that more people would listen more carefully before they start talking [. . . .] When you're listening, let's say, to the [Taku Sugimoto Guitar Quartet], in the first moments, with all your knowing and all our expectations [. . .] you might be a little confused. There's nothing going on. Four guitar players play a few notes every two minutes. That might sound very abstract and very complicated, very intellectual. But in a way it's exactly the opposite. It's very direct, keeping and exploring the tension between notes. When you have a piece of paper and you start drawing, this nothing, this white can be very frightening, just to put the first drop of ink or of color or of anything. So that means this nothing is very, very powerful. And to deal with that, and to play with that or, in other words, to listen to this nothing, that's thrilling, I think. That's really thrilling.

—Günter Müller[9]

> Live completely alone for four days
> without food
> in complete silence, without much movement.
> Sleep as little as necessary,
> think as little as possible.
>
> After four days, late at night,
> without conversation beforehand
> play single sounds.
>
> WITHOUT THINKING what you are playing
> close your eyes,
> just listen.

—Karlheinz Stockhausen[10]

# II. Modes of Listening

## Introduction

For centuries, European art music prescribed a particular mode of listening exemplified by the ritual of the concert hall: In a closed space, separated from the outside world and the sonic domain of everyday life, a silent audience, seated some distance from a stage, listened to performers on that stage produce a narrow range of timbres on a limited array of musical instruments. In the second half of the 20th century, these listening conventions were mapped onto popular musics; and today, despite differences in genre and venue, they continue to define the ideal mode of listening to music, whether it be classical, jazz, rock, etc. Yet contemporary musical practices and technologies have problematized this traditional mode of auditory apprehension and have necessitated a new discourse around listening.

Radio and sound recording radically changed the act of listening to music, and altered the very nature of music as well. Music could now be detached from its source, from its ties to any particular setting and location. This made possible at least two new modes of listening. On the one hand, it allowed what Pierre Schaeffer termed "acousmatic listening": listening to sound without any visual clue to its source. This shift was not only phenomenological but ontological as well. Thus, instead of existing as mere reproductions of live events, recordings disclosed ontologically distinct and autonomous soundworlds. In Schaeffer's view, this afforded a new kind of experience: that of pure sound. On the other hand, recorded sound allowed music to infiltrate the spaces of everyday life, making possible "ambient" listening, music heard as an accompaniment to mundane activity: driving, shopping, working, etc. This idea was already envisioned in the early 1920s by Erik Satie and Darius Milhaud, who produced what they called "furniture music," "music that would be a part of the surrounding noises and that would take them into account."[1] But it took the technology of recording to fully realize this idea.

Already in the 1940s, theorists such as Theodor Adorno and Aldous Huxley noted the pernicious ideological effects of such passive listening. Indeed, the Muzak Corporation had already begun using background music to regulate mood and increase worker productivity. Despite Muzak's ubiquity and corporate success, the term "Muzak" quickly became a kind of musical insult, signifying bad music and a bad listening experience. Nonetheless, in the 1970s, progressive rock and experimental music composer Brian Eno began to see the liberatory possibilities of "Ambient" listening, the ways in which it afforded listeners a new experience of music and sonic space. The advent of the Walkman stirred similar reactions. Critics complained about its anti-social aspects. Yet, theorists such as Iain Chambers saw in it the possibility of actively producing a soundtrack for one's daily perambulations.

The advent of recording had an effect not only on listening practices but also on what sounds could be heard as music. Recording equipment allowed one to amplify and focus upon previously unheard or inconspicuous sounds. Moreover, as recorded entities, the sounds of trains or frogs, for example, could be placed on par with sounds made by violins or trumpets. From there, it was a short step to begin to perceive environmental sound aesthetically, radically transforming the nature of musical sound and composition. "This blurring of the edges between music and environmental sounds," wrote R. Murray Schafer in 1973, "is the most striking feature of twentieth century music."[2]

Within this new context—opened up by John Cage—Pauline Oliveros, J.K. Randall, and others began to extend not only Cage's compositional ideas but also his vernacular discursive style, which, however informal, helped admit into musical discourse a vast experiential domain foreclosed by traditional musical and musico-logical approaches. Oliveros' musical phenomenology demanded an expanded sonic depth-of-field that took what traditionally might be considered distractions (the bulldozer outside, the radio playing in the next room) to be a significant part of listening, composing, and writing. For Randall, the act of consuming "Some Warm Pepsi and Part Of A Baloney Sandwich" was not outside but within the experiential totality of listening to Wagner's *Götterdämmerung*.

The advent of recording and broadcasting forever altered the experience of listening and drew attention to the act of listening itself. Contemporary music reflects these phenomenological changes and continues to work through the prob-lems and possibilities inherent in these new modes of listening.

## NOTES

1. Erik Satie as quoted by Fernand Léger in Alan M. Gillmor, *Erik Satie* (Boston: Twayne, 1988), 232.
2. See Schafer, chap. 7, above.

# 12

## *Visual and Acoustic Space*

### MARSHALL McLUHAN

A profoundly influential theorist of late 20th century media, Marshall McLu-han (1911–1980) examined the ways in which communication and informa-tion technologies transform human subjectivity and community. His conception of "the global village"—the retribalization of the human race via a world network of electronic media—anticipated the Internet by nearly two decades. Throughout his career, McLuhan argued that radio, television, computers, and other electronic technologies are essentially prosthetic devices that vastly extend the human nervous system.

Indeed, throughout his work, McLuhan was interested in the human per-ceptual apparatus, the ways in which our senses (and their technological extensions) shape and are shaped by their environment. In this essay, writ-ten in the late 1970s, McLuhan contrasts the different worlds proper to sight and hearing. He argues that, while visual culture has dominated Western thought, perception, and imagination since ancient Greece, the late 20th century witnessed a rapid shift toward a very different mode of perception, that of the acoustic or auditory.

While in elementary school, Jacques Lusseyran was accidentally blinded. He found himself in another world of collision and pressure points. No longer could he pick his way through the ordinary "neutral" world of reflected light. It was the same environment that we are all born into but now it came to him demanding explora-tion:

> Sounds had the same individuality as light. They were neither inside nor out-side, but were passing through me. They gave me my bearings in space and put me in touch with things. It was not like signals that they functioned but like replies . . .
>
> But most surprising of all was the discovery that sounds never came from one point in space and never retreated into themselves. There was the sound,

its echo, and another sound into which the first sound melted and to which it had given birth, altogether an endless procession of sounds . . .

Blindness works like dope, a fact we have to reckon with. I don't believe there is a blind man alive who has not felt the danger of intoxication. Like drugs, blindness heightens certain sensations, giving sudden and often disturbing sharpness to the senses of hearing and touch. But, most of all, like a drug, it develops inner as against outer experience, and sometimes to excess . . .[1]

We, who live in the world of reflected light, in visual space, may also be said to be in a state of hypnosis. Ever since the collapse of the oral tradition in early Greece, before the age of Parmenides, Western civilization has been mesmerized by a picture of the universe as a limited container in which all things are arranged according to the vanishing point, in linear geometric order. The intensity of this conception is such that it actually leads to the abnormal suppression of hearing and touch in some individuals. (We like to call them "bookworms.") Most of the information we rely upon comes through our eyes; our technology is arranged to heighten that effect. Such is the power of Euclidean or visual space that we can't live with a circle unless we square it.[2]

But this was not always the expected order of things. For hundreds of thousands of years, mankind lived without a straight line in nature. Objects in this world resonated with each other. For the caveman, the mountain Greek, the Indian hunter (indeed, even for the latter-day Manchu Chinese), the world was multicentered and reverberating. It was gyroscopic. Life was like being inside a sphere, 360 degrees without margins; swimming underwater; or balancing on a bicycle. Tribal life was, and still is, conducted like a three-dimensional chess game; not with pyramidal priorities. The order of ancient or prehistoric time was circular, not progressive. Acoustic imagination dwelt in the realm of ebb and flow, the *logos*. For one day to repeat itself at sunrise was an overwhelming boon. As this world began to fill itself out for the early primitive, the mind's ear gradually dominated the mind's eye. Speech, before the age of Plato, was the glorious depository of memory.

Acoustic space is a dwelling place for anyone who has not been conquered by the one-at-a-time, uniform ethos of the alphabet. It exists in the Third World and vast areas of the Middle East, Russia, and the South Pacific. It is the India to which Gandhi returned after twenty years in South Africa, bringing with him the knowledge that Western man's penchant for fragmentation would be his undoing. There are no boundaries to sound. We hear from all directions at once. But the balance between inner and outer experience can be precise. If our eardrums were tuned any higher we would hear molecules colliding in the air or the roaring rush of our own blood. Sound comes to us from above, below, and the sides. As Lusseyran says, it passes through us and is rarely limited by the density of physical objects. Most natural materials act as a tuning fork. The human baby cannot move out into the environment until sound teaches depth—which the child adapts to the demands of Euclidean or visual space later on.

Each of these modalities is a sensory preference of the culture. For the society that accepts it, that modality, whether acoustic or visual, is the foundation on which it recognizes its own perception of sanity. But we wish to advance an idea that you, the reader, won't in all probability, initially accept. And that is for several thousand years, at least, man's sensorium, or his seat of perceptive balance, has been out of plumb.

The term *sensus communis* in Cicero's time meant that all the senses, such as seeing, hearing, tasting, smelling, and touch, were translated equally into each other. It was the Latin definition of man in a healthy natural state, when physical and psychic energy were constant and distributed in a balanced way to all sense areas.[3] In such a condition it is rather difficult to hallucinate. In any cultural arrangement, trouble always occurs when only one sense is subjected to a barrage of energy and receives more stimulus than all the others. For modern Western man that would be the visual state.

As psychologists understand sense ratios, overstimulation and understimulation can cause thought and feeling to separate. Sleeping may be regarded as a dimming down of one or two sensory inputs. Hypnosis, on the other hand, is a steady assault on one sense, like a tribal drumbeat. Modern torturers in Chile break down prisoners by putting them in cells where everything—walls, furniture, utensils, window covers—is painted white. In Vietnam, Communist interrogators discovered (as police interrogators everywhere) that unexpected beatings and random electric shocks create sharp peaks of floating anxiety and subsequently a ready uncritical conviction.

Without being aware of it, North Americans have created the same kind of violence for themselves. Western man thinks with only one part of his brain and starves the rest of it. By neglecting ear culture, which is too diffuse for the categorical hierarchies of the left side of the brain, he has locked himself into a position where only linear conceptualization is acceptable.

Euclid and Newton fixed Western man's body in rigid space and oriented him toward the horizon.[4] As neurosurgeon Joseph Bogen puts it, the linear sequential mode of the left hemisphere underlies language and analytical thought. The right hemisphere of the brain, which is principally concerned with pattern recognition of an artistic and holistic quality, grasps the relationship between diverse parts readily and is not bound up with a rigid sequence of deductions. The intellectual legacy of Euclid and Newton therefore is a substitution of perspective for qualitative thinking, which is always composed of multi-sensual elements.

Everything in life after the Greeks was reduced to the uniform and the homogenous, Swift's island of Laputa. Thought had to have a beginning, a middle, and an end. No thesis was acceptable unless all ideas were interconnected to project an e-x-t-e-n-d-e-d point of view, which is the interior structure of the essay, we might add.

If you think of every human sense as creating its own space, then the eye creates a space where there can only be one thing at a time. The eye acts as a machine—like a camera. Light focused on the back of the eye ensures that two objects will not occupy the same place at the same time. The mind teaches the eye to see an object right side up, on a plane and in perspective space. As children, when perspective (or the vanishing point) arrives—when we learn to focus an inch or two in front of the page—we learn to read and write. The phonetic alphabet gives us a point of view since it promotes the illusion of removing oneself from the object.

It would almost seem that the very physiology of the eye promotes the idea that everything is in sequence—that is, in its proper place, at the proper time, and in linear relationship. The kind of mentality that prompted Shakespeare's King Lear to divide his kingdom among his daughters, to abstract himself from the medieval perception that England was contained in himself is more modern than tribal. What we are saying is that the human eye appears to be the father of linear logic. Its very nature encourages reasoning by exclusion: something is either in that space or it isn't.

The constraints of Western logic are tied to our sense of sequential relationships—logic made visual. The middle ground, however accounted for initially, is eventually excluded. It is either-or. If your culture nurtures you to favor the eye, your brain has difficulty giving equal weight to any other sense bias. You are trapped by visual only assumptions. For centuries, the Japanese, unlike Westerners, have treasured the pictorial space between objects in a painting, the *ma;* and have viewed such space as more dominant than all objects portrayed. Like the yin/yang complementarity of wave/particle in atomic physics.

Anyone who has been involved in gestalt, or studied primitive societies—once he or she gets over the impulse to measure these societies with Western templates—is aware that either-or is not the only possibility. Both-and can also exist. People who have not been exposed to the phonetic alphabet, that is, the "uncivilized," can easily entertain two diametric possibilities at once. Edmund Carpenter pointed out to us that the Inuits, or the Eskimos, cannot visualize in two dimensions. If they are asked to draw the animals they hunt on a flat surface, the result—to our eyes—is often grotesque. But ask them to draw the same figure on, let us say, the rounded surface of a walrus tusk, and the etched drawing will take on three-dimensional life as you roll the tusk in your fingers.

[. . . . H]ere we have a clue to the mentality of the pre-literate, that world of oral tradition that we eventually left behind about the end of the Hellenic period. It is the mentality of the multitude, or as Yeats put it: everything happening at once, in a state of constant flux. For the genuinely tribal man there is no causality, nothing occurring in a straight line. He turns aside from the habit of construing things chronologically—not because he can't, but as Edmund Carpenter says, because he doesn't want to.

Carpenter advises us that the Trobriander Islanders only recognize now, the eternal present. Bronislaw Malinowski and Dorothy Lee, who studied these people, discovered that they disdained the concept of *why.* European man to them was hung up on the idea of setting priorities, of making past and future distinctions. "To the Trobriander, events do not fall of themselves into a pattern of cause and effect as they do for us. We in our culture automatically see and seek relationships, not essence. We express relationship mainly in terms of cause or purpose . . . ."[5] The Trobriander is only interested in experiencing the current essence of a person or object. He is interested in his yams, his stone knife, his boat, as those objects are today. There is no such thing as a "new" or an "old" boat, a blooming yam or a decayed one. There is no past or future, only the essence of being that exists now. The Trobriander, like the Inuit, directly experiences a sense of timelessness, so he is never bothered by such questions as "who created the creator." The English language, in fact most Western languages, suggests through its tense structure that reality can only be contained in the concept of a past, a present, and a future which rather incongruously implies that man is capable, like a god, of standing outside the time continuum. The hubris of Western man might very well lie in the priority-setting propensity for quantitative reasoning [. . . .]

To summarize, visual space structure is an artifact of Western civilization created by Greek phonetic literacy. It is a space perceived by the eyes when separated or abstracted from all other senses. As a construct of the mind, it is continuous, which is to say that it is infinite, divisible, extensible, and featureless— what the early Greek geometers referred to as *physis*. It is also connected (abstract figures with fixed boundaries, linked logically and sequentially but having no visible grounds), homogeneous (uniform everywhere), and static (qualitatively unchangeable). It is like the "mind's eye" or visual imagination which dominates the thinking of literate Western people, some of whom demand ocular proof for existence itself.

Acoustic space structure is the natural space of nature-in-the-raw inhabited by non-literate people. It is like the "mind's ear" or acoustic imagination that dominates the thinking of pre-literate and post-literate humans alike (rock video has as much acoustic power as a Watusi mating dance). It is both discontinuous and nonhomogeneous. Its resonant and interpenetrating processes are simultaneously related with centers everywhere and boundaries nowhere. Like music, as communications engineer Barrington Nevitt puts it, acoustic space requires neither proof nor explanation but is made manifest through its cultural content. Acoustic and visual space structures may be seen as incommensurable, like history and eternity, yet, at the same time, as complementary, like art and science or biculturalism.

Occasionally, certain persons in history have been in the right place and time to be truly bicultural. When we say bicultural we mean the fortune to have a foot placed, as it were, in both visual and acoustic space, like Hemingway in his Cuban village hideaway or Tocqueville in America. Marco Polo was such a one. The Phoenicians, the earliest cultural brokers between East and West, having brought a cuneiform method of accounting to the Egyptians and the phonetic alphabet to the Greeks, were likewise blessed.

The phonetic alphabet underlies all of Western linguistic development.[6] By the time it had gone through the Greeks and Romans and reasserted itself in the print literature of the Renaissance, Western sense ratios had been firmly altered. The Greeks gave a new birth to the alphabet as a mode of representation having neither visual nor semantic meaning. Egyptian ideographs, for instance, were directly related to particular sensuous sounds and actions, with unique graphic signs. On the other hand, the matrix of the Greek alphabet could be used to translate alien languages back and forth without changing the form and number (twenty-four) of the original alphabetic characters. It became the first means of translation of knowledge from one culture to another. The reader in the process became separated from the original speaker and the particular sensuous event. The oral tradition of the early Greek dramatists, of the pre-Socratics, and Sophocles, gave way very gradually to the written Pan-European tradition and set the emotional and intellectual posture of the West in concrete, as it were. We were "liberated" forever from the resonating magic of the tribal word and the web of kinship.

The history of the Western world since the time of Aristotle has been a story of increasing linguistic specialism produced by the flat, uniform, homogeneous presentation of print. Orality wound down slowly. The scribal (or manuscript) culture of the Middle Ages was inherently oral/aural in character. Manuscripts were meant to be read aloud. Church chantry schools were set up to ensure oral fidelity. The Gutenberg technology siphoned off the aural-tactile quality of the Ancients, systemized language, and established heretofore unknown standards for pronunciation and meaning. Before typography there was no such thing as bad grammar.

After the public began to accept the book on a mass basis in the fourteenth and fifteenth centuries—and on a scale where literacy mattered—all knowledge that could not be so classified was tucked away into the new "unconscious" of the folk tale and the myth, there to be resurrected later as the Romantic Reaction.

But since World War I and the advent of those technical wavesurfers Marconi and Edison, the rumbles of aural-tactility, the power of the spoken word, have been heard. James Joyce in *Finnegans Wake,* celebrated the tearing apart of the ethos of print by radio, film (television), and recording. He could easily see that Goebbels and his radio loudspeakers were a new tribal echo. And you may be sure that emerging mediums such as the satellite, the computer, the data base, teletext-videotext, and the international multi-carrier corporations, such as ITT, GTE, and AT&T, will intensify the attack on the printed word as the "sole" container of the public mentality, without being aware of it of course. By the twenty-first century, most printed matter will have been transferred to something like an ideographic microfiche as only part of a number of data sources available in acoustic and visual modes. This new interplay between word and image can be understood if we realize that our skulls really contain two brains straining to be psychically united [. . . .]

## NOTES

1. Lusseyran, *And There Was Light*, tr. Elizabeth Cameron (Boston: Little, Brown, 1963), pp. 23–24, 48–49.
2. F. M. Cornford, "The Invention of Space," *Essays in Honour of Gilbert Murray* (London: Allen and Unwin, 1936), pp. 215–235.
3. Cicero's training, through Plato's disciples, was influenced by an earlier religious usage that *logos* (a primitive utterance of the word) structured the *kosmos* and infused man's being with a wise concept of world order or common sense. *Heraclitus: The Cosmic Fragments*, ed. Geoffrey S. Kirk (London: Cambridge University Press, 1954), pp. 70, 396, 403. Also, Harold Innis in *Empire and Communications* (London: Oxford University Press, 1951), p. 76, says "The structure of man's speech was an embodiment of the structure of the world." Cicero's rhetorical theory, as an interchange of both thought and feeling (*inventio, dispositio, elocutio, memoria* and *pronuntia*) became the academic anchor for the medieval trivium; for a form of summation consult Marcus Tullius Cicero, *De Oratore*, trs. E. W. Sutton and H. Rackham (Cambridge: Harvard University Press, 1967), pp. 97–109.
4. Cornford, "The Invention of Space," p. 219.
5. The eternal present: Summarized from an extended exchange between Edmund Carpenter and Marshall McLuhan during a student discussion of Carpenter's first draft essay "Thinking Through Language," at the Centre for Culture and Technology, University of Toronto. Also, cf. Dorothy Lee, "Lineal and Nonlineal Codifications of Reality," *Explorations in Communication: An Anthology*, pp. 136–154.
6. Eric Havelock, "Origins of Western Literacy," in *Ontario Institute for Studies in Education*, Monograph Series no. 14 (Toronto: 1971), p. 43.

# 13

# The Politics of Hearing

## HANNS EISLER AND THEODOR ADORNO

Theodor Adorno (1903–1969) was among the most important and influential German philosophers of the 20th century. A founding member of the Frankfurt School for Social Research, Adorno's work offers a consistent critique of contemporary culture and society aimed at resisting its ideology and deep irrationality. With the rise of Hitler, Adorno and many of his Frankfurt School colleagues were exiled in the United States. Adorno found himself in the peculiar position of living in Hollywood, the heart of what he called "the culture industry," which he came to see as a form of nearly totalitarian social control. Music figures centrally in Adorno's writing, and avant-garde music serves as one of the few forces of resistance to "the culture industry." An accomplished pianist, Adorno studied composition with Alban Berg and was a lifelong advocate for Schoenberg's music.

Hanns Eisler (1898–1962) studied with Arnold Schoenberg, but later rejected contemporary classical music as elitist, turning instead to the composition of populist worker's songs, often with lyrics penned by Bertolt Brecht. Like Adorno, Eisler fled Hitler's Germany and landed in Hollywood. During his ten years there, he composed scores for several major films. In 1947, Eisler became the first Hollywood artist to be called before McCarthy's Committee on Un-American Activities. He was subsequently deported and spent the rest of his life in East Germany, whose national anthem he composed.

*Composing for the Films* was first published in 1947 under Eisler's name alone, due to Adorno's fear of political reprisal. The book argues that, in the cinema, sound and music should play a critical role in relationship to image and action. In this short excerpt, the authors reflect on the profound differences between auditory and visual perception and sound a note of caution about the politics of hearing and listening.

The function of music in the cinema is one aspect—in an extreme version—of the general function of music under conditions of industrially controlled cultural con-

sumption. Music is supposed to bring out the spontaneous, essentially human element in its listeners and in virtually all human relations. As the abstract art *par
excellence*, and as the art farthest removed from the world of practical things it is
predestined to perform this function. The human ear has not adapted itself to the
bourgeois rational and, ultimately, highly industrialized order as readily as the eye,
which has become accustomed to conceiving reality as made up of separate
things, commodities, objects that can be modified by practical activity. Ordinary
listening, as compared to seeing, is 'archaic'; it has not kept pace with technological progress. One might say that to react with the ear, which is fundamentally a
passive organ in contrast to the swift, actively selective eye, is in a sense not in
keeping with the present advanced industrial age and its cultural anthropology.[1]

For this reason acoustical perception preserves comparably more traits of
long bygone, pre-individualistic collectivities than optical perception. At least two
of the most important elements of occidental music, the harmonic-contrapuntal
one and that of its rhythmic articulation, point directly to a group modelled upon
the ancient church community as its only possible inherent 'subject.' This direct
relationship to a collectivity, intrinsic in the phenomenon itself, is probably connected with the sensations of spatial depth, inclusiveness, and absorption of individuality, which are common to all music.[2] But this very ingredient of collectivity,
because of its essentially amorphous nature, leads itself to deliberate misuse for
ideological purposes. Since music is antithetical to the definiteness of material
things, it is also in opposition to the unambiguous distinctness of the concept. Thus
it may easily serve as a means to create retrogression and confusion, all the more
so because, despite its nonconceptual character, it is in other respects rational-
ized, extensively technified, and just as modern as it is archaic. This refers not only
to the present methods of mechanical reproduction, but to the whole development
of post-medieval music. Max Weber even terms the process of rationalization the
historical principle according to which music developed. All middle-class music
has an ambivalent character.[3] On the one hand, it is in a certain sense precapitalis-
tic, 'direct,' a vague evocation of togetherness; on the other hand, because it has
shared in the progress of civilization, it has become reified, indirect, and ultimately
a 'means' among many others. This ambivalence determines its function under
advanced capitalism. It is *par excellence* the medium in which irrationality can be
practiced rationally.

It has always been said that music releases or gratifies the emotions, but
these emotions themselves have always been difficult to define. Their actual content seems to be only abstract opposition to prosaic existence. The greater the
drabness of this existence, the sweeter the melody. The underlying need
expressed by this inconsistency springs from the frustrations imposed on the
masses of the people by social conditions. But this need itself is put into the service of commercialism. Because of its own rationality, so different from the way it
is perceived, and its technical malleability, music can be made to serve regression
'psychotechnically' and in that role is more welcomed in proportion as it deceives
its listeners in regard to the reality of everyday existence.

Such tendencies affect culture as a whole, but they manifest themselves with
particular blatancy in music. The eye is always an organ of exertion, labor, and
concentration; it grasps a definite object. The ear of the layman, on the other hand,
as contrasted to that of the musical expert, is indefinite and passive. One does not

have to open it, as one does the eye, compared to which it is indolent and dull. But this indolence is subject to the taboo that society imposes upon every form of laziness. Music as an art has always been an attempt to circumvent this taboo, to transform the indolence, dreaminess, and dullness of the ear into a matter of concentration, effort, and serious work. Today indolence is not so much overcome as it is managed and enhanced scientifically. Such a rationally planned irrationality is the very essence of the amusement industry in all its branches. Music perfectly fits the pattern.

## NOTES

1. A remark of Goethe's confirms this. 'According to my father everyone should learn to draw, and for that reason he had great regard for Emperor Maximilian, who was said to have given explicit orders to that effect. He also more seriously urged me to practice drawing than music, which; on the other hand, he recommended to my sister, even keeping her at the piano for a good part of the day, in addition to her regular lessons.' (*Dichtung und Wahrheit,* Part I, Book IV.) The boy, visualized by the father as a representative of progress and enlightenment, is supposed to train his eye, while the girl, who represents historically outmoded domesticity and has no real share in public life and economic production, is confined to music, as was generally the case with young upper-class women in the nineteenth century, quite apart from the role of music throughout oriental society.

2. Cf. Ernst Kurth: *Musikpsychologie,* Berlin, 1931, pp. 116-36: e.g. 'There is not only the perceptual space that is drawn into musical expression from outside; there is also a space for inner listening, which is an autonomous musico-psychological phenomenon' (p. 134); or: 'The spatial impressions of music also claim their independence; it is essential . . . that they should not arise by the detour of any perceptual image. They pertain to energetic processes, and are autogenous' (p. 135).

3. This perhaps helps to explain why modern music meets with so much greater resistance than modern painting. The ear clings to the archaic essence of music, while music itself is involved in the process of rationalization.

# 14

# *Acousmatics*

## PIERRE SCHAEFFER

The founder of *musique concrète* (see the introduction to Section I), Pierre Schaeffer (1910–1995) is equally important as a theorist of musical listening. Trained as a radio engineer and announcer, Schaeffer was fascinated by the fact that radio and recording made possible a new experience of sound—what he called "reduced listening" or "acousmatic listening"—that disclosed a new domain of sounds—"*objets sonores*" or sonorous objects, the objects of "acousmatic listening."

Like many post-War French intellectuals, Schaeffer was attracted to the philosophy of Edmund Husserl, founder of "phenomenology." Phenomenology disregards the traditional philosophical distinctions between "subject" and "object," "appearance" and "reality" and instead attempts simply to describe the contents of experience without reference to its source or subjective mode (e.g., dreaming, waking, etc.). In the case of sound, for example, instead of distinguishing sounds with reference to their sources (the sound *of* a guitar, the sound *of* a violin), phenomenology attempts to "reduce" (separate or distill) signal from source, and to restrict itself to describing the differences among sounds themselves. For Schaeffer, technologies such as radio and the phonograph made palpable this phenomenological experience, which was already envisioned by the Pythagoreans, among the first European musical theorists. These technologies effectively subvert the hierarchical relationship of source to signal, allowing sounds themselves (the sonorous objects) to have their own existence distinct from their sources. In this chapter from his *magnum opus*, *Treatise on Musical Objects*, Schaeffer introduces the concepts of "acousmatic listening" and the "sonorous object."

## The Relevance of an Ancient Experience

*Acousmatic*, the *Larousse* dictionary tells us, is the: "*Name given to the disciples of Pythagoras who, for five years, listened to his teachings while he was hidden behind a curtain, without seeing him, while observing a strict silence."* Hidden from their eyes, only the voice of their master reached the disciples.

It is to this initiatory experience that we are linking the notion of acousmatics, given the use we would like to make of it here. The *Larousse* dictionary continues: *"Acousmatic, adjective: is said of a noise that one hears without seeing what causes it."* This term [. . .] marks the perceptive reality of sound as such, as distinguished from the modes of its production and transmission. The new phenomenon of telecommunications and the massive diffusion of messages exists only *in relation to* and *as a function of* a fact that has been rooted in human experience from the beginning: natural, sonorous communication. This is why we can, without anachronism, return to an ancient tradition which, no less nor otherwise than contemporary radio and recordings, gives back to the ear alone the entire responsibility of a perception that ordinarily rests on other sensible witnesses. In ancient times, the apparatus was a curtain; today, it is the radio and the methods of reproduction, along with the whole set of electro-acoustic transformations, that place us, modern listeners to an invisible voice, under similar conditions.

## Acoustic and Acousmatic

We would utilize this experience erroneously if we subjected it to a Cartesian decomposition by distinguishing the "objective"—what is behind the curtain—from the "subjective"—the reaction of the auditor to these stimuli. In such a perspective, it is the so-called "objective" elements that contain the references of the elucidation to be undertaken: frequencies, durations, amplitudes . . .; the curiosity put into play is that of acoustics. In relation to this approach, acousmatics corresponds to a reversal of the usual procedure. Its interrogation is symmetrical: it is no longer a question of knowing how a subjective listening interprets or deforms "reality," of studying reactions to stimuli. It is the listening itself that becomes the origin of the phenomenon to be studied. The concealment of the causes does not result from a technical imperfection, nor is it an occasional process of variation: it becomes a precondition, a deliberate placing-in-condition of the subject. It is *toward it*, then, that the question turns around: "What am I hearing? . . . What exactly are you hearing"—in the sense that one asks the subject to describe not the external references of the sound it perceives but the perception itself.

Nonetheless, acoustics and acousmatics are not opposed to each other like the objective and the subjective. If the first approach, starting with physics, must go as far as the "reactions of the subject" and thereby integrate, in the end, the psychological elements, the second approach must in effect be unaware of the measures and experiences that are applicable only to the physical object, the "signal" of acousticians. But for all that, its investigations, turned toward the subject, cannot abandon its claim to *an objectivity that is proper to it*: if what it studies were reduced to the changing impressions of each listener, all communication would become impossible; Pythagoras' disciples would have to give up naming, describing, and understanding what they were hearing *in common*; a particular listener would even have to give up understanding himself from one moment to the next. The question, in this case, would be how to rediscover, through confronting subjectivities, something several experimenters might agree on.

pierre schaeffer • 77

## The Acousmatic Field

In the sense of acoustics, we started with the physical signal and studied its trans-formations via electro-acoustic processes, in tacit reference to the norms of a sup-posedly known listening—a listening that grasps frequencies, durations, etc. By contrast, the acousmatic situation, in a general fashion, symbolically precludes any relation with what is visible, touchable, measurable. Moreover, between the experience of Pythagoras and our experiences of radio and recordings, the differ-ences separating direct listening (through a curtain) and indirect listening (through a speaker) in the end become negligible. Under these conditions, what are the characteristics of the current acousmatic situation?

### a) *Pure Listening*

For the traditional musician and for the acoustician, an important aspect of the recognition of sounds is the identification of the sonorous sources. When the latter are effectuated without the support of vision, musical conditioning is unsettled. Often a surprise, sometimes uncertain, we will discover that much of what we thought was heard was in reality only seen, and explicated, through the context. This is why certain sounds produced by instruments as different as string instru-ments and wind instruments can be confused.

### b) *Listening to Effects*

In listening to sonorous objects [*objets sonores*] whose instrumental causes are hidden, we are led to forget the latter and to take an interest in these objects for themselves. The dissociation of seeing and hearing here encourages another way of listening: we listen to the sonorous forms, without any aim other than that of hearing them better, in order to be able to describe them through an analysis of the content of our perceptions.

In fact, Pythagoras' curtain is not enough to discourage our curiosity about causes, to which we are instinctively, almost irresistibly drawn. But the repetition of the physical signal, which recording makes possible, assists us here in two ways: by exhausting this curiosity, it gradually brings the sonorous object to the fore as a perception worthy of being observed for itself; on the other hand, as a result of ever more attentive and more refined listenings, it progressively reveals to us the richness of this perception.

### c) *Variations in Listening*

Furthermore, since these repetitions are brought about in physically identical conditions, we become aware of the variations in our listening and better under-stand what is in general termed its "subjectivity." This does not refer, as one might perhaps tend to think, to an imperfection or a kind of "fuzziness" [*flou*] that would scramble the clarity of the physical signal; but rather to particular clarifications or precise directions that reveal, in each case, a new aspect of the object, toward which our attention is deliberately or unconsciously focused.

### d) *Variations in the Signal*

Finally, we should mention the special possibilities we have for intervening in the sound, the implementation of which accentuates the previously described features of the acousmatic situation. We have focused on the physical signal fixed on a disk or magnetic tape; we can act on it, dissect it. We can also make different recordings of a single sonorous event, approaching the sound at the moment of its taping [*prise de son*] from various angles, just as one can film a scene using different shots [*prise de vues*]. Assuming that we limit ourselves to a single recording, we can still read the latter more or less quickly, more or less loudly, or even cut it into pieces, thereby presenting the listener with several versions of what was originally a unique event. What does this deployment of diverging sonorous effects from a single material cause represent, from the point of view of the acousmatic experience? What correlation can we expect between the modifications that are imposed on what is recorded on the tape and the variations in what we are hearing?

## On the Sonorous Object: What It Is Not

We have spoken at several points of the sonorous object, utilizing a notion that has already been introduced, but not clarified. It is clear, in light of the present chapter, that we were able to propose this notion in advance only because we were implicitly referring to the acousmatic situation that has just been described. If there is a sonorous object, it is only insofar as there is a blind listening [*écoute*] to sonorous effects and contents: the sonorous object is never revealed clearly except in the acousmatic experience.

Given this specification, it is easy for us to avoid erroneous responses to the question raised at the end of the preceding paragraph.

a) *The sonorous object is not the instrument that was played.*

It is obvious that when we say "That's a violin" or "That's a creaking door," we are alluding to the *sound* emitted by the violin, to the *creaking* of the door. But the distinction we would like to establish between the instrument and the sonorous object is even more radical: if someone plays us a tape which records a sound whose origin we are unable to identify, what are we hearing? Precisely what we are calling a sonorous object, independent of any causal reference, which is designated by the terms *sonorous body*, *sonorous source* or *instrument*.

b) *The sonorous object is not the magnetic tape.*

Although it is materialized by the magnetic tape, the object, as we are defining it, is not on the tape either. What is on the tape is only the magnetic trace of a signal: a *sonorous support* or an *acoustic signal*. When listened to by a dog, a child, a Martian, or the citizen of another musical civilization, this signal takes on another meaning or sense. The object is not an object *except* to our listening, it is relative to it. We can act on the tape physically, cutting it, modifying its replay speed. Only the act of listening by a listener [*seule l'écoute d'un auditeur*] can provide us with an account of the perceptible result of these manipulations. Coming from a world in which we are able to intervene, the sonorous object is nonetheless *contained entirely in our perceptive consciousness*.

pierre schaeffer • 79

c) *A few centimeters of magnetic tape can contain a number of different sonorous objects.*

This remark follows from the preceding one. The manipulations just mentioned do not modify *a* sonorous object having an intrinsic existence. They have *created other objects* from it. There is, of course, a *correlation* between the manipulations to which one subjects a tape or its diverse conditions of reading, the conditions of our listening and the perceived object.

A simple correlation? Not at all, it must be expected. Suppose, for example, that we listened to a sound recorded at normal speed, then slowed down, then again at normal speed. The slowed-down portion, acting like a magnifying glass in relation to the temporal structure of the sound, will have allowed us to discern certain details—of grain, for example—which our listening, thus alerted and informed, will rediscover in the second passage at normal speed. We must let ourselves be guided here by the evidence, and the very way we have had to formulate our supposition dictates the response: it is indeed the *same* sonorous object, subjected to different means of observation, that we are comparing to itself, original and transposed. But what makes it one and the same object is precisely our will to comparison (and also the fact that the operation to which we have subjected it, in this very intention to compare it to itself, has modified it, without rendering it unrecognizable).

Suppose now that we play this slowed-down sound to an unwarned listener. Two cases can arise. Either the listener will still recognize the instrumental origin and, at the same time, the manipulation; for him there will be *an original sonorous source* that in fact *he does not hear*, but to which, however, his listening refers him: what he hears is effectively a *transposed version*. Or else he will not identify the real origin, will not suspect the transposition, and he will then hear *an original sonorous object*, which will be so *automatically.* (It cannot be a question of an illusion or a lack of information, since in the acousmatic attitude our perceptions cannot rest on anything external.) Inversely, for those of us who have just subjected the sonorous object to one or more transpositions, it is likely that there will be a unique object and its different transposed versions. However, it may also happen that, abandoning any intention to comparison, we attach ourselves exclusively to one or the other of these versions, in order to make use of them, for example, in a composition; they will then become for us so many original sonorous objects, completely independent of their common origin.

We could devote ourselves to similar analyses of other types of manipulations (or variations of the act of recording [*prise de son*]) which, as a function of our intention, our knowledge, and our prior training, will have as their result either variations of a single sonorous object, or the creation of diverse sonorous objects. With the slowing-down, we have voluntarily chosen a modification that lends itself to equivocation. Other manipulations can transform an object in such a way that it becomes impossible to grasp any perceptible relations between the two versions. In this case, we will not speak of the permanence of a single sonorous object, if the identification no longer rests on anything but the recollection of the diverse operations to which "something that was on the magnetic tape" was subjected. If it is impossible for a listener to recognize a kinship between the diverse sonorous results—even guided by recollections and a will to comparison—we will say that the manipulations of a single signal have given way to diverse sonorous objects, whatever our intention may have been.

d) *But the sonorous object is not a state of the mind* [*âme*].

To avoid confusing it with its physical cause or a "stimulus," we seemed to have grounded the sonorous object on our subjectivity. But—our last remarks already indicate this—the sonorous object is not modified for all that, neither with the variations in listening from one individual to another, nor with the incessant variations in our attention and our sensibility. Far from being subjective (in the sense of individuals), incommunicable, and practically ungraspable, sonorous objects, as we shall see, can be clearly described and analyzed. We can gain knowledge of them. We can, we hope, transmit this knowledge.

Our rapid examination of the characteristics of the sonorous object reveals this ambiguity: as an objectivity linked to a subjectivity, it will surprise us only if we obstinately insist on opposing "psychologies" and "external realities" as antinomic. Theories of knowledge did not have to wait for the sonorous object to perceive the contradiction that we are indicating here, and which is not revealed in the acousmatic situation as such [. . . .]

## The Originality of the Acousmatic Procedure

Our approach is thus distinguished from the spontaneous instrumental practice in which [. . .] everything is given at once: the instrument, as the element and means of a musical civilization, and the corresponding virtuosity, and thus a certain structuration of the music extracted from it. Nor do we any longer lay claim to "the most general instrument that exists"; what we are aiming at, in fact, and which follows from the preceding remarks, is the most general musical situation that exists. We can now describe it explicitly. We have at our disposal the generality of sounds—at least in principle—without having to produce them; all we have to do is push the button on a tape recorder. Deliberately forgetting every reference to instrumental causes or preexisting musical significations, we then seek to devote ourselves entirely and exclusively to *listening*, to discover the instinctive paths that lead from the purely "sonorous" to the purely "musical." Such is the suggestion of acousmatics: to deny the instrument and cultural conditioning, *to put in front of us the sonorous and its musical "possibility."*

One more remark before finishing [. . . .] In the course of this chapter, we have already begun to *hear* with another ear [. . . .] The interest of this remark is not a matter of pure form: it consists in noting that the operative technique has itself created the conditions of a new listening. Let us give audio-visual techniques what is owed to them: we expect from them unheard-of sounds, new timbres, deafening plays—in a word, instrumental progress. Indeed, they provide all that, but very quickly we no longer know what to do with it all; these new instruments are not added easily to the old ones, and the questions they pose singularly disrupt received notions. The tape recorder has the virtue of Pythagoras' curtain: if it creates new phenomena to observe, it creates above all new conditions of observation [. . . .]

# 15

## *Profound Listening and Environmental Sound Matter*

### FRANCISCO LÓPEZ

The work of Spanish sound artist Francisco López (1964– ) grows out of his experience as an entomologist. While doing fieldwork in Latin American rainforests, López was struck by the connection between the rainforest soundscape and Pierre Schaeffer's concept of "acousmatic listening." Though rainforests are full of sound, the sources of these sounds (insects, birds, monkeys, etc.) remain largely hidden. Over the past two decades, López's work as a sound artist has exploited this connection between field recordings and acousmatic listening. He considers himself an ecologist; yet rejects many of the assumptions and practices of the Acoustic Ecology movement and its founder, R. Murray Schafer. In this piece, López rejects the idea that sound recording can ever be simply representational and argues instead that it is always a creative act. López's recordings are nearly all "untitled" in an effort to call our attention to the sounds themselves rather than to their sources. For the same reason, he asks that audience members wear blindfolds during his live performances. In this discussion of his 1997 recording *La Selva* (composed entirely of field recordings from the La Selva rainforest reserve in Costa Rica), López summarizes his compositional philosophy and theory of listening.

Many nature recordings as well as some current sound art embody an aesthetic that is governed by traditional bioacoustic principles, which emphasize procedural, contextual, or intentional levels of reference. Whenever there is such a stress on the representational/relational aspect of nature recordings, the meaning of the sounds is diminished, and their inner world is dissipated.

Counter to this trend, I believe in the possibility of a "blind" listening, a pro-found listening freed as much as possible from such constraints. This form of listening doesn't negate what is *outside* the sounds but explores and affirms all that is *inside* them. This purist, absolute conception is an attempt at fighting against the dissipation of this inner world.

## Nature Sound Environments vs. Bioacoustics

My approach departs from traditional bioacoustics, which follows a reductive interpretation of nature recordings. This discipline focuses on capturing the sounds produced by different animal species, mainly for identification purposes [. . . .] The sounds of many animal species are included in the recordings that constitute my work, *La Selva*, and they have even been identified, but none of them has been singled out in the processes of recording and editing. With traditional bioacoustics, the aim of which is scientific, the calls, songs, or other sounds of a certain species are usually isolated from the "background" sound of its environment in both the recording and the editing processes, and the contrast between the foregrounded species and its background is even further enhanced.

In *La Selva* the sound-producing animal species appear together with other accompanying biotic and non-biotic components that inhere in the sound environment. Any resulting distinction between foreground and background was not arranged purposefully but emerged incidentally, due to the location of the microphones, as might occur with our ears. My attention was "focused" on the sound environment as a whole, which is one of the reasons why there are no indexes on the CD. I wanted to discourage a focal listening centered on the entrances of species or other sonic events.

The habitual focus on animals as the main elements in a sound environment is particularly limiting. Not only are non-biotic sound sources evident in many nature environments (rainfall, rivers, storms, wind), but there is also a type of sound-producing biotic component that exists in almost every environment and that is usually overlooked: plants. In most cases—especially forests—what we tend to refer to as the sound of rain or wind might more aptly be called the sound of plant leaves and branches.

If our reception of nature sounds were more focused on the environment as a whole rather than on the organisms we perceive to be most similar to us, we would be more likely to take the bioacoustics of plants into account. Further, a sound environment is the consequence not only of all its sound-producing components, but also of all its sound-transmitting and sound-modifying elements. The birdsong we hear in the forest is as much a consequence of the trees or the forest floor as it is of the bird. If we listen attentively, the topography, the degree of humidity of the air, or the type of materials in the topsoil become as essential and defining of the sonic environment as the sound-producing animals that inhabit a certain space [. . . .]

In my work with nature sound environments, I have moved away from the rationalizing and categorizing of these aural entities. I prefer this environmental perspective not because it is more "complete" or more "realistic" but because it encourages a perceptual shift from the recognition and differentiation of sound sources to the appreciation of the resulting sound matter. As soon as the call is in the air, it no longer belongs to the frog that produced it.

## The Illusion of Realism or the Fallacy of the "Real"

The recordings that are featured on *La Selva* have not been modified or subjected to any process of mixing or additions. One might say that this work features "pure" nature sound environments, as is often claimed on commercially released nature recordings. But I believe this obscures a series of questions that have to do with our sense of reality and our notions about its representation in sound recordings. In some of the nature recordings that attempt to convey an easy sense of natural-ness, various animal vocalizations are mixed over a background matrix of environ-mental sound. As in the case of traditional bioacoustics, in which sounds are isolated, this artificial mixing approach of massive inclusion could be criticized as being unreal or hyperreal. Yet we should then consider on which grounds are we criticizing this tricky departure from reality.

Since the advent of digital recording technology (with all its concomitant sound-quality improvements), it has become all the more evident, in our attempt at apprehending the sonic world around us, that the microphones we use are not only our basic interfaces, they are non-neutral interfaces. The way different micro-phones "hear" varies so significantly that they can be considered as a first trans-formational step in the recording process. The consequences of the choices made regarding which microphones will be used are more dramatic than, for example, a further re-equalization of the recordings in the studio.

Yet even if we don't subtract or add anything to the recording, we cannot avoid imposing on it our version of what we consider to be reality. Attempts have been made to circumvent this problem by means of technological improvements. The ambisonics surround sound system, for example, is foreseen as a means of *repro-ducing* soundscapes, conveying a more realistic sense of envelopment and an illu-sion of "being there." Although I appreciate the palette of new sound nuances and the "spaceness" facilitated by these technological improvements, it isn't "realism" that I'm after in my work. But this evocation of place seems frequently to be an objective in the creation of nature recordings.

Only I don't think "reality" is being reproduced with these techniques; rather, a hyperreality is being constructed. The carefully recorded, selected, and edited sound environments that we are able to comfortably enjoy in our favorite armchairs offer an enhanced listening experience, one that we would likely not have if we were hearing those sounds in the "real" world. Ironically, it is often these nonrealis-tic effects that give this kind of sound work its appeal, as they satisfy our expecta-tions of how "the real thing" sounds. I don't mean to suggest that the recorded version is better. Rather, I want to suggest that it is not a version but a different entity with its own inherent value.

Sound editing seems to be another unavoidable obstacle in the attempt to portray aural reality. Whereas the "microphone interface" transfigures the spatial and material characteristics of sound, editing affects its temporality. This process has already begun to take place during the act of recording in that there is always a start and an end for the recording. In most cases, further "time windows" are created in the editing process when a new start and a new end are established for the sound fragment. Also, when we have several sound fragments, we create a montage.

If it is naturalness that we are after in our sound work, what kind of editing makes a piece sound more "real"? David Dunn has challenged the decision often made in nature recording to eliminate human-made sounds. He contends that the elision of sound fragments of natural environments that contain human sonic intrusions (aircraft, road traffic, etc.)—by not recording them or editing them out—is a "false representation of reality" that "lures people into the belief that these places still fulfill their romantic expectations."[1]

But I think the problem goes beyond the issue of phonographic falsification. Our bodies and imaginations engage in sonic transcription and reproduction more than the machines we have invented for these purposes. For instance, we can have a much more striking perception of such a human sonic intrusion than does a microphone, or not perceive it at all, both in the moment it is heard and in the traces it has left in our memory. Do we always realize when there's some distant traffic noise if our attention is focused on an insect call? Do we remember the nearby voices of people when we are recalling a day we enjoyed the sound of the rain in the forest? If not, was our experience—or what we have retained of it—false? Even if our level of consciousness includes both the traffic and the insect, do we have to embrace both of them in representing reality? Because this perceptual ambiguity is at the basis of our apprehension of "reality," I don't think a recording that has been "cleaned up" of human-made sounds is any more false than one that hasn't.

I don't believe that there is such a thing as the "objective" apprehension of sonic reality. Regardless of whether or not we are recording, our minds conceptualize an ideal of sound. And not only do different people listen differently, but the very temporality of our presence in a place is a form of editing. The spatial, material, and temporal transfigurations exist independently of phonography. Our idea of the sonic reality, even our fantasy about it, *is* the sonic reality each one of us possesses [. . . .]

## This is Not La Selva: Sound Matter vs. Representation

"This is not a pipe"

—René Magritte

What you hear on *La Selva* is not La Selva. That is, *La Selva* (the musical piece) is not a representation of La Selva (the reserve in Costa Rica). While it certainly contains elements that can be understood as representational, the musical piece is rooted not in a documentary approach but in a notion of "sound matter" [. . . .]

What I'm defending here is the transcendental dimension of the sound matter *itself*. In my conception, sound recording does not document or represent a richer and more significant "real" world. Rather, it focuses on the inner world of sounds. When the representational/relational level is emphasized, sounds acquire a restricted meaning or a goal, and this inner world is dissipated. I'm thus straightforwardly endorsing Pierre Schaeffer's concepts of the "sound object" and of "reduced" or "acousmatic" listening.[2] I prefer the term "matter" to "object," because I think it better reflects the continuity of the sonic material one finds in sound environments, a continuity affirmed by the non-representational approach to sound recording. I also prefer the term "profound" to the term "reduced" because the latter connotes simplification.

The richness of this sound matter in nature is astonishing, but to appreciate it in depth we have to face the challenge of profound listening. We have to shift the focus of our attention and understanding from representation to being [. . . .]

## Environmental Acousmatics: The Hidden Cicada Paradox

Acousmatics, or the rupture of the visual cause-effect connection between the sound sources and the sounds themselves, can contribute significantly to the "blindness" of profound listening. Like most tropical rain forests, La Selva is a dynamic example of what we could call "environmental acousmatics." There are many sounds in the forest, but one rarely has the opportunity to see the sources of most of those sounds. This is not only because the multitude of animals are hidden in the foliage. The foliage also obscures itself, concealing myriad plant sound sources, caused not only by wind or rain but by falling leaves and branches—a frequent occurrence in that forest.

Many animals in La Selva live in this acousmatic world, in which the rule is not to see their conspecifics, predators, or preys, but just to hear them. This acous-matic feature is best exemplified by one of the most characteristic sounds of La Selva: the strikingly loud and harsh song of the cicadas. During the day, this is probably the sound that typically would most naturally stand in the foreground of the sonic field. You hear it with an astonishing intensity and proximity. Yet, like a persistent paradox, you never see its source.

## A Non-Bucolic Broadband World

Nature sound environments are often characterized as tranquil places, peaceful islands of quietude in a sea of rushing, noisy, human-driven habitats [. . . .] While this notion might be true for certain natural environments and under certain conditions, I think it contributes to a restricted and bucolic view of nature that I don't share. Like many other tropical rain forests, La Selva is quite a noisy place. The diverse sounds of water (rain, watercourses), together with the sound web created by the intense calls of insects or frogs and plant sounds, make up a wonderfully powerful broadband sound environment of thrilling complexity. The textures are extremely rich, with multiple layers that merge with each other and reveal themselves by addition or subtraction, challenging one's perception and also the very notion of what an individual sound might be.

This contributes to expanding our aural understanding of nature, not by denying stillness but by embracing a more inclusive conception, freed of our judgment and reductive categorization. I'm certainly in favor of defending the "pristine" sound quality of natural environments, but for this reason: I think we should avoid the sound intrusion that leads to sonic homogenization, thus conserving the diversity of sounds in the world. In that spirit, I also support the preservation and enhancement of the diversity of human-made sound environments and devices. The value we assign to sound environments is a complex issue that we shouldn't simplify. Under some circumstances, nature can also be considered to be an intrusion in human-made sound environments. In this sense, my approach is as futurist as it is environmentalist [. . . .]

I consider *La Selva* to be a piece of music, but not in the classical sense of the word. Nor do I subscribe to the traditional concept of what is considered to be musical in nature, or how nature and music have been coupled—for example, the search for melodic patterns, comparisons between animal sounds and musical instruments, or "complementing" nature sounds with "musical" ones. To me, a waterfall is as musical as a birdsong.

I believe in expanding and transforming our concept of music through nature (and through "non-nature"), not in the absolute assignment of sounds to music (either in any restricted traditionally academic sense or in the Cagean universal version). Rather, it is my belief that music is an aesthetic (in its widest sense) perception/understanding/conception of sound. It's our *decision*—subjective, intentional, non-universal, not necessarily permanent—that converts nature sounds into music. We don't need to transform or complement the sounds. Nor do we need to pursue a universal and permanent assignment. It will arise when our listening moves away and is freed from being pragmatically and representationally oriented. And attaining this musical state requires a profound listening, an immersion in the *inside* of sound matter.

## NOTES

1. David Dunn, "Nature, Sound Art, and the Sacred," in *The Book of Music and Nature*, ed. David Rothenberg and Marta Ulvaeus (Middletown, CT: Wesleyan University Press, 2001), pp. 95–107.
2. See chap. 14, above.

# 16

# *Adequate Modes of Listening*

## OLA STOCKFELT

Music theorist Ola Stockfelt (1953– ) writes on soundscapes, background music, and the history of musical listening. In this article, he shows that modern life requires us to cultivate a variety of modes of listening, no one of which has any inherent priority. Hence, Stockfelt challenges Theodor Adorno's notion (developed most explicitly in his *Introduction to the Sociology of Music*) that only a focused, expert listening is an adequate and properly critical one. Throughout the piece, Stockfelt invokes a central thesis of philosophical hermeneutics, arguing that different listening practices effectively recompose any given piece of music and, therefore, that the nature of the musical work is always in flux.

Towards evening, I am totally exhausted, but I can finally sink into the seat and relax. The roar of the engines and the hiss from the vents is almost deafening. Under normal circumstances, I detest those sounds, but now they give me the marvelous confirmation that I have made it—I have finally got past all those unexpected and absurd obstacles that forced me to run around and around, all day, in the heat, from office to office and from airport to airport, even though I had my reservation and was ready to depart in the morning. Between this buzz and the noise from fellow passengers, mad individual flute tones find their way to me, tones that further confirm my impression that I have finally reached a place where I can relax. It takes a few minutes before I can even muster the attention to listen to what is actually being played: it is the first movement of Mozart's Symphony no. 40, the "Great G-minor," in an arrangement for flute soloist and some kind of rock group. The flutist seems totally unengaged; as do the other musicians, when it is even possible to distinguish what they are playing. Moreover, the arranger has mutilated the movement quite brutally—large sections are simply absent. As long as I wasn't listening closely, it was perfect music for the situation, but now I start to be both irritated and interested—and not at all at home any more.

What does it mean to treat good music like that? [. . . .]

Western industrialized nations today form a more or less homogeneous culture dominated musically by European and North American "art music" and Anglo-American popular music. Through the phonograph record, radio, and television, the same music is to a great extent scattered across the entire world.[1] Each hearing person who listens to the radio, watches TV, goes to the movies, goes dancing, eats in restaurants, goes to supermarkets, participates in parties, has built up, has been *forced* (in order to be able to handle her or his perceptions of sound)—to build up an appreciable competence in translating and using the music impressions that stream in from loudspeakers in almost every living space. Such competence results not primarily from any formalized schooling but from different everyday learning processes as we teach ourselves which of the sounds that ebb and surge across the modern cityscape at every instant of the day should be clustered together and understood as music and which should be understood as something else; which different types of music correlate with which activity and which subculture; which type of intramusical meanings attach to different types of sound in different musical contexts. The mass-media musical mainstream (in the widest sense of the phrase) has hence become something of a nonverbal lingua franca, one common cultural repertoire transcending traditional culture, class, and age boundaries.[2] Alongside this common cultural competence, many listeners also live in one or several more or less profiled subcultures with a more specialized musical language.[3]

At the same time, the same listeners have the competence to use the same type of music, even the same piece of music, in a variety of different ways in different situations. The symphony that in the concert hall or on earphones can give an autonomous intramusical experience, tuning one's mood to the highest tension and shutting out the rest of the world, may in the café give the same listeners a mildly pleasant, relaxed separation from the noise of the street. At the movies (like the use of Mozart's Symphony no. 40's first movement in a James Bond film)[4] or on television (like the main theme from the same movement in the introduction trailer for the 1987 world ice hockey championships in Vienna), parts of the same work may clearly designate the persons and environments shown according to categories of class and cultural status. And on the car radio in rush hour traffic (if the radio can't be shut off) the same music may constitute an annoying hazard to road safety.

In this way, the situation in which one encounters music conditions the music itself. Particularly with regard to music within the communal repertoire, one can even assume that daily listening is often *more conditioned by the situation in which one meets the music than by the music itself, or by the listener's primary cultural identity,* at least within that more or less homogeneous cultural sphere that comprises Western industrialized environments. Which mode of listening the listener adopts in a given situation depends mainly on how the listener chooses to listen— that is, which mode of listening he or she chooses to develop or adopt. And yet this choice is neither totally free nor accidental.

*In part,* every mode of listening demands a significant degree of competence on the part of the listener (and the competence will not be less by being shared by many), and no listener can have an infinite repertoire of modes of listening. The mode of listening a listener can adopt is in this way limited by the competences in modes of listening that he or she possesses or can develop in a given situation

[. . . .] *In part,* not every mode of listening is in any immediate way adaptable to every type of sound structure or even to every type of musical work [. . . .] *In part,* different modes of listening are in different ways more or less firmly connected to specific listening situations. For example, to dance during a symphony concert (practically impossible because of the fixed seats) is to commit a gaffe, a breach of social convention, even if one is hearing Viennese waltzes or other music originally meant to accompany dancing. It is likewise inappropriate to sink into prolonged intramusical contemplation when one is squeezed into a 7-11-type convenience store. *In part,* finally, the listener's choice of strategies is not entirely free. It can be impossible, for example, to choose to listen in an autonomously reflexive mode if too many other things are competing for attention, and impossible to refuse to listen—to dishearken—to very strong and profiled sounds, or to musemes with a special significance for the listener.[5] Different listeners are also conscious to different degrees of their own choice of mode of listening, and are moreover able to adapt a chosen mode of listening in different situations in relation to different types of sound structures [. . . .]

Today, one can hear almost any style of music in any surrounding and in any situation. The sound of big opera ensembles can be fitted onto a windsurfing board, and the sound of a nylon-stringed guitar can fill a football stadium; one can listen to march music in the bathtub and salon music in the mountains. This state of affairs is still quite novel. Not that long ago, one was obliged to go to the opera to hear opera, and the only way to hear the guitar was to sit rather close to the performer. Various musical styles were implicitly bound to specific environments and specific relationships between the performer and the listener [. . . .]

Each style of music, even if it can make an appearance almost anywhere today, is shaped in close relation to a few environments. In each genre, a few environments, a few situations of listening, make up the constitutive elements in this genre: "The distance between musician and audience, between spectator and spectator, the overall dimension of the events are often fundamental elements in the definition of a genre, and often guide the participants, in the right or wrong way in determining what they should expect about other rules of genre; often 'how you are seated' says more about the music that will be performed than a poster does."[6]

Such an environment can be concretely tangible, like a concert hall, a *palais de danse,* or a church; but it may also be more difficult to localize. Loudspeakers constitute a sort of musical environment, just as one can say that in certain contexts "radio offerings" in their own right constitute a musical environment—not as tangible as a church but not less real.

For recently produced works of music, the style-specific and genre-specific environments have often been identical. Music that is intended for performance in a concert hall has been produced for the concert hall situation. For music mainly targeted toward play on car stereos, one can, for instance, use small speakers that simulate car stereos during the mixing. For works of music that have existed for a longer time, however, the discrepancy can be considerable: this is the case, for example, when liturgical or predominantly dance music is performed in the concert hall for a seated public engaged in aesthetic contemplation. In these instances the changed situation of listening has meant greater or lesser changes in the work of music as sound and especially in the *perceived* work of music.[7]

For each musical genre, a number of listening situations in a given historical situation constitute the genre-specific relation between music and listener. These determine the genre-defining property and the ideal relation between music and listener that were presumed in the formation of the musical style—in the composing, the arranging, the performance, the programming of the music. I have chosen to call these *genre-normative listening situations.*

Genre-normative listening situations are not absolute but are perpetually changing in tandem with the changes in society, in the same way that musical styles change. The private music rooms of late eighteenth-century connoisseurs, for example, engendered a totally different relationship between the listener and the music from those attaining in the opera hall or concert hall, relationships that in their turn differed from those characteristic of the bourgeois salon and restaurant. These different situations hence demanded or made possible different types of musical performance (in spite of the fact that the works being performed might be identical on paper). The situations, and the different performances, also demanded or made possible different modes of listening, and hence resulted in different musical experiences.

Consequently, each genre also has a number of *genre-normative modes of listening,* and even these have changed over time in relationships corresponding to styles of music, to choices of strategies of the listener, to the genre-normative situations of listening, and to a series of social factors. The reflexive, active attitude of musicians to music is a mode of listening that is probably (to some extent) common to almost all forms of "music" (for instance, if one also counts electronic music composers as performing musicians). Other normative modes of listening, like the normative user situations, can almost become defining characteristics for other genres of music.

I have chosen to call each listening in a genre-normative listening situation with its situation-associated genre-normative mode of listening *adequate listening.* Adequate listening hence occurs when one listens to music according to the exigencies of a given social situation and according to the predominant sociocultural conventions of the subculture to which the music belongs.

As a rule, a genre comprises several types of adequate listening. The person who performs music listens with a different type of concentration than do people who are simply listening; but both types of listening can surely be adequate to the genre. Both those who are caught up in the music and dance wildly out on the floor and those who stand close to the stage and concentrate, admiring and studying the virtuosity of the solo guitarist, show adequate attitudes at a blues-rock concert; on the other hand, someone who leans back and with half-closed eyes tries to follow the tonal and thematic tension, relations, and dissolutions is probably not listening adequately.

*To listen adequately hence does not mean any particular, better, or "more musical," "more intellectual," or "culturally superior" way of listening. It means that one masters and develops the ability to listen for what is relevant to the genre in the music, for what is adequate to understanding according to the specific genre's comprehensible context.* Adequate listening is not a prerequisite of assimilating or enjoying music, of learning how to recognize musical styles, or how to create meaning for oneself from what music expresses; it *is* a prerequisite of using music as a language in a broader sense, as a medium for real communication from composer, musician, or programmer to audience/listener. In live situations, an adequately listening audience may also be the prerequisite for the performers' ability to perform genre-adequate music in genres that build on reciprocal communication between executors and listeners. Adequate listening, with adequate modes of listening in an adequate situation, is a normative part of music genre, in the same way that sounding material is.

Adequate listening is, like all languages, always the result of an informal (although sometimes formalized) contract between a greater or smaller group of people, an agreement about the relation of the musical means of expression to this group's picture of the world. Adequate listening is hence always in the broadest sense ideological: it relates to a set of opinions belonging to a social group about ideal relations between individuals, between individuals and cultural expression, and between the cultural expressions and the construction of society [. . . .]

[A]utonomous reflexive listening is not the only adequate listening to develop and establish itself: people have listened adequately to different music in a number of different ways, even though not all these modes of listening were carried on in a formalized fashion into the present. There has never been only *one* adequate autonomous listening in existence—disagreement between different theoretical schools can be seen as oppositions between different autonomous adequacy ideals that can, perhaps by splitting hairs, be said to constitute different musical genres within the frame of one and the same musical style.

Analysis of a musical genre, or of a work in a musical genre, must contain and be based on analysis of the listening adequate to that genre, of the music as it is experienced as adequate to the genre in the normative listening situations, with an adequate mode of listening, adequate extramusical connotations, and adequate simultaneous activities—this is a prerequisite for the possibility of analyzing the "right" piece of music. However, for analyses of everyday music listening, this is not always enough. Analysis of music in everyday listening situations must be based on listening adequate to the given situation. Such adequacy is not determined by the music style in and of itself, or by the genre within which the music style was created, or by the genre to which it primarily belongs today, but rather by the location of the music in the specific situation. That location determines, for instance, who can fulfill the role of "transmitter" in "the musical communication chain." When analyzing background music that targets a general audience in a specific situation, one might therefore develop a strategy of making the music understandable as it is meant to be made understandable by the arranger and programmer. An analysis based on a one-sided, concentrated, autonomous listening will be an analysis of the wrong object, even if the music analyzed originally was created for such a mode of listening. This constraint naturally creates special methodological problems, inasmuch as an adequately adapted "background listening" makes continuous reflexive consciousness impossible. An analysis must therefore begin from such shifts between modes of listening, between foreground and background [. . . .]

Hence we must develop our competence reflexively to control the use of, and the shifts between, different modes of listening to different types of sound events. In the same way that we must listen to the urban soundscape as "music" in order to make it more human, thereby developing the competence to draw up active goals for the "composition" of a more human sound environment, we must develop the competence to listen to that music precisely *as* a part of the sounds-cape in order to explain and change the position of the music in this soundscape. Insofar as we strive to understand today's everyday music and want to develop pedagogical programs with real relevance to those who will live and participate in this musical life, we must develop our own reflexive consciousness and competence as active "idle listeners."

## NOTES

1. See Roger Wallis and Krister Malm, *Big Sounds from Small People: The Music Industry in Small Countries* (New York: Pendragon, 1984), and Jeremy Tunstall, *The Media Are American: Anglo-American Media in the World,* Communication and Society series (New York: Columbia University Press, 1977).
2. Philip Tagg convincingly demonstrates both the common competence of adequately understanding and contextually placing different musical structures through the process of reflexive listening and the fact that listeners for the most part understand the musical semiotic content in such situations in the same way, across cultural areas in other ways considerably separated (Tagg and Clarida, unpublished report on listeners' responses to film and television title themes).
3. See Ulf Hannerz's discussion of "cultural repertoires" in Hannerz, "Research in the Black Ghetto: A Review of the Sixties," *Discovering Afro-America,* ed. Roger D. Abrahams and John F. Szwed (Leiden: International Studies in Sociology and Social Anthropology, E. J. Brill, 1975), and Hannerz, "Delkulturerna och helheten" ("Subcultures and the Totality"), *Kultur och medvetande (Culture and Consciousness),* ed. Ulf Hannerz, Rita Liljeström, and Orvar Löfgren (Göteborg: Akademilitteratur, 1982).
4. *The Living Daylights,* 1988.
5. Minimal fragments of musical meaning. See Philip Tagg, *Kojak, 50 Seconds of Television Music—toward the Analysis of Affect in Popular Music* (Göteborg: Skrifter från Musikvetenskapliga institutionen vid Göteborgs Universitet No. 2, 1979)—Trans.
6. Franco Fabbri, "A Theory of Musical Genres: Two Applications," *Popular Music Perspectives,* ed. David Horn and Philip Tagg (Göteborg and Exeter: International Association for the Study of Popular Music, 1981), 57.
7. One could even say that changes in the listening situation, and therefore in the modes of listening, have created totally new works of music—in cases where the sounding structure in the original context wasn't being perceived as music.

# 17

# *Ambient Music*

## BRIAN ENO

Throughout his career, Brian Eno (1948– ; see also chaps. 22 and 34) has consistently challenged the distinctions between art music and popular music, musician and non-musician. A founding member of the British pop group Roxy Music in the early 1970s, Eno went on to become a successful solo artist and producer, working on records by Talking Heads, David Bowie, U2, Laurie Anderson, and others. He is also a noted sound and video artist who has exhibited audio-visual installations for more than two decades. In the mid 1970s, intrigued by the possibilities of environmental music but critical of its actual commercial use by the Muzak Corporation and others, Eno worked to produce a more rich and subtle form that he called "Ambient Music," which he first explored on a series of solo records (*Discreet Music*, *Music for Airports*, *Music for Films*, *On Land*, etc.).

In 1978 I released the first record which described itself as Ambient Music, a name I invented to describe an emerging musical style.

It happened like this. In the early seventies, more and more people were changing the way they were listening to music. Records and radio had been around long enough for some of the novelty to wear off, and people were wanting to make quite particular and sophisticated choices about what they played in their homes and workplaces, what kind of sonic mood they surrounded themselves with.

The manifestation of this shift was a movement away from the assumptions that still dominated record-making at the time—that people had short attention spans and wanted a lot of action and variety, clear rhythms and song structures and, most of all, voices. To the contrary, I was noticing that my friends and I were making and exchanging long cassettes of music chosen for its stillness, homogeneity, lack of surprises, and most of all, lack of variety. We wanted to use music in a different way—as part of the ambience of our lives—and we wanted it to be continuous, a surrounding.

At the same time there were other signs on the horizon. Because of the development of recording technology, a whole host of compositional possibilities that were quite new to music came into existence. Most of these had to do with two closely related new areas—the development of the texture of sound itself as a focus for compositional attention, and the ability to create with electronics virtual acoustic spaces (acoustic spaces that don't exist in nature).

When you walk into a recording studio, you see thousands of knobs and controls. Nearly all of these are different ways of doing the same job: they allow you to do things to sounds, to make them fatter or thinner or shinier or rougher or harder or smoother or punchier or more liquid or any one of a thousand other things. So a recording composer may spend a great deal of her compositional energy effectively inventing new sounds or combinations of sounds. Of course, this was already well known by the mid sixties: psychedelia expanded not only minds but recording technologies as well. But there was still an assumption that playing with sound itself was a "merely" technical job—something engineers and producers did—as opposed to the serious creative work of writing songs and playing instruments. With Ambient Music, I wanted to suggest that this activity was actually one of the distinguishing characteristics of new music, and could in fact become the main focus of compositional attention.

Studios have also offered composers virtual spaces. Traditional recording put a mike in front of an instrument in a nice-sounding space and recorded the result. What you heard was the instrument and its reverberation in that space. By the forties, people were getting a little more ambitious, and starting to invent technologies that could supplement these natural spaces—echo chambers, tape delay systems, etc. A lot of this work was done for radio—to be able to "locate" characters in different virtual spaces in radio dramas—but it was popular music which really opened the subject up. Elvis and Buddy and Eddy and all the others sang with weird tape repeats on their voices—unlike anything you'd ever hear in nature. Phil Spector and Joe Meek invented their own "sound"—by using combinations of overdubbing, home-made echo units, resonant spaces like staircases and lift-shafts, changing tape-speeds and so on, they were able to make "normal" instruments sound completely new. And all this was before synthesizers and dub reggae . . .

By the early seventies, when I started making records, it was clear that this was where a lot of the action was going to be. It interested me because it suggested moving the process of making music much closer to the process of painting (which I thought I knew something about). New sound-shaping and space-making devices appeared on the market weekly (and still do), synthesizers made their clumsy but crucial debut, and people like me just sat at home night after night fiddling around with all this stuff, amazed at what was now possible, immersed in the new sonic worlds we could create.

And immersion was really the point: we were making music to swim in, to float in, to get lost inside.

This became clear to me when I was confined to bed, immobilized by an accident in early 1975. My friend Judy Nylon had visited, and brought with her a record of 17th-century harp music. I asked her to put it on as she left, which she did, but it wasn't until she'd gone that I realized that the hi-fi was much too quiet and one of the speakers had given up anyway. It was raining hard outside, and I could hardly hear the music above the rain—just the loudest notes, like little crystals, sonic icebergs rising out of the storm. I couldn't get up and change it, so I just lay there waiting for my next visitor to come and sort it out, and gradually I was seduced by this listening experience. I realized that this was what I wanted music to be—a place, a feeling, an all-around tint to my sonic environment.

After that, in April or May of that year, I made *Discreet Music*, which I suppose was really my first Ambient record (though the stuff I'd done with the great guitarist Robert Fripp before that gets pretty close). This was a 31-minute piece (the longest I could get on a record at the time) which was modal, evenly textured, calm and sonically warm. At the time, it was not a record that received a very warm welcome, and I probably would have hesitated to release it without the encouragement of my friend Peter Schmidt, the painter. (In fact, it's often been painters and writers—people who use music while they work and want to make for themselves a conducive environment—who've first enjoyed and encouraged this work.)

In late 1977 I was waiting for a plane in Cologne airport. It was early on a sunny, clear morning, the place was nearly empty, and the space of the building (designed, I believe, by the father of one of the founders of Kraftwerk) was very attractive. I started to wonder what kind of music would sound good in a building like that. I thought, "It has to be interruptible (because there'll be announcements), it has to work outside the frequencies at which people speak, and at different speeds from speech patterns (so as not to confuse communication), and it has to be able to accommodate all the noises that airports produce. And, most importantly for me, it has to have something to do with where you are and what you're there for—flying, floating and, secretly, flirting with death." I thought, "I want to make a kind of music that prepares you for dying—that doesn't get all bright and cheerful and pretend you're not a little apprehensive, but which makes you say to yourself, 'Actually, it's not that big a deal if I die.'"

Thus was born the first Ambient record—*Music for Airports*—which I released on my own label (called Ambient Records, of course). The inner sleeve of that release carried my manifesto:

### Ambient Music

The concept of music designed specifically as a background feature in the environment was pioneered by Muzak Inc. in the fifties, and has since come to be known generically by the term Muzak. The connotations that this term carries are those particularly associated with the kind of material that Muzak Inc. produces—familiar tunes arranged and orchestrated in a lightweight and derivative manner. Understandably, this has led most discerning listeners (and most composers) to dismiss entirely the concept of environmental music as an idea worthy of attention.

Over the past three years, I have become interested in the use of music as ambience, and have come to believe that it is possible to produce material that can be used thus without being in any way compromised. To create a distinction between my own experiments in this area and the products of the various purveyors of canned music, I have begun using the term Ambient Music.

An ambience is defined as an atmosphere, or a surrounding influence: a tint. My intention is to produce original pieces ostensibly (but not exclusively) for particular times and situations with a view to building up a small but versatile catalogue of environmental music suited to a wide variety of moods and atmospheres.

Whereas the extant canned music companies proceed from the basis of regularizing environments by blanketing their acoustic and atmospheric idiosyncrasies, Ambient Music is intended to enhance these. Whereas conventional background music is produced by stripping away all sense of doubt and uncertainty (and thus all genuine interest) from the music, Ambient Music retains these qualities. And whereas their intention is to "brighten" the environment by adding stimulus to it (thus supposedly alleviating the tedium of routine tasks and levelling out the natural ups and downs of the body rhythms), Ambient Music is intended to induce calm and a space to think.

Ambient Music must be able to accommodate many levels of listening attention without enforcing one in particular; it must be as ignorable as it is interesting.

September 1978

Like a lot of the stuff I was doing at the time, this was regarded by many English music critics as a kind of arty joke, and they had a lot of fun with it. I'm therefore pleased that the idea has stuck around so long and keeps sprouting off in all sorts of directions: it comes back round to me like Chinese Whispers—unrecognizable but intriguing. Those early seeds (there were only four releases on the original Ambient Records label—*On Land* and *Music for Airports* by me, *The Plateaux of Mirror* by Harold Budd and *Day of Radiance* by Laraaji) have contributed to a rich forest of music.

(1996)

# 18

## *The Aural Walk*

### IAIN CHAMBERS

Along with Stuart Hall and Dick Hebdige, Iain Chambers (1949– ) is a leading figure in the influential "Birmingham School" of cultural studies. Like Hebdige, Chambers has a particular interest in the circulation of music and its role in the construction of identity. His books include *Urban Rhythms: Pop Music and Popular Culture* (1985) and *Popular Culture: The Metropolitan Experience* (1986).

The following piece considers the transformation of listening practices made possible by portable musical technologies such as the Walkman. It responds to a common criticism of the Walkman: that it encourages an aggressively private listening experience. Chambers argues that, however private, portable stereos provide the listening subject with a tool for mediating his or her public experience, transforming it from a passive one into an active one. On Chambers' view, the Walkman allows us to shape our audio-visual experience and thus to produce a soundtrack for our everyday lives.

"One hundred solitudes form the whole of the city of Venice—this is its spell. An image for the man of the future." Nietzsche's observation refers not to the 'lonely crowd,' that spectre of collective angst, nor to Poe's Man of the Crowd, who found a vicarious vitality among the throng, but to the artifice of luxurious solitude: solitude as the most exquisite refinement of all urban design. Could it be that we come to the city in order to achieve solitude? Such has been the unspoken premise of the modern city of utopian individualism. By solitude I do not mean isolation. Isolation is a state of nature: solitude is the work of culture. Isolation is an imposition, solitude a choice.

—Brian Hatton[1]

The Sony Walkman. Launched on the world in the spring of 1980, this urban, hi-fi, gadget was based on an idea that came to Akio Morita, President of Sony, while, rather appropriately, walking in New York. Over the decade and now into the nineties the Walkman has offered access to a portable soundtrack that, unlike the transistor radio, car stereo and the explicitly opposed intention of the bass-boosted "ghetto blaster" or "boogie box," is, above all, an intensely private experience. However, such a refusal of public exchange and apparent regression to individual solitude also involves an unsuspected series of extensions. With the Walkman there is simultaneously a concentration of the auditory environment and an extension of our individual bodies.

For the meaning of the Walkman does not necessarily lie in itself—it sits there, neat, usually black, often wrapped in leather, and quite oblivious—but in the extension of perceptive potential. People who walk around with a Walkman might simply seem to signify a void, the emptiness of metropolitan life, but that little black object can also be understood as a pregnant zero, as the link in an urban strategy, a semiotic shifter, the crucial digit in a particular organisation of sense. For the idea of the void, of nothing, always introduces us to the paradox that nothing can only be known by knowing nothing, that is, something.[2] So we might suggest that the apparent vacuity of the Walkman opens up the prospect of a passage in which we discover, as Gilles Deleuze reminds us in *Logique du sens* (1969), those other cities that exist inside the city. There we move along invisible grids where emotional energies and the imaginary flow, and where the continual slippage of sense maintains the promise of meaning.

In the manifest refusal of sociability the Walkman nevertheless reaffirms participation in a shared environment. It directly partakes in the changes in the horizon of perception that characterise the late twentieth century, and which offers a world fragmenting under the mounting media accumulation of intersecting signs, sounds and images. With the Walkman strapped to our bodies we confront what Murray Schafer in his book *The Tuning of the World* calls a "soundscape," a soundscape that increasingly represents a mutable collage: sounds are selected, sampled, folded in and cut up by both the producers (DJs, rap crews, dub masters, recording engineers) and the consumers (we put together our personal play lists, skip some tracks, repeat others, turn up the volume to block out the external soundtrack or flip between the two).[3] Each listener/player selects and rearranges the surrounding soundscape, and, in constructing a dialogue with it, leaves a trace in the network.

The Walkman, like the transistor radio, the portable computer, the mobile phone and, above all, the credit card, is a privileged object of contemporary nomadism. Yet, as Chantal de Gournay has pointed out, while the computer and global credit status transmit you through a-topic space in a "virtual," rather than a corporeal, reality, where time is "fatal" and space incidental, the Walkman, on the contrary, draws the world into you, reaffirms your body, and laconically signals a "diasporic identity" put together in transit.[4] Like Walter Benjamin's description of the Parisian arcades that let light into their interiors, the Walkman brings the external world into the interior design of identities.

In this mobile, wrap-around world, the Walkman, like dark glasses and iconoclastic fashion, serves to set one apart while simultaneously reaffirming individual contact to certain common, if shifting, measures (music, fashion, aesthetics, metropolitan life . . . and their particular cycles of mortality). So the Walkman is both a mask and a masque: a quiet putting into act of localised theatrics. It reveals itself as a significant symbolic gadget for the nomads of modernity, in which music on the move is continually being decontextualised and recontextualised in the inclusive acoustic and symbolic flux of everyday life.[5] Still, if the Walkman so far represents the ultimate form of the art of transit, it also represents the ultimate musical means in mediating the ambient. For it permits the possibility, however fragile and however transitory, of imposing your soundscape on the surrounding aural environment and thereby domesticating the external world: for a moment it can all be brought under the STOP/START, FAST FORWARD, PAUSE and REWIND buttons.

The fascination of the image of the Walkman, apart from the inner secret it brazenly displays in public (what is s/he listening to?), is the ambiguous position that it occupies between autism and autonomy: that ambiguous mixture of danger and saving power, to paraphrase Heidegger's quotation from Hölderlin, that characterises modern technology. Therefore, to understand the Walkman involves multiplying on it diverse points of view, and appreciating that it does not subtract from sense but adds to and complicates it. Pursuing this we might say that our relationship to the Walkman "will be free if it opens our human existence to the essence of technology."[6] By "essence" (*Wesen*) Heidegger intends something that endures through time, that dwells in the present, that offers a "sense" of technology that is not merely reducible to the "technological." Despite the nostalgia for authenticity that permeates Heidegger's discourse we can nevertheless bend his words in a suggestive direction. To the question what is technology and, in this particular case, the Walkman, we can answer that it is simultaneously a technical instrument and a cultural activity. To continue with the German philosopher's concerns, the Walkman is an instrument and activity that contributes to the casting into sense, to the re-presenting, or en-framing (*Ge-stell*), of the contemporary world. In retracing the etymology of "technology" back to the Greek *techné* and its ancient connection to the arts, to *poiesis* and knowledge, Heidegger suggests a wider frame for thinking its sense, its particular truth.

However, as both instrument and activity, the Walkman is not simply an instrument that reveals the enduring truth of technology and being; it is also an immediate historical reality and practice. As part of the equipment of modern nomadism it contributes to the prosthetic extension of mobile bodies caught up in a decentred diffusion of languages, experiences, identities, idiolects and histories that are distributed in a tendentially global syntax. The Walkman encourages us to think inside this new organisation of time and space. Here, for example, the older, geometrical model of the city as the organiser of space has increasingly been replaced by chronometry and the organisation of time. The technology of space has been supplemented and increasingly eroded by the technology of time: the "real time," the "nanoseconds" of computer chips and monitor blips, of transitory information on a screen, of sounds snatched in the headphones. It leads to the emergence of a further dimension. "Speed suddenly returns to become a *primitive force* beyond the measure of both time and space."[7]

To travel, and to perform our *travail*, in this environment we plug in, choosing a circuit. Here, as opposed to the discarded "grand narratives" (Lyotard) of the city, the Walkman offers the possibility of a micro-narrative, a customised story and soundtrack, not merely a space but a place, a site of dwelling. The ingression of such a privatised habitat in public spaces is a disturbing act. Its uncanny quality lies in its deliberate confusion of earlier boundaries, in its provocative appearance "out of place." Now, the confusion of "place," of voices, histories and experiences speaking "out of place" forms part of the altogether more extensive sense of contemporary semantic and political crisis. A previous spatial hierarchy has had increasingly to confront an excess of languages emerging out of the histories and languages of feminism, sexual rights, ethnicity, race and the environment that overflow and undercut its authority. The Walkman is therefore a political act? It is certainly an act that unconsciously entwines with many other micro-activities in conferring a different sense on the *polis*. In producing a different sense of space and time, it participates in rewriting the conditions of representation: where "representation" clearly indicates both the semiotic dimensions of the everyday *and* potential participation in a political community.

In Bruce Chatwin's marvelous book *The Songlines* we are presented with the idea that the world was initially sung into being.

> I have a vision of the Songlines stretching across the continents and ages; that wherever men have trodden they have left a trail of song (of which we may, now and then, catch an echo); and that these traits must reach back, in time and space, to an isolated pocket in the African savannah, where the First Man opening his mouth in defiance of the terrors that surrounded him, shouted the opening stanza of the World Song, "I AM!".[8]

The Nietzschean vision of the world, that is, a world of our making, dependent on our activity and language for its existence, is here laid out as the human adventure in which the movements of peoples, and the rigours and rhythms of bodies, limbs and voice, set the patterns, the design, the nomination, of the land, the country, our home. The religious aura of this nomadism has clearly waned in the more secular networks of Western society. Perhaps it still continues to echo inside the miniaturised headphones of modern nomads as the barely remembered traces of a once sacred journey intent on celebrating its presence in a mark, voice, sign, symbol, signature, to be left along the track.

## NOTES

1. Brian Hatton, "From Neurosis to Narrative," in Linda Brown and Deyan Sudjic, eds., *Metropolis. New British Architecture and the City*, London, ICA, 1988.

2. See Brian Rotman's interesting study of the question, *Signifying Nothing: The Semiotics of Zero*, London, Macmillan, 1987.

3. R. Murray Schafer, *The Tuning of the World*, New York, Alfred Knopf, 1977.

4. Chantal de Gournay, "Citadins et nomads. L'espace public à l'épreuve des technologies de communication mobile," paper given at the Centre de Sociologie de l'Innovation of the École Nationale Supérieure des Mines, Paris, 9 January 1992.

5. Shuhei Hosokawa, "The Walkman Effect," *Popular Music* 4, 1984, pp. 171–3. This is a brilliant, pioneering essay on the question of the Walkman. It is extracted from a full-length study in Japanese: Shuhei Hosokawa, *Walkman no Shûjigaku*, Tokyo, Asahi Shuppan, 1981.

6. Martin Heidegger, "The Question Concerning Technology," in Martin Heidegger, *The Question Concerning Technology and Other Essays*, New York, Harper & Row, 1977, p. 3.

7. Paul Virilio, *Lo spazio critico*, Bari, Dedalo, 1988, p. 15; *L'Espace critique*, Paris, Christian Bourgois, 1984.

8. Bruce Chatwin, *The Songlines*, London, Picador, 1988, p. 314.

# 19

## *Some Sound Observations*

### PAULINE OLIVEROS

Composer Pauline Oliveros (1932– ) played a key role in the development of a range of contemporary musical practices: tape music, electronic music, experimental music, minimalism, World Music, and Ambient music. In the early 1960s, she co-founded the San Francisco Tape Music Center, one of the first electronic music studios in the United States. She is well known for a series of haunting electronic pieces (among them *Alien Bog*, *Beautiful Soop*, and *Bye, Bye Butterfly*) that make use of analog electronics and tape delay systems. More recently, Oliveros has built her music around drones generated by her just-tuned and often electronically processed accordian. Throughout her career, Oliveros has actively advocated for the recognition of women composers both in her writings and through the Pauline Oliveros Foundation, inaugurated in 1985. The following piece was comissioned by *Source*, a San Francisco-based magazine that documented the American experimental music scene in the late 1960s. The article exemplifies Oliveros' lifelong investigation into the process of listening, its centrality to composition, and its importance for a holistic conception of human existence.

As I sit here trying to compose an article for *Source*, my mind adheres to the sounds of myself and my environment. In the distance a bulldozer is eating away a hillside while its motor is a cascade of harmonics defining the space between it and the Rock and Roll radio playing in the next room. Sounds of birds, insects, children's voices and the rustling of trees fleck this space.

As I penetrate the deep drone of the bulldozer with my ear, the mind opens and reveals the high pitched whine of my nervous system. It reaches out and joins the flight of an airplane drone, floats down the curve of Doppler effect.

Now, fifteen minutes since the beginning of this writing, the bulldozer has stopped for a while. The freeway one-half mile away, unmasked, sends its ever-shifting drone to join with the train whistle from Encinitas.

The bulldozer starts again moving the air like an audible crooked staircase before reaching its full power. As I lean on my wooden table, my arm receives sympathetic vibrations from the low frequencies of the bulldozer, but hearing seems to take place in my stomach. A jet passes over. Some of its sound moves through my jawbone and out the back of my neck. It is dragging the earth with it.

I would like to amplify my bowl of crackling, shaking jello. (Once in 1959 a bulldozer came through the side of my house while I was eating lunch. The driver looked at me, backed out, and continued to operate the bulldozer.)

I would like to amplify the sound of a bull dozing.

The bulldozer has stopped again. On the other side of the freeway, a dog repeats a high bark which curves downward. My dog has a tinkling collar. I would like to find a free way.

Three days ago at UC Davis, I experienced a magnificent performance of Bob Ashley's *Wolfman.* My ears changed and adapted themselves to the sound pressure level. All the wax in my ears melted. After the performance, ordinary conversation at two feet away sounded very distant. Later, all ordinary sounds seemed heightened, much louder than usual. Today I can still feel *Wolfman* in my ears. MY EARS FEEL LIKE CAVES. Monday I am going to hear *Wolfman* again. It will be the fourth time I've heard *Wolfman,* and I can't wait to hear the feedback dripping from his jaws again.

My present bulldozer has started and stopped again. A faraway jet simulates a fifty foot tabla, accompanied by an infinite freeway tamboura.

I am tired of writing this article, but not of the opportunity it is giving me to listen and remember. My chair is creaking as restlessness grows. I wonder what God's chair sounds like? I would like to amplify it. I would like to amplify a spider spinning its web.

Loren Rush calls his new work Theater of the Mind. Since last night, he is still playing and singing in the theater of my mind.

The bulldozer remains silent. A very low frequency is shaking my belly. (7 Hz at high intensity can make you sick or kill you.) It is an automobile becoming more apparent as it passes, now accented by a motorbike.

(Once in a half-waking state, my head was held hard against a wall by the sound of a model airplane motor. I thought some cosmic dentist was drilling for my mind's tooth.)

The breeze is rising and blowing my papers about the table. The rustling in the trees sounds like tape hiss until it mixes with the next plane overhead.

Recently, a young man described his experience working in proximity to jet engines. After overcoming fear of the sound, he began to find sounds to listen to, such as small tinklings within the engine.

Why can't sounds be visible? Would the feedback from ear to eye cause fatal oscillation? Can you remember the first sound you ever heard? What is the first sound you remember hearing?

Why shouldn't a music department in a university devote itself entirely to music since 1950? Without a substantial body of new literature and instrumentation, the symphony and opera will become defunct—dead horses in the 21st Century. Who cares.

I often think of the title of one of La Monte Young's pieces which I have not yet had the pleasure of hearing: *The Second Dream of the High Tension Wire.*

In the Schwann long-playing record catalog there are special sections for railroads, sound effects, sports cars, test records, and honky-tonk piano, but none for electronic music.

When a concert pianist is on tour, he usually finds a tuned Steinway grand piano to play. What kind of sound system does the electronic musician find?

When I stopped writing yesterday, I went on listening. I attended dinner in a Syrian restaurant and ate a concert with my *Wolfman* ears. The house lights dimmed to a singing SCR (Silicon Controlled Rectifier). Spots came up and the bassoon soloist walked on the stage, bowed to the applause, walked off again and told someone to turn off the heating fan which was playing a duet with the SCR. He returned, bowed again to the new round of applause. His taped accompaniment began. I heard trees rustling in the speakers.

Loren Rush has synthesized a bassoon sound at the artificial intelligence center at Stanford. With John Chowning's programming, he can make it move in circles, ellipses, or figure-eights around two speakers. He can make the synthesized bassoon do a *glissando.* Loren has a lecture entitled "A Day in the Life of a Plastic Bassoon."

Next, a quiet trio played in the manner of Morton Feldman: accented, perfectly-cued car drones.

I listened to a Schubert octet in the recording engineer's sound booth. The speakers added their characteristics to the orchestration. As we watched the audience, the engineer said, "Those people are not listening to the music as it was intended. They should be having dinner."

I am inside my house now. Outside, sounds are attenuated by the insulation. I hear a dripping faucet and the ticking of my cuckoo clock. They combine and are joined by the refrigerator. The planes from Palomar Airport dwindle in through the furnace openings.

I have listened to many refrigerators. There is often a flickering between the sixth and seventh harmonic. Once, while in the process of drinking ouzo with David, Bob, and Orville, a refrigerator sent its harmonics out to surround my head with circles, ellipses, and figure-eights.

In 1963 I made a tape piece for dancer Elizabeth Harris. It was made from piano sounds. On the night of the first performance, I stood in the wings prepared to start the tape recorder. Suddenly, I heard the opening sounds of my piece, but the tape transport was not moving. The dance involved a mobile that was suspended from a strand of piano wire. When the mobile was lowered, it moved like a pendulum, causing the piano wire to vibrate.

In New York, Terry Riley led me fifteen blocks out of our way to hear a building ventilator. I wonder what microbes hear?

Sitting in a parking lot on my third day of article writing. I could listen to the stereophony of car starter gagglings, motor wigglings, door squeals, and "bllaps" forever. It's almost like Debussy, compared to Saturday's Wagnerian bulldozer.

The best part of Lincoln Center is the tunnel from the IRT to the Beaumont Theater. Walking toward the theater, my footsteps greeted me from the approaching wall; midway, they followed me from the opposite wall. I listened to this more than one hundred and fifty times—an Alice in Tunnelland—while moving from the saga of subway sound to Brechtian music drama.

"If the moon is ever visited, one feature of its environment will be known beforehand with certainty; the wastes will be noiseless except for vibration transmitted through the solid surface. Since there is no gaseous atmosphere, there can be no tread of footsteps heard, no rustle of clothing, and if an obstruction is dynamited, the debris will fly apart silently as in a dream." (Edgar Villchur: *Reproduction of Sound*)

During the quiet evening of a summer vacation near the Feather River Canyon, Lynn, Bob, and I wanted to play music. We decided to read John Cage's *Atlas Eclipticalis* from the original score, which was shining brightly above.[1] The canyon creatures joined us as we played, and we played until our awareness became imbedded in the canyon and summoned a ghostly, floating train, an apparition of metal meeting metal, reflected doubly, triply, endlessly from the canyon, from the mind, from the flickering passenger windows, the rumbling ties, OUR EARS FELT LIKE CANYONS. We didn't speak until morning.

One's ideas about music can change radically after listening to recorded works at fast forward or rewind on a tape recorder. Ramón Sender arranged Wagner's *Ring Cycle* by a series of re-recordings at fast forward to four successive clicks. "The auditory basis of obstacle detection by bats was independently recognized in 1932 by a Dutch zoologist, Sven Dijkgraaf, who made a careful study of these faint, audible clicks and noted how closely they were correlated with the echo-location of obstacles. This is an example of the need for care, patience, and appropriate conditions if one is to notice and enjoy some of the more fascinating facets of the natural world." (Donald R. Griffin: *Echoes of Bats and Men*)

According to Loren Rush, the reason for studying counterpoint is that you may have to teach it some day.

"Airborne sound waves are reflected back almost totally from the water, and underwater sound is equally well reflected back downward from the surface . . . once proper equipment was available for converting underwater sound to audible airborne sound . . . underwater listening became refined enough and common enough to reveal the immense variety of sounds used by marine animals." (Ibid)

In most schools and universities the language laboratories are better equipped for sound processing and modifications than the music departments.

Human hearing is non-linear. Our ears are less sensitive to low and high frequencies approaching the limits of audibility. Our ears are most sensitive at about 3000 Hz where some people can hear collisions of air molecules.

A fast sweep of the audio range by a tone generator can produce a click.

"Some animals, notably insects, do not have ears in their heads but in such unlikely places as legs (some crickets) or the thorax, the 'middle' portions of the insect body to which the legs attach (some grasshoppers)." (Bergeijk, Pierce & David, *Waves and the Ear*)

I stopped writing yesterday in order to go on listening. Monday's performance of *Wolfman* was somewhat marred because the sponsors failed to provide proper speakers and amplifiers. I heard Wolfman's ghost drooling feedback.

Many music departments are more concerned with analysis than communication.

When I was sixteen, my accordion teacher taught me to hear combination tones. The accordion is particularly able to produce them if you squeeze hard enough. From that time, I wished for a way to eliminate the fundamental tones so I could listen only to the combination tones. When I was thirty-two, I began to set signal generators beyond the range of hearing and to make electronic music from amplified combination tones. I felt like a witch capturing sounds from a nether realm.

In one electronic studio I was accused of black art, and the director disconnected line amplifiers to discourage my practices, declaring that signal generators are of no use above or below the audio range because you can't hear them. Since all active processing equipment contains amplifiers, I found that I could cascade two pieces of equipment and get enough gain for my combination tones to continue my work, plus the addition of various amplifier characteristics as orchestration. I worked there for two months, and, for recreation, would ride my bicycle to the town power plant where I would listen for hours to the source of my newly-found powers.

Saturday's bulldozer has gone away. The birds and insects share the air with waxing, waning plane and car drones. The insects are singing in the supersonic range. I hear their combination tones while the insects probably hear the radio frequency sounds created by motor drones, but not the fundamentals. If we could hear the micro-world, we would probably hear the brain functioning.

## NOTES

1. [*Atlas Eclipticalis* is a graphic score rendered from star charts —Eds.]

# 20

# *Compose Yourself*

## J. K. RANDALL

An American composer of electronic and acoustic music, J.K. Randall (1929– ) taught at Princeton University from 1957 until his retirement in 1991. Through his compositions and writings, one can trace a path from "total serialism" to "experimental music." Randall was an associate editor at the prestigous journal *Perspectives of New Music*, where parts of "Compose Yourself" first appeared in 1972. Its informal and iconclastic style caused a prominent patron of the journal to withdraw his financial support. Formally, the piece is more like a poem or a musical composition than an essay. None-theless, it presents a careful and articulate phenomenological description that refuses to separate listening (in this case, to Richard Wagner's *Götter-dämmerung*) from the totality of bodily and conscious experience.

## ACT II SCENE I ARISES OUT OF ITS OWN VORSPIEL

there's been a *prelude, and towards the end of it the curtain went up and then the moon came out plötzlich. What you're hearing now—(there's Alberich hassling Hagen)—is a repeated chord in the clarinets. That's about the size of it. Well yes, the 4th horn is laying down a low A underneath (which gets itself goosed*[1] *every so often by a pizzicato)—and there's that scrabbly lick*[2] *in the violas for a moment; but mostly the clarinets repeating a chord. That's about it—about the size of it. Hear it now?*

{You want the *whole* picture? Oh come on. Yes, sure there was an Act One before this and a stretch of Vorspiel before that. But since then there's been Some Warm Pepsi and Part Of A Baloney Sandwich—I mean like about 3/5 of a Generationgap has transpired since then man {What do you mean, "worse than that"? . . . . . What about yesterday? . . . . . Last week? . . . . . Yesterday and last week both? . . . . . .Three whole mothers? . . . . . No, sorry; I wasn't around {(—Now look. Here's this clarinet chord. Hear it? (—See: here. Start from it. (—And let's get down to it before it catches up with last week

## OK, let's lay it out straight: it's a diminished-seventh chord

{don't panic, Culture fans: so help me, this one's even been identified at the
Curtis Institute {somewhere towards the back of the manual, kiddies: under
"Weird Chords And Other Embarrassments". (Thank God they all resolve.)
(Of course, This One doesn't): but that's Genius for you, kiddies: different
rules for different people (and more sex too!! {don't flip, cats, "o₇" in the fake-
book

## a diminished-seventh chord which can be heard as

{that's right, gramps: the one that delivered the mustache[3], back there when
flicks really flicked {yes, madam, and successfully impersonated Death[4] in
over two hundred cantatas of J. S. Bach, back before Albert Schweitzer saved
Africa {right on, brothersister, the one that Ben Boretz generated the *Tristan*
Metaprelude out of (—*generating cycles, cycles of cycles, cycles of cyclecy-
cles, layers*

## can be heard

*within metalayers; burying an Old Warhorse and resurrecting a new world,*

## *can be heard as*

*a new way of constructing, of imagining—a new slicing of Space & Time,
brothersister; the Old slicings not merely*

## Can Be Heard As A Just Previously[5]

*shuffled around sisterbrother but dissolved, metavaried; and the New rig*]

## Can *Be Heard As A just Previously Heard Evolution*[5]-In-

{(oh alrighta'ready: so get your hair out of your eyes long enough to find the
First Fret on G and on high E; no, lay off the low E—it'll still be there when
you come down—and blow me just the top five strings. (Sure the low A is for
real: I've given you that horn note free for nothing just to let you know where
I'm at. Sounds pretty groovy? (Better use your own lyrics though: Alberich is
a temporarily oppressed superfink, and Hagen blows cowhorn

## EVOLUTION–IN–TIME TEMPORALLY COMPRESSED[4].

{—He means the moontune: the one in thirds, in the violins, with that weird high A.
—You mean the one that plötzliched?
—Yeah that's the one: think about it: (sort of all
                                    scrunched
                                    up

]APPENDIX

*-orously imagined, lovingly defined (—not pos-*
*tures, but reconstruction within, sitherbrosters;*

*—not slogans, but reconstruction without*

*(—metavariations*
*Brithersostered,*

*(sotherbristers)*

## NOTES

1. (pfung! ; !pfung(
2. fibbadibba dooooooo
3. (chuggathuggashuggafuggachuggathuggashuggafugga)
4. {*ooo! freaky*
5. tra-la la la dabatabada tra-la la la dabatabada tra-

Today our acoustic technology is beginning to restore the ancient union of words and music, but especially the tape recorder has brought back the voice of the bard.

—Marshall McLuhan[1]

No generation of composers has been exposed to as much different music as we have, thanks to the technology of recording and the resulting boom in the quantity of music available. Twenty or thirty years ago you had to bend over backward to find a record from Bali. Today, media's gone nuts. We're just trying to incorporate these different elements that are available to us.

—John Zorn[2]

The phonograph does not hear as do ears that have been immediately trained to filter voices, words, and sounds out of noise; it registers acoustic events as such.

—Friedrich Kittler[3]

The microphone is an instrument which acts toward the ear as the microscope does to the eye. It will render evident to us sounds that are otherwise absolutely inaudible. I have heard myself the tramp of a little fly across a box with a tread almost as loud as that of a horse across a wooden bridge.

—W.H. Preece (1878)[4]

Technology precedes artistic invention (as much as we artists would like to think it's the other way around!). First came the electric guitar and *then* came rock and roll.

—John Adams[5]

The gramophone record is in fact a very mixed blessing [. . . . I]ts tendency [is] to emphasize the product status of the music engraved upon it [. . . . T]he idea becomes subtly implanted, not necessarily deliberately, that in owning a record one somehow owns a piece of the work itself [. . . .] The record also has the undesirable effect, especially in many modern works where a degree of choice is left to the performer, and in improvised music, of fixing one particular version to the exclusion of all other possibilities [. . . .]

—Christopher Small[6]

[T]he whole culture of listening to records I don't understand. Where do you look? Do you stare at a wall when you listen to records? Normally, what do record buyers do? Do they buy the record, take it home, put it on for the next . . . I mean, they can last for 74 minutes! Do they sit there for 74 minutes, they don't do the dishes, just sit and look at something, or close their eyes? [. . . .] If you could only play a record *once,* imagine the intensity you'd have to bring to the listening! In the same way that if I play something I can only play it once. There might be a great similarity between each time I play, but I cannot repeat what I play. If you could only listen to it once, don't you think it might concentrate the eardrums?

—Derek Bailey[7]

[D]ocuments such as tape-recordings of improvisation are essentially empty, as they preserve chiefly the form that something took and give at best an indistinct hint as to the feeling and cannot of course convey any sense of time and place [. . . I]t is impossible to record with any fidelity a kind of music that is actually derived from the room in which it is taking place—its size, shape, acoustical properties, even the view from the window [. . . .T]his music is not ideal for home listening. It is not a suitable background for social intercourse. Besides, this music does not *occur* in a home environment, and its force depends to some extent on public response.

—Cornelius Cardew[8]

I hate going to improvised music concerts [. . . .] I just want to buy the record. I mean, you've got people who are playing for you who have years and years of thought and trial and error with this form of music. What they're giving you is information so dense that, unless you're fucking brilliant, you're not going to get all the possible trains of thought that are going on there.

—Jim O'Rourke[9]

The studio must be like a living thing. The machine must be live and intelligent. Then I put my mind into the machine by sending it through the controls and the knobs or into the jack panel. The jack panel is the brain itself, so you've got to patch up the brain and make the brain a living man, but the brain can take what you're sending into it and live.

—Lee "Scratch" Perry[10]

The esthetic of the fabrication defect will re-utilize the sonorous trash (everyday symphony), be they conventional or unconventional instruments (for example: toys, cars, whistles, saws, hertz orchestra, street noises, etc.) [. . . .] It will recycle the alphabet of emotions contained in songs and musical symbols of the First World, that sealed each marked step of our affective and emotional life. They will be put to use in small "cells" of "plagiarized" material. This deliberate practice unleashes an esthetic of plagiarism, an esthetic of *arrastão* [a dragnet: technique used in urban robbery. A small group fan out and then run furiously through a crowd, taking people's money, jewelry, bags, sometimes even clothes] that ambushes the universe of well-known and traditional music. We are at the end, thus of the composer's era, inaugurating the plagi-combinator era.

—Tom Zé[11]

The concept of owning music is really falling apart [. . . .] T]here is simply no technological backing for the traditional concepts anymore. Playback, storing, copying, distributing music is effortless. Music spreads like a virus. In the longterm, recorded music will be available to anyone, anytime [. . . .] From an artistic standpoint, being able to tap into millions of other users' record collections and bootleg archives is unprecedented and fantastic.

—Sebastian Oschatz of Oval[12]

# III. Music in the Age of Electronic (Re)production

## Introduction

Music has always inhabited the space between nature and technology, intuition and artifice. It is said to be rooted in the heartbeat and the voice; but it is no less bound up with the history of the machine. "The moment man ceased to make music with his voice alone, the art became machine-ridden," noted cultural historian Jacques Barzun in his introduction to the Columbia-Princeton Electronic Music Center's first concert in 1961. "Orpheus's lyre was a machine, a symphony orchestra is a regular factory for making artificial sounds, and a piano is the most appalling contrivance of levers and wires this side of the steam engine."[1]

Experimental practices in contemporary music have exploited both sides of the nature/technology opposition, and, in the process, have unsettled that very opposition and any stable conception of "music." When John Cage, R. Murray Schafer, and Pauline Oliveros opened music to "environmental sound," they did so largely via the tape recorder, arguably the most revolutionary piece of technology in the history of music. Pierre Schaeffer and Brian Eno have shown how the tape recorder and subsequent recording media created a world of virtual sound, a realm of sonic simulacra detached from any specific moment, site, or source. By the same token, the microphone hears neither *what* the ear hears nor *how* it hears. It is what Marshall McLuhan calls a technological prosthesis, an extension of the human nervous system that retrains the ear and triggers in us a new auditory awareness and a new set of auditory desires.

In the mid-1960s and early 1970s, these technological developments began to undermine the category of musical "authenticity." This had a particularly unsettling effect on both classical music and popular musics, both of which place a premium on *presence*, the realness of the singular live event.[2] In 1964, the celebrated pianist Glenn Gould scandalized the classical music establishment when he gave up public performance in favor of the recording studio. For Gould, the perfect performance could only be created in the studio, pieced together from multiple takes. Hence, for Gould, "the authentic" was a technological product. A few years later, Miles Davis began to undermine the category of "authenticity" in jazz. While jazz largely defined itself by virtuosic playing "in the moment," Davis began to create music by recording extended improvisations and then handing them over to his producer, Teo Macero, to edit and reassemble as he wished. At the same time, from within a tradition obsessed with origins, the natural, and the spiritual, reggae producers such as King Tubby and Lee "Scratch" Perry invented "dub," a new music that gleefully exploited the capacities of the recording studio to create immersive and mystical electronic spaces by fracturing, magnifying, and multiplying the vocal and instrumental moments of an original reggae track.

Recording began as a reproduction of the live act. Yet, today, the recorded event has all but displaced the live event as primary. Glenn Gould's intervention within classical music was already well under way within rock and pop. As soon as rock performers discovered the magic of the recording studio, live performance became, at best, a simulation of the recorded instance. If the classical tradition resisted this move and rock and pop were ambivalent about it, new musics rooted in electronics positively embraced it. Disco, dub, HipHop, House, Techno—all of these musics begin with and are built from samples, slices of recorded sound.

With the rise of a musical culture built around recording and sampling, traditional conceptions of the author and the work began to come under strain. As Chris Cutler and others note, the origins of the modern notion of the "author" and the "work" are coincident with the origin of capitalism. An author is the producer of a unique, fixed, and bounded work that bears his or her signature; and copyright laws insure and protect that property. As soon as recording becomes primary, the recorded entity begins to live a public life of its own apart from its author and becomes available for appropriation and reinscription by others. It's no surprise, then, that HipHop, for example, has been plagued by litigation concerning copyright infringement. In Cutler's view (one shared by many HipHop producers and musicians such as John Oswald and Negativland), copyright laws are no longer appropriate to a new technological and musical setting that makes the entire archive of recorded sound available for use and reuse. Hence the culture of the remix, which appropriates and alters an "original recording," itself often a remix, producing a *mise en abime* that endlessly defers any originary instance.[3]

Musical technologies are constantly reappropriated and redirected to ends and uses other than those originally intended. The "electric guitar" began as an amplified guitar and ended up as an entirely different instrument. The multi-track tape recorder was soon taken out of the hands of the engineer and placed into the hands of the composer. In the hands of the HipHop DJ, the turntable was transformed from a "record player" into a live sampler and percussion instrument. And the computer glitch, once an unwanted digital error, has become desirable sound material for many producers of contemporary electronica. Like the recorded sample, musical technology as a whole ceases to have any given or fundamental use value, but instead is laid open to endless transformation and redirection.

## NOTES

1. See chap. 53.
2. See Simon Reynolds, "Post-Rock," chap. 52. Also see Evan Eisenberg, *The Recording Angel: Explorations in Phonography* (New York: McGraw-Hill, 1987) and Theodor Gracyk, *Rhythm & Noise: An Aesthetics of Rock* (Durham, NC: Duke University Press, 1996).
3. See also Simon Reynolds, "Versus: The Science of Remixology," *Pulse!* (May 1996); "In the Mix: DJ Culture and Remixology, 1993–97," in *Generation Ecstasy* (Boston: Little Brown, 1998); and Christoph Cox, "Versions, Dubs, and Remixes: Realism and Rightness in Aesthetic Interpretation," in *Interpretation and Its Objects: Studies in the Philosophy of Michael Krausz*, ed. Andreea Deciu Ritivoi (Amsterdam: Rodopi, 2003).

# 21

# *The Prospects of Recording*

## GLENN GOULD

Glenn Gould (1932–1982) was among the leading classical pianists of the 20th century. A child prodigy, he performed with the Toronto Symphony at the age of 16 and, at 22, signed a recording contract with Columbia Master-works. Later that year (1955), he made a recording of Bach's *Goldberg Variations* that quickly became an international bestseller. Over the next decade, Gould toured Europe, the Soviet Union, and the United States, performing with the world's greatest orchestras. Then, in 1964, he abruptly announced his retirement from public performance. Gould's withdrawal from the stage was prompted in part by his feeling that public performance was demeaning, and in part by his desire to dedicate more of his time to writing and producing radio documentaries. Yet it was also driven by his view that the live concert had been eclipsed by audio recording, which could produce perfect, ideal performances that highlighted the work itself rather than the performer and his or her virtuosity. In this 1966 essay, Gould explores the vast changes in musical ontology, phenomenology, production, and listening brought about by audio recording.

In an unguarded moment some months ago, I predicted that the public concert as we know it today would no longer exist a century hence, that its functions would have been entirely taken over by electronic media. It had not occurred to me that this statement represented a particularly radical pronouncement. Indeed, I regarded it almost as self-evident truth and, in any case, as defining only one of the peripheral effects occasioned by developments in the electronic age. But never has a statement of mine been so widely quoted—or so hotly disputed [. . . .]

### A Change of Acoustic

If we were to take an inventory of those musical predilections most characteristic of our generation, we would discover that almost every item on such a list could be attributed directly to the influence of the recording. First of all, today's listeners have come to associate musical performance with sounds possessed of characteristics which two generations ago were neither available to the profession nor wanted by the public—characteristics such as analytic clarity, immediacy, and indeed almost tactile proximity. Within the last few decades the performance of music has ceased to be an occasion, requiring an excuse and a tuxedo, and accorded, when encountered, an almost religious devotion; music has become a pervasive influence in our lives, and as our dependence upon it has increased, our reverence for it has, in a certain sense, declined. Two generations ago, concertgoers preferred that their occasional experience of music be fitted with an acoustic splendor, cavernously reverberant if possible, and pioneer recording ventures attempted to simulate the cathedrallike sound which the architects of that day tried to capture for the concert hall—the cathedral of the symphony. The more intimate terms of our experience with recordings have since suggested to us an acoustic with a direct and impartial presence, one with which we can live in our homes on rather casual terms [. . . .]

## An Untapped Repertoire

From a musicological point of view, the effort of the recording industry on behalf of Renaissance and pre-Renaissance music is of even greater value. For the first time, the musicologist rather than the performer has become the key figure in the realization of this untapped repertoire; and in place of sporadic and, often as not, historically inaccurate concert performances of a Palestrina mass or a Josquin chanson, or whichever isolated items were heretofore considered approachable and not too offensively pretonal, the record archivists have documented a new perspective for the history of music.

The performer is inevitably challenged by the stimulus of this unexplored repertoire. He is also encouraged by the nature of studio techniques to appropriate characteristics that have tended for a century or two to be outside his private preserve. His contact with the repertoire he records is often the result of an intense analysis from which he prepares an interpretation of the composition. Conceivably, for the rest of his life he will never again take up or come in contact with that particular work. In the course of a lifetime spent in the recording studio he will necessarily encounter a wider range of repertoire than could possibly be his lot in the concert hall. The current archival approach of many recording companies demands a complete survey of the works of a given composer, and performers are expected to undertake productions of enormous scope which they would be inclined to avoid in the concert hall, and in many cases to investigate repertoire economically or acoustically unsuitable for public audition—the complete piano works of Mozart which Walter Gieseking undertook for Angel, for instance.

But most important, this archival responsibility enables the performer to establish a contact with a work which is very much like that of the composer's own relation to it. It permits him to encounter a particular piece of music and to analyze and dissect it in a most thorough way, to make it a vital part of his life for a relatively brief period, and then to pass on to some other challenge and to the satisfaction of some other curiosity. Such a work will no longer confront him with a daily challenge. His analysis of the composition will not become distorted by overexposure, and his performance top-heavy with interpretative "niceties" intended to woo the upper balcony, as is almost inevitably the case with the overplayed piece of concert repertoire [. . . .]

## The Splendid Splice

Of all the techniques peculiar to the studio recording, none has been the subject of such controversy as the tape splice. With due regard to the not-so-unusual phenomenon of a recording consisting of single-take sonata or symphony movements, the great majority of present-day recordings consist of a collection of tape segments varying in duration upward from one twentieth of a second. Superficially, the purpose of the splice is to rectify performance mishaps. Through its use, the wayward phrase, the insecure quaver, can, except when prohibited by "overhang" or similar circumstances of acoustical imbalance, be remedied by minute retakes of the offending moment or of a splice segment of which it forms a part. The antirecord lobby proclaims splicing a dishonest and dehumanizing technique that purportedly eliminates those conditions of chance and accident upon which, it can safely be conceded, certain of the more unsavory traditions of Western music are founded. The lobbyists also claim that the common splice sabotages some unified architectural conception which they assume the performer possesses.

It seems to me that two facts challenge these objections. The first is that many of the supposed virtues of the performer's "unified conception" relate to nothing more inherently musical than the "running scared" and "go-for-broke" psychology built up through decades of exposure to the *loggione* of Parma and their like. Claudio Arrau was recently quoted by the English journal *Records and Recordings* to the effect that he would not authorize the release of records derived from a live performance since, in his opinion, public auditions provoke stratagems which, having been designed to fill acoustical and psychological requirements of the concert situation, are irritating and antiarchitectural when subjected to repeated playbacks. The second fact is that one cannot ever splice style—one can only splice segments which relate to a conviction about style. And whether one arrives at such a conviction pretaping or posttaping (another of the time-transcending luxuries of recording: the posttaping reconsideration of performance), its existence is what matters, not the means by which it is effected.

A recent personal experience will perhaps illustrate an interpretative conviction obtained posttaping. A year or so ago, while recording the concluding fugues from volume 1 of *The Well-Tempered Clavier*, I arrived at one of Bach's celebrated contrapuntal obstacle courses, the fugue in A minor. This is a structure even more difficult to realize on the piano than are most of Bach's fugues, because it consists of four intense voices that determinedly occupy a register in the center octaves of the keyboard—the area of the instrument in which truly independent voice leading is most difficult to establish. In the process of recording this fugue we attempted eight takes. Two of these at the time were regarded, according to the producer's notes, as satisfactory. Both of them, number 6 and number 8, were complete takes requiring no inserted splice—by no means a special achievement, since the fugue's duration is only a bit over two minutes. Some weeks later, however, when the results of this session were surveyed in an editing cubicle and when takes 6 and 8 were played several times in rapid alternation, it became apparent that both had a defect of which we had been quite unaware in the studio: both were monotonous.

Each take had used a different style of phrase delineation in dealing with the thirty-one-note subject of this fugue—a license entirely consistent with the improvisatory liberties of baroque style. Take 6 had treated it in a solemn, legato, rather pompous fashion, while in take 8 the fugue subject was shaped in a prevailingly staccato manner which led to a general impression of skittishness. Now, the fugue in A minor is given to concentrations of strettos and other devices for imitation at close quarters, so that the treatment of the subject determines the atmosphere of the entire fugue. Upon most sober reflection, it was agreed that neither the Teutonic severity of take 6 nor the unwarranted jubilation of take 8 could be permitted to represent our best thoughts on this fugue. At this point someone noted that, despite the vast differences in character between the two takes, they were performed at an almost identical tempo (a rather unusual circumstance, to be sure, since the prevailing tempo is almost always the result of phrase delineation), and it was decided to turn this to advantage by creating one performance to consist alternately of takes 6 and 8.

Once this decision had been made, it was a simple matter to expedite it. It was obvious that the somewhat overbearing posture of take 6 was entirely suitable for the opening exposition as well as for the concluding statements of the fugue, while the more effervescent character of take 8 was a welcome relief in the episodic modulations with which the center portion of the fugue is concerned. And so two rudimentary splices were made, one which jumps from take 6 to take 8 in bar 14 and another which at the return to A minor (I forget in which measure, but you are invited to look for it) returns as well to take 6. What had been achieved was a performance of this particular fugue far superior to anything that we could at the time have done in the studio. There is, of course, no reason why such a diversity of bowing styles could not have been applied to this fugue subject as part of a regulated a priori conception. But the necessity of such diversity is unlikely to become apparent during the studio session, just as it is unlikely to occur to a performer operating under concert conditions. By taking advantage of the posttaping afterthought, however, one can very often transcend the limitations that performance imposes upon the imagination.

When the performer makes use of this postperformance editorial decision, his role is no longer compartmentalized. In a quest for perfection, he sets aside the hazards and compromises of his trade. As an interpreter, as a go-between serving both audience and composer, the performer has always been, after all, someone with a specialist's knowledge about the realization or actualization of notated sound symbols. It is, then, perfectly consistent with such experience that he should assume something of an editorial role. Inevitably, however, the functions of the performer and of the tape editor begin to overlap. Indeed, in regard to decisions such as that taken in the case of the abovementioned A-minor fugue, it would be impossible for the listener to establish at which point the authority of the performer gave way to that of the producer and the tape editor, just as even the most observant cinema goer cannot ever be sure whether a particular sequence of shots derives from circumstances occasioned by the actor's performance, the exigencies of the cutting room, or the director's a priori scheme. That the judgment of the performer no longer solely determines the musical result is inevitable. It is, however, more than compensated by the overwhelming sense of power which editorial control makes available to him [. . . .]

## The "Live" Performance on Records

Before examining the larger ramifications for the future of recording, I should like to consider here some hardy strains of argument that perennially decry the influence of recording upon standard items of the repertoire and upon the hierarchy of the musical profession.

These arguments sometimes overlap each other, and it can become rather difficult to detect the area of protest with which each is concerned. However, under a general heading of "humanitarian idealism" one might list three distinguishable subspecies, which can be summarized as follows: (1) An argument for aesthetic morality: Elisabeth Schwarzkopf appends a missing high C to a tape of *Tristan* otherwise featuring Kirsten Flagstad, and indignant purists, for whom music is the last blood sport, howl her down, furious at being deprived a kill. (2) Eye versus ear orientation: a doctrine that celebrates the existence of a mystical communication between concert performer and public audience (the composer being seldom mentioned). There is a vaguely scientific pretension to this argument, and its proponents are given to pronouncements on "natural" acoustics and related phenomena. (3) Automation: a crusade which musicians' union leaders currently share with typesetters and which they affirm with the fine disdain of featherbedding firemen for the diesel locomotive. In the midst of a proliferation of recorded sound which virtually erases earlier listening patterns, the American Federation of Musicians promotes that challenging motto "Live Music Is Best"—a judgment with the validity of a "Win with Willkie" sticker on the windshield of a well-preserved '39 LaSalle.

As noted, these arguments tend to overlap and are often joined together in celebration of occasions that afford opportunity for a rearguard holding action. Among such occasions, none has proved more useful than the recent spate of recorded "live" performances—events which straddle two worlds and are at home in neither. These events affirm the humanistic ideal of performance; they eschew (so we are told!) splices and other mechanical adventures, and hence are decidedly "moral"; they usually manage to suppress a sufficient number of pianissimo chords by an outbreak of bronchitis from the floor to advertise their "live"-ness and confirm the faith of the heroically unautomated.

They have yet another function, which is, in fact, the essence of their appeal for the short-sellers: they provide documentation pertaining to a specific date. They are forever represented as occasions indisputably of and for their time. They spurn that elusive time-transcending objective which is always within the realization of recorded music. For all time, they can be examined, criticized, or praised as documents securely located in time, and about which, because of that assurance, a great deal of information and, in a certain sense, an emotional relation, is immediately available. With regard to the late Dutch craftsman who, having hankered to take upon himself the mantle of Vermeer, was martyred for a reluctance to live by the hypocrisy of this argument, I think of this fourth circumstance—this question of historical date—as the van Meegeren syndrome.

Hans van Meegeren was a forger and an artisan who for a long time has been high on my list of private heroes. Indeed, I would go so far as to say that the magnificent morality play which was his trial perfectly epitomizes the confrontation between those values of identity and of personal-responsibility-for-authorship which post-Renaissance art has until recently accepted and those pluralistic values which electronic forms assert. In the 1930s van Meegeren decided to apply himself to a study of Vermeer's techniques and—for reasons undoubtedly having more to do with an enhancement of his ego than with greed for guilders—distributed the works thus achieved as genuine, if long lost, masterpieces. His prewar success was so encouraging that during the German occupation he continued apace with sales destined for private collectors in the Third Reich. With the coming of VE Day, he was charged with collaboration as well as with responsibility for the liquidation of national treasures. In his defense van Meegeren confessed that these treasures were but his own invention and, by the values this world applies, quite worthless—an admission which so enraged the critics and historians who had authenticated his collection in the first place that he was rearraigned on charges of forgery and some while later passed away in prison.

The determination of the value of a work of art according to the information available about it is a most delinquent form of aesthetic appraisal. Indeed, it strives to avoid appraisal on any ground other than that which has been prepared by previous appraisals. The moment this tyranny of appraisaldom is confronted by confused chronological evidence, the moment it is denied a predetermined historical niche in which to lock the object of its analysis, it becomes unserviceable and its proponents hysterical. The furor that greeted van Meegeren's conflicting testimony, his alternate roles of hero and villain, scholar and fraud, decisively demonstrated the degree to which an aesthetic response was genuinely involved.

Some months ago, in an article in the *Saturday Review*, I ventured that the delinquency manifest by this sort of evaluation might be demonstrated if one were to imagine the critical response to an improvisation which, through its style and texture, suggested that it might have been composed by Joseph Haydn. (Let's assume it to be brilliantly done and most admirably Haydnesque.) I suggested that if one were to concoct such a piece, its value would remain at par—that is to say, at Haydn's value—only so long as some chicanery were involved in its presentation, enough at least to convince the listener that it was indeed by Haydn. If, however, one were to suggest that although it much resembled Haydn it was, rather, a youthful work of Mendelssohn, its value would decline; and if one chose to attribute it to a succession of authors, each of them closer to the present day, then—regardless of their talents or historical significance—the merits of this same little piece would diminish with each new identification. If, on the other hand, one were to suggest that this work of chance, of accident, of the here and now, was not by Haydn but by a master living some generation or two before his time (Vivaldi, perhaps), then this work would become—on the strength of that daring, that foresight, that futuristic anticipation—a landmark in musical composition.

And all of this would come to pass for no other reason than that we have never really become equipped to adjudicate music per se. Our sense of history is captive of an analytical method which seeks out isolated moments of stylistic upheaval—pivot points of idiomatic evolution—and our value judgments are largely based upon the degree to which we can assure ourselves that a particular artist participated in or, better yet, anticipated the nearest upheaval. Confusing evolution with accomplishment, we become blind to those values not explicit in an analogy with stylistic metamorphosis.

The van Meegeren syndrome is entirely apropos of our subject, because the arguments contra the prospects of recording are constructed upon identical criteria. They rely, most of all, upon a similar confirmation of historical data. Deprived of this confirmation, their system of evaluation is unable to function; it is at sea, derelict amidst an unsalvageable debris of evidence, and it casts about in search of a point by which to take a bearing. When recordings are at issue, such a point cannot readily be found. The inclination of electronic media is to extract their content from historic date. The moment we can force a work of art to conform to our notion of what was appropriate to its chronology, we can attribute to it, arbitrarily if necessary, background against which in our analysis it can be portrayed. Most aesthetic analysis confines itself to background description and avoids the foreground manipulation of the object being analyzed. And this fact alone, discarding the idle propaganda of the public relations machines, accounts for the endorsement of the recorded public event. Indirectly, the real object of this endorsement is a hopelessly outmoded system of aesthetic analysis—a system incapable of a contribution in the electronic age but the only system for which most spokesmen of the arts are trained.

Recordings produced in a studio resist a confirmation of such criteria. Here date is an elusive factor. Though a few companies solemnly inscribe the date of the studio sessions with each recorded package, and though the material released by most large companies can, except perhaps in the case of reissues, be related to a release number that will suggest an approximate date to the aficionado, it is possible that the music heard on that recording will have been obtained from sessions held weeks, months, or indeed years apart. Those sessions may easily have been held in different cities, different countries, taped with different equipment and different technical personnel, and they may feature performers whose attitudes to the repertoire under consideration have metamorphosed dramatically between the taping of the first note and the last. Such a recording might currently pose insuperable contractual problems, but its complicated gestation would be entirely consistent with the nature of the recording process.

It would also be consistent with that evolution of the performing musician which recording necessitates. As the performer's once-sacrosanct privileges are merged with the responsibilities of the tape editor and the composer, the van Meegeren syndrome can no longer be cited as an indictment but becomes rather an entirely appropriate description of the aesthetic condition in our time. The role of the forger, of the unknown maker of unauthenticated goods, is emblematic of electronic culture. And when the forger is done honor for his craft and no longer reviled for his acquisitiveness, the arts will have become a truly integral part of our civilization [. . . .]

**The Participant Listener**

At the center of the technological debate, then, is a new kind of listener—a listener more participant in the musical experience. The emergence of this mid-twentieth-century phenomenon is the greatest achievement of the record industry. For this listener is no longer passively analytical; he is an associate whose tastes, preferences, and inclinations even now alter peripherally the experiences to which he gives his attention, and upon whose fuller participation the future of the art of music waits.

He is also, of course, a threat, a potential usurper of power, an uninvited guest at the banquet of the arts, one whose presence threatens the familiar hierarchical setting of the musical establishment. Is it not, then, inopportune to venture that this participant public could emerge untutored from that servile posture with which it paid homage to the status structure of the concert world and, overnight, assume decision-making capacities which were specialists' concerns heretofore?

The keyword here is "public." Those experiences through which the listener encounters music electronically transmitted are not within the public domain. One serviceable axiom applicable to every experience in which electronic transmission is involved can be expressed in that paradox wherein the ability to obtain in theory an audience of unprecedented numbers obtains in fact a limitless number of private auditions. Because of the circumstances this paradox defines, the listener is able to indulge preferences and, through the electronic modifications with which he endows the listening experience, impose his own personality upon the work. As he does so, he transforms that work, and his relation to it, from an artistic to an environmental experience.

Dial twiddling is in its limited way an interpretative act. Forty years ago the listener had the option of flicking a switch inscribed "on" and "off" and, with an up-to-date machine, perhaps modulating the volume just a bit. Today, the variety of controls made available to him requires analytical judgment. And these controls are but primitive, regulatory devices compared to those participational possibilities which the listener will enjoy once current laboratory techniques have been appropriated by home playback devices.

It would be a relatively simple matter, for instance, to grant the listener tape-edit options which he could exercise at his discretion. Indeed, a significant step in this direction might well result from that process by which it is now possible to disassociate the ratio of speed to pitch and in so doing (albeit with some deterioration in the quality of sound as a current liability) truncate splice-segments of interpretations of the same work performed by different artists and recorded at different tempos. Let us say, for example, that you enjoy Bruno Walter's performance of the exposition and recapitulation from the first movement of Beethoven's Fifth Symphony but incline toward Klemperer's handling of the development section, which employs a notably divergent tempo. (I happen to like both performances all the way through, but there's no accounting for taste.) With the pitch-speed correlation held in abeyance, you could snip out these measures from the Klemperer edition and splice them into the Walter performance without having the splice produce either an alteration of tempo or a fluctuation of pitch. This process could, in theory, be applied without restriction to the reconstruction of musical performance. There is, in fact, nothing to prevent a dedicated connoisseur from acting as his own tape editor and, with these devices, exercising such interpretative predilections as will permit him to create his own ideal performance [. . . .]

### En Route to a Stylistic Mix

The listener's splice prerogative is but one aspect of that editorial mix which recorded music encourages. In terms of its unselfconscious juxtaposition of a miscellany of idioms, it will have an effect similar to that which André Malraux—in his *Voices of Silence*—attributes to art reproductions. One result of this stylistic permissiveness will be a more tolerant regard for the artistic by-products of those cultures which are, from our Western point of view, chronologically "out of sync." The transmission of events and sounds around our planet has forced us to concede that there is not just one musical tradition but, rather, many musics, not all of which are concerned—by our definition of the word—with tradition [. . . .]

Through simultaneous transmissions, through radio and television particularly, the art of such a [culture] becomes for those of us on the outside rather too easily accessible. Such media encourage us to invoke comparisons between the by-products of such a culture and those to which our own very different orientation gives rise. When we find that the expression of that culture represents what seem to us archaic ideologies, we condemn it as old-fashioned or sterile, or puritanical, or as possessed of any other limitation from which we consider ourselves emancipated. With simultaneous transmission we set aside our touristlike fascination with distant and exotic places and give vent to impatience at the chronological tardiness the natives display. To this extent, Professor McLuhan's concept of the "global village"—the simultaneity of response from McMurdo Sound to Murmansk, from Taiwan to Tacoma—is alarming. There just could be some fellow at McMurdo, "out of sync" and out of touch, revivifying C major as Mozart never dreamed of!

But these intrusions pertain only to those media developments that reproduce images or sounds instantaneously. Recordings arouse very different psychological reactions and should always be considered with this proviso in mind. Whereas simultaneous reception reveals differences on a current, comparative, indeed competitive basis, the preservation of sound and image makes possible the archival view, the unimpassioned reflection upon the condition of a society, the acceptance of a multifaceted chronological concept. Indeed, the two utilizations of electronic transmission—for clarification of present circumstances occasioned by radio and television and for indefinite future re-examination of the past permitted by recording—are antidotal. The recording process, with its encouragement of a sympathetic "after-the-fact" historical view, is the indispensable replenishment of that deteriorating tolerance occasioned by simultaneous transmission. Just as simultaneous reception tends to provoke unproductive comparisons and encourages conformity, preservation and archival replay encourage detachment and nonconformist historical premises.

In my opinion, the most important of the missing links in the evolution of the listener-consumer-participant, as well as the most persuasive argument for the stylistic mix, is to be found in that most abused of electronic manifestations—background sound. This much-criticized and often misunderstood phenomenon is the most productive method through which contemporary music can confide its objectives to a listening, consuming, Muzak-absorbing society. Cunningly disguised within the bland formulae from which background sounds are seemingly concocted is an encyclopedia of experience, an exhaustive compilation of the clichés of post-Renaissance music. Moreover, this catalogue provides a cross-referenced index which permits connections between stylistic manifestations with fine disregard for chronological distinction. Within ten minutes of restaurant Muzak one can encounter a residue of Rachmaninoff or a blast of Berlioz proceeding without embarrassment from the dregs of Debussy. Indeed, all the music that has ever been can now become a background against which the impulse to make listener-supplied connections is the new foreground [. . . .]

There is an interesting correlation between the neutrality of this background vocabulary—the unobtrusiveness of its contribution—and the fact that most background music is conveyed through recordings. These are in fact two complementary facets of the same phenomenon. For since the recording does not depend, as does the concert, upon the mood of a special occasion, and relies instead upon relating to a general set of circumstances, it exploits in background music those abilities through which that phenomenon is able to draw, without embarrassment, upon an incredible range of stylistic reference—summoning to the contemporary world idiomatic references from earlier times, placing them in a context in which, by being accorded a subdivided participation, they achieve a new validity.

. Background music has been attacked from many quarters—by Europeans as a symptom of the decadence of North American society, by North Americans as a product of megalopolitan conformity. Indeed, it is perhaps accepted at face value only in those societies where no continuing tradition of Occidental music is to be found.

Background music, of course, confirms all the argumentative criteria by which the opponents of musical technology determine their judgments. It has no sense of historic date—the fact that it is studio produced and the stylistic compote of its musical substance prevent this; the personnel involved are almost always anonymous; a great deal of overtracking and other electronic wizardry is involved in its making—hence such arguments as those of automation, aesthetic morality, and the van Meegeren syndrome find in background music a tempting target. This target, however, protected at present by commercial rather than aesthetic considerations, is immune to attack.

Those who see in background music a sinister fulfillment of the Orwellian environment control assume that it is capable of enlisting all who are exposed to it as proponents of its own vast cliché. But this is precisely the point! Because it can infiltrate our lives from so many different angles, the cliché residue of all the idioms employed in background becomes an intuitive part of our musical vocabulary. Consequently, in order to gain our attention any *musical* experience must be of a quite exceptional nature. And meanwhile, through this ingenious glossary, the listener achieves a direct associative experience of the post-Renaissance vocabulary, something that not even the most inventive music appreciation course would be able to afford him.

## Music's Role in an Electronic Age

As this medium evolves, as it becomes available for situations in which the quite properly self-indulgent participation of the listener will be encouraged, those venerable distinctions about the class structure within the musical hierarchy—distinctions that separated composer and performer and listener—will become outmoded. Does this, then, contradict the fact that since the Renaissance the separation of function (specialization) has been the professional lot and that the medieval status of the musician, one who created and performed for the sake of his own enjoyment, has long since been supplanted by our post-Renaissance orgy of musical sophistication? I should say that these two concepts are not necessarily contradictory.

This overlapping of professional and lay responsibility in the creative process does tend to produce a set of circumstances that superficially suggests the largely unilateral participation of the pre-Renaissance world. In fact, it is deceptively easy to draw such parallels, to assume that the entire adventure of the Renaissance and of the world which it created was a gigantic historical error. But we are not returning to a medieval culture. It is a dangerous oversimplification to suggest that under the influence of electronic media we could retrograde to some condition reminiscent of the pre-Renaissance cultural monolith. The technology of electronic forms makes it highly improbable that we will move in any direction but one of even greater intensity and complexity; and the fact that a participational overlapping becomes unashamedly involved with the creative process should not suggest a waning of the necessity for specialized techniques.

What will happen, rather, is that new participation areas will proliferate and that many more hands will be required to achieve the execution of a particular environmental experience. Because of this complexity, because so many different levels of participation will, in fact, be merged in the final result, the individualized information concepts which define the nature of identity and authorship will become very much less imposing. Not that this identity reduction will be achieved without some harassment from those who resent its implications. After all, what are the batteries of public relations men, advertising executives, and press agents doing if not attempting to provide an identification for artist and producer in a society where duplication is everywhere and where identity in the sense of information about the authors means less and less?

The most hopeful thing about this process—about the inevitable disregard for the identity factor in the creative situation—is that it will permit a climate in which biographical data and chronological assumption can no longer be the cornerstone for judgments about art as it relates to environment. In fact, this whole question of individuality in the creative situation—the process through which the creative act results from, absorbs, and re-forms individual opinion—will be subjected to a radical reconsideration.

I believe the fact that music plays so extensive a part in the regulation of our environment suggests its eventual assumption of a role as immediate, as utilitarian, as colloquial as that which language now plays in the conduct of our daily lives. For music to achieve a comparable familiarity, the implications of its styles, its habits, its mannerisms, its tricks, its customary devices, its statistically most frequent occurrences—in other words, its clichés—must be familiar and recognized by everyone. A mass recognition of the cliché quotient of a vocabulary need not suggest our becoming saturated with the mundanities of those clichés. We do not value great works of literature less because we, as men in the street, speak the language in which they happen to be written. The fact that so much of our daily conversation is concerned with the tedious familiarities of common courtesy, the mandatory conversation openers about the weather and so on, does not for a moment dull our appreciation of the potential glories of the language we use. To the contrary, it sharpens it. It gives us background against which the foreground that is the habitat of the imaginative artist may stand in greater relief. It is my view that in the electronic age the art of music will become much more viably a part of our lives, much less an ornament to them, and that it will consequently change them much more profoundly.

If these changes are profound enough, we may eventually be compelled to redefine the terminology with which we express our thoughts about art. Indeed, it may become increasingly inappropriate to apply to a description of environmental situations the word "art" itself—a word that, however venerable and honored, is necessarily replete with imprecise, if not in fact obsolete, connotations.

In the best of all possible worlds, art would be unnecessary. Its offer of restorative, placative therapy would go begging a patient. The professional specialization involved in its making would be presumption. The generalities of its applicability would be an affront. The audience would be the artist and their life would be art.

# 22

## *The Studio as Compositional Tool*

### BRIAN ENO

Brian Eno (1948– ; see also chaps. 17 and 34) is a key figure in the shift from "composer" and "musician" to "producer" in contemporary electronic culture. Drawing lessons from a genealogy of visionary producers—Phil Spector, Joe Meek, George Martin, Teo Macero, Brian Wilson, Lee "Scratch" Perry, and others—Eno was struck early on by the extraordinary creative potential of the recording studio, its ability to construct new sonic worlds. Here, he offers a brief history of the "studio as instrument" and meditates on the ways in which this instrument has shaped modern music and sonic cognition.

The first thing about recording is that it makes repeatable what was otherwise transient and ephemeral. Music, until about 1900, was an event that was perceived in a particular situation, and that disappeared when it was finished. There was no way of actually hearing that piece again, identically, and there was no way of knowing whether your perception was telling you it was different or whether it was different the second time you heard it. The piece disappeared when it was finished, so it was something that only existed in time.

The effect of recording is that it takes music out of the time dimension and puts it in the space dimension. As soon as you do that, you're in a position of being able to listen again and again to a performance, to become familiar with details you most certainly had missed the first time through, and to become very fond of details that weren't intended by the composer or the musicians.

The effect of this on the composer is that he can think in terms of supplying material that would actually be too subtle for a first listening. Around about the 1920s—or maybe that's too early, perhaps around the '30s—composers started thinking that their work was recordable, and they started making use of the special liberty of being recorded.

I think the first place this had a real effect was in jazz. Jazz is an improvised form, primarily, and the interesting thing about improvisations is that they become more interesting as you listen to them more times. What seemed like an almost arbitrary collision of events comes to seem very meaningful on relistening. Actually, almost any arbitrary collision of events listened to enough times comes to seem very meaningful. (There's an interesting and useful bit of information for a composer, I can tell you.) I think recording created the jazz idiom, in a sense; jazz was, from 1925 onwards, a recorded medium, and from '35 onwards I guess—I'm not a jazz expert by any means—it was a medium that most people received via records. So they were listening to things that were once only improvisations for many hundreds of times, and they were hearing these details as being compositionally significant.

Now, let's talk about another aspect of recording, which I call the detachable aspect. As soon as you record something, you make it available for any situation that has a record player. You take it out of the ambience and locale in which it was made, and it can be transposed into any situation. This morning I was listening to a Thai lady singing; I can hear the sound of the St. Sophia Church in Belgrade or Max's Kansas City in my own apartment, and I can listen with a fair degree of conviction about what these sounds mean. As Marshall McLuhan said, it makes all music all present. So not only is the whole history of our music with us now, in some sense, on record, but the whole global musical culture is also available. That means that a composer is really in the position, if he listens to records a lot, of having a culture unbounded, both temporally and geographically, and therefore it's not at all surprising that composers should have ceased writing in a European classical tradition, and have branched out into all sorts of other experiments. Of course, that's not the only reason that they did, either.

So, to tape recording: till about the late '40s, recording was simply regarded as a device for transmitting a performance to an unknown audience, and the whole accent of recording technique was on making what was called a "more faithful" transmission of that experience. It began very simply, because the only control over the relative levels of sounds that went onto the machine was how far they were from the microphone-like device. The accent was on the performance, and the recording was a more or less perfect transmitter of that, through the cylinder and wax disc recording stages, until tape became the medium by which people were recording things.

The move to tape was very important, because as soon as something's on tape, it becomes a substance which is malleable and mutable and cuttable and reversible in ways that discs aren't. It's hard to do anything very interesting with a disc—all you can do is play it at a different speed, probably; you can't actually cut a groove out and make a little loop of it. The effect of tape was that it really put music in a spatial dimension, making it possible to squeeze the music, or expand it.

Initially tape recording was a single track, all the information contained and already mixed together on that one track. Then in the mid-'50s experiments were starting with stereo, which was not significantly different. The only difference was that you had two microphones pointing to your ensemble, and you had some impression of a real acoustic—sound came to you from two different sources as you listened. Then came three-track recording; it allowed the option of adding another voice or putting a string section on, or something like that. Now this is a significant step, I think; its the first time it was acknowledged that the performance isn't the finished item, and that the work can be added to in the control room, or in the studio itself. For the first time composers—almost always pop composers, as very few classical composers were thinking in this form—were thinking, "Well, this is the music. What can I do with it? I've got this extra facility of one track." Tricky things start getting added. Then it went to four-track after that, and the usual layout for recording a band on four track at that time [. . . .]

From that impulse two things happened: you got an additive approach to recording, the idea that composition is the process of adding more, which was very common in early '70s rock (this gave rise to the well-known and gladly departed orchestral rock tradition, and it also gave rise to heavy metal music—that sound can't be got on simpler equipment); it also gave rise to the particular area that I'm involved in: in-studio composition, where you no longer come to the studio with a conception of the finished piece. Instead, you come with actually rather a bare skeleton of the piece, or perhaps with nothing at all. I often start working with no starting point. Once you become familiar with studio facilities, or even if you're not, actually, you can begin to compose in relation to those facilities. You can begin to think in terms of putting something on, putting something else on, trying this on top of it, and so on, then taking some of the original things off, or taking a mixture of things off, and seeing what you're left with—actually constructing a piece in the studio.

In a compositional sense this takes the making of music away from any traditional way that composers worked, as far as I'm concerned, and one becomes empirical in a way that the classical composer never was. You're working directly with sound, and there's no transmission loss between you and the sound—you handle it. It puts the composer in the identical position of the painter—he's working directly with a material, working directly onto a substance, and he always retains the options to chop and change, to paint a bit out, add a piece, etc.

Compare that to the transmission intervals in a classical sequence: the composer writes a piece of music in a language that might not be adequate to his ideas—he has to say this note or this one, when he might mean this one just in between, or nearly this one here. He has to specify things in terms of a number of available instruments. He has to, in fact, use a language that, like all languages, will shape what he wants to do. Of course, any good composer understands that and works within that framework of limitations. Finally he has something on the page, and by a process this arrives at a conductor. The conductor looks at that, and if he isn't in contact with the composer, his job is to make an interpretation of it on the basis of what he thinks the composer meant, or whatever it is *he'd* like to do. There's very likely another transmission loss here—there won't be an identity between what he supposes and what the composer supposes. Then the conductor has the job of getting a group of probably intransigent musicians to follow his instructions, to realize this image of the music he has. Those of you who work with classical musicians know what a dreadful task this is, not to be wished on anyone.

So they come up with something. One can see there's not necessarily an identity between what the composer—or the conductor—thought, and what they did, so that's three transmission losses. I'd argue there is another one in the performance of the piece: since you're not making a record, you're not working in terms of a controlled acoustic, and you're not working in a medium that is quite so predictable as a record. If I make a record, I assume it's going to be the same every time it's played. So I think there is a difference *in kind* between the kind of composition I do and the kind a classical composer does. This is evidenced by the fact that I can neither read nor write music, and I can't play any instruments really well, either. You can't imagine a situation prior to this where anyone like me could have been a composer. It couldn't have happened. How could I do it without tape and without technology?

One thing I said about the traditional composer was that he worked with a finite set of possibilities; that is, he knew what an orchestra was composed of, and what those things sounded like, within a range. If you carry on the painting analogy, it's like he was working with a palette, with a number of colors which were and weren't mixable. Of course, you can mix clarinets and strings to get different sounds, but you're still dealing with a range that extends from here to here. It's nothing like the range of sounds that's possible once electronics enter the picture. The composer was also dealing with a finite set of relationships *between* sounds; the instruments are only so loud, and that's what you're dealing with, unless you stick one out in a field and one up close to your ear. It was out of the question that he could use something, for example, as the Beach Boys once did—making the sound of someone chewing celery the loudest thing on a track.

Of course, everyone is constrained in one way or another, and you work within your constraints. It doesn't mean that suddenly the world is open, and we're going to do much *better* music, because we're not constrained in certain ways. We're going to do *different* music because we're not constrained in certain ways—we operate under a different set of constraints [. . . .]

# 23

# *Bettered by the Borrower: The Ethics of Musical Debt*

## JOHN OSWALD

Since the early 1980s, Canadian multi-media artist John Oswald (1953– ) has played saxophone in the free improvising trio CCMC and recorded with improvisers Henry Kaiser, Jim O'Rourke, John Zorn, and others. Yet he is best known for his practice of "plunderphonics": the sampling and radical re-editing of pop recordings. Inspired by the cut-up methods of William S. Burroughs and James Tenney's 1961 sampling composition *Collage #1 ("Blue Suede")*, Oswald began experimenting with musical cut-ups in the early 1970s and issuing these cut-up compositions on cassette via his own Mystery Tapes label. In 1989, Oswald released the CD *Plunderphonic*, which presented inventive and humorous remixes of recordings by Dolly Parton, Michael Jackson, Bing Crosby, The Beatles, Glenn Gould, Public Enemy, James Brown, and others. The cover featured a collaged photo of Michael Jackson as a nude woman. Though the CD was given away for free and all the samples were fully credited, Oswald was threatened with a lawsuit by the Canadian Recording Industry Association for infringing the copyrights of their clients CBS Records and Michael Jackson. He was forced to destroy all remaining copies of the CD and was prohibited from distributing or reproducing it. Oswald continued to make legal plunderphonics compositions, filling commissions by Hal Willner, the Berlin Opera, the Kronos Quartet, the Grateful Dead, and others. In 2002, the Seeland label released the *69 Plunderphonics 96* box set, which included the original *Plunderphonic* CD and a number of Oswald's other plunderphonics experiments. In this article, written shortly before the release of the *Plunderphonic* CD, Oswald meditates on the nature of music in the age of analog and digital reproduction.

Musical instruments produce sounds. Composers produce music. Musical instruments reproduce music. Tape recorders, radios, disc players, etc., reproduce sound. A device such as a wind-up music box produces sound and reproduces music. A phonograph in the hands of a "HipHop/scratch" artist who plays a record like an electronic washboard with a phonographic needle as a plectrum, produces sounds which are unique and *not* reproduced—the record player becomes a musical instrument. When tape recorders, basically designed for documentation and reproduction, became available in the '40s, a few individuals, like Pierre Schaeffer in France, began transforming the recordings, distorting them into something new, producing music through them as if the tape recorders were magnetic violins. Even earlier, composer John Cage was specifying the use of radios and phonographs as musical instruments.

Quite often the sounds found emanating from phonographic and radio musical instruments have some prior ownership. These previous creators (including those who give credit to a divine source) have copyright: a charter of control over the commercial and moral implications of reproduction. But some sources continue to maintain a "finders-keepers" ethic.

## The Right of Copy

In 1976, ninety-nine years after Edison went into the record business, the U.S. Copyright Act was revised to protect sound recordings for the first time. Before this, only written music was considered eligible for protection. Forms of music that were not intelligible to the human eye were deemed ineligible. The traditional attitude was that recordings were not artistic creations, but "mere uses or applications of creative works in the form of physical objects." For instance, Charles Ives' Symphony No. 3 was published and copyrighted in 1947 by Arrow Music Press Inc. That the copyright was assigned to the publisher instead of the composer was the result of Ives' disdain for copyright in relation to his own work, and his desire to have his music distributed as widely as possible. He at first self-published and distributed volumes of his music free of charge. In the postscripts of *114 Songs* he refers to the possessor as the *gentle borrower*.

Later in his life Ives did allow for commercial publication, but always assigned royalties to other composers. Ives admired the philosophy of Ralph Waldo Emerson who, in his essay "Quotation and Originality," said, "What you owe to me— you will vary the phrase—but I shall still recognize my thought. But what you say from the same idea, will have to me also the expected unexpectedness which belongs to every new work of Nature."

The real headache for the writers of copyright has been the new electronic contrivances, including digital samplers of sound and their accountant cousins, computers. The electronic brain business is cultivating, by grace of its relative youth, pioneering creativity and a corresponding conniving ingenuity, "the intimate cultural secretions of electronic, biological, and written communicative media."[1]

## "Blank Tape is Derivative, Nothing of Itself"[2]

While the popular intrigue of computer theft has inspired cinematic and paperback thrillers, the robbery of music is restricted to elementary poaching and blundering innocence. The plots are trivial. The Disney cable channel accuses Sony of conspiring with consumers to let them make unauthorized Mickey mice by taping TV broadcasts on videocassette.

The dubbing-in-the-privacy-of-your-own-home controversy is actually the tip of a hot iceberg of rudimentary creativity. After decades of being the passive recipients of music in packages, listeners now have the means to assemble their own choices, to separate pleasures from the filler. They are dubbing a variety of sounds from around the world, or at least from the breadth of their record collections, making compilations of a diversity unavailable from the music industry, with its circumscribed policy of only supplying the common denominator.

Former Beatle George Harrison was found guilty of an indiscretion in choosing a vaguely familiar sequence of pitches. He was nailed in court for subconsciously plagiarizing the 1962 tune "He's So Fine" by the Chiffons in his song "My Sweet Lord" (1970).

Yet the Beatles are an interesting case of reciprocity between fair use and the amassing of possession and wealth. "We were the biggest nickers in town. Plagiarists extraordinaire," says Paul McCartney.[3] He owns one of the world's most extensive song catalogs, including a couple of state anthems. John Lennon incorporated collage technique into pieces like "Revolution #9," which contains dozens of looped unauthorized fragments taped from radio and television broadcasts.

### The Commerce of Noise

The precarious commodity in music today is no longer the tune. A fan can recognize a hit from a ten-millisecond burst. One studio-spawned mass-market recording firm called the Art of Noise strings atonal arrays of timbres along an always inevitable beat—the melody is often retrofitted.

Singers with *original* material aren't studying Bruce Springsteen's melodic contours; they're trying to *sound* just like him. And sonic impersonation is quite legal. While performing rights organizations continue to farm for proceeds to tunesters and poetricians, those who are really shaping the music—the rhythmatists, timbralists and mixologists under various monikers—have rarely been given compositional credit.

I found this comment on PAN, a musicians' computer network bulletin board, during a forum in January '86:

> Various DX7 programmers have told me that they "bury" useless data in their sounds so that they can prove ownership later. Sometimes the data is obvious, like weird keyboard scalings on inaudible operators, and sometimes it's not, like the nonsense characters (I seem to recall someone once thought they were Kanji) in a program name. Of course, any pirate worth his salt would find all these things and change them. . . . Synth programmers are skilled craftspeople, just like violin makers, so if they go to the trouble of making new and wonderful sounds that other people can use, they should be compensated for their efforts. Unfortunately it's not as easy as just selling the damn violin.

### The Cross-Referencing Blues

Musical language has an extensive repertoire of punctuation devices but nothing equivalent to literature's " " quotation marks. Jazz musicians do not wiggle two fingers of each hand in the air, as lecturers sometimes do, when cross-referencing during their extemporizations, as on most instruments this would present some technical difficulties.

Without a quotation system, well-intended correspondences cannot be distinguished from plagiarism and fraud. But anyway, the quoting of notes is but a small and not significant portion of common appropriation.

Am I underestimating the value of melody writing? Well, I expect that before long we'll have marketable expert tune-writing software which will be able to generate the banalities of catchy permutations of the diatonic scale in endless arrays of tuneable tunes, from which a not-necessarily-affluent songwriter can choose; with perhaps a built-in checking lexicon of used-up tunes which would advise Beatle George not to make the same blunder again.

In his speculative story *Melancholy Elephants*,[4] Spider Robinson writes about the pros and cons of rigorous copyright. The setting is half a century from now. The story centers on one person's opposition to a bill which would extend copyright to perpetuity. In Robinson's future, composition is already difficult, as most works are being deemed derivative by the copyright office. The Harrison case is cited as an important precedent:

> Artists have been deluding themselves for centuries with the notion that they create. In fact they do nothing of the sort. They discover. Inherent in the nature of reality are a number of combinations of musical tones that will be perceived as pleasing by a human central nervous system. For millennia we have been discovering them, implicit in the universe—and telling ourselves that we "created" them.

## Hands-On Listening

Sounding utensils, from the erh-hu to the Emulator, have traditionally provided such a potential for varied expression that they have not in themselves been considered musical manifestations. This is contrary to the great popularity of generic instrumental music ("The Many Moods of 101 Strings," "Piano for Lovers," "The Trucker's DX-7," etc.), not to mention instruments which play themselves, the most pervasive example in recent years being preprogrammed rhythm boxes. Such devices, as found in lounge acts and organ consoles, are direct kin to the juke box: push a button and out comes music. J.S. Bach pointed out that with any instrument "all one has to do is hit the right notes at the right time and the thing plays itself." The distinction between sound producers and sound reproducers is easily blurred, and has been a conceivable area of musical pursuit at least since John Cage's use of radios in the Forties.

Just as sound producing and sound reproducing technology become more interactive, listeners are once again, if not invited, nonetheless encroaching upon creative territory. This prerogative has been largely forgotten in recent decades: gone are the days of lively renditions on the parlor piano.

Computers can take the expertise out of amateur music-making. A current *music-minus-one* program retards tempos and searches for the most ubiquitous chords to support the wanderings of a novice player. Some audio equipment geared for the consumer inadvertently offers interactive possibilities. But manufacturers have discouraged compatibility between their amateur and pro equipment.

Passivity is still the dominant demographic. Thus the atrophied microphone inputs which have now all but disappeared from premium stereo cassette decks.

## Starting From Scratch

As a listener my own preference is the option to experiment. My listening system has a mixer instead of the one-choice-only function of a receiver; an infinitely variable-speed turntable, filters, reverse capability, and a pair of ears.

An active listener might speed up a piece of music in order to more clearly perceive its macrostructure, or slow it down to hear articulation and detail more precisely. One might trace "the motifs of the Indian raga Darbari over Senegalese drumming recorded in Paris and a background mosaic of frozen moments from an exotic Hollywood orchestration of the 1950s, a sonic texture like a 'Mona Lisa' which, in close-up, reveals itself to be made up of tiny reproductions of the Taj Mahal."[5]

During World War II concurrent with Cage's re-establishing the percussive status of the piano, Trinidadians were discovering that discarded oil barrels could be cheap, available alternatives to their traditional percussion instruments which were, because of the socially invigorating potential, banned. The steel drum eventually became a national asset. Meanwhile, back in the States, *scratch* and *dub* have, in the eighties, percolated through the black American ghettoes, for perhaps similar reasons. Within an environmentally imposed limited repertoire of possessions a portable disco may have a folk music potential exceeding that of the guitar. Pawned and ripped-off electronics are usually not accompanied by users' guides with consumer warnings like "this blaster is a passive reproducer." Any performance potential found in an appliance is often exploited.

Referring to DJ Francis Grasso at the Salvation Club in New York in the mid-seventies, Albert Goldman writes in *Disco* that "Grasso invented the technique of 'slipcueing': holding the disc with his thumb whilst the turntable whirled beneath, insulated by a felt pad. He'd locate with an earphone the best spot to make the splice then release the next side precisely on the beat. . . . His tour de force was playing two records simultaneously for as long as two minutes at a stretch. He would super the drum break of 'I'm a Man' over the orgasmic moans of Led Zeppelin's 'Whole Lotta Love' to make a powerfully erotic mix . . . that anticipated the formula of bass drum beats and love cries . . . now one of the cliches of the disco mix."[6]

Thus the sound of music conveyed with a new authority over the airwaves is dubbed, embellished and manipulated in kind.

## Aural Wilderness

The reuse of existing recorded materials is not restricted to the street and the esoteric. The single guitar chord occurring infrequently on Herbie Hancock's hit arrangement "Rockit" was not struck by an in-studio union guitarist but was sampled directly from an old Led Zeppelin record. Similarly, Michael Jackson unwittingly turns up on Hancock's followup clone "Hard Rock." Now that keyboardists are getting instruments with the button for this appropriation built in, they're going to push it, easier than reconstructing the ideal sound from oscillation one. These players are used to fingertip replication, as in the case of the organ that had the titles of the songs from which the timbres were derived printed on the stops.[7]

Charles Ives composed in an era in which much of music existed in the public domain. Public domain is now legally defined, although it maintains a distance from the present which varies from country to country. In order to follow Ives' model we would be restricted to using the same oldies which in his time were current. Nonetheless, music in the public domain can become very popular, perhaps in part because, as *This Business of Music*[8] puts it, "The public domain is like a vast national park without a guard to stop wanton looting, without a guide for the lost traveler, and in fact, without clearly defined roads or even borders to stop the helpless visitor from being sued for trespass by private abutting owners."

Professional developers of the musical landscape know and lobby for the loopholes in copyright. On the other hand, many artistic endeavors would benefit creatively from a state of music without fences, but where, as in scholarship, acknowledgement is insisted upon.

### The Medium is Magnetic

Piracy or plagiarism of a work occur, according to Milton, "if it is not bettered by the borrower." Stravinsky added the right of possession to Milton's distinction when he said, "A good composer does not imitate; he steals." An example of this better borrowing is Jim Tenney's "Collage 1" (1961), in which Elvis Presley's hit record "Blue Suede Shoes" (itself borrowed from Carl Perkins) is transformed by means of multi-speed tape recorders and razorblade.

Tenney took an everyday music and allowed us to hear it differently. At the same time, all that was inherently Elvis radically influenced our perception of Jim's piece.

*Fair use* and *fair dealing* are respectively the American and the Canadian terms for instances in which appropriation without permission might be considered legal. Quoting extracts of music for pedagogical, illustrative and critical purposes has been upheld as legal fair use. So has borrowing for the purpose of parody. Fair dealing assumes use which does not interfere with the economic viability of the initial work.

In addition to economic rights, an artist can claim certain moral rights to a work. Elvis' estate can claim the same rights, including the right to privacy, and the right to protection of "the special significance of sounds peculiar to a particular artist, the uniqueness of which might be harmed by inferior unauthorized recordings which might tend to confuse the public about an artist's abilities."

My observation is that Tenney's "Blue Suede" fulfills Milton's stipulation; is supported by Stravinsky's aphorism; and does not contravene Elvis' morality.

### Hitting Back the Parade

The property metaphor used to illustrate an artist's rights is difficult to pursue through publication and mass dissemination. The Hit Parade publicly promenades the aural floats of pop. As curious tourists, should we not be able to take our own snapshots ("tiny reproductions of the Taj Mahal") rather than be restricted to the official souvenir postcards and programs?

All popular music is (as is all folk music by definition) essentially, if not legally, existing in a public domain. Listening to pop music isn't a matter of choice. Asked-for or not, we're bombarded by it. In its most insidious state, filtered to an incessant bassline, it seeps through apartment walls and out of the heads of Walkpeople. Although people in general are making more noise than ever before, fewer people are making more of the total noise; specifically, in music, those with megawatt PAs, triple-platinum sales, and heavy rotation. Difficult to ignore, pointlessly redundant to imitate: how does one not become a passive recipient?

As oceanographer Bob Ballard of the Deep Emergence Laboratory described their plan to apprehend the Titanic once it had been located at the bottom of the Atlantic, "You pound the hell out of it with every imaging system you have."

## NOTES

1. This is Chris Cutler's poignant phrase, from *File Under Popular* (New York: Auto-nomedia, 1993), which also includes a good analysis of attempted definitions of popular music: "There can be no such thing as a finished or definitive piece of music. At most there could be said to be 'matrices' or 'fields.' Consequently there is also no element of personal property, though there is of course individual contribution." (p. 26).

2. David Horowitz of Warner Communications quoted in "The War Against Home Tap-ing," *Rolling Stone* (Sept. 16, 1982): 62.

3. Quoted in *Musician* (February 1985), p. 62.

4. From Spider Robinson, *Melancholy Elephants* (New York: Penguin Books, 1984).

5. Quoted from Jon Hassell's essay "Magic Realism" [liner notes to *Aka-Darbari-Java (Magic Realism)*, Editions EG EEGCD-31—Eds.], this passage refers in an evocative way to some appropriations and transformations in Hassell's recordings. In some cases this type of use obscures the identity of the original and at other times the sources are recognizable.

6. [Albert Goldman, *Disco* (New York: Hawthorn Books, 1978), 115.—Eds.]

7. I have been unable to relocate the reference to this device which had, for example, a "96 Tears" stop. According to one source it may have been only a one-off mockup in ads for the Roland Juno 60 synthesizer.

8. Sidney Schemel and William Krasilovsky, *This Business of Music*, 5th ed. (New York: Watson-Guptill, 1985).

# 24

# *Plunderphonia*

## CHRIS CUTLER

Chris Cutler (1947– ) has been a key figure in vanguard music for more than three decades. In 1971, he began playing drums for experimental rock outfit Henry Cow, which combined rock, improvised music, avant-garde composition, and left-wing politics, and collaborated with like-minded groups such as Soft Machine, Slapp Happy, and Gong. Following Henry Cow's dissolution in 1978, Cutler went on to found a number of other groups (Art Bears, Cassiber, etc.) and to perform with Pere Ubu and The Residents. In the past two decades, he has been a significant presence on the British free improvisation scene, working with Eddie Prévost, Eugene Chadbourne, Fred Frith, Zeena Parkins, and others.

Cutler has been equally important as a musical organizer, distributor, and theorist. In 1978, he formed "Rock in Opposition," a collective of musicians dedicated to resisting the power of the commercial music industry. The same year, he founded Recommended Records, "an alternative, independent, non-commercial record distribution, mailorder network and label." Cutler's essays have consistently pursued the ideal of a genuinely democratic culture. In this article, Cutler places sampling and "plunderphonics" in historical perspective, examining the ways in which recording and musical technology have altered the very nature of music and musical practice.

Until 1877, when the first sound recording was made, sound was a thing predicated on its own immediate disappearance; today it is increasingly an *object* that will outlast its makers and consumers. It declines to disappear, causing a great weight of dead music to press upon the living. What to do with it? An organic response has been to recycle, an answer strenuously resisted by traditional music thinking. Yet, plagiarism, once rejected as insupportable, has today emerged both as a standard procedure and as a consciously self-reflexive activity, raising vexed debates about ownership, originality, copyright, skill and cultural exhaustion. This essay attempts to sketch the history of plunderphonics and relate it to the paradigm shift initiated by the advent of sound recording.

## Introduction

*"Sounds like a dive downwards as a sped up tape slows rapidly to settle into a recognisable, slightly high-pitched Dolly Parton. It continues to slow down, but more gradually now. The instruments thicken and their timbres stretch and richen. Details unheard at the right speed suddenly cut across the sound. Dolly is changing sex; she's a man already; the backing has become hallucinatory and strange. The grain of the song is opened up and the ear, seduced by detail, lets a throng of surprising associations and ideas fall in behind it. The same thing is suddenly very different. Who would have expected this extraordinary composition to have been buried in a generic country song, 1000 times heard already and 1000 times copied and forgotten?"*

So I hear John Oswald's version of Dolly Parton's version of "The Great Pretender," effectively a recording of Oswald playing Parton's single once through, transformed via varispeed media (first a high speed cassette duplicator, then an infinitely variable speed turntable, finally a hand-controlled reel-to-reel tape—all seamlessly edited together). Apart from the *economy* of this single procedure of controlled deceleration, which is, as it were, *played* by Oswald, no modifications have been made to the original recording. However, although the source is plainly fixed and given, the choice, treatment and reading of this source are all highly conscious products of Oswald's own intention and skill. So much so indeed that it is easy to argue that the piece, although "only" Parton's record, undoubtedly forms, in Oswald's version, a self-standing composition with its own structure and logic—both of which are profoundly different from those of the original. Oswald's "Pretender" would still work for a listener who had never heard the Parton version, and in a way the Parton version never could. Though the Parton version is, of course, *given*—along with and against the plundered version. What Oswald has created—created because the result of his work is something startlingly new—is a powerful, aesthetic, significant, polysemic but highly focused and enjoyable sound artefact; both a source of direct listening pleasure and (for our purposes) a persuasive case for the validity and eloquence of its means.

John Oswald's "Pretender" and other pieces—all originated from existing copyright recordings but employing radically different techniques—were included on an EP and later a CD, *Plunderphonic*. Both were given away free to radio stations and the press. None was sold. The liner note reads: "This disc may be reproduced but neither it, nor any reproductions of it are to be bought or sold. Copies are available only to public access and broadcast organisations, including libraries, radio or periodicals." The 12" EP, consisting of four pieces—"Pretender" (Parton), "Don't" (Presley), "Spring" (Stravinsky), "Pocket" (Basie)—was made between 1979 and 1988 and released in May 1988, with some support from the Arts Council of Canada. The CD, containing these and 20 other pieces was realised between 1979–89 and released on October 31st 1989 and was financed entirely by Oswald himself. Between Christmas Eve 1989 and the end of January 1990 all distribution ceased and all extant copies were destroyed. Of all the plundered artists it was Michael Jackson who pursued the CD to destruction. Curiously Jackson's own plundering, for instance the one minute and six seconds of The Cleveland Symphony Orchestra's recording of Beethoven's Ninth which opens Jackson's "Will You Be There?" on the CD *Dangerous*, for which Jackson claims no less than six credits, including composer copyright (adding plagiarism to sound piracy), seems to have escaped his notice.

## Necessity and Choice (Continued)

In 1980 I wrote that "From the moment of the first recording, the actual performances of musicians on the one hand, and all possible sound on the other, had become the proper matter of music creation."[1] I failed, however, to underline the consequence that "all sound" has to include other people's already recorded work; and that when all sound is just raw material, then recorded sound is *always* raw—even when it is cooked. This omission I wish now in part to redress.

Although recording offered all audible sound as material for musical organisation, art music composers were slow to exploit it, and remain so today. One reason is that the inherited paradigms through which art music continues to identify itself have not escaped their roots in notation, a system of mediation which determines both what musical material is available and what possible forms of organisation can be applied to it. The determination of material and organisation follows from the character of notation as a discontinuous system of instructions developed to model visually what we know as melody, harmony and rhythm represented by, and limited to, arrangements of *fixed tones* (quantised, mostly 12 to an octave) and *fixed durations* (of notes and silences). Notation does not merely quantise the material, reducing it to simple units but, constrained by writability, readability and playability, is able to encompass only a very limited degree of complexity within those units. In fact the whole edifice of western art music can be said, after a fashion, to be constructed upon and through notation,[2] which, amongst other things, *creates* "the composer" who is thus constitutionally bound to it.

No wonder then that recording technology continues to cause such consternation. On the one hand it offers control of musical parameters beyond even the wildest dreams of the most radical mid-20th century composer; on the other it terminally threatens the deepest roots of the inherited art music paradigm, replacing notation with the direct transcription of performances and rendering the clear distinction between performance and composition null.

Perhaps this accounts for the curious relationship between the art music world and the new technology which has, from the start, been equivocal or at least highly qualified (Edgard Varèse and later Karlheinz Stockhausen notably excepted). And it is why the story I shall have to tell is so full of tentative high art experiments that seem to die without issue and why, although many creative innovations in the new medium were indeed made on the fringes of high art, their adoption and subsequent extension has come typically through other, less ideologically intimidated (or less paradigmatically confused?) musical genres. Old art music paradigms and new technology are simply *not able* to fit together.[3]

For art music then, recording is inherently problematic—and surely plunderphonics is recording's most troublesome child, breaking taboos art music hadn't even imagined. For instance, while plagiarism was already strictly off limits (flaunting non-negotiable rules concerning originality, individuality and property rights), plunderphonics was proposing routinely to appropriate as its raw material not merely other people's tunes or styles but finished recordings of them! It offered a medium in which, far from art music's essential creation *ex nihilo*, the origination, guidance and confirmation of a sound object may be carried through *by listening alone*.

The new medium proposes, the old paradigms recoil. Yet I want to argue that *it is precisely in this forbidden zone that much of what is genuinely new in the creative potential of new technology resides*. In other words, the moral and legal boundaries which currently constitute important determinants in claims for musical legitimacy, impede and restrain some of the most exciting possibilities in the changed circumstances of the age of recording. History to date is clear on such conflicts: the old paradigms will give way. The question is—to what?

One of the conditions of a new art form is that it produce a metalanguage, a theory through which it can adequately be described. A new musical form will need such a theory. My sense is that Oswald's *Plunderphonic* has brought at last into sharp relief many of the critical questions around which such a theory can be raised. For by coining the name, Oswald has identified and consolidated a musical practice which until now has been without focus. And like all such namings, it seems naturally to apply retrospectively, creating its own archaeology, precursors and origins.

## Originality

Of all the processes and productions which have emerged from the new medium of recording, plunderphonics is the most consciously self-reflexive; it begins and ends only with recordings, with the *already played*. Thus, as I have remarked above, it cannot help but challenge our current understanding of originality, individuality and property rights. To the extent that sound recording as a medium negates that of notation and echoes in a transformed form that of biological memory, this should not be so surprising.[4] In ritual and folk musics, for instance, originality as we understand it would be a misunderstanding—or a transgression—since proper performance is repetition. Where personal contributions are made or expected, these must remain within clearly prescribed limits and iterate sanctioned and traditional forms.

Such musics have no place for genius, individuality or originality as we know them or for the institution of intellectual property. Yet these were precisely the concepts and values central to the formation of the discourse that identified the musical, intellectual and political revolution that lay the basis for what we now know as the classical tradition. Indeed they were held as marks of its superiority over earlier forms. Thus, far from describing *hubris* or transgression, originality and the individual voice became central criteria of value for a music whose future was to be marked by the restless and challenging pursuit of progress and innovation. Writing became essential, and not only for transmission. A score was an individual's signature on a work. It also made unequivocal the author's claim to the legal ownership of a sound blueprint. "Blueprint" because a score is mute and others have to give it body, sound, and meaning. Moreover, notation established the difference and immortality of a work in the abstract, irrespective of its performance.

## Copyright

The arrival of recording, however, made each performance of a score as permanent and fixed as the score itself. Copyright was no longer so simple.[5] When John

Coltrane recorded his version of "My Favourite Things" (1961), a great percentage of which contains no sequence of notes found in the written score, the assigning of the composing rights to Rogers and Hammerstein hardly recognises the compositional work of Coltrane, Garrison, Tyner and Jones. A percentage can now be granted for an "arrangement" but this doesn't satisfy the creative input of such performers either. Likewise, when a collective improvisation is registered under the name, as often still occurs, of a bandleader, nothing is expressed by this except the power relations pertaining in the group. Only if it is registered in the names of all the participants, are collective creative energies honoured—and historically, it took decades to get copyright bodies to recognise such "unscored" works, and their status is still anomalous and poorly rated.[6] Still, this is an improvement: until the mid 1970s, in order to claim a composer's copyright for an improvised or studio originated work, one had to produce some kind of score constructed from the record—a topsy-turvy practice in which the music created the composer. And to earn a royalty on a piece which started and ended with a copyright tune but had fifteen minutes of free improvising in the middle, a title or titles had to be given for the improvised parts or all the money would go to the author of the bookending melody. In other words, the response of copyright authorities to the new realities of recording was to cobble together piecemeal compromises in the hope that, between the copyrights held in the composition and the patent rights granted over a specific recording, most questions of assignment could be adjudicated—and violations could be identified and punished. No one wanted to address the fact that recording technology had called not merely the mechanics but the adequacy of the prevailing *concept* of copyright into question.

It was Oswald, with the release of his not-for-sale EP and then CD who, by naming, theorising and defending the use of "macrosamples" and "electroquotes," finally forced the issue. And it was not so much that the principles and processes involved were without precedent but rather that through Oswald they were at last brought together in a focused and fully conscious form.

The immediate result was disproportionate industry pressure, threats and the forcible withdrawal from circulation and destruction of all extant copies. This despite the fact that the CD in question was arguably an original work (in the old paradigmatic sense), was not for sale (thereby not exploiting other people's copyrights for gain) and was released precisely to raise the very questions which its suppression underlined but immediately stifled. Nevertheless, the genie was out of the bottle.

The fact is that, considered as raw material, a recorded sound is technically indiscriminate of source. All recorded sound, as recorded sound, is information of the same quality. A recording of a recording is just a recording. No more, no less. We have to start here. Only then can we begin to examine, as with photomontage (which takes as its strength of meaning the fact that a photograph of a photograph is—a photograph) how the message of the medium is qualified by a communicative intent that distorts its limits. Judgements about what is plagiarism and what is quotation, what is legitimate use and what, in fact if not law, is public domain material, cannot be answered by recourse to legislation derived from technologies that are unable even to comprehend such questions. When "the same thing" is so different that it constitutes a new thing, it isn't "the same thing" anymore—even if, like Oswald's hearing of the Dolly Parton record, it manifestly is the "same thing" and no other. The key to this apparent paradox lies in the protean self-reflexivity of recording technology, allied with its elision of the acts of production and reproduction—both of which characteristics are incompatible with the old models, centred on notation, from which our current thinking derives, and which commercial copyright laws continue to reflect.

Thus plunderphonics as a practice radically undermines three of the central pillars of the art music paradigm: *originality* (it deals only with copies), *individuality* (it speaks only with the voice of others), and *copyright* (the breaching of which is a condition of its very existence).

### Recording History: The Gramophone

As an attribute unique to recording, the history of plunderphonics is in part the history of the self-realisation of the recording process; its coming, so to speak, to consciousness.[7] Sound recording began with experiments in acoustics and the discovery that different pitches and timbres of sound could be rendered visible, most notably in 1865 by Leon Scott de Martinville attaching a stylus to a membrane, causing the membrane to vibrate with a sound and allowing it to engrave its track on a glass cylinder coated with lampblack moving at a fixed speed. Such experiments were conducted only to convert otherwise invisible, transient sound into a "writing" (phono-graph means "voice-writer"), a fixed visible form that would allow it to be seen and studied. It was some ten years before it occurred to anyone that by simply reversing the process the sound thus written might be recovered. And it wasn't until the late 1870s that the first, purely mechanical phonograph was constructed, without clear purpose, speculatively appearing as a "dictaphone," sonic snapshot device, novelty item or talking doll mechanism. Interestingly all Edison's early cylinders were recording devices as well as reproducing devices, but he quickly lost the initiative to the mass reproducible flat Berliner disc, which was only a reproductive medium. Its mass production however fed the growing consumer market for music recordings. Though its reproductive quality was poorer than the Edison cylinder, the disc was cheaper and more accessible, and in the hands of entrepreneurs and users music quickly became the primary content of recorded media—a process accelerated after the electrification of the whole process in 1926 which resulted in improved recording techniques, superior reproductive quality and increasing uninterrupted playing times. The breakthrough for the record as a producing (as opposed to reproducing) medium, didn't come until 1948, in the studios of French Radio, with the birth of *musique concrète*. There were no technological advances to explain this breakthrough, only a thinking advance; the chance interpenetrations of time, place and problematic.

The first *concrète* pieces, performed at the *Concert de Bruits* in Paris by engineer/composer Pierre Schaeffer, were made by manipulating gramophone records in real time, employing techniques embedded in their physical form: varying the speed, reversing the direction of spin, making "closed grooves" to create repeated ostinati etc. Within two years the radio station, in the face of resistance from Schaeffer, had reequipped the studio with tape recorders; and Schaeffer, now head of the Groupe de Musique Concrète, continued to develop the same aesthetic of sound organisation and to extend the transformational procedures learned through turntable manipulations with the vastly more flexible resources of magnetic tape. Other composers began to experiment with disc manipulation around the same time, including Tristram Cary in London and Mauricio Kagel in Buenos Aires. Tape had completely displaced direct-to-disc recording by 1950 and the studio that was to become an instrument was the tape studio. Disc experiments seemed merely to have become a primitive forerunner to tape work. It is curious that, in spite of the intimacy of record and recording, the first commercially available *musique concrète* on disc was not released until 1956.

## Tape

Where the gramophone was an acoustic instrument, the magnetic recorder, also invented at the end of the nineteenth century, was always electrical. The gramophone, however, had numerous initial advantages: it was easier to amplify (the energy of the recoverable signal was greater to start with), and as soon as Émile Berliner replaced the cylinder with the disc and developed a process to press copies from a single master (1895), records were easy to mass produce. Wire—and then tape—were both much more difficult. For these and other reasons, tape was not regularly employed in music until after the Second World War, when German improvements in recording and playback quality and in stable magnetic tape technology were generally adopted throughout the world. Within five years tape had become standard in all professional recording applications.

The vinyl disc meanwhile held its place as the principle commercial playback medium and thus the ubiquitous public source of recorded sound. This division between the professionally productive and socially reproductive media was to have important consequences, since it was on the gramophone record that music appeared in its public, most evocative form; and when resonant cultural fragments began to be taken into living sound art, it was naturally from records, from the "real" artefacts that bricoleurs would draw. But before we get to this part of the story, I want to take a quick look at plundering precedents in some other fields.

## History/Plunder

From early in the twentieth century conditions existed that one would expect to have encouraged sound plundering experiments as a matter of course. First, the fact of sound recording itself, its existence, its provision of a medium which offers the sonic simulacrum of an actual sound event in a permanent and alienable form. Moreover, in principle, a sound recording, like a photograph, is merely surface. It has no depths, reveals no process and is no palimpsest. It's just there; always the first, always a copy. It has no aura, nor any connection to a present source. And with its special claims toward objectivity and transparency, the tongue of a recording is always eloquently forked and thus already placed firmly in the realm of art.[8]

Secondly, montage, collage, borrowing, bricolage have been endemic in the visual arts since at least the turn of the century. The importation of readymade fragments into original works was a staple of cubism (newspaper, label samples, advertising etc.), futurism and early soviet art. Dada took this much further (Kurt Schwitters above all and the photomontagists) and as early as 1914 Marcel Duchamp had exhibited his bottle rack, a work in which, for the first time, a complete unmodified object was simply imported whole into an "art space." Yet strangely it waited 25 years for John Cage in his *Imaginary Landscape No.1* (1939) to bring a gramophone record into a public performance as an instrument—and he still only used test tones and the effect of speed changes.

Having said this, I recently learned that at a Dada event in 1920 Stefan Wolpe used eight gramophones to play records at widely different speeds simultaneously—a true precedent, but without consequences; and of course Ottorino Respighi did call for a gramophone recording of a nightingale in his 1924 *Pina di Roma*—a technicality this, but imaginative nonetheless (though a bird call would have sufficed). Moreover, Darius Milhaud (from 1922), László Moholy-Nagy at the Bauhaus (1923) and Edgard Varèse (1936) had all experimented with disc manipulation, but none eventually employed them in a final work. Paul Hindemith and Ernst Toch did produce three recorded "studies" (*Grammophonmusik*, 1929-30), but these have been lost, so it is difficult to say much about them except that, judging from the absence of offspring, their influence was clearly small.[9] More prescient, because the medium was more flexible, were sound constructions made by filmmakers in the late 1920s and 1930s, using techniques developed for film, such as splicing and montaging, and working directly onto optical film soundtrack—for instance, in Germany, Walter Ruttman's *Weekend* (1928) and Fritz Walter Bischoff's lost sound symphony, *Hallo! Hier Welle Erdball* (1928); and, in Russia, constructivist experiments including G. V. Alexandrov's *A Sentimental Romance* (1930) and Dziga Vertov's *Enthusiasm* (1931). There had also been some pieces of film music which featured "various treatments of sound recordings . . . probably created with discs before being transferred to celluloid—by such composers as Yves Baudrier, Arthur Honnegger and Maurice Jaubert."[10]

The ideas were around, but isolated in special project applications. And strangely, optical recording techniques developed for film in the 1920s, although endowed with many of the attributes of magnetic tape, simply never crossed over into the purely musical domain, despite Edgard Varèse's visionary proposal in 1940 for an optical sound studio in Hollywood—a proposal which, needless to say, was ignored.

With so many precedents in the world of the visual arts, and the long availability of the means of direct importation and plunder, it does seem surprising that it took so long for there to be similar developments in the world of music. And when, at last, the first clear intimations of the two principle elements crucial to plunderphonic practice did arrive, they arrived in two very different spheres, each surrounded by its own quite separate publicity and theory. The key works were Pierre Schaeffer's early experiments with radio sound archive discs (e.g. *Étude aux tourniquets*, 1948) and John Cage's unequivocal importation of readymade material into his *Imaginary Landscape No.4* (1951) for twelve radios—where all the sounds, voices and music were plundered whole, and at random, from the ionosphere. In 1955, *Imaginary Landscape No. 5* specified as sound material forty-two gramophone records. Thus, although Schaeffer used pre-recorded materials, these were "concrete" sounds, not already recorded compositions; while Cage made his construction out of "copyright" works, although this fact was purely incidental to the intention of the piece.

It wasn't until 1961 that an unequivocal exposition of plunderphonic techniques arrived in James Tenney's celebrated *Collage No.1 ("Blue Suede")*, a manipulation of Elvis Presley's hit record "Blue Suede Shoes." The gauntlet was down; Tenney had picked up a "non art," lowbrow work and turned it into "art"; not as with scored music by writing variations on a popular air, but simply by subjecting a gramophone record to various physical and electrical procedures.

Still no copyright difficulties.

## To Refer or Not to Refer

Now, it can easily be argued that performances with—and recordings which comprise—ready-made sounds, including other people's completed works, reflect a concern endemic in twentieth-century art with art media in and of themselves apart from all representational attributes. This can take the form, for instance, of an insistence that all that is imitation can be stripped away, leaving only sensual and essential forms with no external referents; or a belief that all semiotic systems consist of *nothing but* referentiality—signalled by the addition, as it were, of imaginary inverted commas to everything. But it is only a loss of faith, or illusion, or nerve, that stands between this century's younger belief in "pure" languages and today's acceptance of the "endless play of signification." Moreover, plunderphonics can be linked, historically and theoretically, to both perceptions. Thus a recording may be considered as no more than the anonymous carrier of a "pure"—which is to say a non-referential—sound; or it may be an instance of a text that *cannot exist without reference*. In the first way, as Michel Chion's "Ten Commandments For an Art of Fixed Sounds" makes clear, the composer "distinguishes completely sounds from their sonic source . . . he has done with mourning the presence of the cause."[11] Here the goal is to "purify" the sound, to strip it of its origin and memories (though it may well be that that same erased origin remains still to haunt it). In the second way, the recording—for instance a sample—may be no more than a fragment, a knowing self reference, a version, and may be used to point at this very quality in itself.

As a found (or stolen) object, a sound is no more than available—for articulation, fragmentation, reorigination; it may be given the form of pure "acousmatics" or made an instance of the availability and interchangeability—the *flatness*—of a recording, its origin not so much erased as rendered infinitely relative. These applications, of course, do not exhaust it: as a pirated cultural artefact, a found object, as debris from the sonic environment, a plundered sound also holds out an invitation to be used *because* of its cause and because of all the associations and cultural apparatus that surround it. And surely, what has been done with "captured" visual images (Warhol, Rauschenberg, Lichtenstein)—or with directly imported objects (Duchamp, the mutilated poster works of Harris, Rotella, De la Villegle and others)—all of which *depend upon* their actuality and provenance (as ready-mades)—can equally be done with captured "images" of sound.

Plundered sound carries, above all, the unique ability not just to *refer* but to *be*; it offers not just a new means but a new meaning. It is this dual character that confuses the debates about originality which so vex it.

## High and Low

Popular musics got off to a slow start with sound piracy. Nevertheless they soon proved far more able to explore its inherent possibilities than art musics, which even after fifty years of sporadic experiment remained unable rigorously so to do. It is interesting perhaps that Tenney, who made the most radical essay into unashamed plunder, chose popular music as his primary source. In a later piece, *Viet Flakes*, from 1967, he mixed pop, classical and Asian traditional musics together and in so doing drew attention to another significant facet of the life of music on gramophone records, namely that, in the same way that they conceal and level their sources, records as objects make no distinction between "high" and "low" culture, "art" and "pop."[12] A record makes all musics equally accessible—in every sense. No special clothes are needed, no expensive tickets need be bought, no travel is necessary, one need belong to no special interest or social group, nor be in a special place at a special time. Indeed, from the moment recordings existed, a new kind of "past" and "present" were born—both immediately available on demand. Time and space are homogenised in the home loudspeaker or the headphone, and the pop CD costs the same as the classical CD and probably comes from the same shop. All commodities are equal.

For young musicians growing up in the electric recording age, immersed in this shoreless sea of available sound, electronics, Maltese folk music, bebop, rhythm and blues, show tunes, film soundtracks and the latest top ten hit were all equally on tap. Tastes, interests, studies could be nourished at the pace and following the desire of the listener. Sounds, techniques and styles could flit across genres as fast as you could change a record, tune a dial or analyse and imitate what you heard. A kind of sound intoxication arose. Certainly it was the ideas and applications encountered in recorded music of all types which led a significant fringe of the teenage generation of the late 1960s into experiments with sound, stylistic bricolage, importations, the use of noise, electronics, "inappropriate" instruments and—crucially—recording techniques.[13] The influence of art music and especially the work of Varèse, Schaeffer, Stockhausen and others cannot be overestimated in this context and, more than anything, it would be the crossplay between high and low art that would feature increasingly as a vital factor in the development of much innovative music. In plunderphonics too, the leakages—or maybe simply synchronicities—between productions in what were once easily demarcated as belonging in high or low art discourses, are blatant. Indeed, in more and more applications, the distinction is meaningless and impossible to draw.

But there are simpler reasons for the special affinity between low art and plundering. For instance, although the first plunder pieces (viz. the early *concrète* and the Cage works mentioned) belonged firmly in the art camp, blatant plundering nevertheless remained fairly off limits there, precluded essentially by the non-negotiable concern with originality and peer status—and also with the craft aspect of creating from scratch: originating out of a "creative centre" rather than "just messing about with other people's work." The world of low art had few such scruples: indeed, in a profound sense plundering was endemic to it—in the "folk" practices of copying and covering for instance (few people played original compositions), or in the use of public domain forms and genres as vessels for expressive variation (the blues form, jazz interpretations, sets of standard chord progressions and so on). The twentieth-century art kind of originality and novelty simply was not an issue here. Moreover, in the "hands on," low expectation, *terra nova* world of rock, musicians were happy to make fools of themselves "rediscovering America" the hard way.

What I find especially instructive was how, in a sound world principally mediated by recording, the high and low art worlds increasingly appropriated from one another. And how problems that were glossed over when art was art and there was no genre confusion (like Tenney's appropriation of copyrighted, but lowbrow, recordings) suddenly threatened to become dangerously problematic when genres blurred and both plunder and original began to operate in the same disputed (art/commercial) space.

## Low Art Takes a Hand

Rock precedents for pure studio tapework come from Frank Zappa, with his decidedly Varèse-esque concrete pieces on the albums *Absolutely Free*, *Lumpy Gravy* and *We're Only In It For The Money*, all made in 1967 (*We're Only In It For The Money* also contains an unequivocally plundered Surf music extract) and The Beatles' pure tapework on "Tomorrow Never Knows" from the 1966 album *Revolver*. "Revolution No 9" on *The White Album* is also full of plundered radio material. In the early 1960s radios were ubiquitous in the high art world and in some intermediary groups such as AMM and Faust (in the latter, on their second UK tour, guest member Uli Trepte played "Space Box"—a shortwave radio and effects—as his main instrument).

Such examples—taken in combination with, firstly, the increasing independence, confidence and self-consciousness of some rock musicians; secondly, a generation of musicians coming out of art schools; furthermore, the mass availability of ever cheaper home recording equipment; and, finally, a climate of experiment and plenitude—made straightforward plunder inevitable. This promise was first substantially filled by The Residents. Their second released album, *Third Reich and Roll* (1975), a highly self-reflexive commentary on rock culture and hit records, curiously employed a technique analogous to that used by Stockhausen in 1970 for his Beethoven Anniversary recording, *Opus 1970*, which had nothing to do with influence and everything to do with the medium. What Stockhausen had done was to prepare tapes of fragments of Beethoven's music which ran continuously throughout the performance of the piece. Each player could open and shut his own loudspeaker at will and was instantaneously to "develop" what he heard instrumentally (condense, extend, transpose, modulate, synchronise, imitate, distort). To different ends The Residents followed a similar procedure: instead of Beethoven, they copied well known pop songs to one track of a four-track tape and then played along with them (transposing, modulating, distorting, commenting on, intensifying), thus building up tracks. Though they subsequently erased most of the source material, you can often, as with *Opus 1970*, still hear the plundered originals breaking through.

In 1977 it was The Residents again who produced the first unequivocal 100% plunder to come out of pop, following in the high art footsteps of James Tenney's Presley-based *Collage No.1*, and the later, more successful 1975 work *Omaggio a Jerry Lee Lewis* by American composer Richard Trythall (plundered from various recordings of Lewis's "Whole Lotta Shakin' Goin' On"). Trythall comments: "Like the table or newspaper in a cubist painting, the familiar musical object served the listener as an orientation point within a maze of new material . . . the studio manipulations . . . carried the source material into new, unexpected areas, while maintaining its past associations."[14] The Residents' work was a 7-inch single titled "Beyond The Valley Of A Day In The Life" and subtitled "The Residents Play The Beatles/The Beatles Play The Residents." It came packaged as an art object in a numbered, limited edition and hand-silkscreened cover, but was sold to—and known by—a rock public. One side of this single was a cover version of The Beatles song "Flying." The other was pure plunderphonics. This whole side was assembled from extracts dubbed off Beatles records, looped, multitracked, composed with razor blades and tape. It is an ingenious construction, and remains a landmark.

## Sampling and Scratching

Although there were some notable experiments and a few successful productions, tape and disc technologies made plundering difficult and time consuming and thus suitable only for specific applications. What brought plundering to the centre of mass consumption low art music was a new technology that made sound piracy so easy that it didn't make sense *not* to do it. This development was digital sampling, launched affordably by Ensoniq in the mid-1980s. Digital sampling is a purely electronic digital recording system which takes samples or "vertical slices" of sound and converts them into binary information, into data, which tells a sound producing system how *to reconstruct*, rather than *reproduce* it. Instantly.

At a fast enough sampling rate the detailed contours of a sound can be so minutely traced that playback quality is compatible with any analogue recording system. The revolutionary power associated with a digital system is that the sound when stored consists of information in a form that can be transformed, edited or rewritten electronically, without "doing" anything to any actual analogue recording but only to a code. This really is a kind of a writing. When it is stored, modified or reproduced, no grooves, magnetised traces or any other contiguous *imprint* link the sound to its means of storage (by imprint I mean as when an object is pressed into soft wax and leaves its analogue trace). It is stored rather as discrete data, which act as *instructions* for the eventual reconstruction of a sound (as a visual object when electronically scanned is translated only into a binary code). Digital sampling allows any recorded sound to be linked to a keyboard or to a MIDI trigger and, using electronic tools (computer software), to be stretched, visualised on screen as waveforms and rewritten or edited with keys or a light pencil. All and any parameters can be modified and any existing electronic processing applied. Only at the end of all these processes will an audible sound be recreated. This may then be listened to and, if it is not what is wanted, reworked until it is and only then saved. It means that a work like Cage's four minute long *Williams Mix* (1952, the first tape collage made in America) which took a year to cut together, could now be programmed and executed quite quickly using only a domestic computer.

The mass application is even more basic. It simply puts any sound it records—or which has been recorded and stored as software—on a normal keyboard, pitched according to the key touched. The user can record, model and assign to the keys any sounds at all. At last here is a musical instrument which is a recording device and a performing instrument—*whose voice is simply the control and modulation of recordings*. How could this technology not give the green light to plundering? It was so simple. No expertise was needed, just a user friendly keyboard, some stuff to sample (records and CDs are easy—and right there at home), and plenty of time to try things out. Producing could be no more than critical consuming; an empirical activity of Pick'n'Mix. Nor was that all. Sampling was introduced into a musical climate where low art plundering was already deeply established in the form of "scratching"—which in its turn echoed in a radically sophisticated form the disc manipulation techniques innovated in high culture by Hindemith and Koch, Milhaud, Varèse, Honegger, Kagel, Cary, Schaeffer, Knizac et al., but now guided by a wholly different aesthetic.

## From Scratch

The term *scratching* was coined to describe the practice of the realtime manipulation of 12" discs on highly-adapted turntables. It grew up in US discos where DJs began to programme the records they played, running them together, cutting one into another on beat and in key, superimposing, crossfading and so on. Soon this developed to the point where a good DJ could play records as an accompanying or soloing instrument, along with a rhythm box, other tracks or singing. New and extended techniques emerged—for instance the rhythmic slipping of a disc to and fro rapidly by hand on a low friction mat to create rhythms and cross rhythms—alongside old *concrète* techniques: controlled-speed alterations and *sillons fermés* riffs. ("Two manual decks and a rhythm box is all you need. Get a bunch of good rhythm records, choose your favourite parts and groove along with the rhythm machine. Using your hands, scratch the record by repeating the grooves you dig so much. Fade one record into the other and keep that rhythm box going. Now start talking and singing over the record with your own microphone. Now you're making your own music out of other people's records. That's what scratching is."— sleeve note to Malcolm McLaren's B-BU-BUFFALO GALS, 1982).

It was only after scratching had become fashionable in the mid-1970s in radical black disco music that it moved back toward art applications, adopted quite brilliantly by Christian Marclay. Marclay used all the above techniques and more, incorporating also an idea of Milan Knizac's, who had been experimenting since 1963 with deliberately mutilated discs, particularly composite discs comprising segments of different records glued together. Of course everything Marclay does (like Knizac) is 100% plundered, but on some recordings he too, like John Oswald on his seminal *Plunderphonic* recordings, creates works which, echoing Tenney and Trythall, concentrate on a single artist, thus producing a work which is about an artist and made only from that artist's sonic simulacrum. Listen, for instance, to the "Maria Callas" and "Jimi Hendrix" tracks on *More Encores* (subtitled "Christian Marclay plays with the records of Louis Armstrong, Jane Birkin & Serge Gainsbourg, John Cage, Maria Callas, Frederic Chopin, Martin Denny, Arthur Ferrante & Louis Teicher, Fred Frith, Jimi Hendrix, Christian Marclay, Johann Strauss, John Zorn").

Marclay rose to prominence as a member of the early 1980s New York scene, on the experimental fringe of what was still thought of unequivocally as low art. He emerged from the context of disco and scratching, not *concrète* or other artworld experiments with discs (though they were part of his personal history). His cultural status (like the status of certain other alumni of the New York school such as John Zorn) slowly shifted, from low to high, via gallery installations and visual works and through the release of records such as *Record Without A Cover* (1985), which has only one playable side (the other has titles and text pressed into it) and comes unwrapped with the instruction: "Do not store in a protective package." Or the 1987 grooveless LP, packaged in a black suede pouch and released in a limited and signed edition of 50 by Ecart Editions. Marclay's work appears as a late flowering of an attenuated and, even at its height, marginal high art form, reinvented and reinvigorated by low art creativity. It traces the radical inter-penetrations of low and high art in the levelling age of sound recording; the swing between high art experiment, low art creativity and high art reappropriation, as the two approach one another until, at their fringes, they become indistinguishable. This *aesthetic levelling is a property of the medium* and this indistinguishability signals not a collapse but the coming into being of a new aesthetic form.

## Oswald Plays Records

Curiously, the apotheosis of the record as an instrument—as the raw material of a new creation—occurred just as the gramophone record itself was becoming obsolete and when a new technology that would surpass the wildest ambitions of any scratcher, acousmaticist, tape composer or sound organiser was sweeping all earlier record/playback production systems before it. Sampling, far from destroying disc manipulation, seems to have breathed new life into it. Turntable techniques live on in live House and Techno. Marclay goes from strength to strength, more credits for "turntables" appear on diverse CDs and younger players like Otomo Yoshihide are emerging with an even more organic and intimate relation to the record/player as an expressive instrument.[15]

It is almost as if sampling had recreated the gramophone record as a craft instrument, an analogue, expressive voice, made authentic by nostalgia. Obsolescence empowers a new mythology for the old phonograph, completing the circle from passive repeater to creative producer, from dead mechanism to expressive voice, from the death of performance to its guarantee. It is precisely the authenticity of the 12" disc that keeps it in manufacture; it has become anachronistically indispensable.

## Disc-Tape-Disc

Applications of a new technology to art are often first inspired by existing art paradigms, frequently simplifying or developing existing procedures. Then new ideas emerge that more directly engage the technology for itself. These arise as a product of use, accident, experiment or cross fertilisation—but always through hands-on interaction. New applications then feed back again into new uses of the old technologies and so on. For a long time such dynamic inter-penetrations can drive aspects of both. Painting and film, for instance, have just such a productive history. A similar process could be traced in the tension between recording and performance. A particularly obvious example of this is the way that hard cuts and edits made with tape for musical effect inspire *played* "edits"—brilliantly exemplified in the work of John Zorn. This process can be traced more broadly, and more profoundly, in the growth and refinement of the new sound aesthetic itself, which from its origins in the crisis in art music at the turn of the century through to contemporary practices in many fields, is characterised by the dynamic interactions between fluid and fixed media. New instrumental techniques inform, and are informed by, new recording techniques. Each refines a shared sonic language, sets problems, makes propositions. Each takes a certain measure of itself from the other, both living and dead: "Records are . . . dead" as Christian Marclay carefully points out.[16]

## More Dead Than Quick

What is essential—and new—is that by far the largest part of the music that we hear is recorded music, live music making up only a small percentage of our total listening. Moreover, recording is now the primary medium through which musical ideas and inspiration spread (this says nothing about quality, it is merely a quantitative fact). For example, one of the gravitational centres of improvisation—which is in every respect the antithesis of fixed sound or notated music—is its relation to recorded sound, including recordings of itself or of other improvisations. This performance-recording loop winds through the rise of jazz as a mass culture music, through rock experiments and on to the most abstract noise productions of today. Whatever living music does, chances are that the results will be recorded— and this will be their immortality. In the new situation, *it is only what is* not *recorded that belongs to its participants while what is recorded is placed inevitably in the public domain.*

Moreover, as noted earlier, recorded music leaves its genre community and enters the universe of recordings. As such the mutual interactions between composers, performers and recordings refer back to sound and structure and not to particular music communities. Leakage, seepage, adoption, osmosis, abstraction, contagion: these describe the life of sound work today. They account for the general aesthetic convergence at the fringes of genres once mutually exclusive—and across the gulf of high and low art. There is a whole range of sound work now about which it simply makes no sense to speak in terms of high or low, art or popular, indeed where the two interpenetrate so deeply that to attempt to discriminate between them is to fail to understand the sound revolution which has been effected through the medium of sound recording.

Plunderphonics addresses precisely this realm of the recorded. It treats of the point where both public domain and contemporary sound world meet the transformational and organisational aspects of recording technology; where listening and production, criticism and creation elide. It is also where copyright law from another age can't follow where—as Oswald himself remarked—"If creativity is a field, copyright is the fence."[17]

## Pop Eats Itself

I want now to look at some of the many applications of plundering beyond those of directly referential or self-reflexive intent like those of Tenney, Trythall, The Residents, Oswald and Marclay.

First, and most obvious, is the widespread plundering of records for samples that are recycled on HipHop, House and Techno records in particular, but increasingly on pop records in general. This means that drum parts, bass parts (often loops of a particular bar), horn parts, all manner of details (James Brown whoops etc.) will be dubbed off records and built up layer by layer into a new piece. This is essentially the same procedure as that adopted by The Residents in their Beatles piece, except that nowadays the range and power of electronic treatments is far greater than before and the results achieved of far greater technical complexity. Rhythms and tempi can be adjusted and synchronised, pitches altered, dynamic shape rewritten and so on. Selections sampled may be traceable or untraceable, it need not matter. Reference is not the aim so much as a kind of creative consumerism, a bricolage assembly from parts. Rather than start with instruments or a score, you start with a large record and CD collection and then copy, manipulate and laminate.

Moral and copyright arguments rage around this. There have been several high profile copyright infringement cases, and since 1990 bigger studios have employed departments to note and clear all samples and register and credit all composers, artists and original recording owners. "Sampling licences" are negotiated and paid for. This is hugely time consuming and slightly ridiculous and really not an option for amateurs and small fish. Oswald's CD *Plexure* (1993), for instance, has so many tiny cuts and samples on it that, not only are their identities impossible to register by listening, but compiling credit data would be like assembling a telephone directory for a medium sized town. Finding, applying, accounting and paying the 4000-plus copyright and patent holders would likewise be a full-time occupation, effectively impossible. Therefore such works simply could not exist. We have to address the question whether this is what we really want.

For now I am more interested in the way pop really starts to eat itself. Here together are cannibalism, laziness and the feeling that everything has already been originated, so that it is enough now endlessly to reinterpret and rearrange it all. The old idea of originality in *production* gives way to another (if to one at all) of originality in *consumption*, in hearing.

### Cassiber

Other applications use plundered parts principally as sound elements which relate in a constitutive or alienated way to the syntax of a piece. They may or may not carry referential weight, this being only one optional attribute which the user may choose to employ. The Anglo-German group Cassiber (comprising Chris Cutler, Heiner Goebbels and Christoph Anders) uses just such techniques in which samples act both as structure and as fragments of cultural debris. Cassiber creates complexities; no piece is reducible to a score, a set of instructions, a formula. Simultaneity and superimposed viewpoints are characteristic of much of the work—as is the tension between invention and passion on the one hand and "dead" materials on the other.

When the group was formed, singer Christoph Anders worked with a table stacked with prepared cassettes, each containing loops or raw extracts taken from all manner of musics (on one Cassiber piece, there might be fragments of Schubert, Schoenberg, The Shangri-La's, Maria Callas and Them). The invention of the sampler put in his hands a similar facility, except with more material and infinitely greater transformational power, all accessible immediately on a normal keyboard. It means that, in a way impossible—though desired—before, they can be played. They can be as unstable as any performed musical part—and as discontinuous.

Cassiber's use of familiar fragments, though these are often recognisable—and thus clearly referential—doesn't depend on this quality which is accepted merely as a possible aspect, but rather on their musical role within the piece. Where House and Rap use samples to reinforce what is familiar, Goebbels and Anders use them to make the familiar strange, dislocated, more like debris—but (and this is the key) as structural rather than decorative debris. It is an affect only plundered materials can deliver.[18]

## The Issue

What is the issue? Is it whether *sound* can be copyrighted or snatches of a performance? If so, where do we draw the line—at length or recognisability? Or does mass-produced, mass-disseminated music have a kind of folk status? Is it so ubiquitous and so involuntary (you *have* to be immersed in it much of your waking time) that it falls legitimately into the category of "public domain"? Since violent action (destruction of works, legal prohibition, litigation and distraint) have been applied by one side of the argument, these are questions we cannot avoid.

## A Brief Review of Applications

A. *There It Is*: There are cases such as that of Cage, in *Imaginary Landscapes 4* and *5*, where materials are all derived directly from records or radio and subjected to various manipulations. Though there are copyright implications, the practice implies that music picked randomly "out of the air" is simply there. Most of Cage's work is more a kind of listening than of producing.

B. *Partial Importations*: An example of partial importation is *My Life In The Bush Of Ghosts* (David Byrne and Brian Eno) and the work of Italians Roberto Musci and Giovanni Venosta. In both cases recordings of ethnic music are used as important voices, the rest of the material being constructed around them. The same might be done with whale songs, sound-effects records and so on. I detect political implications in the absence of copyright problems on such recordings. At least, it is far from obvious to me why an appeal to public domain status should be any more or less valid for "ethnic" music than it is for most pop—or any other recorded music.

C. *Total Importation*: This might rather be thought of as interpretation or re-hearing of existing recordings. Here we are in the territory of Tenney, Trythall, The Residents, Marclay and quintessentially, of plunderphonic pioneer John Oswald. Existing recordings are not randomly or instrumentally incorporated so much as they become the simultaneous subject and object of a creative work. Current copyright law is unable to distinguish between a plagiarised and a new work in such cases, since its concerns are still drawn from old pen and paper paradigms. In the visual arts Duchamp with readymades, Warhol with soupcans and Brillo boxes, Lichtenstein with cartoons and Sherry Levine with re-photographed "famous" photographs are only some of the many who have, one way or another, broached the primary artistic question of "originality," which Oswald too can't help but raise.

D. *Sources Irrelevant*: This is where recognition of parts plundered is not necessary or important. There is no self-reflexivity involved; sound may be drawn as if "out of nothing," bent to new purposes or simply used as raw material. Also within this category falls the whole mundane universe of sampling or stealing "sounds": drum sounds (not parts), guitar chords, riffs, vocal interjections etc., sometimes creatively used but more often simply a way of saving time and money. Why spend hours creating or copying a sound when you can snatch it straight off a CD and get it into your own sampler-sequencer?

E. *Sources Untraceable*: These are manipulations which take the sounds plundered and stretch and treat them so radically that it is impossible to divine their source at all. Techniques like this are used in electronic, concrete, acousmatic, radiophonic, film and other abstract sound productions. Within this use lies a whole universe of viewpoints. For instance, the positive exploration of new worlds of sound and new possibilities of aestheticisation—or the idea that there is no need to originate any more, since what is already there offers such endless possibilities—or the expression of an implied helplessness in the face of contemporary conditions, namely, everything that can be done has been done and we can only rearrange the pieces.

This is a field where what may seem to be quite similar procedures may express such wildly different understandings as a hopeless tinkering amidst the ruins or a celebration of the infinitude of the infinitesimal.

**Final Comments**

Several currents run together here. There is the technological aspect: plundering is impossible in the absence of sound recording. There is the cultural aspect: since the turn of the century the importation of readymade materials into artworks has been a common practice, and one which has accumulated eloquence and significance. The re-seeing or re-hearing of familiar material is a well-established practice and, in high art at least, accusations of plagiarism are seldom raised. More to the point, the two-way traffic between high and low art (each borrowing and quoting from the other) has proceeded apace. Today it is often impossible to draw a clear line between them—witness certain advertisements, Philip Glass, Jeff Koons, New York subway graffiti.

It seems inevitable that in such a climate the applications of a recording technology that gives instant playback, transposition and processing facilities will not be intimidated by the old proscriptions of plagiarism or the ideal of originality. What is lacking now is a discourse under which the new practices can be discussed and adjudicated. The old values and paradigms of property and copyright, skill, originality, harmonic logic, design and so forth are simply not adequate to the task. Until we are able to give a good *account* of what is being done, *how* to think and speak about it, it will remain impossible to adjudicate between legitimate and illegitimate works and applications. Meanwhile outrages such as that perpetrated on John Oswald will continue unchecked [. . . .]

**NOTES**

1. Chris Cutler, "Necessity and Choice in Musical Forms," *File Under Popular: Theoretical and Critical Writings on Music* (New York: Autonomedia, 1993), 33.
2. As I have argued in "Necessity and Choice in Musical Forms," section II (i).

3. There were sporadic experiments, as we shall see, and notably Varèse grasped the nettle early. Pierre Schaeffer made the radical proposal, but precisely from his work as an engineer, and not as a product of the art music tradition. A few followed—Stockhausen, Berio, Nono and others—and new schools formed which in part or whole abandoned mediating notation (*musique concrète* and electronic, tape, acousmatic and electroacoustic musics, for example), but these too tried to retain, as far as possible, the old status and values for their creators, merely replacing the score with direct personal manipulation, and continuing to make the same claims to originality, personal ownership, creation *ex nihilo*, etc. John Cage was an interesting exception: his originality and individuality being claimed precisely in their negation.

4. For the full argument, see "Necessity and Choice in Musical Forms," Section III (ii).

5. The first Copyright Act in England was passed in 1709. The current Act dates from 1988 and includes rights of the author to remuneration for all public performances (including broadcasts, jukeboxes, Muzak, fairground rides, concerts, discotheques, film, TV and so on) as well as for recordings of all kinds. The recording is copyrighted separately from the composition, so that every individual recording of a composition also has an owner.

6. Most copyright bodies still discriminate between works which earn a lot by the minute ("serious" composed works) and those which earn a little (pop music, for instance and improvised-compositions). Criteria for making such decisions vary, reflecting the prejudices of the day.

7. Which is to say, where it raises questions that reflect upon its own identity.

8. And through its documentary authenticity also in the realm of the political, as the purity of the retouched photograph and doctored tape attest.

9. Hugh Davies recently brought to my attention a notice from a 1993 conference in Berlin where it was reported that in the mid-1980s Hindemith's discs had been offered to the director of a German musicological institute. He refused them and their current whereabouts remain unknown.

10. Hugh Davies, "A History of Sampling," *unfiled: Music Under New Technology* (ReR/ Recommended Sourcebook 0401), 11–12.

11. Michel Chion, *L'Art des sons fixés* (Fontaine: Editions Metamkine/Nota Bene/Sono-Concept, 1991), 22.

12. I shall treat the quotation marks as read from here on.

13. See Cutler "The Residents," "Necessity and Choice," and "Progressive Music in the UK," in *File Under Popular*.

14. Richard Trythall, programme note on *Omaggio a Jerry Lee Lewis*, on Various Artists, *CMCD: Six Classic Concrete, Electroacoustic, and Electronic Works 1970–1990*, ReR CMCD.

15. Hear, for instance, Otomo's Ground Zero recording *Revolutionary Peking Opera*, ReR GZ1 CD.

16. From an interview with J. Dean Kuipers in *Ear* magazine (1993).

17. From the *Plunderphonic* CD booklet.

18. For example "Start the Show" from the CD *A Face We All Know*, ReRCD (1989).

# 25

# *Operating System for the Redesign of Sonic Reality*

## KODWO ESHUN

Kodwo Eshun (1968– ) is a music journalist, art critic, and theorist of techno-culture. Along with colleagues such as Mark Sinker, Greg Tate, John Corbett, Erik Davis, and Paul D. Miller, Eshun helped to define the concept of "Afrofuturism," which marks out a lineage of black artists (Sun Ra, George Clinton, Lee "Scratch" Perry, Alice Coltrane, Samuel R. Delany, Octavia Butler, Derrick May, etc.) for whom black identity is fundamentally connected with science fiction and electronic technology. Eshun rejects the stereotypical view that black artists uniquely embody "soul," "authenticity," "reality," and "humanism." Instead, he uncovers, in Afrofuturism, a view of the black artist as posthuman cyborg.

[. . . .] At the Century's End, the Futurhythmachine has 2 opposing tendencies, 2 synthetic drives: the Soulful and the Postsoul. But then all music is made of both tendencies running simultaneously at all levels, so you can't merely *oppose* a humanist r&b with a posthuman Techno.

Disco remains the moment when Black Music falls from the grace of gospel tradition into the metronomic assembly line. Ignoring that disco is therefore *audibly* where the 21st C begins, 9 out of 10 cultural crits prefer their black popculture humanist, and emphatically 19th C. Like Brussels sprouts, humanism is good for you, nourishing, nurturing, soulwarming and from Phyllis Wheatley to R. Kelly, present-day r&b is a perpetual fight for human status, a yearning for human rights, a struggle for inclusion within the human species. Allergic to cybersonic if not to sonic technology, mainstream American media—in its drive to banish alienation, and to recover a sense of the whole human being through belief systems that talk to the 'real you'—compulsively deletes any intimation of an AfroDiasporic futurism, of a 'webbed network' of computerhythms, machine mythology and conceptechnics which routes, reroutes and crisscrosses the Black Atlantic. This digital diaspora connecting the UK to the US, the Caribbean to Europe to Africa, is in Paul

Gilroy's definition a 'rhizomorphic, fractal structure', a 'transcultural, international formation.'[1]

The music of Alice Coltrane and Sun Ra, of Underground Resistance and George Russell, of Tricky and Martina, comes from the Outer Side. It alienates itself from the human; it arrives from the future. Alien Music is a synthetic recombinator, an applied art technology for amplifying the rates of becoming alien. Optimize the ratios of excentricity. Synthesize yourself.

From the outset, this Postsoul Era has been characterized by an extreme indifference towards the human. The human is a pointless and treacherous category.

And in synch with this posthuman perspective comes Black Atlantic Futurism. Whether it's the AfroFuturist *concrète* of George Russell and Roland Kirk, the Jazz Fission of Teo Macero and Miles Davis, the World 4 Electronics of Sun Ra and Herbie Hancock, the Astro Jazz of Alice Coltrane and Pharoah Sanders, the cosmophonic HipHop of Dr Octagon and Ultramagnetic MCs, the post-HipHop of The Jungle Brothers and Tricky, the Spectral Dub of Scientist and Lee Perry, the off-world Electro of Haashim and Ryuichi Sakamoto, the despotic Acid of Bam Bam and Phuture, the sinister phonoseduction of Parliament's Star Child, the hyper-rhythmic psychedelia of Rob Playford and Goldie, 4 Hero and A Guy Called Gerald, Sonic Futurism always adopts a cruel, despotic, amoral attitude towards the human species [. . . .]

*More Brilliant than the Sun's* achievement, therefore, is to design, manufacture, fabricate, synthesize, cut, paste and edit a so-called artificial discontinuum for the Futurhythmachine.

Rejecting today's ubiquitous emphasis on black sound's necessary ethical allegiance to the street, this project opens up the new plane of Sonic Fiction, the secret life of forms, the discontinuum of AfroDiasporic Futurism, the chain reaction of PhonoFiction. It moves through the explosive forces which technology ignites in us, the temporal architecture of inner space, audiosocial space, living space, where postwar alienation breaks down into the 21st C alien.

From Sun Ra to 4 Hero, today's alien discontinuum therefore operates not through continuities, retentions, genealogies or inheritances but rather through intervals, gaps, breaks. It turns away from roots; it opposes common sense with the force of the fictional and the power of falsity.

One side effect of the alien discontinuum is the rejection of any and all notions of a compulsory black condition. Where journalism still insists on a solid state known as 'blackness', *More Brilliant* dissolves this solidarity with a corpse into a *fluid*arity maintained and exacerbated by soundmachines.

Today's cyborgs are too busy manufacturing themselves across timespace to disintensify themselves with all the Turing Tests for transatlantic, transeuropean and transafrican consciousness: affirmation, keeping it real, representing, staying true to the game, respect due, staying black. Alien Music today deliberately fails all these Tests, these putrid corpses of petrified moralism: it treats them with utter indifference; it replaces them with nothing whatsoever.

It deserts forever the nauseating and bizarre ethic of 'redemption'.

AfroDiasporic Futurism has assembled itself along inhuman routes, and it takes artificial thought to reveal this. Such relief: jaws unclench, as conviction collapses.

Where crits of CyberCult still gather, 99.9% of them will lament the disembodiment of the human by technology. But machines *don't* distance you from your emotions, in fact quite the opposite. Sound machines make you feel *more* intensely, along a broader band of emotional spectra than ever before in the 20th Century.

Sonically speaking, the posthuman era is not one of disembodiment but the exact reverse: it's a *hyperembodiment*, via the Technics SL 1200. A non-sound scientist like Richard Dawkins 'talks very happily about cultural viruses,' argues Sadie Plant, 'but doesn't think that he himself is a viral contagion.'[2] Migrating from the lab to the studio, Sonic Science not only talks about cultural viruses, it is itself a viral contagion. It's a sensational infection by the spread of what Ishmael Reed terms antiplagues.[3]

Machine Music doesn't call itself science because it controls technology, but because music is the artform most thoroughly undermined and recombinated and reconfigured by technics. Scientists set processes in motion which swallow them up: the scientist's brain is caught up in the net. Acid's alien frequency modulation turns on its DJ-producers Phuture and Sleezy D and begins to 'stab your brain' and 'disrupt thought patterns' [. . . .]

Alien Music is all in the breaks: the distance between Tricky and what you took to be the limits of Black Music, the gap between Underground Resistance and what you took Black Music to be, between listening to Miles & Macero's "He Loved Him Madly" and crossing all thresholds with and through it, leaving every old belief system: rock, jazz, soul, Electro, HipHop, House, Acid, drum'n'bass, electronics, Techno and dub—forever.

### NOTES

1. Paul Gilroy, *The Black Atlantic* (London: Verson, 1993), p. 4.
2. Sadie Plant, Matthew Fuller, *Alien Underground Version 0.1* (Spring 1995).
3. Ishmael Reed, *Mumbo Jumbo* (Alison & Busby, 1978), p. 6.

# Part Two
# PRACTICES

When, at the end of the Middle Ages, the Occident attempted to notate musical discourse, it was actually only a sort of shorthand to guide an accomplished performer, who was otherwise a musician of oral and traditional training. These graphic signs were sufficiently imprecise to be read only by an expert performer and sufficiently precise to help him find his place if, by mishap, he had a slip of memory [. . . .] Later on, the appearance of the musical staff on the one hand, and symbols of time duration on the other, made it possible to move to real notation which reflects with exactitude the whole of the musical material presented in this manner. At this point in history it does not seem as if the contemporaries of that time fully realised the consequences of their discovery. For in actual fact, from that moment on, a musical work was no longer strictly musical; it existed outside of itself, so to speak, in the form of an object to which a name was given: the score. The score very soon ceased to be the mere perpetuator of tradition, to become the instrument of elaboration of the musical work itself.

—Jacques Charpentier[1]

[W]hen you get right down to it, a composer is simply someone who tells other people what to do. I find this an unattractive way of getting things done. I'd like our activities to be more social—and anarchically so.

—John Cage[2]

My desire was not to "compose" but to project sounds into time, free from a compositional rhetoric that had no place here.

—Morton Feldman[3]

Music is not painting, but it can learn from this more perceptive temperament that waits and observes the inherent mystery of its materials, as opposed to the composer's vested interest in his craft [. . . .] The painter achieves mystery by allowing what he is doing to be itself. In a way, he must step aside in order to be in control. The composer is just learning to do this. He is just beginning to learn that controls can be thought of as nothing more than accepted practice.

—Morton Feldman[4]

I find [John Cage's notion of "chance composition"] so highly unproductive, because "chance" is not an aesthetic category [. . . .] Composing by chance is not composing at all. Composing [. . .] means to put things together.

—Pierre Boulez[5]

John Cage and Earle Brown have carried the cut-up method much further in music than I have in writing.

—William S. Burroughs[6]

A composition must make possible the freedom and dignity of the performer. It should allow both concentration and release.
No sound or noise is preferable to any other sound or noise.
Listeners should be as free as the players.

—Christian Wolff[7]

I am personally astounded that even today one does not play Kandinsky or Miro, even though it would be so simple and easy to do so.

—Roman Haubenstock-Ramati[8]

Both aleatory and indeterminism are words which have been coined [. . .] to bypass the word improvisation and as such the influence of non-white sensibility.

—Anthony Braxton[9]

As a result of the impasse in serial music, as well as other causes, I originated in 1954 a music constructed from the principle of indeterminism; two years later I named it "Stochastic Music" [. . . .N]atural events such as the collision of hail or rain with hard surfaces, or the song of cicadas in a summer field [. . . .] are made out of thousands of isolated sounds; this multitude of sounds, seen as a totality, is a new sonic event. This mass event is articulated and forms a plastic mold of time which itself follows aleatory and stochastic laws [. . . .] Everyone has observed the sonic phenomena of a political crowd of dozens or hundreds of thousands of people. The human river shouts a slogan in a uniform rhythm. Then another slogan springs from the head of the demonstration; it spreads towards the tail, replacing the first. A wave of transition thus passes from the head to the tail. The clamor fills the city, and the inhibiting force of voice and rhythm reaches a climax. It is an event of great power and beauty in its ferocity. Then the impact between the demonstrators and the enemy occurs. The perfect rhythm of the last slogan breaks up in a huge cluster of chaotic shouts, which also spreads to the tail. Imagine, in addition, the reports of dozens of machine guns and the whistle of bullets adding their punctuations to this total disaster. The crowd is then rapidly dispersed, and after sonic and visual hell follows a detonating calm, full of despair, dust, and death. The statistical laws of these events, separated from their political or moral context, are the same as those of the cicadas or the rain. They are the laws of the passage from complete order to total disorder in a continuous or explosive manner. They are stochastic laws [. . . .] For some time now I have been conducting these fascinating experiments in instrumental works; but the mathematical character of this music has frightened musicians and has made the approach especially difficult.

—Iannis Xenakis[10]

With the early Oval works, we used random processes like sampling prepared CDs. We mostly prepared them without even having heard the material in normal playback mode. It was exactly like John Cage said: We never would have been able to come up with these samples by means of any inspiration or composition. These samples were not imaginable beforehand [. . . .] The sensibility of working with rhythms and digital sound glitches is educated by exposure to random sounds and structures.

—Sebastian Oschatz of Oval[11]

# IV. The Open Work

## Introduction

Earle Brown's composition *December 1952* consists of a single page with a scattering of horizontal and vertical bars of varying size and thickness. Suspended on the white page, the delicate black bars seem to be floating toward or away from the viewer like stars seen from a spacecraft. Accompanying the score is a brief set of notes offering open-ended instructions: "For one or more instruments and/or sound-producing media [. . . .] The composition may be performed in any direction from any point in the defined space for any length of time [. . . .]"[1]

Inspired by jazz improvisation and the paintings of Piet Mondrian and Jackson Pollack, Brown aimed to produce visually compelling scores that would provoke classical performers to improvise, a skill that had diminished in importance since the late 19th century. "I couldn't understand why classical musicians couldn't improvise, and why so many looked down on improvisation," Brown noted. "The whole series [of pieces] *October, November,* and *December* [*1952*] was progressively trying to get them free of having to have every little bit of information before they had confidence enough to play."[2]

Brown's compositions and those of contemporaries such as John Cage, Christian Wolff, Karlheinz Stockhausen, and Henri Pousseur marked a radical shift in contemporary classical music—a shift that Chris Cutler (see chap. 24) sees as marking the boundary between two technological eras: the age of print and the age of recording, the former favoring fixed, bounded works, the latter fluid, open ones. The conventional score presents a "closed work." It uniquely determines pitch, rhythm, meter, instrumentation, and formal shape, offering only a little latitude for performer interpretation (for example, with regard to tempo and dynamics). But in the 1950s and '60s, Brown, Cage, Wolff and others began to produce genuinely "open" works that gave enormous freedom to performers. Given the score and instructions for *December 1952*, for example, two faithful "realizations" (as such performances came to be called) could be radically different musical experiences.

Though such "open" compositions come in a tremendous variety of forms, John Cage helpfully sorted them into two general categories. His own *Music of Changes* (1951) exemplifies one of these. Composed by tossing coins to determine pitch, duration, and attack, it is "indeterminate with respect to composition"; but, since, once chosen by the composer, these elements are fixed, the piece is "determinate with respect to its performance." Scores such as Brown's represent another category: compositions that are "determinate with respect to their composition" but "indeterminate with respect to their performance."

"Graphic scores" such as *December 1952* offer performers a radical degree of freedom. Composers such as Pierre Boulez and Karlheinz Stockhausen came to advocate a more modest form of performance indeterminacy they termed "aleatory" composition. The opening section of Boulez's *Third Piano Sonata* consists of standard musical notation distributed over 10 sheets of paper, which the performer can arrange in any sequence he or she likes. Stockhausen's *Klavierstück XI* consists of 19 discrete passages of notation scattered over a single large sheet of paper. The performer is instructed to begin wherever his or her eye falls on the page and then proceed to any other passage as he or she wishes. The performance ends when any one passage has been played three times.

Within classical music, "open" composition had a relatively short life span, virtually disappearing during the mid-1970s. But, subsequently, these strategies came to be adopted by musicians and performers in other musical domains, particularly in jazz, improvised music, and electronic music. Composer-improvisors such as Anthony Braxton, John Zorn, Lawrence "Butch" Morris, Fred Frith and others developed a range of open-ended compositional strategies intended to guide improvisation: graphic scores, cue cards, hand signals, and various other rules and guidelines that constrain but do not uniquely determine the outcome of a performance. Braxton has also embraced another radical procedure introduced by Cage in which two independent compositions can be played simultaneously. Electronic music has become increasingly fascinated with the creative indeterminacies of electronic systems and equipment (see chaps. 36 and 57). The San Francisco quartet DISC, for example, performs live sets using randomly chosen commercial CDs that they deliberately damage and then use as improvisatory material.

Of course, "open" strategies are not unique to music. There have been parallel developments in literature, film, architecture, and the fine arts. Indeed, philosophers Umberto Eco and Gilles Deleuze have suggested that open art forms express something characteristic of contemporary culture in general. If the classic "closed work" expressed the closed system of Newtonian physics and a God-centered universe, "open works" express the indeterminate world of quantum physics and a post-theological universe, an authorless world without a unique origin, essence, or end.[3] Whatever one thinks of this historical/philosophical thesis, it is clear that "open" composition productively challenges traditional conceptions of the composer and the work, and the roles of the performer and the audience as well.

## NOTES

1. Earle Brown, *Folio* (1952–53) and *Four Systems* (1954) (New York: Associated Music Publishers, 1961).
2. Liner notes to *Earle Brown: Works for Piano 1951–1995*, David Arden (New Albion NA082).
3. See Eco's "The Poetics of the Open Work" (chap. 26, below) and Gilles Deleuze, *Difference and Repetition*, trans. Paul Patton (New York: Columbia University Press, 1994), 66–69.

# 26

# The Poetics of the Open Work

## UMBERTO ECO

Umberto Eco (1932– ) is one of Europe's leading intellectuals. Trained in medieval philosophy and aesthetics, Eco went on to become an influential cultural critic and theorist, publishing books on literary interpretation, linguistics, semiotic theory, and pop culture. In the mid-1950s, while working as cultural director at RAI, Italy's state radio-television network, Eco encountered the composer Luciano Berio, who had recently established an electronic music studio upstairs from Eco's office. Berio's indeterminate compositions prompted Eco to think about the history and theory of what Eco would term "the open work": works of art that call upon performers, readers, viewers, or listeners to complete or to realize them. According to Eco, works of art reflect the intellectual worldviews of their time; and "indeterminate" composition represents in music the post-theological, open-ended universe of Einstein, Heisenberg, and Bohr. The following essay was written in 1959, in the early days of indeterminate composition. The much more radically open compositions of John Cage, Christian Wolff, Roman Haubenstock-Ramati, Cornelius Cardew, Earle Brown, and others would push Eco's argument even further.

A number of recent pieces of instrumental music are linked by a common feature: the considerable autonomy left to the individual performer in the way he chooses to play the work. Thus he is not merely free to interpret the composer's instructions following his own discretion (which in fact happens in traditional music), but he must impose his judgment on the form of the piece, as when he decides how long to hold a note or in what order to group the sounds: all this amounts to an act of improvised creation. Here are some of the best known examples of the process.

(1) In *Klavierstück XI*, by Karlheinz Stockhausen, the composer presents the performer a single large sheet of music paper with a series of note groupings. The performer then has to choose among these groupings, first for the one to start the piece and, next, for the successive units in the order in which he elects to weld them together. In this type of performance, the instrumentalist's freedom is a func-

tion of the "combinative" structure of the piece, which allows him to "mount" the sequence of musical units in the order he chooses.

(2) In Luciano Berio's *Sequenza for solo flute*, the composer presents the performer a text which predetermines the sequence and intensity of the sounds to be played. But the performer is free to choose how long to hold a note inside the fixed framework imposed on him, which in turn is established by the fixed pattern of the metronome's beat.

(3) Henri Pousseur has offered the following description of his piece *Scambi*:

Scambi is not so much a musical composition as a *field of possibilities*, an explicit invitation to exercise choice. It is made up of sixteen sections. Each of these can be linked to any two others, without weakening the logical continuity of the musical process. Two of its sections, for example, are introduced by similar motifs (after which they evolve in divergent patterns); another pair of sections, on the contrary, tends to develop towards the same climax. Since the performer can start or finish with any one section, a considerable number of sequential permutations are made available to him. Furthermore, the two sections which begin on the same motif can be played simultaneously, so as to present a more complex structural polyphony. It is not out of the question that we conceive these formal notations as a marketable product: if they were tape-recorded and the purchaser had a sufficiently sophisticated reception apparatus, then the general public would be in a position to develop a private musical construct of its own and a new collective sensibility in matters of musical presentation and duration could emerge.

(4) In Pierre Boulez's *Third Sonata for piano*, the first section (*Formant 1: Antiphonie*) is made up of ten different pieces on ten corresponding sheets of music paper. These can be arranged in different sequences like a stack of filing cards, though not all possible permutations are permissible. The second part (*Formant 2: Trope*) is made up of four parts with an internal circularity, so that the performer can commence with any one of them, linking it successively to the others until he comes round full circle. No major interpretative variants are permitted inside the various sections, but one of them, *Parenthèse*, opens with a prescribed time beat, which is followed by extensive pauses in which the beat is left to the player's discretion. A further prescriptive note is evinced by the composer's instructions on the manner of linking one piece to the next (for example, *sans retenir, enchaîner sans interruption*, and so on).

What is immediately striking in such cases is the macroscopic divergence between these forms of musical communication and the time-honored tradition of the classics. This difference can be formulated in elementary terms as follows: a classical composition, whether it be a Bach fugue, Verdi's *Aïda*, or Stravinsky's *Rite of Spring*, posits an assemblage of sound units which the composer arranged in a closed, well-defined manner before presenting it to the listener. He converted his idea into conventional symbols which more or less oblige the eventual performer to reproduce the format devised by the composer himself. Whereas the new musical works referred to above reject the definitive, concluded message and multiply the formal possibilities of the distribution of their elements. They appeal to the initiative of the individual performer, and hence they offer themselves, not as finite works which prescribe specific repetition along given structural coordinates, but as "open" works, which are brought to their conclusion by the performer at the same time as he experiences them on an aesthetic plane.[1]

To avoid any confusion in terminology, it is important to specify that here the definition of the "open work," despite its relevance in formulating a fresh dialectics between the work of art and its performer, still requires to be separated from other conventional applications of this term. Aesthetic theorists, for example, often have recourse to the notions of "completeness" and "openness" in connection with a given work of art. These two expressions refer to a standard situation of which we are all aware in our reception of a work of art: we see it as the end product of an author's effort to arrange a sequence of communicative effects in such a way that each individual addressee can refashion the original composition devised by the author. The addressee is bound to enter into an interplay of stimulus and response which depends on his unique capacity for sensitive reception of the piece. In this sense the author presents a finished product with the intention that this particular composition should be appreciated and received in the same form as he devised it. As he reacts to the play of stimuli and his own response to their patterning, the individual addressee is bound to supply his own existential credentials, the sense conditioning which is peculiarly his own, a defined culture, a set of tastes, personal inclinations, and prejudices. Thus his comprehension of the original artifact is always modified by his particular and individual perspective. In fact, the form of the work of art gains its aesthetic validity precisely in proportion to the number of different perspectives from which it can be viewed and understood. These give it a wealth of different resonances and echoes without impairing its original essence; a road traffic sign, on the other hand, can only be viewed in one sense, and, if it is transfigured into some fantastic meaning by an imaginative driver, it merely ceases to be *that* particular traffic sign with that particular meaning. A work of art, therefore, is a complete and *closed* form in its uniqueness as a balanced organic whole, while at the same time constituting an *open* product on account of its susceptibility to countless different interpretations which do not impinge on its unadulterable specificity. Hence every reception of a work of art is both an *interpretation* and a *performance* of it, because in every reception the work takes on a fresh perspective for itself.

Nonetheless, it is obvious that works like those of Berio and Stockhausen are "open" in a far more tangible sense. In primitive terms we can say that they are quite literally "unfinished": the author seems to hand them on to the performer more or less like the components of a construction kit. He seems to be unconcerned about the manner of their eventual deployment. This is a loose and paradoxical interpretation of the phenomenon, but the most immediately striking aspect of these musical forms can lead to this kind of uncertainty, although the very fact of our uncertainty is itself a positive feature: it invites us to consider *why* the contemporary artist feels the need to work in this kind of direction, to try to work out what historical evolution of aesthetic sensibility led up to it and which factors in modern culture reinforced it. We are then in a position to surmise how these experiences should be viewed in the spectrum of a theoretical aesthetics [. . . .]

In every century the way that artistic forms are structured reflects the way in which science or contemporary culture views reality. The closed, single conception in a work by a medieval artist reflected the conception of the cosmos as a hierarchy of fixed, preordained orders. The work as a pedagogical vehicle, as a monocentric and necessary apparatus (incorporating a rigid internal pattern of meter and rhymes) simply reflects the syllogistic system, a logic of necessity, a deductive consciousness by way of which reality could be made manifest step by step without unforeseen interruptions, moving forward in a single direction, proceeding from first principles of science which were seen as one and the same with the first principles of reality. The openness and dynamism of the Baroque mark, in fact, the advent of a new scientific awareness: the substitution of the *tactile* by the *visual* (meaning that the subjective element comes to prevail) and attention is shifted from the *essence* to the *appearance* of architectural and pictorial products. It reflects the rising interest in a psychology of impression and sensation—in short, an empiricism which converts the Aristotelian concept of real substance into a series of subjective perceptions by the viewer. On the other hand, by giving up the essential focusing center of the composition and the prescribed point of view for its viewer, aesthetic innovations were in fact mirroring the Copernican vision of the universe. This definitively eliminated the notion of geocentricity and its allied metaphysical constructs. In the modern scientific universe, as in architecture and in Baroque pictorial production, the various component parts are all endowed with equal value and dignity, and the whole construct expands towards a totality which is near to the infinite. It refuses to be hemmed in by any ideal normative conception of the world. It shares in a general urge toward discovery and constantly renewed contact with reality.

In its own way the "openness" that we meet in the decadent strain of Symbolism reflects a cultural striving to unfold new vistas. For example, one of [Stéphane] Mallarmé's projects for a pluridimensional deconstructible book envisaged the breaking down of the initial unit into sections which could be reformulated and which could express new perspectives by being deconstructed into correspondingly smaller units which were also mobile and reducible. This project obviously suggests the universe as it is conceived by modern, non-Euclidean geometries.

Hence it is not overambitious to detect in the poetics of the "open" work—and even less so in the "work in movement"[2]—more or less specific overtones of trends in contemporary scientific thought. For example, it is a critical commonplace to refer to the spatiotemporal continuum in order to account for the structure of the universe in [James] Joyce's works. Pousseur has offered a tentative definition of his musical work which involves the term "field of possibilities." In fact, this shows that he is prepared to borrow two extremely revealing technical terms from contemporary culture. The notion of "field" is provided by physics and implies a revised vision of the classic relationship posited between cause and effect as a rigid, one-directional system: now a complex interplay of motive forces is envisaged, a configuration of possible events, a complete dynamism of structure. The notion of "possibility" is a philosophical canon which reflects a widespread tendency in contemporary science: the discarding of a static, syllogistic view of order, a corresponding devolution of intellectual authority to personal decision, choice, and social context.

If a musical pattern no longer necessarily determines the immediately following one, if there is no tonal basis which allows the listener to infer the next steps in the arrangement of the musical discourse from what has physically preceded them, this is just part of a general breakdown in the concept of causation. The two-value truth logic which follows the classical *aut-aut* [either/or], the disjunctive dilemma between *true* and *false*, a fact and its contradictory, is no longer the only instrument of philosophical experiment. Multivalue logics are now gaining currency, and these are quite capable of incorporating *indeterminacy* as a valid stepping-stone in the cognitive process. In this general intellectual atmosphere, the poetics of the open work is peculiarly relevant: it posits the work of art stripped of necessary and foreseeable conclusions, works in which the performer's freedom functions as part of the *discontinuity* which contemporary physics recognizes, not as an element of disorientation, but as an essential stage in all scientific verification procedures and also as the verifiable pattern of events in the subatomic world.

From Mallarmé's *Livre* to the musical compositions which we have considered, there is a tendency to see every execution of the work of art as divorced from its ultimate definition. Every performance *explains* the composition, but does not *exhaust* it. Every performance makes the work an actuality, but is itself only complementary to all possible other performances of the work. In short, we can say that every performance offers us a complete and satisfying version of the work, but at the same time makes it incomplete for us, because it cannot simultaneously give all the other artistic solutions which the work may admit.

Perhaps it is no accident that these poetic systems emerge at the same period as the physicists' principle of *complementarity*, which rules that it is not possible to indicate the different behavior patterns of an elementary particle simultaneously. To describe these different behavior patterns, different *models*, which Heisenberg has defined as adequate when properly utilized, are put to use, but, since they contradict one another, they are therefore also complementary.[3] Perhaps we are in a position to state that for these works of art an incomplete knowledge of the system is in fact an essential feature in its formulation. Hence one could argue, with Bohr, that the data collected in the course of experimental situations cannot be gathered in one image, but should be considered as complementary, since only the sum of all the phenomena could exhaust the possibilities of information[4] [. . . .]

It would be quite natural for us to think that this flight away from the old, solid concept of necessity and the tendency toward the ambiguous and the indeterminate reflect a crisis of contemporary civilization. Or, on the other hand, we might see these poetical systems, in harmony with modern science, as expressing the positive possibility of thought and action made available to an individual who is open to the continuous renewal of his life patterns and cognitive processes. Such an individual is productively committed to the development of his own mental faculties and experiential horizons. This contrast is too facile and Manichean. Our main intent has been to pick out a number of analogies which reveal a reciprocal play of problems in the most disparate areas of contemporary culture and which point to the common elements in a new way of looking at the world.

What is at stake is a convergence of new canons and requirements which the forms of art reflect by way of what we could term *structural homologies*. This need not commit us to assembling a rigorous parallelism—it is simply a case of phenomena like the "work in movement" simultaneously reflecting mutually contrasted epistemological situations, as yet contradictory and not satisfactorily reconciled. Thus the concepts of "openness" and dynamism may recall the terminology of quantum physics: indeterminacy and discontinuity. But at the same time they also exemplify a number of situations in Einsteinian physics.

The multiple polarity of a serial composition in music, where the listener is not faced by an absolute conditioning center of reference, requires him to constitute his own system of auditory relationships.[5] He must allow such a center to emerge from the sound continuum. Here are no privileged points of view, and all available perspectives are equally valid and rich in potential. Now, this multiple polarity is extremely close to the spatiotemporal conception of the universe which we owe to Einstein. The thing which distinguishes the Einsteinian concept of the universe from quantum epistemology is precisely this faith in the totality of the universe, a universe in which discontinuity and indeterminacy can admittedly upset us with their surprise apparitions, but in fact, to use Einstein's words, do not presuppose a God playing random games with dice but the Divinity of Spinoza, who rules the world according to perfectly regulated laws. In this kind of universe, relativity means the infinite variability of experience as well as the infinite multiplication of possible ways of measuring things and viewing their position. But the objective side of the whole system can be found in the invariance of the simple formal descriptions (of the differential equations) which establish once and for all the relativity of empirical measurement.

This is not the place to pass judgment on the scientific validity of the metaphysical construct implied by Einstein's system. But there is a striking analogy between his universe and the universe of the work in movement. The God in Spinoza, who is made into an untestable hypothesis by Einsteinian metaphysics, becomes a cogent reality for the work of art and matches the organizing impulse of its creator.

The *possibilities* which the work's openness make available always work within a given *field of relations.* As in the Einsteinian universe, in the "work in movement" we may well deny that there is a single prescribed point of view. But this does not mean complete chaos in its internal relations. What it does imply is an organizing rule which governs these relations. Therefore, to sum up, we can say that the *work in movement* is the possibility of numerous different personal interventions, but it is not an amorphous invitation to indiscriminate participation. The invitation offers the performer the chance of an oriented insertion into something which always remains the world intended by the author.

In other words, the author offers the interpreter, the performer, the addressee a work *to be completed.* He does not know the exact fashion in which his work will be concluded, but he is aware that once completed the work in question will still be his own. It will not be a different work, and, at the end of the interpretative dialogue, a form which is *his* form, will have been organized, even though it may have been assembled by an outside party in a particular way that he could not have foreseen. The author is the one who proposed a number of possibilities which had already been rationally organized, oriented, and endowed with specifications for proper development.

Berio's *Sequenza*, which is played by different flutists, Stockhausen's *Klavierstück XI*, or Pousseur's *Mobiles*, which are played by different pianists (or performed twice over by the same pianists), will never be quite the same on different occasions. Yet they will never be gratuitously different. They are to be seen as the actualization of a series of consequences whose premises are firmly rooted in the original data provided by the author.

This happens in the musical works which we have already examined, and it happens also in the plastic artifacts we considered. The common factor is a mutability which is always deployed within the specific limits of a given taste, or of predetermined formal tendencies, and is authorized by the concrete pliability of the material offered for the performer's manipulation. [Bertolt] Brecht's plays appear to elicit free and arbitrary response on the part of the audience. Yet they are also rhetorically constructed in such a way as to elicit a reaction oriented toward, and ultimately anticipating, a Marxist dialectic logic as the basis for the whole field of possible responses.

All these examples of "open" works and "works in movement" have this latent characteristic which guarantees that they will always be seen as "works" and not just as a conglomeration of random components ready to emerge from the chaos in which they previously stood and permitted to assume any form whatsoever.

Now, a dictionary clearly presents us with thousands upon thousands of words which we could freely use to compose poetry, essays on physics, anonymous letters, or grocery lists. In this sense the dictionary is clearly open to the reconstitution of its raw material in any way that the manipulator wishes. But this does not make it a "work." The "openness" and dynamism of an artistic work consist in factors which make it susceptible to a whole range of integrations. They provide it with organic complements which they graft into the structural vitality which the work already possesses, even if it is incomplete. This structural vitality is still seen as a positive property of the work, even though it admits of all kinds of different conclusions and solutions for it.

The preceding observations are necessary because, when we speak of a work of art, our Western aesthetic tradition forces us to take "work" in the sense of a personal production which may well vary in the ways it can be received but which always maintains a coherent identity of its own and which displays the personal imprint that makes it a specific, vital, and significant act of communication. Aesthetic theory is quite content to conceive of a variety of different poetics, but ultimately it aspires to general definitions, not necessarily dogmatic or *sub specie aeternitatis*, which are capable of applying the category of the "work of art" broadly speaking to a whole variety of experiences, which can range from the *Divine Comedy* to, say, electronic composition based on the different permutations of sonic components.

We have, therefore, seen that (i) "open" works, insofar as they are *in movement*, are characterized by the invitation to *make the work* together with the author and that (ii) on a wider level (as a sub*genus* in the *species* "work in movement") there exist works which, though organically completed, are "open" to a continuous generation of internal relations which the addressee must uncover and select in his act of perceiving the totality of incoming stimuli. (iii) *Every* work of art, even though it is produced by following an explicit or implicit poetics of necessity, is effectively open to a virtually unlimited range of possible readings, each of which causes the work to acquire new vitality in terms of one particular taste, or perspective, or personal *performance* [. . . .]

umberto eco • **173**

This doctrine can be applied to all artistic phenomena and to art works throughout the ages. But it is useful to have underlined that now is the period when aesthetics has paid especial attention to the whole notion of "openness" and sought to expand it. In a sense these requirements, which aesthetics have referred widely to every type of artistic production, are the same as those posed by the poetics of the "open work" in a more decisive and explicit fashion. Yet this does not mean that the existence of "open" works and of "works in movement" adds absolutely nothing to our experience [. . . .] While aesthetics brings to light one of the fundamental demands of contemporary culture, it also reveals the latent possibilities of a certain type of experience in every artistic product, independently of the operative criteria which presided over its moment of inception.

The poetic theory or practice of the "work in movement" senses this possibility as a specific vocation. It allies itself openly and self-consciously to current trends in scientific method and puts into action and tangible form the very trend which aesthetics has already acknowledged as the general background to performance. These poetic systems recognize "openness" as *the* fundamental possibility of the contemporary artist or consumer. The aesthetic theoretician, in his turn, will see a confirmation of his own intuitions in these practical manifestations: they constitute the ultimate realization of a receptive mode which can function at many different levels of intensity.

Certainly this new receptive mode vis-à-vis the work of art opens up a much vaster phase in culture and in this sense is not intellectually confined to the problems of aesthetics. The poetics of the "work in movement" (and partly that of the "open" work) sets in motion a new cycle of relations between the artist and his audience, a new mechanics of aesthetic perception, a different status for the artistic product in contemporary society. It opens a new page in sociology and in pedagogy, as well as a new chapter in the history of art. It poses new practical problems by organizing new communicative situations. In short, it installs a new relationship between the *contemplation* and the *utilization* of a work of art.

Seen in these terms and against the background of historical influences and cultural interplay which links it by analogy to widely diversified aspects of the contemporary world view, the situation of art has now become a situation in the process of development. Far from being fully accounted for and catalogued, it deploys and poses problems in several dimensions. In short, it is an "open" situation, *in movement*. A work in progress.

## NOTES

1. Here we must eliminate a possible misunderstanding straightaway: the practical intervention of a "performer" (the instrumentalist who plays a piece of music or the actor who recites a passage) is different from that of an interpreter in the sense of consumer (somebody who looks at a picture, silently reads a poem, or listens to a musical composition performed by somebody else). For the purposes of aesthetic analysis, however, both cases can be seen as different manifestations of the same interpretative attitude. Every "reading," "contemplation," or "enjoyment" of a work of art represents a tacit or private form of "performance."

2. [Works, such as Pousseur's *Scambi*, that are essentially incomplete, that call upon the performer or auditor to collaborate with the composer in realizing them.—Eds.]

3. Werner Heisenberg, *Physics and Philosophy* (London: Allen and Unwin, 1959), chap. 3.

4. Niels Bohr, in his epistemological debate with Einstein (see P. A. Schlipp, ed., *Albert Einstein: Philosopher-Scientist* [Evanston, Ill.: Library of Living Philosophers, 1949]). Epistemological thinkers connected with quantum methodology have rightly warned against an ingenuous transposition of physical categories into the fields of ethics and psychology (for example, the identification of indeterminacy with moral freedom; see P. Frank, *Present Role of Science*, Opening Address to the Seventh International Congress of Philosophy, Venice, September 1958). Hence it would not be justified to understand my formulation as making an analogy between the structures of the work of art and the supposed structures of the world. Indeterminacy, complementarity, noncausality are not *modes of being* in the physical world, but *systems for describing* it in a convenient way. The relationship which concerns my exposition is not the supposed nexus between an "ontological" situation and a morphological feature in the work of art, but the relation between an operative procedure for explaining physical processes and an operative procedure for explaining the processes of artistic production and reception. In other words, the relationship between a *scientific methodology* and a *poetics*.

5. On this "*éclatement multidirectionnel des structures*," see A. Boucourechliev, "Problèmes de la musique moderne," *Nouvelle Revue Française* (December-January, 1960-1).

# 27

# *Composition as Process:*
# *Indeterminacy*

## JOHN CAGE

In the late 1940s, John Cage (1912–1992; see also chaps. 6 and 33) discovered Zen Buddhism, which profoundly influenced his aesthetic worldview. His Zen practice sparked a philosophical commitment to "nonintention," the affirmation of life as it is rather than the desire to improve upon it. In the wake of this realization, Cage developed a range of techniques that would allow him to relinquish control over his compositions and to place himself in the role of listener and discoverer rather than that of creator. In the 1950s, he introduced "indeterminacy" and "graphic notation" into contemporary musical practice, using coin tosses, the *I Ching*, star maps, and other devices to make compositional choices and to spark performers to make choices of their own. Cage's famous "silent" piece *4' 33'* (1952) aimed at allowing audiences to experience non-intentional sound as musical. Non-intention was also fostered by the technique of "simultaneity," which called for several compositions to be performed at once, producing unexpected sonic conjunctions.

In this essay, Cage criticizes indeterminate compositions—such as his own *Music of Changes* (1951), composed by the tossing of coins—that are "indeterminate with respect to their composition" but "determinate with respect to their performance." Such compositions do not allow the same freedom to the performer that they allow to the composer. Hence, Cage favors a more radical indeterminacy: compositions that are "indeterminate with respect to their performance."

This article is the text of a lecture delivered in 1958, a year before the publication of Eco's essay. Like Eco (see chap. 26), Cage begins with the example of Stockhausen's *Klavierstück XI*. But Cage goes on to affirm a conception of the musical work that is more radically "open" than Eco's, a conception of the musical work that would lead the way from "indeterminate" to "experimental" composition: compositions that are not *objects* but *proc-*

*esses*. This lecture was first published in Cage's collection *Silence*, where it appeared in extremely small type and was prefaced by this note: "The excessively small type in the following pages is an attempt to emphasize the intentionally pontifical character of this lecture."

This is a lecture on composition which is indeterminate with respect to its performance. The *Klavierstück XI* by Karlheinz Stockhausen is an example. *The Art of the Fugue* by Johann Sebastian Bach is an example. In *The Art of the Fugue*, structure, which is the division of the whole into parts; method, which is the note-to-note procedure; and form, which is the expressive content, the morphology of the continuity, are all determined. Frequency and duration characteristics of the material are also determined. Timbre and amplitude characteristics of the material, by not being given, are indeterminate. This indeterminacy brings about the possibility of a unique overtone structure and decibel range for each performance of *The Art of the Fugue*. In the case of the *Klavierstück XI*, all the characteristics of the material are determined, and so too is the note-to-note procedure, the method. The division of the whole into parts, the structure, is determinate. The sequence of these parts, however, is indeterminate, bringing about the possibility of a unique form, which is to say a unique morphology of the continuity, a unique expressive content, for each performance.

The function of the performer, in the case of *The Art of the Fugue*, is comparable to that of someone filling in color where outlines are given. He may do this in an organized way which may be subjected successfully to analysis. (Transcriptions by Arnold Schoenberg and Anton Webern give examples pertinent to this century.) Or he may perform his function of colorist in a way which is not consciously organized (and therefore not subject to analysis)—either arbitrarily, feeling his way, following the dictates of his ego; or more or less unknowingly, by going inwards with reference to the structure of his mind to a point in dreams, following, as in automatic writing, the dictates of his subconscious mind; or to a point in the collective unconscious of Jungian psychoanalysis, following the inclinations of the species and doing something of more or less universal interest to human beings; or to the "deep sleep" of Indian mental practice—the Ground of Meister Eckhart— identifying there with no matter what eventuality. Or he may perform his function of colorist arbitrarily, by going outwards with reference to the structure of his mind to the point of sense perception, following his taste; or more or less unknowingly by employing some operation exterior to his mind: tables of random numbers, following the scientific interest in probability; or chance operations, identifying there with no matter what eventuality.

The function of the performer in the case of the *Klavierstück XI* is not that of a colorist but that of giving form, providing, that is to say, the morphology of the continuity, the expressive content. This may not be done in an organized way: for form unvitalized by spontaneity brings about the death of all the other elements of the work. Examples are provided by academic studies which copy models with respect to all their compositional elements: structure, method, material, and form. On the other hand, no matter how rigorously controlled or conventional the structure, method, and materials of a composition are, that composition will come to life if the form is not controlled but free and original. One may cite as examples the sonnets of Shakespeare and the *haikus* of Basho. How then in the case of the *Klavierstück XI* may the performer fulfill his function of giving form to the music? He must perform his function of giving form to the music in a way which is not consciously organized (and therefore not subject to analysis), either arbitrarily, feeling his way, following the dictates of his ego, or more or less unknowingly, by going inwards with reference to the structure of his mind to a point in dreams, following, as in automatic writing, the dictates of his subconscious mind; or to a point in the collective unconscious of Jungian psychoanalysis, following the inclinations of the species and doing something of more or less universal interest to human beings; or to the "deep sleep" of Indian mental practice—the Ground of Meister Eckhart—identifying there with no matter what eventuality. Or he may perform his function of giving form to the music arbitrarily, by going outwards with reference to the structure of his mind to the point of sense perception, following his taste; or more or less unknowingly by employing some operation exterior to his mind: tables of random numbers, following the scientific interest in probability; or chance operations, identifying there with no matter what eventuality.

However, due to the presence in the *Klavierstück XI* of the two most essentially conventional aspects of European music—that is to say, the twelve tones of the octave (the frequency characteristic of the material) and regularity of beat (affecting the element of method in the composing means), the performer—in those instances where his procedure follows any dictates at all (his feelings, his automatism, his sense of universality, his taste)—will be led to give the form aspects essentially conventional to European music. These instances will predominate over those which are unknowing where the performer wishes to act in a way consistent with the composition as written. The form aspects essentially conventional to European music are, for instance, the presentation of a whole as an object in time having a beginning, a middle, and an ending, progressive rather than static in character, which is to say possessed of a climax or climaxes and in contrast a point or points of rest.

The indeterminate aspects of the composition of the *Klavierstück XI* do not remove the work in its performance from the body of European musical conventions. And yet the purpose of indeterminacy would seem to be to bring about an unforeseen situation. In the case of *Klavierstück XI*, the use of indeterminacy is in this sense unnecessary since it is ineffective. The work might as well have been written in all of its aspects determinately. It would lose, in this case, its single unconventional aspect: that of being printed on an unusually large sheet of paper which, together with an attachment that may be snapped on at several points enabling one to stretch it out flat and place it on the music rack of a piano, is put in a cardboard tube suitable for safekeeping or distribution through the mails.

This is a lecture on composition which is indeterminate with respect to its performance. The *Intersection 3* by Morton Feldman is an example. The *Music of Changes*[1] is not an example. In the *Music of Changes*, structure, which is the division of the whole into parts; method, which is the note-to-note procedure; form, which is the expressive content, the morphology of the continuity; and materials, the sounds and silences of the composition, are all determined. Though no two performances of the *Music of Changes* will be identical (each act is virgin, even the repeated one, to refer to René Char's thought), two performances will resemble one another closely. Though chance operations brought about the determinations of the composition, these operations are not available in its performance. The function of the performer in the case of the *Music of Changes* is that of a contractor who, following an architect's blueprint, constructs a building. That the *Music of Changes* was composed by means of chance operations identifies the composer with no matter what eventuality. But that its notation is in all respects determinate does not permit the performer any such identification: his work is specifically laid out before him. He is therefore not able to perform from his own center but must identify himself insofar as possible with the center of the work as written. The *Music of Changes* is an object more inhuman than human, since chance operations brought it into being. The fact that these things that constitute it, though only sounds, have come together to control a human being, the performer, gives the work the alarming aspect of a Frankenstein monster. This situation is of course characteristic of Western music, the masterpieces of which are its most frightening examples, which when concerned with humane communication only move over from Frankenstein monster to Dictator.

In the case of the *Intersection 3* by Morton Feldman, structure may be viewed as determinate or as indeterminate; method is definitely indeterminate. Frequency and duration characteristics of the material are determinate only within broad limits (they are with respect to narrow limits indeterminate); the timbre characteristic of the material, being given by the instrument designated, the piano, is determinate; the amplitude characteristic of the material is indeterminate. Form conceived in terms of a continuity of various weights—that is, a continuity of numbers of sounds, the sounds themselves particularized only with respect to broad range limits (high, middle, and low)—is determinate, particularly so due to the composer's having specified boxes as time units. Though one might equally describe it as indeterminate for other reasons. The term "boxes" arises from the composer's use of graph paper for the notation of his composition. The function of the box is comparable to that of a green light in metropolitan thoroughfare control. The performer is free to play the given number of sounds in the range indicated at any time during the duration of the box, just as when driving an automobile one may cross an intersection at any time during the green light. With the exception of method, which is wholly indeterminate, the compositional means are characterized by being in certain respects determinate, in others indeterminate, and an interpenetration of these opposites obtains which is more characteristic than either. The situation is therefore essentially non-dualistic; a multiplicity of centers in a state of non-obstruction and interpenetration.

The function of the performer in the case of the *Intersection 3* is that of a photographer who on obtaining a camera uses it to take a picture. The composition permits an infinite number of these, and, not being mechanically constructed, it will not wear out. It can only suffer disuse or loss. How is the performer to perform the *Intersection 3*? He may do this in an organized way which may be subjected successfully to analysis. Or he may perform his function of photographer in a way which is not consciously organized (and therefore not subject to analysis) either arbitrarily, feeling his way, following the dictates of his ego; or more or less unknowingly, by going inwards with reference to the structure of his mind to a point in dreams, following, as in automatic writing, the dictates of his subconscious

john cage • 179

mind; or to a point in the collective unconsciousness of Jungian psychoanalysis, following the inclinations of the species and doing something of more or less universal interest to human beings; or to the "deep sleep" of Indian mental practice— the Ground of Meister Eckhart—identifying there with no matter what eventuality. Or he may perform his function of photographer arbitrarily, by going outwards with reference to the structure of his mind to the point of sense perception, following his taste; or more or less unknowingly by employing some operation exterior to his mind: tables of random numbers, following the scientific interest in probability; or chance operations, identifying there with no matter what eventuality.

One evening Morton Feldman said that when he composed he was dead; this recalls to me the statement of my father, an inventor, who says he does his best work when he is sound asleep. The two suggest the "deep sleep" of Indian mental practice. The ego no longer blocks action. A fluency obtains which is characteristic of nature. The seasons make the round of spring, summer, fall, and winter, interpreted in Indian thought as creation, preservation, destruction, and quiescence. Deep sleep is comparable to quiescence. Each spring brings no matter what eventuality. The performer then will act in any way. Whether he does so in an organized way or in any one of the not consciously organized ways cannot be answered until his action is a reality. The nature of the composition and the knowledge of the composer's own view of his action suggest, indeed, that the performer act sometimes consciously, sometimes not consciously and from the Ground of Meister Eckhart, identifying there with no matter what eventuality.

This is a lecture on composition which is indeterminate with respect to its performance. *Indices* by Earle Brown is not an example. Where the performance involves a number of players, as it does in the case of *Indices*, the introduction of a score—that is, a fixed relation of the parts—removes the quality of indeterminacy from the performance. Though tables of random numbers (used in a way which introduces bias), brought about the determinations of the composition (structure, method, materials, and form are in the case of *Indices* all thus determined), those tables are not available in its performance. The function of the conductor is that of a contractor, who, following an architect's blueprint, constructs a building. The function of the instrumentalists is that of workmen who simply do as they are bid. That the *Indices* by Earle Brown was composed by means of tables of random numbers (used in a way which introduces bias) identifies the composer with no matter what eventuality, since by the introduction of bias he has removed himself from an association with the scientific interest in probability. But that the notation of the parts is in all respects determinate, and that, moreover, a score provides a fixed relation of these parts, does not permit the conductor or the players any such identification. Their work is laid out before them. The conductor is not able to conduct from his own center but must identify himself insofar as possible with the center of the work as written. The instrumentalists are not able to perform from their several centers but are employed to identify themselves insofar as possible with the directives given by the conductor. They identify with the work itself, if at all, by one remove. From that point of view from which each thing and each being is seen as moving out from its own center, this situation of the subservience of several to the directives of one who is himself controlled, not by another but by the work of another, is intolerable.

(In this connection it may be remarked that certain Indian traditional practices prohibit ensemble, limiting performance to the solo circumstance. This solo, in traditional Indian practice, is not a performance of something written by another but an improvisation by the performer himself within certain limitations of structure, method, and material. Though he himself by the morphology of the continuity brings the form into being, the expressive content does not reside in this compositional element alone, but by the conventions of Indian tradition resides also in all the other compositional elements.)

The intolerable situation described is, of course, not a peculiarity of *Indices*, but a characteristic of Western music, the masterpieces of which are its most imposing examples, which, when they are concerned not with tables of random numbers (used in a way which introduces bias) but rather with ideas of order, personal feelings, and the integration of these, simply suggest the presence of a man rather than the presence of sounds. The sounds of *Indices* are just sounds. Had bias not been introduced in the use of the tables of random numbers, the sounds would have been not just sounds but elements acting according to scientific theories of probability, elements acting in relationship due to the equal distribution of each one of those present—elements, that is to say, under the control of man.

This is a lecture on composition which is indeterminate with respect to its performance. The *4 Systems* by Earle Brown is an example. This piece may be performed by one or several players. There is no score, either for the solo circumstance or for that of ensemble. The quality of indeterminacy is for this reason not removed from the performance even where a number of players are involved, since no fixed relation of the parts exists. The original notation is a drawing of rectangles of various lengths and widths in ink on a single cardboard having four equal divisions (which are the systems). The vertical position of the rectangles refers to relative time. The width of the rectangles may be interpreted either as an interval where the drawing is read as two-dimensional, or as amplitude where the drawing is read as giving the illusion of a third dimension. Any of the interpretations of this material may be superimposed in any number and order and, with the addition or not of silences between them, may be used to produce a continuity of any time-length. In order to multiply the possible interpretations the composer gives a further permission—to read the cardboard in any of four positions: right side up, upside down, sideways, up and down.

This further permission alters the situation radically. Without it, the composition was highly indeterminate of its performance. The drawing was not consciously organized. Drawn unknowingly, from the Ground of Meister Eckhart, it identified the composer with no matter what eventuality. But with the further permission— that of reading the cardboard right side up, upside down, sideways, up and down— the drawing became that of two different situations or groups of situations and their inversions. Inversions are a hallmark of the conscious mind. The composer's identification (though not consciously so according to him) is therefore no longer with no matter what eventuality but rather with those events that are related by inversion. What might have been non-dualistic becomes dualistic. From a non-dualistic point of view, each thing and each being is seen at the center, and these centers are in a state of interpenetration and non-obstruction. From a dualistic point of view, on the other hand, each thing and each being is not seen: relationships are seen and interferences are seen. To avoid undesired interferences and to make one's intentions clear, a dualistic point of view requires a careful integration of the opposites.

If this careful integration is lacking in the composition, and in the case of *4 Systems* it is (due to the high degree of indeterminacy), it must be supplied in the performance. The function of the performer or of each performer in the case of *4 Systems* is that of making something out of a store of raw materials. Structure, the division of the whole into parts, is indeterminate. Form, the morphology of the continuity, is also indeterminate. In given interpretations of the original drawing (such as those made by David Tudor sufficient in number to provide a performance by four pianists lasting four minutes) method is determinate and so too are the amplitude, timbre, and frequency characteristics of the material. The duration characteristic of the material is both determinate and indeterminate, since lines extending from note-heads indicate exact length of time, but the total length of time of a system is indeterminate. The performer's function, in the case of *4 Systems* is dual: to give both structure and form; to provide, that is, the division of the whole into parts and the morphology of the continuity.

Conscious only of his having made a composition indeterminate of its performance, the composer does not himself acknowledge the necessity of this dual function of the performer which I am describing. He does not agree with the view here expressed that the permission given to interpret the drawing right side up, upside down, and sideways, up and down obliges the integration of the opposites: conscious organization and its absence. The structural responsibility must be fulfilled in an organized way, such as might be subjected successfully to analysis. (The performers in each performance have, as a matter of record, given to each system lengths of time which are related as modules are in architecture: fifteen seconds and multiples thereof by two or four.) The formal responsibility must be fulfilled in one or several of the many ways which are not consciously organized. However, due to the identification with the conscious mind indicated in *4 Systems* by the presence of inversions, though not acknowledged by the composer, those ways which are not consciously organized that are adjacent to the ego are apt to be used, particularly where the performer wishes to act in a way consistent with the composition as here viewed. He will in these cases perform arbitrarily, feeling his way, following the dictates of his ego; or he will perform arbitrarily, following his taste, in terms of sense perception.

What might have given rise, by reason of the high degree of indeterminacy, to no matter what eventuality (to a process essentially purposeless) becomes productive of a time-object. This object, exceedingly complex due to the absence of a score, a fixed relation of the parts, is analogous to a futurist or cubist painting, perhaps, or to a moving picture where flicker makes seeing the object difficult.

From the account which appears to be a history of a shift from non-dualism to dualism (not by intention, since the composer does not attach to the inversions the importance here given them, but as a by-product of the action taken to multiply possibilities) the following deduction may be made: To ensure indeterminacy with respect to its performance, a composition must be determinate of itself. If this indeterminacy is to have a non-dualistic nature, each element of the notation must have a single interpretation rather than a plurality of interpretations which, coming from a single source, fall into relation. Likewise—though this is not relevant to *4*

*Systems*—one may deduce that a single operation within the act of composition itself must not give rise to more than a single notation. Where a single operation is applied to more than one notation, for example to those of both frequency and amplitude characteristics, the frequency and amplitude characteristics are by that operation common to both brought into relationship. These relationships make an object; and this object, in contrast to a process which is purposeless, must be viewed dualistically. Indeterminacy when present in the making of an object, and when therefore viewed dualistically, is a sign not of identification with no matter what eventuality but simply of carelessness with regard to the outcome.

This is a lecture on composition which is indeterminate with respect to its performance. *Duo II for Pianists* by Christian Wolff is an example. In the case of *Duo II for Pianists*, structure, the division of the whole into parts, is indeterminate. (No provision is given by the composer for ending the performance.) Method, the note-to-note procedure, is also indeterminate. All the characteristics of the materials (frequency, amplitude, timbre, duration) are indeterminate within gamut limitations provided by the composer. The form, the morphology of the continuity, is unpredictable. One of the pianists begins the performance: the other, noticing a particular sound or silence which is one of a gamut of cues, responds with an action of his own determination from among given possibilities within a given time bracket. Following this beginning, each pianist responds to cues provided by the other, letting no silence fall between responses, though these responses themselves include silences. Certain time brackets are in zero time. There is no score, no fixed relation of the parts. *Duo II for Pianists* is evidently not a time-object, but rather a process the beginning and ending of which are irrelevant to its nature. The ending, and the beginning, will be determined in performance, not by exigencies interior to the action but by circumstances of the concert occasion. If the other pieces on the program take forty-five minutes of time and fifteen minutes more are required to bring the program to a proper length, *Duo II for Pianists* may be fifteen minutes long. Where only five minutes are available, it will be five minutes long.

The function of each performer in the case of *Duo II for Pianists* is comparable to that of a traveler who must constantly be catching trains the departures of which have not been announced but which are in the process of being announced. He must be continually ready to go, alert to the situation, and responsible. If he notices no cue that fact itself is a cue calling for responses indeterminate within gamut limitations and time brackets. Thus he notices (or notices that he does not notice) a cue, adds time bracket to time bracket, determines his response to come (meanwhile also giving a response), and, as the second hand of a chronometer approaches the end of one bracket and the beginning of the next, he prepares himself for the action to come (meanwhile still making an action), and, precisely as the second hand of a chronometer begins the next time bracket, he makes the suitable action (meanwhile noticing or noticing that he does not notice the next cue), and so on. How is each performer to fulfill this function of being alert in an indeterminate situation? Does he need to proceed cautiously in dualistic terms? On the contrary, he needs his mind in one piece. His mind is too busy to spend time splitting itself into conscious and not-conscious parts. These parts, however, are still present. What has happened is simply a complete change of direction. Rather than making the not-conscious parts face the conscious part of the mind, the conscious part, by reason of the urgency and indeterminacy of the situation, turns towards the not-conscious parts. He is therefore able, as before, to add two to two to get four, or to act in organized ways which on being subjected to analysis successfully are found to be more complex. But rather than concentrating his attention here, in the realm of relationships, variations, approximations, repetitions, logarithms, his attention is given inwardly and outwardly with reference to the structure of his mind to no matter what eventuality. Turning away from himself and his ego-sense of separation from other beings and things, he faces the Ground of Meister Eckhart, from which all impermanencies flow and to which they return. "Thoughts arise not to be collected and cherished but to be dropped as though they were void. Thoughts arise not to be collected and cherished but to be dropped as though they were rotten wood. Thoughts arise not to be collected and cherished but to be dropped as though they were pieces of stone. Thoughts arise not to be collected and cherished but to be dropped as though they were the cold ashes of a fire long dead." Similarly, in the performance of *Duo II for Pianists*, each performer, when he performs in a way consistent with the composition as written, will let go of his feelings, his taste, his automatism, his sense of the universal, not attaching himself to this or to that, leaving by his performance no traces, providing by his actions no interruption to the fluency of nature. The performer therefore simply does what is to be done, not splitting his mind in two, not separating it from his body, which is kept ready for direct and instantaneous contact with his instrument.

This is a lecture on composition which is indeterminate with respect to its performance. That composition is necessarily experimental. An experimental action is one the outcome of which is not foreseen. Being unforeseen, this action is not concerned with its excuse. Like the land, like the air, it needs none. A performance of a composition which is indeterminate of its performance is necessarily unique. It cannot be repeated. When performed for a second time, the outcome is other than it was. Nothing therefore is accomplished by such a performance, since that performance cannot be grasped as an object in time. A recording of such a work has no more value than a postcard; it provides a knowledge of something that happened, whereas the action was a non-knowledge of something that had not yet happened.

There are certain practical matters to discuss that concern the performance of music the composition of which is indeterminate with respect to its performance. These matters concern the physical space of the performance. These matters also concern the physical time of the performance. In connection with the physical space of the performance, where that performance involves several players (two or more), it is advisable for several reasons to separate the performers one from the other, as much as is convenient and in accord with the action and the architectural situation. This separation allows the sounds to issue from their own centers and to interpenetrate in a way which is not obstructed by the conventions of European harmony and theory about relationships and interferences of sounds. In the case of the harmonious ensembles of European musical history, a fusion of sound was of the essence, and therefore players in an ensemble were brought as close together as possible, so that their actions, productive of an object in time, might be effective. In the case, however, of the performance of music the composition of which is indeterminate of its performance so that the action of the players is productive of a process, no harmonious fusion of sound is essential. A non-obstruction of sounds is of the essence. The separation of players in space when there is an ensemble is useful towards bringing about this non-obstruction and interpenetration, which are of the essence. Furthermore, this separation in space will facilitate the independent action of each performer, who, not constrained by the performance of a part which has been extracted from a score, has turned his mind in the direction of no matter what eventuality. There is the possibility when people are crowded together that they will act like sheep rather than nobly. That is why separation in space is spoken of as facilitating independent action on the part of each performer. Sounds will then arise from actions, which will then arise from their own centers rather than as motor or psychological effects of other actions and sounds in the environment. The musical recognition of the necessity of space is tardy with respect to the recognition of space on the part of the other arts, not to mention scientific awareness. It is indeed astonishing that music as an art has kept performing musicians so consistently huddled together in a group. It is high time to separate the players one from another, in order to show a musical recognition of the necessity of space, which has already been recognized on the part of the other arts, not to mention scientific awareness. What is indicated, too, is a disposition of the performers, in the case of an ensemble in space, other than the conventional one of a huddled group at one end of a recital or symphonic hall. Certainly the performers in the case of an ensemble in space will be disposed about the room. The conventional architecture is often not suitable. What is required perhaps is an architecture like that of Mies van der Rohe's School of Architecture at the Illinois Institute of Technology. Some such architecture will be useful for the performance of composition which is indeterminate of its performance. Nor will the performers be huddled together in a group in the center of the audience. They must at least be disposed separately around the audience, if not, by approaching their disposition in the most radically realistic sense, actually disposed within the audience itself. In this latter case, the further separation of performer and audience will facilitate the independent action of each person, which will include mobility on the part of all.

There are certain practical matters to discuss that concern the performance of music the composition of which is indeterminate with respect to its performance. These matters concern the physical space of the performance. These matters also concern the physical time of the performance. In connection with the physical time of the performance, where that performance involves several players (two or more), it is advisable for several reasons to give the conductor another function than that of beating time. The situation of sounds arising from actions which arise from their own centers will not be produced when a conductor beats time in order to unify the performance. Nor will the situation of sounds arising from actions which arise from their own centers be produced when several conductors beat different times in order to bring about a complex unity to the performance. Beating time is not necessary. All that is necessary is a slight suggestion of time, obtained either from glancing at a watch or at a conductor who, by his actions, represents a watch. Where an actual watch is used, it becomes possible to foresee the time, by reason of the steady progress from second to second of the second hand. Where, however, a conductor is present, who by his actions represents a watch which moves not mechanically but variably, it is not possible to foresee the time, by reason of the changing progress from second to second of the conductor's indications. Where this conductor, who by his actions represents a watch, does so in relation to a part rather than a score—to, in fact, his own part, not that of another—his actions will interpenetrate with those of the players of the ensemble in a way which will not obstruct their actions. The musical recognition of the necessity of time is tardy with respect to the recognition of time on the part of broadcast communications, radio, television, not to mention magnetic tape, not to mention travel by air, departures and arrivals from no matter what point at no matter what time, to no matter what point at no matter what time, not to mention telephony. It is indeed astonishing that music as an art has kept performing musicians so consistently beating time together like so many horseback riders huddled together on one horse. It is high time to let sounds issue in time independent of a beat in order to show a musical recognition of the necessity of time which has already been recognized on the part of broadcast communications, radio, television, not to mention magnetic tape, not to mention travel by air, departures and arrivals from no matter what point at no matter what time, to no matter what point at no matter what time, not to mention telephony.

## NOTES

1. [A 1951 composition by Cage composed in part by tossing coins in the manner of the *I Ching*, the ancient Chinese book of oracles.—Eds.]

# 28

# Visual Sounds:
# On Graphic Scores

## CHRISTOPH COX

In this short piece, philosopher, critic, and aesthetic theorist Christoph Cox (1965– ) presents an introduction to "graphic scores"—scores that forgo traditional musical symbols in favor of novel graphic elements that are intended to stimulate open-ended musical performance and improvisation. "Graphic scores" lead to a radical indeterminacy that pushes the traditional musical score to its limit, beyond which composition gives way to free improvisation. Such scores also highlight the synaesthetic aspects of musical notation, which calls upon musicians to render visual symbols as sounds. As such, they represent a prominent aspect of contemporary art: the shift to multimedia aesthetic practices.

"All art constantly aspires towards the condition of music," the British aesthete Walter Pater wrote in 1888. Pater's remark captured the spirit of 19th-century aesthetics, which glorified music as the most ethereal and transcendent of the arts. Less than a century after Pater's declaration, however, this view was turned on its head, as avant garde composers began imagining a music that aspired to the condition of painting. Morton Feldman, John Cage, Cornelius Cardew, Anthony Braxton and others dedicated their works to painters and started to conceive the visual aspect of musical composition—the writing of a score—no longer merely as a means to an end but as an end in itself. Abandoning traditional musical notation, Earle Brown's score for *December 1952* (1952)—a single white page with a scattering of horizontal and vertical bars—bears a striking resemblance to Piet Mondrian's early abstract canvases. Recalling the Constructivist paintings of Kasimir Malevich, the lines, angles and circles that make up the score for Cardew's massive *Treatise* (1963–67) are designed to "produce . . . in the reader, without any sound, something analogous to the experience of music." Of his "visually notated" *Composition 10*—all asterisks, arrows, and doodles—Braxton wrote: "A given performance . . . should reveal its actual visual material . . . which is to say, one should be able to actually see as well as hear [the piece]."

Fascination with the visual arts did not alone account for the proliferation of graphic scores in the 1950s, '60s and '70s. Practical, musical considerations played a role as well. The emergence of electronic and tape music in the 1950s called for new notational techniques. How to score factory noises, or the sweeps and squiggles of sine tones? More often than not, composers opted for a direct visual translation of the sonic material. Hence the scores for Karlheinz Stockhausen's *Kontakte* (1968) or Bernard Parmegiani's *Violostries* (1964) exhibit the kind of "seismographic" notation prophesied by Edgard Varèse decades earlier.

Deeper philosophical and political concerns also contributed to the move away from conventional staff notation. Politicized composers such as Cardew rejected the traditional score for supporting a hierarchical division of labor that required performers to subject themselves to the will of the composer. In contrast, the indeterminacy of graphic notation helped to dissolve this hierarchy, instead fostering an active collaboration between the two parties. Cage came to a similar realization, deeming his early "chance" composition *Music of Changes* (1951) "inhuman" for its strict regulation of performance. In response, he set to work on a series of graphic scores that culminated in the astonishing *Concert for Piano and Orchestra* (1957–58), a compendium of graphic elements, instructions and variables that indicates only the rough parameters of its realization.

This interest in blurring the boundaries between composition and improvisation reveals the influence of jazz. Indeed, the generation of the '50s and '60s was raised in jazz's golden age; and graphic scores mark a meeting point between the European and the African-American musical traditions. Brown was trained as a jazz musician; and Cardew's democratic sensibilities led him to abandon the world of classical music to join the improvising ensemble AMM. From the other side, inspired by Cage, Brown and Feldman, Anthony Braxton turned to graphic notation as a way to structure the sonic chaos of free jazz and to provide a meditative focal point for collective improvisation.

So what does graphic music sound like? It's hard to say, since the latitude given to the performers means that no two realizations of the same composition are likely to sound the same. Moreover, these pieces are often "scored" for "unspecified instruments" and few give any indication of how long it should take to play them. Nevertheless, performances of graphic compositions tend to be spacious and intriguing, full of odd sounds that fly around like the brush strokes of an Action Painter or the lines and marks of a master calligrapher.

# 29

## Transformations and Developments of a Radical Aesthetic

### EARLE BROWN

Along with Morton Feldman and Christian Wolff, Earle Brown (1926–2002) was a prominent member of the "New York School," a group of composers centered around John Cage in New York City during the 1950s and loosely affiliated with the "New York School" visual artists (Mark Rothko, Jackson Pollock, Philip Guston, Alexander Calder, David Smith, and others). Brown's *Folio* and *Four Systems* (1952–54) contain some of the earliest, most abstract, and most radical "graphic scores" (see chap. 28). Trained in both the classical and jazz traditions, Brown aimed to revive the lost tradition of improvisation among classical musicians. His graphic scores also reflect his close connection to the visual arts. As he explains here, Brown particularly admired the work of Alexander Calder, whose floating mobiles slowly drift, presenting ever-new aspects. Much of Brown's career was dedicated to producing this "open," "mobile form" in music. In this retrospective essay, Brown presents and explains his aesthetic philosophy.

### Aesthetic Bio

[. . . .] The earliest, and still the predominant influences on my conceptual attitude toward art, were the works of Alexander Calder and Jackson Pollock, which I remember first seeing around 1948 or 1949: the integral but unpredictable "floating" variations of a mobile, and the contextual "rightness" of the results of Pollock's directness and spontaneity in relation to the materials and his particular image of the work—as a total space (of time).

Aspects of these two kinds of work have been integral to my own work since 1950. In Calder, the construction of units and their placement in a flexible situation that subjects the original relationships to constant and virtually unpredictable, but inherent, change (the movement of the units as well as the movement of the viewer) led me to construct units of rhythmic groups (with assigned intensities but "open" timbre possibilities subject to an independent timbral-density plan), modify them according to [. . .] "generative" techniques, and assemble them rather arbitrarily—accepting the fact that all possible assemblages were inherently possible and valid [. . . .]

In highly experimental works from 1952 and 1953, collected and published as *Folio* and *Four Systems* (subtitled "experiments in notation and performance process"), the Alexander Calder-inspired "mobility" finally found a practical (for *me*) notational expression. The scores were in different invented notations of a highly ambiguous graphic nature, subject to a number of different—but all inherently valid—realizations.

I felt that the realizable concepts of physical and conceptual "mobility" in relation to the graphic input by *me* was a practical and creatively ambiguous stimulus to performer involvement and sonic creativity. This is not an abandonment of composer responsibility but the musical result inherent in a provoked, multicreative, "synergistic" interaction of the composer's concept, the graphic score, the performer's realization, and the audience. Not one of them is independent of the others; there exists, rather, a truly collaborative, creative *synergy* ("Synergy" is the subtitle of *November 1952*, from *Folio*).

The notation used for *Music for Cello and Piano* (1954-55) is developed from the graphic experiments of *Folio*. It is highly composed and notationally explicit, but is written in what I call a "time notation" because of its lack of dependence on any rational metric system, and its reliance upon the performers' actions, relative to their "time sense" of the visually ambiguous graphic relationships. The notation intentionally encourages varying realizations of the given material—between the instruments in any one performance, and from performance to performance—while at the same time presenting the performers with an unequivocal basic graphic situation. It is now usually called "proportional" notation.

There are two very different notations used in *Hodograph I*. The first is the "time notation" of *Music for Cello and Piano*, called "explicit" in the preface to the work (explicit insofar as frequency, intensity, timbre, modes of attack, and *relative* duration are given). The second notation is called "implicit," in that it *implies* the amount and character of activity—all of the above characteristics of the sound—by means of line drawings. There are three fifteen-second "implicit" areas in the score, which sporadically interrupt the "explicit" areas. The use of line drawings in my work goes back to my attempts in 1950 and 1951 to produce pieces in which decisions as to the validity and rational function of details, such as pitch and vertical correspondences (in general, the editorial aspects of composing), were minimized as much as possible, and qualities of spontaneity and immediacy were considered to be the most direct and essential aspects of the work. It was an attempt to realize graphically the essence of the piece, the initial intuitive conception, before it was molded to conform to technical and aesthetic concepts of structure, form, continuity, art, beauty, and other acquired habits and prejudices of taste and training. These pieces (for piano and string quartet) are in standard notation and are to be performed as is usual, but were written in an extremely rapid, direct, and intuitive manner: the entire piece would be sketched within a few moments (relative frequencies, intensities, durations, and contours) and then notated, or "punctuated," as music. It was an attempt to bring the time needed to compose the piece closer to the time needed to perform the piece. Similar graphic "generalizations" are the first stages in most of my works. In *Hodograph I* the "implicit" areas are sketched by me in much the same way (different in every area in every printed score) but are "punctuated" and realized in sound by the performers. The juxtaposition of the two notations produces a result that is a spontaneous correlation between the performers and their individual responses, and the varying degrees of ambiguity in the notations.

My interest in notational ambiguities, mobile scores, spontaneity in the compositional and performance processes, "objectively" acquired structure, and the use of what has been called the "inarticulate, transitive" sounds of instruments, grows out of a larger interest in hearing the tentative and unforeseeable situations that may occur in a relatively unconditioned event involving sounds in an implicit context. A totally unconditioned event is probably not possible: one's first impulse and first actions inevitably condition the work to some extent, but the conditioning of subsequent compositional actions can, to varying degrees, inhibit or release the work as an entity. What interests me is to find the degree of conditioning (of conception, of notation, and of realization) that will balance the work between the points of control and noncontrol. At that point, the work, the performer, and I will most clearly exist—both as entities and identities.

A meeting with John Cage in 1951, in Denver, was of considerable importance to me. It was my first contact with anyone else who was consciously working in what I felt to be the "poetic atmosphere" of the Calder and Pollock work. Cage at this time was composing *Music of Changes*, and using chance as a technique for constructing the work. This was a striking confirmation to me that the arts in general were beginning to consciously deal with the given materials and, to varying degrees, liberate them from the inherited "functional" concepts of control . . . the affirmative act of "relinquishing the initiative to the words themselves," as Mallarmé suggested . . . the experience of the results being an affirmative act of appreciation, and not dependent upon logical context. It is a vague, general realization by artists such as Joyce, Gertrude Stein, and many painters and poets, that no two people experience or understand the same artistic information in the same way. "Multi-ordinal" creation, understanding, and appreciation are indigenous to the human mind. Artists began to approach ambiguity and abstraction in reaction to this realization.

Although I am in complete sympathy with the utilization of so-called "chance"—as in some painting, dance, and music—I am personally much more inclined to utilize procedures in which spontaneous and immediate involvement spontaneously condition and uncondition the result [. . . .]

### Notebook Excerpts

~Chaos is a state of *seeming* unrelatedness. . . . Actually, there is no such thing as chaos except as a saturation point of comprehensibility, which is somewhere between here and infinity . . . and always sliding about between [. . . .]

~This (proportional) notation and how it can go together with time is sufficiently and excitingly mysterious to me. I have considerable difficulty in imagining the sound when seeing the piece of paper. This in itself is a delightful place to be [. . . .]

~There is no such thing as irrationality or incongruity in music, other than the mathematical or associational . . . only associational if one is listening historically. There is nothing rational in music because there is nothing to be known about any sound except to hear it . . . which has become difficult because of the arbitrary assignment of theories to what is natively meaningless. To work with the meaninglessness is to work with meaning in its true light of infinity. Apart from the general prevailing indolence, the difficulty people experience in experiencing this music is directed expectancy . . . which is, to a degree, natural.

~I have always found that the most enlivening thing about art, or anything else, is its mystery and its being beyond my particular experiential conditioning and, therefore, understanding. There is, of course, no such thing as complete understanding but there comes to be a familiarity and acceptance of something that one spends time with, which might as well be called understanding. When this occurs, the mystery and the real poetic life go out of it . . . not out of the work but out of my response to it and what is left is the form, the technique, and a poetry that is no longer vital. There is a great deal of admirable form, technique, and non-vital poetry that I can admire as such, intellectually, but find completely unrewarding poetically.

~With *Folio* I intentionally extended the compositional aspect and the performance process as far out of normal realms as I could . . . just short of producing nothing at all. Within the same year I wrote works having extremes of finite control and extremes of infinite ambiguity, knowing full well that what I was looking for lay somewhere in between. (I wrote a note to myself at that time, which was to the effect that truth lies at a point somewhere on the arc stretched between two extremes of a paradox, and that point is always fluctuating . . . as I was.)

**Instructions for *Twenty-five Pages***

The twenty-five pages may be played in any sequence; each page may be performed either side up; events within each two-line system may be read as in either treble or bass clef; the total duration of the piece is between 8'20" and 25', based on probable but not compulsory extremities of 5" and 15" per two-line system. A time structure in terms of seconds per two-line system may be preset by the performer, obtained from the composer, or arrived at spontaneously during the performance. The indicated note durations are precise relative to each other and to the eventual time value assigned to each line system.

"Impossible" hand spreads may be broken, arpeggio-fashion, and played as rapidly as possible, from top to bottom, bottom to top, from the center outward or from the outward extremes to the center.

Indicated tones that are below the keyboard range may be considered as, in fact, unplayable, and omitted if that particular event is played as being in the bass clef. Another arrangement of the pages may find these notes again within the range of the keyboard.

It will be seen that the basic "mobile" elements of the piece (page sequence and inversion, clef disposition and time) admit of a considerable number of different presentations of this material. All of these possibilities are valid within the total concept of the work, provided that once a selection from the range of possibilities has been made it be executed with devotion and accuracy in regard to the durations, attacks, and intensities. The variable factors are to be dealt with to any degree of simplicity or complexity interesting to the performer.

The piece may be played by any number of pianos up to 25.

## The General Movement

The general movement, in all the arts, is toward the presentation of an "actual" event rather than a remembered or "representational" event. The materials become progressively more freed from subservience to the "history" of their usage and less dependent upon the inherited semantic function (a function based on the commonly understood and accepted habits of the past). The presentation of an "actual" event attempts to bring the "audience" and the work together in/at the same "time"—to close the gap between art (reflection) and life (*being* . . . in the moment and not somewhere else).

This development has made a lot of people very nervous because of their experience of not being able to control or foresee or accept the *non*-control and the *not*-foreseen as it happens to them every day (it is understandably nerve-wracking in daily life if you have an inflexible attitude and a certainty as to the functional and useful purpose of your activities as they (should) march convincingly toward your goal). A certain type of artist has accepted such goal-oriented functionalism, and it is an honorable endeavor but it is based on an acceptance of the idea that we can know something and know how to make someone else know it. This kind of knowing that anybody can have just by deciding to . . . . There is variety in what various people decide upon knowing and it is sometimes interesting but never profound. "Do you know do you know or do you know because I tell you so?" (Gertrude Stein); "because I" or you or somebody else "tell(s) you so" is never enough.

The "freeing of the materials" has come about because of (some) artists realizing that the material *is* free and that any definition or condition that is imposed upon it is only an imaginary and momentarily effective illusion. Much of art is based on such illusory thinking, and this is perfectly proper to art of the past or present that is illustrative of exterior "reality" and based upon a currently acceptable vocabulary of "expressive," inherited concepts of "reality," and conceivable relationships within observable limits. This is a functional, useful, consciously communicable, "common denominator" approach to art, and may actually be the true, or at least the original, description of "art"—the involvement of an imaginative artisan wishing to produce an object that would function usefully and/or poetically as a "finely wrought" example of skill, taste, intellect, and imagination.

The more recent developments in art find the artist no longer content with the inherited vocabulary nor with his ability to acquire skill in the manipulation of his "craft." There is a desire to remake or review the entire world of possibilities, from its primary components and qualities . . . to discover what is or might be possible rather than to condition the possibilities of discovery by imposing rational causality directives, as the artist understands them. This dissatisfaction with second-hand experience, the desire for "freedom from the known," is neither negativistic nor escapist but is, on the contrary, a commitment to the feeling (intuitive) that everything is meaningful and valuable (infinitely) if one is sufficiently unqualified by Pavlovian response patterns to experience the *now* of it!

### Calder Piece

[. . . .] Those who are familiar with my work are aware that the original impulse and influence that led me to create "open form" musical works (which, in 1952, I called "mobile compositions") came from observing and reflecting on the aesthetic nature and lifelike qualities of the mobiles of Alexander Calder [. . . .]

In Paris (in 1963) I began the work [*Calder Piece*] for the Quartet with the idea that it would be "conducted" by a mobile in the center of the space, with the four percussionists placed equidistantly, in four corners, around it; the varying configurations of the elements of the mobile being "read" by the performers, and the evolving "open form" of each performance being a function of the movements of the mobile, and subject to the scoring and "choreography" of the performers' movements. It is a very intricate "feedback" condition between the mobile, the score, and the performers.

The practicality of this whole thing was of course dependent upon the hope that Calder would find this collaboration interesting and create a mobile for it [. . .] Sandy was immediately intrigued and excited by the idea, and [. . .] everything was happily agreed to [. . . .]

The final scoring of the piece had to wait for the mobile to be finished because various aspects of the score and performance were directly based on the number and color of the elements and their physical placement in the structure of the mobile (however, it turned out to be "Calder Red," which called for some hasty rethinking on my part). It was not until 1966 that everything came together and the work was finished. Sandy named the mobile "Chef d'Orchestre."

*Calder Piece* was first performed at the Théâtre de l'Atelier in Paris early in 1967. In addition to the mobile functioning as a "conductor," the scoring calls for the musicians to actually use it as a featured percussion instrument. One is not conditioned to tolerate the striking of a Work of Art, and the sounds of breath-holding could be heard in the audience when the musicians first approached and played on the mobile. (It just occurred to me that striking a conductor is not very traditional, either.) [. . . .]

### Further Thoughts on Calder

In recognizing the bottle drier as a beautiful "work" (author unknown), and accepting it as Art, Duchamp began a tremendously important aesthetic transformation—not destroying Art but adding profoundly to the expansion of the Art mentality, as Calder did. The acceptance of diverse elements, created by the artist, situated in a spatial relationship, subject to unforeseeable but necessarily relevant and integral variations of that original relationship (a condition of "mobility"), is a profound realization that a "work of art" must not necessarily be static, but through the artist's foresight and acceptance of lifelikeness in the initial conception of the work, all unforeseeable transformations of the relationships in that unique "mobile" construction are valid. This is an enormous revelation . . . it brings the heretofore static visual art experience into a vital relationship to the "time arts" . . . theatre, music.

Calder establishes a general density
of motion for each mobile, then
he leaves it on its own.

The objects inhabit a halfway station
between the servility of a statue
and the independence of nature.

—Jean-Paul Sartre

Brown establishes a general density of
potential for each composition, then
he leaves it on its own.

The sonic elements inhabit a halfway station
between the servility of form
and the independence of nature.

—E. B. (excusez-moi, J.-P.)

# 30

## *The Game Pieces*

### JOHN ZORN

Since the early 1970s, composer and saxophonist John Zorn (1953– ) has been the ringleader of New York's "downtown" music scene. He has led a range of groups (among them Naked City, Masada, Painkiller, Spy vs. Spy, and News for Lulu) and has composed chamber music, film soundtracks, and electronic music. Zorn's music is relentlessly genre-crossing and referential, combining (often in a single piece) elements of free jazz, punk rock, cartoon music, cool jazz, klezmer, Heavy Metal, and avant-garde composition. Here, Zorn introduces his famous "game pieces," which consciously draw upon the "open" techniques of John Cage, Earle Brown, Karlheinz Stockhausen, Cornelius Cardew, and others to shape the performances of improvising musicians. After an initial introduction, Zorn discusses this compositional practice with Christoph Cox.

From 1974 until about 1990, a large part of my compositional time was spent devising music for improvisers, what I now call "game pieces."[1] Tying together loose strings left dangling by composers such as Earle Brown, Cornelius Cardew, John Cage, and Stockhausen, I began to work out complex systems harnessing improvisers in flexible compositional formats. Working on a blackboard, ideas would come slowly, often staying on the board for months before all the various elements seemed balanced and complete. I tried to make every piece a world in itself, and often they took over a year to write. These pieces have somehow lasted, taking on a life of their own and they are now used in schools, improvisation workshops and are performed monthly from Tokyo to Berlin, San Francisco to Sydney. They have become my most often played compositions, but there continues to be a mystery about them, an enigma.

Many people have wondered why I have deliberately chosen not to publish (or even write down) the rules to these pieces, preferring to explain them myself in rehearsal as part of an oral tradition. The reasons are many. There is a lot more to these pieces than just the rules. For one thing, the choosing of players has always been a crucial part of the performance process and the art of choosing a band and being a good band leader is not something you can impart on paper in a written preface to the score. Although these pieces were written in the abstract and can be done essentially by anyone, they were not written in a vacuum. They were originally created to harness the personal languages of a new school of improvisers working together in the East Side of Lower Manhattan. Players that I worked with closely and often.

To do this music properly is to do it with a community of like-minded musicians and an understanding of tactics, personal dynamics, instrumentation, aesthetics and group chemistry. It's about cooperation, interaction, checks and balances, tension and release and many more elusive, ineffable things both musical and social. First and foremost it's about playing good music. I have no problem with people doing this music (after all, music is meant to be played), as long as they realize the difference between amateur/outlaw versions (without my presence) and the more "authorized" versions I organize myself. These pieces can go where anyone wants to take them, and since they live on in the underground as part of an oral/aural tradition, this becomes one of the dangers as well as part of the fun. Nevertheless there can be no such thing as a definitive version and I'm sometimes pleasantly surprised by tapes of renegade versions I receive in the mail [. . . .]

**How do you situate your game pieces in relation to the tradition of "open works" pioneered in the 1950s by John Cage, Earle Brown, Karlheinz Stockhausen and others?**

The exciting thing about that music was its flexibility in terms of performance. It could be different every time. One of the problems that both Earle Brown and John Cage came up against was a certain friction and resistance from classical players to work in those kinds of open contexts. Cage perversely thrived on that friction between what *he* wanted and what *they* didn't want to do. There was a drama about it. And he could kind of sit there and laugh about it in some Zen-like fashion. I don't think Earle had that same kind of sense of humor. I think he was a little more tormented by it.

**He also had a background in jazz . . .**

. . . which Cage clearly did not. For many years, Cage was very resistant to improvisation. It's interesting that the word "improvisation" was very dirty in the classical music world of the 60s. It was almost as if it was an insult to the composer if someone used the word "improvisation." I can understand why composers at that time felt compelled to justify their work with intellectual systems and words such as "aleatoric," "intuitive," and "indeterminate." They were trying to justify to the critical community that this was not "improvised music"—music that the performers were making up as they went along—but music that was truly envisioned by a musical mind and then passed down to the performers.

My particular thrust in writing the game pieces—as with all of my music—is to engage, inspire, and enthrall a group of musicians into doing music that *they* are excited about, so that that excitement is passed on to the audience. It's crucial that there's a close relationship and a dialogue between performer and composer. For me, this is the most crucial relation in music-making. And I think that's why Stockhausen, Kagel, Cage, Partch and eventually even Reich and Glass formed their own ensembles—steady musicians who continued to work with their music, and who understood what they wanted. There's a lot more to music than what's on the page, in *any* music of *any* kind. What's on the page is just a sketch. You get as close as you can. But you *want* to leave things open to performers in any music, or you end up with something that's just so dictatorial. Music that's overmarked is often more than daunting to the performer. It becomes impossible. You don't want a machine to be playing this stuff. It's got to be *human*. You want to give the option for the musicians on the stage to be able to express their creativity in some kind of way, whether it's in fingering or phrasing or dynamics or whatever. I feel very strongly that there is an interaction between what's on the page and the musician that's playing it, and that there should be a level of creativity involved.

**When Brown wrote his open compositions, he was trying to get classical musicians to improvise, to contribute to the shaping of the piece. You, however, are writing for a group of skilled improvisers.**

Exactly. When Stockhausen and Cage created their own units, they were initiating a very eloquent dialogue between composer and performer. I took the whole process one step further, in terms of "the open work," in that, when I write music, I write music for performers, for a community of players of which I, too, am a member.

**Do you write music for *specific* performers?**

Well, not specific players in the way that Duke Ellington wrote for Johnny Hodges. I write for specific *kinds* of musicians that have specific *kinds* of skills. It's a community. But the critical thing is really the interaction between what's on the page and the musicians who are playing it. The page has got to inspire the musician. They've got to look at the page and say: "Wow, this is amazing. This is fucking difficult. But I can do it, and it's worth the time it takes to learn it." What you get on the stage, then, is not just someone reading music but a *drama*. You get a *human* drama. You get *life itself*, which is what the ultimate musical experience is: it's life. Musicians relating to each other, through music.

In my case, the first musicians that I became involved with were musicians that very much loved to improvise. They were musicians that were excited by the work of Stockhausen and Cage and Earle Brown. They were also excited by the work of Albert Ayler, Anthony Braxton, Leo Smith and Ornette Coleman. They were excited by the work of film soundtrack composers like Bernard Hermann and Jerry Goldsmith. They were also excited by World Music from Bali, Africa and Japan . . . . It was the recording explosion. We were the generation that benefited from that. And we looked for like-minded musicians to work with.

When I picked up the saxophone, I was not trying to put myself into a "jazz" context but into a context where I could work down and dirty with other musicians, workshopping, improvising, talking about ideas—*that* was what the "downtown" scene was all about. The old-fashioned concept of the ivory tower composer coming in with a book of compositions and then passing the tablets down from Mount Sinai did not work in that world. I knew that. I had no right to bring my compositions in unless I understood what was going on and could devise something that could not be a result of pure improvisation, something that could only happen in a context that I had created . . . something new, something different, and, of course, something that they would want to play. That meant it had to be both challenging and fun. If it was too simple, the players would get bored. If it was too complicated, they would get lost. It was very much a matter of balance. It was also important to me to get improvisers to focus on making each moment something special. In a sense, these early lessons in composing for improvisers defined my entire compositional style. I always write from the perspective of a player. I want to excite the performer and have that excitement passed on to the listener, and I want each moment of each piece I write to be something special.

## How do the game pieces instantiate and foster these ideals?

The game pieces came about from being an improviser and working with improvisers. I learned very early that it is not very exciting for an improviser to be told what to play, especially when what you can make up yourself is more interesting than what's been written for you to play. I wanted to find something to harness the personal languages that the improvisers had developed on their own, languages that were so idiosyncratic as to be almost unnotateable (to write it down would be to ruin it). The answer for me was to deal with *form*, not with *content*, with *relationships*, not with *sound*. Instructions in these early game pieces do not have musicians on the stage relating to *sound*. They have musicians on the stage relating to *each other*. The improvisers on the stage were *themselves* the sound.

I worked it out slowly. At first, each new piece focused on different areas of improvisation that I thought were critical. The *Lacrosse* piece from 1976 is about concentrating ideas in short statements (sound events), as a way of stopping people from just closing their eyes and blowing, going on and on with the same idea. With the piece *Pool* (1979), a prompter was introduced who initiated radical changes of information by cued downbeats. *Track and Field* (1981) added open game systems: trading, duos, etc. This kind of "game" idea was also used by Cardew and Pauline Oliveros. But for them a single idea would constitute the whole piece, a kind of Fluxus event that would say "look at any player in the group and play a duo with them." That might be the whole piece. I took that *kind* of idea and incorporated it into a larger context where it was just one of maybe 30 ideas that could be used at any time, cued by members of the group. There was always a critical moment in rehearsal, about half way through, where the performers began to crack up, laughing partly in exhilaration, partly in exasperation over rules that were right on the edge of impossibility. It was at these moments that I knew the piece was going to be a success. I tried to create a context where anything could happen at any moment, and everybody had equal control. It was the players themselves who were making the decisions. If there was something you wanted to have happen, you could make it happen. And so the pieces slowly evolved into complex on-and-off systems, dealing only with *when* musicians play and *with whom*. Musicians relating to musicians.

These sorts of ideas were also used by Stockhausen, for example, in *Plus-Minus* (1963) or *Kurzwellen* (1968). Instructions such as "play higher than the sound you're hearing on the radio, play lower than the sound, imitate the sound" were very open in a sense, but still related to sound, and were still tied to a timeline. Even in Earle Brown's music you were presented with a timeline. There would be a series of events that could happen in any order, but, within each event, it was *all written*. There always seemed to be information that needed to be completed for the piece to be finished. Similarly, my early game pieces often included long lists of player permutations. *Klarina* (1974) is a complex list of all the possible combinations of three players who perform on three different instruments each. *Archery* (1979) included a series of all the possible solo, duo, and trio combinations for 12 players, which ended up being 200-some odd combinations; and you had to complete them all to finish the piece! Eventually I saw this as a bit restrictive, and I eliminated the timeline, so that the players could end the piece at any time. What remained were scores that did not refer to *sound* or *time*—two parameters traditionally inseparable from the art of music—but were a complex set of rules that, in a sense, turned players on and off like toggle switches to such a complicated degree that it didn't really matter what the content was. The music could go just about anywhere. The piece was still itself. Game pieces can sound like anything and last any length depending on the players and the moment, but they always somehow retain their own identity, the way baseball differs from croquet.

Over the years, the systems became more flexible, more varied. Post-*Cobra* (1984) game pieces began to give options to the players in terms of determining content, through the use of modifiers, which specified different parameters of sound. Each of these twists and wrinkles were devised through practicum. By seeing how players responded to various cues and situations in performance, I could come up with new ideas and situations that were unique and exciting to play. Although elements of the game pieces repeat from piece to piece, they were always contextualized and recontextualized in new ways within each piece. Each piece is a different world, and indeed, it is a mistake to play *Cobra* like it was *Archery*, or *Ruan Lingyu* (1987) like it was *Xu Feng* (1985).

In these later compositions, players are asked to relate more and more to sound in spontaneously constructing pieces. Abstract parameters like high, low, loud or quiet (in *Xu Feng*) were later joined (in *Bezique* [1989]) by specific genres like, blues, soundtrack, mood, classical, and jazz as moments that could be called upon by any player at any time, orchestrated spontaneously and cued at the prompter's downbeat. It is interesting to see the progression. In *Bezique*, each player in the group has a chance to completely organize an ordering of sound events—to "compose" a piece themselves. When each player has completed their successive piece, the performance is over. We have come full circle here, with a triumphant return to both the timeline and the world of sound. Perhaps it is fitting that *Bezique*, which consists almost entirely of sound modifiers, is one of my last explorations of the game piece medium, as in it, improvisers have themselves become composers.

## NOTES

1. [*Baseball* (1976), *Lacrosse* (1976), *Dominoes* (1977), *Curling* (1977), *Golf* (1977), *Hockey* (1978), *Cricket* (1978), *Fencing* (1978), *Pool* (1979), *Archery* (1979), *Tennis* (1979), *Track and Field* (1980), *Jai Alai* (1980), *Goi* (1981), *Croquet* (1981), *Locus Solus* (1982), *Sebastopol* (1983), *Rugby* (1983), *Cobra* (1984), *Xu Feng* (1985), *Hu Die* (1986), *Ruan Lingyu* (1987), *Hwang Chin-ee* (1988), *Bezique* (1989), *Que Tran* (1990)—Eds.]

# 31

## *Introduction to* Catalog of Works

### ANTHONY BRAXTON

Composer, reed player, and musical philosopher Anthony Braxton (1945– )
came to prominence in the 1960s as a key member of the Association for
the Advancement of Creative Musicians (AACM), a collective of Chicago
musicians dedicated to African-American avant garde music. The AACM's
members came out of the "jazz" tradition, but most rejected the term "jazz"
in favor of the terms "creative music" or "great black music." Braxton is often
associated with "free jazz"; yet he has always looked for ways to restrain
the anarchy of free jazz by way of various compositional procedures. His
work is influenced equally by jazz history and by the compositional methods
of Cage, Brown, and Stockhausen. Since the late 1960s, Braxton's composition titles have consisted of abstract diagrams and number-letter combinations, reflecting his joint interests in graphic composition and esoteric
spiritual traditions. Each of Braxton's compositions (which now number more
than 300) provides a set of open structures and parameters for collective
improvisation. In the mid-1980s, he began "collaging" his compositions,
embedding one composition in another and calling upon performers to play
different compositions simultaneously—a technique pioneered by Cage. In
this piece, Braxton presents his conception of musical collage and simultaneity, and the holistic worldview from which it springs.

The body of "musics" that make up this Catalog of Works represent the "best I
could do" when confronted with the incredible gifts of beauty that the Masters have
given us in the phenomenon we call music. I perceive this effort as an evolving
MULTI-LOGIC sound universe that demonstrates sonic unification on three primary planes of perception dynamics—abstract realization, concrete realization
and intuitive realization. All of these matters are part of the wonderful world of
sound wonder and beauty—I am so grateful for music and the "act of thinking
about music/feeling." Life on earth would be impossible without music—our species could not exist without love and compassion. All of these matters are related.

The construction of this body of works has been my main preoccupation since 1967 and as such it is my responsibility to present this material as correctly as possible—THAT IS: it is important for the reader to understand the overcontext that gives this material its "perceived meaning" (LIFE). This is necessary because all of these works are part of one organic sound world state—and all of these efforts seek to affirm my life experiences: that being, what I have learned and experienced in my actual (REAL) life—as perceived from my value systems— rather than from imposed social and/or political values. This difference is important and must be taken into account or real penetration (insight) into this material could be "complex" (smile). As such, I would like to establish a general overview about this material for future musicologists and musician/interpreters so that any person interested in my work will have some idea of my values and "way of being." My comments in these notes will apply to every composition in this catalog—and will encompass all additional entries I hope to add. Indeed, I am really commenting on the aesthetic tenet axioms of my music system/platform (life).

The most important feature of the body of material that must first be understood is that this information represents the vibrational fluid and atomic structural ingredients of one dynamic sound state (intention). That is, I have approached this material with respect to my needs as an instrumentalist as well as composer. With this effort I have tried to erect a "perception context" that respects and allows for both disciplines (improvisational/fluid musics and notated/stable musics) to exist and evolve—as unified and independent realities (with its own secrets and particulars). I have designed this material as an affirmation of "SOUND" AND MUSIC SCIENCE—as a response to the great African, European, and Asian men and women who have clarified the profound "beauty" of that which we call music. There are no words to adequately express my gratitude to the heavens for the fact of "reception and definition." Music is profoundly interwoven into the total experience of existence.

There are four fundamental postulates that must be understood about this material if my objectives are to be respected (or understood), that being:

I.  **All compositions in my music system connect together**

II. **All instrumental parts in my group of musics are autonomous**

III. **All tempos in this music state are relative (negotiable)**

IV. **All volume dynamics in this sound world are relative**

Let me clarify:

A. a) **All compositions in my music system can be executed at the same time/moment.** That is, this material in its entirety can be performed together as one state of being—at the same time (in whole or in part—in any combination). This option is the aesthetic conceptual/vibrational/fulfillment of my music.

b) **Shorter works can also be positioned into larger works—into any section of a given "host" composition.**

c) **Isolated parts from a given structure can be positioned into other structures—or one structure—as many times as desired.**

d) **Any section (part) of any structure can be taken and used repeatedly by itself or with another structure—or structures.**

B. a) **All instrumental parts in these groups of compositions are changeable—that is, any instrumental part can be used by any instrument—or instruments.** Or any section from a given structure can be spliced out and integrated into another structure. What this means is that the harmonic reality of a given structure has vertical, linear, and correspondence realities (logics) that transcend any one plane of definition. All notated pitches in this music state involve only the primary imprint reality of a given form—as viewed from its origin/identity instrumentation. Every part can also be utilized (or "adopted") by any instrument or instrumentation. In other words, every solo piece can be an orchestra piece—in any order or sequence. Every orchestral instrumental part can be taken away from its "identity territory" and used by itself or with another piece or pieces.

b) **A given performer or group of performers can take any part of any composition (or compositions) and use that material as solo or combination material.** A given performer can sequence parts of different compositions into one music/type for one musician or for as many musicians as desired. Structural material used in this manner becomes a reservoir of structural and conceptual possibilities—including traditional interpretation.

C. a) **All tempos in my music system are relative.** That is—the initial "indicated" tempo of a given composition is only a point of definition for the unified imprint state of that work and is not intended as the only option. What this means is that the "life" of a given structure in this system has limitless possibilities—"settings" or "colors."

b) **Every composition in this music world can be executed in any tempo**—in the same way that a composition of Duke Ellington's can be played as a ballad or as a fast piece. Primary tempo designations are also included so that the interpreter can have every option available.

c) **Each composition contains open duration spaces where time/space adjustments and parameters can be treated creatively.**

D. a) **All volume dynamics in this universe of music are relative.** What this means is that volume adjustments can be made when two or more given instrumentalists perform (execute) different compositions together.

b) **Each person can respect his or her physical and vibrational particulars when dealing with the physical demands (and challenges) of the music.**

c) **Performers are encouraged to look for "affinities" and "composite sound states" based on the collective dynamics of the ensemble.** All of these matters will affect the music in every way.

The reality of this system seeks to establish fresh concepts about structure (FORM) and participation dynamics. What this means is that architecture and vibrational properties in this sound world are designed to establish **1) an individual reality context** (i.e., solo manipulations and strategies); **2) a collective or ensemble reality context** (i.e., interactive strategies for large and small ensemble groups); and finally, **3) a correspondence reality context** (one that establishes the interconnection logics—"WORLDS"—between structures).

I would also like to make four additional comments about this material to hopefully give insight into those things I would want any person interested in my music system to know about.

My comments are:

a. **Have fun with this material and don't get hung up with any one area.**

b. **Don't misuse this material to have only "correct" performances without spirit or risk.** Don't use my work to "kill" young aspiring students of music (in other words—don't view this material as only a technical or emotional noose that can be used to suppress creativity). If the music is played too correctly it was probably played wrong.

c. **Each performance *must* have something unique.** I say take a chance and have some fun. If the instrumentalist doesn't make a mistake with my materials, I say "Why!? NO mistake—NO work!" If a given structure concept has been understood (on whatever level) then connect it to something else, something different—be creative (that's all I'm writing).

d. **Finally, I recommend as few rehearsals as possible so that everyone will be slightly nervous**—and of course put in "emergency cues" just in case anything goes wrong. Believe me there will be days when nothing works at all. Also try and keep the music "on the line" to maintain the "spark of invention," and be sure to keep your sense of humor.

Good Luck,

Anthony Braxton
Mills College 1988

P.S. (and please don't make the music too "cutesy")

In 1952, with Morton Feldman, Christian Wolff, Earle Brown, and David Tudor, I had taken steps to make a music that was just sounds, sounds free of judgments about whether they were "musical" or not, sounds free of memory and taste (likes and dislikes), sounds free of fixed relations between two or more of them (musical syntax, or glue, as Henry Cowell called it when he introduced one of our concerts in the fifties at the New School). Since the theory of conventional music is a set of laws exclusively concerned with "musical" sounds, having nothing to say about noises, it had been clear from the beginning that what was needed was a music based on noise, on noise's lawlessness. Having made such an anarchic music, we were later able to include in its performance even so-called musical sounds. The next steps were social, and they are still being taken. We need first of all a music in which not only are sounds just sounds but in which people are just people, not subject, that is, to laws established by any one of them even if he is "the composer" or "the conductor." Finally (as far as I can see at present), we need a music which no longer prompts talk of audience participation, for in it the division between performers and audience no longer exists: a music made by everyone.

—John Cage[1]

Formerly, whenever anyone said the music I presented was experimental, I objected. It seemed to me that composers knew what they were doing and that the experiments that had been made had taken place prior to the finished works, just as sketches are made before paintings and rehearsals precede performances [. . . .] Now, on the other hand, times have changed; music has changed; and I no longer object to the word "experimental." I use it in fact to describe all the music that especially interests me and to which I am devoted, whether someone else wrote it or I did. What has happened is that I have become a listener and the music has become something to hear [. . . .] Those involved with the composition of experimental music find ways and means to remove themselves from the activities of the sounds they make [. . . .] And what is the purpose of writing music? One is, of course, not dealing with purposes but dealing with sounds. Or the answer must take the form of paradox: a purposeful purposelessness or a purposeless play.

—John Cage[2]

My past experience was not to "meddle" with the material, but use my concentration as a guide to what might transpire. I mentioned this to Stockhausen once when he asked me what my *secret* was. "I don't push the sounds around." Stockhausen mulled this over, and asked: "Not even a little bit?"

—Morton Feldman[3]

In 1965 I joined a group of four musicians in London who were giving weekly performances of what they termed "AMM Music," a very pure form of improvisation operating without any formal system or limitation. The four original members of AMM came from a jazz background; when I joined in I had no jazz experience whatever, yet there was no language problem. Sessions generally lasted about two hours with no formal breaks or interruptions, although there would sometimes occur extended periods of close to silence [. . . .] Informal "sound" has a power over our emotional responses that formal "music" does not, in that it acts subliminally rather than on a cultural level. This is a possible definition of the area in which AMM is experimental. We are searching for sounds and for the responses that attach to them, rather than thinking them up, preparing them and producing them. The search is conducted in the medium of sound and the musician himself is at the heart of the experiment.

—Cornelius Cardew[4]

If I push one button, a pure tone comes out, but if I dare to push two or three at a time, the sounds react to one another and become somewhat distorted. Things also change a lot depending on how hard I push the buttons. And of course, the speakers and other parts of the sound system change the tones, too. I can only control about half of the sounds, so I can't predict what will happen: it's like an accident.

—Sachiko M on her improvisatory practice with oscillators[5]

I wish to get away from the paradigm of music as language-like, the aesthetics that believe music, or art in general, is a form of communication. My favorite metaphor for explaining what I'm after is a tree in a meadow: the tree is just standing there, it's not a message for you, but looking at it, you may think about a lot of things, feel a lot of things. So in a way I'm trying to do music that exists like a tree. When you associate things with what you hear, visualizing this or that, language gets back into the game and destroys the possibility of perceiving the existence of sound, its "being like this."

—Bernhard Günter[6]

My whole generation was hung up on the 20 to 25 minute piece. It was our clock. We all got to know it, and how to handle it. As soon as you leave the 20–25 minute piece behind, in a one-movement work, different problems arise. Up to one hour you think about form, but after an hour and a half it's scale. Form is easy—just the division of things into parts. But scale is another matter. You have to have control of the piece—it requires a heightened kind of concentration. Before, my pieces were like objects; now, they're like evolving things.

—Morton Feldman[7]

The virtual work is "open" by design. Every actualization reveals a new aspect of the work. Some systems not only manifest a combination of possibilities but encourage the emergence of absolutely unpredictable forms during the process of interaction. Thus creation is no longer limited to the moment of conception or realization; the virtual system provides a machine for generating events.

—Pierre Lévy[8]

# V. Experimental Musics

## Introduction

On May 10, 1979, Alvin Lucier strung an 80-foot wire under the rotunda of the U.S. Customs House in New York City. With the help of a sine wave oscillator and an electromagnet, the wire was set in motion and then amplified, filling the space with a rich, raspy drone. "The wire played itself," remarked Lucier. "All changes in volume, timbre, harmonic structure, rhythmic and cyclic patterning, and other sonic phenomena were brought about solely by the actions of the wire itself."[1]

Lucier's *Music on a Long Thin Wire* is an exemplary instance of experimental music. While often used to characterize unusual or avant-garde music of any sort, the phrase "experimental music" refers more specifically to a particular genre of vanguard music initially developed in Britain and the United States during the 1960s. John Cage succinctly characterized experimental music as a musical action "the outcome of which is not foreseen."[2] More generally, the experimental "composer" (a term that experimental music pushes to its limit) designs a set of initial conditions (technical, sonic, conceptual, verbal, social, etc.) and then leaves them to unfold more or less on their own. In Morton Feldman's phrase, the experimental composer/performer tries "not to 'meddle' with the material," not "to push the sounds around."[3] Experimental music, then, invites us into an autonomous world of evolving sounds rather than one that is constructed (composed) for us in advance.

Many indeterminate compositions ("graphic scores" in particular) probably fit Cage's description of experimental music. Yet the two practices have different socio-musical origins and represent distinctly different aesthetics. Indeterminacy emerged from the 1950s classical avant garde, and represents a move away from the highly structured musical world of serialism. By contrast, experimental music has its origins in 1960s counterculture, and emerges as much from conceptual and performance art as from the then current compositional practices. It is fundamentally interested in the issue of *process*: in the procedures for generating sound and in the life of sounds once they have come into the world. For many experimental composers/musicians, this emphasis on process is an attempt to counteract the reification of sound and music, the tendency within modernity to transform unfolding processes into discrete products, to render becoming as being.[4] In the same way, experimental composers/musicians tend to be interested in the materiality of sound rather than its musical meaning. And they tend to be less interested in virtuoso performance—experimental pieces are often designed for amateur or non-musicians—than in fostering virtuoso listening.

Umberto Eco (see chap. 26) conceived indeterminacy as a cultural analog to the scientific shift from a closed, Newtonian physics to an open, quantum physics. Along the same lines, one might say that experimental music figures the shift from the classical *physical* worldview of the seventeenth and eighteenth centuries (which also gave rise to the classical musical work) to the *biological, evolutionary,* and even *cybernetic* worldviews of the 19th, 20th, and 21st centuries.[5] Brian Eno (chap. 34) and David Toop (see chap. 36) note that a piece of experimental music tends to operate like an evolutionary process. It begins with a specific set of sonic characteristics and organizational structures that are then submitted to random, chance, or algorithmic mutations and/or environmental effects that cause the original parameters to drift. This process is usually open-ended, without any necessary stopping point. If the traditional composer is akin to an omnipotent God, who structures and controls all aspects of a musical performance, the experimental composer is in the position of the ordinary human being, who may initiate events but is powerless to control their destiny. No longer purely a maker, the experimental composer becomes him- or herself an observer.

Along with electronic music, experimental music has had a profound impact on music outside the classical domain. Eno himself played a significant role, here. An admirer of Cage and a sometime member of the Scratch Orchestra, Eno, along with King Crimson guitarist Robert Fripp, began, in the early 1970s, to experiment with electronic systems that drastically altered the rock material fed into them.[6] In 1975, Eno founded the Obscure record label (a subsidiary of British pop giant Island Records), which introduced rock audiences to the works of many experimental composers, among them Cage, Gavin Bryars, and Christopher Hobbs. Since then, the influence of the early experimentalists and their procedures can be discovered in fringe pop, rock, punk, HipHop, and electronica. Post-punk rockers Jim O'Rourke and Sonic Youth, for example, have noted the importance to their work of composers such as Cage, David Behrman, Cornelius Cardew, and Alvin Lucier.[7] The influence of new software and the ramifying rhizome of the internet have also provided new resources for process composition (see Toop, chap. 36). The electronica outfit Oval, for example, now produces, in addition to finished CDs, algorithmic software to be used by its audiences to compose their own Oval music. And turntablism and remix culture in general are engaged in a process of ongoing recomposition that transforms recordings from finished products to sonic material that is perpetually in-process. Like the biological, electronic, and cybernetic processes it affirms, then, experimental music itself continues to ramify in the world, reappearing in ever-new manifestations.

## NOTES

1. Alvin Lucier, liner notes to *Music on a Long Thin Wire* (Lovely Music LCD 1011).
2. See chap. 27, above, and the epigraph to Michael Nyman, "Towards (a Definition of) Experimental Music," chap. 32, below.
3. Morton Feldman, *Give My Regards to Eighth Street: Collected Writings of Morton Feldman,* ed. B. H. Friedman (Cambridge, MA: Exact Charge, 2002), 142–43. In this respect, wind chimes and Aeolian harps can be considered precursors to experimental musical practices.
4. See the classic discussion of this tendency and reification in general in Georg Lukacs, "Reification and the Consciousness of Proletariat," *History and Class Consciousness,* trans. Rodney Livingstone (Cambridge, MA: MIT Press, 1971), 83–222.
5. On this shift in the sciences, see, for example Ernst Mayr, *One Long Argument: Charles Darwin and the Genesis of Modern Evolutionary Thought* (Cambridge, MA: Harvard University Press, 1991), chaps. 4–5.
6. Hear, for example, Fripp and Eno's *No Pussyfooting*, Editions EG EEGCD2.
7. Jim O'Rourke, personal communication. Hear also Sonic Youth, *Goodbye 20ᵗʰ Century*, SYR 4.

# 32

# *Towards (a Definition of) Experimental Music*

## MICHAEL NYMAN

A successful composer of minimalist music and film scores, Michael Nyman (1944– ) began his career in the early 1960s as a musicologist specializing in Baroque music. A few years later, he became a music critic for *The Spectator*, where, in a 1968 article, he was the first to use the term "minimalism" to describe a musical style. Nyman's work as a critic brought him into contact with the "experimental" music scenes that had sprung up in England and the United States during the 1960s. In 1974, writing in the midst of this musical revolution, Nyman published his genre-defining study *Experimental Music: Cage and Beyond*. Following its publication, Nyman himself became a prolific composer, writing minimalist music inflected with elements of medieval, Renaissance, baroque, and classical music. Nyman scored eleven films for the British film director Peter Greenaway and wrote the soundtrack for Jane Campion's Academy-Award winning film *The Piano*. In the following piece, drawn from the opening chapter of *Experimental Music*, Nyman catalogs the defining features of "experimental music."

Objections are sometimes made by composers to the use of the term *experimental* as descriptive of their works, for it is claimed that any experiments that are made precede the steps that are finally taken with determination, and that this determination is knowing, having, in fact, a particular, if unconventional, ordering of the elements used in view. These objections are clearly justifiable, but only where, as among contemporary evidences in serial music, it remains a question of making a thing upon which attention is focused. Where, on the other hand, attention moves towards the observation and audition of many things at once, including those that are environmental—becomes, that is, inclusive rather than exclusive—no question of making, in the sense of forming understandable structures, can arise (one is a tourist), and here the word 'experimental' is apt, providing it is understood not as descriptive of an act to be later judged in terms of success and failure, but simply as of an act the outcome of which is unknown. What has been determined?

John Cage (1955)

[. . . .] I shall make an attempt to isolate and identify what experimental music is [. . . .] Since, as the Chinese proverb has it, 'One showing is worth a hundred sayings' I propose to take a practical instance—Cage's *4′33″*—dating from the same inauguration period of experimental music as the [statement] quoted above, and use it as a point of reference. I have selected the so-called silent piece not because it is notorious (and misunderstood) but simply because it is the most empty of its kind and therefore for my purposes the most full of possibilities. It is also—certainly for Cage—a work that has outlived its usefulness, having been overtaken by the revolution it helped to bring about. ('I no longer need the silent piece' Cage said in an interview in 1966.) I shall build the discussion around Cage's questioning of the traditional unities of composing, performing and listening: 'Composing's one thing, performing's another, listening's a third. What can they have to do with one another?' In normal circumstances it might seem puzzling to make this separation, but even at such an early point in the history of experimental music *4′33″* demonstrates very clearly what composition, realization and audition may or may not have to do with one another [. . . .]

## Composing

### Notation

The published score of *4′33″* bears the numbers I, II, III, each marked 'TACET' and each given a duration in minutes and seconds which together add up to four minutes thirty-three seconds. A secondary part of the notation tells the performer that the piece may be done on any instrument, for any length of time. Since 'tacet' is the notation which informs a player that he should play nothing during a movement, the performer of *4′33″* is asked to make no sounds in the three timed sections.

As notation, then, *4′33″* is early evidence of the radical shift in the methods and functions of notation that experimental music has brought about. A score may no longer 'represent' sounds by means of the specialized symbols we call musical notation, symbols which are read by the performer who does his best to 'reproduce' as accurately as possible the sounds the composer initially 'heard' and then stored. Edgard Varèse once drew attention to some of the disadvantages of the mechanics of traditional notation: with music 'played by a human being you have to impose a musical thought through notation, then, usually much later, the player has to prepare himself in various ways to produce what will—one hopes—emerge as that sound.' *4′33″* is one of the first in a long line of compositions by Cage and others in which something other than a 'musical thought' (by which Varèse meant a pattern of sounds) is imposed through notation. Cornelius Cardew wrote in 1963: 'A composer who hears sounds will try to find a notation for sounds. One who has ideas will find one that expresses his ideas, leaving their interpretation free, in confidence that his ideas have been accurately and concisely notated.'

*Processes*

Experimental composers are by and large not concerned with prescribing a defined *time-object* whose materials, structuring and relationships are calculated and arranged in advance, but are more excited by the prospect of outlining a *situation* in which sounds may occur, a *process* of generating action (sounding or otherwise), a *field* delineated by certain compositional 'rules'. The composer may, for instance, present the performer with the means of making calculations to determine the nature, timing or spacing of sounds. He may call on the performer to make split-second decisions in the moment of performance. He may indicate the temporal areas in which a number of sounds may be placed. Sometimes a composer will specify situations to be arranged or encountered before sounds may be made or heard; at other times he may indicate the number and general quality of the sounds and allow the performers to proceed through them at their own pace. Or he may invent, or ask the performer to invent, particular instruments or electronic systems.

Experimental composers have evolved a vast number of processes to bring about 'acts the outcome of which are unknown' (Cage). The extent to which they are unknown (and to whom) is variable and depends on the specific process in question. Processes may range from a minimum of organization to a minimum of arbitrariness, proposing different relationships between chance and choice, presenting different kinds of options and obligations [. . . .]

1. Chance determination processes

These were first used by Cage who still favours them—the *I Ching* (the ancient Chinese Book of Oracles) used to answer questions about the articulation of his material (*Music of Changes*, 1951, *Mureau*, 1971); observation of the imperfections on paper (*Music for Piano*, 1952-6); the random overlaying of shapes printed on perspex and readings taken to make various determinations (*Variations I-III* and *VI*, 1958-67); a star map (*Atlas Eclipticalis*, 1961-2) and the computer (*HPSCHD*, 1969). Other composers have also used this type of chance process: random number tables or the telephone directory are to be used in La Monte Young's *Poem* (1960), and in Christopher Hobbs' *Voicepiece* (1968) random techniques are used to produce a programme of vocal action for each individual performer. George Brecht uses shuffled cards in *Card Piece For Voices* (1959) as does Cage in *Theatre Piece* (1960). The importance of Cage's chance methods of the early 50s, according to Dick Higgins, lay in the placing of the 'material at one remove from the composer by allowing it to be determined by a system he determined. And the real innovation lies in the emphasis on the creation of a system' (or process).

2. People processes

These are processes which allow the performers to move through given or suggested material, each at his own speed. Morton Feldman was certainly the first to use this procedure in *Piece for Four Pianos* (1957); Cardew uses it in all seven paragraphs of *The Great Learning* (1968-71). It could of course be used to establish the determinations of chance processes. One particular form of this process, where each person reads the same notation, has been described by Michael Parsons:

> The idea of one and the same activity being done simultaneously by a number of people, so that everyone does it slightly differently, 'unity' becoming 'multiplicity', gives one a very economical form of notation—it is only necessary to specify one procedure and the variety comes from the way everyone does it differently. This is an example of making use of 'hidden resources' in the sense of natural individual differences (rather than talents or abilities) which is completely neglected in classical concert music, though not in folk music.

Differences of ability account for the (possible) eventuality of players getting lost in Frederic Rzewski's *Les Moutons de Panurge* (1969) (once you're lost you're encouraged to stay lost) and the (probable) deviations from the written letter of the classics by the members of the Portsmouth Sinfonia.

3. Contextual processes

These are concerned with actions dependent on unpredictable conditions and on variables which arise from within the musical continuity. The selection of new pitches in *The Great Learning* Paragraph 7 is an example of this process, originated by Christian Wolff whose music presents a comprehensive repertoire of contextual systems. One of the 'movements' of *Burdocks* (1970), for instance, is for an orchestra made up of at least fifteen players, each of whom chooses one to three sounds, fairly quiet. Using one of these each time, you have to play as simultaneously as possible with the next sound of the player nearest to you; then with the next sound of the next nearest player; then with the next nearest after him, and so forth until you have played with all the other players (in your orchestra, or if so determined beforehand, with all players present), ending with the player farthest away from you [. . . .]

4. Repetition processes

These use extended repetition as the sole means of generating movement—as, for example, in John White's *Machines*, in the 'gradual process music' of Steve Reich, Terry Riley's *Keyboard Studies*, or a piece like Hugh Shrapnel's *Cantation I* (1970). Riley's *In C* (1967) and Paragraph 2 of Cardew's *The Great Learning* use repetition within a 'people' process (or vice versa). In repetition processes the 'unforeseen' may arise (*pace* Feldman) through many different factors, even though the process may, from the point of view of structure, be totally foreseen.

5. Electronic processes

[. . .] A straightforward example [of an electronic process] is David Behrman's *Runthrough* (1970). This asks only for a particular electronic set-up consisting of generators and modulators with dials and switches and a photocell distributor which three or four people use for improvisation. Behrman writes that 'because there is neither a score nor directions, any sound which results from any combination of the switch and light positioning remains part of the "piece". (Whatever you do with a surfboard in the surf remains a part of surfboarding.)' [. . . .]

## Identity

The identity of a composition is of paramount importance to [avant-garde composers such as] Boulez and Stockhausen, as to all composers of the post-Renaissance tradition. But identity takes on a very different significance for the more open experimental work, where indeterminacy in performance guarantees that two versions of the same piece will have virtually no perceptible musical 'facts' in common. With a score like Cardew's *Treatise* (1963-6) aural recognizability is both impossible and irrelevant since the (non-musical) graphic symbols it contains have no meanings attached to them but 'are to be interpreted in the context of their role in the whole'. The performer may choose to realize for example, as a circle, some sort of circular sound, movement or gesture; but it is more likely that he will interpret it in a 'non-representational' way by a melody, or silence, or counting, or turning off the lights, or tuning in to a radio signal, or whatever. Each performer is invited by the absence of rules to make personal correlations of sight to sound. These will naturally change from one performance to another, whose time scale will be totally different. What price identity here with a score which is in no way a compendium or reduction of all possible realizations? [. . . .]

Difficulties also arise when one tries to explain the most open processes. A description of a particular performance may tell you little of its musical concepts, and a description of the score may tell you too much about possible interpretations to be of any use. With Cage's *Cartridge Music*, Behrman's *Runthrough* or Lucier's *Vespers* the difficulties are less obvious because the type of sound in any one version will be recognizably similar to that of another (though a lot of other aspects will be different). But separate performances of Cage's *Fontana Mix* (1958) or of Cardew's *Treatise* may exhibit no family likenesses. Cage's own tape collage versions (available on record ironically) are only *versions*, momentary isolations or interruptions of an unrestricted process; they in no way constitute the identity of the process called *Fontana Mix* [. . . .]

## Time

The attitude towards time expressed by *4' 33"* had its origins in the rhythmic structures that Cage worked with in the thirties and forties and it became the basis of all Cage's music which involves the measurement (exact or approximate) of time. This attitude was of such fundamental importance to experimental music that the composer Robert Ashley could state with certainty (in 1961):

> Cage's influence on contemporary music, on 'musicians' is such that the entire metaphor of music could change to such an extent that—time being uppermost as a definition of music—the ultimate result would be a music that wouldn't necessarily involve anything but the presence of people . . . It seems to me that the most radical redefinition of music that I could think of would be one that defines 'music' without reference to sound.

Time may initially be nothing more than a frame to be filled. 'Form is the length of programmed time' declared Christian Wolff [. . . .] Needless to say this has nothing to do with partial or incomplete performances: processes are by definition always in motion and can be equally well expressed in two minutes or twenty-four hours. 'Beginnings and ends are not points on a line but limits of a piece's material . . . which may be touched at any time during the piece. The boundaries of the piece are expressed, not at moments of time which mark a succession, but as margins of a spatial projection of the total sound structure.' (Christian Wolff) [. . . .]

One can distinguish a number of methods of releasing time in experimental music. A time frame may be chosen at random and then filled with sounds. Or temporal determinations may be made by some method or other and then measured according to any time units whatsoever, from the shortest possible to the longest possible. For Cage's *Atlas Eclipticalis* or La Monte Young's *Poem* (to name but two) 'the duration may be anything from no time to any time'. The work may last the duration of a natural event or process—the time it takes birthday cake candles to burn out (George Brecht's *Candle Piece for Radios*) or the time it takes for swung microphones to come to rest (Steve Reich's *Pendulum Music*). Or the duration may be determined simply by the time it takes to work through the given material. In some pieces (such as Reich's *Phase Patterns*, Gavin Bryars' *Jesus' Blood Never Failed Me Yet* or Christopher Hobbs' *The Remorseless Lamb*) the working-through may be similar to that of traditional music but in Paragraphs 2, 6 or 7 of *The Great Learning*, or in Riley's *In C*, where each performer moves through at his own speed, the duration of the piece is dependent on the inner workings of the process [. . . .]

As an example of how a 'working-through' notation is experienced as time there is the story that Dick Higgins tells of a performance of a piece by George Brecht given by Cage's class at the New School for Social Research around 1958. Each performer had to do two different things once only, and Cage suggested that they should do them in the dark so that they could not tell, visually, when the piece was over. 'The result was extraordinary,' says Higgins, 'both for its own sake and for the extraordinary intensity that appeared in waves, as we wondered whether the piece was over or not, what the next thing to happen would be.' Afterwards the performers were asked how long they thought they had been in the dark; guesses ranged from four to twenty-four minutes: the actual duration had been nine minutes. Perhaps this kind of experiential time was what was in Feldman's mind when he spoke of working with 'Time in its unstructured existence . . . how Time exists before we put our paws on it . . . our minds, our imagination, into it.'

## Performing

Experimental music thus engages the performer at many stages before, above and beyond those at which he is active in traditional Western music. It involves his intelligence, his initiative, his opinions and prejudices, his experience, his taste and his sensibility in a way that no other form of music does, and his contribution to the musical collaboration which the composer initiates is obviously indispensable. For while it may be possible to view some experimental scores only as concepts, they are, self-evidently (specific or general), directives for (specific or general) action. Experimental music has, for the performer, effected the reverse of Duchamp's revolution in the visual arts. Duchamp once said that 'the point was to forget *with my hand* . . . I wanted to put painting once again at the service of my mind.' The *head* has always been the guiding principle of Western music, and experimental music has successfully taught performers to remember with their hands, to produce and experience sounds physiologically.

## Tasks

The freedom of action that experimental scores give may be to some extent an illusion [. . . .] People tend to think that since, within the limits set by the composer, anything may happen, the resulting music will therefore be unconsidered, haphazard or careless. The attitude that experimental music breeds amongst its best performers/composers/listeners is not what Cage called 'carelessness as to the result' but involvement and responsibility of a kind rarely encountered in other music [. . . .]

## The Game Element

The tasks which the co-ordination processes of Christian Wolff set the player are of a different order. *For 1, 2, or 3 People* (1964) contains four symbols which mean: (1) play after a previous sound has begun, hold till it stops; (2) start anytime, hold until another sound starts, finish with it; (3) start at the same time (or as soon as you are aware of it) as the next sound, but stop before it does; (4) start anytime, hold till another sound starts, continue holding anytime after that sound has stopped. The fact that notations like these give the players no advance warning led David Behrman to write:

> The player's situation might be compared to that of a ping-pong player awaiting his opponent's fast serve: he knows what is coming (the serve) and knows what he must do when it comes (return it); but the details of how and when these take place are determined only at the moment of their occurrence.

Dick Higgins coined the term 'Games of Art' in connection with certain forms of experimental music, and Professor Morse Peckham has written:

> The role of the game player is to present his opponent, who may be himself, as in solitaire or fishing, with an unpredicted situation which will force him to behave in a particular way; while the player faced with such a situation has as his role the task of rearranging the situation so that the tables are turned. Playing a game involves continuous risk-running. The rules place limits on what may be done, but more importantly, they provide guides to improvisation and innovation. Behaviour is aimed at following rules in predictable situations and interpreting rules in unpredicted ones. Hence, an important ingredient of game playing consists of arguments about how the rules should be interpreted.

## Rules and Their (Subjective) Interpretation

Peckham was writing about games in general, but what he has to say is very relevant to the mainly solitaire-type games of experimental music. The composer

michael nyman • **215**

gives the performer freedoms, which may take him further than the composer may have envisaged: 'I think composition is a serious occupation and the onus is on the performer to show the composer some of the implications and consequences of what he has written, even if from time to time it may make him (the composer of course) look ridiculous. What he writes and what you read are two different things.' (John Tilbury, 1969) [. . . .]

Just as the interpretation of the rules may be taken out of the composer's hands and become the private concern of the performer, so may the rules themselves. Some pieces intentionally make explicit the subjectivity which is at the root of a large number of experimental scores. Giuseppe Chiari's instructions for his *Lavoro* (1965) provide a simple example: 'All round the performer are many different things placed in the most complete disorder. He arranges them in the proper order. He follows his own idea of what their proper order is' [. . . .]

*The Instrument as Total Configuration*

[. . . . In experimental music] the use of a musical instrument need not be limited by the boundaries erected by tradition. Experimental music exploits an instrument not simply as a means of making sounds in the accepted fashion, but as a total configuration—the difference between 'playing the piano' and the 'piano as sound source'.

In the past, piano music viewed the keyboard-hammer-string mechanism from the vantage-point of the keyboard alone. (There have been exceptions, of course—Chopin's view of the art of pedalling as a 'sort of breathing' and Debussy's desire to 'forget that the piano has hammers'.) Experimental composers have extended the functions of the basic mechanism. They have brought about alteration of timbre by inserting objects between the strings (Cage's prepared piano) and by applying various electronic treatments of which the simplest is amplification. The piano becomes more than ever before a keyboard-operated percussion instrument. Cage devised the prepared piano as a one-man percussion band and Steve Reich describes his *Phase Patterns* as 'literally drumming on the keyboard' [. . . .]

Once you move to the exterior of the piano you find a number of wooden and metal surfaces which can be 'played'. Again it was Cage who pioneered this with the accompaniment to *The Wonderful Widow of Eighteen Springs* (1942) which is performed by the percussive action of the fingertips and knuckles on the closed keyboard lid. When you have realised that the piano does have an outside then a series of extensions of the concept 'piano' become possible. The instrument can be seen as just a large brown, mainly wooden object, on legs with wheels, of a particular shape, having curious mechanical innards and serving as a musical instrument. The inner mechanism may be completely disregarded (does it then cease to be a piano?—any complex object has a number of uses, most of them only partial) so that the piano can be treated as an object with surfaces to be hit or painted, have things thrown at, left on, hidden in, moved about or fed with hay [as in La Monte Young's *Piano Piece for David Tudor No. 1* (1960)]. (Needless to say it is in no sense a definition of experimental music that pianos should be used in this way—Feldman's keyboard writing, for instance, has always been every bit as 'sensitive' and 'musical' as Debussy's or Webern's.)

Cardew's *Memories of You* (1964), for piano solo, sums up this new approach to the piano. Its notation consists of a series of immature grand piano outlines on or off which tiny circles are placed. Each circle gives the location of a sound relative to a grand piano: the sound begins and/or ends at that point. Different kinds of circle indicate whether the sounds are to be made at floor level, above floor level or both. It is not specified whether the sounds are to be made on or with the piano, or with other instruments, or whether the sounds should be 'musical' or made on or with the environment. Thus the piano becomes a kind of 'umbrella' covering a range of sounding activities whose only direct connection with the piano may be the fact that they take place with reference to the 'piano space'.

## Music as Silence, Action, Observations—and Sounds

[In experimental music] the performer is not obliged to begin from the traditional starting point of causing sounds to be made and heard by means of a musical instrument. For when [the performer of *4′33″*] does not need to make sounds to give a musical performance; when Cage declares 'Let the notations refer to what is to be done, not to what is heard, or to be heard' [. . .]; when Ashley refers to time, not sounds, as the ruling metaphor of music; and when the slow-motion procedure of [Takehisa] Kosugi's *Anima 7* could be applied to any action—then we realize that in experimental music sounds no longer have a pre-emptive priority over not-sounds. Seeing and hearing no longer need to be considered separately, or be combined into 'music theatre' as an art-form separate from, say, instrumental music (as it tends to be with the avant garde). Theatre is all around us, says Cage, and it has always hung around music—if only you let your attention be 'distracted' from the sounds: Cage prefers the sight of the horn player emptying out the spit from his instrument to the sounds the orchestra is making; you may prefer to watch Bernstein with the volume control turned down to zero.

## Who Are the Performers?

Understandably, in view of the kind of tasks set, the extraordinary range of often demanding musical and para-musical skills called upon, experimental music has developed its own breed of performers and tightly-knit performing groups—Tudor, Rzewski, Tilbury, Cage, Cardew, [Howard] Skempton, Feldman (even), the Sonic Arts Union and the Scratch Orchestra, to whom experimental music is more than just a 'kind of music' to be performed; rather, a permanent creativity, a way of perceiving the world. Significantly only Tilbury and (in the earlier part of his career) Tudor in this list are strictly *performers only*; all the others are composers who took up performance—perhaps to protect their scores from the misunderstandings their very openness may encourage, or because they were attracted by the freedoms they allowed, or simply because the most direct way of realizing their performance-proposals was to realize them themselves. And in the same way, some performers, seeing how little work the act of composition may involve, have in turn become composers. The work of Rzewski and the Scratch Orchestra in the late sixties went a long way towards channelling and releasing the creativity everybody has within them.

michael nyman • 217

## Listening

The third component of Cage's compositional 'trinity', listening, implies the presence of someone involved in seeing and hearing. But need this be 'the audience' as we have come to consider it? For experimental music emphasizes an unprecedented fluidity of composer/performer/listener roles, as it breaks away from the standard sender/carrier/receiver information structure of other forms of Western music.

In experimental music the perceiver's role is more and more appropriated by the performer—not only in scores like Toshi Ichiyanagi's *Sapporo* (1962) which has a sign which tells the player to listen to what other players are doing, or in music like Christian Wolff's which needs a high degree of listening and concentration. Dick Higgins' account of the Brecht performance in the dark at the New School showed that the task (of performing two actions) had become less important for the individual than the perceptual and experiential situation that was brought about. (This does of course leave room for perceiving to be done by any 'audience' that may happen to be present.) And if the performer's participation is passive, involving observation rather than action, the work is not invalidated or changed. For Cage at least experimental music is not concerned with 'communication' as other music is considered to be. He once said: 'We are naïve enough to believe that words are the most efficient form of communication.' On another occasion he is reported to have said: 'Distinguish between that "old" music you speak of which has to do with *conceptions* and their *communication*, and this new music, which has to do with *perception* and the arousing of it in us. You don't have to fear from this new music that something is bad about your liking your own music.'

A task may have a far greater value for the performer than it has for the audience. Certain tasks may seem hermetically sealed to the listener, self-evident games whose rules are not publicly available, mysterious rites with professionally guarded secrets. For the performer the tasks may be self-absorbing, or of only private significance, so that the question of 'projection' is not part of his concern [. . . .]

The tasks of experimental music do not generally depend on, and are not markedly changed by, any response from an audience, although the atmosphere in which these tasks are accomplished may be completely changed by audience response. Experimental music has, if nothing else, at least the virtue of persistence which keeps it going throughout any uncalled-for reactions it quite often provokes. Hostile listeners quite often consider that their protest sounds are just as good as those of the performers; John Tilbury pointed out the difference on one such occasion: that whereas the audience's sounds were uncontrolled, instinctive gut-reactions, the performer knew exactly what he was doing, producing his sounds with consideration and control.

What then is the function of the audience in experimental music? Does 'listening's a third' in fact leave nothing for the listener to do? Quite the contrary the listener, too, has a far more creative and productive role than he had before. This follows from Cage's rejection of the notion of entertainment as 'being done to':

> Most people think that when they hear a piece of music, they're not doing anything but that something is being done to them. Now this is not true, and

we must arrange our music, we must arrange our art, we must arrange everything, I believe, so that people realize that they themselves are doing it, and not that something is being done to them.

Cage is not giving a mandate for audience participation: he is aiming at the fullest possible engagement of the listener and the testing of his perceptual faculties [. . . .]

*Focus*

[. . . .] Cage's crucial decentralization of musical and physical space brings music more into line with painting: 'Observe that the enjoyment of a modern painting carries one's attention not to a centre of interest but all over the canvas and not following any particular path. Each point on the canvas may be used as a beginning, continuing, or ending of one's observation of it.' So that if the listener does not have anything done *to* him, since the composer has not arranged things so that everything is done *for* him, the responsibility for how he hears or sees is placed firmly on the functioning of his own perception. The listener should be possessed ideally of an open, free-flowing mind, capable of assimilating in its own way a type of music that does not present a set of finalized, calculated, pre-focused, projected musical relationships and meanings. The listener may supply his own meanings if that is what he wants; or he may leave himself open to taking in any eventuality, bearing in mind George Brecht's proviso that any 'act of imagination or perception is in itself an arrangement, so there is no avoiding anyone making arrangements'. Since the listener may not be provided with the structural signposts (of various shapes and sizes, pointing in various directions) that he is given in other music, everyone has, according to Cage, the opportunity of 'structuring the experience differently from anybody else's in the audience. So the less we structure the occasion and the more it is like unstructured daily life, the greater will be the stimulus to the structuring faculty of each person in the audience. *"If we have done nothing then he will have everything to do.'"* (My italics) [. . . .]

*The Musical Consequences*

[. . . .] Cage:

I would assume that relations would exist between sounds as they would exist between people and that these relationships are more complex than any I would be able to prescribe. So by simply dropping that responsibility of making relationships I don't lose the relationship. I keep the situation in what you might call a natural complexity that can be observed in one way or another.

[. . . .] And this is the effect that processes have in experimental music: they are the most direct and straightforward means of simply setting sounds in motion; they are impersonal and external and so they do not have the effect of organizing sounds and integrating them, of creating relationships of harmony as the controlling faculty of the human mind does. If a composer sets up a process which allows each player to move through the material at his own speed, for example, it is impossible for him to draw things together into some kind of calculated image, a particular effect or pattern of logical connections. Rise and fall, loud and soft, may occur but they occur spontaneously, so that the old (and new) 'music of climax' is no longer the prevailing model. For all things are now equal and no one thing is given any priority over any other thing.

Merce Cunningham summed up the implications of this situation where priorities no longer exist, where every item is of equal value, as early as 1952:

Now I can't see that crisis any longer means a climax, unless we are willing to grant that every breath of wind has a climax (which I am), but then that obliterates climax being a surfeit of such. And since our lives, both by nature and by the newspapers, are so full of crisis that one is no longer aware of it, then it is clear that life goes on regardless, and further that each thing can be and is separate from each and every other, viz: the continuity of the newspaper headlines. Climax is for those who are swept by New Year's Eve.

One of the automatic consequences, so it appears, of the musical processes employed by experimental composers, is the effect of flattening out, de-focusing the musical perspective. This flatness may be brought about in a situation ranging from uniformity and minimum change—for example, the music of Steve Reich or John White, which consists of a constant or near-constant band of sound from which inessentials have been removed, to one of maximum change and multiplicity—for instance in Cage or the Scratch Orchestra where no attempt is made to harmonize or make coherent any number of hermetic and self-contained 'compartments'. (Cage said in 1961: 'We know two ways to unfocus attention: symmetry is one of them; the other is the over-all where each small part is a sample of what you find elsewhere. In either case, there is at least the possibility of looking anywhere, not just where someone arranged you should.')

Form thus becomes an assemblage, growth an accumulation of things that have piled-up in the time-space of the piece. (Non- or omni-directional) *succession* is the ruling procedure as against the (directional) *progression* of other forms of post-Renaissance art music. What the painter Brian O'Doherty wrote of Feldman's music can be seen to apply to the music of other experimental composers: 'Sounds do not progress, but merely heap up and accumulate in the same place (like Jasper Johns' numbers). This blurs and obliterates the past, and obliterating it, removes the possibility of a future.'

'What is, or seems to be, new in this music? [asked Christian Wolff in 1958]. One finds a concern for a kind of objectivity, almost anonymity—sound come into its own. The "music" is a resultant existing simply in the sounds we hear, given no impulse by expressions of self or personality. It is indifferent in motive, originating in no psychology nor in dramatic intentions, nor in literary or pictorial purposes. For at least some of these composers, then, the final intention is to be free of artistry and taste. But this need not make their work "abstract", for nothing, in the end, is denied. It is simply that personal expression, drama, psychology, and the like are not part of the composer's initial calculation: they are at best gratuitous.'

# 33

## *Introduction to* Themes & Variations

### JOHN CAGE

The tradition of "experimental music" extends back to Erik Satie, Charles Ives, Edgard Varèse, Henry Cowell, and Harry Partch. Yet John Cage (1912–1992; see also chaps 6 and 27) is undoubtedly the father of contemporary experimental music. It was Cage who defined experimental music not simply as music containing novel elements but as music that initiates sonic processes the outcomes of which are not known in advance. Cage's ideas and compositional practices remain revolutionary today and are constantly revisited by experimental composers and improvisers. In the following piece (the introduction to a 1982 collection of "mesostic" writings titled *Themes & Variations*), Cage sums up his aesthetic philosophy and worldview in a series of poetic aphorisms.

Nonintention (the acceptance of silence) leading to nature; renunciation of control; let sounds be sounds.

Each activity is centered in itself, i.e., composition, performance, and listening are different activities.

(Music is) instantaneous and unpredictable; nothing is accomplished by writing, hearing, or playing a piece of music; our ears are now in excellent condition.

A need for poetry.

Joyce: "Comedy is the greatest of arts because the joy of comedy is freest from desire and loathing."

Affirmation of life.

Purposeful purposelessness.

Art = imitation of nature in her manner of operation.

Coexistence of dissimilars; multiplicity; plurality of centers; "Split the stick, and there is Jesus."

Anonymity or selflessness of work (i.e., not self-expression).

A work should include its environment, is always experimental (unknown in advance).

Fluent, pregnant, related, obscure (nature of sound).

Empty mind.

No ideas of order.

No beginning, middle, or end (process, not object).

Unimpededness and interpenetration; no cause and effect.

Indeterminacy.

Opposites = parts of oneness.

To thicken the plot (Ramakrishna); his answer to the question: Why, if God is good, is there evil in the world?

Adventure (newness) necessary to creative action.

If the mind is disciplined (body too), the heart turns quickly from fear towards love (Eckhart).

Anything can follow anything else (providing nothing is taken as the basis).

Influence derives from one's own work (not from outside it).

Chance operations are a useful means; moksha.

Being led by a person, not a book; artha.

Love.

Right and wrong.

Non-measured time.

Process instead of object.

America has a climate for experimentation.

World is one world.

History is the story of original actions.

Move from zero.

All audible phenomena = material for music.

Impossibility of errorless work.

Spring, Summer, Fall, Winter (Creation, Preservation, Destruction, Quiescence).

Possibility of helping by doing nothing.

Music is not music until it is heard.

Music and dance together (and then other togethers).

Men are men; mountains are mountains before studying Zen. While studying Zen, things become confused. After studying Zen, men are men; mountains are mountains. What is the difference between before and after? No difference. Just the feet are a little off the ground (Suzuki).

If structure, rhythmic structure.

Boredom plus attention = becoming interested.

Principle underlying all of the solutions = question we ask.

Activity, not communication.

The nine permanent emotions (the heroic, the mirthful, the wondrous, the erotic; tranquility; sorrow, fear, anger, the odious).

The practicality of changing society derives from the possibility of changing the mind.

The giver of gifts (returning to the village having experienced no-mindedness).

Studying being interrupted.

Nothing-in-between.

Object is fact not symbol (no ideas).

Poetry is having nothing to say and saying it; we possess nothing.

Uncertainty of future.

Noises (underdog); changing music and society.

Not working = knowing. Working = not knowing.

Distrust of effectiveness of education.

HCE

It is, is cause for joy.

Earth has no escape from Heaven (Eckhart).

Mobility, immobility.

Highest purpose = no purpose. Vision = no vision. (In accord with nature.)

We are the oldest at having our airway of knowing nowness (Gertrude Stein).

Fluency in and out.

No split between spirit and matter.

Importance of being perplexed. Unpredictability.

Not being interrupted by shadows (by environment).

Theatre is closer to life than art or music.

Devotion.

Enlightened = not enlightened. Learning = learning we're not learning.

Breaking rules.

No use for value judgments.

We are all going in different directions.

Importance of no rules.

Going to extremes (Yuji Takahashi).

Absence of boredom.

Anarchy.

Meaninglessness as ultimate meaning.

Mind can change.

To do more rather than less.

To sober and quiet the mind thus making it susceptible to divine influences.

The means of thinking are exterior to the mind.

Art is criminal action.

Love = leaving space around loved one.

Utilities, not politics (intelligence; problem solving). Anarchy in a place that works.

Not just self- but social-realization.

Unemployment (cf. artists).

Giving up ownership, substituting use.

Whole society (including, e.g., the mad: they speak the truth).

Religious attitude (George Herbert Mead); world consciousness.

More with less.

Music is permanent; only listening is intermittent (Thoreau).

Invention.

Not things, but minds.

Dealing with 1, not 2.

To make a garden empty-minded.

Music = no music.

Inclusive, not exclusive: aperiodic; no vision, etc.

Objective within; going in all directions.

Demilitarization of language (no government).

A music that needs no rehearsal.

Feet on the ground.

To set all well afloat. (Thoreau: Yes and No are lies. The only true answer will set all well afloat.)

Art's self-alteration.

Impossibility of repeated actions; loss of memory. To reach these two's a goal (Duchamp).

Complexity of nature; giving up simplicity of soul, vision, etc.

Constellation of ideas (five as a minimum).

Problems of music (vision) only solved when silence (non-vision) is taken as the basis.

Giving unto others what they wish to be given, not what you would wish to be given (alteration of the Golden Rule).

Use all solutions; do everything!

Inactivity (the camera).

Goal is not to have a goal.

# 34

## Generating and Organizing Variety in the Arts

### BRIAN ENO

In the late 1960s and throughout the 1970s, as his successful career in pop music was getting underway, Brian Eno (1948– ; see also chaps. 17 and 22) was immersed in the British "experimental music" scene. He performed in Cornelius Cardew's Scratch Orchestra and Gavin Bryars's Portsmouth Sinfonia—experimental orchestras that welcomed amateur musicians. In 1975, Eno founded Obscure Records, a label dedicated to the dissemination of experimental music by composers such as Bryars, Christopher Hobbs, David Toop, Max Eastley, John Adams, Michael Nyman, Harold Budd, and others. In its first year, Obscure issued Eno's own experimental work, *Discreet Music*, which explored his interest in self-generating and self-regulating systems. In the following essay, written in 1976, Eno draws on cybernetic theory and evolutionary biology to contrast experimental composition and performance with its classical antecedents.

A musical score is a statement about organization; it is a set of devices for organizing behaviour toward producing sounds. That this observation was not so evident in classical composition indicates that organization was not then an important focus of compositional attention. Instead, the organizational unit (be it the orchestra or the string quartet or the relationship of a man to a piano) remained fairly static for two centuries while compositional attention was directed at using these given units to generate specific results by supplying them with specific instructions.

In order to give more point to the examination of experimental music that follows, I should like to detail some of the aspects and implications of the paradigm of classical organization—the orchestra. A traditional orchestra is a ranked pyramidal hierarchy of the same kind as the armies that existed contemporary to it. The hierarchy of rank is in this pattern: conductor, leader of the orchestra; section principals; section subprincipals; and, finally, rank-and-file members. Occasionally a soloist will join the upper echelons of this system; and it is implied, of course, that the composer with his intentions and aspirations has absolute, albeit temporary, control over the whole structure and its behaviour. This ranking, as does military ranking, reflects varying degrees of responsibility; conversely, it reflects varying degrees of constraint on behavior. Ranking has another effect: like perspective in painting, it creates "focus" and "point of view." A listener is given the impression that there are a foreground and a background to the music and cannot fail to notice that most of the "high-responsibility" events take place in the foreground, to which the background is an ambience or counterpoint.[1] This is to say that the number of perceptual positions available to the listener is likely to be limited. The third observation I should like to make about the ranking system in the orchestra is this: it predicates the use of trained musicians. A trained musician is, at the minimum, one who will produce a predictable sound given a specific instruction. His training teaches him to be capable of operating precisely like all the other members of his rank. It trains him, in fact, to subdue some of his own natural variety and thus to increase his reliability (predictability).

I shall be using the term *variety* frequently in this essay and I should like to attempt some definition of it now. It is a term taken from cybernetics (the science of organization) and it was originated by W. R. Ashby.[2] The *variety* of a system is the total range of its outputs, its total range of behavior. All organic systems are probabilistic: they exhibit variety, and an organism's flexibility (its adaptability) is a function of the amount of variety that it can generate. Evolutionary adaptation is a result of the interaction of this probabilistic process with the demands of the environment. By producing a *range* of outputs evolution copes with a *range* of possible futures. The environment in this case is a *variety-reducer* because it "selects" certain strains by allowing them to survive and reproduce, and filters out others. But, just as it is evident that an organism will (by its material nature) and must (for its survival) generate variety, it is also true that this variety must not be unlimited. That is to say, we require for successful evolution the transmission of *identity* as well as the transmission of *mutation*. Or conversely, in a transmission of evolutionary information, what is important is not only that you get it right but also that you get it slightly wrong, and that the deviations or mutations that are useful can be encouraged and reinforced.

My contention is that a primary focus of experimental music has been toward its own organization, and toward its own capacity to produce and control variety, and to assimilate "natural variety"—the "interference value" of the environment. Experimental music, unlike classical (or avant-garde) music, does not typically offer instructions toward highly specific results, and hence does not normally specify wholly repeatable configurations of sound. It is this lack of interest in the *precise* nature of the piece that has led to the (I think) misleading description of this kind of music as *indeterminate*. I hope to show that an experimental composition aims to set in motion a system or organism that will generate unique (that is, not necessarily repeatable) outputs, but that, at the same time, seeks to limit the range of these outputs. This is a tendency toward a "class of goals" rather than a particular goal, and it is distinct from the "goalless behaviour" (indeterminacy) idea that gained currency in the 1960s.

I should like to deal at length with a particular piece of experimental music that exemplifies this shift in orientation. The piece is Paragraph 7 of *The Great Learning*[3] by Cornelius Cardew, and I have chosen this not only because it is a compendium of organizational techniques but also because it is available on record[4] [. . . .] I should point out that implicit in the score is the idea that it may be performed by *any* group of people (whether or not trained to sing). The version available on record is performed by a mixed group of musicians and art students, and my experience of the piece is based on four performances of it in which I have taken part.

Cardew's score is very simple. It is written for any group of performers (it does not require trained singers). There is a piece of text (from Confucius) which is divided into 24 separate short phrases, each of one to three words in length. Beside each phrase is a number, which specifies the number of repetitions for that line, and then another number telling you how many times that line should be sung loudly. The singing is mostly soft.

All singers use exactly the same set of instructions. They are asked to sing each line of the text the given number of times, each time for the length of a breath, and on one note. The singers start together at a signal, and each singer chooses a note for the first line randomly, staying on it until the completion of the repetitions of the line.

The singer then moves on to the next line, choosing a new note. The choice of this note is the important thing. The score says: "Choose a note that you can hear being sung by a colleague. If there is no note, or only the note you have just been singing, or only notes that you are unable to sing, choose your note for the next line freely. Do not sing the same note on two consecutive lines. Each singer progresses through the text at his own speed."

A cursory examination of the score will probably create the impression that the piece would differ radically from one performance to another, because the score appears to supply very few *precise* (that is, quantifiable) constraints on the nature of each performer's behavior, and because the performers themselves (being of variable ability) are not "reliable" in the sense that a group of trained musicians might be. The fact that this does not happen is of considerable interest, because it suggests that *somehow a set of controls that are not stipulated in the score arise in performance* and that these "automatic" controls are the real determinants of the nature of the piece.

In order to indicate that this proposition is not illusory, I now offer a description of how the piece might develop if *only* the scored instructions affected its outcome. I hope that by doing this I shall be able to isolate a difference between this hypothetical performance and a real performance of the piece and that this difference will offer clues as to the nature of the "automatic" controls.

*Hypothetical performance.* The piece begins with a rich sustained discord ("choose any note for your first note"). As the point at which singers move onto their next line and next note is governed by individual breath lengths ("sing each line for the length of a breath"), it is probable that they will be changing notes at different times. Their choice of note is affected by three instructions: "do not sing the same note on two consecutive lines," "sing a note that you can hear," and, if for some reason neither of these instructions can be observed, "choose your next note freely." Now, let's propose that there are twenty singers, and that by some chance they have all chosen different first notes. Presumably one of them reaches the end of his first line before any other singer. As he cannot repeat his own previous note, he has an absolute maximum of nineteen notes to choose from for his "next note." He chooses one, and reduces the "stock" of notes available to nineteen. The next singer to change has a choice of eighteen notes. By a continuation of this procedure, one would expect a gradual reduction of different notes in the piece until such time as there were too few notes available for the piece to continue without the arbitrary introduction of new notes in accordance with the third of the three pitch instructions. With a larger number of singers this process of reduction might well last throughout the piece. So, in this hypothetical performance, the overall shape of the piece would consist of a large stock of random notes thinning down to a small, even, occasionally replenished stock of equally random notes (as they are either what is left of the initial stock or the random additions to it).

*Real performance.* The piece begins with the same rich discord and *rapidly* (that is, before the end of the first line is reached) thins itself down to a complex but not notably dissonant chord. Soon after this, it "settles" at a particular level of variety that is much higher than that in the hypothetical performance and that tends to revolve more or less harmonically around a drone note. This level of variety is fairly closely maintained throughout the rest of the piece. It is rare that performers need to resort to the "choose your next note freely" instruction, and, except in the case of small numbers of singers, this instruction appears to be redundant.[5] This is because new notes are always being introduced into the piece regardless of any intention on the part of individual performers to do so. And this observation points up the presence of a set of "accidents" that are at work to replenish the stock of notes in the piece. The first of these has to do with the "unreliability" of a mixed group of singers. At one extreme it is quite feasible that a tone-deaf singer would hear a note and, following the primary pitch instruction to "sing any note that you can hear," would, "match" it with a new note. Another singer might unconsciously transpose a note into an octave in which it is easier for him to sing, or might sing a note that is harmonically a close relative (a third or a fifth) to it. A purely external physical event will also tend to introduce new notes: the phenomenon of beat frequency. A *beat frequency* is a new note formed when two notes close to each other in pitch are sounded. It is mathematically and not harmonically related to them. These are three of the ways by which new material is introduced.

Apart from the "variety-reducing" clauses in the score ("sing a note that you can hear," "do not sing the same note on two consecutive lines"), some others arise in performance. One of these has to do with the acoustic nature of the room in which the performance is taking place. If it is a large room (and most rooms that can accommodate performances on the scale on which this piece normally occurs are large), then it is likely to have a *resonant frequency*. This is defined as the pitch at which an enclosure resonates, and what it means in practice is this: a note sounded at a given amplitude in a room whose resonant frequency corresponds to the frequency of the note will *sound louder* than any other note at the same amplitude. Given a situation, then, where a number of notes are being sounded at fairly even amplitude, whichever one corresponds to the resonant frequency of the room will sound louder than any of the others. In Paragraph 7 this fact creates a statistical probability that the piece will drift toward being centered on an environmentally determined note. This may be the drone note to which I alluded earlier.

Another important variety reducer is preference ("taste"). Because performers are often in a position to choose between a fairly wide selection of notes, their own cultural histories and predilections will be an important factor in which "strains" of the stock they choose to reinforce (and, by implication, which they choose to filter out). This has another aspect; it is extremely difficult unless you are tone deaf (or a trained singer) to maintain a note that is very discordant with its surroundings. You generally adjust the note almost involuntarily so that it forms some harmonic relationship to its surroundings. This helps explain why the first dissonant chord rapidly thins out.

In summary, then, the generation, distribution, and control of notes within this piece are governed by the following: one specific instruction ("do not sing the same note on two consecutive lines"), one general instruction ("sing any note that you can hear"), two physiological factors (tone-deafness and transposition), two physical factors (beat frequencies and resonant frequency), and the cultural factor of "preference." Of course, there are other parameters of the piece (particularly amplitude) that are similarly controlled and submit to the same techniques of analysis, and the "breathing" aspects of the piece might well give rise to its most important characteristic—its meditative calm and tranquillity. But what I have mentioned above should be sufficient to indicate that something quite different from classical compositional technique is taking place: the composer, instead of ignoring or subduing the variety generated in performance, has constructed the piece so that this variety is really the substance of the music.

Perhaps the most concise description of this kind of composition, which characterizes much experimental music, is offered in a statement made by the cybernetician Stafford Beer. He writes: "Instead of trying to specify it in full detail, you specify it only somewhat. You then ride on the dynamics of the system in the direction you want to go."[6] In the case of the Cardew piece, the "dynamics of the system" is its interaction with the environmental, physiological, and cultural climate surrounding its performance.

The English composer Michael Parsons provides another view on this kind of composition:

The idea of one and the same activity being done simultaneously by a number of people, so that everyone does it slightly differently, "unity" becoming "multiplicity," gives one a very economical form of notation—it is only necessary to specify one procedure and the variety comes from the way everyone does it differently. This is an example of making use of "hidden resources" in the sense of natural individual differences (rather than talents or abilities) which is completely neglected in classical concert music, though not in folk music.[7]

This movement toward using natural variety as a compositional device is exemplified in a piece by Michael Nyman called *1-100* (Obscure 6). In this piece, four pianists each play the same sequence of one hundred chords descending slowly down the keyboard. A player is instructed to move on to his next chord only when he can no longer hear his last. As this judgment is dependent on a number of variables (how loud the chord was played, how good the hearing of the player is, what the piano is like, the point at which you decide that the chord is no longer audible), the four players rapidly fall out of sync with one another. What happens after this is that unique and delicate clusters of up to four different chords are formed, or rapid sequences of chords are followed by long silences. This is an elegant use of the compositional technique that Parsons has specified, not least because it, like the Cardew piece, is extremely beautiful to listen to—a factor that seems to carry little critical weight at present.

Composition of this kind tends to create a perceptual shift in a listener as major as (and concomitant with) the compositional shift. It is interesting that on recordings, these two pieces both have "fade" endings (the Cardew piece also has a fade beginning), as this implies not that the piece has finished but that it is *continuing out of earshot*. It is only rock music that has really utilized the compositional value of the fade-out: these pieces use it as a convenience in the sense that both were too long for a side of a record. But a fade-out is quite in keeping with the general quality of the pieces and indicates an important characteristic that they share with other experimental music: that the music is a section from a hypothetical continuum and that it is not especially directional: it does not exhibit strong "progress" from one point (position, theme, statement, argument) to a resolution. To test the validity of this assumption, imagine a fade-out ending halfway through Beethoven's Ninth Symphony. Much of the energy of classical music arises from its movement from one musical idea to another—the theme and variation idea—and this movement is directional in the sense that the history and probable futures of the piece have a bearing on the perception of what one is hearing at the present.

Experimental music, however, has become concerned with the simultaneous permutation of a limited number of elements at a moment in time as well as the relations between a number of points in time. I think also that it has tended to reduce the time-spans over which compositional ideas are developed; and this has led to the use of cyclic forms such as that in Gavin Bryars' *Jesus' Blood Never Failed Me Yet.* (It is interesting that this piece, Paragraph 7, and *1-100* are all based on "found material"; and in each case the focus of the composer's attention is toward *reorganizing* given material. There is a special compositional liberty in this situation.)

I do not wish to subscribe to the view that the history of art is a series of dramatic revolutions where one idea overthrows another. I have made some distinctions between classical and experimental compositional techniques, and between the perceptual modes that each encourages in a listener, but I do not wish to propose that the development from one to the other is a simple upward progression. I have ascribed characteristics to these two musics as though they were mutually exclusive, when virtually any example will show that aspects of *each* orientation exist in any piece. What I am arguing for is a view of musical development as a process of generating new hybrids. To give an example: one might propose a "scale of orientations" where, on the right hand, one placed the label "Tending to subdue variety in performance" and, on the left, "Tending to encourage variety in performance." It would be very difficult to find pieces that occupied the extreme polarities of this scale, and yet it is not difficult to locate distinct pieces at points along the scale. A classical sonata, if only by virtue of the shortcomings of musical notation, allows some variety in performance.[8] On the other (left) hand, the most random of *random music* (whatever that term meant) is constrained in its range by all sorts of factors down to the straightforward laws of physics. So we might place the Cardew piece toward the left, but not as far left as, say, a free-jazz improvisation. A scale of this kind does not tell us much about the music that we place on it, but its function is to remind us to think in terms of hybrids rather than discontinuities.

Given the above reservation about polarizing musical ideas into opposing camps, I should now like to describe two organizational structures. My point is not that classical music is one and contemporary music the other, but that each is a group of hybrids tending toward one of the two structures. At one extreme, then, is this type of organization: a rigidly ranked, skill-oriented structure moving sequentially through an environment assumed to be passive (static) toward a resolution already defined and specified. This type of organization regards the environment (and its variety) as a set of emergencies and seeks to neutralize or disregard this variety. An observer is encouraged (both by his knowledge of the ranking system and by the differing degrees of freedom accorded to the various parts of the organization) to direct his attention at the upper echelons of the ranks. He is given an impression of a hierarchy of value. The organization has the feel of a well-functioning machine: it operates accurately and predictably for one class of tasks but it is not adaptive. It is not self-stabilizing and does not easily assimilate change or novel environmental conditions. Furthermore, it requires a particular type of instruction in order to operate. In cybernetics this kind of instruction is known as an *algorithm*. Stafford Beer's definition of the term is "a comprehensive set of instructions for reaching a known goal"; so the prescription "turn left at the lights and walk twenty yards" is an algorithm, as is the prescription "play a C-sharp for a quaver followed by an E for a semiquaver."[9] It must be evident that such specific strategies can be devised only when a precise concept of form (or identity, or goal, or direction) already exists, and when it is taken for granted that this concept is static and singular.

Proposing an organizational structure opposite to the one described above is valueless because we would probably not accord it the name *organization:* whatever the term does connote, it must include some idea of constraint and some idea of identity. So what I shall now describe is the type of organization that typifies certain organic systems and whose most important characteristics hinge on this fact: that changing environments require adaptive organisms. Now, the relationship between an organism and its environment is a sophisticated and complex one, and this is not the place to deal with it. Suffice it to say, however, that an adaptive organism is one that contains built-in mechanisms for monitoring (and adjusting) its own behaviour in relation to the alterations in its surroundings. This type of organism must be capable of operating from a different type of instruction, as the real coordinates of the surroundings are either too complex to specify, or are changing so unpredictably that no particular strategy (or specific plan for a particular future) is useful. The kind of instruction that is necessary here is known as an *heuristic*, and is defined as "a set of instructions for searching out an unknown goal by exploration, which continuously or repeatedly evaluates progress according to some known criterion."[10] To use Beer's example: if you wish to tell someone how to reach the top of a mountain that is shrouded in mist, the heuristic "keep going up" will get him there. An organism operating in this way must have something more than a centralized control structure. It must have a responsive network of subsystems capable of autonomous behaviour, and it must regard the irregularities of the environment as a set of opportunities around which it will shape and adjust its own identity.

What I have tried to suggest in this essay is a technique for discussing contemporary music in terms of its functioning. I have concentrated primarily on one piece of music because I wanted to show this technique at work on one specific problem and because I feel that the technique can thereafter quite easily be generalized to deal with other activities. I do not wish to limit the scope of this approach to music, although because music is a social art that therefore generates some explicit organizational information, it lends itself readily to such analysis. I have in the past discussed not only the fine arts but also, for example, the evolution of contemporary sporting practices and the transition from traditional to modern military tactics by asking the same kinds of questions directed at the organizational level of the activities. It does not surprise me that, at the systems level, these apparently disparate evolutions are very accurate analogues for each other.

In his book *Man's Rage for Chaos* Morse Peckham writes: "Art is the exposure to the tensions and problems of the false world such that man may endure exposing himself to the tensions and problems of the real world."[11] As the variety of the environment magnifies in both time and space and as the structures that were thought to describe the operation of the world become progressively more unworkable, other concepts of organization must become current. These concepts will base themselves on the assumption of change rather than stasis and on the assumption of probability rather than certainty. I believe that contemporary art is giving us the feel for this outlook.

## NOTES

1. This ranking is most highly developed in classical Indian music, where the tamboura plays a drone role for the sitar. I think it no coincidence that Indian society reflected the same sharp definition of roles in its caste system.

2. W. Ross Ashby, *An Introduction to Cybernetics* (1956; reprint ed., London: University Paperbacks, 1964).

3. Each paragraph corresponds to one in the Confucian classic of the same title.

4. [Currently available on CD as Cornelius Cardew and the Scratch Orchestra, *The Great Learning*, Organ of Corti 21—Eds.]

5. A number of the score instructions seem redundant; all of those concerning the leader, for example, make almost no difference to the music.

6. Stafford Beer, *Brain of the Firm: The Managerial Cybernetics of Organization* (London: Allen Lane, 1972), 69.

7. Michael Parsons, quoted in Michael Nyman, *Experimental Music: Cage and Beyond* (see chap. 32, above).

8. It is interesting to observe that the sound of a string orchestra results from minute variations of tuning, vibrato, and timbre. This is why electronic simulations of strings have not been notably successful.

9. Beer, *Brain of the Firm*, 305.

10. Beer, *Brain of the Firm*, 306.

11. Morse Peckham, *Man's Rage for Chaos* (New York: Schocken Books, 1967), 314.

# 35

# A Scratch Orchestra: Draft Constitution

## CORNELIUS CARDEW

Cornelius Cardew (1936–81) was a central figure in British vanguard music during the 1960s and '70s. From 1958 to 1960, he worked as an assistant to Karlheinz Stockhausen and György Ligeti at the newly established Studio for Electronic Music in Cologne. While in Cologne, Cardew witnessed a set of concerts by John Cage and David Tudor that deeply affected him, leading him to view the European avant-garde tradition as elitist and moribund. (Cardew later wrote a polemical book titled *Stockhausen Serves Imperialism*.) He abandoned serial composition and turned to indeterminate and experimental approaches. In 1965, Cardew joined the free improvising collective AMM, for which he wrote his massive graphic score *Treatise* (1963-67). In 1969, Cardew founded the Scratch Orchestra, a large, experimental musical ensemble composed of musicians and non-musicians. A few years later, Cardew came to see even the Scratch Orchestra as too musically insular and elitist. He began composing in a Romantic, populist folk style and later joined the political rock band People's Liberation Music. Cardew's life was cut short in 1981 when he was killed by a hit-and-run driver. In the following piece, he defines the term "Scratch Orchestra" and describes its experimental procedures.

*Definition*: A Scratch Orchestra is a large number of enthusiasts pooling their resources (not primarily material resources) and assembling for action (music-making, performance, edification).

*Note:* The word music and its derivatives are here not understood to refer exclusively to sound and related phenomena (hearing, etc.). What they do refer to is flexible and depends entirely on the members of the Scratch Orchestra.

*The Scratch Orchestra* intends to function in the public sphere, and this function will be expressed in the form of—for lack of a better word—concerts. In rotation (starting with the youngest) each member will have the option of designing a concert. If the option is taken up, all details of that concert are in the hands of that person or his delegates; if the option is waived the details of the concert will be determined by random methods, or by voting (a vote determines which of these two). The material of these concerts may be drawn, in part or wholly, from the basic repertory categories outlined below.

## 1. Scratch music

Each member of the orchestra provides himself with a notebook (or Scratchbook) in which he notates a number of accompaniments, performable continuously for indefinite periods. The number of accompaniments in each book should be equal to or greater than the current number of members of the orchestra. An accompaniment is defined as music that allows a solo (in the event of one occurring) to be appreciated as such. The notation may be accomplished using any means—verbal, graphic, musical, collage, etc.—and should be regarded as a period of training: never notate more than one accompaniment in a day. If many ideas arise on one day they may all be incorporated in one accompaniment. The last accompaniment in the list has the status of a solo and if used should only be used as such. On the addition of further items, what was previously a solo is relegated to the status of an accompaniment, so that at any time each player has only one solo and that his most recent. The sole differentiation between a solo and an accompaniment is in the mode of playing.

The performance of this music can be entitled *Scratch Overture*, *Scratch Interlude* or *Scratch Finale* depending on its position in the concert.

## 2. Popular Classics

Only such works as are familiar to several members are eligible for this category. Particles of the selected works will be gathered in Appendix 1. A particle could be: a page of score, a page or more of the part for one instrument or voice, a page of an arrangement, a thematic analysis, a gramophone record, etc.

The technique of performance is as follows: a qualified member plays the given particle, while the remaining players join in as best they can, playing along, contributing whatever they can recall of the work in question, filling the gaps of memory with improvised variational material.

As is appropriate to the classics, avoid losing touch with the reading player (who may terminate the piece at his discretion), and strive to act concertedly rather than independently. These works should be programmed under their original titles.

## 3. Improvisation Rites

A selection of the rites in *Nature Study Notes* will be available in Appendix 2. Members should constantly bear in mind the possibility of contributing new rites. An improvisation rite is not a musical composition; it does not attempt to influence the music that will be played; at most it may establish a community of feeling, or a communal starting-point, through ritual. Any suggested rite will be given a trial run and thereafter left to look after itself. Successful rites may well take on aspects of folklore, acquire nicknames, etc.

Free improvisation may also be indulged in from time to time.

## 4. Compositions

Appendix 3 will contain a list of compositions performable by the orchestra. Any composition submitted by a Member of the orchestra will be given a trial run in which all terms of the composition will be adhered to as closely as possible. Unless emphatically rejected, such compositions will probably remain as compositions in Appendix 3. If such a composition is repeatedly acclaimed it may qualify for inclusion in the Popular Classics, where it would be represented by a particle only, and adherence to the original terms of the composition would be waived.

## 5. Research Project

A fifth repertory category may be evolved through the Research Project, an activity obligatory for all the members of the Scratch Orchestra, to ensure its cultural expansion.

*The Research Project.* The universe is regarded from the viewpoint of travel. This means that an infinite number of research vectors are regarded as hypothetically travellable. Travels may be undertaken in many dimensions, e.g. temporal, spatial, intellectual, spiritual, emotional. I imagine any vector will be found to impinge on all these dimensions at some point or other. For instance, if your research vector is the *Tiger*, you could be involved in time (since the tiger represents an evolving species), space (a trip to the zoo), intellect (the tiger's biology), spirit (the symbolic values acquired by the tiger) and emotion (your subjective relation to the animal).

The above is an intellectual structure, so for a start let's make the research vector a word or group of words rather than an object or an impression etc. A record of research is kept in the Scratchbook and this record may be made available to all.

From time to time a journey will be proposed (Journey to Mars, Journey to the Court of Wu Ti, Journey to the Unconscious, Journey to West Ham, etc.). A discussion will suffice to provide a rough itinerary (e.g. embarkation at Cape Kennedy, type of vehicle to be used, number of hours in space, choice of a landing site, return to earth or not, etc.).

Members whose vectors are relevant to this journey can pursue the relevance and consider the musical application of their research; members whose vectors are irrelevant (research on rocket fuels won't help with a journey to the Court of Wu Ti) can put themselves at the disposal of the others for the musical realization of their research.

A date can be fixed for the journey, which will take the form of a performance.

*Conduct of research.* Research should be through direct experience rather than academic; neglect no channels. The aim is: by direct contact, imagination, identification and study to get as close as possible to the object of your research. Avoid the mechanical accumulation of data; be constantly awake to the possibility of inventing new research techniques. The record in the Scratchbook should be a record of your activity rather than an accumulation of data. That means: the results of your research are in you, not in the book.

*Example:*

| Research vector | Research record |
|---|---|
| *The Sun* | *29.vi. Looked up astronomical data in* EB *& made notes to the accpt of dustmotes (symbol of* EB*) and sunbeams* |
| | *1-28. viii. Holiday in the Bahamas to expose myself to the sun* |
| | *29.vii. Saw 'the Sun' as a collection of 6 letters and wrote out the 720 combinations of them.* |
| | *1.viii. Got interested in Sun's m. or f. gender in different languages, and thence to historical personages regarded as the Sun (like Mao Tse-Tung). Sought an astrological link between them.* |
| Astrology | 3.viii. Had my horoscope cast by Mme Jonesky of Gee's Court. |
| | etc. |

(note that several vectors can run together)
(the facing page should be left blank for notes on eventual musical realizations)

*Spare time activity* for orchestra members: each member should work on the construction of a unique mechanical, musical, electronic or other instrument.

## APPENDICES

Appendix 1 *Popular Classics:*
Particles from:  Beethoven, *Pastoral Symphony*
 Mozart, *Eine Kleine Nachtmusik*
 Rachmaninov, *Second Piano Concerto*
 J. S. Bach, *Sheep may safely graze*
 Cage, *Piano Concert*
 Brahms, *Requiem*
 Schoenberg, *Pierrot Lunaire*
 etc.
(blank pages for additions)

Appendix 2 *Improvisation Rites from the book 'Nature Study Notes'* (two examples must suffice):
1. Initiation of the pulse
Continuation of the pulse
Deviation by means of accentuation, decoration, contradiction
—HOWARD SKEMPTON

14. All seated loosely in a circle, each player shall write or draw on each of the ten fingernails of the player on his left.

No action or sound is to be made by a player after his fingernails have received this writing or drawing, other than music.

Closing rite: each player shall erase the marks from the fingernails of another player. Your participation in the music ceases when the marks have been erased from your fingernails.

(Groups of two or more late-comers may use the same rite to join in an improvisation that is already in progress.)

(blank pages for additions)

—RICHARD REASON

Appendix 3 *List of compositions:*
La Monte Young, *Poem*
Von Biel, *World II*
Terry Riley, *In C*
Christopher Hobbs, *Voicepiece*
Stockhausen, *Aus den Sieben Tagen*
Wolff, *Play*
Cage, *Variations VI*
etc.
(blank pages for additions)

Appendix 4 *Special Projects and supplementary material*
(blank pages)

[. . . .]

# 36

## The Generation Game: Experimental Music and Digital Culture

### DAVID TOOP

David Toop (1949– ; see also chap. 51) is among the most innovative and wide-ranging writers on contemporary music. His pioneering book on HipHop, *Rap Attack*, first appeared in 1984. A decade later, Toop published *Ocean of Sound* (1995), a poetic survey of contemporary musical life from Debussy through Ambient, Techno, and drum 'n' bass. Since the 1970s, Toop has also been an important presence on the British experimental and improvised music scene. With sound artist Max Eastley, he recorded *New and Rediscovered Musical Instruments* for Brian Eno's Obscure label in 1975. Over the past decade, he has released eight other solo albums and collaborated with an extraordinary variety of musicians, among them John Zorn, Evan Parker, Derek Bailey, Scanner, Flying Lizards, Prince Far-I, Witchman, and others. In 2001, Toop curated *Sonic Boom*, the UK's largest-ever exhibition of sound art; and in 2002, he curated the double-CD set *Not Necessarily English Music: A Collection of Experimental Music from Great Britain, 1960-1977*. In this article, Toop examines the ways in which the Internet and digital technology are making possible a renewal of experimental musical activity.

In 1986, Jae-eun Choi, a Korean artist and film maker, initiated a series of experiments that she calls the World Underground Project. She buried sheets of Japanese paper in the soil of 11 locations around the world. The first pieces were excavated from the site in Kyong-Ju, Korea, after four years. Others, including those buried at sites in Kenya, France and Italy, were still underground in 1998. Japanese paper begins with a strong character, before a single mark is made on, or into its surface. The absorbency and texture encourages accident and generates unpredictability. Those sheets that were excavated had been transformed by the years of their interment into gorgeous maps of organic growth [. . . .]

Now think about Japanese paper in relation to compact discs. Unless the silver disc malfunctions or aborts, the promise of this carrier is to remain true to an original state throughout its so-called life. False optimism, no doubt, but aside from the occasions when they go drastically wrong, CDs don't exhibit the slight variations in playback sound and gradual deteriorations and fluctuations that characterise vinyl and tape. A CD is more or less a dead thing, or seems that way until it really dies.

At the polar opposite of that inertia is Christian Marclay's *Record Without A Cover*. Marclay's instruction in how to initiate the process of *Record Without A Cover* was embossed on the surface of the vinyl: "Do not store in a protective package." I've had mine since the mid-80s. Two years ago I used to lay it on a pile of 12" singles by the window. Heat absorbent black vinyl, it made an attractively warm bullseye on which our cat would sit and gaze out of the window at birds in the cherry tree. A lot of unmentionable stuff got embedded into the grooves through that particular example of functionality, and when she was out trying to catch those birds, sunshine warped the disc into a picturesque wave. And then there's the dust, collecting on the record, as a record of my ambivalent attitude to order.

Just from a simple instruction, a supposedly 'final' artefact is transformed into an ongoing musical piece that the initiator cannot control. Like an awful lot of music enthusiasts, in my own house I'm vanishing into a vast housing estate of miniature tower blocks built from CDs. The more oppressive this static, one-sided arrangement seems to become, the more I'm interested in the idea of a music that can generate itself over time, giving itself up to the user in the way that Jae-eun Choi's Japanese paper surrenders to a colony of micro-organisms under the earth [. . . .]

An email from Richard Ross, programmer for Markus Popp's Oval Process, asks me a question: "I was wondering what constituted generative music, and were computers necessary? I came to the conclusion," he writes from California, "that if you dispensed with computers as a component of it, then things like windchimes and Aeolian harps might arguably fall into that camp. Other possibilities might be Cage's *Imaginary Landscape No. 4* as a live performance. If generative music is music created on the fly, by some kind of rule-based system, then these things follow very loose sort of rules, but rules none the less."

In issue five of *Musics* magazine, published in 1976, sound sculptor Max Eastley wrote a short history of Aeolian harps, including the story of St. Dunstan, who narrowly avoided incineration at the stake in the Middle Ages for the suspiciously demonic crime of making a harp that played by itself. Eastley also related the interesting case of Ichabod Angus Mackenzie, a sculptor and musician who produced 53 wind sound sculptures in 1934. "During an interview he was asked if it disturbed him to leave his instruments performing alone without a human audience," Eastley wrote. "He replied, 'That's up to humans. They're never without an audience.'"

This raises some of the core issues challenged by 20th century music, and 20th century thought in general: the relationship of the composer to the audience, for example, or the use of chance and accident in the creation of music; the construction of feedback systems or self-generating and adaptive mechanisms that shape sound; the exertion or abdication of control of a musical result; the modelling of music based on ecosystems and similar complex environments and the setting in motion of events that question the definition of music as a cultural production distinguished from noise or unorganised sound by human agency and intentionality.

In the 21st century, such ideas have been expanded dramatically by the evolution of the Internet, itself a self-propagating Web lacking any central control. *Sound Drifting* was a large scale generative sound installation curated by Colin Fallows and Heidi Grundmann for the Ars Electronica 99 festival. A web of sub-projects, sourced from six different countries, could be heard simultaneously and continuously, either onsite in Linz, Austria, online as a virtual installation and on air via Austrian National Radio [. . . .]

"More recently," the introduction to *Sound Drifting* explained, "there has been a growing interest in generative systems by artists working with the Internet, especially using sound, but increasingly with the appropriation of games software, search engines and so forth. Some of this work is highly critical of the ubiquity and unseemly power of generative systems in modern decision making. But the most conspicuous cultural use of generative systems has been in the field of music—which means that the word 'generative,' when used in relation to sound, usually causes people to think of music. However, although some music drifted in, *Sound Drifting* was not about 'music'—nor was it conceived as a concert hall, showcase or gallery space for the works of individual artists. *Sound Drifting* was about networking, communication and collaboration; about control-sharing between artists, users and machines; about letting go of one's own art and making ecological use of existing things; about listening to the world without adding to it; about the different concepts of duration and evolving processes at work in the material and immaterial realities of which we are part; about the aesthetics of different but connectable sounds, images, texts appearing on line—on air—on site as fugitive interfaces to a complex, invisible and not yet properly understood system of data processing."

In March [2001], Brian Eno gave a lecture at the ICA in London, linking his ideas on generative music with the model of John Conway's Game of Life. Conway, a Cambridge mathematician, invented Life as a cellular automaton, a game regulated by three logical rules: (1) Every counter with two or three neighboring counters survives to the next generation (i.e., the next move). (2) Every counter with zero or one neighbors 'dies' (of loneliness), and every counter with four or more neighbors dies (of overcrowding). (3) Every empty cell with exactly three neighboring occupied cells gives birth to a new counter. "With these simple rules of birth, survival and death," Paul Davies wrote in *God and the New Physics*, "Conway and his colleagues have discovered the most astonishing richness and variety in the evolution of certain counter configurations." In other words, out of a set of very basic conditions, or limitations, surprising events will emerge.

A week after his lecture, sitting in a patch of sunlight outside his studio, speaking on his mobile, Brian Eno talks about connections between that proposition, developed from ideas investigated by mathematicians such as John Von Neumann and Stanislas Ulam, and the compositions that first sparked his interest in generative music. "I think the Steve Reich pieces and Terry Riley's *In C*," he says. "I would call those the predecessors of this. I would say anything where the com-

david toop • 241

poser doesn't specify a thing from the top down. What I think is different about generative music is that instead of giving a set of detailed instructions about how to make something, what you do instead is give a set of conditions by which something will come into existence."

The Steve Reich pieces he refers to are the early voice works for tape—*It's Gonna Rain* and *Come Out*—both of which explore the strange accretion of phenomena that occurs when two identical tape loops play in synch but then run progressively out of phase due to slight variations in motor speed in the tape machines. "I thought the economy of them was so stunning," says Eno. "There's so little there. The complexity of the piece appears from nowhere. You think, my God, it's so elegant to make something like that. Of course, I was hearing this at the time when 24-track recording had appeared and people were making huge, vast, heavy, soggy pieces of music with no economy whatsoever. Suddenly to hear this Reich piece, which I thought was the most beautiful listening experience, and to realise that it was made from just a few molecules of sound. That really impressed me" [. . . .]

A day after our first chat about this subject (though in retrospect, all our conversations over the years seem to have been about this subject), Eno comes back to me with an aphorism: "Generative music is like trying to create a seed, as opposed to classical composition which is like trying to engineer a tree." Gardening and engineering are key metaphors. "I think one of the changes of our consciousness of how things come into being, of how things are made and how they work," he says, "is the change from an engineering paradigm, which is to say a design paradigm, to a biological paradigm, which is an evolutionary one. In lots and lots of areas now, people say, How do you create the conditions at the bottom to allow the growth of the things you want to happen? So a lot of the generative music thing is much more like gardening. When you make a garden, of course you choose some of the things you put in, and of course you have some degree of control over what the thing will be like, but you never know precisely. That's the wonderful thing about gardening. It responds to conditions during its growth and it changes and it's different every year [. . . .]

In the late 1960s and early 1970s, collaborative group music was one of the most powerful available tools for experimenting with new models of society, forms through which individual expression might thrive within collective organisations [. . . .] During the period in the late 1960s when he shifted his group, Spontaneous Music Ensemble, away from the compositional models of Ornette Coleman, Eric Dolphy and George Russell into uncharted territory, [John] Stevens began to formulate pieces that could help musicians who were new to this way of playing (and that included just about everybody back then). *Click Piece*, for example, was a simple instruction to play the shortest sound possible on your instrument. The difficulty of this varied from instrument to instrument, player to player, and quite a considerable amount of concentration was needed to pare each sound down to its smallest event and keep it there. As a player, you became aware of the way in which a group sound was emerging only after some time had elapsed. The paradox lay in the way that a complex group interaction, quite ravishing to listen to on occasions, could emerge from individual self-absorption. The piece seemed to develop with a mind of its own and almost as a by-product, the basic lessons of improvisation—how to listen and how to respond—could be learned through a careful enactment of the instructions.

Evan Parker remembers the way in which his duo with John Stevens pushed this atomistic way of playing to a limit. "The moments of interaction got shorter and shorter," he says. "You couldn't go any further than that." So a method that stimulated considerable variety in a large group comprising players of mixed ability and experience, quickly became an unproductive limitation for a duo of two well-matched, skilful and confident musicians.

I put it to Parker that Brian Eno's gardening analogy might be applied to his solo playing for soprano saxophone along with many of the theories of webs, swarms and emergent phenomena found in books such as Kevin Kelly's *Out Of Control: The New Biology Of Machines*. "We all are delighted if we can find some way of talking about something that is very difficult to talk about," he admits. "Fractal maths and chaos theory are very useful for talking about the solo playing, though of course the number of calculations involved to arrive at a fractal diagram or drawing is probably a magnitude of millions different from the number of calculations involved in me playing a solo. But in the sense that the whole design is built up from one calculation, the output of which becomes the input for the next calculation, there is in some way a connection with the way I work in the solo thing. I set up loops of stuff and then observe the loop and listen closely to the loop and say, ah, now I'll emphasise that note, or now I'll bring out that difference tone, or I'll try and put something underneath it in relation to that or on top. Gradually the centre of attention in the loop shifts somewhere else. The loop suddenly is a different loop. It's something that's still bearing fruit for me. I'm not saying that's exclusively the method I'm using in solo playing but it's the core method."

This sets up a complex feedback system between the saxophone and independently functioning regions of his own distributed consciousness, enabled by Parker's circular breathing and his knowledge of the overtones available through advanced fingering techniques. "Absolutely," he agrees. "It's the key notion of the 20th century. I'm not an expert on cybernetics but bringing an ability to generalise about feedback is a 20th century phenomenon. Before that there were specific applications but I don't think there was a general awareness of how many control systems can be analysed in terms of the feedback between inputs and outputs. Its certainly high on my list of analytical tools."

In 1966 and 1967, Pauline Oliveros produced two tape pieces—*Alien Bog* and *Beautiful Soop*—using Don Buchla's "Buchla Box" 100 Series synthesizer and her own tape delay system. Working at the Tape Music Center at Mills College in Oakland, she had been influenced by the sounds of frogs living in the pond outside her window at Mills. Tape delay systems were means of creating unpredictable variety in music. Terry Riley's system, the time lag accumulator, was a technological equivalent of the feedback system later developed by Evan Parker and one of the inspirations behind Brian Eno's use of tape loops.

For Eno, the system that allowed him to create *Discreet Music* was fine, except it was limited to the length of a vinyl LP. "All of those phase systems," he says, "they're theoretically endless, generating new stuff as they go, new combinations. I always wanted that kind of music—not only *Discreet Music* but the things that followed it like *Music For Airports*—to be endless pieces. I saw them more like paintings, just things that stayed in place, than compositions, things that had a structure to them. I was always looking for creating, not a recording of the results of the generative process, but creating a generating machine itself." This led to his use of Tim Cole's Koan software, a program he had hunted for in research centres in Stanford and Palo Alto but failed to find.

The desire to make a music that exists in a state of being, theoretically without beginning or end, is paralleled by Evan Parker's interest in relatively long forms and their relationship to improvising. "What happens when you work with the longest elements?" asks Parker. "Maybe you're not improvising anymore. You're just remembering." That dialectic, at the core of his music, contributes to the subjective impression in the listener that something is alive and growing, like a timelapse photograph of plant growth, one of the creatures grown in the "garden of unearthly delights" by William Latham's computational breeding program or the volatile communities generated by Conway's Game Of Life.

The observation of nature, either through bioacoustic study, environmental sound recording or ecology, has led some musicians to the creation of emergent systems based on non-human source material. Mamoru Fujieda, for example, wired up plants using a Plantron interface devised by botanist Yuji Dogane. The data collected by electrodes recording changes to the surface electric potential of the plant leaves was converted to MIDI and then transformed into melodic patterns using MAX, the graphical music programming environment developed by Miller Puckette and other authors at IRCAM in 1986.

While Fujieda translates plant activity firmly into the human sphere, Michael Prime's work is more of an intuitive mapping of the interface between humans and non-human species. As in Fujieda's *Pattern Of Plants*, Prime, a member of London Improv group Morphogenesis, uses a bioactivity translator. This controls oscillators which are used as sound sources. His *L-fields*, a work for hallucinogenic plants, is named after studies in voltage potential made in the 1930s and 40s by a Yale scientist, Dr. Harold S. Burr. According to Prime, speaking in an interview with Francois Couture of Québec radio: "He had several local trees connected to voltage meters for a period of years, and discovered that their voltage potentials varied not only with periods of light and dark, but also with the cycles of the moon, magnetic storms and sunspots. The fields of humans varied not just with these natural rhythms, but also according to mental state, health, presence of cancer, etc. He finally postulated that these fields were not just a pattern produced by living organisms, but were also the morphogenetic blueprint that controlled their development."

Prime describes his use of a bioactivity translator as occupying "a kind of hinterland between composition, improvisation and process/generative music." One of his inspirations is the musical use of human brainwaves explored by Alvin Lucier, Richard Teltelbaum and David Rosenboom in the late 1960s, another version of generative music that relates to speculations made by Evan Parker about the role of left brain/right brain activity during his solo performances. In a sense, Prime simply plugs into biological activity and during the period in which he is plugged in, the unpredictable and inevitably mysterious signals given off by plants both create and are folded into Prime's soundscape. The intricacy and alien beauty of bioacoustic feedback systems such as the hunting relationship between bats and moths—the bat tracking moths with ultrasonic pulses, the moths using evasive flying measures whenever they hear ultrasound—can suggest new ways of "growing" music.

Pieces like "Chaos & The Emergent Mind Of The Pond," created by sound recordist and composer David Dunn in 1990, are illustrations of the way in which "shaped" soundscapes can become a category of found art that links to generative work of all kinds.

In his book, *Why Do Whales And Children Sing?*, Dunn quotes the anthropologist and musician Steven Feld, whose research and recording among the Kaluli people of Papua New Guinea and the rainforest in which they live has drawn new maps of the relationship between favoured sound patterns, aesthetic preferences and social relations. "Steven Feld describes the New Guinea rainforest as a world of coordinated alarm clocks," writes Dunn, "an intersection of millions of simultaneous cycles all refusing to ever start or stop at the same point." In books such as *Music Grooves*, co-authored with Charles Keil, Feld has written extensively about valued sonic qualities among the Kaluli, including ". . . interaction of patterned and random sounds; playful accelerations, lengthenings and shortenings; and the fission and fusion of sound shapes and phrases into what electroacoustic composer Edgard Varèse called the 'shingling' of sound layers across pitch space."

Feld's observation of simultaneous cycles working out of phase, or the Kaluli love of "in-sync, out-of-phase patterning" recalls Brian Eno's enthusiasm for *In C*, *It's Gonna Rain* and Paragraph Seven of *The Great Learning*. One of the most enthralling examples of this phenomenon can be heard when large groups of frogs are calling, each frog responding to another, calls sometimes falling in perfect synchronisation, moving in and out of phase, then falling suddenly silent for reasons a human can't divine. David Dunn has extrapolated from his recordings of this emergent mind to develop a series of real-time multi-channel electroacoustic performances and installations for live computers.

"They explore the global behaviour of hyper-chaotic analogue circuits modelled in the digital domain," he tells me, via email from New Mexico. "These circuits exhibit an immense range of sonic behaviour, all generated from the equivalent of three sinewave oscillators linked together in a feedback path that exhibits two of the essential traits of a chaotic system: non-linearity and high sensitivity to initial conditions. The emergent complexity results from the dynamical attributes of cross-coupled chaotic states interacting in a multidimensional phase space [. . . .]"

"My main question on generative music is: can we trust machines to create for us?" asks David Rothenberg, musician and author of *Hand's End: Technology And The Limits Of Nature*. The life's work of John Cage could be interpreted as that question almost in reverse: can we trust humans to create music? Through the influence of books as much as anything else—the oracular hexagrams of the *I Ching*, James Joyce's *Finnegans Wake* and the writings of Gertrude Stein—Cage arrived at *The Music Of Changes* in 1951, a composition he described in *Musicage*, his conversations with Joan Retallack, as "where the process of composing was changed from making choices to asking questions."

Although Cage's ghost is present almost anywhere we care to look, his philosophy of nonintentionality has become a resource, rather than a way of life, for many musicians currently working with electronic media. As a member of the think-tank (also including architect Paul Shepheard, landscape architect Georgina Livingston, digital sound artist Joel Ryan and Brian Eno) that offered guidance to Jem Finer in his development of the *Longplayer* project, I remember a phase during which Finer considered using a segment of Cage's prepared piano music as the source material to feed through SuperCollider, the real time sound synthesis program developed by James McCartney. The intention of *Longplayer* was to generate a piece of music that would last for 1000 years, using SuperCollider's capacity to loop small segments of music and gradually move the start point of the loop, with each new loop applying the same process to itself to create a nest of loops, all working within the differing boundaries of its parent loop to create constant evolution. Fascinating, but though informed by Cage, perhaps not a particularly Cageian way to compose [. . . .]

Issues of intentionality, linearity and the model of active composer and passive listener are being challenged by software and software users yet held in place by the dominant carrier of music, the compact disc. "Our minds have become nodes in the expanding space of the Internet," wrote Kim Cascone for the liner notes to *Selected Random Works*, released on Ritornell, "connecting freely with other nodes in a rhizomatic manner. Comparing this fluidic, smooth space with the linear space of the audio compact disc, we find that a linear model of time has been imposed onto an inherently non-linear medium."

Live streaming, installations, MIDI files and the release of authored software, rather than finished product, offer ways around this contradiction, though the effect at the moment can feel and sound like the aimless exploration of a huge choice of possibilities, something like the experiments of the 1960s when the excitements of process and change could obscure the imperatives of making music that was worth a second listen [. . . .]

There is a significant difference between software programs such as Logic Audio or Cubase, basically emulations of the recording studio, and more open applications such as MAX/MSP, Cloud Generator developed by Curtis Roads and John Alexander, or interesting curiosities such as Akira Rabelais's Argeïphontes Lyre (elliptically explained to me by Rabelais by means of a lengthy chunk of Greek mythology). Composers who have devoted a lifetime to compositional methods that go beyond the customary means of committing sound to tape, its equivalents or emulations, are increasingly important in this shifting field: Iannis Xenakis, for example, for his theory of stochastic processes, derived from mathematician Jacques Bernouilli's "law of large numbers" or the cybernetic and entropic compositions of Roland Kayn [. . . .]

For Markus Popp of Oval, one of the most important factors in his recent trajectory is the presentation of his Oval Process software, developed with Richard Ross, as an interactive installation object. "That is this tangible interface," he says, speaking from his studio in Berlin, "declaring the interface public domain and just handing it over to the audience or whoever is present at the given time of the exhibition or wherever the unit is on display. This is one aspect of it, and the other aspect, which might even be considered the stronger statement is, of course, the available audio content which is on my CD, which is a quite vigorous statement against the typical productivity work flow in music."

He describes his [. . .] recent CDs—*ovalprocess* (2000) and [. . .] *Commers* (2001)—as the tangible front end of an attempt to introduce an alternative rhetoric to the production of electronic music. At the same time, Oval Process is a statement to encourage non-expert audiences [. . . .]

Like Japanese paper buried underground, the final organisation of the music is relinquished by its maker, though the elements remain intact. Popp seems to interpret the current situation in music as a moment for making statements that jump out of established historical frameworks, for when people are confronted by music designed to grow and evolve beyond the composer's intentions or even understanding, the old science fiction anxieties still recur [. . . .]

[N]otation is to improvisation as the portrait is to the living model.

—Ferruccio Busoni[1]

(a) Western "classical" music demands a solution to most of the technical problems of making music *before* the music can be performed. Whereas—although most improvised musics demand a high level of technical competence—the elaboration of a theme, on a chord sequence or the direct response of musical dialogue, demands the application of "problem-solving" techniques *within* the actual performance. (b) In improvised music there is a creative and inter-active dialogical relationship between performers, whereas a composed work acts as a medium between the various instrumental components. The relationship between musicians loses its social significance; lessened by the agency of an external element, e.g., the composition.

—Eddie Prévost[2]

Music was born free, and to win freedom is its destiny.

—Ferrucio Busoni[3]

I'm attracted to improvisation because of something I value. That is a freshness, a certain quality that can only be obtained by improvisation, something you cannot possibly get by writing. It is something to do with the "edge." Always being on the brink of the unknown and being prepared for the leap. And when you go out there you have all your years of preparation and all your sensibilities and your prepared means, but it is a leap into the unknown.

—Steve Lacy[4]

That's the great thing about improvisation. Or *playing*—"improvisation" has got that heavy sound to it. Playing is really subversive of virtually everything. So you clamp it down, like the industry's clamped down on it. I mean they don't want improvisation, naturally. You can't make money out of this shit where you don't know what's going to happen from one minute to another. So, the process has been, of course, to nail it all down. But then the subversiveness gets into the technology, so even a guy doing a mix, you can't nail him down. There are guys improvising remixing a record. And that's where the life is in music. It always seems like it's the vein, the conduit for life in the music. That appetite seems to me to be always to do with changing things, which is often to do with fucking things up.

—Derek Bailey[5]

Free Improvisation is almost by definition outsider music, opposed to capitalist business-as-usual. Improvisers want to explore the possibilities of the instant—in this space, using these instruments, with this audience (or lack of it) [....] Free Improvisation doesn't guarantee any particular sound or mood, it produces a question mark rather than a commodity.

—Ben Watson[6]

It's like, everybody wanted to use freedom as a context to *freak out*, and that was not what I was talking about. One of the problems of collective improvisation, as far as I'm concerned, is that people who use anarchy or collective improvisation will interpret that to mean

"Now I can kill you"; and I'm saying, wait a minute! [. . . . I]f you look back at the last twenty years, what has freedom meant? For a great many people, so-called freedom music is more limiting than bebop, because in bebop you can play a ballad or change the tempo or key. So-called freedom has not helped us as a family, as a collective, to understand responsibility better [. . . .] So the notion of freedom that was being perpetrated in the sixties might not have been the healthiest notion [. . . .] I'm not opposed to the *state* of freedom [. . . .] But fixed and open variables, with the fixed variables functioning from fundamental value systems—that's what freedom means to me.

—Anthony Braxton[7]


I have turned more and more toward precise musical notation to insure that the improvisor is consciously and psychically tuned in to the overall structure of a piece. On first glance this approach would seem to inhibit the improvisor. This is a valid criticism, but I believe that this inhibition is now a real necessity when one perceives that "free" or "open" improvisation has become a cliché, a musical dead end.

—Anthony Davis[8]


There's no such thing as freedom without some kind of control, at least self-control or self-discipline [. . . .] Coltrane did a lot of experimenting in that direction [. . .] even though it gave an impression of freedom, it was basically a well thought out and highly disciplined piece of work.

—Elvin Jones[9]


[A] musical score is written to keep the performer from playing what he already knows and leads him to explore other new ideas and techniques.

—Elliott Carter[10]


I'm really honest when I say that, for me a performance, I put the guitar on the table, I get it all working and I go off, do something, and then it's 8 o'clock, it's time to play and I kind of look at the guitar in horror at that point and I really don't have a single idea. I'd go further and say that when my hand descends to play the very first notes of a performance I still don't have any ideas. As the hand or the fingers are just beginning to touch the strings ideas begin to come and then you just take it from whatever happens at that stage.

—Keith Rowe[11]


My improvisations are based on shifting many or singular sounds around in contrasting, delightful, agonising, abrupt, slow, hilarious, too fast, fat—to name but a few—combinations. Overall working sensually while perverting perception; sound in all its physicality; running with the surprises is therefore of the essence. Usually, the performance space and myself are the only players of course, so [performing with the electronic orchestra] MIMEO is a glorious treat, as I'm allowed to take one sonic role/layer/job at a time, find a hole or make one, colour it pink or translucent, divert the whole mass down another road, slab, be part of an organism that makes a piece of music, rather than a single source.

—Kaffe Matthews[12]

# VI. Improvised Musics

## Introduction

The scene is a small pub on a busy London street in August 1992.[1] Taped to the outside window is a handwritten sign announcing a duo performance by guitarist Derek Bailey and percussionist John Stevens. Inside the pub, Bailey walks in, sits down, and strums his guitar for a moment. It's not clear just when the performance begins. Stevens is still adjusting his kit; but Bailey seems to have crossed over from tuning up to performing. Although he's playing a traditional hollow-body electric guitar, Bailey calmly draws from the instrument an array of unexpected sounds: atonal chords, scraped lines, ringing feedback, and a scattering of harmonics. When Stevens finally joins in, his fluttering hands produce tumbling metallic textures, a meterless assortment of clattering bells, rapid rolls, and punctuating thuds. There's clearly no overarching plan here. Rather, the performance is guided purely by the moment-to-moment interaction of the two musicians. Forty-five minutes later, the performance ends as informally as it began with a nod from the performers and applause from the small but attentive audience.

Bailey is one of the founders and premier players of this form of music, developed in Britain and Europe in the mid-1960s and generally termed "free improvisation" or "improvised music." Its American counterpart, inaugurated several years earlier by Ornette Coleman, Cecil Taylor, and Albert Ayler, generally falls under the name "free jazz." Free jazz and improvised music did away with the strict forms of jazz and classical music (tonality, chord changes, formal shape and structure, etc.). They abolished the traditional hierarchy of instrumentation in jazz, classical, rock, and pop, allowing any instrument to become an equal partner in improvisation with any other. In short, free jazz and improvised music abandoned virtually every prop or anchor for improvisation in order to spur musicians to play genuinely in the moment, relying solely on their ingenuity and their instantaneous responses to the contributions of fellow performers. This urge toward improvisatory exploration encouraged performers to go beyond the established practices of instrumental technique to develop "extended" techniques: wind players employ new fingerings and ways of blowing to produce microtones, chords, harmonics, and vocal elements such as pops and growls; percussionists strike or rub their instruments in unorthodox places and ways, and often incorporate found objects; string players prepare their instruments with nuts, bolts, and other gadgets to drastically alter their sonic characteristics; etc.

Like composers and performers of experimental music, many practitioners of free jazz and improvised music insist on the importance of the transitory moment. They affirm the value of a musical *community* in opposition to a music *industry* that solely values objects and commodities. For many, the improvised musical performance serves to create—in the midst of existing hierarchical social relations—a utopian space, a genuinely democratic realm full of cooperation, coexistence, and intersubjective exchange. Without established musical or social props, everything is held together by these intersubjective relations among performers, lines of connection that are both as strong and as fragile as a spider's web, and, as such, constantly under construction and repair.

Free jazz and improvised music share a number of musical and social imperatives, particularly a striving for "freedom" conceived both musically and politically. Yet the two forms represent relatively distinct strands, distinguished largely by the contexts of their development. Free jazz is inextricably bound up with the politics of race in the United States. Its ancestry lies in the history of African-American music, from blues and gospel to swing and bebop. Like these earlier forms, free jazz represents the transformation of a history of oppression into a kind of transcendence and even ecstasy. Historically, free jazz performances are often characterized by extraordinarily high levels of musical energy, the creation of colossal sound masses that bind musicians and audience members together in an awesome experience of collective power. Improvised music, on the other hand, is more distinctly European and modernist in origin, reflecting the dual musical influences of jazz (e.g., John Coltrane, Eric Dolphy, Albert Ayler) and the classical avant-garde (e.g., Anton Webern, Karlheinz Stockhausen, John Cage), and loosely connected to anarchist and Marxist political theory. In comparison with free jazz, improvised music is often more sober, dispassionate, and informal, guided less by musical expression than by sonic exploration.

Since the 1960s, the lineages of free jazz and improvised music have continued and have generated new offshoots. Improvised musics have enjoyed a resurgence in the past decade. In downtown New York, a new generation of musicians (among them Charles Gayle, David S. Ware, Matthew Shipp, William Parker, and Susie Ibarra) has created a vibrant free jazz scene. In Britain, Europe, and Japan, an older generation of free improvisers (e.g., Han Bennink, Peter Brötzmann, Evan Parker, Keith Rowe) performs regularly with younger players (e.g., Otomo Yoshihide, Sachiko M, DJ Olive, Marcus Schmickler), often armed with computers, samplers, and turntables instead of saxophones or double basses. The past decade has also seen the emergence of "free rock" and "free folk," terms that attempt to mark the ways in which outfits such as The No-Neck Blues Band, Jackie-O Motherfucker, and Sunburned Hand of the Man have infused rock with the spirit of free improvisation. Though the lines between improvised music, experimental music, and electronic music are increasingly blurry, improvising musicians remain distinctly committed to the risks and rewards of live performance premised only on in-the-moment decisions and interactions.

## NOTES

1. The description here is based on the video *Gig*, issued by Derek Bailey's Incus label in 1996.

# 37

# *Change of the Century*

## ORNETTE COLEMAN

Along with Cecil Taylor and Albert Ayler, Ornette Coleman (1930– ) launched the "free jazz" revolution in the late 1950s and early 1960s. Coleman's first two recordings, *Something Else!* (1958) and *Tomorrow is the Question* (1959) made a stir. But it was his arrival in New York in 1959 and the series of records that followed (boldly titled *The Shape of Jazz to Come* [1959], *Change of the Century* [1959], *This is Our Music* [1960], and *Free Jazz* [1960]) that profoundly shook the jazz world. On these records, Coleman and his quartet improvised without preset chord progressions (indeed, without a chordal instrument such as piano or guitar). *Free Jazz* employed a double quartet that improvised collectively without preset key, melody, chord changes, or meter, producing an abstract sonic experience analogous to the Jackson Pollock painting featured on the album's cover. Though lambasted and ridiculed by the jazz mainstream, Coleman's approach deeply influenced young experimentalists such as the Association for the Advancement of Creative Musicians (AACM), as well as jazz veterans such as John Coltrane, whose 1965 release *Ascension* took collective improvisation into even wilder territory. In the following piece, drawn from the liner notes to *Change of the Century*, Coleman gives his own account of his free jazz practice.

Some musicians say, if what I'm doing is right, they should never have gone to school.

I say, there is no single *right* way to play jazz. Some of the comments made about my music make me realize though that modern jazz, once so daring and revolutionary, has become, in many respects, a rather settled and conventional thing. The members of my group and I are now attempting a break-through to a new, freer conception of jazz, one that departs from all that is "standard" and cliché in "modern" jazz.

Perhaps the most important new element in our music is our conception of *free* group improvisation. The idea of group improvisation, in itself, is not at all new; it played a big role in New Orleans' early bands. The big bands of the swing period changed all that. Today, still, the individual is either swallowed up in a group situation, or else he is out front soloing, with none of the other horns doing anything but calmly awaiting their turn for *their* solos. Even in some of the trios and quartets, which permit quite a bit of group improvisation, the final effect is one that is imposed beforehand by the arranger. One knows pretty much what to expect.

When our group plays, before we start out to play, we do not have any idea what the end result will be. Each player is free to contribute what he feels in the music at any given moment. We do not begin with a preconceived notion as to what kind of effect we will achieve. When we record, sometimes I can hardly believe that what I hear when the tape is played back to me is the playing of my group. I am so busy and absorbed when I play that I am not aware of what I'm doing at the time I'm doing it.

I don't tell the members of my group what to do. I want them to play what they hear in the piece for themselves. I let everyone express himself just as he wants to. The musicians have complete freedom, and so, of course, our final results depend entirely on the musicianship, emotional make-up and taste of the individual member. Ours is at all times a group effort and it is only because we have the rapport we do that our music takes on the shape that it does. A strong personality with a star-complex would take away from the effectiveness of our group, no matter how brilliantly he played.

With my music, as is the case with some of my friends who are painters, I often have people come to me and say, "I like it but I don't understand it." Many people apparently don't trust their reactions to art or to music unless there is a verbal *explanation* for it. In music, the only thing that matters is whether you *feel* it or not. You can't intellectualize music; to reduce it analytically often is to reduce it to nothing very important. It is only in terms of emotional response that I can judge whether what we are doing is successful or not. If you are touched in some way, then you are *in* with me. I love to play for people, and how they react affects my playing.

[. . . .I]n a certain sense there really is no start or finish to any of my compositions. There is a continuity of expression, certain continually evolving strands of thought that link all my compositions together. Maybe it's something like the paintings of Jackson Pollock.

# 38

# *Free Improvisation*

## DEREK BAILEY

Guitarist Derek Bailey (1930– ) is among the founders of "free improvisation," a musical practice linked to, but genealogically and sonically distinct
from, "free jazz." On the one hand, as Bailey contends here, "free improvisation" is the world's oldest form of music-making, predating jazz, the modernist avant-garde, and experimental music by millenia. On the other hand,
he acknowledges that "free improvisation" also names a musical practice
that emerged in Britain and Europe in the early 1960s inspired by jazz and
free jazz, and also by Arnold Schoenberg's atonal music, Anton Webern's
serial compositions, the indeterminate and experimental work of composers
such as Earle Brown and John Cage, and other sources. Where "free jazz"
players tend to affirm their ties to jazz and to African-American heritage,
"free improvisers" generally resist explicit connections to "idiomatic" musical traditions, jazz included.

   For more than four decades, Bailey has been one of the leading practitioners of "free improvisation." He has performed in an astonishing variety
of contexts, from improvisations with African, Brazilian, and Burmese percussionists and sessions with buto and tap dancers to recordings with British
drum 'n' bass producers and Japanese noise musicians. In 1970, Bailey
founded the Incus record label to document performances of "free improvisation"; and, from 1977 through the early 1990s, he hosted Company Week,
an annual gathering that brought together improvisers of all stripes for what
were often first-time encounters. The following excerpts are taken from Bailey's key book, *Improvisation: Its Nature and Practice in Music*, which originated as a series of television interviews with improvising musicians. Here,
Bailey and his compatriots offer an account of the emergence of free improvisation and a description of its characteristic musical strategies.

## Free

Freely improvised music, variously called 'total improvisation,' 'open improvisation,' 'free music,' or perhaps most often simply, 'improvised music,' suffers from—

and enjoys—the confused identity which its resistance to labeling indicates. It is a logical situation: freely improvised music is an activity which encompasses too many different kinds of players, too many different attitudes to music, too many different concepts of what improvisation is, even, for it all to be subsumed under one name. Two regular confusions which blur its identification are to associate it with experimental music or with avant-garde music. It is true that they are very often lumped together but this is probably done for the benefit of promoters who need to know that the one thing they do have in common is a shared inability to hold the attention of large groups of casual listeners. But although they might share the same corner of the marketplace they are fundamentally quite different to each other. Improvisors might conduct occasional experiments but very few, I think, consider their work to be experimental. Similarly, the attitudes and precepts associated with the avant-garde have very little in common with those held by most improvisors. There are innovations made, as one would expect, through improvisation, but the desire to stay ahead of the field is not common among improvisors. And as regards method, the improvisor employs the oldest in music-making.

The lack of precision over its naming is, if anything, increased when we come to the thing itself. Diversity is its most consistent characteristic. It has no stylistic or idiomatic commitment. It has no prescribed idiomatic sound. The characteristics of freely improvised music are established only by the sonic-musical identity of the person or persons playing it.

Historically, it pre-dates any other music—mankind's first musical performance couldn't have been anything other than a free improvisation—and I think that it is a reasonable speculation that at most times since then there will have been some music-making most aptly described as free improvisation. Its accessibility to the performer is, in fact, something which appears to offend both its supporters and detractors. Free improvisation, in addition to being a highly skilled musical craft, is open to use by almost anyone—beginners, children and non-musicians. The skill and intellect required is whatever is available. It can be an activity of enormous complexity and sophistication, or the simplest and most direct expression: a lifetime's study and work or a casual dilettante activity. It can appeal to and serve the musical purposes of all kinds of people and perhaps the type of person offended by the thought that 'anyone can do it' will find some reassurance in learning that Albert Einstein looked upon improvisation as an emotional and intellectual necessity.[1]

The emergence of free improvisation as a cohesive movement in the early sixties and its subsequent continuous practice has excited a profusion of sociological, philosophical, religious and political explanations, but I shall have to leave those to authors with the appropriate appetite and ability. Perhaps I can confine myself to the obvious assumption that much of the impetus toward free improvisation came from the questioning of musical language. Or more correctly, the questioning of the 'rules' governing musical language. Firstly from the effect this had in jazz, which was the most widely practised improvised music at the time of the rise of free improvisation, and secondly from the results of the much earlier developments in musical language in European straight music, whose conventions had, until this time, exerted a quite remarkable influence over many types of music, including most forms of improvisation to be found in the West.

Two important pieces of reading concerning free improvisation are Leo Smith's book *Notes: 8 Pieces* and Cornelius Cardew's 'Towards an Ethic of Improvisation,' which is from his *Treatise Handbook* [. . . .] Each of these documents is written by a musician with a great deal of experience of free improvisation and they write of it with insight and pertinence. They are however totally different from each other. Smith speaks of free improvisation almost exclusively as an extension of jazz and Cardew considers it mainly in terms of European philosophy and indeterminate composition. And both accounts are valid, each reflecting perfectly one of the twin approaches to free improvisation which took place in the sixties [. . . . T]hese documents also indicate that for musicians of integrity, in either field, wishing for a direct, unadulterated involvement in music, the way to free improvisation was the obvious escape from the rigidity and formalism of their respective musical backgrounds.

Opinions about free music are plentiful and differ widely. They range from the view that free playing is the simplest thing in the world requiring no explanation, to the view that it is complicated beyond discussion. There are those for whom it is an activity requiring no instrumental skill, no musical ability and no musical knowledge or experience of any kind, and others who believe it can only be reached by employing a highly sophisticated, personal technique of virtuosic dimensions. Some are attracted to it by its possibilities for musical togetherness, others by its possibilities for individual expression. There is, as far as I know, no general view to be given. So I propose to base my account of free improvisation largely on my own playing experiences within the music. Objectivity will, I am sure, be quite beyond me, but whenever possible I shall quote other views and opinions. I should emphasise that it is not my intention to try and present an overall picture of the free music scene, nor to give a definitive account of the groups mentioned. I intend only to point to certain aspects of certain groups and situations which seem to me to illustrate some of the central tenets of free improvisation.[2]

## Joseph Holbrooke[3]

This group, which existed from 1963 to 1966, initially played conventional jazz and by 1965 was playing totally improvised pieces. From then on it continued to play both totally improvised and part-improvised pieces. The musicians in the group were Gavin Bryars, who was then a bass player, Tony Oxley the percussionist, and myself. The stages of our collective development from playing a standard idiomatic improvisation[4] through to playing freely improvised music seemed at the time, and even more so in retrospect, almost imperceptible. As far as one can tell, they consisted in accepting the implications of the most logical and appropriate developments in our playing, and following where they led [. . . .]

Initially, we were playing fairly conventionally in a jazz manner. The improvisation was on set chord sequences, usually jazz standards, and played in time. But it seems that almost from the very beginning there was a movement to expand these boundaries. The regular metre was always under attack; systematically so when Tony Oxley evolved a method of super-imposing a different time feel over the original, creating not a poly-rhythmic effect but a non-rhythmic effect. He and Bryars practised working with this until the feeling of a regular pulse was totally removed. Additionally, harmonic experiments were taking place, an example of which is a composition of Bryars', a more or less conventional tune in 3/4 time, in which the soloist improvised not on the chord being played but on the following chord, the chord about to played. We were also following at that time certain aspects of the recorded work of Scott LaFaro and John Coltrane. All these moves constituted an attack on the harmonic and rhythmic framework within which we were working but when we did eventually break that framework it was once again only through gradual, not wholesale, moves. One of the first of these was to break the metre down. Having reached the point where the aural effect we were achieving was one of playing out of time it began to seem almost perverse not to actually play out of time. A soloist would now stay on each chord for as long as he wished to improvise on it, making the change to the next chord how and when he wished, taking his accompanists with him. Tony Oxley: 'This was rhythmically very useful to me. It was a release from the dogma of the beat.' The move away from a set harmonic sequence was to modal playing. The vehicles for this were usually either John Coltrane pieces from that period or a series of modal pieces written at that time by all three of us. We spent much time playing modally, and our earliest 'free' improvisations had a definite modal orientation.

This was probably the easiest way to start. Except, of course, that it wasn't free. It was modal. Still, it provided a base from which we could explore rhythmic and scalar relationships fairly freely. In order to escape the constant threat of the eternally suspended resolution we turned our attention to intervallic manipulation of pitch. Our influences here were partly a belated interest in Webern and partly some aspects of John Coltrane's improvisations. The main stimulus, however, was to escape from the lack of tension endemic in tonal or modal pitch constructions. The 'tension and release' myth upon which most scalar and arpeggio patterns, phrases and designs are based seemed to us no longer valid. In these closed systems there is a circular quality to the improvisation which means that the release is built into the tension, that the answer is contained in the question. The effect is of slackness, blandness. The modal setting particularly, without the restriction or discipline of an idiom, seemed to invite a facile, vacuous type of improvisation. It was to escape from this that we turned to a more atonal, non-causal organisation of the pitch. Much of our language now was arrived at by the exclusion of the elements we didn't want, which very often turned out to be mainstays of our previous tonal language, and by a much more consistent use of the more 'dissonant' intervals. There was some use of serial devices.

Bryars introduced what he describes as 'the serial equivalent of a free jazz ballad'. We each had a series of notes, with alternatives, and each note was held as long as the player wished. So there was a continuous changing harmony. There were attempts to improvise serially. Working in 3 or 4 note cells, 1 or 2 notes being held in common between successive cells. Oxley at this time started to change his instrument from a kit designed to supply set rhythmic patterns to one with an increased potential for varied sounds, timbres and percussive effects. An example of this is the occasion when, after hearing Bryars' newly acquired record of Cage's *First Constructions in Metal,* Oxley, impressed by the gong glissando effect, tried to find a way to emulate it. This he eventually did by tying a piece of cloth to a cymbal in such a way as to be able to bend the cymbal after it had been struck. It was probably years later that we discovered that the gong gliss effect was created by immersing it in water. But this was the sort of thing that was influencing the music we played. About his bass playing at this time, Bryars says: 'I very often played chords on the bass: triple stops, double stops, I always played 3 finger pizzicato, and I played horizontally across the strings like a flamenco guitarist. Ascending was usually in fast runs, descending in disjunct leaps. Scale steps going up and large steps down. But when these things became clichés I can remember consciously trying to drop them. I would at all times try and avoid playing the pulse of the music.'

These were some of the means by which we reacted against the restrictions of the inherited improvising language, its nostalgia, and looked for fresher, less worn material with which to work. By this time most of the music was collectively improvised and solos were unaccompanied. Such accompaniment as happened was a sort of occasional commentary from the other instruments.

So the whole was somewhat atonal in character, played in a discontinuous, episodic manner, with two instruments—amplified guitar and percussion—matched to the volume of a very softly played double-bass. But the experience of playing freely soon had the effect, as it always does, of producing a set of characteristics unique to that particular grouping of musicians and of producing an identity only a small proportion of which was established by the technical, purely musical constituents [. . . .]

### Solo

Improvisors are, as a rule, musically gregarious, preferring to work with other musicians in any combination from duo up to quite inexplicably large ensembles. For most people improvisation, although a vehicle for self expression, is about playing with other people and some of the greatest opportunities provided by free improvisation are in the exploration of relationships between players. In this respect solo improvisation makes no sense at all. However, at some time or other, most improvisors investigate the possibility of playing solo [. . . .]

For me there has always been an attraction in solo playing, perhaps partly explained by the nature and tradition of the guitar, the instrument I play. But when, around 1970/71 after a period of some years playing in improvising groups of many different styles and sizes, I turned almost exclusively to solo improvising, I did so out of necessity. The need, after a considerable time thinking only in group terms, was to have a look at my own playing and to find out what was wrong with it and what was not wrong with it. I wanted to know if the language I was using was complete, if it could supply everything that I wanted in a musical performance. The ideal way of doing this, perhaps the only way, it seemed to me, was through a period of solo playing. Alternating periods of group playing with solo playing is something I have tried to maintain ever since [. . . .]

The most obvious differences to group improvisation—greater cohesiveness and easier control for the soloist—are not, in improvisation, necessarily advantages and an even greater loss, of course, is the unpredictable element usually provided by other players. In this situation the language becomes much more important and there will be times in solo improvisation when the player relies entirely on the vocabulary used. At such times, when other more aesthetically acceptable resources such as invention and imagination have gone missing, the vocabulary becomes the sole means of support. It has to provide everything needed to sustain continuity and impetus in the musical performance. This, it seems to me, is where the main danger in solo improvisation arises.

Improvising alone, before an audience, is not without its terrors. The temptation, when nothing else seems to be offering itself, to resort to tried and proven procedures, to flog those parts of the performance which are most palatable to an audience—and no musician who has spent time playing in public is in any doubt about what they are—is not easily resisted and it is clear that in solo improvising, as with a great deal of performed music, audience response can be the cause of rituals and formulae being repeatedly trotted out long after they have lost any musical motivation. At this point the credibility of the activity is in the balance and maintaining it simply depends on the courage of the player. Once solo playing descends to being the recycling of previously successful formulae its relevance to improvisation becomes pretty remote [. . . .]

The developments in my playing following on from those described in the [section] on Joseph Holbrooke continued along the same lines and for the same reasons: to find a way of dealing with a freely improvised situation in which a conventional vocabulary proved inadequate [. . . .]

Beyond the immediate influence of the musicians I was playing with, the bases of my improvising language came from an interest in the music of Schoenberg's pre-serial, 'free' atonal period, the later music of Webern and also certain early electronic music composers. (Musicians who shared, it is fairly safe to say, a deep antipathy to anything remotely connected with improvisation.) Apart from the fact that I liked the stuff, I thought (and I still think) that intervallic manipulation of pitch is less restricting and more productive than other ways of pitch management, and that the very clearly differentiated changes of timbre which characterised some early electronic music was the sort of thing which could assist in assembling a language that would be literally disjointed, whose constituents would be unconnected in any causal or grammatical way and so would be more open to manipulation. A language based on malleable, not pre-fabricated, material. Generally I was looking, I think, to utilise those elements which stem from the concepts of unpredictability and discontinuity, of perpetual variation and renewal first introduced into European composition at the beginning of the 20th century.

But this 'improvising language' was, of course, superimposed upon another musical language; one learned, also empirically, over many years as a working musician. Working musicians, those found earning a living in night clubs, recording studios, dance halls and any other place where music has a functional role, spend very little time, as I remember it, discussing 'improvising language,' but anyone lacking the ability to invent something, to add something, to improve something would quickly prove to be in the wrong business. In that world, improvisation is a fact of musical life. And it seems to me that this bedrock of experience, culled in a variety of situations, occasionally bubbles up in one way or another, particularly playing solo. Not affecting specifics like pitch or timbre or rhythmic formulations (I've yet to find any advantage in quoting directly any of the kinds of music I used to play) but influencing decisions that affect overall balance and pace—judging what will work. The unexpected, not to say the unnerving, can also occasionally appear. Recently, it seems to me, some reflection of the earliest guitar music I ever heard occasionally surfaces in my solo playing; music I have had no connection with, either as listener or player, since childhood.

Once a vocabulary of some homogeneity is assembled and is working and has proved to be usable in a playing situation, material can be included, at least for a period, from any source. And that's a necessity, because the need for material is endless. A feeling of freshness is essential and the best way to get that is for some of the material to be fresh. In a sense it is change for the sake of change. Change for the sake of the benefits that change can bring [. . . .]

Solo playing, in fact, has produced some remarkable, even spectacular, performances, usually of a dense, furiously active nature: a panic of loneliness; a manic dialogue with the phantom other; virtuosic distortions of natural bodily functions unequalled since the days of La Petomaine. Missing, is the kind of playing which produces music independent of the characteristics of instruments or even individual styles ('. . . who played that? . . .'), unidentifiable passages which are the kind of magic only possible, perhaps, in group playing [. . . .]

Perhaps I have given the impression that there is no forward planning, no overall structure, no 'form'. Adverse criticism of free improvisation—pretty nearly the only kind available—almost always aims itself at the same two or three targets and the clear favourite of these is 'formlessness'. As the criteria for assessing a piece of music, any piece of music, is usually inherited from the attitudes and prejudices handed down by the mandarins of European straight music this is to be expected. Nowhere is the concept of form as an ideal set of proportions which transcend style and language clung to with such terrified tenacity as by the advocates of musical composition. 'The necessity for design and balance is nowhere more imperative than in music, where all is so fleeting and impalpable—mere vibrations of the tympanic membrane.' Although written many years ago, that is still probably a fairly accurate indication of the importance attached to form by those people concerned with composed music. Even in those parts of contemporary composition where the earlier types of overall organisation no longer serve, a great deal of ingenuity is exercised in finding something upon which the music can be 'based'. Myths, poems, political statements, ancient rituals, paintings, mathematical systems; it seems that any overall pattern must be imposed to save music from its endemic formlessness.

There is no technical reason why the improvisor, particularly the solo improvisor, should not do the same thing. Most musical form is simple, not to say simpleminded. But generally speaking, improvisors don't avail themselves of the many 'frameworks' on offer. They seem to prefer formlessness. More accurately, they prefer the music to dictate its own form.

In practice, this works in many ways and, as the subconscious aim is probably to invent a form unique to every performance, giving a precise account of the complex forces that govern the shape and direction of an improvisation, even if such a thing is possible, would have no general significance. But there is a forward-looking imagination which, while mainly concerned with the moment, will prepare for later possibilities. Rather in the way that memory works, perhaps, a piece can be criss-crossed with connections and correspondences which govern the selection and re-selection of events as well as guiding the over-all pacing of the piece. Simultaneously, events remembered and events anticipated can act on the present moment. As Evan Parker says: 'Improvisation makes its own form'; and similarly, Carl T. Whitmer: 'In expansion the form is generated.' Frank Perry, the percussionist: 'For me, improvisation has meant the freeing of form that it may more readily accommodate my imagination.'

The need to isolate and examine the problems of language, to connect and to extend it, are adequately answered by solo playing. But solo playing for the improvisor can be more than that and above all can offer a method by which one can work continuously on all aspects of a body of music; an uninterrupted activity which relies not on time and place or structured opportunities for its occasion or on any of the different levels of acceptance and approval upon which performed music usually depends for its viability, but relies only on the player's ability to develop his music, to maintain its evolution, and so guarantee his own continuing involvement.

Maintaining solo playing which remains meaningful from an improvising point of view is an elusive business, not least because the easier it becomes to play solo the harder it becomes to improvise solo, but it provides many rewards and is, at times, essential.

But ultimately the greatest rewards in free improvisation are to be gained in playing with other people. Whatever the advantages to solo playing there is a whole side to improvisation; the more exciting, the more magical side, which can only be discovered by people playing together. The essence of improvisation, its intuitive, telepathic foundation, is best explored in a group situation. And the possible musical dimensions of group playing far outstrip those of solo playing.

Paradoxically, perhaps, I have found that the best base from which to approach group playing is that of being a solo improvisor. Having no group loyalties to offend and having solo playing as an ultimate resource, it is possible to play with other musicians, of whatever persuasion, as often as one wishes without having to enter into a permanent commitment to any stylistic or aesthetic position. This might be, I think, the ideal situation for an improvisor.

## Objections

Perhaps this is a good point at which to acknowledge that the world is not divided into improvisors, those who can, and non-improvisors, those who cannot. There are, of course, musicians who can improvise, who have considerable experience of improvisation, and who have found it, for various reasons, unacceptable to them. What follows is a transcription of a conversation between Gavin Bryars and myself in which he describes his disenchantment with improvisation. I think it also indicates one of the main differences between a composer's and an improvisor's attitude towards making music.

*I decided to stop working as a practicing musician, to give up the playing job I was doing and go into teaching. For some time before that I had been getting more and more interested in theoretical aspects of music. I had been reading Cage and had been involving myself more in questions of aesthetics and composition. This was the general background. But I can point to certain specific occasions which I can now recognise as being significant in my turning from improvisation.*

*One of them was the last time Joseph Holbrooke played together. There had been quite a long gap, maybe months, since we had worked together and because of the demands of teaching I had not spent very much time practising the bass. When we played together regularly I was always playing, but on this occasion I think I had lost touch with the instrument a bit. And the fact that I was called upon to play just as we used to play and the fact that I was neither emotionally nor physically trained for it meant that the experience was inadequate and that I was trying to recapture something that had been happening in the past. And that seemed morally wrong. Then I witnessed some of the things that were going on in the London scene at that time. There was a bass player, for instance, who by his performance convinced me that he had no idea of what he was doing. I had always been insistent that technically I had to know exactly what I was doing on the instrument. Just achieving the 'general effect' type of playing didn't interest me. And he was doing his fantastic runs and so on and although it sounded in the genre, the appropriate thing in the context, as far as I could see he had no idea what he was doing—he was a clown. He had no conceptual awareness of what he ought to be doing. I thought he was playing a part. And when I realised that it was possible for someone to sham like that it depressed me immensely and I never played my own bass again after that. I have played other basses in a number of fairly undemanding situations but from then on I did no further work on the bass, and my own bass, which at that time needed repairing, still needs repairing. Later, after going to America and studying with Cage, and returning here and joining in, on live electronics, etcetera, some of the playing that was going on around 1967 and 68 I was becoming more and more ideologically opposed to improvisation. I began to find improvisation a dead end. I could only get out of improvisation what I brought into it [. . . .] It was not possible to transcend the situation I was playing in.*

*Now on the other hand, I found that by composing I could. Composing, I could reach conceptions that I could never reach in a limited, defined, performing time. I couldn't reach an equal conceptual excellence in improvising as in composing [. . . .]*

In the time you are referring to, the late 60s, there was a lot of confusion between free improvisation and free jazz. To a lesser extent it still exists. In fact free improvisation is very often confused in its identity or in its attempt to find an identity. Yet I think there is a type of playing which it is appropriate to describe as free improvisation. But it does seem difficult, firstly to get hold of it, and secondly, to keep hold of it. The tendency is often for the music to slide off into some more readily identifiable area, jazz or comedy or into very obvious forms such as you described. Another aspect of the same problem is that the longer you play in the same situation or group—and this certainly applies to playing solo—the less appropriate it becomes to describe the music as 'free' anything. It becomes, usually, very personalised, very closely identified with the player or group of players. And then you suddenly find yourself in the business of peddling 'my music'. But I believe that that ossifying effect can be counteracted by playing with as many different sorts of improvisor as possible.

*One of the main reasons I am against improvisation now is that in any improvising position the person creating the music is identified with the music. The two things are seen to be synonymous. The creator is there making the music and is identified with the music and the music with the person. It's like standing a painter next to his picture so that every time you see the painting you see the painter as well and you can't see it without him. And because of that the music, in improvisation, doesn't stand alone. It's corporeal. My position, through the study of Zen and Cage, is to stand apart from one's creation. Distancing yourself from what you are doing. Now that becomes impossible in improvisation. If I write a piece I don't even have to be there when it is 'played.' They are conceptions. I'm more interested in conception than reality. Because I can conceive of things that don't have any tangible reality. But if I'm playing them, if I'm there at the same time, then that's real. It's not a conception.*

A lot of improvisors find improvisation worthwhile, I think, because of the possibilities. Things that can happen but perhaps rarely do. One of those things is that you are 'taken out of yourself.' Something happens which so disorientates you that, for a time, which might only last for a second or two, your reactions and responses are not what they normally would be. You can do something you didn't realise you were capable of. Or you don't appear to be fully responsible for what you are doing. Two examples of this might be the production by some member of the group of something so apt or so inappropriate that it momentarily overwhelms your sensibility—and the results of this type of thing are literally incalculable. Another example, on a totally different time scale, might be Joseph Holbrooke where three people produced over a period of years something they could not have achieved individually or, in fact, could not have expected to achieve collectively. Aren't these things which it is impossible to identify with? Wouldn't this be an example of improvisation producing something not totally determined by the players? [. . . .]

*But in the act of the music being made there is no discrimination between the music made and the people making it. The music doesn't exist elsewhere as some general concept* [. . . .]

Some years later Gavin resumed improvising. In 1991 he [. . .] gave his current views on improvisation.

*My ambivalent feelings about improvisation are still there and some of my conceptual objections to it still remain. In a way my ongoing caveats about improvisation no longer come from a possible hostility between the improvisor and the composer, but rather stem from my perception of difficulties within the activity of improvisation itself* [. . . .]

*My main objections to improvisation have not been eradicated, they have been assimilated into a broader musical practice. The principal conceptual difficulties still remain for me: that of the personalising of music, and of the unity of performer and music. I find it above all uncomfortable to watch improvisors work, and I find recordings of improvisations seldom rewarding. If I have to experience improvisation I would rather it be as a player than from the outside* [. . . .]

### Limits and Freedom

In all its roles and appearances, improvisation can be considered as the celebration of the moment. And in this the nature of improvisation exactly resembles the nature of music. Essentially, music is fleeting; its reality is its moment of performance. There might be documents that relate to that moment—score, recording, echo, memory—but only to anticipate it or recall it.

Improvisation, unconcerned with any preparatory or residual document, is completely at one with the non-documentary nature of musical performance and their shared ephemerality gives them a unique compatibility. So it might be claimed that improvisation is best pursued through its practice in music. And that the practice of music is best pursued through improvisation [. . . .]

## NOTES

1. Alexander Moszkowski reported that in 1919 Einstein told him '. . . improvisation on the piano was a necessity of his life. Every journey that takes him away from the instrument for some time excites a home-sickness for his piano, and when he returns he longingly caresses the keys to ease himself of the burden of the tone experiences that have mounted up in him, giving them utterance in improvisations.' *Conversations with Einstein*, published 1921.

2. Nor is it my intention to make a contribution to the increasingly frequent re-writing of the history of the beginnings of free improvisation, except perhaps to mention that my first involvement with it—which left me totally confused and alienated—was in 1957. It was a confrontation which has no musical significance in this account, but it does provide some evidence that free improvisation wasn't 'started' by anybody.

3. The group's name came from Tony Oxley although it could quite easily have come from Gavin Bryars who at that time was beginning to show what was to become a lasting interest in early 20th century English music. Joseph (sometimes Josef) Holbrooke, once described as the 'cockney Wagner,' was a composer of prodigious output who, although creating something of a stir in his own lifetime has been almost totally ignored since. Investigations about him produced different dates for his birth (1875 or 1878) and different dates for his death (1958 or 1961) raising the consideration that there might be more than one Joseph Holbrooke, a speculation reinforced by the staggering amount of music published under that name. It seemed a good cover for our activities.

4. ["Idiomatic improvisation (. . .) is mainly concerned with the expression of an idiom—such as jazz, flamenco, or baroque—and takes its identity and motivation from that idiom. Non-idiomatic improvisation has other concerns and is most usually found in so-called 'free' improvisation and, while it can be highly stylised, is not usually tied to representing an idiomatic identity," Derek Bailey, from the "Introduction" to *Improvisation*, xi–xii.—Eds.]

# 39

# Little Bangs: A Nihilist Theory of Improvisation

## FREDERIC RZEWSKI

Frederic Rzewski (1938– ) has been a leading figure in avant-garde, experimental, and improvised music for more than four decades. In the late 1950s, he befriended John Cage and key members of Cage's circle, among them Christian Wolff, David Tudor, and David Behrman. Rzewski received a Fulbright fellowship in 1960 to travel to Rome, where he made his reputation as a virtuoso avant-garde pianist, debuting compositions by Stockhausen and others. Yet, by the mid-1960s, Rzewski's interests had turned to free improvisation. In 1966, along with a group of American expatriates in Rome, he formed the collective Musica Elettronica Viva (MEV), which dedicated itself to a bruitist improvisatory practice that employed everyday objects and makeshift live electronics. During his time with MEV, Rzewski's approach to music became increasingly political. He came to see improvisation as a way to break down the boundaries between musicians and non-musicians, performers and audience members. By the decade's end, Rzewski had left MEV to focus on the composition of explicitly political works such as *Attica* (1972), *Coming Together* (1972), and *The People United Will Never Be Defeated* (1975) that were increasingly Romantic and populist, reflective of Rzewski's growing worries about the elitism of avant-garde and experimental practices. Since 1977, Rzewski has taught composition at the Liège Conservatory in Belgium. In this piece, he reflects back upon the ethics and politics of free improvisation, and the ways in which it models everyday experience, time, and causality.

[. . . .] In the fall of 1968, I was living in Rome and working with a group of musicians, Musica Elettronica Viva. We were all composers, but were also very intensely interested in exploring the relatively new field of free improvisation.

I had just bought a Philips microcassette recorder, which had just appeared on the market, and was having a lot of fun with it. (I used it, for example, in improvised performances to make very quick loops by alternating the toggle switch between "play" and "rewind" positions.)

I was walking down the street in Trastevere one morning when I saw Steve Lacy, one of our group's members at the time, coming out of a bar. Without thinking, I went up to him, took out my little recorder, and said: "Steve, in fifteen seconds, tell me the difference between composition and improvisation."

Without hesitation, Steve replied: "In fifteen seconds, the difference between composition and improvisation is that in composition you have all the time you want to think about what to say in fifteen seconds, while in improvisation you have only fifteen seconds." (Later I timed his recorded answer with a stopwatch and found that it took exactly fifteen seconds.) Elegant as this formulation is, it clearly does not tell the whole story, nor could this story be told in fifteen seconds except perhaps as an endless succession of fifteen-second variations on this theme.

One could say that composition is a process of selectively storing and organizing information accumulated from the past, so that it becomes possible to move ahead without having constantly to reinvent the wheel. Improvisation, on the other hand, is more like garbage removal: constantly clearing away the accumulated perceptions of the past, so that it becomes possible to move ahead at all.

The most basic technique of composition is that of transferring information from short-term memory to long-term: remembering an idea long enough so that one can write it down. This process of transference is also one of translation: re-forming an impulse or feeling so that it can be expressed in some kind of symbolic language. The most basic technique of improvisation is that of short-circuiting this process of conservation: forgetting—momentarily at least—everything that is not relevant to the objective of expressing an idea immediately in sound. This process has more to do with spontaneous reflexes than with language.

Composition is the result of an editing process in which one's impulses are passed through the critical filter of the conscious mind: only the "good" ideas are allowed to pass through. Improvisation is more like free association, in which ideas are allowed to express themselves without having to pass this test, somehow avoiding the barriers erected by consciousness.

Improvisation is a game that the mind plays with itself, in which an idea is allowed to enter the playing field, in order to be kicked around in pleasing patterns for a moment before being substituted by another idea. The first idea is unintentional, an error, a wrong note, a fumble in which the ball is momentarily lost, a momentary surfacing of an unconscious impulse normally kept under cover. The play to which it is subjected is the graceful recovery of the fumbled ball, a second "wrong" note that makes the first one seem right, the justification for allowing the idea to be expressed in the first place [. . . .]

In Lacy's view [. . .], there would seem to be no difference between composition and improvisation, except for one of duration in the preparation of the act. In that case, improvisation would fall into the category of "real-time composition," an idea widely accepted in the 1960s, which had legal as well as aesthetic consequences. By this was meant: music that is composed at the same time that it is performed, rather than previous to the performance, as normally happens.

If there were a machine that could write the music down as fast as it was played, or even as soon as ideas appeared in the player's mind, then there would, in fact, be no difference between these two things. But such machines, though crude, do already exist, and clearly they change nothing.

Writing is not merely a mechanical process like sound recording, but something that goes on in the brain, before any mechanical activity. Even in the experimental *écriture automatique* of the surrealists, there is a time interval, however small, before the hand executes the necessary maneuvers that record the symbols generated by the brain's nervous impulses.

Composition and improvisation, however related, however inseparable in fact, remain two quite different, even contrary, mental processes. If composition has to do with remembering, and improvisation with forgetting, it is hard to imagine one without the other, since both of these things are fundamental to the brain's activity. Furthermore, both of these things must be very common, potentially understandable by everybody, in much the same way that everybody who dreams is potentially a poet. (Pablo Neruda in his autobiography relates an encounter with a young worker on a train who, recognizing the famous poet, tells him that he too wished to be a poet, rather than a simple worker. Neruda replies that he is in fact a poet, since he, like everybody, dreams—the only difference being that poets simply remember their dreams long enough to write them down.) [. . . .]

An improvised piece of music is held to be "free." A written piece is assumed to be "structured." Depending on one's point of view, freedom or structure might be considered to be desirable or undesirable qualities, "good" or "bad" according to the circumstances surrounding the performance, and according to one's beliefs about what makes music good or bad.

In the 1960s, in radical circles of the "free music" movement, *freedom* was an ethical and political, as well as an aesthetic, concept. Free music was not merely a fashion of the times, and not merely a form of entertainment. It was also felt to be connected with the many political movements that at that time set out to change the world—in this case, to free the world from the tyranny of outdated traditional forms.

Free improvisation was viewed as the possible basis for a new form of universal communication, through the spontaneous and wordless interaction of improvising musicians of different traditions. (There are intriguing echoes of Wagner in this notion.)

Although many interesting results in this collective experiment were achieved, this movement had neither the time nor the resources to carry this research very far, precisely because its success depended upon changing the world, something that did not happen, and could not have happened at the time. There were some lasting effects nonetheless, and in a small way, at least, the world *was* changed.

The most basic propositions of free improvisation, if they could be expressed in words, might be:

(1) Anything can, and does, happen at any time.
(2) At the same time, things happen in predictable chains, according to predetermined conditions and agreed-upon conventions.
(3) These chains are constantly being broken, according to changes in conditions. Our expectations of what must or will happen also change.
(4) At any moment, my activity or inactivity may influence, actively or passively, the state of the whole.

(5) At the same time, my perception of this state may influence my activity.

(6) A circular causality may exist between present and future, so that not only does the present influence the future, but the future influences the present.

(7) Likewise, the past determines the present, but the present also constantly changes the past (something which, according to Augustine, even God cannot do).

In music, it is possible to express experiences convincingly, which, if expressed in words, appear meaningless. An example would be time flowing backwards. An event, the end of a melody, is perceived before the event that preceded it. We know what is coming, and time is reversed. In this respect again, music resembles dream. (We have all had ecstatic dreams, in which we seem to be out of time or out of space.) [. . . .]

Ecstasy, a state of perception in which one seems to be outside of oneself, or to be in more than one place at the same time, is a fundamental element of free improvisation. (In live electronics especially, when the sound that I produce reaches me from a loudspeaker on the other side of the room, I may have the experience of hearing myself in two different places.)

*Time is not just a linear sequence, in which the past conditions the future. It is also a continuous present, in which each moment is a new beginning . . . Each moment is a reenactment of creation . . . The universe of improvisation is constantly being created; or rather, in each moment a new universe is created . . . Although events may seem to succeed each other in an orderly way, each one somehow growing out of the one that preceded it, there is no reason why this must necessarily be so . . . At any moment, an event may occur for no reason at all, with no relation at all to the preceding event . . . In this universe each moment is an entelechy, with both its cause and its end contained in itself.*

In free improvisation this autonomy of the moment, in which things happen for no reason at all and lead nowhere, is fundamental. Nor is there any reason why my thoughts should follow a logical order. They may be constantly interrupted, forgotten as soon as they occur, and lead to nothing.

This universe—unlike the physical universe, which is presumably the effect of one primal cause, or Big Bang—is an endless series of "little bangs," in which new universes are constantly being created. The new universe may appear to follow smoothly from the old one, or it may have nothing to do with it. In this way, improvisation resembles real life in the real world, unlike most written music, in which the interruptions of real life have been edited out.

In improvised music, we can't edit out the unwanted things that happen, so we just have to accept them. We have to find a way to make use of them and, if possible, to make it seem as if we actually wanted them in the first place. And in a way, we actually *did* want them, because if we didn't want these unwanted things to happen, we wouldn't improvise in the first place. That is what improvisation is about [. . . .]

Written music often follows the form of the syllogism: A, then B, and A again. Everyday real life, although it may have an orderly sequence, seldom has this symmetrical character. One of the things that makes written music pleasing is the violation of such symmetry. A situation is set up in which a symmetrical repetition or balancing phrase is expected. This expectation is then partly satisfied, but also partly frustrated (see, for example, the scherzo from Beethoven's *Hammerklavier* sonata). Sometimes written music succeeds in reproducing the tentative, groping quality of certain moments of a typical improvisation (see, for example, the largo movement from the *Hammerklavier*).

On the other hand, a basic device of improvised music is to introduce a pre-composed pattern unexpectedly, at a moment when anything at all might happen. Such epiphanies of order in the midst of chaos also seem to relate a seemingly formless groping to a larger world in which things make sense.

But the basic subject matter of improvisation is the precariousness of existence, in which anything, death or disease, for example, could interrupt the continuity of life at any time. The attitude of the improviser could, in this respect, be said to be tragic. The tragic situation is precisely that in which a sudden change in power relationships may intervene at any time, causing pain or death for some, and pleasure for others (especially for the impartial observer).

[. . . .] Because improvisation resembles ordinary real life in its precariousness and unpredictability, it contains a necessary element of realism, with which many people can immediately identify, even if the musical language is strange to them. (For this reason, the radical, free music of the 60s and 70s, even though its harmonic language was often as difficult and obscure as the most cerebral written compositions of the same period, was able to attract a much larger audience than did its classical counterpart.)

Because improvisation resembles real life, it can illuminate this real life. It can make us aware that the surface of rationality that covers this reality may be only an illusion. This reality that seems to flow smoothly along familiar lines, behaving predictably in accordance with familiar causal patterns, may be only a small part— that part that I choose to perceive—of a greater reality in which most things happen without cause.

Why, indeed, must events have causes? Why assume that there is an "unknown" cause rather than *no* cause? Why must the universe be comprehensible to my limited human mind? Is it not simpler to admit that, among the vast quantities of data that confront my consciousness at every moment, only a tiny part may be said to be rational?

Most of my experience does not happen for a reason. It just happens. Only a few things happen in an orderly, rational sequence. But these are the things that occupy most of my attention, because they are the things I can control.

Music can expand our awareness of the irrational, dark side of reality. It can make us aware, if only vaguely, of the possibility of other universes right under our noses, in which our human systems of rational organization do not apply. Such little universes may appear and disappear at any moment, and presumably at any point in space. The improvising musician simply gives them a voice.

Anything can, and does, happen once. Furthermore, it must be so. Somewhere in the universe there must be a place where things fall up, people get younger, balloons inflate by themselves, and dead dogs get up and walk.

Paradise is now, and can be only now. The question that tormented Pascal— why humans perpetually exile themselves from this Paradise—has never been answered. People continue to choose to live in the Hell of the past, or the Purgatory of the future. For some reason they prefer renunciation or postponement to immediate gratification.

For some reason they also appear to prefer an existing unequal society, in which there is a possibility of greater domination, to a more equal one in which domination is diminished.

I believe these two things are somehow connected. The difficulty of living in the present moment is somehow related to the difficulty of creating an egalitarian society. Both of these things are perceived as ideals, only partially attainable, if at all, in reality. Improvised music has something to do with both of them. Certainly it has to do with being present. It also has to do with democratic forms and equality, at least in a group situation. It can function as a kind of abstract laboratory in which experimental forms of communication can be tried without risk of damage to persons. The great improvised music of the twentieth century may be remembered by future generations as an early abstract model in which new social forms were first dimly conceived.

Improvisation tells us: *Anything is possible—anything can be changed—now.*

The world can be changed without having to change human nature. Humans are perfectly all right the way they are. They mostly get along fine, without anyone telling them how to do it. They tend not to bump into one another walking on the street. They feed, nurse, and help each other. Most of their transactions happen easily, quickly, unconsciously, efficiently, and without money. Families and villages across the world can be examples of a society in which complexity is achieved without despotism, equality without violence.

Change of some kind is inevitable. We have to be ready for anything. The potential for new forms of intolerance on a mass scale is as great as it ever was. But the beautiful nonviolent revolution is also more needed than ever. (Where there is danger, says Hölderlin, the Saving also grows: *Wo Gefahr ist, wächst das Rettende auch.*)

Great social movements do not have clearly definable causes. Although not totally free of causality, they nevertheless happen spontaneously. No individual can foresee them completely (which is precisely what improvisation is all about). And if there *is* ultimately some kind of peaceful transition to more generous forms of social organization, music—and improvised music in particular—will play an important role in this process, as it has done in the past.

# 40

## Improvised Music after 1950: Afrological and Eurological Perspectives

### GEORGE E. LEWIS

Improviser-trombonist, composer, and computer/installation artist George E. Lewis (1952– ) studied composition with Muhal Richard Abrams at the AACM (Association for the Advancement of Creative Musicians) School of Music in Chicago. Over the course of his career, Lewis has played swing with the Count Basie Band, composed and performed experimental music and free jazz with Anthony Braxton, Derek Bailey, John Zorn, and Musica Elettronica Viva, premiered computer compositions at IRCAM (Institut de Recherche et Coordination Acoustique/Musique) and STEIM (Studio voor Elektro-Instrumentale Muziek), and debuted multi-media installations at The Kitchen. In this essay, Lewis examines the turn to improvisation in post-1950 American and European art music, highlighting the important, but generally disavowed, influence of jazz on this turn. He goes on to compare and contrast the contemporary Euro-American approach to improvisation with the improvisatory practice embedded in African-American musics.

Since the early 1950s controversy over the nature and function of improvisation in musical expression has occupied considerable attention among improvisers, composers, performers, and theorists active in that sociomusical art world that has constructed itself in terms of an assumed high-culture bond between selected sectors of the European and American musical landscapes. Prior to 1950 the work of many composers operating in this art world tended to be completely notated, using a well-known, European-derived system. After 1950 composers began to experiment with open forms and with more personally expressive systems of notation. Moreover, these composers began to designate salient aspects of a composition as performer-supplied rather than composer-specified, thereby renewing an interest in the generation of musical structure in real time as a formal aspect of a composed work.

After a gap of nearly one hundred and fifty years, during which real-time generation of musical structure had been nearly eliminated from the musical activity of this Western or "pan-European" tradition, the postwar putative heirs to this tradition have promulgated renewed investigation of real-time forms of musicality, including a direct confrontation with the role of improvisation. This ongoing reappraisal of improvisation may be due in no small measure to musical and social events taking place in quite a different sector of the overall musical landscape. In particular, the anointing, since the early 1950s, of various forms of "jazz," the African-American musical constellation most commonly associated with the exploration of improvisation in both Europe and America, as a form of "art" has in all likelihood been a salient stimulating factor in this reevaluation of the possibilities of improvisation.

Already active in the 1940s, a group of radical young black American improvisers, for the most part lacking access to economic and political resources often taken for granted in high-culture musical circles, nonetheless posed potent challenges to Western notions of structure, form, communication, and expression. These improvisers, while cognizant of Western musical tradition, located and centered their modes of musical expression within a stream emanating largely from African and African-American cultural and social history. The international influence and dissemination of their music, dubbed "bebop," as well as the strong influences coming from later forms of "jazz," has resulted in the emergence of new sites for transnational, transcultural improvisative musical activity.

In particular, a strong circumstantial case can be made for the proposition that the emergence of these new, vigorous, and highly influential improvisative forms provided an impetus for musical workers in other traditions, particularly European and American composers active in the construction of a transnational European-based tradition, to come to grips with some of the implications of musical improvisation. This confrontation, however, took place amid an ongoing narrative of dismissal, on the part of many of these composers, of the tenets of African-American improvisative forms.

Moreover, texts documenting the musical products of the American version of the move to incorporate real-time music-making into composition often present this activity as a part of "American music since 1945," a construct almost invariably theorized as emanating almost exclusively from a generally venerated stream of European cultural, social, and intellectual history—the "Western tradition." In such texts, an attempted erasure or denial of the impact of African-American forms on the real-time work of European and Euro-American composers is commonly asserted.

This denial itself, however, drew the outlines of a space where improvisation as a theoretical construct could clearly be viewed as a site not only for music-theoretical contention but for social and cultural competition between musicians representing improvisative and compositional modes of musical discourse. The theoretical and practical positions taken with regard to improvisation in this post-1950 Euro-American tradition exhibit broad areas of both confluence and contrast with those emerging from musical art worlds strongly influenced by African-American improvisative musics.

This essay attempts to historically and philosophically deconstruct aspects of the musical belief systems that ground African-American and European (including European-American) real-time music-making, analyzing the articulation and resolution of both musical and what were once called "extramusical" issues. This analysis adopts as critical tools two complementary connotative adjectives, "Afrological" and "Eurological." These terms refer metaphorically to musical belief systems and behavior which, in my view, exemplify particular kinds of musical "logic." At the same time, these terms are intended to historicize the particularity of perspective characteristic of two systems that have evolved in such divergent cultural environments.

Improvisative musical utterance, like any music, may be interpreted with reference to historical and cultural contexts. The history of sanctions, segregation, and slavery, imposed upon African Americans by the dominant white American culture, has undoubtedly influenced the evolution of a sociomusical belief system that differs in critical respects from that which has emerged from the dominant culture itself. Commentary on improvisation since 1950 has often centered around several key issues, the articulation of which differs markedly according to the cultural background of the commentators—even when two informants, each grounded in a different system of belief, are ostensibly discussing the same music.

Thus, my construction of "Afrological" and "Eurological" systems of improvisative musicality refers to social and cultural location and is theorized here as historically emergent rather than ethnically essential, thereby accounting for the reality of transcultural and transracial communication among improvisers. For example, African-American music, like any music, can be performed by a person of any "race" without losing its character as historically Afrological, just as a performance of Karnatic vocal music by Terry Riley does not transform the raga into a Eurological music form. My constructions make no attempt to delineate ethnicity or race, although they are designed to ensure that the reality of the ethnic or racial component of a historically emergent sociomusical group must be faced squarely and honestly.

In developing a hermeneutics of improvisative music, the study of two major American postwar real-time traditions is key. These traditions are exemplified by the two towering figures of 1950s American experimental musics—Charlie "Bird" Parker and John Cage. The work of these two crucially important music-makers has had important implications not only within their respective traditions but intertraditionally as well. The compositions of both artists are widely influential, but I would submit that it is their real-time work that has had the widest impact upon world musical culture. The musics made by these two artists, and by their successors, may be seen as exemplifying two very different conceptions of real-time music-making. These differences encompass not only music but areas once thought of as "extra-musical," including race and ethnicity, class, and social and political philosophy.

## Bird

In the musical domain, improvisation is neither a style of music nor a body of musical techniques. Structure, meaning, and context in musical improvisation arise from the domain-specific analysis, generation, manipulation, and transformation of sonic symbols. Jazz, a largely improvisative musical form, has long been explicitly and fundamentally concerned with these and other structural issues. For African-American improvisers, however, sonic symbolism is often constructed with a view toward social instrumentality as well as form. New improvisative and compositional styles are often identified with ideals of race advancement and, more importantly, as resistive ripostes to perceived opposition to black social expression and economic advancement by the dominant white American culture.

Ebullient, incisive, and transgressive, the so-called "bebop" movement brought this theme of resistance to international attention. Influencing musicality worldwide, the movement posed both implicit and explicit challenges to Western notions of structure, form, and expression. In the United States, the challenge of bop, as exemplified by the work of Charlie "Bird" Parker, Dizzy Gillespie, Thelonious Monk, Bud Powell, and Kenny "Klook" Clarke, obliged the dominant European-American culture to come to grips, if not to terms, with Afrological aesthetics [. . . .]

In *Blues People*, Amiri Baraka (then LeRoi Jones) asserts that bebop "had more than an accidental implication of social upheaval associated with it."[1] For the bebop musicians this upheaval had a great deal to do with the assertion of self-determination with regard to their role as musical artists. While jazz has always existed in the interstices between Western definitions of concert music and entertainment, between the commercial and the experimental, challenging the assigned role of the jazz musician as entertainer created new possibilities for the construction of an African-American improvisative musicality that could define itself as explicitly experimental [. . . .]

## Cage

In a 1972 essay contrasting composition with improvisation, musicologist Carl Dahlhaus summarizes the former as an autonomous, internally consistent structure, fully worked-out and written out, and designed to be realized by a performer in a process separate from that of the work itself.[2] Already by the 1950s, the work of John Cage presented an explicit challenge to this notion of composition. Like Bird, the activity of Cage and his associates, such as Christian Wolff, David Tudor, Morton Feldman, and Earle Brown, had profound and wide-ranging influence not only in the musical, literary, and visual domains but socially and culturally as well. The musical and theoretical work of these composers can be credited with radically reconstructing Eurological composition; the trenchancy of this reconstruction involved in large measure the resurrection of Eurological modes of real-time musical discourse, often approaching an explicitly improvisative sensibility [. . . .]

In his important manifesto, *Silence* (1961), Cage declares that "an experimental action is one the outcome of which is not foreseen" and is "necessarily unique."[3] Cage's notion of spontaneity and uniqueness was informed by his studies of Zen, and in particular by his attendance at Daisetz Suzuki's early 1950s lectures on that subject in New York City. At the same time, in terms of social location, composers such as Cage and Morton Feldman located their work as an integral part of a sociomusical art world that explicitly bonded with the intellectual and musical traditions of Europe. The members of this art world, while critiquing aspects of contemporary European culture, were explicitly concerned with continuing to develop this "Western" tradition on the American continent. The composer's "History of Experimental Music in the United States" identifies as relevant to his concerns both European and American composers and artists, including the European Dada movement, composers such as Debussy and Varèse, and later European experimentalists such as Pierre Boulez, Karlheinz Stockhausen, Luigi Nono, and Luciano Berio.[4] Among the American composers that Cage mentions as being part of America's "rich history" of music are Leo Ornstein, Dane Rudhyar, Lou Harrison, Harry Partch, and Virgil Thomson.

Though these and other composers do earn criticism, the only indigenous music that receives sharp denunciation from Cage is the African-American music that he frequently refers to as "hot jazz." Criticizing the expression of Henry Cowell's interest in this and other American indigenous traditions, Cage appropriates the then-current conventional wisdom about the opposition between "jazz" music and "serious" music: "Jazz per se derives from serious music. And when serious music derives from it, the situation becomes rather silly."[5]

We may regard as more rhetorical device than historical fact Cage's brief account of the origins of jazz. In any event, despite such declarations as "the world is one world now" or "when I think of a good future it certainly has music in it but it doesn't have one kind . . . it has all kinds," it is clear that Cage has drawn very specific boundaries, not only as to which musics are relevant to his own musicality but as to which musics suit his own taste.[6] The Cageian tendency is to confront this contradiction through the use of terms that essentially exnominate or disguise his likes and dislikes as such: "some music . . . which would not be useful to me at all might be very useful to someone else."[7]

The composer does, however, make allowance for the fact that others may draw different boundaries: "I can get along perfectly well without any jazz at all; and yet I notice that many, many people have a great need for it. Who am I to say that their need is pointless?"[8] This basic reference to freedom of choice, however, can hardly be extrapolated to argue that Cage is characterizing himself as possessing a culturally diverse musical sensibility. Rather, the composer is reaffirming a relatively mundane truism concerning the diversity of personal taste, while simultaneously making clear that, for him, a "need for jazz" would indeed be pointless.

## Exnomination

Despite Cage's disavowal of jazz, however, the historical timeline shows that Cage's radical emphasis upon spontaneity and uniqueness—not generally found in either American or European music before Cage—arrives some eight to ten years after the innovations of bebop. And it is certain that bebop, a native American music with a strong base in New York City, was well known to what has come to be known as the "New York School" of artists and musicians of which Cage and Feldman were part. In the case of visual artists from that social circle, such as Jackson Pollock and Franz Kline, the connection with jazz has been remarked upon in a number of essays.[9]

The composer Anthony Braxton's pithy statement concerning the disavowal of Afrological forms by the art world that nurtured Cage's work advances the essential issue directly: "Both aleatory and indeterminism are words which have been coined . . . to bypass the word improvisation and as such the influence of non-white sensibility."[10] Why improvisation and non-white sensibility would be perceived by anyone as objects to be avoided can usefully be theorized with respect to racialized power relations.

Commentators such as the media critic John Fiske [. . . .] have identified "whiteness" as an important cultural construct in American society [. . . .] For Fiske, whiteness is "not an essential racial category that contains a set of fixed meanings, but a strategic deployment of power. . . . The space of whiteness contains a limited but varied set of normalizing positions from which that which is not white can be made into the abnormal; by such means whiteness constitutes itself as a universal set of norms by which to make sense of the world."[11] Fiske identifies "exnomination" as a primary characteristic of whiteness as power: "Exnomination is the means by which whiteness avoids being named and thus keeps itself out of the field of interrogation and therefore off the agenda for change. . . . One practice of exnomination is the avoidance of self-recognition and self-definition. Defining, for whites, is a process that is always directed outward upon multiple 'others' but never inward upon the definer."[12]

It is my contention that, circumstantially at least, bebop's combination of spontaneity, structural radicalism, and uniqueness, antedating by several years the reappearance of improvisation in Eurological music, posed a challenge to that music which needed to be answered in some way. All too often, the space of whiteness provided a convenient platform for a racialized denial of the trenchancy of this challenge, while providing an arena for the articulation of an implicit sensibility which I have termed "Eurological."

The anthropologist and improviser Georgina Born presents the circumstantial case:

> Some of the main elements of experimental music practice—improvisation, live group work, the empirical use of small, commercial electronics in performance—were pioneered in the jazz and rock of the 1950s and 1960s. Moreover, the politics of experimental music are similar to those of the advanced black jazz of the 60s. Its musical collectivism, for example, was prefigured by the Chicago black musicians' cooperative, the Association for the Advancement of Creative Musicians (AACM), which became a model for later progressive, cooperative music organizations. The fact that these influences often remain unacknowledged and subterranean, even within experimental music, signals their status as deriving from an "other" culture and the reluctance of the postmodern sphere of legitimate music to admit its indebtedness to the "other."[13]

Texts appropriating the term "experimental music" construct this classification as denoting a particular group of postwar music-makers who come almost exclusively from either European or European-American heritage. Coded qualifiers to the word music—such as "experimental," "new," "art," "concert," "serious," "avant-garde," and "contemporary"—are used in these texts to delineate a racialized location of this tradition within the space of whiteness; either erasure or (brief) inclusion of Afrological music can then be framed as responsible chronicling and "objective" taxonomy [. . . .]

george e. lewis • 277

Clearly jazz must have been a powerful force in postwar improvisative music, since so many fledgling Eurological improvisers needed to distance themselves from it in one way or another. In this regard, the ongoing Eurological critique of jazz may be seen as part of a collective project of reconstruction of a Eurological real-time musical discipline. This reconstruction may well have required the creation of an "other"—through reaction, however negative, to existing models of improvisative musicality [. . . .]

## Spontaneity

Spontaneity is an important value for improvisers working in both Eurological and Afrological forms, though the definition of spontaneity certainly differs according to tradition. Following Cage, [musicologists Elliott] Schwartz and [Daniel] Godfrey affirm that the result of a musical experience created through indeterminate means is meant to be "immediate, spontaneous, and unique: a ritual celebration, not a fixed art object bounded by predetermined relationships or notational strait-jackets."[14]

Notions of uniqueness and the unforeseen, however, are hardly unique to Eurological indeterminacy. Saxophonist Steve Lacy observed that "you have all your years of preparation and all your sensibilities and your prepared means but it is a leap into the unknown."[15] Many commentators have identified the uniqueness of an improvisation as a highly prized goal among African-American improvisers. [Paul] Berliner quotes the trumpeter Doc Cheatham, whose work straddles the pre- and postwar eras, to the effect that Armstrong and others of comparable creative ability would "play fifteen or thirty different choruses, and they would never play the same thing . . . Every time they'd play a tune, the solo would be different."[16] A similar sentiment was expressed with Coltrane's amazement at how Gillespie could play the introduction to "I Can't Get Started" differently every time.[17]

Despite the statements of these and other highly experienced improvisers who have gone on record with their experiences of uniqueness and discovery, a number of composers and theorists working in Eurological music have asserted a quite different view of the same music. The cognitive psychologist John Sloboda maintains that jazz improvisers use "a model which is, in most cases, externally supplied by the culture."[18] Lukas Foss has asserted that in improvisation, "one plays what one already knows."[19]

This viewpoint, which has attained the status of conventional wisdom in some circles, is similar to Schwartz and Godfrey's claim that "Cage's indeterminacy should be distinguished from improvisation, in that the latter is directed to a known end."[20] Cage's own statement that "improvisation is generally playing what you know" leads naturally to his opinion that improvisation "doesn't lead you into a new experience"[21] [. . . .]

Buried within [the] Eurological definition of improvisation is a notion of spontaneity that excludes history or memory. In this regard, "real" improvisation is often described in terms of eliminating reference to "known" styles. Among the styles that are already "known," "jazz" is the most often cited in the literature on the subject—perhaps by reason of its role as epistemological other [. . . .] The inescapable conclusion from a Eurological standpoint is that jazz, whose character is "known," cannot be truly spontaneous or original. Moreover, jazz's supposed dependence upon memorized motifs prevents it from exemplifying "true" improvisation—despite its practitioners' experience of it [. . . .]

As with any music, close listening and analysis of improvised music requires attention to information at different laminar depths. Thus, each of the numerous released recordings of, say, Coltrane's "Giant Steps," regarded at the level of individual passages, is the result of careful preparation [. . . .] At the same time, each improvisation, taken as a whole, maintains its character as unique and spontaneous.

The Eurological notion of pure spontaneity in improvisation fails to account for this temporally multilaminar aspect of an improvisation. By fixing upon the surface level of immediate spontaneity, unsullied by reference to the past or foreshadowing of the future, the reduction of the notion of improvisative spontaneity to the present moment insists on ephemerality. In its extreme form this notion requires that an improvisation be done once and never heard in any form again. [Larry] Solomon's insistence that a recorded improvisation, "upon replay, is no longer an improvisation" reduces experienced immediacy on the part of both listeners and improvisers to an infinitely small "now," a Euclidean point, excluding both the past and the future.[22]

However, listeners have heard some recorded improvisations literally thousands of times. The performances are learned by heart, yet even after many years, new layers of meaning are spontaneously discovered. While a memorized improvisation is, taken note by note, utterly predictable, these recorded versions often seem to renew themselves when viewed in a more expansive temporal context. Moreover, improvisers are hearing their music at the same time as any potential listener; in this sense, the experiences of improviser and listener are similar [. . . . I]t seems clear that the listener also improvises, posing alternative paths, experiencing immediacy as part of the listening experience.

The elimination of memory and history from music, emblematic of the Cageian project, may be seen as a response to postwar conditions. Seen in historical terms, the decline of improvisation in European music in the nineteenth and early twentieth centuries would seem to preclude any identification of exclusively or even primarily European antecedents for Eurological improvised music. In such an atmosphere, the postwar modernist emphasis of musicians such as Cage on "the present," deemphasizing memory and history, would appear to be a natural response to the impossibility of discovering such antecedents on the part of those for whom the preservation of European purity of musical reference would be a prime concern.

This response to historical conditions, moreover, may be viewed not only in terms of the more usually theorized postwar modernist desire to be made new through "negation of the principles of the previous tradition" but, again, with respect to the quintessentially American myth of the frontier, where that which lies before us must take precedence over "the past."[23] On the other hand, the African-American improviser, coming from a legacy of slavery and oppression, cannot countenance the erasure of history. The destruction of family and lineage, the rewriting of history and memory in the image of whiteness, is one of the facts with which all people of color must live. It is unsurprising, therefore, that from an ex-slave's point of view an insistence on being free from memory might be regarded with some suspicion—as either a form of denial or of disinformation.

george e. lewis • 279

## Improvised Music

[. . . . A] field termed "improvised music" has arisen and come to some prominence in the period since 1970. I would identify improvised music as a social location inhabited by a considerable number of present-day musicians, coming from diverse cultural backgrounds and musical practices, who have chosen to make improvisation a central part of their musical discourse. Individual improvisers are now able to reference an intercultural establishment of techniques, styles, aesthetic attitudes, antecedents, and networks of cultural and social practice [. . . .]

The incorporation and welcoming of agency, social necessity, personality and difference, as well as strong relationship to popular and folk cultures, are some of the features of improvised music which distinguish it as a field from Eurological work "incorporating" or "using" improvisation, or featuring "indeterminancy" or aleatoric practices. In my own view, the development of the improviser in improvised music is regarded as encompassing not only the formation of individual musical personality but the harmonization of one's musical personality with social environments, both actual and possible. This emphasis on personal narrative is a clear sign of the strong influence of the Afrological on improvised music.

One important model in the area of improvised music is the sort of "open" improvisation practiced by members of the Association for the Advancement of Creative Musicians (AACM), the African-American musicians' collective widely recognized for the variety of innovative musical ideas promulgated by its membership since its inception in 1965 on Chicago's nearly all-black South Side. The "AACM model" stresses a composer-improviser orientation and the importance of asserting the agency, identity, and survival of the African-American artist [. . . .]

Another important and very different model of "improvised music" is practiced by the European "free" improvisors [. . . .] Reflecting the diverse backgrounds of its participants, this group often blends personal narrative reminiscent of an Afrological perspective with sonic imagery characteristic of European forms spanning several centuries, and [. . .] places great emphasis on the social necessity for the role of improvisor [. . . .] In this regard it becomes entirely probable that the direct use of the term "improvised music" in the sense that I am using it here began among this group of European improvisors. The term was adopted, I believe, not to distinguish it from jazz in the sense of critique, but to better reflect the European improvisors' sense of having created a native model of improvisation, however influenced by Afrological forms.

A third strain within improvised music is the so-called "downtown (New York) school," whose music is often timbrally and dynamically disjunctive, with rapid and frequent changes of mood and extremes of dynamics, extensive use of timbres reminiscent of rock, and strong interface with popular culture. Again, the emphasis here on personality in improvisation is Afrological in nature; this group, in my view, has attempted to come to terms with the innovations of Cage in terms of time, spontaneity and memory, while declining to accept Cage's critique of jazz and improvisation.

In recent years, moreover, the emergence of musicians who do not claim roots in either European or American forms has further served to identify improvised music's transcultural nature, [. . .] pointing up the dangers of essentialist thinking with regard to the connection between music, race and national origin [. . . .]

## Freedom

The advent of various strains of "free" improvisation—including "free" jazz, which emerged in the early 1960s, as well as the European "free" improvisation which emerged in several cultural strata in the 1970s—placed "freedom" back on the musical agenda. In the case of "free" jazz, the tumultuous push for human rights in the United States had clear analogues in the music, as remarked upon by politically active musicians such as Archie Shepp. With regard to the improvisations of musicians such as Vinko Globokar and Cornelius Cardew, where improvisation itself became a symbol for freedom, the events of May 1968 in Paris and other European capitals could be seen as germane.[24]

As with the theme of spontaneity, notions of freedom and control differ markedly between Eurological and Afrological viewpoints. "Free jazz" was, as one can readily observe from the drummer Arthur Taylor's interviews with Afrological improvisers, quite controversial among jazz musicians.[25] Whatever the viewpoints of the musicians on free jazz itself, the responses of several improvisers on the topic of "freedom" are instructive. In particular, the Eurological discourse concerning "rules" for improvisation is almost entirely absent. Rather, the improvisers seem to agree that freedom in Afrological improvisation is perceived as being possible only through discipline, defined as technical knowledge of music theory and of one's instrument as well as thorough attention to the background, history, and culture of one's music [. . . .]

Among improvisers from the Eurological standpoint, freedom is sometimes framed in terms of European music's traditional composer-to-performer hierarchy. According to [Mildred Portney] Chase, "improvisation is the free zone in music, where anything is permitted and considered acceptable. You are responsible only to yourself and to the dictates of your taste."[26] Similarly, preparation for improvisation is described in terms of the need to "free ourselves from those negative attitudes that inhibit us."

A much more widespread view that has evolved in Eurological music circles with regard to improvisation is the notion that, to be musically coherent, improvisation cannot be left as "free," but must instead be "controlled" or "structured" in some way. The composer and critic Tom Johnson's characterization of Cage's indeterminacy is typical: "Cage began referring to work indeterminate of its performance because to have called his work 'improvisations' would have implied that the performers were not guided by goals and rules."[27] Another reason for asserting this necessity for rules is exemplified in the complaint by Berio that "improvisation presents a problem in that there's no true unanimity of discourse among the participants, only, once in a while, a unity of behavior"[28] [. . . .]

In any event, performer choice and "intuition" systems, as promulgated by Stockhausen and other Eurological composers, do indeed turn out to be somewhat different from improvisation in the Afrological sense. These systems seem to take account of the absence of pedagogy in the Eurological music education system with regard to improvisation. At the very least, they are designed to compensate for this lack by mitigating, for the performer, the "terrifying prospect of being free to play whatever comes to mind," by providing material to supplement or even to supplant the performer's own creative lexicon.[29]

My own view is that in analyzing improvisative musical activity or behavior in structural terms, questions relating to how, when, and why are critical. On the other hand, the question of whether structure exists in an improvisation—or for that matter, in any human activity—often begs the question in a manner that risks becoming not so much exegetic as pejorative. It should be axiomatic that, both in our musical and in our human, everyday-life improvisations, we interact with our environment, navigating through time, place, and situation, both creating and discovering form. On the face of it, this interactive, form-giving process appears to take root and flower freely, in many kinds of music, both with and without preexisting rules and regulations.

## Personality

One important aspect of Afrological improvisation is the notion of the importance of personal narrative, of "telling your own story." Berliner's subchapter on this topic identifies this metaphor of the story as underlying the structural process of many improvisers.[30] Erroll Garner encapsulates this viewpoint well: "If you take up an instrument, I don't care how much you love somebody, how much you would like to pattern yourself after them, you should still give yourself a chance to find out what you've got and let that out."[31]

Part of telling your own story is developing your own "sound." An Afrological notion of an improviser's "sound" may be seen as analogous to the Eurological concept of compositional "style," especially in a musically semiotic sense. Moreover, for an improviser working in Afrological forms, "sound," sensibility, personality, and intelligence cannot be separated from an improviser's phenomenal (as distinct from formal) definition of music. Notions of personhood are transmitted via sounds, and sounds become signs for deeper levels of meaning beyond pitches and intervals. The saxophonist Yusef Lateef makes it plain: "The sound of the improvisation seems to tell us what kind of person is improvising. We feel that we can hear character or personality in the way the musician improvises"[32] [. . . .]

Eurological improvisers have tended to look askance on the admission of personal narrative into improvisative activity. I believe that, for postwar Eurological improvisers, the ideas of Cage have, again, had the greatest impact in this regard: "What I would like to find is an improvisation that is not descriptive of the performer, but is descriptive of what happens, and which is characterized by an absence of intention."[33] Interviewing the members of AMM, the composer Christopher Hobbs states that one of the joys of listening to the group is that "you can't distinguish who is playing what, and that it is completely unimportant one way or the other."[34] British composer Gavin Bryars, who moved away from improvisation during the 1970s, maintained that "one of the main reasons I am against improvisation now is that in any improvising position the person creating the music is identified with the music. . . . It's like standing a painter next to his picture so that every time you see the painting you see the painter as well and you can't see it without him"[35] [. . . .]

At the same time, though the members of the innovative improvisation group Musica Elettronica Viva (including pianist Alvin Curran, electronic improviser Richard Teitelbaum, trombonist Garrett List, and pianist Frederic Rzewski) have all had close associations with Cage, their ideas about group improvisation—as with other "post-Cage improvisers" such as Malcolm Goldstein—seem to part company with Cage's views. Frederic Rzewski's "Description and Analysis of a Process" maintains that the music of MEV is "based on friendship. This element of friendship is communicated in the music; it cannot be concealed."[36]

Earlier in this passionate, brilliant, yet somewhat rambling treatise, Rzewski states that "Any unfriendly act on the part of some individual threatens the strength of the music we are all trying to create."[37] Malcolm Goldstein is even more direct than Rzewski, maintaining, with Erroll Garner, that the improvisative act demands from the improviser that an answer be created to this important question: "Who are you? How do you think or feel about this moment/sounding?"[38] Perhaps the most trenchant conception of what improvisation can be is to be found in this testament by Charlie Parker: "Music is your own experience, your thoughts, your wisdom. If you don't live it, it won't come out of your horn."[39] The clear implication is that what you do live does come out of your horn.

## NOTES

1. LeRoi Jones, *Blues People* (New York: William Morrow, 1963), 188.
2. Carl Dahlhaus, "Was heisst improvisation?" *Neue Zeitschrift für Music* 133, no. 9 (1972): 9–23.
3. John Cage, *Silence: Lectures and Writings by John Cage* (Hanover, NH: University Press of New England/Wesleyan University Press, 1973), 39.
4. John Cage, "History of Experimental Music in the United States," in *Silence*, 67–75.
5. Cage, *Silence*, 72.
6. Cage, *Silence*, 75, and Cage in Kostelanetz, *Conversing with Cage* (New York: Limelight, 1987), 257.
7. Cage in Kostelanetz, *Conversing with Cage*, 257.
8. Cage in Kostelanetz, *Conversing with Cage*, 257.
9. See Chad Mandeles, "Jackson Pollack and Jazz: Structural Parallels," *Arts Magazine* 57 (1981): 139.
10. Anthony Braxton, *Tri-Axium Writings*, volume 1 (Dartmouth: Synthesis/Frog Peak, 1985), 366.
11. John Fiske, *Media Matters: Everyday Culture and Political Change* (Minneapolis: University of Minnesota Press, 1994), 42.
12. Fiske, *Media Matters*, 42.
13. Georgina Born, *Rationalizing Culture: IRCAM, Boulez, and the Institutionalization of the Musical Avant-Garde* (Berkeley: University of California Press, 1995), 351 n29.
14. Elliott Schwarz and Daniel Godfrey, *Music Since 1945: Issues, Materials and Literature* (New York: Schirmer, 1993), 92.
15. Steve Lacy, quoted in Derek Bailey, *Improvisation: Its Nature and Practice in Music* (New York: Da Capo, 1992), 57–58.
16. Paul Berliner, *Thinking in Jazz* (Chicago: University of Chicago Press, 1994), 268.
17. Quoted in Berliner, *Thinking in Jazz*, 269.
18. John Sloboda, *The Musical Mind: The Cognitive Psychology of Music* (Oxford: Oxford University Press, 1985), 141.
19. Lukas Foss quoted in David Cope, *New Directions in Music* (Madison: Brown and Benchmark, 1993), 127.
20. Schwartz and Godfrey, *Music Since 1945*, 92.
21. John Cage quoted in Kostelanetz, *Conversing with Cage*, 223.
22. Larry Solomon, "Improvisation II," *Perspectives of New Music* 24, no. 2 (1985): 226.
23. Born, *Rationalizing Culture*, 40.
24. Vinko Globokar, "Reflexionen Über Improvisation," in *Improvisation und neue Musik: Acht Kongressreferate* (Mainz: Schott, 1979), 25–41.
25. Arthur Taylor, *Notes and Tones: Musician-to-Musician Interviews* (New York: Da Capo, 1993).

26. Mildred Portney Chase, *Improvisation: Music from the Inside Out* (Berkeley: Creative Arts, 1988), 15.

27. Tom Johnson, *The Voice of New Music: New York City 1972–1982* (Eindhoven, Netherlands: Het Apollohuis, 1989), 207–208.

28. Luciano Berio, *Two Interviews* (London: Marion Boyars, 1985), 81.

29. Christopher Small, *Music of the Common Tongue: Survival and Celebration in Afro-American Music* (London: Calder, 1987), 302.

30. Berliner, *Thinking In Jazz*, 210.

31. Erroll Garner quoted in Taylor, *Notes and Tones*, 97.

32. Yusef Lateef, "The Pleasures of Voice in Improvised Music," *Views on Black American Music* 3 (1985–88), 44.

33. John Cage quoted in Kostelanetz, *Conversing with Cage*, 222.

34. Barney Childs and Christopher Hobbs, eds, "Forum: Improvisation," *Perspectives of New Music* 21 (1982–83): 40.

35. Gavin Bryars quoted in Bailey, *Improvisation*, 115. [See chap. 38, above.—Eds.]

36. Frederic Rzewski, "Description and Analysis of a Process," unpublished, obtained from the author, 1968, 3.

37. Rzewski, "Description and Analysis of a Process," 3.

38. Malcolm Goldstein, *Sounding the Full Circle* (Sheffield, England: Goldstein/Frog Peak, 1988), 10.

39. Charlie Parker, quoted in Michael Levin and John S. Wilson, "No Bop Roots in Jazz: Parker," *Down Beat* 61, no. 2 (1994): 24.

The form of their pieces is always flat. They are not interested in building to climaxes, or in manipulating tension and relaxation, or in working with large contrasts of any kind. They keep their music flat, never allowing it to rise above or fall below a certain plane. In a way, this flatness is related to the idea of "all over" painting. In both cases, there is an attempt to make all areas of the form equal in importance. The term "static" is often used in reference to their music, since it never leaves this one level and never seems to be moving toward anything. Traditionally this word has been considered derogatory when applied to music, and in many quarters it still is. But in listening to the music of these composers, one soon discovers that static does not necessarily mean boring, the way we always thought it did. Many interesting things can happen all on one plane. A pitch changes slightly, a rhythm is altered, something fades in or out. They are not big changes, but they are changes, and there are more than enough of them to sustain one's interest, provided that he can tune in on this minimal level.

—Tom Johnson on musical minimalism[1]

[In the early 1960s] I was noticing that things didn't sound the same when you heard them more than once. And the more you heard them, the more different they did sound. Even though something was staying the same, it was changing. I became fascinated with that [. . . .] In those days the first psychedelic experiences were starting to happen in America, and that was changing our concept of how time passes, and what you actually hear in music.

—Terry Riley[2]

In Zen they say: If something is boring after two minutes, try it for four. If still boring, try it for eight, sixteen, thirty-two, and so on. Eventually one discovers that it is not boring at all but very interesting.

—John Cage[3]

I have often tried to explain that my music is a reaction against the romantic and expressionistic musical past, and that I'm seeking something more objective, something that doesn't express my emotions, something that doesn't try to manipulate the emotions of the listener either, something outside myself.

Sometimes I explain that my reasons for being a minimalist, for wanting to work with a minimum of musical materials, is because it also helps me to minimize arbitrary self-expression.

Sometimes I say, "I want to find the music, not to compose it."

Sometimes I talk about mathematics and formulas, and how these things provide a means of avoiding subjective decisions and permitting objective logical deductions

Sometimes I quote my teacher Morton Feldman who said so often, "Let the music do what it wants to do."

Sometimes I draw a parallel with the way John Cage used chance, which was also an attempt to base his music on something outside of himself.

Sometimes I talk about all these things, and think that surely everyone will understand what I'm doing and why I am doing it, but whatever I say there are questions: What am I supposed to feel? How can music be impersonal like that? Don't you want to express something? Etc. etc. The idea of music as self-expression is so ingrained in the music education of almost everyone that people become totally disoriented when you try to take it away.

Then one day, frustrated by my inability to communicate my esthetic goals to a group of students, I just said "I am *not* interested in *autobiography.*"

—Tom Johnson[4]


In black culture, repetition means that the thing *circulates* (exactly in the manner of any flow [. . .]) there is an equilibrium. In European culture, repetition must be seen to be not just circulation and flow but accumulation and growth. In black culture, the thing (the ritual, the dance, the beat) is "there for you to pick it up when you come back to it." If there is a goal (*Zweck*) in such a culture, it is always deferred; it continually "cuts" back to the start, in the musical meaning of "cut" as an abrupt, seemingly unmotivated break (an accidental *da capo*) with a series already in progress and a willed return to a prior series [. . . .] The "cut" overtly insists on the repetitive nature of the music, by abruptly skipping back to another beginning which we have already heard. Moreover, the greater the insistence on the pure beauty of repetition, the greater the awareness must also be that repetition takes place not on a level of musical development or progression, but on the purest tonal and timbral level.

—James A. Snead[5]


Certain modern musicians oppose the transcendent plan(e) of organization, which is said to have dominated all of Western classical music, to the immanent sound plane, which is always given along with that to which it gives rise, brings the imperceptible to perception, and carries only differential speeds and slownesses in a kind of molecular lapping: *the work of art must mark seconds, tenths and hundreds of seconds.* Or rather it is a question of a freeing of time, Aeon, a nonpulsed time for a floating music, as Boulez says, an electronic music in which forms are replaced by pure modifications of speed. It is undoubtedly John Cage who first and most perfectly deployed this fixed sound plane, which affirms process against all structure and genesis, a floating time against pulsed time or tempo, experimentation against any kind of interpretation, and in which silence as sonorous rest also marks the absolute state of movement.

—Gilles Deleuze and Félix Guattari[6]


And you thought Carl Orff had found an easy way to make a living!

—Glenn Gould upon hearing Terry Riley's *In C*[7]

# VII. Minimalisms

## Introduction

A dense and raspy drone pours from the speakers like a tidal wave. At first, the tone is monolithic, sheer force without detail or definition. As the sound fills the space, textures and intervals begin to emerge from, and recede back into, the immense rush of sound. At the core of the drone, a violin and a viola cycle continuously, at times sounding like organs, at other times like foghorns or whistles. Voices intermittently enter and drop out, punctuated by an almost subliminal patter of hand drums. Strings and voices all waver around the drone, at times swerving slightly up or down, occasionally jumping to a higher harmonic. Immersed in the drone, temporal recollection and anticipation seem to fall away, and one comes to focus on the moment, on each new texture and interval. Beginnings and endings come to seem unimportant, and one can imagine this music carrying on forever.[1]

Whether organized around a drone or a pulse, classic minimalism replaced the teleology of harmonic development with a music of ec-static repetition. It turned away from the modernist classical music of the era and instead allied itself with the earthy discourse of '60s counterculture.[2]

From its inception, minimalism actively blurred the boundaries between "high" and "mass" culture, "classical" and "popular" music. Many of its practitioners (e.g., Terry Riley, Steve Reich, Philip Glass, and, later, Glenn Branca, Arnold Dreyblatt, and Rhys Chatham) formed and trained small groups more akin to rock or jazz bands than classical ensembles. Breaking with the decorum of the concert hall, the minimalists forged connections with the icons of art pop and found a new fan base in rock clubs. Theatre of Eternal Music violist John Cale provided the backdrop for the Velvet Underground's late '60s psychedelia. In the '70s and '80s, David Bowie, Brian Eno, and David Byrne developed a fascination with the music of Philip Glass that eventually led to direct collaborations. Rhys Chatham and Glenn Branca fused minimalism with punk rock and recruited members of Sonic Youth, Mars, Swans, and Band of Susans. Today, the cultural ties between minimalist composers and popular music have never been stronger, thanks largely to the influence of Techno and its offshoots.

Despite the tag (never favored by its practitioners), "minimalism" contains a wealth of resources, allowing each generation to interpret it differently. Early minimalism drew inspiration from Indian ragas, Indonesian gamelan, and West African drumming; today, minimalism sounds at home among the denizens of the datascape attuned to the buzz and crackle of cybernetic paraphernalia. In both cases, the essential impulse is the same. Steve Reich, for example, was certainly inspired by Balinese gamelan and Ghanaian drumming; but, years before dub and HipHop, he also made pioneering use of tape effects and studio manipulations. Though composed for marimbas and bongos instead of samplers and sequencers, the kind of layered, modular repetition later fostered by Reich and Glass is the stuff of which Techno is made.

Techno's minimalism recapitulates the sonic and social spirit of early minimalism, offering a repetitive, psychedelic provocation for mind-expansion and all-night partying. Yet, through Techno and beyond it, minimalism has also provided new resources for sound artists who are as likely to present their work in galleries as in clubs. For artists such as Ryoji Ikeda and Carsten Nicolai, minimalist repetition provides a means of slowing down the data flow and focusing the listener's attention on the nature of sound and signal.

Post-rock artists such as Tortoise and Papa M, ambient artists such as Thomas Köner, Tetsu Inoue, and Main, and jazz groups such as The Necks employ minimalist strategies as a means of escape from the verse/chorus/verse song form so common in pop, rock, and jazz (see Reynolds, chap. 52). Where the traditional rock song is always invested in the logic of tension and release, build-up, climax, and dénouement, minimalism has fostered a new interest in what philosophers Gilles Deleuze and Félix Guattari call the "plateau," "a continuous, self-vibrating region of intensities whose development avoids any orientation toward a culmination point or external end."[3]

## NOTES

1. The description above is based on the only publicly-available recording of the Theatre of Eternal Music (a.k.a. the Dream Syndicate), *Inside the Dream Syndicate, Vol. I: Day of Niagara (1965)* (Table of the Elements, 2000). Whether this music is properly attributed to La Monte Young or to the quintet (which included John Cale, Tony Conrad, Angus MacLise, and Marian Zazeela) is still an open question.

2. Portions of this introduction are drawn from Christoph Cox, "Remix and Match," *Artforum* (March 1999), 35.

3. Gilles Deleuze and Félix Guattari, *A Thousand Plateaus*, trans. Brian Massumi (Minneapolis: University of Minnesota Press, 1987), 22. Deleuze and Guattari draw this term and description from Gregory Bateson's description of Balinese culture.

# 41

# *Rap, Minimalism, and Structures of Time in Late Twentieth-Century Culture*

### SUSAN McCLARY

One of the founders of the "New Musicology," Susan McClary (1946– ) refuses to treat music as an autonomous domain and instead focuses on the socio-political contexts and significations of music, both classical and popular. McClary's groundbreaking book, *Feminine Endings: Music, Gender, and Sexuality* (1991), re-reads the history of music, from Monteverdi and Bizet through Madonna and Diamanda Galas, as gendered in both form and content. In the following piece, McClary poses the historical and anthropological question "Why is repetition so prevalent in the music of the late 20th century?" In response, she offers a genealogy of musical minimalisms that situates them in relationship to the cultural crises of the 20th century.

[. . . .] Imagine that a traveler from one-hundred years ago arrives at our doorstep and asks us why the music of the late twentieth century operates so frequently on the basis of cyclic repetition. Not just the rap and dance genres of popular culture, but also minimalism—perhaps the single most viable extant strand of the Western art-music tradition. So ubiquitous are these patterns that they appear even in the soundtracks to historical films: recall, for example, Michael Nyman's soundtrack to *The Piano,* the minimalist score of which was designed to conjure up the mid-nineteenth-century Romanticism of, say, Schumann.[1]

The proliferation of such patterns across genres has not been noticed very much, in large part because they do not share the same audiences. The devoted fans of Goldie or Missy "Misdemeanor" Elliott don't usually attend Steve Reich concerts, nor do many of the symphony subscribers who admire the works of John Adams involve themselves in the dance-club scene or participate in raves. At my local record store, you must descend two full flights of stairs from the bins containing CDs by Terry Riley to find those featuring Ice Cube. This spatial separation prevents any accidental contamination of one clientele with the unintelligible noises of another—only those intrepid souls committed to crossing over make the effort to bridge this physical enactment of cultural hierarchy. And when you finally present your eclectic selection at the cash register, the check-out clerks eye you with suspicion; sometimes they even ask if you know what you're buying or if you've just grabbed items at random.

Yet the genres often sound astonishingly similar, especially in their ways of structuring time. Let me offer some brief examples:

1. P.J. Harvey, "The Dancer," *To Bring You My Love*, 1995
2. Philip Glass, "Hymn to Aten," *Akhnaten*, 1984
3. Tupac Shakur, "Tradin' War Stories," *All Eyez On Me*, 1996
4. Prodigy, "Climbatize," *The Fat of the Land*, 1997
5. Glass, "Northern Tibet," *Kundun*, 1997

This is the music of our own time—not the only kind, to be sure, but these figure among the most pervasive. We do not have to descend at all into the deep well of the past in order to make contact with its practitioners and audiences; we ourselves should qualify as native informants. If we cannot answer such questions, then who can? Musicologists tend to trust the eye-witness accounts of previous generations when they address the music of their time, yet we defer passively to the future for judgment concerning that of our own moment.[2] So let me pose my ethnographic questions: why does so much of our music work this way? What kinds of needs do these patterns satisfy?

Allow me to anticipate some objections. Left to our own devices, we probably would not ask these questions of ourselves: to those of us invested in any of the genres to which I refer, distinctions count for far more than resemblance. Only listeners not familiar with Tupac Shakur or Philip Glass would privilege the repetitive procedures within which each operates; indeed, a knowledgeable fan or connoisseur might scoff at the idea of dwelling on that most elementary level of activity. To anyone, acquainted with a whole range of rap groups or minimalist composers, what matters are not stylistic similarities, but rather the particularities of Tupac's latest posthumous release, the haunting beauty of the harmonic changes in Glass's most recent collaboration with Robert Wilson, *Monsters of Grace*. To a large extent, the structures of repetition used by these artists have ceased to register as significant: they constitute merely the neutral ground of basic assumptions up against which the actual music occurs. Consequently, we (and I include here relative experts) might well prove inarticulate or downright antagonistic when faced with this line of questioning.

Yet a time-traveler from one-hundred years ago would no doubt insist on interrogating precisely these issues. We can now look back to the 1800s, to what must have seemed then like the infinite variety of symphonic possibilities, and recognize that they all shared an investment in dynamic narratives of subjective struggle towards triumph; we may identify them now as all participating in a specifically nineteenth-century cultural agenda. Indeed, that peculiar way of structuring time (mostly unremarked by commentators of the period) may now qualify as far more important for purposes of cultural history than the manifest content of any given symphony.[3] If the ideological priorities of late Romantic music appear relatively obvious from our vantage point, so too our own characteristic habits would seem absolutely fundamental to anyone transported from a previous time [. . . .]

Consequently, instead of simply asking *us* why our music works as it does, I will try to imagine explaining to someone from the outside how things got to be this way. No one a century ago could have predicted the shape of music today: how did it get to be this way? Strange to say, it proves nearly as difficult to account for our own predicament as for that of an earlier period, for which the receding years have filtered out many of the elements that make everyday life so complex, leaving behind for analysis—for better or worse—only those artifacts that managed somehow to survive [. . . .]

I will begin, then, by considering the dislodging of what would have seemed to nineteenth century Europeans a structure of time as pervasive as a fact of nature: the narrative orientation not only of operas but also of symphonies and quartets. At the peak of what appeared its greatest triumph, however—the period of the gigantic instrumental epics of Mahler and Bruckner—this model came under exceptionally vicious attack. And not from another cultural stratum: no, this was an insider job, perpetrated by those whose training had prepared them to inherit and pass on this tradition, so rich with the accreted wisdom of centuries.

Schoenberg, for instance, sought to strip away from his work all vestiges of convention, which he regarded as repressive ideology, and he plunged inward to cultivate what he took as authentic, intensely organic subjectivity: indeed, a subjectivity capable of producing its own self-generated objectivity. Cultural critic Theodor Adorno, who worked closely with the musicians of the Second Viennese School, explained why Schoenberg fought so vehemently against instances of repetition: if we understand a piece of music as an allegory of personal development, then any reiteration registers as regression—as a failure or even a refusal to keep up the unending struggle for continual growth demanded for successful self-actualization. Similarly, reliance on cultural conventions—even those responsible for nineteenth-century symphonies—betrays for Schoenberg/Adorno an intolerable concession to pressures to conform to the outside world. Schoenberg's embattled Self thus enacts a scenario of extreme insularity, admitting neither reference to the previously existing musical codes that make communication feasible nor to the redundancy that offers the listener internal structural markers; it glorifies a Self so resistant to the constraints of normative social interaction and accepted definitions of reason that it became—and quite deliberately so—indistinguishable from manifestations of madness.[4]

But Schoenberg's was not the only apocalyptic agenda of the early 1900s. Stravinsky's heresy, by contrast, raged against the fetish of individualistic interiority Schoenberg held in common with the Romantic tradition; in place of allegories of exquisitely wrought Selfhood, he offered collective, ritualized violence. Disdaining the bourgeois sensibility given voice by classic forms, he hurled the primitivism of *Rite of Spring* at scandalized Parisian audiences: *this*—not pretty, cleaned-up images of love, duty, and self-expression—was Stravinsky's vision of humanity (revealed here just as Freud was unmasking the anarchic substructure of the unconscious). Civilization and its discontents had become too burdensome; urban artists coveted the freedom they imagined as the birthright of tribal peoples.[5]

Predictably, Adorno critiqued Stravinsky severely—not for his dissonance or departure from traditional practices, but for the hypnotic effect of his repetitious ostinato patterns, which Adorno heard as seducing listeners into passive acceptance of the most barbarous elements of encroaching totalitarianism.[6] He believed that when audiences give up the admittedly difficult task of critical thinking, then the path is paved for demagogues like Hitler or Stalin. To Adorno, Schoenberg's music posed fierce challenges to keep the mind alert and behavior autonomous; from that point of view, Stravinsky seemed to cast his lot in with group-incited hedonism and potential atrocity.

We do not have to accept these arguments as somehow or other *true*, but they do offer insight into why musical repetition became a moral battlefield in the 1920s. Schoenberg's position, which came to prevail within the North American academy, has strongly influenced the training of young musicians. This training accounts in part for the automatic reaction against musical styles that operate according to repetition, though many of the musicians who parrot the condemnation of repetition could not reconstruct the prehistory of this controversy: they know only that *repetition is bad*.

But the repetition in today's music does not descend directly from Stravinskian ostinatos—except perhaps for the memorable leitmotiv for the shark in *Jaws.* In certain respects, minimalist composers owe more to Schoenberg. To be sure, his declared war on repetition would seem to move us further away from the cyclicism of today's music. In retrospect, however, we might argue that the very fanaticism with which Schoenberg's atonal followers strove to enforce his radical position eventually helped to precipitate its opposite: the oedipal child rebels by acting out precisely the worst nightmare of the too-strict parent, and High Modernism's stringent prohibition inadvertently goaded a later generation to embrace obsessive repetition.[7]

Yet repetitive structures signify more than a simple reaction formation—an arbitrary strategy for refuting paternal serialists. Nor does it necessarily align itself with fantasies of primitivism, as did Stravinsky's *Rite-of-Spring* ostinatos. But in order to explain more fully for this phenomenon we have to entertain the idea that the European classical tradition has ceased to occupy the mainstream, that it no longer qualifies as the protagonist in the history of music—not even in the West. In other words, my answer to our time traveler will require a very different account of music of the last hundred years than the one typically delineated in textbooks titled *Twentieth-Century Music.*[8]

Two other musical traditions have played unexpected but starring roles in the development of our music—both introduced into the West largely as a result of the imperialist projects that led Europe to hold dominion over the rest of the globe during the nineteenth century. For conquest, it seems, cuts both ways: if the West prevailed economically and politically, the attractions of some of its plunder proved irresistibly seductive. Bizet's opera *Carmen* presciently staged in 1875 some of this cultural reversal, as an aristocratic soldier in a colonial army falls under the sway of native customs: his lofty sentiments and proper operatic idiom wilt before the sensual license of "gypsy" music. And like Don José, audiences—including even listeners as sophisticated as Tchaikovsky and Nietzsche—confessed themselves spellbound by Carmen's exotic utterances, even though her French-composed songs and dances represented World Music at third remove at best.[9] The glories of the symphonic legacy began to feel like the White Man's Burden.[10]

In 1889, to celebrate the centennial of its Revolution, France hosted the Exhibition Universelle, at which it displayed the acquisitions of its century of colonial expansion. A young French composer happened to wander into the Indonesian Pavilion, where he encountered a performance by a gamelan—a percussion ensemble from Java. The shimmering sounds themselves captivated his ear, but the Indonesian fashion of shaping time impressed him even more. Instead of the goal-oriented trajectories of the music he knew, Claude Debussy heard the gamelan playing what Javanese musicians would recognize as complex interlocking cycles related to Indonesian philosophies of life.[11] Although he had little interest in the metaphysics that generated these patterns, he perceived in this music a radically different mode of temporality from the one inscribed in European practices. This experience helped Debussy to transform his *modus operandi* as he experimented—along with Satie and Ravel—with how to structure sound without recourse to the postponed gratification of tonal harmony or the promise of climax. If previous composers had sought exotic color in superficial references to the Orient, sprinkled innocuously on top of a securely European tonal framework, Debussy increasingly accepted as his structural premise the Asian structures of time he had stumbled upon by accident at a world's fair.[12]

As it turns out, Debussy was just the first of a distinguished line of Western composers drawn not only to Asian musical practices, but also to the philosophies and theologies that sustain them: to name but a few, Colin McPhee, Lou Harrison, Benjamin Britten, and John Cage. Even quintessential modernists such as Pierre Boulez and Karlheinz Stockhausen have featured gamelan-inspired textures or foregrounded the recitation of Hindu mantras in their work. The list would also include a virtual *Who's Who* of 1960s minimalism: La Monte Young, Terry Riley, Pauline Oliveros, Laurie Anderson, and Philip Glass.[13] Thus, a colonialist enterprise that set off to impose European values on the rest of the globe also produced the reverse effect, as an increasing number of the West's most creative artists—weary of what they perceived as the cul-de-sac of the European tradition and its attendant ideologies—jumped ship.[14] Several of these went far beyond the simple imitation of alien musical styles: compelled first by the non-violent and non-linear cyclic sound-patterns they heard, they eventually converted to Buddhism and now strive to live their lives in accordance with its precepts.

The public, however, felt the impact of Asian influences on Western music in the 1960s not through the work of these still-obscure experimentalists, but rather through the rock music that was quickly becoming an international *lingua franca*. Most famously, the Beatles—a band that began its career with covers of Chuck Berry songs—suddenly started weaving sitars and trance-like passages into their albums: a move very much in keeping with the Counterculture's fascination with alternative (ahem) drug-induced modes of consciousness. To be sure, although some disciples of the Counterculture studied with gurus and undertook pilgrimages, many responded to this engagement with Eastern references as the latest fad, as an accessory like hash brownies. Still, regardless of intentions, whether lofty or fashion-driven, the cyclic patterning of Asian music infiltrated Western culture in general, and its sounds became part of the overall range of possibilities available to musicians. The Beatles' *Sgt. Pepper* begat Led Zeppelin's "Kashmir," to say nothing of the exotic references in everything from Metallica to Beck to Madonna, who actually sings in Sanskrit [ . . . in *Ray of Light*].

But the musical framework onto which these specifically Asian characteristics were grafted—namely the blues—was itself already posited on repetitive proce-dures. For the other tradition that has come to dominate the music of our century is a legacy of the people who were transported to the Americas against their wills from West Africa.

Christopher Small, in his magnificent *Music of the Common Tongue,* traces how inherited musical practices have enabled African-Americans to survive the brutal conditions of slavery and other forms of social oppression throughout the last four centuries.[15] James Snead and Henry Louis Gates, Jr. have further theo-rized the centrality of repetition in African-based cultural forms, literary as well as musical. An earlier generation of critics, most of them trained to privilege structural complexity and innovation in their aesthetic judgments, often decried what they perceived as the simple-mindedness of African-American music and literature. But Small, Snead, Gates, Samuel Floyd, Tricia Rose, Robert Walser, and others have explained how these practices work to maintain a sense of community through the recycling of materials, while individual artists "signify" imaginatively on those famil-iar materials.[16]

Most listeners did not await the verdicts of these cultural theorists, however, before embracing African-based music. Narrative accounts of music in the twenti-eth century ought to (but rarely do) find at their core the succession of Black genres that stamped themselves indelibly on the lives of generation after genera-tion: ragtime, blues, jazz, R&B, gospel, doowop, soul, rock, reggae, funk, disco, rap. This, I would argue, is the most important tributary flowing into today's music.

[. . . .] Yet my time-traveler from 1900 would no doubt profess astonishment that this displacement of European by African-based musics in Western culture could have occurred. To be sure, Dvorak had suggested Black music as the obvi-ous source for a genuinely American musical language, but few composers took his recommendation seriously.

A large part of the explanation for this startling cultural emergence has to do, of course, with the exceptional vitality, creativity, and power of musicians working within these idioms. But quality alone does not guarantee reception—especially when it springs from a long marginalized, even despised segment of the popula-tion. What kinds of conditions allowed for the displacement of a dominant tradition by one of negative prestige?

Recall that turn-of-the-century European composers chose to depart radically from the conventions sustaining their customary relationship with audiences. This widespread crisis took place at the same moment as the emergence of unantici-pated technologies: sound recording and radio. Suddenly, the performance by an improvising musician could be heard directly, without the previously-necessary mediation of notation. Details such as quality of voice, rhythmic nuance, expres-sive gesture could be captured and circulated far beyond the musician's actual location. At the moment these technologies appeared, European composers had their minds set on alienating their usual audience. Black popular music stepped in to fill the resulting vacuum, and the 1920s proclaimed themselves worldwide The Jazz Age.

Perhaps the single most important feature of twentieth-century musical culture is its gradual but pervasive African-Americanization. If we are subjected to debates about the value of gangsta rap, most of the alternatives available are other genres that can trace themselves back to blues. Given its ubiquity, black pop music would seem to be the element most clearly responsible for converting our collective sense of time from tortured heroic narratives to cycles of kinetic pleasure. As Prince sings, "There's joy in repetition!" One can even perceive a strong influence of African-based patterning in both the experimental music and rock of the 1960s—the time when the influence of Asian practices is most explicit. The blues and its descendants had predisposed both rockers and minimalist composers to experience time in this way, even if their attraction to Buddhism or Hindu mysticism led them to propose a somewhat different lineage.

How, then, do we explain this structure of feeling so prevalent in our own moment? [. . . .] The postmodernists claim this propensity for repetition as a reaction against the formalist excesses of High Modernism, and they rightly draw parallels between the minimalist art of, say, Andy Warhol and the music of Glass or Reich. Whether multiple images of Marilyn Monroe or self-replicating cycles of arpeggios, the underlying structure operates according to an additive process rather than either a traditional mode of representation or the abstraction of mid-century artworks. Certain postmodernist philosophers, especially Gilles Deleuze and Jean-François Lyotard, have sought to valorize the repetitive, ecstatic structures of time in our moment; they theorize it as a new mode of consciousness, only now becoming intelligible up against the dialectical individualism of the recent past.[17]

Yet many still resist what they perceive as the dire implications of repetitive formations. Much of this criticism continues the line of argumentation first articulated by Adorno against what he heard variously as reification in Schubert's crystalline structures, Wagner's flashcard leitmotivs, and the robotic jitterbug rhythms of jazz. Thus Fredric Jameson decries the absence of depth in today's artworks, and Jean Baudrillard lays the blame at the feet of advertising strategies, which produce desire by bombarding the population with slogans, trademarks, and rootless (if spellbinding) imagery[18] [. . . .]

By contrast, my convoluted genealogy would have to include Stravinsky's primitivism; Debussy's escape from European narrativity into Indonesian temporalities; the global circulation of blues and jazz made possible by sound technologies; Benjamin Britten's use of gamelan-inspired sonorities as symbols of alternative sexualities;[19] Aaron Copland's redeployment of Stravinskian ostinatos to construct the still-prevailing semiotics of the American West; the attempts by a succession of youth cultures to reclaim their bodies through the rhythms of Swing, 50s rock 'n' roll, disco, or Techno; the drug-induced mysticism of the Counterculture and the trance-states sought by New Age devotees in their preference for drone-based musics; the cyclic processes explored by feminist musicians searching for alternatives to what they perceive as the violence of dominant procedures;[20] the virtuosity of Ravi Shankar, who influenced Coltrane, Glass, and the Beatles; the yearning of composers of the 1970s to reconnect with the audiences estranged by the Modernists; the attractiveness of Buddhist philosophies to many Westerners burned out on materialist consumption; the disco movement that emerged from gay venues to challenge rock's self-proclaimed authenticity and that continues in the various versions of dance-club music; the aggressive international music business which makes the world's music available as commodity, simultaneously homogenizing and diversifying cultural forms; a commitment to ecology, which inspired *Koyaanisqatsi,* Eno's Ambient music, and the Grateful Dead; the technologies of sampling and digital arrangement that greatly facilitate repetitive constructions; the griot and gospel-preaching traditions that inform the cultural practice of rap.[21]

In other words, the structures of repetition that characterize so much of our music testify to the complex, unpredictable history of our century. As the poststructuralists might say, this condition is overdetermined—that is, it owes its emergence to countless moments of creativity, accidents of reception, strange correspondences between distant sensibilities, contributions from long-ignored minorities, and much more. Like all cultural moments, ours has both utopian and dystopic elements,[22] which is why we must continue to strive to make sense of it and debate as participants each new option as it appears.

Very deep indeed is the well of our own era. Too many possible explanations jostle for our attention, all of them accompanied by fiercely contested cultural baggage. Yet the fact that we cannot reduce the phenomenon of cyclic structures to the effect of a single cause does not make it arbitrary or meaningless—quite the contrary. Answers may present themselves more easily some time in the future when our particular set of conventions begin to give way to others. At that point, another flurry of debates will point up explicitly what has become exhausted, what is still held as valuable about these repetitive schemata.

The historian of the future will have the luxury of looking back on our era, to see what turns out to have been important after all. That historian, however, will no doubt yearn to have experienced what it was like to be alive at this very moment, trying to make sense of the bewildering profusion of musical practices and critical opinions. That's why it's so important for us to perform—if only from time to time—an anthropology of ourselves. For there's no time like the present.

## NOTES

1. Similarly, the soundtrack for *Angels and Insects* used minimalist patterning to represent the nineteenth century.

2. When I was receiving my training in the 1960s, the profession still regarded nineteenth-century music as too close for serious scrutiny. The journal *19th-Century Music* began only in the late 1970s, and scholars have started to tackle early twentieth-century repertories only since the late 1980s.

3. It takes a great deal of effort to teach advanced graduate students how to interpret the particularities of a nineteenth-century score (a skill that the most casual concert-goer of the 1890s would have assumed as basic), but today's public-radio subscribers happily tune in for interchangeable instances of a repertory that guarantee in advance the quality of motion to which they are addicted.

4. Theodor W. Adorno, "Arnold Schoenberg, 1874-1951," *Prisms,* trans. Samuel Weber and Shierry Weber (Cambridge, Mass.: MIT Press, 1981), 147–72. For more on this cultural moment and its motivations see Friedrich A. Kittler, *Discourse Networks, 1800/1900,* trans. Michael Metteer and Chris Cullens (Stanford: Stanford University Press, 1990) and Andreas Huyssen, *After the Great Divide: Modernism, Mass Culture, Postmodernism* (Bloomington: Indiana University Press, 1986).

5. A good deal has been written recently on the relationship between early twentieth-century Modernism and this primitivist projection. See, for instance, Marianna Torgovnick, *Gone Primitive: Savage Intellects, Modern Lives* (Chicago: University of Chicago Press, 1990).

6. Adorno pits Stravinsky and Schoenberg against each other in *Philosophy of Modern Music,* trans. Anne G. Mitchell and Wesley V. Blomster (New York: Seabury Press, 1973). For another point of view, see Richard Taruskin, *Stravinsky and the Russian Traditions,* 2 vols. (Berkeley and Los Angeles: University of California Press, 1996). In his novel of 1924, *The Magic Mountain,* Thomas Mann too focuses on what was already seen among German intellectuals as the widespread refusal of the Enlightenment project in the wake of the Great War. Mann's Hans Castorp—a young man of privilege who has trained to work as an engineer—becomes absorbed in the repetitive daily regimen in a tubercular sanitarium and gradually abandons his sense of teleology. In his text Mann devotes many long passages to discussing the philosophical and social implications of these two ways of experiencing time. Interestingly, the character who consistently advocates the progress-model of time is also associated with Satan—as was, of course, Faust's Mephistopheles.

7. For more on this set of reactions, see my "Terminal Prestige: The Case of Avant-Garde Music Composition," *Cultural Critique 12* (Spring 1989), 57–81.

8. See, for instance, Robert P. Morgan, *Twentieth-Century Music* (New York: W.W. Norton, 1991). Only a few books attempt to cross between the continuation of the European art tradition and popular music. See John Rockwell, *All American Music* (New York: Vintage Books, 1983) and David Toop, *Ocean of Sound: Aether Talk, Ambient Sound and Imaginary Worlds* (London and New York: Serpents Tail, 1995).

9. See my *Georges Bizet: Carmen* (Cambridge: Cambridge University Press, 1993).

10. See the comparison between Bizet and Wagner in the opening sections of Friedrich Nietzsche, *The Case of Wagner,* trans. Walter Kaufmann (New York: Vintage Books, 1967).

11. Judith Becker, Gregory Bateson, and Clifford Geertz have all written extensively about Indonesian modes of temporality.

12. For more on the specific responses to the gamelan in the music of Debussy and subsequent composers, see Mervyn Cooke, "The East in the West: Evocations of the Gamelan in Western Music," in *The Exotic in Western Music,* ed. Jonathan Bellman (Boston: Northeastern University Press, 1998), 258–80.

13. For more on the musical procedures of these musicians, see Wim Mertens, *American Minimal Music,* trans. J. Hautekiet (London: Kahn & Averill; White Plains, NY: Pro/Am Music Resources Inc., 1983).

14. [. . . . Thomas] Mann's *The Magic Mountain* recognizes as early as 1924 this pull of the East, as he traces the appeal of repetitive time-structures to Asia and to the disenchantment of so many with European ideals concerning science and progress. See especially the chapter titled "Encyclopaedic."

15. Christopher Small, *Music of the Common Tongue: Survival and Celebration in Afro-American Music* (London: John Calder, 1987; rev. ed., Hanover, N.H.: Wesleyan University Press, 1998).

16. James Snead, "On Repetition in Black Culture," *Black American Literature Forum 15,* no. 4 (1981), 146-54; Henry Louis Gates, Jr., *The Signifying Monkey: A Theory of African-American Literary Criticism* (Oxford: Oxford University Press, 1988); Samuel A. Floyd, Jr., *The Power of Black Music: Interpreting Its History from Africa to the United States* (Oxford: Oxford University Press, 1995); Tricia Rose, *Black Noise: Rap Music and Black Culture in Contemporary America* (Hanover, N.H.: Wesleyan University Press, 1994); Robert Walser, "Rhythm, Rhyme, and Rhetoric in the Music of Public Enemy," *Ethnomusicology 39/ 2* (1995), 193–218.

17. Gilles Deleuze, *Difference and Repetition*, trans. Paul Patton (New York: Columbia University Press, 1994); Deleuze and Félix Guattari, *A Thousand Plateaus: Capitalism and Schizophrenia*, trans. Brian Massumi (Minneapolis: University of Minnesota Press, 1987); Jean-François Lyotard, *The Postmodern Condition: A Report on Knowledge*, trans. Geoff Bennington and Brian Massumi (Minneapolis: University of Minnesota Press, 1984) and "Several Silences," in his *Driftworks*, trans. Joseph Maier (New York: Semiotext(e), 1984), 91–110.

18. See, for instance, Fredric Jameson, "Postmodernism and Consumer Society," and Jean Baudrillard, "The Ecstasy of Communication," both in Hal Foster, ed., *The Anti-Aesthetic: Essays on Postmodern Culture* (Port Townsend, Wash.: Bay Press, 1983). See also the extended Adorno-like critique of repetition in Jacques Attali, *Noise: The Political Economy of Music*, trans. Brian Massumi (Minneapolis: University of Minnesota Press, 1985).

19. Philip Brett, "Eros and Orientalism in Britten's Operas," in *Queering the Pitch: The New Gay and Lesbian Musicology,* ed. Brett, Elizabeth Wood, and Gary C. Thomas (London and New York: Routledge, 1994), 235–56. See also Cooke, "The East in the West."

20. See the discussions in my *Feminine Endings: Music, Gender, and Sexuality* (Minneapolis: University of Minnesota Press, 1991).

21. Tricia Rose argues persuasively that we must locate rap in the intersection between traditional practices and state-of-the-art technology. See her *Black Noise.*

22. See the concluding section of Mertens, *American Minimal Music,* 113-24.

**298** • audio culture

# 42

# Thankless Attempts at a Definition of Minimalism

## KYLE GANN

Through his regular contributions to *The Village Voice* and *The New York Times*, Kyle Gann (1955– ) has been a tireless advocate for minimalist and post-minimalist music. He is the author of *The Music of Conlon Nancarrow* (1995), *American Music in the 20th Century* (1997), and articles on La Monte Young, Rhys Chatham, Henry Cowell, John Cage, and others. A composer of microtonal music, Gann draws equally from the American experimental tradition and from Hopi, Zuni, and Pueblo Indian musics. What follows is Gann's attempt to pinpoint the defining features of minimalist music and to distinguish several of its distinct strands.

What is minimalism? What constitutes a minimalist work? [. . . .]

There have even been thirty years of carping about the term minimalism, which was coined apparently by Michael Nyman in 1968, though Tom Johnson (as music critic for the *Village Voice* in New York) has also staked such a claim. Many of the original minimalist works last for hours and contain thousands of notes: how, disbelievers claim, can we call such grandiose music minimalist?

Well, it's pretty simple, really. Minimalist music, at least originally, tended to restrict itself to a tiny repertoire of pitches and rhythmic values, like the F Dorian scale and steady 8th-notes of Philip Glass's *Music in Fifths*. The length of the works actually underlines the intense restriction of materials: you might write a four-minute piece using only seven pitches and no one would notice, but write a 30-minute piece, and the austere limitations become a major phenomenon of the composition.

Moreover, minimalism borrowed its name from the eponymous art movement, and there are clear parallels between the quasi-geometric linearity and predictability of Philip Glass's and Steve Reich's notes with the clean geometric lines and simple optical illusions of a Frank Stella or Sol Lewitt. One visual-art tome describes minimalist art as that which is "barren of merely decorative detail, in which geometry is emphasized and expressive technique avoided."[1] That's a fairly precise, if incomplete, description of most early minimalist music. K. Robert Schwarz quotes La Monte Young's definition as "That which is made with a minimum of means," which applies if by "means" you mean pitches and rhythmic values, not necessarily number of notes and stretches of time.[2]

Moreover, as Wittgenstein emphasized, the use of a word is its meaning. Most culturally literate people by now know that the word has been used to describe the musics of Young, Reich, and Glass. Pragmatically speaking, its meaning is circumscribed by at least their music of the 1960s and 1970s. To deny the term's usefulness at this point would be as futile as going back and arguing that we shouldn't call Monet's paintings Impressionistic. Other terms have been advanced: "trance music," "hypnotic music," "process music," "modular music," and, more pejoratively, "wallpaper music" and "going-nowhere music." Some of these are too vague, others too specific, and none is as precise and flexible at once as minimalism.

Composer John Adams [. . .] has stated three cut and dried criteria for what constitutes a minimalist piece: regular, articulated pulse; the use of tonal harmony with slow harmonic rhythm; and the building of large structures through repetition of small cells.[3] That certainly covers a lot of the public perception of minimalism. It ties together Riley's *In C* and *A Rainbow in Curved Air*, Glass's *Music in Fifths* and *Einstein on the Beach*, and Reich's *Drumming* and *Music for 18 Musicians*.

What it specifically (and intentionally) leaves out is the sine-tone installations of La Monte Young, and the related drone music of the Theatre of Eternal Music, which contain neither regular pulse nor repetitive pitch cells. Personally, for me, Young's *Composition 1960 No. 7*, which consists of the pitches B and F-sharp and the notation "to be held for a long time," must be regarded as a seminal work, perhaps *the* seminal work, of minimalism. I have trouble with a definition that omits that piece, and also with one that omits the drone music of Phill Niblock and the slow, ambling chord progressions of Harold Budd [. . . .]

Let's consider for a moment the ideas, devices, and techniques through which early minimalist music found expression:

1. *Static harmony:* Starting with Young's *Composition 1960 No. 7*, the minimalist tendency to stay on one chord, or to move back and forth among a small repertoire of chords, has marked most minimalist music, including Reich's *Piano Phase*, *Drumming*, and *Octet*. Glass's early ensemble works tended to stay within one scale rather than harmony—not necessarily a tenable distinction. In minimalist music this harmony is almost always related to the diatonic scale or mode—though there are important exceptions, such as Phill Niblock's music and James Tenney's *Chromatic Canon*, which applies a minimalist process to a 12-tone row.

2. *Repetition:* This is perhaps the most stereotypical aspect of minimalist music, the tendency that audiences superficially associate with its stuck-in-the-groove quality. It first appears in Terry Riley's tape pieces from 1963: *Mescalin Mix* and *The Gift*. Many minimalist works do not use repetition, however: Young's completely static sine-tone installations (except in the most microscopic acoustic sense), Tom Johnson's and Jon Gibson's permutational pieces, Phill Niblock's drone works.

3. *Additive process*: Minimalist works tended to start with a basic repeated pattern and add on in one of two ways. Either the pattern would be lengthened by adding additional notes or measures or phrases in usually a 1, 1+2, 1+2+3, 1+2+3+4 kind of way (*Music in Fifths*; Frederic Rzewski's *Les Moutons des Panurge*, *Attica*, and *Coming Together*; and later Carl Stone's electronic *Shing Kee*), or else by slowing down existing patterns ([Reich's] *Music for Mallet Instruments, Voice, and Organ*); or else a certain recurring duration would begin with silence and add notes with each recurrence (*Drumming*).

Because of additive process and other types of linear process detailed below, minimalist music was often called "Process Music"—a perfectly viable term and an interesting subject in its own right, but not a term that can be considered exactly coextensive with minimalism.

4. *Phase-shifting* : This technique, of two identical phrases played at the same time but at slightly different tempos so as to go out of phase with each other, was most characteristic of Reich's works of the 1960s and early 1970s: *Piano Phase*, *Come Out*, *It's Gonna Rain*, and *Drumming*. This technique had antecedents in Henry Cowell's *New Musical Resources* and Conlon Nancarrow's tempo explorations. Though not widely used in minimalist works per se, it survived as an important archetype in postminimal music (e.g. William Duckworth's *Time Curve Preludes*, John Luther Adams's *Dream in White on White*, Kyle Gann's, *Time Does Not Exist*).

5. *Permutational process*: Composers who wanted slightly less obvious melodic progressions, like Jon Gibson in his *Melody* (1975) and *Call* (1978), and Tom Johnson in his *Nine Bells*, would sometimes turn to systematic permutations of pitches.

6. *Steady beat*: Certainly many of the most famous minimalist pieces relied on a motoric 8th-note beat, although there were also several composers like Young and Niblock interested in drones with no beat at all. We can at least say that it was a near-universal trait of minimalism to never use a wide variety of rhythms; you might proceed in 8th-notes, or 8ths and quarters, or whole notes with fermatas, but you do not get the kind of mercurial rhythmic variety one would hear in any 19th-century classical composition. Perhaps "steady-beat-minimalism" is a criterion that could divide the minimalist repertoire into two mutually exclusive bodies of music, pulse-based music versus drone-based music.

7. *Static instrumentation*: The early minimalist ensembles, starting with *In C* and the Theatre of Eternal Music and continuing through the Reich and Glass ensembles, were all founded on a concept of everyone playing all the time; the minimalist concept of instrumentation is based on the idea of music being a ritual in which everyone participates equally, not on the classical European paradigm of the painter's palette in which each instrument adds its dash of color where needed. Minimalist ensembles (and postminimalist and totalist after them) hardly ever display the traditional give-and-take of a classical chamber group. In these days of amplification, which has been applied to minimalist works from the beginning, this makes minimalism, in my view, the beginning of a new and more economical symphonic tradition that can dispense with that labor-intensive, economically inefficient dinosaur, the orchestra.

8. *Linear transformation*: This is a generalization of processes such as additive structure above. Many of the minimalists have cultivated a fascination with lin-

ear motion from one musical state to another, such as Niblock's slow mutations from maximum in-tuneness to maximum dissonance or vice versa, or James Tenney's motion from tonality to atonality in his *Chromatic Canon*, and the linear acceleration of his *Spectral Canon for Conlon Nancarrow* (1974), an indisputably minimalist work and a very important one.

9. *Metamusic*: For awhile in the '70s it seemed that Steve Reich's chief preoccupation was the unintended acoustic details that arose (or were perceived) as a side effect of strictly carried-out processes. These included soft melodies created by the overtones of played notes, which Reich referred to as "metamusic," and even reinforced with notated instrumental melodies in such works as his *Octet*. One could say that the overtone phenomena buzzing above the slowly glissandoing drones of Phill Niblock's music, and even the changing overtone patterns heard as you walk through a La Monte Young sine-tone installation, constitute metamusic as well.

10. *Pure tuning*: It's noteworthy that minimalism started, in the musics of Young, Tony Conrad, and the Theatre of Eternal Music, as a slowed-down exploration of pure frequency ratios, resonant intervals outside the 12-pitch piano scale; Phill Niblock's music and much of Terry Riley's continue this feature as well. One could make an argument that the true minimalist music, hardcore minimalism, is in pure tunings. But since Glass and Reich have always been happy with the equal-tempered scale, this would be a hard sell.

11. *Influence of non-Western cultures*: This is far from a universal component of minimalism, nor a necessary one, but composers who started on the minimalist path had no European precedent to look to for examples of repetition or harmonic stasis, and typically turned eastward. It is significant that Young, Riley, and Glass were inspired by Indian classical music, and that Reich studied African drumming. And minimalism led directly to a much greater absorption of non-Western aesthetics and techniques by younger composers of the next generation. In a way, minimalism created a bridge over which American composers could rejoin the rest of the non-European world.

This is hardly a complete list of techniques and features of minimalist music, but it does constitute a family of character traits. No minimalist piece uses all of these, but I could hardly imagine calling a piece minimalist that didn't use at least a few of them. (If anyone can identify such a work, contact me and I'll add its traits to the list.)

Looking, however, to the opposite bank of minimalism, we find that many of these traits can be found in music that was influenced by minimalism, that grew out of minimalist practice, but that has departed so far from what we think of as minimalist as to no longer justify the name. For instance, many works that I consider postminimalist are characterized by steady beats, static harmony, and additive structures. For that reason, I like to add one delimiting feature to my own personal definition of minimalism:

12. *Audible structure*: For me, the thing that *Drumming, In C, Attica, Composition 1960 No. 7, Einstein on the Beach*, Budd's *The Pavilion of Dreams*, and all the other classic minimalist pieces shared was that their structure was right on the surface, that you could tell just from listening, often just from the first audition, what the overall process was. It seemed to me that part of minimalism's early mystique

was to have no secrets, to hold the music's structure right in the audience's face, and have that be listened to.

## NOTES

1. Kenneth Baker, *Minimalism* (New York: Abbeville Press, 1988).
2. K. Robert Schwarz, *Minimalists* (London: Phaidon, 1996), 9.
3. John Adams, "In Conversation with Jonathan Sheffer," *Perceptible Processes: Minimalism and the Baroque*, ed. Claudia Swan et al. (New York: Eos, 1997), 76.

# 43

## *Music as a Gradual Process*

### STEVE REICH

Steve Reich (1936– ) is one of the four major early minimalist composers. He studied philosophy as an undergraduate and went on to study composition, first at Julliard and then at Mills College and the San Francisco Tape Music Center, hotbeds for early experimental music in America. In 1970, Reich traveled to Accra to study Ghanaian drumming. Upon his return to the U.S., he began performing with a Balinese gamelan in Seattle. His early tape pieces, *It's Gonna Rain* (1965) and *Come Out* (1966), stand at the origin of both minimalist and experimental musical practices. Drawing from his experiences with African and Balinese musics, Reich's early instrumental pieces, particularly his music for percussion, foreground the phased repetition and accumulation of small rhythmic cells. In this 1969 manifesto, Reich succinctly proclaims his commitment to repetition and audible process in music.

I do not mean the process of composition, but rather pieces of music that are, literally, processes.

The distinctive thing about musical processes is that they determine all the note-to-note (sound-to-sound) details and the overall form simultaneously. (Think of a round or infinite canon.)

I am interested in perceptible processes. I want to be able to hear the process happening throughout the sounding music.

To facilitate closely detailed listening a musical process should happen extremely gradually.

Performing and listening to a gradual musical process resembles:

- pulling back a swing, releasing it, and observing it gradually come to rest;
- turning over an hour glass and watching the sand slowly run through to the bottom;
- placing your feet in the sand by the ocean's edge and watching, feeling, and listening to the waves gradually bury them.

Though I may have the pleasure of discovering musical processes and composing the musical material to run through them, once the process is set up and loaded it runs by itself.

Material may suggest what sort of process it should be run through (content suggests form), and processes may suggest what sort of material should be run through them (form suggests content). If the shoe fits, wear it.

As to whether a musical process is realized through live human performance or through some electro-mechanical means is not finally the main issue. One of the most beautiful concerts I ever heard consisted of four composers playing their tapes in a dark hall. (A tape is interesting when it's an interesting tape.)

It is quite natural to think about musical processes if one is frequently working with electro-mechanical sound equipment. All music turns out to be ethnic music.

Musical processes can give one a direct contact with the impersonal and also a kind of complete control, and one doesn't always think of the impersonal and complete control as going together. By "a kind" of complete control I mean that by running this material through this process I completely control all that results, but also that I accept all that results without changes.

John Cage has used processes and has certainly accepted their results, but the processes he used were compositional ones that could not be heard when the piece was performed. The process of using the *I Ching* or imperfections in a sheet of paper to determine musical parameters can't be heard when listening to music composed that way. The compositional processes and the sounding music have no audible connection. Similarly in serial music, the series itself is seldom audible. (This is a basic difference between serial—basically European—music and serial—basically American—art, where the perceived series is usually the focal point of the work.)

What I'm interested in is a compositional process and a sounding music that are one and the same thing.

James Tenney said in conversation, "Then the composer isn't privy to anything." I don't know any secrets of structure that you can't hear. We all listen to the process together since it's quite audible, and one of the reasons it's quite audible is, because it's happening extremely gradually.

The use of hidden structural devices in music never appealed to me. Even when all the cards are on the table and everyone hears what is gradually happening in a musical process, there are still enough mysteries to satisfy all. These mysteries are the impersonal, unintended, psychoacoustic by-products of the intended process. These might include sub-melodies heard within repeated melodic patterns, stereophonic effects due to listener location, slight irregularities in performance, harmonics, difference tones, and so on.

Listening to an extremely gradual musical process opens my ears to *it*, but *it* always extends farther than I can hear, and that makes it interesting to listen to that musical process again. That area of every gradual (completely controlled) musical process, where one hears the details of the sound moving out away from intentions, occurring for their own acoustic reasons, is *it*.

I begin to perceive these minute details when I can sustain close attention and a gradual process invites my sustained attention. By "gradual" I mean extremely gradual; a process happening so slowly and gradually that listening to it resembles watching a minute hand on a watch—you can perceive it moving after you stay with it a little while.

Several currently popular modal musics like Indian classical and drug-oriented rock and roll may make us aware of minute sound details because in being modal (constant key center, hypnotically droning and repetitious) they naturally focus on these details rather than on key modulation, counterpoint and other peculiarly Western devices. Nevertheless, these modal musics remain more or less strict frameworks for improvisation. They are not processes.

The distinctive thing about musical processes is that they determine all the note-to-note details and the overall form simultaneously. One can't improvise in a musical process—the concepts are mutually exclusive.

While performing and listening to gradual musical processes one can participate in a particular liberating and impersonal kind of ritual. Focusing in on the musical process makes possible that shift of attention away from *he* and *she* and *you* and *me* outward toward *it*.

# 44

# *Basic Concepts of Minimal Music*

## WIM MERTENS

A second-generation minimalist composer, Wim Mertens (1953– ) is also an important theorist of musical minimalism. His book, *American Minimal Music*, was one of the earliest, and certainly the most philosophically astute, studies of the four classic minimalist composers: La Monte Young, Terry Riley, Steve Reich, and Philip Glass. In this excerpt from that book, Mertens considers the nature of structure, time, and memory in minimalist composition, contrasting the dialectical and teleological nature of traditional classical music with the non-dialectical, static character of minimalist music.

By the designations *American Minimal Music* or "Repetitive Music" one usually understands the music of the composers La Monte Young, Terry Riley, Steve Reich and Philip Glass. These four American composers were the first to apply consistently the techniques of repetition and minimalism in their works. Their music developed in the 1960s in America, and during the seventies became very successful in Europe as well [. . . .]

It might be useful to consider the difference between the use of repetition or techniques of repetition in traditional Western music and American repetitive music.

The use of repetition is not new at all. What is new is only the global musical *context* in which it is used, and it is only this situation that allows us to distinguish between American repetition and repetition in classical music. In traditional music, repetition is used in a preeminently *narrative* and *teleological* frame,[1] so that musical components like rhythm, melody, harmony and so on are used in a causal, prefigured way, so that a musical perspective emerges that gives the listener a non-ambivalent orientation and that attempts to inform him of *meaningful* musical *contents*.

The traditional work is *teleological* or end-orientated, because all musical events result in a directed end or synthesis. The composition appears as a musical product characterized by an organic totality. By the underlying dynamic, dramatising construction, a directionality is created that presumes a *linear memory* in the listener, that forces him or her to follow the linear musical evolution. Repetition in the traditional work appears as a *reference to what has gone before,* so that one has to remember what was forgotten. This demands a learned, serious and concentrated, memory-dominated approach to listening. The music of the American composers of repetitive music can be described as non-narrative and a-teleological. Their music discards the traditional harmonic functional schemes of tension and relaxation and (currently) disapproves of classical formal schemes and the musical narrative that goes with them (formalizing a tonal and/or thematic dialectic). Instead there appears non-directed evolution in which the listener is no longer submitted to the constraint of following the musical evolution [. . . .]

The differences one can find in the compositional techniques that Young, Riley, Glass and Reich use, in no way obscure the broad similarities in the basic mechanics of their music and its ideological connotations. These are most easily delineated by setting them against the traditional romantic-dialectical musical model.

There is only a very tenuous polemical relationship between repetitive music and romantic-dialectical music—in fact, the guiding principles of the latter have simply been ignored. But on the other hand, it is clear that repetitive music can be seen as the final stage of an anti-dialectic movement that has shaped European avant-garde music since Schoenberg, a movement that reached its culmination with John Cage, even though his music has a very obvious polemical-intellectual background and orientation completely absent from repetitive music. So, bearing in mind the way in which repetitive music had adopted certain avant-garde ideas, it is possible to evaluate critically the struggle between the avant-garde and the dialectical model. Thus the real importance of repetitive music lies in the way in which it represents the most recent stage in the continuing evolution of music since Schoenberg.

One can, of course, approach the phenomenon of repetitive music from a number of different angles—for instance, one could focus on the restorative features of its musical language, such as the restoration of tonality or the emphasis on rhythmic pulse, or the choice of easily recognisable sound images. But such an approach seems superficial and defensive, because no matter how consistently composers of repetitive music have spoken out against the intellectualism of the avant-garde (which for Reich, includes Webern and Cage), they cannot escape its influence.

Another possible line of investigation would have been to draw attention to the open influence of non-European, so-called primitive music. La Monte Young has been influenced by Japanese Gagaku theatre and Indian raga music; and he and Terry Riley are both disciples of the Indian raga master Pandit Pran Nath. Philip Glass has based his rhythmic systems on the additive time-structures of tabla music; and Steve Reich had adopted certain rhythmic principles from the music of Ghana and the Ivory Coast, and also from Balinese Gamelan music. But this use of non-European techniques should not be regarded as the foundation of their work, but rather as a symptom of the ability of the modern culture industry to annex a foreign culture, strip it of its specific social-ideological context and incorporate it into its own culture products.

In the analysis which follows, traditional dialectical music will be compared and contrasted with non-dialectical repetitive music from a number of different viewpoints. For instance, one finds that in repetitive music the concept of *work* has been replaced by the notion of *process,* and that no one sound had any greater importance than any other. And as Ernst Albrecht Stiebler wrote: "It is a characteristic of repetitive music that nothing is being expressed: it stands only for itself."

Traditional dialectical music is representational: the musical form relates to an expressive content and is a means of creating a growing tension; this is what is usually called the "musical argument." But repetitive music is not built around such an "argument"; the work is non-representational and is no longer a medium for the expression of subjective feelings. Glass has written that "This music is not characterized by argument and development. It has disposed of traditional concepts that were closely linked to real time, to clock-time. Music is not a literal interpretation of life and the experience of time is different. It does not deal with events in a clear directional structure. In fact there is no structure at all." And additionally, that "Music no longer has a mediative function, referring to something outside itself, but it rather embodies itself without any mediation. The listener will therefore need a different approach to listening, without the traditional concepts of recollection and anticipation. Music must be listened to as a pure sound-event, an act without any dramatic structure."

In the *Village Voice,* Ron Rosenbaum, the critic, wrote of an anti-apocalyptical music with an extra-historical experience of time, brought about by discarding teleological and dramatic elements. La Monte Young has removed finality, the apocalypse, from his music, and what is left is mere duration and stasis, without beginning or end: eternal music. In fact, Young has said that his *Dream House* project is a permanent, continuous work that has no beginning and goes on indefinitely.

The conventional idea of the musical work as a totality is no longer valid, since a repetitive work is essentially a process, a music whose function is not to represent something outside itself but only to refer to its own creation. [Ivanka] Stoianova has spoken of ". . . generating the present at each moment. Aimless wandering without beginning, multidirectional motion without cause or effect." And, of course, this omni-directionality makes causal relationships impossible. A work becomes a process when it relates only to itself. The most important characteristic of musical process as defined by Reich is that it determines simultaneously both the note-to-note details and the overall form. Reich believes in the work's gradual inevitability: "Once the process is set up and loaded, it runs by itself." Subjective intervention is strictly ruled out in favour of a complete determinacy. Reich calls this a particularly liberating and impersonal ritual—he nominally controls everything that happens in the compositional process but also accepts everything that results without further modification. Like Reich, Glass rejects any structure that exists outside the musical process—the process has to generate its own structure: "My music has no overall structure but generates itself at each moment."

In process music, structure is secondary to sound; the two coincide only in so far as the process determines both the sound and the overall form. Repetitive music is mono-functional and sounds are not programmed to achieve a final solution of the opposition between material and structure. In dialectical music the real drama lies in the opposition between form and content and the final resolution of this opposition. But with the removal of logical causality sound becomes autonomous, so that in a process work no structure exists before sound: *it* is produced at each moment. Reich has said that he readily accepts any unplanned acoustical effects that arise in the course of the process. These are also important to Glass who said that "What is important is the immediate physiological effect on the listener." And La Monte Young, in particular, experimented with these physiological effects; he wrote about the *Well-Tuned Piano,* his most far-reaching attempt to systematize these effects, "that each harmonic interval determines a distinct feeling." What he had in mind was to make a catalogue of intervals and the feelings they produce, so as to be able to calculate a measurable effect that could be made on the listener.

In repetitive music perception is an integral and creative part of the musical process since the listener no longer perceives a finished work but actively participates in its construction. Since there is no absolute point of reference a host of interpretative perspectives are possible. So that goal-directed listening, based as it is on recollection and anticipation, is no longer suitable and must be in favour of a random, aimless listening, traditional recollection of the past being replaced by something akin to a "recollection into the future," actualisation rather than reconstruction. This "forward recollection" removes memory from its privileged position.

Stoianova called this a game of "iterative monadism": what matters is not what the sound may stand for but its physiological intensity, or, as Young puts it: "One must get inside the sound."

American repetitive music is an objective music in that, since no physiological tension is created, there is an ambiguous relationship with the listener. The music exists for itself and has nothing to do with the subjectivity of the listener. The latter's position has become an ambiguous one: on the one hand he is freed of intentionality, but on the other hand he is reduced to a passive role, merely submitting to the process. Reich had this in mind when he remarked that, one can control everything only as long as one is prepared to accept everything.

What is more important: freedom or manipulation? Liberating the listener does not seem to be a major concern of repetitive composers. Since each moment may be the beginning or the end, the listener can choose how long he wants to listen for, but he will never miss anything by not listening. Some people have commented on the bulldozer effect of repetitive music, but this effect is erroneous since repetitive music has brought about a reversal of the traditional position; the subject no longer determines the music, as it did in the past, but the music now determines the subject. This reversal results in a shift towards extra-musical elements. For unlike traditional dialectical music, repetitive music does not represent a physical event but is the actual embodiment of this event.

Though Reich and Glass are somewhat less outspoken about the importance of the aural result, for Young and Riley, this aural result is music's only *raison d'être.* Riley's accumulative processes assume a fundamental distinction between micro-level and macro-level. Continuous change is achieved by inserting new elements into the basic form that is repeated and the pulse displaces attention away from the details of form towards the overall process, so that extreme variations on the micro-level may paradoxically produce an impression of immobility. The very rapid patterns that Riley uses produce slow movements that nevertheless feel like a "vibrating motionless trance," which resembles, as Stiebler noted, a state of weightlessness, which is precisely the effect that Riley intends to achieve. In fact he has said that he considers his music has failed if it cannot bring the listener out of himself. But the opposite process is also possible: La Monte Young has used the static dimension of music as a means of producing in the listener the feeling of motion.

To what extent the adoption of a mystical ideology is an inevitable by-product of the use of repetition is not too clear, though the use of non-European musical elements has certainly led Riley and Young to come under the influence of Eastern ideology. To Riley and Young the aim of music is to get "far out," or as Young put it: "If people don't get carried away by my music it is a failure." For Riley, pulse is a somewhat Eastern method of getting "far out": "You can get as far out as you want by relating to a constant." And the effect of Riley's music is achieved by identification with what he calls the total time process. But the continuous variation in Riley's accumulative process negates itself because of its emptiness and leads one to perceive passing time simply as stasis. Young, on the other hand, refers to identification with sound as such: "To get into the sound: The sound is God, I am the sound that is God." The extended static sounds of La Monte Young's music suggest an anti-apocalyptic time as pure duration. Or as Wolfgang Burde wrote: "Minimal music has discovered the adventure of macro-time and what is required is no longer an analytical approach, but a surrendering to a musical stream that will lead to a new expanded experience of time." Daniel Caux made a similar point when he noted in Riley's music an attempt to hypnotize the listener back into a state of innocence.

For Glass and Reich, the removal of dialectical content from music is in no way connected with mystical ideology. Reich's music assumes neutrality of values as a matter of principle. And while his attempt to use Western sound material in the context of non-Western structural methods seems at first sight to be merely a technical procedure without ideological relevance, the fact that both his and Glass's music takes place in non-dialectical macro-time, brings them very close to the mysticism of Riley and Young. Glass has expressed his opposition to traditional clock-time and denies structured time-relationships and intentionality. In Western music, the musical argument is the result of a dialectical subdivision of time. Yet both Riley and Reich have eliminated this historical negativity: their idea of time is an empty one, and because of this no real change can take place in their music, so that a higher level of macro-time, beyond history, is reached, which has been called *now* or *stasis* or *eternity*. It is this non-historical character of repetitive music that is the real negation of subjectivity. Repetitive music attempts to unite the historical subject with nonhistorical time and it is in this way that repetitive music refers to the mythical ending of history. As the sleeve note of Riley's *Rainbow in Curved Air* says: "And then all wars ended. Arms of every kind were outlawed and the masses gladly contributed them to giant foundries in which they were melted down and the metal poured into the earth. . . . All boundaries were dissolved. . . . The energy from dismantled weapons provided free heat and light. . . . The concept of work was forgotten."

## NOTES

1. The term *teleology* has its origin in the Greek *telos* (purpose) and originally was a concept in natural philosophy referring to certain directednesses that can be distinguished in

nature, and mainly in living nature. Within the modern science of nature a distinction is made between teleology and finality. With teleology, the directedness is defined but one cannot determine scientifically whether there is also an intention behind it. Here the distinction is made between *Zweck* and *Absicht, End* and *Purpose*. We will not retain this distinction, except in the sense of external and internal musical purposes. The external musical directedness corresponds to what is above called *Absicht* and *Purpose*. It includes the expression of feelings, the symbolisation of situations and the imitation of actions. In this sense, teleological music is a music that has a representative function. (Programme music is a particular example of this external directedness). Internal directedness refers to the evolution within the music itself, and not to a representational content directed from the outside. In Western music, this kind of directedness is realized through the strong stress on harmony, which can be seen as an evolutional model aiming at a final climax. Thus, Western music is essentially *dialectical:* development follows from the presence of a conflict between opposites and finally leads to a situation of synthesis, in which conflicts are entirely or partially resolved. This can be called *narrative* by analogy with the evolution of a classical novel, in which the dénouement resolves the conflicts of the plot.

The concepts "teleology" and "narrative" run in parallel so that, as in the case of teleology, a distinction can be made between the narrative in the external and internal sense.

# 45

## LYssophobia: On Four Violins

### (TONY CONRAD, VIOLIN; RECORDED
### 19 DECEMBER 1964)

### TONY CONRAD

Violinist Tony Conrad (1940– ) was a key member of the Theatre of Eternal Music, the drone-based minimalist ensemble centered around La Monte Young in the early 1960s. Indeed it was Conrad, a Harvard-trained mathematician, who introduced Young to the mathematics of the harmonic series that the group so steadfastly explored. After the Theatre of Eternal Music disbanded in 1965, Conrad went on to record with the German art-rock collective Faust and, more recently, with the post-rock duo Gastr del Sol and its members, David Grubbs and Jim O'Rourke. He has also released several recent solo recordings featuring his trademark violin drone. Conrad is also known as a pioneer "structuralist" filmmaker whose debut, *Flicker* (1966), consisted solely of stroboscopic light patterns.

In the following piece, written in 1996 to accompany the release of his 1964 drone composition *Four Violins*, Conrad recalls his experience with the Theatre of Eternal Music, describing the group's musical practice and reflecting on the ways in which it challenged inherited notions of musical authorship and the musical work. With its capitalized "LY," the article's title refers to Conrad's ongoing dispute with La Monte Young, who claims sole authorship of the recordings made by the Theatre of Eternal Music and refuses to release them to the public or to the group's members.

[. . . .] I can't say that my early experiences with the violin were pleasurable, because I always thought the violin sounded so bad. I'm saying that I didn't practice much, if at all, or advance well, even with my own private teacher. An excellent young symphony violinist, Ronald Knudsen, started coming to my house when I was in high school, to teach me, but he soon found that I wasn't going to learn the licks. He advised a better instrument; he made me go back to scales; nothing worked. The saccharine 19th-century salon pieces in my music book could have sung out, if I had played them "expressively," with vibrato; but I hated vibrato. Then Knudsen gave me some 18th-century music, full of double stops, and I discovered what it was like to hear two notes sounding together.

Playing in tune, Knudsen urged, was a matter of playing slowly and listening carefully. And playing ever so accurately in tune made the music sound so much better. Whatever you can play slow, you can easily play fast, he always said. When he found that I was responsive to the intonation exercises he gave me, Knudsen brought me a book on acoustics. I was playing two-part harmony from the Bach Chorales. Then we started spending my whole lesson on long conversations about the harmonic series, scales and tunings, intonation, long durations, careful listening, and the relationship between these ideas and disciplined attention to fundamentals.

Knudsen's wife was Japanese; perhaps this was linked to his almost "Zen" approach to practice. He passed on to me exercises that he had found startling: could I hold one bow stroke for a half minute? a minute? How closely could you learn how long a half minute was? Could I play in tune? I mean, really in tune? And more than one note at a time, which was the only way to really hear intonation most clearly? Were there other notes, scales, harmonic progressions, which could be understood through intonation? If I were really careful, it might take me a long time just to get my violin really in tune. And anything that I could play slow I could play fast; the secret of playing well was playing more slowly [. . . .]

The first recording of Indian music I heard was an Ali Akbar Khan performance on Angel Records, in late 1959. It was electrifying; my recollection is vivid. I had never heard the classical music of another culture before; ethnomusicological recordings were extremely unusual in this time.

The underlying relations among melodic and rhythmic functions, and the role of pitch in establishing a key tone (Sa), are not so terribly different in Indian music and Western common-practice harmony; and the emotional compass of Indian music is fairly coherent and legible to the Western listener (moreso, one might say, than that of Arabic singing, for instance). It was apparent to me upon first listening that the element which enabled the acute focus and unusual emotional intensity of this music was the drone, which expanded attentiveness to intervallic relations while eliminating the function of harmonic motion.

The drone, as a quintessential of Indian musical logic, plays much the same role that the progression $V \to$ I plays in Western music. Each is a core, an armature, which defines the listener's sense of the musical events. Western music, with its ever-present investment in progression, animates a sense of absence—of suspension or expectation. This irresolution corresponds to the conflict that provides a forward impetus in narrative story telling. Indian music also conveys feelings of suspension and resolution, but much differently—and always in the presence of its object. Its operative figure is balance, or repetition, but not absence and conflict.

My response to this music was different from that of my composer friends, all of whom discovered Indian music at about the same time. What most of them found exciting in Indian music was its modal, rhythmic, and ornamental structure. On the other hand, I had been strongly focused upon the intersection of intonation, slow playing, and intervallic (rather than harmonic) listening for some years, and found in Indian music a vindication of my predilection for drone-like performing [. . . .] Feeling the leveraging capability of drone playing in Indian music made me imagine what other new musics might spring from a drone, set within a less authoritarian and tradition-ridden performance idiom.

Around the time I left school and moved to New York, my friend La Monte Young was playing a series of improvisational concerts with several other musicians at a small gallery, called "10-4." I was enraptured to find that he had swerved off in an "oriental" direction: while Young played saxophone (somewhere between Bismillah Khan and Ornette Coleman), Angus MacLise improvised on bongos, Billy Linich (Billy Name) strummed folk guitar, and Marian Zazeela sang drone. All in all, those were hysterical and overwrought concerts; they went on for hours in overdrive, with frequent breaks for the musicians to refresh themselves offstage or in the john. The music was formless, expostulatory, meandering; vaguely modal, arhythmic, and very unusual; I found it exquisite.

What I heard in this music was two parts of what I later saw as three. First, I heard an abrupt disjunction from the post-Cagean crisis in music composition; here the composer was taking the choice of sounds directly in hand, as a real-time physicalized (and directly specified) process—in short, I saw redefinitions of composition, of the composer, and of the artist's relation to the work and the audience. As a response to the un-choices of the composer Cage, here were composerly choices that were specified to a completeness that included and concluded the performance itself.

Secondly, I also heard a composition process which drew upon established vocabularies of traditions, abstracting (or appropriating) the foundations of different musicological (and ethnomusicological) structures, and which worked outward from these linguistic taproots to articulate a (comprehensible) voice in a (new and) invented musical language.

What I did not hear was perhaps the most obvious part of what had appeared here, which was simply that Young had torn a page out of his own history as a jazz musician. He had played, in fact, with Ornette, with Don Cherry [. . .], and with others as a young sax player in the L.A. area. The black players had tried to get Young to "swing"; he would not (or could not), and (like other white 50s jazz musicians in California) went "cool." Young, characteristically, went cooler than any of the rest of them, and started incorporating cool, long spaced-out tones in his classical pieces. His *String Trio* is a kind of hyper-cool California modern classical piece. It was a point of pride, with Young at this time, that he was slow and cool, which brought him to the point of a shared taste with me. Slow, cool, and (which neither of us would have owned up to) nerdy.

Back to the 10-4 Gallery concerts: Though their music was certainly not cool at this point, the group was if nothing else extremely "way-out." I talked to Young, and began to play with the band after the 10-4 concert series ended [. . . .] For the first month I played one drone note, then adding an open fifth for the next month or so. This made Young ecstatic, as he had already composed a piece, *Composition 1960 #7*, which was nothing more than a perfect fifth, marked "to be held for a long time;" and the onus that the ensemble's work might appear to resemble "jazz improvisation" was lifted from him by the device of this nominal contiguity with his neo-dada composition period. Zazeela also held a drone, though it was clear from the first that my presence would introduce entirely new standards of attentiveness to pitch and stability.

John Cage's work and the activities of Fluxus (which were going on all around us) appeared to bring modernism, and the project of an authoritarian musical form based on the sanctity of the score, to a halt. La Monte Young had become notorious as an avatar of this modernist collapse, particularly through his neo-dada compositions (which incorporated unobservable events, were sometimes performed before they were composed, and otherwise exploited logical and textual paradoxes and aporias of the composer-to-performer relation.) [. . . .]

There were three pathways that made sense to the performers of "Dream Music," or the "Theatre of Eternal Music," or "The Dream Syndicate," as I sometimes called it. Happily, what each of these solutions shared was a solid opposition to the North Atlantic cultural tradition of composition.

The first was the dismantling of the whole edifice of "high" culture. Also around this time, I picketed the New York museums and high-culture performance spaces with Henry Flynt, in opposition to the imperialist influences of European high culture. More than that, I had strong sympathies with the aims of Flynt's program, which amounted to the dismantling and dispersion of any and all organized cultural forms. At the time I was also a part of the "Underground Movie" scene, which (as I saw it) reconstructed the movies as a documentary form—a merging of life-aims with movie production. Other counter-cultural components of the Dream Music picture were our anti-bourgeois lifestyles, our use of drugs, and the joy which John Cale and I took in common pop music. Down this pathway there were other fellow travelers, like Andy Warhol and Lou Reed; it led straight to the Velvet Underground, and the melting of art music into rock and roll.

The second solution was to dispense with the score, and thereby with the authoritarian trappings of composition, but to retain cultural production in music as an activity. The music was not to be a "conceptual" activity (either in the sense that Fluxus had exhausted the conceptual approach, or in the sense that "conceptual art" was to retrace a similar terrain seven years later); it would instead be structured around pragmatic activity, around direct gratification in the realization of the moment, and around discipline [. . . .]

At the time, when we played together it was always stressed that we existed as a collaboration. Our work together was exercised "inside" the acoustic environment of the music, and was always supported by our extended discourse pertinent to each and every small element of the totality, both as to each person's performance (the inexorably evolving "improvisation") and as to the ideas which could be attached to the overall sound image. Much of the time, we sat inside the sound and helped it to coalesce and grow around us.

In keeping with the technology of the early 1960s, the score was replaced by the tape recorder. This, then, was a total displacement of the composer's role, from progenitor of the sound to groundskeeper at its gravesite. The recordings were our collective property, resident in their unique physical form at Young and Zazeela's loft, where we rehearsed, until such time as they might be copied for each of us.

The third route out of the modernist crisis was to move away from composing to listening, again working "on" the sound from "inside" the sound. Here I was to contribute powerful tools, including a nomenclature for rational frequency ratios, which ignited our subsequent development [. . . .]

[T]here was a baseline which stabilized the group—our (then) shared conviction that the collaborative composer/performer identity was the way to proceed (historically), and that the mechanism which could make this congruence fruitful would be attention to, and preoccupation with, the sustained *sound itself*. At the point of my arrival in the group, the *sound itself* was "way out," which was incontrovertibly good, but this sound itself had no particular sustained structural integrity or richness. At first, as co-drone (on violin) with Zazeela (on voice), I played an open fifth, as I have mentioned. After a month or two, however, I suggested that I might also some times play another note. What should it be?—And so began our extended discourse on the advisability of each of the various scale degrees. But the evolution of a new argot for this discourse only really got into high gear another month later, some while after I had started playing a third drone note (which we agreed would be a major second or ninth) and our discussions moved on to the fourth note [. . . .]

I played two notes together at all times, so that I heard difference tones vividly in my left ear. The major second, as a consonant interval, has a very deep difference tone, three octaves below the sounded tones. Any change in the pitch of either of the two notes I played would be reflected in a movement of the pitch of the difference tone—but the difference tone would move eight times as fast as the actual pitches. I spent all of my playing time working on the inner subtleties of the combination tones, the harmonics, the fundamentals, and their beats—as microscopic changes in bow pressure, finger placement and pressure, etc., would cause shifts in the sound.

After a while I needed to explain what I was doing to the others, especially as Young had suggested looking for a playable seventh degree. The lowered minor seventh, which he referred to as "bluesy," might—it seemed to me—be identical with the seventh harmonic. The seventh harmonic! How exciting it would be to incorporate accurately tuned intervals which simply do (did) not occur in Western music! I played a seventh harmonic to Young, and he felt it might indeed be the "blue" tone; but how does one tell whether two intervals are the same?

I launched an explication of the scale degrees and their relation to simple numerical frequency ratios. From this point of understanding, it readily followed that we might construct a system of intervals based on the prime numbers 3 and 7, rather than 3 and 5 (which are the foundation for the ordinary diatonic and chromatic scales). The simple arithmetic of composite scale intervals provided us with the makings of a nomenclature, which soon evolved into a fully articulated patois of the Dream sound.

The quality of listening inside the sound, once our playing began to approach rational frequency ratios very closely, became different from other listening experiences. Our unfamiliar intervals, built on tones and timbres which are alien to the vocabulary of 20th century common practice, were surprisingly sonorous—dissonant but not discordant. Ripples of beats, in various ranges of the frequency spectrum, emphasized various aspects of the performance—its focus on timbre, its demands for technical accuracy, and its engagement with rhythm as an aspect of pitch. As I put it at the time, "Pitched pulses, palpitating beyond rhythm and cascading the cochlea with a galaxy of synchronized partials, reopen the awareness of the sine tone—the element of combinatorial hearing. Together and in pairs in all combinations, the partials combine. The ear responds uniquely."[1]

We lived inside the sound, for years. As our precision increased, almost infinitesimal pitch changes would become glaring smears across the surface of the sound. I found that I had to make a very minute pitch adjustment to compensate for the change in the direction of travel of the bow. When John Cale's viola and my violin began to fuse, as though smelted into one soundmass, I felt that the Dream Music had achieved its apogee. Zazeela's voice had grown rock hard, unerring in its pitch control, and unique in its hugeness and stridency of character. The totality of the sound began to outstrip any of our expectations, and to move into new, larger territories with ever more unusual intervallic combinations [. . . .]

## NOTES

1. Tony Conrad, "Inside the Dream Syndicate," *Film Culture* 41 (Summer 1966), 6.

# 46

# *Digital Discipline: Minimalism in House and Techno*

## PHILIP SHERBURNE

Journalist, critic, and DJ Philip Sherburne (1971– ) has written on dance music, DJ Culture, and sound art for *XLR8R*, *Frieze*, *The Village Voice*, *Signal to Noise*, *Parkett*, and other magazines. He curated the CD *Splitting Bits, Closing Loops: Sound on Sound* for *Leonardo Music Journal* and has delivered talks at Tate Modern, the San Francisco Museum of Modern Art, PS1, and other museums and galleries. Writing for *The Wire* in 2001, Sherburne coined the term "MicroHouse" to describe prominent minimalist tendencies in contemporary House and Techno. Here, he offers a genealogy of minimalism in dance music and explores the forces that have driven House, Techno, HipHop, and Garage to "go lean."

Like some microbiotic virus, minimalism is everywhere these days. In popular culture and the lifestyle press, it may not have the same cachet it did in the sans-serif 90s, but from the radio dial to the galleries to underground nightclubs, sonic minimalism is on the upsurge. It's especially prominent in the various forms of electronic dance music—Techno, House, and their "post-Techno" offshoots. To paraphrase New Order, the 80s group who themselves thinned pop music down to its lithe, arpeggiated essence, *everything's gone lean*.

This, in itself, is not news. The origins of most contemporary electronic dance music—found in Kraftwerk's 1974 opus "Autobahn" and updated in the late 80s and early 90s with the streamlined electronic funk of Detroit Techno pioneers like Derrick May and Juan Atkins—emphasized a pared-down palette that cut away all the excesses of a bloating rock and pop tradition. Since then, much dance-floor fare has restrained itself to a limited set of sounds and has produced forms heavily reliant on loops, recurring sequences, and accumulation-through-repetition. These are key tropes in much pop music, but electronic dance music particularly foregrounds the strategies pioneered in the work of so-called minimalist composers like Steve Reich and Philip Glass. Indeed, while it's possible to say that most electronic dance music would be impossible without an emphasis on repetition, beat-oriented electronic music's most avant-garde productions explore the very nature of repetition itself, carrying on the mantle of classical minimalism as a movement delving deep into the heart of form—or, perhaps, skittering across its slick surface.

Of course, classical Minimalism's effects have not been limited to electronic dance music. In the late 1970s, rock music produced its own minimalist reaction to inflated, overproduced mainstream rock. The results, No Wave and punk rock, often made explicit links to the 60s' drone-minimalism tradition, as with Glenn Branca's bands Theoretical Girls and The Static, his guitar orchestras, and the many groups that he influenced. But minimalism in rock—from Sonic Youth to Swans to James Chance—adopted a particularly expressivist stance, marked by noisy outbursts, microtonal experimentation, and a stripped-down, visceral sound, at odds with electronic minimalism's more introspective mechanics. Minimalism also fit rock's functionalist requirements: punk rock's three-chord template, which drew from the blues tradition but ran itself through minimalism's compression engine, guaranteed that its sound could be faithfully replicated by self-taught teenagers playing in basements and VFW halls from Schenectady to San Diego.

Minimalist electronic music, on the other hand, burrowed deeply into the groove to create a particular sort of temporal dislocation which fit with the immersive (and often drug-influenced) needs of the dance floor. Minimalism also satisfied the functionalist requirements of early electronic dance music, which—evolving out of and automating the long, manual mixes pioneered by underground disco DJs like Larry Levan—subsumed all elements to the regulated, mechanized beat. As DJ Culture begat an entire cottage industry of recordings intended solely or primarily for mixing, dance tracks came to be understood as representative of a willfully incomplete form; they came into their own only when paired with other tracks. Minimalism's reliance upon rhythmic and melodic "building blocks"—imagine isolating any single phrase of an early Reich composition, for example—proved the perfect fit for this combinatory form. As Techno produced various offshoots, each one emphasizing a particular stylistic tendency, certain substrains focused on this combinatory approach to an almost exaggerated degree. So while many Detroit Techno producers continued working within the margins of traditional song form, the more Spartan producers in the UK and Sweden, such as Adam Beyer and Surgeon, made an art out of producing microscopic variations on a single rhythmic theme. Records in this tradition were not designed for home listening, but rather as fodder for performance in the hands of the DJ. Indeed, with their strictly codified breakdowns and buildups, records like these are often rightly described as "DJ tools," something like Lego bricks for the selector's toybox.

Today it's impossible to hear Steve Reich's early tape works *Come Out* and *It's Gonna Rain* and not hear the roots—however accidental—of contemporary Techno. The dubbed-out effects as *Come Out* doubles over upon itself, the way that *It's Gonna Rain* breaks down its exposition into a tightly looped 4/4 sequence which itself breaks into smaller and smaller repeating pieces (from "It's gon' rain/it's gon' rain/it's gon' rain/it's gon' rain" to "it's gon'/it's gon'/it's gon'/it's gon'" to "rain/rain/rain/rain")—all of these are key strategies of contemporary dance music. Indeed, vocal tracks like Blackman's 1993 Chicago House tune "I Beat that Bitch with a Bat" cop exactly the same strategy that Reich used to uncover musical rhythms in speech on *Come Out*. (It's ironic that the strategy Reich used to progressive political ends—the speaker of *Come Out* is a young black man recounting political violence—is here appropriated to misogynistic ends, the tracks' debatable camp value notwithstanding.) If the originators of House and Techno were unaware of Reich when they first began sampling and programming their tightly looped progressions, the definitive link was made retroactively when The Orb sampled *Electric Counterpoint* for the club hit "Little Fluffy Clouds" in 1990.

None of this is to suggest that Reich and his contemporaries set out to author the fake book for multiple, amateurist musical traditions. Instead, we might see classic minimalism, especially in its more populist phases as explored by Philip Glass, as fundamental to the creation of a musical grammar that would lead, eventually, to a kind of musical Esperanto—itself fundamental to the DIY zeitgeist of the 80s and 90s.

It's unclear exactly when the term "minimal" crept into Techno's self-description. Techno's origins are best documented in Xeroxed fanzines which were seldom archived, making any definitive research difficult. As early as 1992, though, Simon Reynolds was referring to the work of Detroit Techno pioneers like Derrick May as "elegantly minimalist," in contrast to the rough-and-tumble productions of the UK's breakbeat 'Ardkore movement.[1] Also in 1992, a user on the rec.music. reviews newsgroup, archived by Google, can be found referring to "minimal bleep style," and by 1993 a poster to the alt.rave newsgroup, attempting to make some sense of electronic dance music's proliferation of subgenres, uses "minimal Techno" to describe the work of both Detroit's Carl Craig and Finland's Säkhö label. By 1994—the year that Robert Hood released his *Minimal Nation* EP on Jeff Mills' Axis imprint—the term seems to have caught on as a general descriptor for any stripped-down, Acidic derivative of classic Detroit style. Today, minimalism is second nature, found everywhere from projects like Minimal Man to labels like the economically titled Minimal Records. Minimalism has become so entrenched that it's invoked reflexively, if erroneously: Germany's Areal label, which more than any other Techno imprint is pioneering a fattened-up return to song-form, albeit within the context of repetitive dance floor tracks, goes by the motto, "Advanced Tech-Electronic Minimalism."

It's hard to say *why*, precisely, Techno grew increasingly minimalist in the early 90s. In many ways, it seems to fulfill an almost teleological urge: just as punk rock was driven by a harder/faster/louder impulse that hurtled perpetually toward its final limit (a limit one could argue was reached with Grindcore's double-bass-drum pummel, where the speeds reached seemed to blur into a paradoxical stasis), early 90s Detroit Techno took the repetitive tropes of machine funk (whether Kraftwerk or Giorgio Moroder) and cut away everything but the grinding rhythms. Given the racial politics of Detroit Techno, in which a coterie of mostly black musicians attempted to create an entirely new form of African-American expression, the link to African drumming and its emphasis on polyrhythms can't be ignored. (Perhaps it's no accident that Reich himself studied drumming in Ghana; classic minimalism, after all, took its cues from African, and not Western, musical traditions when it privileged rhythm and repetition over melody and linear progression.) Richie Hawtin's "Afrika," for example—though by a white artist, it falls squarely within the tradition being developed by African-American artists in the early 90s—makes the explicit connection between Techno's minimalistic programming and African percussion.

Minimalism also proved a reaction to certain developments within Techno. In the UK in the early 90s, many of the most popular tunes came from a burgeoning style called "Hardcore" (or "'Ardkore") which emphasized messy excess: cartoony sound effects, goofy sampladelia, and the kind of cultural cross-references that delighted bug-eyed ravers wearing Mickey Mouse gloves. Minimalism's tasteful restraint offered an alternate, and even polemical, position for aesthetes in search of a more refined brand of "intelligent dance music."

In part, minimalism has tended to accompany technological shifts and experiments. Steve Reich's *Come Out* and *It's Gonna Rain* are both dependent upon the medium of magnetic tape, which, as the practitioners of *musique concrète* had demonstrated, proved itself to be a form of musical material in its own right for the ways in which it could be spliced, looped, and delayed. Likewise, early Acid House productions like Phuture's "Acid Tracks" reduced the disco/House form to hitherto unimagined proportions by using the Roland TB-303 bass machine to strip down the track to the most basic of elements: kick drum, cowbell, hand clap, whistle, and the grinding, oscillating bass line that became the signature of the Acid sound. As minimal Techno has evolved, it has tended to follow closely the limits and possibilities of a range of tools, from rudimentary drum machines and sequencers to the popular loop-based performance software Ableton Live, which is designed specifically for the real-time manipulation of pre-recorded loops. The software itself is developed to facilitate the production of minimalistic constructions as opposed to more song-based structures. Contemporary dance music, in this respect, is almost literally hard-wired for minimalism. (This should be no surprise given that musicians are increasingly working as software programmers: one of Ableton's head designers, for instance, is Robert Henke, a pioneer of German minimal Techno who records under the name of Monolake. With musicians increasingly developing their own software tools, a sort of feedback loop occurs whereby the predominant stylistics engender tools designed specifically to further them.)

Another reason for minimalism's spread within dance music is undoubtedly related to the relationship of sound to the body. Whatever repetition's psychological aspects, they are filtered through the body; as any dancer knows, repetition creates a unique sort of corporeal experience wherein the body becomes as if inhabited by the beat. The common practice within House and Techno parties of sustaining an almost unvarying tempo for the duration of the night has the effect—at least ideally—of uniting dancers through the beat, as if joining them into a kind of "desiring machine" ruled by a single pulse. But whereas other minimalist genres like HipHop or dancehall reggae have used looping productions as a backdrop for lyrical virtuosity, minimal Techno corkscrews into the very heart of repetition. Unlike dancehall, there are no "rewinds" in Techno: everything moves forward, but always maintaining the illusion of standing still.

In considering sound and the body, artists have used a similar set of strategies to achieve diametrically opposed ends, especially in recent years. Early minimalist dance music emphasized the rhythmic backbone of disco—cut down to a four-to-the-floor rhythm accented by a handful of off-beats and effects—to create a highly economical form of dance music stripped of anything that might detract from the beat. At the same time, recent developments in "click Techno"—for instance, the profoundly thinned-out tracks highlighted on Mille Plateaux's *Clicks + Cuts* compilations, or Jan Jelinek's densely looped work as Farben, which he explicitly connects to the minimalist tradition via the *moiré* effects in Op Art—could hardly be classified as club music, lacking the forceful rhythmic intensity required to sustain a dance floor. If anything, the latter exists as music in *reaction* to the dance club, an avant-gardist rejection of the obviousness that characterizes most populist dance music.

In minimalism's ubiquity, then, its strategies have turned out to offer solutions to varying, even opposed, sets of problems. If one thing remains constant, though, it's the emphasis on *time*—by cutting out pop music's chord progressions and four-bar structure, and emphasizing gradually evolving rhythmic cycles, both club minimalism and domestic click Techno aim to tap into a continuum that transcends the individual track; indeed, that transcends the individual.

It's worth asking why non-club-oriented productions have retained this focus. The ideology of the nightclub, of course, is that "the party never ends." This is preserved by seamlessly sequencing multiple DJs across the course of the evening who will typically play within well-defined stylistic and tempo parameters; it's augmented by the use of drugs like Ecstasy to help keep partiers going long after normal bedtimes. But non-dancefloor Techno is a kind of pastiche of club music, adopting its form but ignoring its functionalism. It's possible that this represents a resurgence of the modernist ideal of pure formalism—related, of course, to classical minimalism's exploration in the acoustic and psychological properties of repetition. Just as Picasso could exhibit the African mask divorced from its social context as an example of "pure" geometry, domestic Techno seems to pursue ever more specific lines of inquiry into the function of repetition. Consider, for instance, Thomas Brinkmann's *X100* LP, which is built of nothing more than click, tone pulse, and a single bass drum, each element doubled and sent cycling out of phase. Sonically, the record seems like an experiment in phasing—an experiment that creates a profoundly disorienting listening experience, given the way doubled sounds bounce from speaker to speaker, as though the stereo field had been turned into a hall of funhouse mirrors. But the recording's mathematical underpinnings underscore a more clinical interest. Brinkmann calculated the precise number of beats he would need in order for the LP, spinning at 33 RPM, to contain exactly two more bass kicks in one channel than in the other, with the express interest of creating a record whose grooves, on inspection, would yield the unusual image of a pair of overlapping circles.[2] Given Brinkmann's visual emphasis, combined with his mathematical investigations, a vital link becomes clear between what might be called "post-Techno" and the minimalist formalism of visual artists like Agnes Martin. Likewise, Carsten Nicolai, whose audio projects beat (however faintly) with Techno's steady pulse, has explored the austere purity of sinewave formations throughout his career—including the visual output, as raster lines, created by audio signals when routed through video channels. Likewise, his visual works—including a series of paintings based on the idea of the loop—thrum with dots and miniscule lines recalling Martin, while his spartan, scientifically-oriented sculptures and installations suggest Donald Judd's clinical influence.

Minimalism is so prevalent in current pop music that it may be impossible to ascribe any single meaning to it. It's certainly not limited to the world of House and Techno; if anything, it may still be on the ascendant in pop music. For instance, the

Clipse's 2002 tune "Grindin'," produced by The Neptunes, is perhaps the most minimalist track yet to come out of HipHop, itself a genre founded on the surgical strategy of isolating short rhythmic breaks and adding repeating horn stabs or keyboard lines for tone color and intertextual significance. "Grindin'" features a mere handful of percussive sounds, all curiously deadened, to which it adds crystal-clear finger snaps and the swooping, falsetto chorus of "Grindin'," repeated ad nauseum. But in HipHop, minimalism has generally served as a means to an end—a way of creating a functional (and funktional) backdrop for the MC's lyrical material. House and Techno, in contrast, generally devoid of vocals save for the odd sample or refrain, have gone minimal as a means of drawing ever closer to the beat itself, and to the idealized structure that Kodwo Eshun identifies as the "rhythmachine."[3]

Within House and Techno, the very idea of minimalism has lost much of its specificity as variations on reductionist themes—syncopated rhythmic loops using but a handful of drum sounds, washes of chord color, and two- or three-note bass lines—have evolved into a staggering array of styles varying from Chain Reaction's well-known ambient dub-Techno (dubbed "Heroin House" by Reynolds, for its dreamy, horizontal inclinations) to Surgeon's punishing, tribal loopism. Detroit's Jeff Mills is often tagged as a minimalist, despite the fact that his DJ sessions, constructing dangerously top-heavy piles of loops upon loops upon loops, are sonically speaking far more massive than most pop music. Of course, the same could be said as well of early minimalism. As classic Minimalism developed, it grew to emphasize not a minimum of material but a minimum of form, often on a horizontal level, that foregrounded other elements: timbre, texture, and the vertical dimension of the music, which did not so much progress (according to classical/compositional norms) as amass. Then again, Steve Reich continued to be branded as a minimalist long after he'd left behind the experiments in pulse and phasing that led Michael Nyman to coin the term in the first place.

The idea of "minimalism" means different things depending how it's used. On the one hand, there's the stripped-down lucidity of Daniel Bell's work as DBX, in which he crafted tracks so deliriously spare as to be almost physically disorienting—with nothing but the barest of percussion lines and an eerie, disembodied voice, it becomes difficult to orient oneself in space or in time. (Not insignificantly, Richie Hawtin's third album as Plastikman, 1998's *Consumed*, which built upon Bell's ultra-minimal foundation, derived from Hawtin's experience of utter darkness in Canada's northern wilderness.) On the other hand, the polyrhythmic chaos of a track like Robert Hood's "Make a Wish" suggests the density achieved in Reich's most rhythmically convoluted works.

We can say, broadly, that minimalism in House and Techno tends to take one of two paths: either skeletalism or massification. The former term, until now, has tended to be the dominant tradition within minimal House and Techno. Skeletalism is the imperative to carve everything inessential from dance music's pulse, leaving only enough embellishment (syncopation, tone color, effects) to merit the variation. Skeletalism is the teleological impulse driving early Chicago House, Acid, and Detroit Techno to continually do more with less, and it is the defining principle behind the late 90s "clicks and cuts" school to approximate the form of dance music by substitution and implication, swapping out traditional drum samples for equivalent sounds sourced from pared-down white noise: click, glitch, and crackle.

Skeletalism is the sound of DBX's preludes for thump and bleep; it's the sound of Richie Hawtin's bassy, darkly droning mantras; it's the sound of M:I:5's curious collisions of overdriven bass, snare, and guitar samples, which attempt to obliterate white space with bleeding distortion, but still leave the silence between the notes yawning ominously as seismic fissures. Skeletalism almost certainly finds its apogee in Thomas Brinkmann's experiments in abbreviated form, in which Techno's essential form is carved, literally, by cutting vinyl records with a knife and then sequencing the sampled clicks and pops into rudimentary 4/4 pulses.

Massification, on the other hand, represents the strain of electronic dance music that attempts to create extreme densities with a relative paucity of sonic elements. In many ways, this strategy matches the movement of classical minimalism from simplicity toward an ever more complex array of shifting pulses and polyrhythms. It is less apparently minimal than skeletalist tracks, even if it accomplishes its means with few more resources. In the early years of the 21st Century, massification has tended to be the more dynamic area of exploration. Its most distinctive exponent is probably the Chilean/German producer Ricardo Villalobos, whose training in Afro-Cuban percussion has led him to a practice that aims for maximum rhythmic density using only a handful of discrete sounds. Tracks like "Bahaha Hahi" and his remix of Monne Automne's "El Salvador" submerge Techno's all-important downbeat in a roiled sea of offbeats and glancing accents, resulting in a woozy continuum as predictably unpredictable as the surface of choppy water.

Why has Techno, and not drum 'n' bass, earned the "minimalist" tag? After all, drum 'n' bass has kept to the same strategies of repetition, if anything restricting its musical subject matter even more severely by relying extensively on only a handful of classic breakbeats like the famous "Amen" break, which comes from The Winstons' 1969 tune "Amen Brother." Perhaps it's enough to say that upon its emergence, minimal Techno *sounded* minimal—which is to say, minimal Techno's emphasis on empty space between the beats conjured the word in its most literal sense, as opposed to denoting a more academic relationship to classical minimalism. Techno's minimalism resonated more with movements in visual art that emphasized cleanliness of form and a minimum of affect. Minimalism, as a catchword, has come to embody a skeletalist prejudice. Drum 'n' bass, on the other hand, is one of the most "maximal" forms of music out there. In its galloping tempo, its surging waves of bass, and its macho rage, it is all about affect. Minimalism as popularly conceived, then, applies a certain stone-faced (as opposed to screw-faced) poise. This might explain the rise of post-Techno minimalism of the *Clicks + Cuts* series: in the context of a specific class—well educated, enamored with theory, and generally employed in the information economy—minimalism in its most ascetic form fit the day's prohibition on emotion, favoring poise over passion. (It's worth remembering that Detroit Techno's black originators, most of them middle-class, modeled themselves after a "sophisticated," European aesthetic that stood in contrast with stereotypes of inner-city life.)

Skeletalism is also the watchword in current strains of UK Garage (a midtempo hybrid of House and drum 'n' bass). After several years in which UK Garage aimed to reconfigure pop and R&B in line with its idiosyncratic rhythms, producers of the so-called "grime" or "sublow" school—Dizzee Rascal, Wiley, Plasticman, et al.—have stripped away all but the fuzzy bass and overdriven snare drums from their tunes, leaving wide swaths of empty space between the beats. On the surface, this has as much to do with the rise of the MC in UK Garage as any tendency toward silence for silence's sake: essentially the UK's first indigenous manifestation of HipHop, Garage has become the underpinning for a new generation of vocalists rattling off double-time chatter, sometimes composed and sometimes improvised, combining U.S. and Jamaican styles. But U.S. HipHop has always managed to find room for vocalists and busy beats alike, and so it's impossible not to suspect that Garage's newfound leanness has as much to do with its producers' economical infatuations as it has with more utilitarian purposes.

Once again, a dance music form—a form with all the opportunities that technology affords to cram every space with sound—has gone anorexic. The trend seems almost a given. But then again, considering Garage's lyrical turn, one wonders if minimalism reflects a fundamental ambivalence about machine music. Is the urge to pare things down to the absolute minimum born of some distrust of buttons and circuits? When machines (both hardware and software) can cram every nanosecond with noise, is the last refuge of humanity to be found in space, in restraint, and in silence? One wonders if minimalism represents the ultimate human capacity—choice. The ability to leave the blank spaces blank represents the ultimate negative capacity: the will to withhold.

### NOTES

1. Simon Reynolds, "Rrrr-rush!," *Blissout* (http://members.aol.com/blissout/ardkore.htm #rush), originally appeared in *Melody Maker,* June 1992.
2. Philip Sherburne, "Thumbnail Music: Six Artists Talk About Minimalism," *Urban Sounds* 2 no. 1 (http://www.urbansounds.com/us_current/thumbnail/brinkmann_1.html).
3. See chap. 25, above, and Kodwo Eshun, *More Brilliant than the Sun: Adventures in Sonic Fiction* (London: Quartet, 1998), 8.

I foresee a marked deterioration in American music and musical taste, an interruption in the musical development of the country, and a host of other injuries to music in its artistic manifestations, by virtue—or rather by vice—of the multiplication of various music-reproducing machines [. . . .] The ingenuity of a phonograph's mechanism may incite the inventive genius to its improvement, but I could not imagine that a performance by it would ever inspire embryotic Mendelssohns, Beethovens, Mozarts, and Wagners to the acquirement of technical skill, or to the grasp of human possibilities in the art.

—John Philip Sousa (1906)[1]

This made-for-phonograph-record-music [*Originalschallplattenmusik*] was accomplished by superimposing various phonograph recordings and live musical performances, by employing variations in speed, pitch, height and acoustic timbre which are not possible in real performance. The result was an original music which can only be recreated by means of the gramophone apparatus.

—Heinrich Burkhard describing Paul Hindemith's and Ernst Toch's phonograph disc performance, "New Music Berlin 1930"[2]

It was in Jamaica that a record stopped being a finished thing. Instead, in the studio, it became a matrix of sonic possibilities, the raw material for endless "dubs." Thus the concept of the remix was born (several years before similar ideas would dawn on the disco and HipHop DJs). And when a record was played through a sound system, with a deejay toasting over the top, it was no longer a complete piece of music but had become a tool of composition for a grander performance. This was an important change in the status of recorded music, and again something that wouldn't really occur outside Jamaica until disco and HipHop.

—Bill Brewster and Frank Broughton[3]

I've always had this theory that recorded sound is dead sound, in the sense that it's not "live" anymore. Old records have this quality of time past, this sense of loss. The music is embalmed. I'm trying to bring it back to life through my art.

—Christian Marclay[4]

I think the DJ is an archetypal figure that has been throughout human history. It's anyone that's gonna be combining a social situation with music and then setting up a certain parameter of crowd interaction and response, whether that be a shaman or a Roman priest or even, for that matter, government. It's all about reconfiguring and pulling bits and pieces of other things and putting them together and creating a new text that you then send out. So, to me, [using] language is being a DJ. When you're a child, you're absorbing bits and pieces of language around you. Those sit in your head and you slowly are able to speak your own sentences later. It's the same with DJ-ing: you're absorbing these records, these linguistic units, or whatever, and slowly you're able to reconfigure them and to put them out as a stream of sentences, or stream of mixes. The late 20th-century is all about language, to me: codes of information governing behavior, codes governing this, governing that—it's all about these different codes. But the DJ, to me, is a reality hacker. It's someone that can take these codes—and, again, "phonograph" means "writing sound"—the turntable to me is the equivalent of the computer keyboard, because you're taking these different codes and then using them to break through these sort of corporate constructs that society wants to really put on you and then breaking them apart and letting people experience a transcendence in the mix.

—DJ Spooky[5]

An artist is now much more seen as a connector of things, a person who scans the enormous field of possible places for artistic attention, and says, What I am going to do is draw your attention to *this* sequence of things.

—Brian Eno[6]

The work of composing is not one of invention but one of arrangement. All materials being both unique and fundamentally connected, the strategy and art of connecting forms creative work.

—David Shea[7]

[Carl Stalling's music] implies an openness—a non-hierarchical musical overview—typical of today's younger composers but all too rare before the mid-1960s. All genres of music are *equal*—no *one* is inherently better than the others—and with Stalling, all are embraced, chewed up and spit out in a format closer to Burroughs' cut-ups or Godard's film editing of the '60s, than to anything happening in the '40s.

—John Zorn[8]

[On a lot of Miles Davis' records] we would use bits and pieces of cassettes that he would send me and say "Put this in that new album we're working on." I would really shudder. I'd say "Look, where the hell is it going to go? I don't know." He says, "Oh, you know." So he sends me the tape. I listen to it and say, "Oh yeah, maybe we can stick that in here."

—Teo Macero[9]

"The Subliminal Kid" moved in and took over bars cafés and jukeboxes of the world cities and installed radio transmitters and microphones in each bar so that the music and talk of any bar could be heard in all his bars and he had tape recorders in each bar that played and recorded at arbitrary intervals and his agents moved back and forth with portable tape recorders and brought back street sound and talk and music and poured it into his recorder array so he set waves and eddies and tornadoes of sound down all your streets and by the river of all language—Word dust drifted streets of broken music car horns and air hammers—The Word broken pounded twisted exploded in smoke—

—William S. Burroughs[10]

My definition of a Turntablist is a person who uses the turntables not to play music, but to manipulate sound and create music.

—DJ Babu[11]

# VIII. DJ Culture

## Introduction

DJ Rob Swift stands on stage at The Knitting Factory, one of New York City's premier spots for fringe music.[1] Deftly shuffling behind his sound system, he lays identical slabs of vinyl on each of his two turntables. As the beats flow from the left channel, Swift swipes the mixer's crossfader back and forth to cut in slices of music from the right, producing a stuttering echo. Letting the right turntable spin, he runs the record on the left back and forth under the needle to produce rhythmic scratch that syncopates the beat. Standing back for a moment, head bobbing to the beat, he waits for the track to reach a drum break. Then, quickly moving back and forth between the two decks, he begins to transform the breakbeat into a virtuoso percussion improvisation. Though Swift works with only a fragment of the track, it's clear that the audience recognizes the original material and relishes its musical transformations. The sound is all cuts and flows, tiny bits that are constantly hammered in and out of funky grooves.

The term "DJ Culture" emerged in the mid-1990s as a way to describe a range of musics centered on the figure of the DJ as artist: disco, HipHop, House, Techno, drum 'n' bass, and other musical forms. More broadly, it describes the unique musical domain made possible by the culture of recording, a culture in which music and sound circulate as a network of recorded entities detached from the specificity of time, place, and authorship, and all available to become the raw material for the DJ's art.

As a set of musical styles, DJ Culture is quintessentially postmodern, emerging in the 1970s with the extended disco mix, the studio distortions of dub reggae, and the birth of HipHop. Yet, in the more general sense, its roots lie much deeper in the history of the 20th century modernism. In the early 1920s, Bauhaus sculptor, photographer, and painter László Moholy-Nagy had already imagined the *détournement* of the turntable, its transformation from an instrument of musical reproduction into a musical instrument in its own right. In the 1930s, John Cage, Paul Hindemith, and Ernst Toch began to realize Moholy-Nagy's vision. On his earliest gramophone study, *Imaginary Landscape, No. 1*, Cage manipulated variable speed turntables and studio test recordings to produce a ghostly composite of sirens, strummed piano strings, and rumbling percussion. Pierre Schaeffer is surely the godfather of sampling composition. Working with phonograph discs in the 1940s, Schaeffer's compositions consisted entirely of edited bits of found sound. With its rhythmic loops and sharp juxtapositions of train whistles, screeching brakes, and mechanical clatter, Schaeffer's first *musique concrète* composition, *Étude aux chemins de fer* (*Railroad Study*), anticipates HipHop and electronic dance music. In the early 1960s, William S. Burroughs became a DJ of the word, using tape manipulation techniques to cut, splice, and layer his own voice and writing.[2]

From Schaeffer onwards, DJ Culture has worked with two essential concepts: *the cut* and *the mix*. To record is to cut, to separate the sonic signifier (the "sample") from any original context or meaning so that it might be free to function otherwise. To mix is to reinscribe, to place the floating sample into a new chain of signification. The mix is the postmodern moment, in which the most disparate of sounds can be spliced together and made to flow. It is exemplified by those musics of flow: disco, House, and Techno. But the mix is made possible by the cut, that modernist moment in which sound is lifted and allowed to become something else, or is fractured so that it trips and stumbles around the beat. Its forms are HipHop (particularly in its turntablist guise), dub, drum 'n' bass, and contemporary experimentalism by DJs such as Christian Marclay, Philip Jeck, Marina Rosenfeld, and Erik M.

DJ Culture also describes a new modality of audio history and memory. No longer a figure of linear continuity that, ideally, could be recalled in its totality, musical history becomes a network of mobile segments available at any moment for inscription and reinscription into new lines, texts, mixes. In short, musical history is no longer an analog scroll but digital and random access.

"The battle for the immediate future of music will be fought out through the medium of recording," remarked Chris Cutler in a piece that foreshadowed the Napster controversy by decades.[3] Writing in 1982 about the culture of recording in general, Cutler's piece can be read as a DJ Culture manifesto. For Cutler, the cut and the mix make possible a profoundly egalitarian music. Not only does the whole sound world become available for musical use; Cutler also imagines that the culture of recording provides the conditions for a new folk music: an authorless and collective process of musical production that is fluid and ever-changing. For Burroughs, the culture of recording is not so much politically liberatory as politically resistant. It offers neither more nor less than a way to hear critically the voices of dominant culture and to alter and subvert established meanings. Today, one can find advocates of both political positions: on the one hand, in the liberatory imagination of rave culture; and, on the other, in the antinomian practices of Negativland and John Oswald. Whatever one's position, DJ Culture clearly marks out a fundamentally new cultural space. It has altered the very nature of musical production, opened up new channels for the dissemination of music, and activated new modes of listening. It is not surprising, then, that DJ Culture has fostered new social practices and operates on the front lines of cultural politics.

## NOTES

1. This description is based on Rob Swift's solo performance on September 12, 1997, at the second turntablist festival, documented on *Battle Sounds: Turntablist Festival II*.
2. Portions of this introduction appeared previously in Christoph Cox, "Sampling in Classical Music," *Pulse!* (June 2000): 50, and "Abstract Concrete: Francisco López and the Ontology of Sound," *Cabinet* 2 (Spring 2001): 42–45.
3. Chris Cutler, "Necessity and Choice in Musical Forms," in *File Under Popular: Theoretical and Critical Writings on Music* (New York: Autonomedia, 1993), 33. See also chap. 24, above.

# 47

## *Production–Reproduction: Potentialities of the Phonograph*

### LÁSZLÓ MOHOLY-NAGY

Hungarian-born artist and theorist László Moholy-Nagy (1895–1946) was a key figure in European modernism. A photographer, sculptor, filmmaker, painter, typographer, stage designer, and industrial designer, Moholy-Nagy was closely associated with several of the seminal avant-garde art movements of the early 20th century: Dada, Constructivism, De Stijl, and Bauhaus. It was with the Bauhaus that Moholy-Nagy made his reputation and his lasting contributions as an artist, writer, and teacher. With Bauhaus director Walter Gropius, he shared the view that, in association with technology and industry, art could lead the way to a utopian world of beautiful and useful objects and structures.

The following piece is a composite of two texts, "Production—Reproduction" (1922) and "New Form in Music: Potentialities of the Phonograph" (1923), that exemplify Moholy-Nagy's experimental approach to modern technology. Having earlier advocated the use of photography to produce abstract light compositions, Moholy-Nagy suggests here that a similar approach be taken to the phonograph. Instead of using the phonograph simply as a tool of reproduction—a device by which to play recordings—he advocates that it be deployed as a means of musical production. This proposal predates, by several decades, John Cage's experiments with phonographs and phonograph cartridges and, by more than a half century, the turntablist experiments of Grandmaster Flash and Christian Marclay.

[. . . .] Since it is primarily production (productive creation) that serves human construction, we must strive to turn the apparatuses (instruments) used so far only for reproductive purposes into ones that can be used for productive purposes as well. This calls for profound examination of the following questions:

> What is this apparatus (instrument) good for?
> What is the essence of its function?

Are we able, and if so to what end, to extend the apparatus's use so that it can serve production as well?

Let us apply these questions to [an] example [. . .]: the phonograph [. . . .]

So far it has been the job of the phonograph to reproduce already existing acoustic phenomena. The tonal oscillations to be reproduced were incised on a wax plate by means of a needle and then retranslated into sound by means of a microphone (correctly: diaphragm, moving cone).

An extension of this apparatus for productive purposes could be achieved as follows: the grooves are incised by human agency into the wax plate, without any external mechanical means, which then produce sound effects which would signify without new instruments and without an orchestra—a fundamental innovation in sound production (of new, hitherto unknown sounds and tonal relations) both in composition and in musical performance.

The primary condition for such work is laboratory experiments: precise examination of the kinds of grooves (as regards length, width, depth etc.) brought about by the different sounds; examination of the man-made grooves; and finally mechanical-technical experiments for perfecting the groove-manuscript score. (Or perhaps the mechanical reduction of large groove-script records.) [. . . .]

Among present-day musical experiments, an important role is played by researches conducted with amplifiers which open up new paths in the production of acoustic phenomena. The aims of the Italian Bruitists [Russolo and others], in constructing new instruments with new sound-formations, have been substantially fulfilled by experiments with the amplification tube as a specific instrument which permits the production of all sorts of acoustic phenomena. However, this alone does not exhaust the potentialities that might be expected as regards the transformation of music [. . . .]

I have already suggested that the phonograph be transformed from an instrument of reproduction into one of production; this will cause the sound phenomenon itself to be created on the record, which carried no prior acoustic message, by the incision of groove-script lines as required.

Since my description of this process served elsewhere as an example to illustrate another idea, I was very brief in specifying the potentialities, without presenting detailed arguments, for the transformation of our musical conceptions along these lines. In speculative terms, the following is clear:

1. By establishing a groove-script alphabet an overall instrument is created which supersedes all instruments used so far.
2. Graphic symbols will permit the establishing of a new graphic and mechanical scale,[1] that is, the creation of a new mechanical harmony, whereby the individual graphic symbols will be examined and their relations formulated within a rule. (We may allude here to an idea that sounds rather utopian as yet; namely, the transposing of graphic designs into music on the basis of strict regularities of relationships.)
3. The composer would be able to create his composition for immediate reproduction on the disc itself, thus he will not be dependent on the absolute knowledge of the interpretative artist. So far, the latter was in most cases able to smuggle his own spiritual experience into the composition

written in note form. The new potentialities afforded by the phonograph will re-establish the amateurish musical education of our day on a more wholesome basis. Instead of the numerous "reproductive talents," who have actually nothing to do with *real* sound-creation (in either an active or a passive sense), the people will be educated to the *real* reception or creation of music.

4. The introduction of this system in musical performances will also facilitate to a significant degree independence from large orchestral enterprises, and the large-scale distribution of original creations by means of a simple instrument.

(The efficiency of the phonograph has been substantially improved lately by certain technical innovations. Among others, there are two important inventions in this field. One is electrical operation, the other a newly invented diaphragm which ensures almost completely friction-free reproduction of recorded compositions. I think that if we regard these as a necessary condition, then we shall have technically perfect apparatuses within the shortest time.)

I consider that the following practical experiments with the phonograph in the realm of musical composition should be initiated:

1. Since the grooves on the mechanically produced record are microscopic in size, we shall first have to devise a method for reducing by technological means down to the normal size of a present-day record any large-scale groove-script record that can conveniently be worked on by hand. It would be desirable to make a photograph of a present-day (reproductive) record and to make a photo-cliché or photo-engraving of the photograph by a zincographical or galvanoplastical process. Should such a record prove to be just more or less playable, the basis for subsequent work along these lines will be established.

2. Study of the graphic symbols of the most different (simultaneous and isolated) acoustical phenomena. Use of projectors. Film. (Specialist works on physics already include detailed descriptions thereof.)

3. Examination of mechanical, metallic and mineral sounds. From these, attempts to devise—for the time being, in a graphic way—a special language. Special attention to be paid to symbols created by different tonalities.

4. Graphic production of the largest contrasting relations. (Before beginning experiments on the wax plate, it is suggested that one trace with a needle the graphic wave lines of music on a [reproductive] phonograph disc; these lines will become well known to the experimenter who will acquire therefrom a sense for graphic representation.)

5. Finally, there are improvisations on the wax plate to be considered, the phonetic results of which are theoretically unforeseeable, but which may permit us to expect significant incentives since the instrument is rather unknown to us.

## NOTES

1. Our present scale is approximately one thousand years old, and it is not absolutely necessary to be bound by its inadequacies today.

# 48

# The Invisible Generation

## WILLIAM S. BURROUGHS

William S. Burroughs (1914–1997) was the greatest American literary experimentalist of the late 20th century. He was heir to the fortune generated by his grandfather, inventor of the adding machine, precursor to the modern computer. Yet despite this privileged upbringing, Burroughs was a self-described "junky" and "queer" (to cite the titles of his first two books) whose career was spent in self-imposed exile from mainstream American society and culture. After graduating from Harvard in 1936, he landed in New York, where he befriended Allen Ginsberg and Jack Kerouac and became associated with the "Beat Generation." Following the publication of his most famous novel, *Naked Lunch* (1959), Burroughs wrote a trilogy of novels using "the cut-up method." Emulating the techniques of collage in painting and montage in film, Burroughs took a scissors to old and new portions of his writing, and then spliced together the pieces at random to generate new ideas and connections. The technique was not only a tool of literary invention; it was also a response to Burroughs' view that language is an anonymous force of social control, a mind- and action-controlling virus spread through everyday speech and writing, and most glaringly manifested in the mass media. The cut-up method, then, was a means of subverting, or at least resisting, language's normalizing power.

Throughout his later life, Burroughs was a cult figure with a particularly strong standing among musicians. The bands Steely Dan and Soft Machine took their names from Burroughs' novels. Burroughs himself collaborated with Brian Jones (of the Rolling Stones), Ornette Coleman, Laurie Anderson, Psychic TV, the Disposable Heroes of Hiphoprisy, among others. The following text (the epilogue to his cut-up novel *The Ticket that Exploded* [1962]), reveals Burroughs as both a founder of "sound poetry" and a precursor to DJ Culture. In cut-up form, it describes Burroughs' cut-up experiments with tape recorders and reflects upon the profound effects of sound and recording on our daily experience.

what we see is determined to a large extent by what we hear   you can verify this proposition by a simple experiment   turn off the sound track on your television set and substitute an arbitrary sound track prerecorded on your tape recorder street sounds music conversation recordings of other television programs   you will find that the arbitrary sound track seems to be appropriate and is in fact determining your interpretation of the film track on screen people running for a bus in piccadilly with a sound track of machine-gun fire looks like 1917 petrograd   you can extend the experiment by using recorded material more or less appropriate to the film track for example take a political speech on television shut off sound track and substitute another speech you have prerecorded   hardly tell the difference isn't much record sound track of one danger man from uncle spy program run it in place of another and see if your friends can't tell the difference it's all done with tape recorders   consider this machine and what it can do   it can record and play back activating a past time set by precise association a recording can be played back any number of times you can study and analyze every pause and inflection of a recorded conversation why did so and so say just that or this just here play back so and so's recordings and you will find out what cues so and so in you can edit a recorded conversation retaining material which is incisive witty and pertinent   you can edit a recorded conversation retaining remarks which are boring flat and silly   a tape recorder can play back fast slow or backwards you can learn to do these things   record a sentence and speed it up now try imitating your accelerated voice   play a sentence backwards and learn to unsay what you just said . . . such exercises bring you a liberation from old association locks   try inching tape   this sound is produced by taking a recorded text for best results a text spoken in a loud clear voice and rubbing the tape back and forth across the head   the same sound can be produced on a philips compact cassette recorder by playing a tape back and switching the mike control stop start on and off at short intervals which gives an effect of stuttering   take any text speed it up slow it down run it backwards inch it and you will hear words that were not in the original recording new words made by the machine   different people will scan out different words of course but some of the words are quite clearly there and anyone can hear them words which were not in the original tape but which are in many cases relevant to the original text as if the words themselves had been interrogated and forced to reveal their hidden meanings it is interesting to record these words literally made by the machine itself   you can carry this experiment further using as your original recording material that contains no words animal noises for instance record a trough of slopping hogs the barking of dogs   go to the zoo and record the bellowings of Guy the gorilla the big cats growling over their meat goats and monkeys   now run the animals backwards speed up slow down and inch the animals and see if any clear words emerge   see what the animals have to say see how the animals react to playback of processed tape

the simplest variety of cut up on tape can be carried out with one machine like this record any text rewind to the beginning   now run forward an arbitrary interval stop the machine and record a short text wind forward stop record where you have recorded over the original text the words are wiped out and replaced with new words   do this several times creating arbitrary juxtapositions   you will notice that the arbitrary cuts in are appropriate in many cases and your cut up tape makes surprising sense   cut up tapes can be hilariously funny twenty years ago i heard a tape called the drunken newscaster prepared by jerry newman of new york cutting up news broadcasts i can not remember the words at this distance but i do remember laughing until i fell out of a chair paul bowles calls the tape recorder god's little toy maybe his last toy fading into the cold spring air poses a colorless question

any number can play

yes any number can play   anyone with a tape recorder   controlling the sound track can influence and create events   the tape recorder experiments described here will show you how this influence can be extended and correlated into the precise operation   this is the invisible generation he looks like an advertising executive a college student an american tourist doesn't matter what your cover story is so long as it covers you and leaves you free to act you need a philips compact cassette recorder handy machine for street recording and playback   you can carry it under your coat for recording looks like a transistor radio for playback playback in the street will show the influence of your sound track in operation of course the most undetectable playback is street recordings people don't notice yesterday voices phantom car holes in time accidents of past time played back in present time screech of brakes loud honk of an absent horn can occasion an accident here   old fires still catch old buildings still fall or take a prerecorded sound track into the street anything you want to put out on the sublim eire play back two minutes record two minutes mixing your message with the street   waft your message right into a worthy ear   some carriers are much better than others you know the ones lips moving muttering away carry my message all over london in our yellow submarine working with street playback you will see your playback find the appropriate context for example i am playing back some of my dutch schultz last word tapes in the street five alarm fire and a fire truck passes right on cue   you will learn to give the cues you will learn to plant events and concepts after analyzing recorded conversations you will learn to steer a conversation where you want it to go   the physiological liberation achieved as word lines of controlled association are cut will make you more efficient in reaching your objectives   whatever you do you will do it better   record your boss and co-workers analyze their associational patterns learn to imitate their voices oh you'll be a popular man around the office but not easy to compete with   the usual procedure record their body sounds from concealed mikes the rhythm of breathing the movements of after-lunch intestines the beating of hearts now impose your own body sounds and become the breathing word and the beating heart of that organization   become that organization   the invisible brothers are invading present time   the more people we can get working with tape recorders the more useful experiments and extensions will turn up   why not give tape recorder parties every guest arrives with his recorder and tapes of what he intends to say at the party recording what other recorders say to him it is the height of rudeness not to record when addressed directly by another tape recorder and you can't say anything directly have to record it first the coolest old tape worms never talk direct

what was the party like   switch on playback
what happened at lunch   switch on playback

eyes old unbluffed unreadable he hasn't said a direct word in ten years and as you hear what the party was like and what happened at lunch you will begin to see sharp and clear   there was a grey veil between you and what you saw or more often did not see   that grey veil was the prerecorded words of a control machine once that veil is removed you will see clearer and sharper than those who are behind the veil whatever you do you will do it better than those behind the veil this is the invisible generation   it is the efficient generation   hands work and go see some interesting results when several hundred tape recorders turn up at a political rally or a freedom march   suppose you record the ugliest snarling southern law men several hundred tape recorders spitting it back and forth and chewing it around like a cow with the aftosa you now have a sound that could make any neighborhood unattractive   several hundred tape recorders echoing the readers could touch a poetry reading with unpredictable magic and think what fifty thousand beatle fans armed with tape recorders could do to shea stadium several hundred people recording and playing back in the street is quite a happening right there   conservative m.p. spoke about the growing menace posed by bands of irresponsible youths with tape recorders playing back traffic sounds that confuse motorists carrying the insults recorded in some low underground club into mayfair and piccadilly   this growing menace to public order   put a thousand young recorders with riot recordings into the street   that mutter gets louder and louder   remember this is a technical operation one step at a time here is an experiment that can be performed by anyone equipped with two machines connected by extension lead so he can record directly from one machine to the other   since the experiment may give rise to a marked erotic reaction it is more interesting to select as your partner some one with whom you are on intimate terms we have two subjects b. and j.   b. records on tape recorder 1   j. records on tape recorder 2   now we alternate the two voice tracks   tape recorder 1 playback two seconds tape recorder 2 records   tape recorder 2 playback two seconds tape recorder 1 records alternating the voice of b. with the voice of j.   in order to attain any degree of precision the two tapes should be cut with scissors and alternate pieces spliced together   this is a long process which can be appreciably expedited if you have access to a cutting room and use film tape which is much larger and easier to handle   you can carry this experiment further by taking a talking film of b. and talking film of j. splicing sound and image track twenty four alternations per second   as i have intimated it is advisable to exercise some care in choosing your partner for such experiments since the results can be quite drastic b. finds himself talking and thinking just like j.   j. sees b.'s image in his own face   who's face   b. and j. are continually aware of each other   when separated invisible and persistent presence they are in fact becoming each other you see b. retroactively was j. by the fact of being recorded on j.'s sound and image track experiments with spliced tape can give rise to explosive relationships properly handled of course to a high degree of efficient cooperation you will begin to see the advantage conveyed on j. if he carried out such experiments without the awareness of b. and so many applications of the spliced tape principle will suggest themselves to the alert reader suppose you are some creep in a grey flannel suit you want to present a new concept of advertising to the old man it is creative advertising so before you goes up against the old man you record the old man's voice and splices your own voice in expounding your new concept and put it out on the office air-conditioning system splice yourself in with your favorite pop singers    splice yourself in with newscasters prime ministers presidents

why stop there

why stop anywhere

everybody splice himself in with everybody else yes boys that's me there by the cement mixer    the next step and i warn you it will be expensive is programmed tape recorders    a fully programmed machine would be set to record and play back at selected intervals to rewind and start over after a selected interval automatically remaining in continuous operation    suppose you have three programmed machines tape recorder 1 programmed to play back five seconds while tape recorder 2 records    tape recorder 2 play back three seconds while tape recorder 1 records now say you are arguing with your boy friend or girl friend remembering what was said last time and thinking of things to say next time round and round you just can't shut up    put all your arguments and complaints on tape recorder 1 and call tape recorder 1 by your own name    on tape recorder 2 put all the things he or she said to you or might say when occasion arises out of the tape recorders    now make the machines talk    tape recorder 1 play back five seconds tape recorder 2 record    tape recorder 2 play back three seconds tape recorder 1 record    run it through fifteen minutes half an hour    now switch intervals running the interval switch you used on tape recorder 1 back on tape recorder 2    the interval switch may be as important as the context    listen to the two machines mix it around    now on tape recorder 3 you can introduce the factor of irrelevant response so put just anything on tape recorder 3 old joke old tune piece of the street television radio and program tape recorder 3 into the argument

tape recorder 1    waited up for you until two o'clock last night

tape recorder 3    what we want to know is who put the sand in the spinach

the use of irrelevant response will be found effective in breaking obsessional association tracks    all association tracks are obsessional    get it out of your head and into the machines    stop arguing stop complaining stop talking let the machines argue    complain and talk    a tape recorder is an externalized section of the human nervous system    you can find out more about the nervous system and gain more control over your reactions by using the tape recorder than you could find out sitting twenty years in the lotus posture or wasting your time on the analytic couch

listen to your present time tapes and you will begin to see who you are and what you are doing here    mix yesterday in with today and hear tomorrow your future rising out of old recordings    you are a programmed tape recorder set to record and play back

who programs you

who decides what tapes play back in present time

who plays back your old humiliations and defeats holding you in prerecorded preset time

you don't have to listen to that sound    you can program your own playback you can decide what tapes you want played back in present time    study your associational patterns and find out what cases in what prerecordings for playback program those old tapes out it's all done with tape recorders there are many things you can do with programmed tape recorders stage performances programmed at arbitrary intervals so each performance is unpredictable and unique allowing any degree of audience participation readings concerts programmed tape recorders can create a happening anywhere programmed tape recorders are of course essential to any party and no modern host would bore his guests with a straight present time party in a modern house every room is bugged recorders record and play back from hidden mikes and loudspeakers phantom voices mutter through corridors and rooms word visible as a haze tape recorders in the gardens answer each other like barking dogs sound track brings the studio on set you can change the look of a city by putting your own sound track into the streets here are some experiments filming a sound track operations on set find a neighborhood with slate roofs and red brick chimneys cool grey sound track fog horns distant train whistles frogs croaking music across the golf course cool blue recordings in a cobblestone market with blue shutters all the sad old showmen stand there in blue twilight a rustle of darkness and wires when several thousand people working with tape recorders and filming subsequent action select their best sound tracks and film footage and splice together you will see something interesting now consider the harm that can be done and has been done when recording and playback is expertly carried out in such a way that the people affected do not know what is happening thought feeling and apparent sensory impressions can be precisely manipulated and controlled riots and demonstrations to order for example they use old anti-semitic recordings against the chinese in indonesia run shop and get rich and always give the business to another tiddly wink pretty familiar suppose you want to bring down the area go in and record all the ugliest stupidest dialogue the most discordant sound track you can find and keep playing it back which will occasion more ugly stupid dialogue recorded and played back on and on always selecting the ugliest material possibilities are unlimited you want to start a riot put your machines in the street with riot recordings move fast enough you can stay just ahead of the riot surfboarding we call it no margin for error recollect poor old bums caught out in a persian market riot recordings hid under his jellaba and they skinned him alive raw peeled thing writhing there in the noon sun and we got the picture

do you get the picture

the techniques and experiments described here have been used and are being used by agencies official and non official without your awareness and very much to your disadvantage any number can play wittgenstein said no proposition can contain itself as an argument the only thing not prerecorded on a prerecorded set is the prerecording itself that is any recording in which a random factor operates any street recording you can prerecord your future you can hear and see what you want to hear and see the experiments described here were explained and demonstrated to me by ian sommerville of london in this article i am writing as his ghost

look around you look at a control machine programmed to select the ugliest stupidest most vulgar and degraded sounds for recording and playback which provokes uglier stupider more vulgar and degraded sounds to be recorded and play back inexorable degradation look forward to dead end look forward to ugly vulgar playback tomorrow and tomorrow and tomorrow what are newspapers doing but selecting the ugliest sounds for playback by and large if it's ugly it's news and if that isn't enough i quote from the editorial page of the new york daily news we can take care of china and if russia intervenes we can take care of that nation too the only good communist is a dead communist let's take care of slave driver castro next what are we waiting for let's bomb china now and let's stay armed to the teeth for centuries this ugly vulgar bray put out for mass playback you want to spread hysteria record and play back the most stupid and hysterical reactions

marijuana   marijuana   why that's deadlier than cocaine

it will turn a man into a homicidal maniac he said steadily his eyes cold as he thought of the vampires who suck riches from the vile traffic in pot quite literally swollen with human blood   he reflected grimly and his jaw set pushers should be pushed into the electric chair

strip the bastards naked

all right let's see your arms

or in the mortal words of harry j anslinger   the laws must reflect society's disapproval of the addict

an uglier reflection than society's disapproval would be hard to find the mean cold eyes of decent american women to tight lips and no thank you from the shop keeper snarling cops pale nigger killing eyes reflecting society's disapproval fucking queers i say shoot them   if on the other hand you select calm sensible reactions for recordings and playback you will spread calmness and good sense

is this being done

obviously it is not   only way to break the inexorable down spiral of ugly uglier ugliest recording and playback is with counterrecording and playback   the first step is to isolate and cut association lines of the control machine carry a tape recorder with you and record all the ugliest stupidest things cut your ugly tapes in together speed up slow down play backwards inch the tape   you will hear one ugly voice and see one ugly spirit is made of ugly old prerecordings   the more you run the tapes through and cut them up the less power they will have   cut the prerecordings into air into thin air

# 49

---

# Record, CD, Analog, Digital

## CHRISTIAN MARCLAY & YASUNAO TONE

In the late 1970s, concurrent with the birth of HipHop, Christian Marclay (1955– ) pioneered the use of turntables and found recordings to make experimental music in the context of art. John Cage, Paul Hindemith, and Ernst Toch had begun such experiments forty years earlier. Yet it was Marclay who most fully explored this musical terrirory. Inspired by punk rock and by avant-garde art movements such as Dada and Fluxus, Marclay used skipping thrift-store records to produce percussive effects. He cut up and reassembled them into new composites and employed multiple turntables to produce inventive and often humorous collages. Using found records, album covers, audio tapes, and snapshots, Marclay has also produced a body of photographs, sculptures, videos, and installations that have been widely exhibited in galleries and museums.

Yasunao Tone (1935– ) has been producing happenings, experimental music, and digital art for more than four decades. In 1960, with Takehisa Kosugi, Tone formed Group Ongaku, the first collective improvisation ensemble in Japan; and, in 1962, he became an active member of the Japanese wing of Fluxus. Always interested in the manipulation of technology to aesthetic ends, Tone began experimenting with CDs and CD players in the early 1980s. In 1985, he produced his first "wounded CD" by attaching pinhole-punctured transparent tape to commercial CDs in order to override the CD player's error-correction system and produce sporadic bursts of white noise.

In this discussion with the editors of *Music* magazine, Marclay and Tone discuss their work and compare strategies for manipulating analog and digital recordings.

CHRISTIAN MARCLAY: You make CDs skip?
YASUNAO TONE: It's not really skipping. It's distorting information. A CD consists
of a series of samples. You know bytes and bits, right? One byte contains
sixteen bits of information. So, if I block one or two bits, information still

exists—one byte of information—but the numbers are altered so it becomes totally different information. That's the idea. It's not skipping sound.

MARCLAY: So, how do you do it?

TONE: I use Scotch tape. I make many pinholes on bits of Scotch tape which I attach to the CDs.

MARCLAY: I tried doing different things with CDs—scratching the surface or putting a little spray paint on it, different patterns—but just the slightest thing makes . . .

TONE: . . . a big difference.

MARCLAY: Yeah, the machine stops.

TONE: Because error-correcting software is built in.

MARCLAY: Is there a way to take that software out?

TONE: I don't know how to do that, but if you could it would be great [. . . .]

MARCLAY: I like the Scotch tape.

TONE: The Scotch tape enables me to make burst errors without significantly affecting the system and stopping the machine. The error-correcting software constantly interpolates between individual bits of misread information, but if adjacent bits are misread, a burst occurs and the software mutes the output. If a significant number of bursts occur in one frame, the error increases until it eventually overrides the system.

MARCLAY: That's why I like the old-fashioned turntable: because it's so dumb. You can hit it, you can do all these things, and it will never stop playing. The CD players are too smart . . . smart machines.

TONE: But to fight with smart machines you have to be very primitive. The machine's behavior is very peculiar, it cannot decide what to do. Sometimes it proceeds backwards, or it hesitates and searches for the next signal. When the CD player stops or hesitates to advance, I tap it or slightly shake it. This very tiny movement affects the machine's behavior—maybe changing the focal distance of the laser beam—and it recovers from malfunctioning.

MARCLAY: It sounds like a rattlesnake when it's skipping. It has that quality. It is the distinctive CD malfunctioning sound—the sound of a rattlesnake. I was just listening to this CD by DJ Shadow. On the first cut you hear this skipping CD. I think it's the first time I heard that rattlesnake sound in a pop context. Otherwise, I only heard it with you, and Nic Collins, and David Weinstein's band of CD Players, Impossible Music.

TONE: I began to work with CDs in 1985, when the CD player first came out. I think then the machines were more primitive than now. I can still do it, but. . . .

MUSIC: You use a standard machine? You don't alter it at all?

TONE: It's standard. I have two machines. In 1984, I bought the first one to experiment with—I think it's Sharp or something—and then half a year later I bought a different machine. It has better functions for ordinary use, but it's less useful than the first one for me. Within a half year the machines already improved, so I don't think I could use a brand new machine for my performance. I would have to look for old, used ones.

MUSIC: Just like Christian, the turntables you use. . . .

MARCLAY: It's true. The Technics MK2 and MK3, which every DJ swears by, are annoying machines to me. They're too delicate, too limiting for me. The simpler the better.

MUSIC: What kind of turntable do you normally use?

MARCLAY: They're called Califone. They're kind of institutional turntables used by every school in the U.S. They were used for audio-visual presentations, for dance classes and whatever. Built to last, built to be abused by students. They have four different speeds, and I added on and off switches, sometimes an extra tone arm. Otherwise, they're standard.

MUSIC: Christian, in an art context you are situated within a trajectory of Dada, Surrealism, Fluxus, Appropriation. How would you position yourself in a music context, vis-à-vis Experimental, Pop, HipHop, DJ?

MARCLAY: I get my influences from many different places. I'm not very picky about where they come from, whether it's high art or pop culture. That difference has never been important to me. What HipHop DJs were doing had some influence, though I became aware of that work later. My first influences were Cage and some of the Fluxus experiments with sound. Then, *musique concrète* and its experimentation with found sounds. When I became aware of HipHop I could see a natural connection between those two traditions. But, HipHop didn't grow out of that kind of white, nerdy, high art culture. It came out of the streets. It was a simple, direct way to make music. And also a cheap way. Rather than expensive musical instruments, it was just some cheap records and a couple of turntables. There's an economic reason for this happening. And in some strange way these two movements—the Experimental music and the HipHop culture—have kind of grown separately and there are very little interactions between the two, until now. I would like to think that I am in between—neither, nor. I don't try to make pop music and I usually stay away from commercial beats, but my work is informed by the pop music I hear everywhere. It's just a different way of using that material. It's also interesting that my work with records came about just before analog records were replaced by digital technology and sampling. It felt like the industry came out with sampling machines because DJs were sampling. I think the technology was ready to follow in the footsteps of the musical ideas already present.

TONE: Well, you know, it takes a long time to develop digital technology. I don't think they are aware of HipHop or whatever when they are developing something.

MARCLAY: But when they started making their sampling keyboards and stuff, I think maybe there was already that understanding that it was useful to sample because HipHop DJs were doing it.

TONE: Well, the clientele was expected to be not just musicians, but the general public.

MARCLAY: Anybody could become a musician.

TONE: Yeah. Anybody can become a musician. That's something in common between you and me: we use a kind of technique that can be used by any lay people. It doesn't require any special training. That is essentially a Fluxus philosophy.

MARCLAY: And also the Punk philosophy.

TONE: Well, you know, Fluxus came before.

MARCLAY: But, Fluxus was an art movement, and punk was a pop culture phenomenon.

TONE: That's true, but. . . . In the 60s we were transversing many categories [. . . .We] didn't recognize any dichotomy between high and low at that time. These were transversal acts.

MUSIC: We live in a particular, historical moment, with its environment, including the strategy of the avant garde and certain technology which becomes available, not only for the artist, but for others as well.

MARCLAY: When the industry comes up with a machine to record something, it has a very specific use, but the artist has always tried to go beyond what the machine was designed for—like Tone's use of CDs. It's the same with photography. Moholy-Nagy put the camera aside, and started using the *medium* of photography to make photograms. The moment records were invented, people started messing around with them. Again, Moholy-Nagy experimented by modifying the grooves of records, and imagined drawing sounds directly onto the record.

TONE: Even Paul Hindemith. When the record was cylindrical, he played Mozart backwards—actually I don't know if he did it or just proposed it, but it's always like that. A new technology, a new medium appears, and the artist usually enlarges the use of the technology. . . . Deviates.

MARCLAY: Abuse of technology.

TONE: I think deviation of technology. You have to deviate. I call that kind of art *paramedia*. The manufacturers always force us to use a product their way. A medium always has some *telos*; however, people occasionally find a way to deviate from the original purpose of the medium and develop a totally new field. Photographic technology had *telos* to make the image solid, to make shadow and light solid, so the photograph was invented and it's constantly being refined in order to be as accurate as possible. But, artists do not want to just imitate nature. When Man Ray invented solarization, it was a failure in the view of photographic technology, but of course artistically it's much more interesting. Or, *musique concrète*. As soon as the tape recorder was invented, people like Pierre Schaeffer found that by splicing tape and changing its order he could get a different sound than what was originally recorded. So, it's natural for artists to deviate.

MUSIC: I'm interested in how this deviation by the artist affects the chain of manufacturers, marketers, and consumers. For instance, there's a whole new revival of producing turntables. They even make a turntable that plays backwards and has other details that weren't available before. This is partly because the DJ scene is popular, and . . .

MARCLAY: . . . Yeah, now you can buy samples of "record" sounds—HipHop scratches—for your keyboard. You can hear these sounds in advertisements for Coca-Cola or whatever, and so now this dysfunctioning machine sound is being recycled for commercial purposes.

TONE: It's recycled. Reappropriation of artists' appropriations.

MARCLAY: Again an example of the absurdity of wanting to disassociate high and low culture. Another good example is how experimental films from the 70s—Stan Brakhage's fast editing and stuff which had no commercial value—are now being used in every MTV video and every TV ad. And really, who invented this stuff but crazy artists! Somehow the media has reappropriated it and turned it into a commercial. It goes back and forth.

TONE: It's a delusion. It's a deluded form. The manufacturers don't care about the concept.

MARCLAY: It has lost its original meaning. It has become something else.

TONE: Actually, it's totally different. It just looks the same.

MUSIC: You said before that anybody can become a musician and that you both use simple techniques. I hear that in Japan there's this DJ primer for kids to learn how to spin. Any kid can do it. It becomes a sort of commodified popular art form. So how can you radicalize, say, the idea of manipulating records or CDs?

MARCLAY: That's one of the reasons why I don't perform so often anymore. I'm not a very active DJ these days because for me it doesn't have the same meaning as when I did it fifteen years ago when records were the common medium that everybody used at home. Records were considered differently. They were meant to be played from beginning to end, and a DJ just played cuts—one after another—and just worried about transitions. Now the record has become obsolete and CDs have really taken over, even though there is this underground culture of DJs, young kids who are rediscovering vinyl because their first stereo equipment was not a turntable, but a CD player. In Japan they are selling all these black-and-white, throw-away cameras and advertising them with black-and-white images of movie stars from the 40s. It's like the big craze for teenagers to take black-and-white pictures because they don't know black-and-white.

TONE: They thought color pictures were natural.

MARCLAY: They grew up with Fuji colors. It's like re-discovering a poor medium that has a certain fascination. It's a novelty again.

TONE: When a new technology appears which makes old technology obsolete, two typical reactions occur: some artists discover an abnormal use for the new technology in order to expand artistic expression, and sometimes the obsolete technology itself becomes an art form. Christian started working with records just before the appearance of CDs which would soon be making vinyl obsolete. I think you sensed somehow not consciously, but. . . .

MUSIC: Well, even though Christian began manipulating records before CDs were available, his work can be seen now as a reaction to technology, to digital technology. Obviously, you are both more interested in critiquing a medium rather than in cutting-edge technology.

MARCLAY: I remember when my attitude towards the record changed from being this object to be respected, collected and stored for posterity, into a piece of plastic that had no more value than a coffee cup in the gutter. Coming from Switzerland to the United States in the 70s, I noticed that change in attitudes towards objects. I would see records on the street, in the gutter. I would see thousands of records in thrift shops that nobody wanted, that nobody cared about. It was in some way that cultural change that allowed me to see a different attitude towards records, and I pushed in that direction, considering them as just a cheap commodity to be used and abused.

MUSIC: So, in a way you use records just as a Fluxus or Dada artist would use junk?

MARCLAY: Yeah, and the more I used it, the more I started thinking about the object and reflecting on it and playing with its meaning—its cultural value ver-

christian marclay & yasunao tone • 345

sus its commodity value, and how it has affected the way we perceive music and time. And so a lot of my work has been about trying to understand this object.

MUSIC: You have made a few records, too.

MARCLAY: When I made a record, it had to be critical of the vinyl object. It could not only be a document. *Record Without a Cover* was the perfect medium for my ideas, a record that was not about permanence, but about change. It was sold without any protective packaging. By the time you bought it in the store, it was already damaged during shipping and handling. It was a record that threatened everything you were taught about records and how to handle them. It even threatened your needle. You couldn't be a passive listener, you had to be involved. It was intriguing, unstable. It was a record about records.

MUSIC: Earlier you mentioned a CD by DJ Shadow. Of course, a number of DJs are releasing records and CDs now. What do you think of DJs in the recording studio—studio DJs?

MARCLAY: I liked working with records as a performance activity. I used the records in front of people. It was a live event. There are very few recordings because I wasn't really interested in making new records, but more in using "dead" records in a "live" situation. So people understood where the music came from. It was very simple, everybody could understand the process because they knew how to use records. Once you are in a recording studio, you start using all the technology that's available. That technology is not visible or audible necessarily. You get this kind of mystery, in some way a hierarchy. Technology can sometimes create that hierarchy. There's the technicians, the . . .

TONE: . . . composer, conductor, performer, engineer . . .

MARCLAY: . . . And then at the bottom of the pyramid, the listeners, who are just like, "Wow, how did he do this?" I like it better when someone says, "Oh, I could do that." And that's what the old mechanical turntable and vinyl allow me to do. You know, in the 80s everybody wanted to be a guitar player. Now in the 90s, everybody wants to be a DJ. To me the guitar always had a mystery. You had to be really skilled and studied in some ways—even though you had a few illuminated geniuses like Arto Lindsay who just learned by doing it—but there's something about a record and a turntable that seems so easy. I think that's what the big deal is. That's why everyone wants to be a DJ, because it's so easy.

TONE: Well, you're a master. Master of—

MARCLAY: . . . Not a DJ.

TONE: A meta-DJ. I think there's probably a big difference between analog and digital in terms of playing discs. I think digital is basically unpredictable. There are so many bits and bytes of information condensed in one tiny space, and you can't locate which part of the disc produces this sound. But for you, you almost locate, you can actually see the sound. CD players are instructed by the information on the CD—when to stop, how fast to spin—and if you dysfunction that information the disc cannot progress the way the piece goes. So, I do a kind of de-controlling of the sound-producing process, of the system of music itself. Well, it's essentially a Fluxus event. The idea of performance is sort of de-controlled.

MARCLAY: And not knowing the outcome, not being totally in control, and accepting that randomness.

TONE: Basically, as a performance artist we do the same thing, but towards the material I also de-control the material.

MARCLAY: So you're a master of de-controlling?

MUSIC: Tone's a digital master, and Christian's an analog master. [Laughter]

# 50

# Algorithms: Erasures and the Art of Memory

## PAUL D. MILLER

Since his recording debut in 1995, musician, writer, and conceptual artist Paul D. Miller (1970– ) has emerged as one of the most able theorists of DJ Culture. Miller is best known as DJ Spooky, that Subliminal Kid, a producer whose recordings and live performances are firmly rooted in HipHop, Ambient, dub, and drum 'n' bass, but also draw from the history of avant-garde art in the 20th century. His moniker "that Subliminal Kid" is borrowed from a character in William S. Burroughs' cut-up novel *Nova Express*. He has collaborated with composers Iannis Xenakis and Pauline Oliveros, and produced an audio installation based on the work of Marcel Duchamp. Miller has also recently worked with free jazz masters William Parker, Matthew Shipp, Joe McPhee, and Lawrence "Butch" Morris. For Miller, the DJ is not merely an entertainer but an information handler who selects and guides the flow of audio data. The DJ's mix is a composite of fragments drawn from a heterogeneous array of temporal, spatial, and cultural locations. Hence, according to Miller, the DJ regulates not only data but also the construction of time, memory, subjectivity, and experience.

The twentieth century encounter between alphabetic and electronic
faces of culture confers on the printed word a crucial role in staying
the return to the Africa within . . .
                    —Marshall McLuhan, *The Gutenberg Galaxy*

Gimme Two Records and I'll make you a universe . . .
                    —DJ Spooky That Subliminal Kid

One of the first bootleggers, in this case one of the first people to sample music, Lionel Mapleson, used a phonograph recorder given to him by his close personal friend, Thomas Edison, to record extracts of his favorite moments from the various operas that played at New York's Metropolitan Opera house when he was working there during the years 1901–1903. These recordings of various arias comprise the first known texts created by the recording medium (all puns intended). With his recording-phonograph in hand Lionel Mapleson may just have written himself into history books as the first DJ. His phonograph [. . .] was a new way of data-handling that allowed the mechanical implementation of a non-sequential form of text, one including associative trails, dynamic annotations, and cross references—a host of characteristics one finds as common features of computers in our modern hyper-text-formatted world. A journalist writes of the experience of listening to these recordings [. . .]:

> The sense is one of listening from backstage, through a door that keeps opening and closing, to bits and pieces of performances. The vantage point is at a little distance from the singers, and they seem to be heard through a certain amount of backstage clatter; sometimes they move out of line of hearing, and sometimes the noise obscures the voices. But mostly, they can be heard quite well enough for the listener to get a very definite sense of personalities and occasionally of the full impact of virtuosity, that in terms of the opera house today, is quite beyond the wildest imagination . . .

Partitioned subjectivity, cross-fades, sonic shock-wave sounds of seismic bass disruption, pitch, tempo, the inertial drag of bass de-tuned, compressed and pitch-shifted down, drums pitched upwards and downwards, sound as a unified field of spatial representation with its own aural logic, ego become a sonic wave form in the chaotic urban landscape of inner city pressure . . . these are things that go through my mind when I make music. [I] create electronic hybrids (some people still call them songs) that [. . .] create a milieu where a previously interior world could be brought to light through methods like keyboard mapping (delineating zones of aural speed) and time stretching words until they become an elemental part of the song, etc. I [. . .] create music that [. . .] reflect[s] the extreme density of the urban landscape and the way its geometric regularity contours and configures perception [. . . .] To me, assembly is the invisible language of our time and DJing is the forefront art form of the late 20th Century.

**Assemblages are passional, they are compositions of desire. Desire has nothing to do with a natural and spontaneous determination; there is no desire but assembling, assembled, engineered desire [*agençant, agencé, machiné*]. The rationality, the efficiency of an assemblage does not exist without the passions that the assemblage brings into play, without the desires that constitute it as much as it constitutes them . . .**

**—Deleuze and Guattari, *A Thousand Plateaus***

DJ culture—urban youth culture—is all about recombinant potential. It has as a central feature a eugenics of the imagination. Each and every source sample is fragmented and bereft of prior meaning—kind of like a future without a past. The samples are given meaning only when re-presented in the assemblage of the mix. In this way the DJ acts as the cybernetic inheritor of the improvisational tradition of jazz, where various motifs would be used and recycled by the various musicians of the genre. In this case, however, the records become the notes. Also there is the repetitive nature of the music that allows for the unfolding in time of a recursive spatial arrangement of tones whose parallel can be found in the world of architecture, where structural integrity requires the modular deployment of building materials to create a building's framework.

> **Repeating then is every one, repeating then makes a complete history in every one for someone sometime to realise in that one. Repeating is in them of the most delicate shades in them of being and of feeling and so it comes to be clear in each one the complete nature in each one, it comes to be clear in each one the complete nature in each one and others to make a kind of them, a kind of men and women . . .**

> **—Gertrude Stein, *The Making of Americans***

Triggered by the sensuous touch of the DJ's hands guiding the mix, the spectral trace of sounds in your mind that existed before you heard them, telling your memory that the mixed feelings you get, the conflicting impulses you feel when you hear it are impressions—externalized thoughts that tell you you only know that you have never felt what you thought you were feeling because you have never really listened to what you were hearing. The sounds of the ultra-futuristic streetsoul of the urban jungle shimmering at the edge of perception.

> **We have also sound-houses, where we practise and demonstrate all sounds, and their generation. We have harmonies which you have not, of quarter sounds and lesser slides of sounds. Divers instruments of music likewise to you unknown, some sweeter than any you have; together with bells and rings that are dainty and sweet. We represent small sounds as great and deep; likewise great sounds extenuate and sharp; likewise divers tremblings and warblings of sounds, which in their original are entire. We represent and imitate all articulate sounds and letters, and the voices and notes of beasts and birds. We have certain helps which set to the ear do further the hearing greatly. We have also divers strange and artificial echoes, reflecting the voice many times, and as it were tossing it: and some that give back the voice louder than it came; some shriller, and some deeper: yea, some rendering the voice, differing in the letters or articulate sound from that they receive. We have also means to convey sounds in tubes and pipes, in strange lines and distances.**

> **—Francis Bacon, *New Atlantis* (1627 A.D)**

Sound as an isolated object of reproduction, call it our collective memory bank, is the focal point in my work. Like KRS One said a while back, "See how it sound, a little unrational . . ."

Black Americans were sustained and healed and nurtured by the translation of their experience into art, above all in the music . . . All of the intricacy, all of the discipline. All the work that must go into improvisation so that it appears that you've never touched it. Music makes you hungry for more of it. It never really gives you the whole number. It slaps and it embraces, it slaps and it embraces . . . The major things black art has to have are these: it must have the ability to use found objects, the appearance of using found things, and it must look effortless. It must look cool and easy. If it makes you sweat, you haven't done the work. You shouldn't be able to see the seams and stitches.

—Toni Morrison

Beats don't lie and sound is all about flow: don't push the river.

The basic unit of contemporary art is not the idea, but the analysis of and extension of sensations . . .

—Susan Sontag

I consider the mixes created by a DJ to be mood sculptures operating in a recombinant fashion. Based on the notion that all sonic material can be manipulated with the same ease that computers now generate composite images, the DJ combines the musical expression of other musicians with their own and in the process creates a seamless flow of music. In this light, the sample operates as a kind of synecdoche—a focal/coordinate point in the dramaturgical grid of life. Call the mixes and songs generated by the assembly process of DJing and sequencing etc. the social construction of memory [. . . .] A mix, for me, is a way of providing a rare and intimate glimpse into the process of cultural production in the late 20th Century.

Notions of intellectual property and copyright law are brought into question as the communal reception of music takes on the significances of being the sonic equivalent to alchemy. The mix speaks to you of the bricolage of a place where the "self" exists as a deployed network of personae (the Latin root of personae means "that through which sound enters"), music created out of a particular scene or social grouping; and it shows the inexplicable mutability of sound as different people share the memories brought about by the same songs. It demonstrates the uncanny power to metamorphosize, through audio alchemy, the passage of sound into a kind of unspoken story, that like its predecessor, the oral tradition, can pass on "tales" of songs.

In the electronic milieu that we all move in today, the DJ is a custodian of aural history. In the mix, creator and re-mixer are woven together in the syncretic space of the text of samples and other sonic material to create a seamless fabric of sound that in a strange way mirrors the modern macrocosm of cyberspace, where different voices and visions constantly collide and cross-fertilize one another. The linkages between memory, time, and place, are all externalized and made accessible to the listener from the viewpoint of the DJ who makes the mix. Thus, the mix acts as a continuously moving still frame *camera lucida* capturing moment-events. The mix, in this picture, allows the invocation of different languages, texts, and sounds to converge, meld, and create a new medium that transcends its original components. The sum created from this audio collage leaves its original elements far behind.

As a conceptual artist, my work focuses on what I call "Differentiated Being," and its rapport with the electronically accelerated culture of the late 20th Century. The core elements that comprise my "art" are derived from my experiences as a young African-American male living as an object of history rather than its subject, and the social construction of subjectivity. For me, my world represents an artistic attempt at understanding the role of intersubjectivity and the creation of the art object. My work highlights the tenuous relationship of a youth culture based on rapid change, i.e. extreme cultural velocity, a paradigm in which what Lucy Lippard called "the dematerialized art object" holds sway [over] the static art object of the traditional European museum structure.

**He will say, when he wishes to show that I am many, that there are my right parts and my left parts, my front parts and my back parts, likewise upper and lower; all different: for I do, I suppose, partake of multitude.**

**—Plato, *Parmenides***

I feel that because it is in a state of discrepant engagement with modern electro culture, the conventional museum structure is rapidly moving towards a state of desuetude with regards to modern electronic media's impact on the generation to which I belong. Kinetic potential and its manifestation in cultural production are core tenets of my work. A shorthand way of describing its presence in the art objects (some still call them songs) I create would be to see that they focus on "art as potentiality" with regard to a state of being-as-void, or continuous becoming. There are many problems one encounters in the attempt to reconcile conventional "art" with the culture that I call home. But to me, fragmentation is what all of this is about. My work as a DJ is my prime inspiration; and it is the memories that I have gained from my various experiences as a DJ that fuel my inquiry into the art object as a vessel of cultural representation. I do not call my constructs paintings, but rather "objectiles"—that is, objects imbued with an extreme sense of cultural velocity—object + projectile.

In DJ culture music is carried by shards of time—records, CDs, and most popular amongst the initiates, the "mixed tape." All of the previously listed objects are activated by various electronic appliances, thus the kinetic potential—the movement of a static object into a relation of dynamic movement with regards to a social function of electricity—that lies at the center of my oeuvre. To me, the mixed tape is the ultimate example of a new art object. By using a found object—the cassette—that has the ability to hold replicated information, and in turn can be used to reproduce that very same information whenever it is activated: the cassette arrives at a point where it is the electromagnetic equivalent of the blank canvas, and "all the world is in the mix." The mix of found objects or self-generated music that a DJ records to tape, is representative of a style that s/he uses to evoke emotive responses in the listener, thus involving the spectator and creator in a situation where the boundaries dividing the two blur. DJing is also informed by a fluid dialectics of culture that places it at the center of the transition from mimetic to semiotic representation that electronic artforms are highlighting. What these diverse new forms of representation indicate is a migration of human cognitive structures into the abstract "machinery" of the electronic environment.

**I am you, you are me, with language, we are three.**

—**Paul D. Miller**

**Ideas improve, the meaning of words participates in the improvement. Plagiarism is necessary. Progress implies it. It embraces an author's phrase, makes use of his expressions, erases a false idea, and replaces it with the right idea.**

—**Comte de Lautréamont (1870)**

The style a DJ uses is their imprimatur, their way of appropriating the psychological environment that the people that made the records put into their mix, and sharing it with those who attend the performance. In this way the DJ acts as a cipher, translating thought and sound into functional mood units whose accumulated meanings can be found in the audio equivalent of a paratactic structure of linguistic elements or what I like to call "the body telematic," or what Artaud liked to call "the body without organs." In this sense, the records, samples, and various other sonic material the DJ uses to construct their mix act as a sort of externalized memory that breaks down previous notions of intellectual property and copyright law that Western Society has used in the past. It is in this singularly improvisational role of "recombinater" that the DJ creates what I like to call a "post symbolic mood sculpture," or the mix: a disembodied and transient text that mirrors the dematerialized art object mentioned earlier. Operating in a manner that is both enantiamorphic and tesselary, the DJ embodies a telematic relationship where "the sign" becomes sound seeking sense, thus the difference between semiotic and mimetic representation that I mentioned earlier. The implications of this style of creating art are three fold: 1) by its very nature it critiques the entire idea of intellectual property and copyright law, 2) it reifies a communal art value structure in contrast to most forms of art in late capitalist social contexts, 3) it interfaces communications technology in a manner that anthropomorphizes it. In this manner, DJing posits music as an extension of a neurolinguistic relationship of human beings to their, as Marx put it, "alienated life elements." Those "elements," seen through the medium of the mix, reveal to us a place where different voices, rhythms, and tones fuse to create a syncretic flow of sound as externalized memory. They become epiphenomena whose central purpose is to act as a mnemonic device: the social construction of subjectivity is informed by the memories that become the shared text of an attenuated media environment made possible by a variable architecture synthesized from the tones that comprise its forms. C.S. Pierce noted in his idea of semiosis a similar unfolding of human expression, albeit without its cybernetic implications (although they are implicit in his work, I believe), when he wrote back in the 19th century "that since any thought, there must have been a thought, has its analogue in the fact that, since any past time, there must have been an infinite series of times. To say, therefore, that thought cannot happen in an instant, but requires time, is but another way of saying that every thought must be interpreted in another, or that all thought is in signs."

Memory and temporal structure are the new spaces of art to me. Deleuze and Guattari arrive at a similar point in their critique of late capital and schizophrenia with the rhizome structure, a decentered and nonhierarchical form that perfectly illustrates their metaphor for counter culture. Among philosophers like David Hume, Giordano Bruno, Frantz Fanon, Martin Luther King, Friedrich Hegel, Nietzsche, and Malcolm X, a fixation on multiplicity gives their expression all the more immediacy because of its fragmented nature. This, to me is almost the equivalent of time travel along psychological association lines that artists and writers as diverse as Brion Gysin, Sun Ra, Alain Robbe-Grillet, William S. Burroughs, Marcel Duchamp, Rammelzee, Samuel Delaney, H.G. Wells, Greg Tate, Tricia Rose, Grand Master Flash, Sol Lewitt, and Yevgeny Zamyatin, to name a few, have based their works on. Adrift etymologically, the word "phonograph" means "sound writing." In literature, the methodologies used to assemble the mix a DJ creates could be called stream of consciousness narratives (*roman fleuve*), or nonsequential (*roman mallaparte*). The previous meanings, geographic regions, and temporal placement of the elements that comprise the mix, are corralled into a space where the differences in time, place, and culture, are collapsed to create a recombinant text or autonomous zone of expression based on what I like to call "cartographic failure."

**Autonomous zones are interstitial, they inhabit the in-between of socially significant constellations, they are where bodies in the world but between identities go: liminal sites of syncretic unorthodoxy ... Autonomous zones may be thought of, in temporal terms, as shreds of futurity. Like "outside", "future" is only an approximation: there are any number of potential futures in the cracks of the present order, but only a few will actually unfold. Think of autonomous zones in terms of time, but tenseless: time out of joint, in an immanent outside (Nietzsche's untimely).**

**—Brian Masumi, *A Users Guide To Capitalism and Schizophrenia***

All I can say is that in this era of hypermodernity, the current message has been deleted. Any sound can be you. It is through the mix and all that it entails—the re-configuration of ethnic, national, and sexual identity—that humanity will, hopefully, move into another era of social evolution. I can only hope that the world can shift into this new matrix without too much disruption. The other options—genocide, internecine ethnic strife and warfare, the complete destruction of the environment, and the creation of a permanent underclass that doesn't have access to technology—are what the future holds if humanity can't come to grips with these new and explosive forces technology has released in us all.

# 51

# *Replicant: On Dub*

### DAVID TOOP

David Toop (1949– ; see also chap. 36) is among the most innovative and wide-ranging writers on contemporary music. His pioneering book on HipHop, *Rap Attack*, first appeared in 1984. A decade later, Toop published *Ocean of Sound* (1995), a poetic survey of contemporary musical life from Debussy through Ambient, Techno, and drum 'n' bass. Since the 1970s, Toop has also been an important presence on the British experimental and improvised music scene. With sound artist Max Eastley, he recorded *New and Rediscovered Musical Instruments* for Brian Eno's Obscure label in 1975. Over the past decade, he has released eight other solo albums and collaborated with an extraordinary variety of musicians, among them John Zorn, Evan Parker, Derek Bailey, Scanner, Flying Lizards, Prince Far-I, Witchman, and others. In 2001, Toop curated *Sonic Boom*, the UK's largest-ever exhibition of sound art; and in 2002, he curated the double-CD set *Not Necessarily English Music: A Collection of Experimental Music from Great Britain, 1960-1977* (EMF). In this brief excerpt from *Ocean of Sound*, Toop meditates on the history and mind-altering effects of dub, reggae's ghostly other.

Dub music is like a long echo delay, looping through time. Regenerating every few years, sometimes so quiet that only a disciple could hear, sometime shatteringly loud, dub unpicks music in the commercial sphere. Spreading out a song or a groove over a vast landscape of peaks and deep trenches, extending hooks and beats to vanishing point, dub creates new maps of time, intangible sound sculptures, sacred sites, balm and shock for mind, body and spirit.

When you double, or dub, you replicate, reinvent, make one of many versions. There is no such thing as an original mix, since music stored on multi-track tape, floppy or hard disk, is just a collection of bits. The composition has been decomposed, already, by the technology. Dubbing, at its very best, takes each bit and imbues it with new life, turning a rational order of musical sequences into an ocean of sensation. This musical revolution stemmed originally from Jamaica—in particular, the tiny studio once run by the late Osbourne Ruddock, a.k.a. King Tubby, in Kingston. "This is the heart of Kingston 11," Dave Henley wrote, describing the location of Tubby's studio for a reggae fanzine called *Small Axe*. "A maze of zinc fence, potholed roads and suitably dilapidated bungalows. After dark, the streets become remarkably deserted (by Kingston standards, anyway, considering that loafing on the corner is a favourite Jamaican pastime), giving the impression of an eerie tropical ghost town."

Urban, rural, tropic, aquatic, lo-tech, mystical. This was the source mix from which William Gibson drew (sentimentally, some critics think) when adding the humanising element of Rastafari and dub to his *Neuromancer* narrative of tech-Gnosis. When King Tubby first discovered dub, the revelation came, like so many technological discoveries, through an accident. There were other Jamaican recording engineers, of course: Sylvan Morris, Errol T. Thompson and Lloyd "Prince Jammy" James helped to created the sound of albums such as Joe Gibbs's *African Dub All-Mighty* series, or Augustus Pablo's *King Tubby's Meets Rockers Uptown* and *Africa Must Be Free By 1983*. But it was Tubby, cutting discs for Duke Reid at Treasure Isle, who first discovered the thrill of stripping a vocal from its backing track and then manipulating the instrumental arrangement with techniques and effects: drop-out, extreme equalisation, long delay, short delay, space echo, reverb, flange, phase, noise gates, echo feedback, shotgun snare drums, rubber bass, zipping highs, cavernous lows. The effects are there for enhancement, but for a dubmaster they can displace time, shift the beat, heighten a mood, suspend a moment. No coincidence that the nearest approximation to dub is the sonar transmit pulses, reverberations and echoes of underwater echo ranging and bioacoustics. No coincidence, also, that dub originated in a poor section of a city on a Caribbean island.

The first moment of dub has been pursued by reggae historian Steve Barrow through numerous conversations with important reggae record producers such as Bunny Lee. In *Dub Catcher* magazine, Lee conjures some of the excitement of those late-1960s, early-1970s sessions when King Tubby began to experiment with what he termed the "implements of sound": "Tubby's, right," recalls Lee. "With all the bass and drum ting now, dem ting just start by accident, a man sing off key, an' when you a reach a dat you drop out everyting an' leave the drum, an' lick in the bass, an' cause a confusion an' people like it . . . Sometime me an' 'im talk an' me say, 'Drop out now, Tubby!' An' 'im get confuse an' me jus' draw down the whole a the lever . . . you hear 'Pluck' an' jus' start play pure distortion. Me say, 'Yes Tubbs, madness, the people dem like it!' an' just push it right back up . . . An' then Lee Perry do fe 'im share a dub too, ca' 'im an' Tubby's do a whole heap a ting . . . 'im an' Niney [producer nine finger Niney 'the Observer'] an' musician jus' play, an' 'im jus' [makes discordant noises and laughs]. 'Im drunk, drunk yunno—the engineer a go stop 'im an' [he] say, 'You no hear a vibes? Mad sound dat man.' An' when 'im come the people dem like it."

Tubby worked with equipment that would be considered impossibly limited by today's standards, yet his dubs were massive, towering exercises in sound sculpting. Legend records that he cut four dubplates—special, one-off mixes—for his Home Town Hi-Fi System at the end of the 1960s. Playing these instrumental versions at a dance, with U Roy toasting verbal improvisations over the music in real time, he was forced to repeat them all night, dubbing them up live as the crowd went crazy. Tubby worked for some of Jamaica's most creative producers: Lee Perry and Augustus Pablo, in particular, were recording increasingly exotic and distinctive music during the 1970s. On albums such as Perry's *Super Ape* and Pablo's *East of the River Nile*, the mixing board becomes a pictorial instrument, establishing the illusion of a vast soundstage and then dropping instruments in and out as if they were characters in a drama. Lee Perry was a master of this technique, applying it to all his records, whether vocal, dub, instrumental version or talkover, all of them rich in his dub signature of rattling hand drums and scrapers, ghostly voices, distant horn sections, unusual snare and hi-hat treatments, groans and reptilian sibilations, odd perspectives and depth illusions, sound effects, unexpected noises and echoes that repeat to infinity.

Dub also anticipated remix culture. In 1974 Rupie Edwards, a producer of celebrated Jamaican artists such as I Roy, The Ethiopians and Gregory Isaacs, was the first to compile a "version" album—*Yamaha Skank*, twelve different versions of the rhythm of a song called "My Conversation". Although these were not dubs, they grew out of the idea of dubbing a track, shaping and reshaping its "implements of sound" as if music was modelling clay rather than copyright property.

# 52

# *Post-Rock*

## SIMON REYNOLDS

Simon Reynolds (1963– ; see also chap 10) is among the most articulate and wide-ranging of contemporary pop music critics and theorists. A contributing writer at *SPIN*, his articles have appeared in *The Wire, Artforum, The Village Voice, Rolling Stone, The New York Times*, and other magazines. He is the author of two books, *Blissed Out: The Raptures of Rock* (1990) and *Generation Ecstasy: Into the World of Techno and Rave Culture* (1998), and co-author of another, *The Sex Revolts: Gender, Rebellion, and Rock 'n' Roll* (1995). In this essay, originally published in the *Village Voice* in 1995, Reynolds coins the term "post-rock" to refer to the ways in which DJ Culture has infected rock and fundamentally altered some of its defining features.

[. . . .] Post-rock means bands that use guitars but in nonrock ways, as timbre and texture rather than riff and powerchord. It also means bands that augment rock's basic guitar-bass-drums lineup with digital technology such as samplers and sequencers, or tamper with the trad rock lineup but prefer antiquated analog synths and nonrock instrumentation. With its droneswarm guitars and tendency to melt into ambience, post-rock first erodes, then obliterates the song and the voice. By extension, it also parts with such notions as the singer as storyteller and the song as narrative, source of life-wisdom, or site of social resonance. This shift parallels tendencies in the culture (e.g., computer games, virtual reality, designer drugs) that indicate the emergence of a new model of posthuman subjectivity organized around fascination rather than meaning, sensation rather than sensibility.

The more "post" a post-rock band gets, the more it abandons the verse-chorus-verse structure in favor of the soundscape. A band's journey through rock to post-rock usually involves a trajectory from narrative lyrics to stream-of-consciousness to voice-as-texture to purely instrumental music. In the process, there's a dismantling of trad rock's dramatic mechanisms such as "identification" and "catharsis." Instead the listener is plunged into plateau-states of bliss, awe, uncanny-ness, or prolonged sensations of propulsion, ascension, free fall, immersion. In post-rock, "soul" is not so much abolished as radically decentered, dispersed across the entire field of sound, as in club musics like House, Techno, and Jungle, where tracks are less about communication and more like engines for "the programming of sensations" (as Susan Sontag said in 1965 of contemporary art from Rauschenberg to the Supremes). Music that's all surface and no "depth," that has skin instead of soul.

Above all, post-rock abandons the notion of rebellion as we know and love it, in favor of less spectacular strategies of subversion—ones closer to psychic land-scapes of exile and utopia constructed in dub reggae, HipHop, and rave. At the heart of rock 'n' roll stands the body of the white teenage boy, middle finger erect and a sneer playing across his lips. At the center of post-rock floats a phantasmatic un-body, androgynous and racially indeterminate: half ghost, half machine.

Post-rock has its own sporadic but extensive history, which [post-rockers] draw on as much for the suggestiveness of its unrealized possibilities as for actual achievements. In terms of electric guitar, the key lineage runs from the Velvet Underground, through Germany's kosmic rock (Can, Faust, Neu!, Cluster, et al.) and the guitar-loop mosaics of Eno and Fripp, to such late-80s neopsychedeliacs as Jesus & Mary Chain, Spacemen 3, and A.R. Kane. The Velvets melded folkade-lic songcraft with a wall-of-noise aesthetic that was half Phil Spector, half La Monte Young—and thereby invented dronology, a term that loosely describes 50 per cent of today's post-rock activity.

Post-rock emerges from rock's chrysalis when a band's ambitions begin to chafe at the constraints of song and riff. Take Main, an offshoot of the late-80s British indie band Loop, a bunch of longhaired acid freaks with a fetish for the wah-wah pedal. The band's desire to go beyond the Stooges-MC5 matrix expressed itself through covers of Can's "Mother Sky" and the Pop Group's "Thief of Fire," but Loop never quite made the break with rock 'n' roll. Forming Main, singer-guitar-ist Robert Hampson shed both his lank locks and, step by step, every last vestige of rock 'n' roll: first song structure, then backbeat, eventually even distinct chords. Main isn't so much a band as a studio-based research unit dedicated to exploring the electric guitar's spectrum of effects-wracked timbres and tonalities [. . . .]

The other major strand of post-rock endeavor has jettisoned the dronologists' guitar fetish. It also avoids the potential aesthetic backwater of pure ambience by looking outside rock for different forms of kinetic energy. Some, such as Techno-Animal and Scorn, use the looped beats of HipHop and rave; others merge live funk and programmed rhythm [. . . .]

Although these strands stretch across the Atlantic, there are real and telling differences between British and American post-rock, and most of them revolve around British bohemia's susceptibility to the influence of black music, whether African-American, Caribbean, or homegrown. US post-rock can almost be defined by the absence of dub as a living legacy and by its avoidance of HipHop.

Dub's vast impact on British left-field rock goes back to the late-70s, to the kinship punk rockers felt with Rastafarian reggae's spiritual militancy and millen-nial imagery of exile and dread. And so the Clash covered Junior Murvin's "Police and Thieves" and Willie William's "Armagideon Time," while Johnny Rotten went from the metallic KO of Sex Pistols to the antirockist Public Image Ltd., whose *Metal Box/Second Edition* introduced a significant segment of his following to

Lydon's true loves, dub and Can. Brit-bohemia's enduring openness to the Jamaican soundworld, from ska to dub to ragga, explains so much of what's bubbled up from UK subbakulcha in the last two decades [. . . .]

Nearly as influential as dub on the Brit post-rockers is Brian Eno. From the early 70s onward, Eno was, in both theory and practice, connecting the dots between the dub of Lee Perry and King Tubby, Teo Macero's labyrinthine production of Miles Davis, Can's fractal funkadelia, Cluster's Op Art guitar tapestries, and so on. Eno's notions—the studio as instrument, recording as the architectonics of "fictional psycho-acoustic space"—are the organizing principles of post-rock. Most rock producers strive for a glossed-up embellished simulation of the band in performance, but following Eno and dub, post-rock uses effects and processes to sever the link between the sound you hear and the physical act (striking a guitar chord, pounding a drum skin) that produced it.

Dub's fluctuating mix makes the band's presence hazy and miragelike; echo and reverb are used to make each strand of sound occur in its own distinct acoustic space. Sampling and a related technique called "hard disk editing" (where sounds are chopped up and rearranged inside the computer's virtual space) dramatically increase the possibilities for disorientation and displacement. With sampling, what you hear could never possibly have been a real-time event, since it's composed of vivisected musical fragments plucked from different contexts and eras, then layered and resequenced to form a time-warping pseudoevent. You could call it "deconstruction of the metaphysics of presence"; you could also call it magic.

Sampling brings us to HipHop and, once again, the contrast between the avidity of its embrace by British underground rock versus the hesitancy of the US post-rockers [. . . .] In Britain, staying unaware and uninfected by HipHop and its homegrown offshoots (TripHop, drum 'n' bass) can only be achieved by a strenuous feat of cultural inbreeding [. . . .] But in America, where you'd think it'd be even harder to ward off rap's influence, white bohemians shy away, perhaps feeling HipHop is the cultural property of African Americans, and not to be trespassed upon.

As for Techno-rave having any impact on American post-rock, forget it. A cluster of attitudes forms a near impenetrable barrier: the premium on live performance, the lingering legacy of "disco sucks," the hatred of machine rhythms. The upshot of all this is that UK post-rock outfits, influenced by various admixtures of dub, HipHop, and Techno, tend to be sound laboratories for whom live performance is irrelevant, whereas American post-rockers remain deeply committed to the band format and playing live. Instead of drawing on contemporary black and club music, they revisit those brinks in rock history when eggheads pushed rock's envelope beyond the bursting point: Krautrock, obviously, but also Tim Buckley circa *Starsailor*; the Canterbury scene (Soft Machine, Robert Wyatt, Henry Cow); Pere Ubu, Suicide and No Wave; and the freeform passages and proto-Ambient lulls that punctuate the Velvets, Stooges, and MC5, as later developed further by Glenn Branca and Sonic Youth [. . . .]

On both sides of the Atlantic, popular taste and critical opinion clutch tightly to the certainties and satisfactions of song and singer, and their attendant fictions of community and resistance, while the biz demands "charismatic personalities" [. . .] as the focus of its marketing schemes. For post-rock to go mainstream would require a Dylan figure—a Stipe or Vedder, say—shocking his folkie audience by appearing onstage with a sampler, as Dylan did when he went electric. And what is the electric guitar now but the new acoustic guitar, signifier of grit and earth and folk-blood?

A final, emotionally ambivalent thought about the difference between rock and its post-. Let's consider the Stones' "Gimme Shelter," described by Greil Marcus as the greatest piece of recorded rock 'n' roll ever (I agree). Consider specifically the all-too-brief instrumental prequel, the way Keith Richards's soliloquy of a solo conjures a shattering pitch of ecstatic anguish and longing. For a multitude of reasons, the historical conditions that made "Gimme Shelter" not just possible, but of oracular significance, are gone; not only has rock's grand narrative petered out into a delta of microcultures, but the possibility of writing a redemptive narrative itself seems to be fading. A post-rock band would take that intro's appalling poignancy, loop it, stretch it out to six minutes or more, turn it into an environment. Because that limbo-land between bliss-scape and paranoia-scape, narcosis and nightmare is where we who live under the sign of the post- find ourselves.

If you're under ninety, chances are that you've spent most of your life listening to electronic music. The experience that used to be called music up until the 1920s—listening to someone sing or play a musical instrument live and unamplified—actually forms an increasingly minor percentage of our listening experiences now. Instead, we listen to records, or we listen to the radio, or we go to see musicians who transmit electronic signals through electronic PA systems. It might seem extreme to include all the products of the recording age under the umbrella term *electronic music*, but I think it's warranted.

—Brian Eno[1]

The great benefit [of tools like Cubase] is that they remove the issue of skill, and replace it with the issue of judgment. With Cubase or Photoshop, anybody can actually do anything, and you can make stuff that sounds very much like stuff you'd hear on the radio, or looks very much like anything you'd see in magazines. So the question becomes not *whether* you can do it or not, because any drudge can do it if they're prepared to sit in front of the computer for a few days; the question then is: of all the things you can do now, which do you choose to do? This is a whole issue for which there are not manuals!

—Brian Eno[2]

"Stockhausen" and "musique concrète" are clearly the two key words of contemporary Techno.

—Emmanuelle Loubet[3]

Rave music represents a fundamental break with rock, or at least the dominant English Lit and socialist realist paradigms of rock criticism, which focuses on songs and storytelling. Where rock relates an experience (autobiographical or imaginary), rave *constructs* an experience. Bypassing interpretation, the listener is hurled into a vortex of heightened sensations, abstract emotions, and artificial energies [. . . .] Rave provokes this question: is it possible to base a culture around sensations rather than truths, fascination rather than meaning?

—Simon Reynolds[4]

[R]ave is something you immerse yourself into together with other people. There is no guitar hero or rock star or corresponding musical-structural figure to identify with, you just "shake your bum off" from inside the music. You are just one of many other individuals who constitute the musical whole, the whole ground—musical and social—on which you stand. The music is definitely neither melody nor melody plus accompaniment. Nor is it just accompaniment any more than West African polyrhythm, William Byrd's Great Service or Breughel's *Slaughter of the Innocents*. Polarising the issue, you could say that perhaps techno-rave puts an end to nearly four hundred years of the great European bourgeois individual in music, starting with Peri and Monteverdi and culminating with Parker, Hendrix and, Lord preserve us, Brian May, Whitney Houston and the TV spot for Bodyform sanitary towels.

—Philip Tagg[5]

The main culprit in electronic "music" is the term music itself [. . . .] The whole field of electronic music has long since reached a state of pure abstraction and music only survives as a metaphor in software [. . . .] Musical metaphors in software are just providing some means of orientation for people who deal with music as it was [. . . .] I usually don't use the term music too much. I just say "audio".

—Markus Popp of Oval[6]

[We] are on our way to becoming silicon beings—from carbon-based to silicon-based. We're already interfaced with computers and we can't go back [ . . . T]hink of a computer than can download all the music that has ever been done! So then we've got all that as the base for our improvisations. Maybe by then we'll have implants in our ears so that we can hear as low as whales and as high as bats. How's music going to change?

—Pauline Oliveros[7]

Whether you live in Lisbon, London or Lahore, the ordering of things has become a world of possible alternatives. The ordering of sound into musical form is now open to every possibility in the world beyond sound. Once governed by pitch relationships, ordered into an evolving harmonic system, sound might now reflect the extra-musical systems of biology, machines, thought, chance, social relations, chemical effect, political models or body movement.

These are some of the possibilities.

Music can be inspired by a beehive, the malfunction of a machine, an ecosystem, the reflex reactions of another musician, a state of consciousness, a digital glitch, robotics, an ancient divinatory book, an historical incident, the pulse of a city, rhythmic variation, a cinematic mise en scene, a fragment of captured documentation, turbulent water, a particle of speech, a feedback loop, the logic of software, the pattern of the heavens.

Perhaps it starts with a guitar. A sound suddenly exists. A stone in water, over time, furred by green moss. A sheet of metal, over time, mottled and scarred by rust. A slice of bread, over time, growing into a lush forest of mould. A jar of beans, over time, sprouting edible horned crooked limbs.

A crystal garden, the sound grows in reeds and streams, blown like spider web strands, glittering and invisible, pulsing with translucent colour, bubbling and imploding, fraying and powdering. Cloud formations, sound clusters curl and bump, low fat throbs breaking through frost patterns of extruded feedback. Sounds cycle, over time; sounds slither through time, disguised as pitch relationships. Like qualities of air, sounds meet and become each other. The sound seems to rise, to lift, though this is an illusion. Although the sound seems to mirror patterns in the observable world, the sound is learning the order of things. The sound is learning to develop, to think, to live.

—David Toop[8]

# IX. Electronic Music and Electronica

## Introduction

A low electronic hum. A few seconds later, a series of descending, sustained sine tones accumulates on top of it. For a moment, all the sounds seem to be coalescing toward the sense of a chord, only to fuse together into a drone running parallel to the rumble below. Traversed by a spongy, bent bass tone, the sound descends into a slab of white noise. Karlheinz Stockhausen's *Kontakte* comes to mind; or maybe something by Iannis Xenakis. But when this electronic reverie is broken by a fat and bristling 4/4 throb, we realize these guesses are decades off, and that we are listening to electronic music in the wake of Techno.[1]

Panasonic (now Pan Sonic) is among a large and growing body of electronic musicians whose experimental sensibilities reflect the whole history of electronic music, from Schaeffer and Stockhausen to Techno and beyond. They form part of a new breed of electronic experimentalism that is taking place outside of the academy and the pop mainstream alike. *Electronica* represents the unlikely meeting of several genealogical strands: the sonic and intellectual concerns of classic electronic music; the do-it-yourself and bruitist attitudes of punk and industrial music; and beat-driven dance floor sounds from disco through House and Techno.

Classic electronic music sprung up in Europe and the United States during the early 1950s, led by avant-garde composers interested in radical innovation and in more finely controlling their musical materials. Yet, despite the pedigree of its early practitioners, electronic music was, at best, barely tolerated by the classical music establishment; and, for decades, it remained marginal. While progressive rock drew upon many of the latest technological resources, rarely did it fully explore the aesthetic possibilities implicit in early electronic music. Likewise, within the punk and industrial subcultures, noise was tied to rebellion and transgression, and harnessed to conventional rock forms, leaving its sonic ontology unexplored. Finally, the experimental possibilities of beat-driven club music remained subordinate to its utilitarian purpose: its ability to keep people on the dance floor. Only within the past decade has the new audio culture cut fresh paths across and through these musics, hearing in them new possibilities, synthesizing them, and recomposing them in the process.

Pierre Schaeffer's early experiments generated a flurry of excitement about *concrète* techniques and the possibilities of acousmatic listening. Schooled in these techniques, some of Europe's premier composers turned their ears toward a new and different set of possibilities. Moving away from the referentiality of concrete sounds, Stockhausen, Luigi Nono, Luciano Berio, György Ligeti, and others began to delight in the abstract possibilities of the electronic signal. Taking advantage of primitive equipment purpose-built for electronic music and recording (parametric equalizers, ring modulators, plate reverb, etc.), they began to explore pure sine tones and the electronic synthesis of sound. The resulting music was highly abstract, having lost all reference to traditional musical timbres and narrative. Above all, this music was driven by the discovery of a new sonic world inhabited by sounds that had never been heard before.

While producing highly virtuosic music, early electronic music composers were nevertheless constrained to construct their pieces via painstaking tape-manipulation techniques, cutting and splicing tiny sections of recorded electronic material. Expensive and enormous, electronic equipment was confined to well-funded research centers at universities and radio stations. In the mid-1960s, however, Robert Moog and Donald Buchla began to produce small and relatively inexpensive modular synthesizers, opening the world of electronics to rock and jazz. But these early instruments had their limitations. Monophonic keyboards and complex patches made them cumbersome and still slow to work with. In reaction, the music industry moved quickly to produce digital synthesizers with polyphonic keyboards and presets in place of patches. Presets may have been useful for rock and jazz musicians; but they effectively thwarted the sonic experimentation and discovery so valuable to the previous generation.

Fast forward to the early 1990s. A technologically adept generation raised on home computers and video games begins to explore the equipment at its disposal: discarded analogue synths and drum machines picked up at junk shops, DJ equipment, the latest computer hardware, and commercial and homemade software. In their own bedrooms and basements, they began to recapitulate the experiments and discoveries of early electronic music. It's not surprising, then, that this generation has come to hear the whole history of electronic experimentation as vital and contemporary: to learn from Stockhausen, Pauline Oliveros, and David Tudor as well as Kraftwerk, Afrika Bambaataa, and Juan Atkins, and to draw upon these sources to make experimental music that lands squarely between the concert hall and commercial pop radio.

## NOTES

1. The tracks described are "Luotain" and the opening of "Vapina" on Panasonic's *Kulma*, Mute/Blast First 9032.

# 53

## Introductory Remarks to a Program of Works Produced at the Columbia-Princeton Electronic Music Center

### JACQUES BARZUN

Renowned historian Jacques Barzun (1907– ) helped to found the discipline of cultural history. His father, Henri-Martin Barzun, was a noted poet who, as early as 1913, composed Dadaist "simultaneous poems" to be performed with phonographs; and Guillaume Apollinaire, Marcel Duchamp, and Edgard Varèse were regular visitors to the family's Paris home. In 1919, Jacques Barzun moved to the United States to attend Columbia University, where he also received a doctorate, became a professor, and remained until his retirement in 1975. He is the author of more than thirty books of history and criticism, among them *Darwin, Marx, Wagner* (1941), *The House of Intellect* (1959), *Classic, Romantic, Modern* (1961), *The Use and Abuse of Art* (1974), and *From Dawn to Decadence: 1500 to the Present: 500 Years of Western Cultural Life* (2000). An early champion of electronic music, Barzun was invited to introduce the inaugural concerts of music at the Columbia-Princeton Electronic Music Center, established in 1959. The concerts, held at Columbia on May 9 and 10, 1961, featured works by Otto Luening, Vladimir Ussachevsky, Milton Babbitt, Mario Davidovsky, Bülent Arel, and Halim El-Dabh. On each night, Barzun delivered this brief address, offering advice for listening to electronic music. More than forty years later, his advice still seems apt.

Your presence here, at a concert of electronic music, is a compliment to the composers, as well to the Universities that sponsor their work; and while I extend to you a welcome on behalf of the Universities I also wish to convey the composers' hope that you will be as gratified by hearing their works as they are by your willingness to listen.

No doubt your expectations are mixed. You are ready to be surprised, to have your curiosity satisfied, and possibly even to experience snatches of enjoyment as you would at an ordinary concert. If that is your state of mind I am fairly sure you will not be disappointed. But it may be that you are here in a mood of combined trepidation and resistance: this, after all, is the Age of Anxiety . . . Or you may be bent on proving that electronic music is not music—doing this by the most painful test of endurance—or else you may be feeling caught because you have been brought by a friend and friendship is dearer to you than prudence.

If for these or any other reasons you are ill at ease, allow me to suggest a very few considerations which should make you more serene, while leaving you your full freedom of opinion, your entire right to dislike and reject. I suggest, to begin with, that we are not here to like or approve but to understand. And the first step to understanding a new art is to try to imagine why the maker wants it the way it is. That is interesting in itself, even if we ultimately disown the product. To understand in this fashion does not mean to accept passively because someone says that the stuff is new and therefore good, that many believe in it, that it's going to succeed anyway, so it's best to resign oneself to the inevitable. This kind of reasoning has gone on about modern art for some thirty years and nothing has been more harmful to the arts. It is an inverted philistinism, which eliminates judgment and passion just as surely as did the older philistinism of blind opposition to whatever was new.

What then is the decent, reasonable attitude to adopt? Very simple: make the assumption, first, that the old style—whatever it is—has exhausted its possibilities and can only offer repetition or trivial variations of the familiar masterpieces. I do not suggest that you should be convinced that your favorite music is obsolete. I invite you to *assume* that it may be: for by trying to think that it is, as the new composer obviously has done, you will begin to discover what he is up to. By way of encouragement let me remind you that you make this very assumption automatically four or five times in every classical concert, in order to adjust your ear to the changes in style between Bach and Mozart, Mozart and Richard Strauss, and—if you can—between Strauss and Alban Berg. If styles and genres did not suffer exhaustion, there would only be one style and form in each art from its beginnings to yesterday.

But, you may say, electronic music is something else again; it is out of bounds; the jump is too great. There is no semblance of scale, the sounds are new, most of them are in fact noises. Ah noise! Noise is the most constant complaint in the history of music. In the heyday of music it was not only Berlioz and Wagner who were damned as noisy. Mozart before them and Haydn, and even earlier Lully and Handel. I suspect that the reason Orpheus was torn to pieces by women is that he made horrendous noises on his lyre while they were washing clothes at the river in what they thought was melodious silence. The argument of noise is always irrelevant. The true question is: does this noise, when familiar, fall into intelligible forms and impressive contents? To supply the answer takes time. One hearing, two, three, are not enough. Something must change in the sensibility itself, in the way that a foreign language suddenly breaks into meaning and melody after months or years of its being mere noise. As a veteran of the premiere of Stravinsky's *Sacre du Printemps* in Paris, I can testify to the reality of the change. At the end of the piece, the conductor Pierre Monteaux turned around amid the furious howls of the audience and said that since they had liked the piece so much he would play it again. The response was no better and the police had to quell the tumult. But now, fifty years later, the young accept those hammering rhythms and dissonant chords as if they were lullabies. They relish them while dallying in canoes, at the movies to accompany Disney's abstractions, and at the circus, where the music is used for the elephants to dance to.

Associations, in short, and assumptions rule our judgments. They govern our feelings, which we think are altogether spontaneous and truthful. But our sensibility is always more complex and more resourceful that we suppose, and that is why I have ventured to bring to your conscious notice what you knew all the time but might not allow for sufficiently in listening to electronic music for the first time.

The word "electronic" suggests a final objection with which it is well to have come to grips. Most people of artistic tastes share the widespread distrust and dislike of machinery and argue that anything pretending to be art cannot come out of a machine: art is the human product *par excellence*, and electronic music, born of intricate circuits and the oscillations of particles generated by Con Edison, is a contradiction in terms. Here again the answer is simple: the moment man ceased to make music with his voice alone the art became machine-ridden. Orpheus's lyre was a machine, a symphony orchestra is a regular factory for making artificial sounds, and a piano is the most appalling contrivance of levers and wires this side of the steam engine.

Similarly, the new electronic devices are but a means for producing new materials to play with. What matters is not how they are produced but how they are used. And as to that we are entitled to ask the old questions—do we find the substance rich, evocative, capable of subtlety and strength? Do we, after a while, recognize patterns to which we can respond, with our sense of balance, our sense of suspense and fulfillment, our sense of emotional and intellectual congruity? Those are the problems, beyond the technical, which our composers have tried to solve. We shall now attend to their handiwork with pleasure and gratitude (I hope) and certainly with a generous fraction of the patience they have themselves invested in their efforts to please us.

# 54

# *Electronic and Instrumental Music*

## KARLHEINZ STOCKHAUSEN

Karlheinz Stockhausen (1928– ) is perhaps the most important and influential of the European avant-garde composers who emerged after World War
II. He quickly rose to prominence in the early 1950s as a proponent of "total
serialism," which sought to organize all the parameters of music according
to the rules of serial composition. Stockhausen studied briefly at Pierre
Schaeffer's Paris studio, but quickly rejected Schaeffer's *concrète* approach
in favor of electronic music generated from scratch. In 1953, along with Herbert Eimert, Stockhausen founded the Westdeutscher Rundfunk (WDR) studio for electronic music in Cologne, where he produced some of the first
purely electronic compositions and important works such as *Gesang der Jünglinge* (1955–56), *Kontakte* (1959–60), *Telemusik* (1966) and *Hymnen*
(1966–67). Concurrent with his early electronic work, he composed *Klavierstück XI* (1956), among the first and most important examples of "aleatory"
composition. In this article—originally delivered as a lecture in 1958 and
newly translated by Jerome Kohl in collaboration with Suzanne Stephens
and John McGuire—Stockhausen explains the origins and nature of electronic music, and defends its revolutionary features. The essay hearkens
back to Edgard Varèse's call for the "liberation of sound" and to Pierre
Schaeffer's call for a pure music freed from traditional instruments, sonorities, and modes of listening.

I

Electronic music has existed since the year 1953. Thanks to Hanns Hartmann,
General Director of the West German Radio in Cologne, a Studio for Electronic
Music was founded under the direction of Herbert Eimert. Five public presentations in the broadcasting auditorium of the WDR and many radio broadcasts and
public presentations in other cities over the past six years have demonstrated the
results of our work.

How did this music come about?

Since 1950—setting out from the study of scores that were written in the first half of this century—everything that makes European music what it is has been called into question: not only musical language (its grammar, its vocabulary) but also the sound material employed until now, the tones themselves. The historical development of instruments was closely tied to a music that is no longer our music. Since the turn of the century the idea of saying something new has existed, but the old sound symbols continued to be used. In this way a contradiction came into being between the physical nature of the heretofore employed instrumental tones on the one hand, and the new musical conceptions of form on the other.[1]

In "harmonic" ("tonal") music the sound material and the mode of construction of the instruments were in intimate agreement with musical form. The harmony between structure of material and form was definitively destroyed by 12-tone music and its broader consequences in the realm of instrumental music. Precisely for this reason the radical 12-tone music of the first half of this century seems "out of tune," because one operated nonfunctionally with traditional sound material. This contradiction has gained for Expressionist music its best results. In 12-tone composition the harmonic and melodic relationships between the fundamental tones have nothing in common with the microacoustic relationships in the interior of instrumental sounds.

What are the consequences?

What constitutes the difference between instrumental tones, between any perceptible sound events whatever—the violin, the piano, the vowel *a*, the consonant *sh*, the wind?

In 1952–53, in the Groupe pour Musique Concrète in Paris, I made many analyses of instrumental sounds—especially percussion sounds, which were recorded on tape in the Musée de l'Homme—of speech sounds and noises of all kinds. The sounds and noises were recorded in various spaces (anechoic chamber, normally damped room, echo chamber). Electro-acoustic apparatuses (filters, oscillographs, etc.) served to determine attributes of sound. What in music is ordinarily called a "tone"—without questioning what it actually is—proved to be a more or less complex vibrating structure that reaches our ear. Acousticians speak of "sound spectra," and describe them by means of a series of factors in a space-time diagram. Sound analysis with electrical filters is comparable to the analysis of light with the aid of prisms. Physicists today are only slightly interested in the investigation of sound. For theoretical studies in this area, the literature of phonetics has been the most prolific for a long time now.

So the musician—for whom the question of research in sound had become acute for the first time—had to rely to a large extent upon his own practical investigations. He had to enlarge his *métier* and study acoustics in order to get to know his material better. This will become indispensable for all those composers who are not content to accept the sound phenomena as given, but rather wish to resist the dictatorship of the material and extend their own formal conceptions as far as possible into the sounds in order to arrive at a new concordance of material and form: of acoustical microstructure and musical macrostructure.

The existing instrumental sounds are something already preformed, dependent on the construction of the instruments and the manner of playing them: they are "objects." Did today's composers build the piano, the violin or the trumpet? Did they determine how these instruments ought to be played? What does an architect do when he is to build a cantilever bridge, a skyscraper or an aircraft hangar? Does he still use clay, wood and bricks? New forms require prestressed concrete, glass, aluminium—aluminium, glass, and prestressed concrete make the new forms possible.

So the thought arose of giving up preformed instrumental sounds and composing the sounds themselves for a particular composition: artificially assembling them according to the formal laws of this and no other composition. Composing goes one step further than before. The structure of a given composition and the structure of the material employed in it are derived from a single musical idea: structure of material and structure of the work ought to be one.

In short: it has become technically feasible to realize this aim. Practical analyses and studies led us to the idea: if sound spectra can be analysed, perhaps they can also be synthetically generated. Goeyvaerts wrote to me at the time in Paris, that he had made inquiries in Brussels and learned something about generators of sine waves: By all means I ought to set about assembling sound spectra with the aid of such sine generators. In the Paris Club d'Essai, I made the first experiments in the synthetic composition of a sound spectrum with sine oscillators.

In 1953 my work at the Cologne Radio began. Among the sound sources of the Cologne Studio were first of all electronic performance instruments—a melochord and a Trautonium—which served as sound sources in some experiments but then, soon after the idea of sound-spectrum synthesis was adopted, were no longer used.

## II

Before the particulars of this work are described here, I would like first to refer to some compositions for instruments that came into being at this time. They should act as a reminder that the language of new instrumental music and of electronic music is the same (up to now; however, in the long run it will scarcely be possible to keep electronic music free of vulgarization). When visitors come to the Cologne studio to hear electronic music, they very quickly get over the initial shock caused by the unfamiliar sounds and ask why there is no rhythm (they of course mean regular metres with bars having three or four beats), why no melodies, no repetitions, etc. And so the discussion usually doesn't deal at all with electronic music as such, but rather with the manner in which it is composed—the language. For this reason we first play tape recordings of works by Anton Webern that, for example, he had already composed in the year 1910. Then we play newer instrumental compositions by Edgar Varèse, John Cage, Pierre Boulez, Henri Pousseur.

In some instrumental compositions that I had written shortly before beginning to compose with electronic sounds, I made the attempt to integrate all the characteristics of the material into one uniform musical organization—with the exception of instrumental timbres. I had to accept these timbres as given, and it was not possible to produce a relationship, let alone a continuum, between a clarinet tone and a piano tone. The only option was to arrange these instrumental colours in a succession of contrasts—analogous to a colour succession like red–yellow–blue—or by mixtures, something like composing timbral intervals or timbral chords. It was impossible to have all of the various timbres issue from a common embryo, so that a clarinet tone and a piano tone could appear as two different exemplars within one "sound family"—a more comprehensive sound continuum: what a utopian scheme, as long as one has to write for a classical orchestra.

## III

What technique was employed in the sound synthesis for the first electronic studies?

For some decades already there have been electro-acoustic generators, or oscillators, in acoustical laboratories and in the technical divisions of broadcasting institutions. In the beginning we worked only with sine-tone generators. They are called sine-tone generators because the oscillations produced satisfy the sine function. In comparison with any instrumental tone, which has a certain number and a certain selection of "partials" (also called "overtones") in addition to the "fundamental tone," the "sine tone" is a "pure tone" (without "partials"); each "partial" in a "stationary sound spectrum" is such a "sine tone."

The number of partials in a sound spectrum, the frequency of each partial, the amplitude curve of each partial, the duration of each partial in relation to the other partials in their "onset transient" and "decay": these characteristics enable the differentiation of one sound spectrum from another. A sine tone in the middle register sounds somewhat like a flute, which, amongst the orchestral instruments, has the lowest number of partials. Such sine tones were therefore the first elements with which we "com-posed"—in the literal sense: put together—various spectra according to the structural demands of a particular composition. *Therefore every sound is the product of a compositional act.* The composer determines the various properties (also called "parameters").

Practically, the work with sine tones proceeded as follows (even at present, in Cologne we are still forced to work in this complicated manner due to a lack of more suitable equipment): a sine wave is recorded on tape, a second, third and so on are added. In the process, each sine wave receives its own intensity progression through electrical regulation, and then the intensity progression of the entire wave-complex (the "envelope curve") is adjusted once again. The sound's duration is determined by measuring and cutting the tape in centimetre lengths—proceeding from the tape speed, which is 76.2 or 38.1 centimetres per second. In this way, sound after sound is assembled and archived. When all the sounds for a composition have been prepared on tape, the pieces of tape are spliced together according to the score and, if necessary, copied again superimposed by using several synchronized tape recorders. Once the realisation of a piece has been completed, the archived sounds and all intermediate results are erased again; there is therefore no sound catalogue which, after completion of a composition, might perhaps be enriched by some hundred or thousand more sounds "for general use."

It was necessary for the composer of electronic music to have found an adequate form of graphic notation, in order to describe all the details of sound production and assembly.

Obviously, therefore, no instruments—played by some interpreter according to a score—are employed. In electronic music, the interpreter no longer has any function. The composer, in collaboration with some technicians, realizes the entire work. Each working operation can be repeated until the desired precision has been achieved. The first results of the work just described were Eimert's *Glockenspiel*,

Goeyvaert's *Composition No. 5*, Pousseur's *Seismogramme*, Gredinger's *Forman-ten*, and my *Study I* and *Study II*.

This music can only be played back over loudspeakers.

## IV

It is clear that a composer of electronic music should not try to imitate timbres of the traditional instrumentarium or familiar sounds and noises. If, exceptionally, a sound of this kind is required, it would be unfunctional to generate it synthetically: it is recorded where it can most easily be found. If a speechlike sound is to be employed, then it is better to record speech rather than to generate it synthetically. In general, one can already recognize a first criterion of quality in an electronic composition in the extent to which it is kept free of all instrumental or other sound associations. Such associations distract the listener's mind from the autonomy of each sound world presented to him, because he is reminded of bells, organs, birds or water-taps. Associations are created through our experiences and fade away again; they say nothing about the form of a piece of music or about the meaning of the sounds or noises in a particular composition. Hence we ought to draw the obvious conclusion that electronic music sounds best only as electronic music, which is to say that it includes as far as possible only sounds and sound relationships that are unique and free of associations, and that make us believe that we have never heard them before.

However, it is also clear that the diversity of sounds that can be produced electronically is not unlimited. Electronic music as a genre has—in defiance of all our initial notions of abolishing "genres" in the realm of music and of including all possible sound processes—its own phenomenology of sound, which is conditioned not least by loudspeaker playback.

Let's take as an example *Artikulation* by Ligeti. When this piece is performed, the audience always laughs at three points: at the first point heartily, at the second somewhat less so and at the third, they roar with laughter. As they were working on the piece in the studio, the composer and his collaborators laughed as well. Also in new instrumental music, unusual sound combinations stimulate laughter—for example, in the works of the American, Cage. Why is this? Certain sound events are associated with the place and circumstances where they ordinarily occur, and the unusual juxtaposition of sounds and noises that have such associations, as ingredients in the same piece of music, seems comical to begin with. The sound of a pea whistle and the sound of a piano—each by itself—doesn't cause any laughter, but piano tones and pea-whistle tones together in one of Cage's compositions create a comical effect for the audience.

## V

In the existing compositions of electronic music, sounds with harmonic partial-relationships—which by way of comparison can also be described as "vowel sounds"—have been used much less than noises. In Western music, noises have been employed only rarely, and most musicians regard such consonant-like sound events as musically inferior material. Percussion instruments, which produce sound events with only approximate or entirely indeterminate pitch, have been given very little attention until now. For this reason, they have remained at an extremely primitive level in the development of instrument construction. This is accounted for by the one-sided harmonic-melodic development in the realm of fixed fundamental pitches with harmonic partial-tone relationships. For this reason, it can be said that Western music up to this point has been principally a music of vowel sounds, a "music of pitch." The final stage in this development was 12-tone music.

Schönberg wrote a treatise on harmony that referred only to the relationships of fixed frequencies; in the perspective of his time it was of no consequence to take the "consonantal" sound events into consideration and attend, in inseparable connection with harmony, to the questions of metrics, rhythm and dynamics, much less those of sound colouristics. So he and his school were occupied all their lives with problems of a new composition of pitches, in which new laws of equality of rights were formulated, whereas they carried on being slaves of classical metrics, rhythms, dynamics and colouristics which, in virtue of their hierarchical laws, stand in flagrant contradiction to dodecaphonic harmony and melody. For this reason Schönberg's allergy to the concept of "atonal music" is understandable. Today one recognizes that this concept is a harbinger of a fundamental alteration of the conception of musical material: namely, that music with "tones" is a special case as soon as sonic events with constant periodic fundamental vibrations and harmonic partials are fitted into the continuum of all "timbres." In an "atonal" music, then, "tones" simply do not occur, but rather sonic events that are described with the comprehensive term "noises"—therefore aperiodic, "complex" vibrations. For us, vowels and consonants—sounds and noises—are in the first instance nothing but material. Neither the one nor the other of these acoustical phenomena is by nature good or bad. The only crucial thing is what one makes out of them.

Already in the first half of the century the compositions *Ionisation* by Edgar Varèse and *Construction in Metal* by John Cage paved the way for a completely new development, independent of music with tones. The beginnings of *musique concrète* were stimulated by Varèse and Cage, as well.

The category of noises is no less subtly differentiated than the category of sound spectra. On the contrary: In some languages, for example, we find a predominance of unvoiced consonants over vowels. It is natural that in the new musical language the *aperiodic phase relationships determine all aspects of the form—in its details as well as on a larger scale*; in this way periodicity becomes an extreme case of the aperiodic. Consonantal—hence noise-like—sonic phenomena play an especially important role in this; and their significance will increase still further.

As an example I might mention *Scambi* by Henri Pousseur. In this piece, only noises of more or less determinable pitch-register are employed. We speak of noises with different frequency bandwidths and call them "coloured noises." For the production of such "coloured noises" we can in each case superimpose sine waves in dense bundles, but generally we choose a more direct method: the initial material is supplied by a so-called noise generator, which produces "white noise" (the concepts of "white" and "coloured" are borrowed from optics). "White noise" can be described as the simultaneity of all audible vibrations: it sounds like the roar of the sea. From this "white noise" we can filter out frequency bands using all sorts of electrical filters—hence "coloured noises" (consonants like *sh*, *f*, *s*, *ch* etc.

are such "noise spectra"). The sound continuum between the "pure tone" and "white noise" can—for now—be defined such that the "pure tone" is the narrowest "noise band" or, vice versa, that "white noise" is the densest superimposition of "pure tones."

## VI

Where is electronic music produced?

The first studio, as has been said, was founded at the Cologne Radio. This is characteristic. The present-day acoustical communications media at our disposal—and perhaps we are also at theirs—are in the main radio, tape and gramophone record. Tape, gramophone record and radio have profoundly changed the relationship between music and listener. Most music is heard over loudspeakers.

And what have record and radio producers done up to this point? They have reproduced: reproduced music which in past ages was written for the concert hall and opera house; exactly as if the cinema had been content only with photographing old stage plays. And the radio attempts to give these concert and opera newsreports such technical perfection that for the listener differentiating between the original and the copy should become ever less possible: the illusion must be complete. This conscious deception has become ever more perfect, just as with modern printing techniques Rembrandt reproductions are made nowadays which not even an expert can tell from the original any longer. All this is heading toward a society that lives, even culturally, out of cans.

Even though radio had now come to resemble a canning factory, something unforeseen happened: electronic music came into play—a music that proceeded completely functionally out of the specific conditions of broadcasting. It is not recorded with microphones on a stage somewhere in order to be preserved and later reproduced, but rather it comes into existence with the aid of thermionic valves,[3] exists only on tape, and can only be heard over loudspeakers.

Exactly what the birth of a legitimate, functional loudspeaker music means can only be appreciated by those who have once looked through the glass window of a radio- or gramophone-record recording studio where, as in an aquarium, the musicians play literally to the walls for hours on end; with great precision and without spontaneity; without any contact with an audience. And what do they play? Music that was written for quite different purposes, without any thoughts about the radio.

Regardless of how electronic music may presently be judged: its necessity already consists in the sole fact that it shows the way for radiophonic music production. Electronic music no longer employs tape and loudspeaker for reproduction, but rather for production.

The listener at the loudspeaker will sooner or later understand that it makes more sense that music coming from a loudspeaker be music that can be heard only over a loudspeaker and by no other means.

Incidentally, the same problem poses itself today in the case of television. For some time to come we will see television producers employing the new medium unfunctionally, that is to say, wrongly. It will only be used functionally when the camera—which corresponds to the microphone of radio—is used only for topical "live reporting" or not at all, and television-specific electronic-optical compositions are transmitted instead.

## VII

Since the founding of the Cologne studio, further studios for electronic music have been set up: at the Milan radio station under the direction of the composer Luciano Berio, who works there together with the composer Bruno Maderna; at Radio Tokyo, where the young Japanese Toshiro Mayuzumi and Makoto Moroi work; at the Philips factory in Eindhoven, where the composers Henk Badings and Edgar Varèse have worked; at the APELAC company in Brussels—which produces electronic equipment—where the composer Henri Pousseur works; at the Warsaw radio station, where the composers Kotonsky, Krenz and Serocki work; at the Southwest German Radio, Baden-Baden, where the composer Pierre Boulez has recently started to work; at the French Radio, whose studio for *musique concrète* in recent days has ever more frequently been designating itself as a studio for electronic music; at Columbia University, where the composers Vladimir Ussachevsky and Otto Leuning work. More radio stations are currently preparing studios: Radio Stockholm, Radio Helsinki, Radio Copenhagen and the BBC in London.

All of these studios currently work at a very primitive level with equipment that was built for other purposes—for sound analysis or technical measurement—and which are to be found in all electro-acoustic laboratories and broadcasting institutions. This provisional condition is inhibiting, because the imagination of musicians is far in advance of the possibilities for technical realisation, and time and effort do not stand in a reasonable relationship to the result. For purely financial reasons it is still not possible to develop a standardization for studio facilities, even though it is an urgent necessity. In the USA, above all an apparatus has been developed by RCA, the "RCA Mark II Electronic Music Synthesizer," which in my opinion complies very well with the requirements of an electronic music studio. The studio of Columbia University recently obtained the necessary funding and has therefore become the first to have this apparatus at its disposal.

The first experiments with computers (Massachusetts Institute of Technology and the University of Wisconsin, Madison) seem important to me, in that they concentrate composition exclusively on the planning of a work and wish to leave the working out of the realisation, including the automatic production of a structural pattern, to the machines. Perhaps one of the most extreme consequences would be that composers would have to learn to completely change their way of thinking. Whereas heretofore the act of composing in fact consisted in the selection of very specific elements and constellations of elements according to the sonic conception and its presentation in accordance with the material, in the planning for electronic compositional automatons, one would be much less concerned with determining the axioms that define desired results than with determining the axioms of those structures that are *not* desirable. The electronic automaton is constructed for the purpose of composing pieces from a number of elements and rules for associating all possible combinations defined by the composer; therefore the planning work must eliminate all the undesirable combinations down to a few, or even just one, which are to be employed.

## VIII

Does the rise of electronic music foreshadow the end of the era of interpreters? Are performing musicians to be condemned in the future to go on playing only old instrumental music for some "collegium musicum" concerts and in tape-recordings for music museums?

It is a fact that in the evolution of instrumental music the performing musician has been condemned more and more to converting increasingly complicated scores into tones. Musicians became a sort of machine substitute, and finally there no longer remained any room for "free decision," for interpretation in the best sense of the word. It was an entirely natural development that the realisation of sounds was finally transferred to electronic apparatuses and machines. These apparatuses produce the desired results exactly according to technical data; and besides, one does not have to persuade them for hours on end in discussions about the meaning of new music before they will produce a single note.

But it is noteworthy that the same composers who had called electronic music to life, *parallel* to this work in the years since 1956–57, published compositions which present the performing musician with a completely new responsibility. In contrast to electronic music, in which all sonic events are predetermined down to the smallest details and are fixed by technical criteria, in this new instrumental music the performer is granted fields for free, spontaneous decisions, to which machines are not amenable. Human beings have qualities that can never be replaced by a robot; and robots have possibilities that exceed certain limits of human capability, even though—or, more precisely, because—they were invented by humans; they ought to assist humans to obtain ever more more time for the properly human, for creative responsibilities.

Directed chance has recently grown in significance for such compositions, which are to be played by people in the presence of the listeners. The uniqueness of a performance (unrepeatable like the performer himself, who is never the same); the various degrees of freedom of action, experienced by the composer and described in a composition (which the performer responds to intellectually, instinctively or intellectually-instinctively); the determination of the performance duration of a work and even the choice of the number of musicians who are to take part in a performance: all of these are criteria that depend on the performing musicians and give them a degree of responsibility that they never have previously had.

Examples are the *Concert for Piano and Orchestra* (1957–58) by John Cage, which made use of "chance operations" in composition for the first time; the *Third Piano Sonata* (1958) by Pierre Boulez; the work for two pianos, *Mobile* (1958), by Henri Pousseur; and my *Klavierstück XI* (1956).

Apropos of this new instrumental music it has often been said that it involves musical improvisation, such as is familiar from the thorough-bass period or from jazz music. In the works just mentioned, however, it is not the case that the instrumentalist invents something to add to some basic scheme or other provided by the composer—like melodies over a figured bass, like variations on a given basic melody, or like melodic inventions within a given basic rhythmic and harmonic scheme in jazz. The composers of the works mentioned have determined all the elements and the rules of connection. But they have formulated their scores in such a way that at certain points in the course of a work there exists not just one valid option for moving on but rather several equally valid paths are often left open, which can be pursued either during composition or, analogously, in the moment of performance as well (the choice of one path may also be further dependent upon what a simultaneously performing musician is doing, as in Pousseur's piece).

This new kind of instrumental music still must operate with classical instruments. Therefore it momentarily cannot be helped that the initially mentioned contradiction between construction and manner of playing these instruments (as well as the physical structure of their sounds) on the one hand, and the new formal conceptions on the other, now become even more clearly evident than at the time electronic music came into being. This situation is not changed in the least when Cage dismantles classical instruments and has the separate parts blown, knocked, rubbed or bowed. Today it is passé to wish to demonstrate by such methods the "damaging of the world" and "total anarchy." We don't need any more scandals. What we need now more than anything else is a continuum instrument. Through the emergence of a new instrumental music, in fact, it has become meaningful to think about new, suitable instruments, and only now are we slowly realizing how these new instruments might be constructed.

If one believes in the idea of a new instrumental music, one must accept the fact that it will have even more difficulty in prevailing than electronic music. The whole question of whether we are capable of finding and animating a new, irreplaceable form of collective listening through listening to the radio will be dependent exclusively on the composers who work on this new instrumental music. In a way similar to spatial electronic music, some of the new instrumental works functionally incorporate into composition the direction and movement of the sounds in space. A radio transmission—even a two-channel one, as is already possible today—can only convey an approximate idea of this "three-dimensional" music, and people must go into the space where the musicians are playing, if they really want to experience this music.

## IX

In this way instrumental music could hold its own alongside electronic music. In every realm one has to work functionally; every device ought to be employed productively: generators, tape recorders, loudspeakers ought to bring forth what no instrumentalist could ever be capable of playing (and microphones should handed over to the news reporters); score, performer and instrument ought to produce what no electronic apparatus could ever bring forth or imitate or repeat.

Composing electronic music means: describing that which sounds in mechanical and electro-acoustical dimensions and thinking only in terms of machines, electrical apparatuses and circuit diagrams; reckoning with one single production and unlimited repeatability of the composition.

Writing instrumental music—now once more—means: inducing the performer's action by means of optical symbols and appealing directly to the living organism of the musician, to his creative, ever-variable capacity for reaction; enabling multifarious production and unrepeatability from performance to performance.

Then electronic and instrumental music would mutually complement one another, distance themselves ever further and faster from each other—only to awaken the hope of actually meeting occasionally in one work.

The first works in which electronic and instrumental music are combined were premiered in 1958. The idea is to find—beyond contrast, which represents the most rudimentary kind of form—the higher, inherent laws of a bond.

## NOTES

1. See *Die Reihe* 3, p. 23 (in the English edition of *Die Reihe*, p. 20).
2. Now known as *First Construction (in Metal)*—Trans.
3. The English term for the German technical term *Elektronenröhre* is "vacuum tubes"—Trans.

# 55

# Stockhausen vs. the "Technocrats"

## KARLHEINZ STOCKHAUSEN, APHEX TWIN, SCANNER, AND DANIEL PEMBERTON

The music of Karlheinz Stockhausen (1928– ; see chap. 54) profoundly affected art music in the late 20th century. It also became an important influence on the group of electronic music producers who emerged in the 1990s with roots in House and Techno. In 1995, Dick Witts, a reporter for British Radio 3, sent a package to Stockhausen containing music by Aphex Twin ("Ventolin" and "Alberto Balsam"), Plastikman (*Sheet One*), Scanner ("Micrographia," "Dimension," and "Discreet"), and Daniel Pemberton ("Phoenix," "Phosphine," Novelty Track," and "Voices"), and asked him to comment on these pieces. In response to Stockhausen's comments, *The Wire*'s Rob Young met with Aphex Twin, Scanner, and Pemberton (Plastikman was unavailable) to solicit their views on the compositions Stockhausen had recommended to them.

Aphex Twin (a.k.a. Richard D. James, 1971– ) is a producer of "intelligent Techno" and Ambient music who runs the influential Rephlex record label. Plastikman (a.k.a. Richie Hawtin, 1970– ) is an acclaimed DJ and producer of minimalist Techno who also runs the Plus 8 and Minus record labels. Scanner (a.k.a. Robin Rimbaud, 1964– ) made his reputation in the early 1990s by using an airwave scanner to eavesdrop on cellphone conversations and incorporate them into his Ambient, electronic musical sets. Since then, he has emerged as an influential sound artist whose installations have been widely exhibited. Daniel Pemberton (1977– ) is a writer, Ambient producer, and soundtrack composer.

## I. Advice to Clever Children: Stockhausen on the "Technocrats"

*Can we talk about the music we sent you? It was very good of you to listen to it. I wonder if you could give some advice to these musicians.*

I wish those musicians would not allow themselves any repetitions, and would go faster in developing their ideas or their findings, because I don't appreciate at all this permanent repetitive language. It is like someone who is stuttering all the time, and can't get words out of his mouth. I think musicians should have very concise figures and not rely on this fashionable psychology. I don't like psychology whatsoever: using music like a drug is stupid. One shouldn't do that: music is the product of the highest human intelligence, and of the best senses, the listening senses and of imagination and intuition. And as soon as it becomes just a means for ambiance, as we say, environment, or for being used for certain purposes, then music becomes a whore, and one should not allow that really; one should not serve any existing demands or in particular not commercial values. That would be terrible: that is selling out the music.

I heard the piece Aphex Twin of Richard James carefully: I think it would be very helpful if he listens to my work *Song Of The Youth* [*Gesang der Jünglinge*], which is electronic music, and a young boy's voice singing with himself. Because he would then immediately stop with all these post-African repetitions, and he would look for changing tempi and changing rhythms, and he would not allow to repeat any rhythm if it were not varied to some extent and if it did not have a direction in its sequence of variations.

And the other composer—musician, I don't know if they call themselves composers . . .

*They're sometimes called "sound artists". . .*

No, "Technocrats," you called them. He's called Plastikman, and in public, Richie Hawtin. It starts with 30 or 40—I don't know, I haven't counted them—fifths in parallel, always the same perfect fifths, you see, changing from one to the next, and then comes in hundreds of repetitions of one small section of an African rhythm: duh-duh-dum, etc, and I think it would be helpful if he listened to *Cycle* [*Zyklus*] for percussion, which is only a 15 minute long piece of mine for a percussionist, but there he will have a hell to understand the rhythms, and I think he will get a taste for very interesting non-metric and non-periodic rhythms. I know that he wants to have a special effect in dancing bars, or wherever it is, on the public who like to dream away with such repetitions, but he should be very careful, because the public will sell him out immediately for something else, if a new kind of musical drug is on the market. So he should be very careful and separate as soon as possible from the belief in this kind of public.

The other is Robin Rimbaud, Scanner, I've heard, with radio noises. He is very experimental, because he is searching in a realm of sound which is not usually used for music. But I think he should transform more what he finds. He leaves it too much in a raw state. He has a good sense of atmosphere, but he is too repetitive again. So let him listen to my work *Hymnen*. There are found objects—a lot like he finds with his scanner, you see. But I think he should learn from the art of transformation, so that what you find sounds completely new, as I sometimes say, like an apple on the moon.

Then there's another one: Daniel Pemberton. His work which I heard has noise loops: he likes loops, a loop effect, like in *musique concrète*, where I worked in 1952, and Pierre Henry and Schaeffer himself, they found some sounds, like say the sounds of a casserole, they made a loop, and then they transposed this loop. So I think he should give up this loop; it is too old fashioned. Really. He likes train rhythms, and I think when he comes to a soft spot, a quiet, his harmony sounds to my ears like ice cream harmony. It is so kitschy; he should stay away from these ninths and sevenths and tenths in parallel: so, look for a harmony that sounds new and sounds like Pemberton and not like anything else. He should listen to *Kontakte*, which has among my works the largest scale of harmonic, unusual and very demanding harmonic relationships. I like to tell the musicians that they should learn from works which have already gone through a lot of temptations and have refused to give in to these stylistic or to these fashionable temptations . . .

## II. Advice from Clever Children: The "Technocrats" on Stockhausen

*Aphex Twin on* Song Of The Youth

Mental! I've heard that song before; I like it. I didn't agree with him. I thought he should listen to a couple of tracks of mine: "Didgeridoo," then he'd stop making abstract, random patterns you can't dance to. Do you reckon he can dance? You could dance to *Song of the Youth*, but it hasn't got a groove in it, there's no bassline. I know it was probably made in the 50s, but I've got plenty of wicked percussion records made in the 50s that are awesome to dance to. And they've got basslines. I could remix it: I don't know about making it better; I wouldn't want to make it into a dance version, but I could probably make it a bit more anally technical. But I'm sure he could these days, because tape is really slow. I used to do things like that with tape, but it does take forever, and I'd never do anything like that again with tape. Once you've got your computer sorted out, it pisses all over stuff like that, you can do stuff so fast. It has a different sound, but a bit more anal.

I haven't heard anything new by him; the last thing was a vocal record, *Stimmung*, and I didn't really like that. Would I take his comments to heart? The ideal thing would be to meet him in a room and have a wicked discussion. For all I know, he could be taking the piss. It's a bit hard to have a discussion with someone via other people.

I don't think I care about what he thinks. It is interesting, but it's disappointing, because you'd imagine he'd say that anyway. It wasn't anything surprising. I don't know anything about the guy, but I expected him to have that sort of attitude. Loops are good to dance to . . .

He should hang out with me and my mates: that would be a laugh. I'd be quite into having him around.

*Scanner on* Hymnen

It's interesting that I've not heard this before, and maybe Thomas Köner hasn't and so on, but you can relate it to our work. I don't know whether it's conscious or not. I was two years old when this was written! Stockhausen says he don't like repetitions: what I like about repetition is it can draw the listener and lull you into a false sense of security, but when it gets too abstract—this is cut-ups—I find it very difficult to digest over a long period of time. He's a lapsed Catholic, and there's the sense that it's meant to be a religious experience passing through these records, like a purging of the system. Whether you like it or not, you're affected in one way or another. I'd like to hear this live.

I prefer the gentler passages. I do find myself irritated by that barrage of sound against sound over a long period of time: an alternative kind of repetition. That's why I like Jim O'Rourke's work, because it works over long periods.

I wonder about him putting himself into the recording; is it a vanity thing, or part of the process? With the scanner, it's like live editing, which is like this as well. When you scan, if you don't like something you flick between frequencies, when you DJ you cut between records, and it is an art form as a form of live editing . . .

Reminds me of the Holger Czukay LP *Der Osten Ist Rot*, cutting between national anthems, like tuning through a radio: I don't know whether this is actually happening or not. This is very good actually—better than I expected. At the end there's a recording of him breathing. It's quite uncomfortable—like being inside his head.

I take some of what he said about my music to heart. Part of what I'm interested in is transforming material. Lots of the sounds I use are off the scanner or the shortwave radio. Lots of people wouldn't realise that sometimes a bass sound isn't a keyboard bass sound: it's a little blip on the phone. So I do try and transform the material as much as possible. I disagree about repetition: I think, as John Cage said, repetition is a form of change, and it's a concept you either agree or disagree with. I like repetitions; I like Richie Hawtin's work for that very aspect. In a way it is like a religious experience: if his work is about spirituality, then this is a kind of alternative, non-religious spirituality, where you're drawn in by this block of rhythm; it's an incredible feeling, the way it moves you physically, and moves you in a dancefloor as well.

Things like this are designed to be listened to over long periods of time, and sometimes I think it could do with some editing. Most contemporary sound artists are working within a four- to ten-minute time scale, basically. And to be honest, for most people that's enough.

*Daniel Pemberton on* Kontakte

At first I expected someone hitting a piano randomly, but there were happenings in there, with stereo panning and effects. I was very impressed considering the time it was done: the 1960s. He was going on about how everyone's stuff was repetitive, but his stuff is the complete opposite: so unrepetitive that it never really got anywhere. Not necessarily a bad thing, but it didn't have any development in it: sounded like an Old School FSOL. When he recommends *Kontakte* for its "very demanding harmonic relationships," it sounds a bit suspect to me: the whole piece seems to be dealing far more with timbre than with harmonic relationship. It's obviously based around sound, and any harmonics on there, to the non-musical ear, sound like a piano hit randomly. It would be very good to put some HipHop breaks under, actually.

What he said about me was quite funny: he accuses me of old hat . . . I was born in 1977, 25 years after [*Kontakte*], a longer time than I've lived. I'm still learning musical history. If my whole career goes down the pan, at least I've got a future with Mr. Whippy! And for him to call eighths, ninths and tenths "kitschy"! The scales I commonly use aren't too adventurous, but that's because they're the ones that sound nice. The stuff I've done which is unlistenable, I haven't released because no one would enjoy it.

It's good to have other people's views. I ignore them in the sense that I know what I want to do: his criticisms won't make me throw everything away and start working with bizarre new scales and fantastic new instruments. I know what he means about loops though; that's because I haven't got much equipment.

Get a chewn, mate! I think he should develop his music a bit more. Try and repeat some of the ideas, work on them, build them up; you can still change them. He should listen to a track off my forthcoming album, *Homemade*. Stockhausen should experiment more with standard melodies, try and subvert them; he should stop being so afraid of the normal: by being so afraid of the normal he's being normal himself by being the complete opposite. He should try to blend the two together: that would be new and interesting. To me, anyway.

# 56

# *Breakthrough Beats: Rhythm and the Aesthetics of Contemporary Electronic Music*

BEN NEILL

As a composer and performer, Ben Neill (1957– ) routinely crosses the borders between pop, jazz, and experimental music. The leader of La Monte Young's Theatre of Eternal Music Brass Ensemble, Neill has also worked with John Cage, Earle Brown, David Behrman, Pauline Oliveros, and others. Yet Neill is better known for his electronic dance music, his collaborations with DJ Spooky and the Single Cell Orchestra, and his soundtracks for television commercials. He performs on the "mutantrumpet," a hybrid electro-acoustic instrument of his own invention that is fitted with three bells, a trombone slide, and a computer interface. From 1992–98, Neill served as music curator at The Kitchen, New York's premier art and performance space. In this article, he draws on his own experience to reflect on the crucial differences between "high art" and "popular" electronic music.

At this particular moment in the history of computer music, the flow of ideas between high art and popular art seems to have a particular significance. Indeed, the protective parapet that has long kept high art and popular art mutually exclusive seems to be showing signs of vulnerability. It seems that we are about to enter a new cultural architecture that we cannot yet describe; yet we are aware that technology is changing the world and that it will also change the world of computer music.

—Joel Chadabe[1]

Rhythm has always been the life of the party, and now, perhaps more than ever it is the life of the art itself.

—Jon Pareles[2]

What is the distinction between popular and high-art computer music? As Joel Chadabe pointed out in a recent article for *Computer Music Journal*,[3] these are two worlds that rarely intersect, but that seem inevitably drawn together at this juncture in history. The question can be answered in one word—rhythm. It is the beat that draws the dividing line between serious and vernacular, visceral and intellectual. Pulse equals life equals pleasure. While composers used to define themselves in terms of tonal style (atonality, serialism, octatonic, modal, etc.), those distinctions have been largely superseded by rhythmic content. The two worlds of high art and popular electronic music may use slightly different tools, but their aesthetic approaches are most clearly defined in terms of the presence or absence of repetitive beats. Jon Pareles' brilliant *New York Times* article, "The Rhythm Century," explains how rhythm was the "engine of transformation for 20th century music"[4] in everything from *Le Sacre du Printemps* to jazz to the programmed beats of drum 'n' bass and Techno. I believe that this analysis of the last century of music is correct, and that electronic music is no exception to it.

Minimalism changed art music radically in the late 1960s and early 1970s, largely by reintroducing the beat and repetitive structures into the abstract complexity of 1950s serialism and chance-based works. Art music became physical again, connected to pleasure through the visceral elements of World- and popular-music influences. Minimalist composers performed their music using the amplification and instrumentation of current pop music, adding to the pleasure quotient in their works.

> One could imagine that some future history of music will describe the period starting in the late 20th century as follows: "Our current musical language arose in the 1960s and 70s. In its nascent, simplistic state it was at first mistaken for a full blown style in itself, and was termed 'Minimalism.'"[5]

Following on minimalism's groundbreaking innovations, postmodernism gave 1980s art-music composers license to utilize popular culture elements and techniques as never before, and composers such as Glenn Branca, Rhys Chatham, Mikel Rouse, Michael Gordon, Todd Levin and myself borrowed heavily from pop structures. Improvisers such as John Zorn also incorporated popular elements in their works, but used them in a more ironic, detached way, never really embracing popular culture but rather deconstructing or critiquing it from outside.

In the past 10 years, a new breed of composers, with no regard for the former distinctions of pop versus high art, has evolved. Their new aesthetic approach has been made possible by the continuing evolution of computer music technologies that started in the 1970s and 1980s, along with the aesthetic progression of late-20th-century culture into a more global, less Eurocentric form. Many art-music composers scoff at the idea of using regular 4/4 rhythm patterns in their works; current Kitchen curator and composer John King has described this attitude as "the fear of the funk."[6] It is not difficult to understand this bias, since much of the development of 20th-century art music up until minimalism was an evolution toward more and more harmonic, melodic and rhythmic complexity.

> The music schools, the established composers, had been telling youngsters that music, to be valid, should be complex, dissonant, difficult to understand.

ben neill • 387

Throughout the '60s the world of musical composition had been hermetically cut off, by its own choice, from the rest of society.[7]

This attitude is also reminiscent of the bias many classical musicians have traditionally taken toward jazz and improvisation, feeling that it is too vernacular or unsophisticated for their interest. It is no coincidence that the minimalists (e.g. La Monte Young, Terry Riley, Steve Reich, Philip Glass) were also actively involved with jazz and/or various forms of World Music.

The development and evolution of beat construction in current electronic dance music is a highly sophisticated art form in itself, which changes rapidly in its transmission through global networks. Just as composers in earlier historical periods often worked within a given set of large-scale formal parameters (sonata form, dance forms, tone poems, etc.), innovative pop electronic composers use steady pulse, loop-based structures and 4/4 time as a vehicle for a wide range of compositional ideas and innovations. Shifts of tempo, subdivision, sonic manipulation and complex quantization structures are making beat science the new jazz of the 21st century. Much in the same way that jazz soloists listened to each other and incorporated each other's licks into their own solos, beat makers around the world listen and learn from each other through the underground network of DJs, 12-inch white-label vinyl records, mp3s, CD-Rs and the Internet. The artistry of pushing a new style of beat forward is highly refined; at any given time there are many styles being practiced and developed along with new hybrids forming and new genres constantly emerging. Pop electronic music is also rapidly incorporating many elements of art music: experimental live performance techniques (Richie Hawtin, Tortoise, Coldcut), conceptual and process-oriented composition (Thomas Brinkmann, Aphex Twin, Oval), collage (Avalanches, DJ Shadow, DJ Spooky), performance art and theatrical spectacle (Fischerspooner, Rabbit in the Moon) and the extensive use of experimental software and hardware can be seen turning up in clubs and on dance records around the world. The laptop is replacing the acoustic guitar as a primary instrument of expression for scores of new musicians.

The contrasting cultures of high art and popular art reflect the antipodal extremes of a social and cultural order that has been in existence in the western world since the Renaissance.[8]

Having started my career in the postmodern art-music scene of downtown New York in the mid-1980s, I made the emergent global technoculture of DJs, dance-music subgenres and the musical moniker "electronica" my focus starting around 1993. I had incorporated programmed and live repetitive beats into my earliest compositions, mostly presenting these pieces in art-music venues. The opportunity to play my music for a larger, more diverse audience was something I had been searching for; as I understood it, "downtown" music in New York was aimed at making art music a popular form, proving that art had truly been liberated from the confines of the modernist ivory tower, taking the cultural advances of Philip Glass, Laurie Anderson, Steve Reich and Terry Riley to a new level. This approach was not widely recognized by other art-music composers; one of the only others to make the shift to dance music and DJ culture was David Linton, who had drummed with Rhys Chatham in the 1980s and developed a solo interactive drum-performance system around the same time. Linton was responsible for producing such important events as the early Soundlab parties and, more recently, an electronic performance series entitled Unity Gain.

In my position as music curator of the Kitchen from 1992-1998, I gave much of my attention to this new genre of music. The Tone monthly series, co-curated with DJ Spooky and DJ Olive, combined DJs and electronica artists with art-music composers and performers. I saw then in the early 1990s that electronica was the new art music, and that it was important to make the connection between what is and what has been, between the future and the past. My own artistic project over the last 8 years has been to utilize the most sophisticated technologies of experimental art music with my self-designed *mutantrumpet* in the context of electronica's groove-based genres. In other words, I have come down squarely on the side of music with a consistent pulse.

One of the key ideas to come out of recent electronic pop culture is the "rave" sensibility in which the traditional notions of performer and audience are completely erased and redefined. In this type of event, the artists are not the center of attention; instead it is the role of the artist to channel the energy of the crowd and create the proper backdrop for their social interaction. The audience truly becomes the performance, an idea that was explored by the avant-garde for years but did not have the same impact as in the current electronic pop music because of the limited audience for classical avant-garde events [. . . .]

This is another aspect of the difference between art and pop electronic music. At the 2001 Coachella Festival in Indio, California, pop electronic music was presented in a large-scale festival format with eight stages and thousands of people—certainly it was one of the largest electronic-music concerts ever presented in the U.S. While rock bands such as Weezer and Jane's Addiction also performed, the large majority of performers were electronic artists and DJs. Peter Kruder, Doc Martin, Fatboy Slim, the Chemical Brothers, Adam Freeland and St. Germain (one of the only groups to incorporate live instruments), all presented outstanding sets.

For me, however, the unquestionable highlight of the event was a performance by Squarepusher, a.k.a. Tom Jenkinson. His set took place in one of the tents, crowded with approximately 2,500 people, all standing. Jenkinson's set was uncompromisingly experimental in nature. The performance consisted of playback of pre-recorded music; it was essentially a tape-music performance, with little or no sonic manipulation. While many artists and DJs adapt their music to the setting, in this case a huge pop dance event, Squarepusher presented 1 1/2 hours of music in which long stretches of highly processed digital noise and textures that would rival any art-music composer's sonic palette alternated with completely frenzied hyperspeed beats that exceeded 200 beats per minute—hardly dance music as anyone on this planet would recognize it. As I stood in the packed tent, feeling the waves of sonic processing that made my body feel as if it were turning inside out, there came to mind the early works of Edgar Varèse—the stunned audience in the Philips pavilion hearing the *Poème Électronique* for the first time. This truly was a new, exploratory experience, and the audience was an essential part of the innovation. The context was different, however. No longer was this type of music relegated to a rarefied, unique performance situation. Experimentation had fully made its way to popular culture and a mass audience, a significant cultural transmigration from the Varèse performance 50 years ago.

Squarepusher's music and the work of others, including Thomas Brinkmann, Aphex Twin, Richie Hawtin, Richard Devine and the Future Sound of London (to name a few) prove that it is possible for rhythmic electronic-music composers to work with the most abstract sound processes, experimental textures and techniques, as well as rhythmic materials that make references to, but do not fit within, specific pre-existing dance music genres. However, even if electronic art-music composers incorporate rhythmic elements in their works, it is very unusual for their music to be heard outside of the rarefied world of academic computer-music festivals. While popular electronic artists and audiences feel comfortable embracing the experimental sound production methods and ideas of art music, the crossover rarely goes the other way. High-art computer music that has not been directly influenced by minimalism and postmodernism remains elitist and disconnected from the larger cultural sphere, rendering it largely ineffectual as a 21st-century art form. This way of thinking is certainly not limited to electronic-music circles. Many classical music critics have written about the demise of classical music as we know it on a broader scale, and music for theater and film has greatly overshadowed the new orchestral repertoire. This is part of the same cultural phenomenon that is happening in electronic music, but due to the speed that new technologies bring to its production and presentation, electronic music is taking a leading role over acoustic music. I would submit that because of these technological advances, this is a unique moment in history in which music is also leading the visual arts. Electronic-music composers can work in a way very similar to that of painters and sculptors; being self-contained and not relying on others to perform or create one's art speeds up the process greatly.

Like Chadabe, I believe the oppositional situation between high art and pop electronic music is in the process of shifting. However, I see the merger of the two sides a bit differently than he. While his prediction that art music will achieve new levels of accessibility through new interactive technologies may be true (the *Brain Opera* of Tod Machover is a good example of that approach), I believe that pop music will ultimately consume what was known as art music and that we will see a period in which art is consumed and enjoyed by a much wider public than at any time in recent history. There are historical precedents for this; the early operas of Monteverdi were a popular entertainment, as was much of the music of the 19th century, which remains the bulk of classical repertoire.

I believe that this shift is part of a larger cultural change, something that the late writer Terence McKenna described as the Archaic Revival.[9] McKenna suggested that, through the emerging electronic media and connectivity, art would assume a role similar to its position in preliterate societies.

> The zeitgeist of hyperspace that is emerging, initially freighted with technology and cybernetics, requires that it be consciously tuned to an erotic ideal. It is important to articulate the presence of this erotic ideal of the Other early. This is an opportunity to fall in love with the Other, get married and go off to the stars; but it's only an opportunity and not evolutionarily necessary.[10]

The musical equivalent of McKenna's erotic ideal is the steady pulse, the beat. Artists, according to McKenna's view, are the contemporary equivalents of shamans in primitive cultures. Electronic pop music and other forms of digital media art are leading the way in this direction, and thus the prejudice against music with a steady rhythmic pulse is rapidly receding into the past. In the 21st century, pop culture is culture; this is healthy and desirable, and computer technology is facilitating this important progression. Art has spent long enough being cut off from the larger cultural sphere; now it is time for art to be connected in a new way to reflect the connectivity of an increasingly global culture.

## NOTES

1. Joel Chadabe, "Remarks on Computer Music Culture," *Computer Music Journal* 24, No. 4 (2000) p. 9.
2. Jon Pareles, "The Rhythm Century: The Unstoppable Beat," *New York Times* (3 May 1998), Arts and Leisure section, p. 1.
3. Chadabe, "Remarks."
4. Pareles, "The Rhythm Century."
5. Kyle Gann, "Seeds of Minimalism: An Essay on Postminimal and Totalist Music," *Berliner Gesellschaft für Neue Musik* (1998) p. 9.
6. Personal conversation with John King at the Manhattan School of Music Composition Forum, 2001.
7. Gann, "Seeds of Minimalism," p. 11.
8. Chadabe, "Remarks," p. 11.
9. Terence McKenna, *The Archaic Revival* (New York: Harper Collins, 1991).
10. McKenna, *Archaic Revival*, p. 76.

# 57

## The Aesthetics of Failure: "Post-Digital" Tendencies in Contemporary Computer Music

### KIM CASCONE

Composer Kim Cascone (1955– ) is known for his "microsound" compositions, music that explores the textural details of digital sound and that exists
at the intersection of classic electronic music, sound art, and post-Techno.
In the 1980s, Cascone worked as a music editor for film director David Lynch
and founded Silent Records, which featured Ambient recordings by Cascone's own Heavenly Music Corporation (named after an experimental composition by Brian Eno and Robert Fripp). In the mid-1990s, Cascone became
a sound designer for pop producer Thomas Dolby and, later, developed
sound software for computer games. In 2000, Cascone formed the Anechoic
Media label to release his own compositions. In this article, he explores the
aesthetics of what he calls "post-digital" music, which exploits the precariousness of the digital signal and celebrates the sonic effects of digital
glitches, bugs, and errors.

**The digital revolution is over.**

**—Nicholas Negroponte (1998)**[1]

Over the past decade, the Internet has helped spawn a new movement in digital
music. It is not academically based, and for the most part the composers involved
are self-taught. Music journalists occupy themselves inventing names for it, and
some have already taken root: glitch, microwave, DSP, sinecore, and microscopic
music. These names evolved through a collection of deconstructive audio and
visual techniques that allow artists to work beneath the previously impenetrable
veil of digital media. The Negroponte epigraph above inspired me to refer to this
emergent genre as "post-digital" because the revolutionary period of the digital

information age has surely passed. The tendrils of digital technology have in some way touched everyone. With electronic commerce now a natural part of the business fabric of the Western world and Hollywood cranking out digital fluff by the gigabyte, the medium of digital technology holds less fascination for composers in and of itself. [. . . T]he medium is no longer the message; rather, specific tools themselves have become the message.

The Internet was originally created to accelerate the exchange of ideas and development of research between academic centers, so it is perhaps no surprise that it is responsible for helping give birth to new trends in computer music outside the confines of academic think tanks [. . . .] Unfortunately, cultural exchange between non-academic artists and research centers has been lacking. The post-digital music that Max, SMS, AudioSculpt, PD, and other such tools make possible rarely makes it back to the ivory towers, yet these non-academic composers anxiously await new tools to make their way onto a multitude of Web sites [. . . .]

## The Aesthetics of Failure

**It is failure that guides evolution; perfection offers no incentive for improvement.**

**—Colson Whitehead (1999)[2]**

The "post-digital" aesthetic was developed in part as a result of the immersive experience of working in environments suffused with digital technology: computer fans whirring, laser printers churning out documents, the sonification of user-interfaces, and the muffled noise of hard drives. But more specifically, it is from the "failure" of digital technology that this new work has emerged: glitches, bugs, application errors, system crashes, clipping, aliasing, distortion, quantization noise, and even the noise floor of computer sound cards are the raw materials composers seek to incorporate into their music.

While technological failure is often controlled and suppressed—its effects buried beneath the threshold of perception—most audio tools can zoom in on the errors, allowing composers to make them the focus of their work. Indeed, "failure" has become a prominent aesthetic in many of the arts in the late 20th century, reminding us that our control of technology is an illusion, and revealing digital tools to be only as perfect, precise, and efficient as the humans who build them. New techniques are often discovered by accident or by the failure of an intended technique or experiment.

**I would only observe that in most high-profile gigs, failure tends to be far more interesting to the audience than success.**

**—David Zicarelli (1999)**

There are many types of digital audio "failure." Sometimes, it results in horrible noise, while other times it can produce wondrous tapestries of sound. (To more adventurous ears, these are quite often the same.) When the German sound experimenters known as Oval started creating music in the early 1990s by painting small images on the underside of CDs to make them skip, they were using an

kim cascone • 393

aspect of "failure" in their work that revealed a subtextual layer embedded in the compact disc.

Oval's investigation of "failure" is not new. Much work had previously been done in this area such as the optical soundtrack work of László Moholy-Nagy and Oskar Fischinger, as well as the vinyl record manipulations of John Cage and Christian Marclay, to name a few. What is new is that ideas now travel at the speed of light and can spawn entire musical genres in a relatively short period of time.

## Back to the Future

Poets, painters, and composers sometimes walk a fine line between madness and genius, and throughout the ages they have used "devices" such as absinthe, narcotics, or mystical states to help make the jump from merely expanding their perceptual boundaries to hoisting themselves into territories beyond these boundaries. This trend to seek out and explore new territories led to much experimentation in the arts in the early part of the 20th century.

When artists of the early 20th century turned their senses to the world created by industrial progress, they were forced to focus on the new and changing landscape of what was considered "background."

**I now note that ordinarily I am concerned with, focus my attention upon, things or "objects," the words on the page. But I now note that these are always situated within what begins to appear to me as a widening field which ordinarily is a background from which the "object" or thing stands out. I now find by a purposeful act of attention that I may turn to the field as field, and in the case of vision I soon also discern that the field has a kind of boundary or limit, a horizon. This horizon always tends to "escape" me when I try to get at it; it "withdraws" always on the extreme fringe of the visual field. It retains a certain essentially enigmatic character.**

**—Don Idhe (1976)[3]**

Concepts such as "detritus," "by-product," and "background" (or "horizon") are important to consider when examining how the current post-digital movement started. When visual artists first shifted their focus from foreground to background (for instance, from portraiture to landscape painting), it helped to expand their perceptual boundaries, enabling them to capture the background's enigmatic character.

The basic composition of "background" is comprised of data we filter out to focus on our immediate surroundings. The data hidden in our perceptual "blind spot" contains worlds waiting to be explored, if we choose to shift our focus there. Today's digital technology enables artists to explore new territories for content by capturing and examining the area beyond the boundary of "normal" functions and uses of software.

Although the lineage of post-digital music is complex, there are two important and well-known precursors that helped frame its emergence: the Italian Futurist movement at the beginning of the 20th century, and John Cage's composition *4'33"* (1952) [. . . .]

## Snap, Crackle, Glitch

Fast-forwarding from the 1950s to the present, we skip over most of the electronic music of the 20th century, much of which has not, in my opinion, focused on expanding the ideas first explored by the Futurists and Cage. An emergent genre that consciously builds on these ideas is that which I have termed "post-digital," but it shares many names, as noted in the introduction, and I will refer to it from here on out as *glitch*. The glitch genre arrived on the back of the *electronica* movement, an umbrella term for alternative, largely dance-based electronic music (including House, Techno, electro, drum 'n' bass, Ambient) that has come into vogue in the past five years. Most of the work in this area is released on labels peripherally associated with the dance music market, and is therefore removed from the contexts of academic consideration and acceptability that it might otherwise earn. Still, in spite of this odd pairing of fashion and art music, the composers of glitch often draw their inspiration from the masters of 20th century music who they feel best describe its lineage.

*A Brief History of Glitch*

At some point in the early 1990s, Techno music settled into a predictable, formulaic genre serving a more or less aesthetically homogeneous market of DJs and dance music aficionados. Concomitant with this development was the rise of a periphery of DJs and producers eager to expand the music's tendrils into new areas. One can visualize Techno as a large postmodern appropriation machine, assimilating cultural references, tweaking them, and then representing them as tongue-in-cheek jokes. DJs, fueled with samples from thrift store purchases of obscure vinyl, managed to mix any source imaginable into sets played for more adventurous dance floors. Always trying to outdo one another, it was only a matter of time until DJs unearthed the history of electronic music in their archeological thrift store digs. Once the door was opened to exploring the history of electronic music, invoking its more notable composers came into vogue. A handful of DJs and composers of electronica were suddenly familiar with the work of Karlheinz Stockhausen, Morton Subotnick, and John Cage, and their influence helped spawn the glitch movement.

A pair of Finnish producers called Pan Sonic—then known as Panasonic, before a team of corporate lawyers encouraged them to change their name—led one of the first forays into experimentation in electronica. Mika Vainio, head architect of the Pan Sonic sound, used handmade sine-wave oscillators and a collection of inexpensive effect pedals and synthesizers to create a highly synthetic, minimal, "hard-edged" sound. Their first CD, titled *Vakio*, was released in the summer of 1993, and was a sonic shockwave compared to the more blissful strains of Ambient-Techno becoming popular at that time. The Pan Sonic sound conjured stark, florescent, industrial landscapes; test-tones were pounded into submission until they squirted out low, throbbing drones and high-pitched stabs of sine waves. The record label Vainio founded, Sähkö Records, released material by a growing catalog of artists, most of it in the same synthetic, stripped-down, minimal vein.

As discussed earlier, the German project Oval was experimenting with CD-skipping techniques and helped to create a new tendril of glitch—one of slow-moving slabs of dense, flitting textures. Another German group, which called itself

Mouse on Mars, injected this glitch aesthetic into a more danceable framework, resulting in gritty low-fidelity rhythmic layers warping in and out of one another.

From the mid-1990s forward, the glitch aesthetic appeared in various sub-genres, including drum 'n' bass, drill 'n' bass, and TripHop. Artists such as Aphex Twin, LTJ Bukem, Omni Trio, Wagon Christ, and Goldie were experimenting with all sorts of manipulation in the digital domain. Time-stretching vocals and reducing drum loops to eight bits or less were some of the first techniques used in creating artifacts and exposing them as timbral content. The more experimental side of electronica was still growing and slowly establishing a vocabulary.

By the late 1990s, the glitch movement was keeping pace with the release of new features in music software, and the movement began congealing into a rudimentary form. A roster of artists was developing. Japanese producer Ryoji Ikeda was one of the first artists other than Mika Vainio to gain exposure for his stark, "bleepy" soundscapes. In contrast to Vainio, Ikeda brought a serene quality of spirituality to glitch music. His first CD, entitled $+/-$, was one of the first glitch releases to break new ground in the delicate use of high frequencies and short sounds that stab at listeners' ears, often leaving the audience with a feeling of tinnitus.

Another artist who helped bridge the gap between delicate and damaging was Carsten Nicolai (who records and performs under the names Noto and Alva Noto). Nicolai is also a co-founder of Raster-Noton, a German label group that specializes in innovative digital music. In a similar fashion, Peter Rehberg, Christian Fennesz, and the sound/Net art project Farmers Manual are tightly associated with the Mego label located in Vienna. Rehberg has the distinction of having received one of only two honorary Ars Electronica awards in Digital Music for his contribution to electronic music. Over the past few years, the glitch movement has grown to encompass dozens of artists who are defining new vocabularies in digital media. Artists such as immedia, Taylor Deupree, Nobukazu Takemura, Neina, Richard Chartier, Pimmon, *0, Autopoieses, and T:un[k], to name just a few, constitute the second wave of sound hackers exploring the glitch aesthetic [. . . .]

*Power Tools*

Computers have become the primary tools for creating and performing electronic music, while the Internet has become a logical new distribution medium. For the first time in history, creative output and the means of its distribution have been inextricably linked. Our current sonic backgrounds have dramatically changed since *4' 33"* was first performed—and thus the means for navigating our surroundings as well. In response to the radical alteration of our hearing by the tools and technologies developed in academic computer music centers—and a distribution medium capable of shuttling tools, ideas, and music between like-minded composers and engineers—the resultant glitch movement can be seen as a natural progression in electronic music. In this new music, the tools themselves have become the instruments, and the resulting sound is born of their use in ways unintended by their designers. Commonly referred to as sound "mangling" or "crunching," composers are now able to view music on a microscopic level. Curtis Roads coined the term *microsound* for all variants of granular and atomic methods of sound synthesis, and tools capable of operating at this microscopic level are able to achieve these effects.[4] Because the tools used in this style of music embody advanced concepts of digital signal processing, their usage by glitch artists tends to be based on experimentation rather than empirical investigation. In this fashion, unintended usage has become the second permission granted. It has been said that one does not need advanced training to use digital signal processing programs—just "mess around" until you obtain the desired result. Sometimes, not knowing the theoretical operation of a tool can result in more interesting results by "thinking outside the box." As Bob Ostertag notes, "It appears that the more technology is thrown at the problem, the more boring the results" (1998).[5]

> **"I looked at my paper," said Cage. "Suddenly I saw that the music, all the music, was already there." He conceived of a procedure which would enable him to derive the details of his music from the little glitches and imperfections which can be seen on sheets of paper. It had symbolic as well as practical value; it made the unwanted features of the paper its most significant ones—there is not even a visual silence.**
>
> **—David Revill (1999)[6]**

*New Music From New Tools*

Tools now aid composers in the deconstruction of digital files: exploring the sonic possibilities of a Photoshop file that displays an image of a flower, trawling word processing documents in search of coherent bytes of sound, using noise-reduction software to analyze and process audio in ways that the software designer never intended. Any selection of algorithms can be interfaced to pass data back and forth, mapping effortlessly from one dimension into another. In this way, all data can become fodder for sonic experimentation.

Composers of glitch music have gained their technical knowledge through self-study, countless hours deciphering software manuals, and probing Internet newsgroups for needed information. They have used the Internet both as a tool for learning and as a method of distributing their work. Composers now need to know about file types, sample rates, and bit resolution to optimize their work for the Internet. The artist completes a cultural feedback loop in the circuit of the Internet: artists download tools and information, develop ideas based on that information, create work reflecting those ideas with the appropriate tools, and then upload that work to a World Wide Web site where other artists can explore the ideas embedded in the work.

The technical requirements for being a musician in the information age may be more rigorous than ever before, but—compared to the depth of university computer music studies—it is still rather light. Most of the tools being used today have a layer of abstraction that enables artists to explore without demanding excessive technical knowledge. Tools like Reaktor, Max/MSP, MetaSynth, Audiomulch, Crusher-X, and Soundhack are pressed into action, more often than not with little care or regard for the technical details of DSP theory, and more as an aesthetic wandering through the sounds that these modern tools can create.

The medium is no longer the message in glitch music: the tool has become the message. The technique of exposing the minutiae of DSP errors and artifacts for their own sonic value has helped further blur the boundaries of what is to be considered music, but it has also forced us to examine our preconceptions of failure and detritus more carefully.

## Discussion

Electronica DJs typically view individual tracks as pieces that can be layered and mixed freely. This modular approach to creating new work from preexisting materials forms the basis of electronic music composers' use of samples. Glitch, however, takes a more deconstructionist approach in that the tendency is to reduce work to a minimum amount of information. Many glitch pieces reflect a stripped-down, anechoic, atomic use of sound, and they typically last from one to three minutes.

But it seems this approach affects the listening habits of electronica aficionados. I had the experience of hearing a popular sample CD playing in a clothing boutique. The "atomic" parts, or samples, used in composing electronica from small modular pieces had become the whole. This is a clear indication that contemporary computer music has become fragmented, it is composed of stratified layers that intermingle and defer meaning until the listener takes an active role in the production of meaning.

If glitch music is to advance past its initial stage of blind experimentation, new tools must be built with an educational bent in mind. That is, a tool should possess multiple layers of abstraction that allow novices to work at a simple level, stripping away those layers as they gain mastery. In order to help better understand current trends in electronic music, the researchers in academic centers must keep abreast of these trends [. . . .] In this way, the gap can be bridged, and new ideas can flow more openly between commercial and academic sectors.

> We therefore invite young musicians of talent to conduct a sustained observation of all noises, in order to understand the various rhythms of which they are composed, their principal and secondary tones. By comparing the various tones of noises with those of sounds, they will be convinced of the extent to which the former exceeds the latter. This will afford not only an understanding, but also a taste and passion for noises.
>
> —Luigi Russolo (1913)[7]

## NOTES

1. Nicholas Negroponte, "Beyond Digital," *Wired* 6 (12) (1998).
2. Colson Whitehead, *The Intuitionist* (New York: Anchor Books, 1999).
3. Don Idhe, *Listening and Voice: A Phenomenology of Listening* (Athens, Ohio: Ohio University Press, 1976).
4. [See Curtis Roads, *Microsound* (Cambridge, MA: MIT Press, 2001).—Eds]
5. Bob Ostertag, "Why Computer Music Sucks," on-line at http://www.l-m-c.org/uk/texts/ostertag.html
6. David Revill, *The Roaring Silence. John Cage: A Life* (New York: Arcade, 1992).
7. Russolo, *The Art of Noises*, trans. Barclay Brown (New York: Pendragon, 1986).

# Chronology

**1877**
- Thomas Edison invents the phonograph.

**1912**
- Henry Cowell composes *The Tides of Manaunaun*, which utilizes tone clusters.

**1913**
- Luigi Russolo writes *The Art of Noises: Futurist Manifesto*.

**1914**
- Russolo conducts the first public performance of music composed for his *intonarumori* (noise instruments).

**1916**
- In Zurich, Dada artists open the Cabaret Voltaire and experiment with sound poetry and noise music.

**1917**
- Edgard Varèse calls for instruments that would open up "a whole new world of unexpected sounds."
- Erik Satie's ballet *Parade* performed in Paris, with choreography by Diaghilev, a libretto by Cocteau, set design by Picasso, and music by Satie that includes typewriters, ship's whistles, sirens, and revolvers.

**1920**
- Satie and Darius Milhaud compose *Musique d'ameublement* (furniture music).
- Stefan Wolpe employs 8 gramophones to play records simultaneously at different speeds.

**1922–23**
- László Moholy-Nagy calls upon musicians and artists to experiment with phonographs.

**1924**
- Cowell composes *Aeolian Harp*, which calls for the pianist to brush the piano's strings.

**1930**
- Paul Hindemith and Ernst Toch employ superimposed phonograph recordings in live performance.

**1931**
- Varèse composes *Ionisation*, the first European composition written solely for percussion.

**1935**
- The German corporation AEG introduces the first magnetic tape recorder.

**1936**
- Carl Stalling begins composing music for Warner Brothers' cartoons, freely mixing classical, jazz, pop, folk, and country music.

**1938**
- John Cage begins "preparing" the piano by inserting bolts, screws, nuts, and weather stripping into the piano's strings. His most famous "prepared piano" piece, *Sonatas and Interludes*, is composed in 1946.

**1939**
- Cage composes *Imaginary Landscape No. 1* for frequency recordings and variable-speed turntables.

**1948**
- Pierre Schaeffer debuts his first *musique concrète* compositions in a "Concert of Noises" broadcast over French radio.

**1950**
- Schaeffer and Pierre Henry complete *Symphonie pour un homme seul* (*Symphony for a Man Alone*), their *musique concrète* masterpiece.

**1951**
- Cage composes two key indeterminate compositions: *Imaginary Landscape No. 4*, for 12 radios, and *Music of Changes*, composed by tossing coins to determine pitch, duration, and attack.
- Schaeffer and Henry establish a studio at the Radiodiffusion Television Françoise (French Radio-Television) called Groupe de Recherche de Musique Concrète, which soon hosts Pierre Boulez, Karlheinz Stockhausen, Iannis Xenakis and others. (In 1957, the studio would change its name to Groupe de Recherches Musicales [GRM].)
- Werner Meyer-Eppler, Herbert Eimert, and Stockhausen establish an electronic music studio at Westdeutscher Rundfunk (West German Radio) in Cologne. Eschewing concrete sounds for pure electronic synthesis, the studio comes to represent a methodology that rivals *musique concrète*: *elektronische Musik*.

**1952**
- Cage composes the famous "silent piece" *4′33″*, which calls upon the performer to make no intentional sounds, and *Williams Mix*, which cuts up and splices together more than 500 bits of found sound.
- Earle Brown composes *Folio*, a pioneering set of graphic scores that includes *December 1952*.
- Otto Luening and Vladimir Ussachevsky begin to construct an electronic music studio at Columbia University.

**1956**
- Stockhausen completes the electronic composition *Gesang der Jünglinge*.

**1958**
- Varèse composes *Poème électronique* and Xenakis composes *Concret P-H* for the Brussels Exposition's Philips Pavilion, designed by Le Corbusier and Xenakis.

**1957-59**
- At Bell Labs, Max Matthews begins experimenting with computer programs to create sound material.

- Mauricio Kagel composes *Transicion II*, the first piece to call for live tape recorder as part of a performance.
- Ornette Coleman and Cecil Taylor invent free jazz with a string of releases, including Coleman's *Change of the Century* and *The Shape of Jazz to Come* and Taylor's *Looking Ahead!*

**1960**
- Cage composes *Cartridge Music*, for modified phonograph cartridges and contact microphones.
- Stockhausen completes the electronic composition *Kontakte*.
- The conceptual art movement Fluxus gets underway, counting among its members Yoko Ono and La Monte Young, who composes a series of experimental text pieces under the title *Composition 1960*.
- Takehisa Kosugi and Yasunao Tone form Group Ongaku, Japan's first free improvising ensemble.
- Brion Gysin, Ian Sommerville, and William S. Burroughs begin their "cut-up" experiments with magnetic tape.
- As assistant to Stockhausen, Cornelius Cardew realizes Stockhausen's composition *Carré*.
- Coleman's double quartet records *Free Jazz*, which coins the term. Independently, Jamaican-born British saxophonist Joe Harriott records *Free Form*, launching European free jazz.
- Joe Meek and the Blue Men release *I Hear a New World*, which fully exploits the resources of the recording studio in an effort to conjure the sounds of extraterrestrial life.

**1961**
- First concert of works by members of the Columbia-Princeton Electronic Music Center, officially established at Columbia University in 1959 by Luening, Ussachevsky, and Milton Babbitt.
- In Ann Arbor, Michigan, Robert Ashley and Gordon Mumma establish the annual ONCE Festival of experimental music and multi-media performance.
- Terry Riley composes *Mescalin Mix*, an early minimalist composition using overlapping, repeating tape loops.
- Burroughs publishes the second of his "cut-up" novels, *The Ticket that Exploded*, which contains "The Invisible Generation," a primer on his experiments with tape recorders.
- James Tenney composes *Collage No.1 ("Blue Suede")*, a tape collage of Elvis Presley's "Blue Suede Shoes" and perhaps the earliest sampling composition.

**1962**
- Morton Subotnick, Ramon Sender, and Pauline Oliveros found the San Francisco Tape Music Center, inaugurating electronic music's counter-culture.

**1963**
- Derek Bailey, Gavin Bryars, and Tony Oxley form the free improvising ensemble Joseph Holbrooke.

**1964**
- Riley composes *In C*, the first popular classic of music minimalism.
- Young, Marian Zazeela, John Cale, Angus MacLise, and Tony Conrad form the Theatre of Eternal Music, the foundation of drone-based minimalism; and Conrad records *Four Violins*.

- Billed as "The October Revolution In Jazz," Sun Ra, Taylor, Milford Graves, Bill Dixon and others stage the first festival of free jazz.
- Albert Ayler releases the free jazz classic *Spiritual Unity*.
- Superstar classical pianist Glenn Gould announces his retirement from public performance, retreating into the studio to produce ideal performances through studio editing.

## 1965-66
- Oliveros composes the real-time tape-delay compositions *Bye Bye Butterfly* and *I of IV*.
- Subotnick composes the first electronic tape composition designed specifically for home listening, *Silver Apples of the Moon*, which utilizes Donald Buchla's early modular synthesizer, the Buchla Box.
- Steve Reich produces his tape-recorder compositions *It's Gonna Rain* and *Come Out*, early classics of minimalism and experimental music.
- On the South Side of Chicago, a group of African-American experimentalists found the Association for the Advancement of Creative Music (AACM), whose members include Anthony Braxton, Leroy Jenkins, and Leo Smith.
- AACM member Roscoe Mitchell releases his aptly titled record *Sound*.
- Sun Ra releases free jazz classics *The Magic City* and *The Heliocentric Worlds of Sun Ra, Vols. 1 and 2*.
- John Coltrane goes free jazz with his howling double-quartet record *Ascension*.
- Fluxus artist Milan Knizak begins his experiments with altered records—scratching them, burning them, painting on them, punching holes in them, cutting them apart and reassembling them, and then playing them back on a turntable.
- Led by Frederic Rzewski, American expatriates in Rome form the improvising electronic ensemble Musica Elettronica Viva (MEV).
- In London, Keith Rowe, Eddie Prévost, Lou Gare, and Lawrence Sheaff form the improvising ensemble AMM; joined by Cardew the group releases its debut record *AMMusic*, released on the pop music label Elektra and overseen by the producers of Pink Floyd.
- Robert Ashley, Mumma, David Behrman, and Alvin Lucier form the Sonic Arts Union to perform their experimental compositions.
- The Beatles experiment with tape collage on "Tomorrow Never Knows."
- The Beach Boys' Brian Wilson collaborates with Van Dyke Parks on an experimental record to be called *Smile*. The record was never officially released.

## 1967
- Stockhausen composes *Hymnen*, a tape collage of national anthems from around the world.
- Cardew completes his massive graphic score *Treatise*.
- The Velvet Underground releases their debut album *The Velvet Underground and Nico*, featuring minimalist viola drones by Cale.
- *Musique concrète* pioneer Henry records *Messe pour le temps présent*, a *concrète* mass based on pop and rock songs.
- The "Tropicalia" exhibition at Rio de Janeiro's Museum of Modern Art launches Tropicalismo, a multi-media art movement that synthesized pop art, psychedelic rock, Cage's indeterminacy, and other European and North American influences with homegrown concrete poetry, samba, and capoeira.

## 1968
- Bailey, Evan Parker, Hugh Davies, and Jamie Muir form the Music Improvisation Company, a seminal British improvising ensemble.

- German saxophonist Peter Brötzmann releases *Machine Gun*, a founding document of European free jazz.
- Reich writes his minimalist manifesto "Music as a Gradual Process."
- Fred Frith and Tim Hodgkinson form the avant-rock group Henry Cow and play their debut in support of Pink Floyd.
- Stockhausen students Holger Czukay and Irmin Schmidt form the Krautrock quartet Can. Czukay and Rolf Dammers emerge as sampling pioneers on *Canaxis*.
- The Beatles revisit tape collage on "Revolution #9."
- David Tudor composes *Rainforest*, an early masterpiece of live electronic music.
- Frank Zappa releases the rock *concrète* opuses *We're Only In It For the Money* and *Lumpy Gravy*.

## 1969
- In Tokyo, Fluxus veteran Takehisa Kosugi forms the improvising collective Taj Mahal Travelers.
- Cardew convenes the Scratch Orchestra, a large collective of amateur musicians and non-musicians who perform part of his work-in-progress *The Great Learning*. Among the Orchestra's members are Brian Eno and Bryars, who founds his own amateur orchestra, the Portsmouth Sinfonia, the same year.
- Rzewski composes the experimental composition *Les Moutons de Panurge*.
- Jazz composer George Russell records *Electronic Sonata for Souls Loved by Nature*, in which Russell's sextet improvises over "a tape composed of fragments of many different styles of music, avant-garde jazz, ragas, blues, rock, serial music, etc. treated electronically."
- Captain Beefheart records the experimental rock classic *Trout Mask Replica*.

## 1971-72
- Due to internal criticism from communist members, The Scratch Orchestra dissolves and Cardew becomes a devoted Marxist-Leninist. Invited by the BBC to introduce a performance by his former teacher and mentor Stockhausen, Cardew delivers a speech titled "Stockhausen Serves Imperialism."
- Zappa writes an article for *Stereo Review* titled "Edgard Varèse: The Idol of My Youth."

## 1972
- Miles Davis releases *On the Corner*, inspired in equal parts by James Brown and Stockhausen, and assembled in the studio by producer Teo Macero, a student of Varèse.
- King Tubby invents dub (and, in the process, the remix), dropping sounds in and out of the mix and adding reverb and delay to instrumental reggae B-sides.

## 1973
- Canadian composer R. Murray Schafer publishes *The Music of the Environment*, an early version of his magnum opus *The Tuning of the World* (1977), and releases the LP *The Vancouver Soundscape*.
- Eno and Robert Fripp cross rock guitar with experimental tape music on *No Pussy-footing*.
- Formation of the Dada-inspired proto-industrial trio Cabaret Voltaire, which features Chris Watson on tapes and electronics.
- Lee "Scratch" Perry and King Tubby produce the first dub album, The Upsetters' *Blackboard Jungle Dub*.

**1974**

- Michael Nyman publishes *Experimental Music: Cage and Beyond* from inside the British experimental music scene.
- In the early days of disco and HipHop, DJs Kool Herc and Francis Grasso isolate breakbeats and extend them with the use of two turntables.

**1975**

- Eno launches his Obscure record label to bring experimental music to a wider audience.
- Lou Reed releases *Metal Machine Music*, a double-LP of guitar feedback and distortion.

**1976**

- Inspired by the tape cut-ups of Burroughs, British quartet Throbbing Gristle launch Industrial Records and invent industrial music.
- John Zorn composes *Baseball*, the first of his "game pieces."
- Bailey founds Company Week, an annual gathering of free improvisers.
- The Ramones self-titled debut launches punk rock in the United States.

**1977**

- Kraftwerk releases *Trans-Europe Express*, a masterpiece of electronic pop-minimalism that foreshadows Techno.
- DJ Grand Wizard Theodore invents scratching.
- Jacques Attali publishes *Noise: The Political Economy of Music*.
- The Sex Pistols' *Never Mind the Bollocks* and The Clash's self-titled debut launch punk rock in England.
- The Residents record "Beyond the Valley of a Day in the Life," composed of fragments sampled from Beatles records.

**1978**

- Eno produces *No New York*, a compilation that documents New York's experimental No Wave scene, and releases *Music for Airports*, which invents Ambient music.

**1979**

- Art turntablist Christian Marclay begins his early experiments.
- George Lewis releases *Homage to Charles Parker*, featuring key members of the AACM alongside MEV's Richard Teitelbaum.
- The Fatback Band and The Sugar Hill Gang release the first HipHop singles.
- Public Image Ltd releases *Metal Box*, which fuses punk rock, dub, and Krautrock.

**1980–81**

- Glenn Branca's Guitar Army combines punk rock and minimalism, enlisting Thurston Moore and Lee Ranaldo of Sonic Youth, whose debut EP is issued on Branca's Neutral label.
- Sony introduces the Walkman.
- Grandmaster Flash executes the first turntablist masterpiece, "The Adventures of Grandmaster Flash on the Wheels of Steel."
- David Byrne and Eno record *My Life in a Bush of Ghosts*, an album of Fourth World funk built around ethnographic field recordings.
- Burroughs releases a compilation of tape cut-ups, *Nothing Here Now But the Recordings*, on Throbbing Gristle's Industrial Records label.
- Industrial music quintet Einstürzende Neubauten forms in Berlin.

- Under the name Merzbow, Masami Akita begins releasing his noise compositions on cassette.

**1982**
- The first compact discs come on the market.

**1983**
- House music is born in Chicago with Jesse Saunders and Vince Lawrence's "On and On."
- Herbie Hancock's mega-hit "Rockit" mixes jazz and HipHop turntablism.

**1984**
- Zorn composes *Cobra*, the *magnum opus* among his "game pieces."
- The Sound Unity Festival marks a resurgence of free jazz activity in New York City.
- Ensoniq produces the Mirage, the first inexpensive digital sampler.

**1985**
- Techno is launched in Detroit with the release of Model 500's "No UFOs."
- Braxton's classic quartet tours England and documents the concerts on a series of key records for the Leo label.
- Tone begins modifying CDs with pinhole-punctured Scotch tape.
- Lawrence "Butch" Morris releases *Current Trends in Racism in Modern America*, his first recorded "conduction" (conducted improvisation) featuring Zorn, Tone, Frank Lowe, Marclay, Zeena Parkins, and others.
- Marclay releases *Record Without a Cover.*

**1986**
- Miller Puckette develops MAX, which would become the major software tool for live computer improvisation.

**1989**
- John Oswald releases *Plunderphonic*, a CD containing humorous and inventive manipulations of songs by Dolly Parton, Public Enemy, The Beatles, and Michael Jackson. A year later, threatened by lawyers representing Jackson, Oswald is forced to destroy the remaining copies.

**1990**
- Zorn releases *Naked City*, a dizzying mix of jazz, punk rock, film music, Heavy Metal, lounge music, reggae, country, and other styles.
- Sony introduces the recordable CD.

**1992**
- Otomo Yoshihide introduces the turntable into free improvisation on *Ground Zero*.
- Warp Records releases *Artificial Intelligence*, a compilation that establishes the genres of "intelligent Techno" and "electronica."

**1993**
- Robert Hood releases the *Minimal Nation* EP on Jeff Mills' Axis imprint, signaling the arrival of minimal Techno.
- Virgin launches its influential Ambient series, beginning with "A Brief History of Ambient," and continuing with compilations that borrow titles from Cage compositions: "Imaginary Landscapes" and "Music of Changes."

**1994**
- German trio Oval releases *Systemisch*, assembled from fragments of altered and malfunctioning CDs.

- Aphex Twin releases *Selected Ambient Works Volume 2*, a founding document of Ambient electronica.

**1995**
- Simon Reynolds coins the term "post-rock" in articles for the *Village Voice* and *The Wire*.
- The term "turntablism" is coined by DJ Babu of the Beat Junkies crew.
- San Francisco HipHop label Bomb Hip-Hop releases *Return of the DJ Volume I*, the first album to showcase the work of HipHop turntablists.
- David Toop publishes his groundbreaking book *Ocean of Sound*.
- The mysterious Berlin label Basic Channel releases an influential compilation of its dub-soaked House tracks.
- The Internet becomes widely available.
- Albums by Goldie, A Guy Called Gerald, and Spring Heel Jack signal the arrival of Jungle (which is soon rechristened drum 'n' bass).
- Virgin's *Macro Dub Infection* compilation charts dub's influence on drum 'n' bass, post-rock, and HipHop.

**1996**
- Chicago quintet Tortoise issues the key post-rock record *Millions Now Living Will Never Die*.
- Finnish electronica duo Panasonic release *Kulma*.
- DJ Spooky releases his full-length debut, *Songs of a Dead Dreamer*, performs with composer Xenakis, and coins the term "illbient" to refer to his own music and that of Brooklyn DJ outfits Byzar, We, and Sub Dub.
- Bailey releases *Guitar, Drums 'n' Bass*, a collaboration with drum 'n' bass producer DJ Ninj.
- Second-generation minimalist Rhys Chatham records *Hard Edge*, featuring drum 'n' bass rhythms by Apache 61.
- William and Patricia Parker mount the first annual Vision festival, a gathering of free jazz musicians and artists that attracts an avant-rock crowd.

**1997**
- Debut performances by MIMEO, the live electronic music supergroup featuring electronic musicians from classical composition and free improvisation to post-rock and post-Techno.
- Spanish entomologist and sound artist Francisco López releases *La Selva*.

**1998**
- MP3 players come on the market.

**1999**
- Sonic Youth releases *Goodbye 20th Century*, on which the avant-rock quartet, joined by Christian Wolff, Kosugi, and Marclay, perform experimental compositions by Cage, Oliveros, Wolff, Reich, Ono, Cardew and others.
- To accompany its retrospective of Reich's recorded output, Nonesuch releases *Reich Remixed*, a collection of tracks by electronica artists influenced by Reich's minimalism.

**2000**
- Toop curates *Sonic Boom*, a comprehensive sound art exhibit featuring work by Marclay, Renaldo, Scanner, Eno and others.

- The Mille Plateaux label releases *Clicks+Cuts*, an influential compilation of post-digital, minimalist electronica.
- The Australian label Extreme releases *Merzbox*, a 50-CD Merzbow retrospective.
- Free Jazz pianist Matthew Shipp inaugurates the Thirsty Ear label's Blue Series, dedicated to merging free jazz and breakbeat science.
- *The New York Times* reports that, in the previous year, music stores sold more DJ turntables than guitars.

**2001**
- Philip Sherburne coins the term "MicroHouse" to characterize the stripped-down House productions of Vladislav Delay, Jan Jelinek, Thomas Brinkmann, Ricardo Villalobos and others.
- Erstwhile records stages Amplify 01, the first annual summit of the new global Improv.
- Release of *Improvised Music from Japan*, a 10-CD set documenting the burgeoning Japanese Improv scene.

# Glossary

Acousmatic Listening: Term coined by Pierre Schaeffer to describe a listening experience in which sound has been decoupled from its source (also known as "reduced listening").

Acoustic Ecology: Term coined by R. Murray Schafer to refer to research into the effects of the acoustic environment on the creatures living within it.

Additive Synthesis: Sound construction by means of the addition of sine waves to create a complex timbre.

Afrofuturism: A term that describes a genealogy of musicians, writers, filmmakers, and theorists who reject the association of black identity with "nature," "soul," "authenticity," and "the street," and instead connect it with technology, science fiction, and extraterrestrial existence.

Aleatory Composition: Roughly synonymous with indeterminacy. The term is often reserved for the less radical forms of indeterminacy preferred by European composers such as Pierre Boulez and Karlheinz Stockhausen.

Ambient: A term coined by Brian Eno to describe a compositional and listening practice that strives to "tint" the acoustic environment rather to dominate it. Ambient music can incorporate elements of a number of different styles, including jazz, electronica, New Age, modern classical music, and even noise. It is chiefly identifiable as having an overarching atmospheric context.

Analog Synthesizer : A sound-making device that combines various hardware sound-generating modules (oscillators), sound shaping modules (filters), and time shaping modules (voltage controlled amplifiers) and usually driven by a keyboard.

Atonality, Atonal music: Describes a wide range of compositional styles that do not rely on the conventions of tonal harmony and, specifically, do not organize pitches around a tonal center.

Avant-rock: General term for rock music with an experimental edge. Sometimes also called "outrock."

Bauhaus: A modernist school of art, design, and architecture founded in Weimar, Germany in 1919 and closed by the Nazis in 1933. Often driven by utopian social aims, the school encouraged collaborations among the various arts, attempted to dissolve the hierarchy that separated the fine arts from the crafts, and fostered collaborations with industry.

Beat Juggling: The turntablist practice of producing intricate beat patterns by using the crossfader to cut between breakbeats played on each of the two turntables.

Breakbeat: The portion of a track in which all the instruments drop out except the drums. Using two copies of the same record, DJs often extend or loop these portions to form the rhythmic basis of new tracks. Often used to describe the variety of musics that make use of breakbeats, e.g., HipHop, TripHop, and drum 'n' bass.

Breakbeat Science: The art and science of mixing and composing with breakbeats.

Charivari: In early modern Europe, a serenade of noisy music played on pots and pans to signal disapproval of certain marriages or sexual unions.

Clusters, Sound Clusters, Tone Clusters: Groups of adjacent notes played simultaneously.

Computer Music: A compositional practice that uses computer programs to generate sound from scratch, to manipulate existing sounds that have been digitized, or to create sound events in sequential or randomized fashion.

Conduction: A term coined by Lawrence "Butch" Morris to name his practice of conducted improvisation.

Cross Fader: The device on a DJ's mixer that allows him or her to pan the sound from one turntable to the other.

Cut: In DJ Culture, the practice of extracting sound, detaching it from its source or origin via a tape recorder, sampler, turntable and mixer, computer, or other such device.

Dada, Dadaism: A major modernist art movement founded in Zurich and New York in 1915 and remaining active until the early 1920s. Disillusioned by the carnage of World War I, Dada artists lampooned the dominant social and aesthetic values via anarchic theatre, nonsense poems, and the production of collages, photomontages, and ready-mades.

Dancehall: The term originated in the early 1980s as a description of live toasting by a deejay over instrumental reggae tracks. Today's dancehall, sometimes called ragga, features rougher toasting over harsher, more minimal, and often digital beats.

Dance Music: General term for musical styles rooted in club culture and intended for dancing: disco, House, Techno, HipHop, etc.

Deejay: In reggae terminology, the vocalist, MC, or toaster.

Détournement: Literally, to divert or distort. A Situationist tactic by which a given text, image, or piece of music is subversively altered by overlaying it with other texts, images, or sounds, or by incorporating it into a new context that undermines or parodies its original intented meaning or function.

Digital Synthesizer: A sound-making device that combines various software sound-generating modules (oscillators), sound-shaping modules (filters), and time-shaping modules (voltage controlled amplifiers) and usually driven by a keyboard.

DJ: Acronym for "disc jockey." In contemporary music, the term DJ can refer to someone who mixes existing tracks into a set, someone who creates new music with turntables and a mixer, or someone who does both.

DJ Culture: An umbrella term for musics such as disco, dub, HipHop, House, and Techno that are rooted in the art and science of the DJ. More broadly, the term refers to music and sound art that involves the two crucial features of the DJ's art: the cut and the mix.

Drum 'n' Bass: A genre of dance music originally known as Jungle, drum 'n' bass developed in London and Bristol in the early 1990s. Influenced by dub reggae, HipHop, and Techno, it is characterized by rapid digitized breakbeats and a slow bass groove. Among the myriad sub-genres of drum 'n' bass are Jump Up, Techstep, Hardstep, and drill 'n' bass.

Dub: A term that originally designated the instrumental B-side, or "version," of a reggae single intended as a backing track for a deejay. The term came to be associated with the work of producers such as King Tubby and Lee "Scratch" Perry who, via studio effects, turned these versions into works of art in their own right.

Dub Plate: A one-off or limited edition vinyl test pressing. In reggae culture, dub plates are pre-release tracks produced for a DJ to debut at his or her sound system.

Equal Temperament: The dominant tuning system of Western music since the 18th Century in which adjacent notes of the scale are separated by logarithmically equal distances that only approximate the natural harmonic series.

Electro-acoustic: Sometimes uses as a synonym for electronic music composition, the term can also describe compositions that combine the resources of electronic music with traditional acoustic instruments.

Electronic Music: A term designating music made primarily by non-acoustic means such as tape manipulation, analog synthesis, or digital synthesis. More technically, the term names a style of composition that constructs music by additive synthesis instead of by the techniques of *musique concrète*.

Electronica: Electronic music that arises within the context of popular rather than classical music, but that is intended for home listening rather than for the dance floor.

Epistemology, Epistemological: The theory of knowledge. Study of the origins, presuppositions, nature, extent, and veracity of knowledge. More generally, concerned with the nature of knowledge and experience (in contrast with ontology, which is concerned with the nature of being or existence).

Experimental Music: A term coined by John Cage to designate musical acts the outcome of which are not known in advance. Composer Michael Nyman broadened the term to designate a range of compositional strategies that emphasize processes of various kinds (i.e., chance, electronic, human), delight in the unique musical moment, new attitudes toward musical time, composer/audience interaction, etc.

Fourth World: A term coined by composer/trumpeter Jon Hassell to describe an electronic hybrid of ancient and modern, acoustic and digital, composed and improvised, and Eastern and Western musics.

Free Jazz: A form of jazz improvisation not tied to preset chord progressions. The term was initially coined by Ornette Coleman, who titled his 1960 double-quartet record *Free Jazz*.

Free Improvisation: Generally synonymous with "improvised music."

Furniture Music: A form of "background" music conceptualized by composers Erik Satie and Darius Milhaud. A precursor to Brian Eno's Ambient music.

Futurism: The first of the major avant-garde art movements of the 20th century. Launched in 1909 and lasting into the 1920s, Futurism rejected traditional social and aesthetic values and called for a new art that celebrated modern technology, speed, noise, violence, and war. The movement was centered in Italy and Russia, and encompassed painting, sculpture, music, architecture, typography, poetry, cooking, and clothing design.

Glitch, Glitch music: Refers to the work of composers and sound artists who focus on the sonic artifacts (noise, blips, and other "unwanted sounds") produced in the digitization and processing of sound with computers.

Graphic Score: A musical score that consists of idiosyncratic, non-traditional, indeterminate symbols intended to encourage improvisation.

Hermeneutics: A philosophical movement premised on the primacy and irreducibility of interpretation in the understanding of human artifacts (texts, laws, institutions, etc.).

HipHop: An initially African-American form of aesthetic expression that developed in New York in the 1970s. The term originally named three closely related practices: graffiti, break dancing, and rap music. Today, the term is often used as a synonym for rap MCing and/or DJing.

Heavy Metal: A form of rock music characterized by aggressive, driving rhythms, highly amplified guitars, and often dark thematic elements. The style began in the late 1960s/early 1970s with groups such as Black Sabbath and Judas Priest and became more prominent in the late 1970s/early 1980s with groups such as Iron Maiden, Motorhead, Megadeth, and Metallica.

House: A genre of largely instrumental dance music that, in its early years, extended disco tracks and highlighted their more synthetic elements. It is characterized by a 4/4 kick drum pulse, ticking hi hats, and recurrent synthesizer vamps. The name derives from Chicago's Warehouse Club, where the style was first developed in the early 1980s. Since its inception, the genre has splintered into a host of sub-genres, e.g., Deep House, Acid House, Progressive House, Hip House, Micro-House, etc.

Illbient: A term coined by a group of Brooklyn DJs in 1986 to designate a form of dark, urban ambient music that combines elements of dub, drum 'n' bass, HipHop, and *musique concrète*.

Improvised Music: A genre of music related to free jazz but arising out of a different cultural and aesthetic milieu. Where free jazz is rooted in jazz and the history of African-American expression, improvised music more fully reflects the influences of Cageian experimental music and the classical avant-garde.

Indeterminacy: A term that describes the production of musical compositions (1) via chance techniques, or (2) that give performers a great degree of choice as to how to realize them.

Industrial Music: A form of punk rock and experimental electronic music characterized by the use of non-traditional instrumentation ranging from raw materials (glass, metal, wood, etc.) to the tools and machines that process these materials (hammers, drills, presses, etc.) to the manufactured objects themselves (phones, vacuum cleaners, televisions, radios etc.). Industrial music first arose in the mid-1970s with groups such as Cabaret Voltaire, Einstürzende Neubauten, and Throbbing Gristle.

Intelligent Techno, Intelligent Dance Music (IDM): Terms for electronic music rooted in Techno and dance music but intended less for the dance floor than for home listening. The "intelligent" tag stems from the *Artificial Intelligence* compilations, released by Warp in the early 1990s. Related to the slightly broader term "electronica."

Jungle: The original term for what became known as drum 'n' bass. The term refers to a Kingston, Jamaica club known as the Jungle, referenced in an early Jungle track. More recently, Jungle has come to name a darker, rougher form of drum 'n' bass influenced by Jamaican Dancehall.

Just Intonation, Just tuned: An ancient system of tuning in which the intervals are determined by the natural harmonic series. Just intonation is preferred by many minimalist composers for its acoustic purity. See equal temperament.

Krautrock: Term that refers to German rock groups of the late 1960s and 1970s (Can, Tangerine Dream, Faust, Kraftwerk, Neu! and others) that produced progressive rock influenced by minimalism, experimental music, and the classical avant-garde. Sometimes called "*kosmische Musik*," Krautrock is often characterized by an immersive motoric pulse and the creative use of electronics and studio effects.

MC: Acronym for "master of ceremonies." In HipHop, the vocalist or rapper.

Mesostic: A technique for the composition of texts pioneered by John Cage. A variation on acrostic writing, mesostics employ a name or phrase placed vertically down the middle of a page. A new text, read horizontally, is then composed making use of the letters in the vertical row.

Minimalism: A term coined by Michael Nyman and Tom Johnson in 1968 to refer to the early work of American counter-culture composers La Monte Young, Terry Riley, Philip Glass, and Steve Reich. The term generally describes compositions that display some or all of the following features: repetition, often of short modal musical phrases, subtle variation over long periods of time, harmonic stasis, and a steady pulse.

Mix: The fluid stream of music that a DJ creates by juxtaposing and layering tracks.

Mixer: An electronic device for combining several individual signals routed to one or more channels that can then be amplified or recorded.

Mobile Form: A principle of musical structure according to which the sequence and/or makeup of segments of a composition are variable at the time of performance (also known as "open form"). The term was coined by composers who admired the fluidity and indeterminacy of Alexander Calder's mobiles.

Modal Improvisation: A term applied to the improvisational style of saxophonist John Coltrane during his last years, Miles Davis' groups of the late 1960s and early 1970s, and others whose music moved toward harmonic stasis (or, at least, a marked decrease in the harmonic rhythm associated with bebop), and its concomitant extended playing on a single chord-scale.

Modernism: Though the term has a bewildering range of meanings, modernism often refers to a number of key tendencies in 20th century art: abstraction, an emphasis on form rather than meaning or content, a focus on phenomenological experience rather than realism, aesthetic autonomy, utopian progressivism, antipathy to mass culture, etc. The term is also often used as an umbrella term for the group of early 20th century avant-garde art movements that includes Futurism, Cubism, Fauvism, Dada, Bauhaus, etc.

Modernity: A broad historical term that generally encompasses Western history since the European Enlightenment of the 17th and 18th centuries.

Modular Synthesizer: A synthesizer composed of a series of independent circuits, or modules, that can be connected together in various ways to produce sounds.

Monophonic: Literally, "one voice," or an instrument, such as an analog synthesizer, that can only produce one pitch event at a time.

*Musique Concrète*: Music composed by editing recorded sounds. The term was coined by Pierre Schaeffer, a French radio broadcaster who pioneered the technique in the late 1940s.

No Wave: A short-lived musical movement centered in New York's Lower East Side during the late 1970s and early 1980s that merged punk rock with minimalism, experimental music, and performance art. The scene was captured on *No New York*, a compilation produced by Brian Eno in 1978.

*Objet sonore*, Sonorous object: A term coined by Pierre Schaeffer to describe the smallest self-contained particle of a soundscape. Though it may be referential (i.e., a "bell"), it is to be considered as pure sound, independent of it source and of any semantic content.

Onkyo: Literally (in Japanese) "reverberation of sound." The term has come to be applied to an improvisational practice prominent in Japan that explores the fine-grained textural details of acoustic and electronic sound.

Ontology, Ontological: The theory of what exists, of what there is. Inquiry into the very nature of a thing or of Being in general.

Open Work: Umberto Eco coined this term in 1959 to refer to works of literature and music that are, in a sense, deliberately unfinished and that call upon performers, readers, or listeners to complete or realize them.

Patch: A particular configuration of sound generators and sound modifiers on an analog or digital synthesizer.

Phenomenology, Phenomenological: A philosophical methodology founded by Edmund Husserl in the early 20th century, phenomenology attempts to describe the contents of experience irrespective of the sources, reality, truth or falsehood of this experience. Hence, phenomenological description draws no essential distinction between reality and appearance, perception and phantasy.

Plunderphonics: A term invented by Canadian composer John Oswald for his practice of sampling and humorously remixing pop music.

Polyphonic: Literally, "many voices," or an instrument, such as a digital synthesizer, that can produce more than one pitch event at a time.

Post-digital music: see "glitch music."

Postmodernism: Generally refers to a new aesthetic sensibility that emerged in the 1960s, characterized by a breakdown of the boundaries between high art and mass culture, the reemergence of explicit political and social concerns in art, the often ironic juxtaposition of references to heterogeneous historical or cultural styles, the rejection of modernism's utopian progressivism, etc.

Post-rock: A term coined by critic Simon Reynolds in 1995 to describe a form of music that uses rock instrumentation—guitar, bass, drums—in non-rock ways: to produce timbres and textures rather than power chords or melodies. Post-rock reveals the influence of DJ Culture and often supplements rock instrumentation with samplers, sequencers, turntables, and analog synthesizers.

Poststructuralism: An umbrella term for a group of (primarily French) philosophers and cultural theorists who emerged in the 1960s, among them Jacques Derrida, Jean Baudrillard, Michel Foucault, Julia Kristeva, Luce Irigaray, Jean-François Lyotard, and Gilles Deleuze. Poststructuralism is characterized by a rejection of metaphysical entities and epistemological foundations, and the insistence on the irreducible plurality of meaning.

Post-Techno: Any form of electronica genealogically related to Techno but departing from it in one way or another. Akin to "intelligent Techno" or "intelligent dance music."

Powerbook Music: Informal designation for a generation of composers and improvisers whose primary performance instrument is a laptop computer that utilizes various software applications for generating and processing sound.

Preset: A pre-programmed electronic timbre that can be called up quickly in performance on an analog or digital synthesizer.

Producer: Within electronica and DJ Culture, artists are generally termed "producers." The term is deliberately ambiguous, collapsing the traditional distinctions between the "musician" (who plays an instrument), the "composer" (who organizes the overall shape of a piece), the "producer"(who shapes the quality of the recorded sound), and the "engineer" (who handles the technical aspects of recording).

Ragga: Short for raggamuffin. A form closely associated with dancehall reggae.

Rave: A party or sound system usually held at a one-off venue (a warehouse, an open field, etc.) and centered around House, Techno, or drum 'n' bass music spun, often all-night, by a series of DJs.

Rave Culture: A term for the general cultural milieu (clothing, graphic design, drugs) surrounding rave and Techno.

Readerly Text: A term coined by literary theorist Roland Barthes to describe a kind of text that presents itself as a finished product with a self-contained range of meanings, and that limits reading to passive consumption. The term is contrasted with the "writerly text" and the "open work."

Reduced Listening: see "acousmatic listening."

Remix: The creation of a new musical work from pieces of some existing work or works. The remix usually contains some recognizable element of the original piece, though some more extreme remixes alter the original material beyond recognition.

Rhizome: A form of vegetation (such as grass) that has a horizontal, decentralized, connective structure. The term was used more generally by philosophers Gilles Deleuze and Félix Guattari to refer to any entity or collection of entities that exhibits such a structure.

Sample, Sampler, Sampling: A sample is a digital sound file containing a brief sound event, often taken from a piece of recorded music, that is incorporated into a new piece of music. A sampler is a device for capturing and manipulating samples. Sampling refers to the compositional and performance practice of collecting and utilizing digital sound files. The practice of sampling usually involves digitizing sounds from vinyl records, recording them *in situ*, and/or sharing them with other composers.

Semiotics: Semiotics is the science of signs (linguistic, gestural, visual, auditory, etc.) and their contextual meaning. The term is often used synonymously with structuralism and/or poststructuralism.

Sequencer: A piece of hardware or software that allows recorded sound elements to be played back in the exact sequences and relationships in which they were arranged.

Serialism: Often used as a synonym for 12-tone composition, the term is more properly used to describe a compositional technique that extends Schoenberg's 12-tone methodology to other musical parameters, such as pitch, rhythm, dynamics, register, and even timbre. An order of succession is established for any or all of these elements; and these successions are then repeated throughout the composition.

Schizophonia: A term coined by R. Murray Schafer to refer to the split between an original sound and its electro-acoustic reproduction.

Scratching: A turntablist technique originally developed by Grand Wizard Theodore that is performed by moving a vinyl record back and forth under the stylus, creating a distinctive percussive sound that has come to be associated with HipHop. There are many different types of scratch, including the crab, flare, orbit, strobe, twiddle, and others—names that refer to the scratch's sound, the hand motions and equipment set-up required to produce it, or the name of the DJ who developed it.

Selector: In reggae culture, the term for a DJ or person who plays records.

Signifier: The sensuous, material element of a sign, e.g., the particular sound of a spoken word considered separately from its meaning or reference.

Situationism: An artistic and political movement active in France during the 1960s. Situationists rejected the pervasive, media-dominated, capitalist commodity culture (which they dubbed "the society of the spectacle") and sought to subvert it via art and political action.

Soundscape: A term coined by R. Murray Schafer to describe a sound environment, either in the natural world or in any recorded medium.

Sound art: General term for works of art that focus on sound and are often produced for gallery or museum installation.

Sound System: From Jamaican reggae practice, the term describes a mobile DJ set-up that would provide open-air dance parties. Each sound system was run by a DJ or group of DJs who developed a particular style and competed with other DJs and sound systems.

Stochastic Music: A term coined by Iannis Xenakis to describe his use of models from probability theory in the composition of musical works.

Structural Listening: Diametrically opposed to Ambient listening, structural listening is concerned with the overall structure of a musical work and the logical relationship among its parts. The philosopher and music theorist Theodor Adorno considered this the only fully adequate mode of listening to music.

Structuralism: An intellectual movement centered in France during the 1950s and 1960s. Structuralism attempted to provide a general methodology for the human sciences based on the model of Saussure's linguistics, according to which language has meaning not by reference to a non-linguistic reality but by reference to differences and oppositions within the linguistic system itself.

Techno: An evolution of House developed in Detroit in the early 1980s, Techno is often faster than House and more mechanical, minimalist, dystopian, and futuristic. Early Techno combined the cyborg futurism of Kraftwerk and Afrika Bambaataa with the funk of George Clinton and Parliament. The term is sometimes used loosely as an umbrella term for contemporary electronic dance music.

Texture: Generally, texture refers to the quality of a sound or series of sounds that is a product of its pitch(es), timbre, and loudness. It can also refer to the quality of sound produced by a given combination of instruments, voices, or electronic sounds.

Timbre: Term that refers to the subjective qualities of a tone that are a function of its overtone content. Sometimes called "tone color."

Toasting: In reggae culture, the term for rapping or MCing.

Tonality, Tonal music: A term describing the harmonic conventions of most Western music (classical and popular) from the 18th Century to the present. Tonal music is music organized around a center, called the "tonic," and the scale of which the tonic is the principal tone. Also known as "functional harmony" and "common-practice" harmony.

Total Serialism: A term that usually refers to musical composition in which three or more sets of musical parameters are serialized (see "serialism" and "12-tone composition").

Track: Within DJ Culture, the term "track" means a particular piece of music. This usage derives from the terminology of audio recording, where "tracks" are the particular components of a song (the drum track, the guitar track, etc.) that are recorded independently of one another and then mixed together by the engineer. In DJ Culture, the term "track" is preferred to the term "song" because tracks are often seen not as completed entities but as sets of elements to be combined with other such elements by the DJ in the creation of a mix.

TripHop: A term coined in the early 1990s to describe the moody, downtempo HipHop of acts such as Massive Attack and Portishead, and releases on the Mo'Wax label.

Turntablism, Turntablist: A term first coined in 1995 by DJ Babu to describe a form of music in which turntables are used not merely as a device of reproduction (something with which to play recorded music) but as a device of production (something with which to manipulate sound and create music).

12-tone composition: A compositional technique developed by Arnold Schoenberg around 1920 as a way of treading a middle ground between traditional tonality and atonal composition. Schoenberg's method permits the composition of a work in which all pitches are related to a fixed ordering of the twelve chromatic tones. This "series" or "row" sets the basic intervallic character of the piece, and any vertical or horizontal construction of pitches will relate to the original row by one of four transformations: transposition, retrograde, inversion, or retrograde inversion.

Writerly Text: A term coined by literary theorist Roland Barthes to describe a kind of text that discourages the reader from passively consuming it and encourages the reader actively to contribute to its production of meaning. (See "readerly text" and "open work.")

# Selected Discography

## I. Music and Its Others: Noise, Sound, Silence
- Ashley, Robert, *Wolfman*, Alga Marghen ALGA 048.
- Borbetomagus, *Borbetomagus*, Agaric 1980.
- Cage, John, *48:15 (Nine Versions of 4' 33" by John Cage)*, Korm Plastics KP 3005.
- Chartier, Richard, *Of Surfaces*, LINE 008.
- Cowell, Henry, *New Music: Piano Compositions*, New Albion NA 103.
- Disinformation, *R&D2*, Ash International ASH 9.2.
- Duncan, John, *The Crackling*, Trente Oiseaux TOC961.
- Einstürzende Neubauten, *Strategies Against Architecture, Vol. I*, Mute CDSTUMM14.
- Günter, Bernhard, *Un Peu de Neige Salie*, Trente Oiseaux TOCSE01.
- JLIAT, *Still Life #5: 6 Types of Silence*, Edition XI.
- López, Francisco, *Untitled 74*, Authorised Version AV009.
- Malfatti, Radu, *Die Temperatur der Bedeutung/Das Profil des Schweigens*, Edition Wandelweiser EWR 9801.
- Merzbow, *Merzbox Sampler*, Extreme XLTD 003.
- Reed, Lou, *Metal Machine Music*, BMG ND 90670.
- Schafer, R. Murray and the World Soundscape Project, *The Vancouver Soundscape*, Cambridge CSR-2CD 9701.
- Throbbing Gristle, *D.O.A.: The Third and Final Report of Throbbing Gristle*, Mute 1094CD.
- Varèse, Edgard, *Arcana/Amériques/Ionisation/Offrandes/Density 21.5/Octandre/Intégrales*, New York Philharmonic/Ensemble InterContemporain, Pierre Boulez, Sony SMK 45844.
- Various, *Futurism and Dada Reviewed*, Les Temps Modernes LTM 2301.
- Various, *An Anthology of Noise and Electronic Music, Vol. 1*, Sub Rosa SR190.
- Various, *Lowercase Sound* and *Lowercase Sound 2002*, Bremsstrahlung 001/002.
- Xenakis, Iannis, *Electronic Music*, Electronic Music Foundation EMF CD 003.

## II. Modes of Listening
- Aphex Twin, *Selected Ambient Works, Vol. II*, Sire/Warner Bros 9 45482.
- Carter, Chris, *Outside the Circle of Fire*, Touch TO 37.
- Eno, Brian, *Ambient 1: Music for Airports*, Editions EG EEGCD 17.
- Eno, Brian, *Ambient 4: On Land*, Editions EG EEGCD 20.
- Ferrari, Luc, *Presque Rien*, INA-GRM INA C 2008.
- Lucier, Alvin, *Vespers and Other Early Works*, New World NW80604.
- Oliveros, Pauline, *Deep Listening*, New Albion NA022.
- López, Francisco, *La Selva*, V2_Archief V228.
- Satie, Erik, *Socrate*, Ensemble Erwartung, Bernard Degraupes, FNAC 592292.
- Schaeffer, Pierre, *L'Ouevre Musicale*, INA-GRM INA C 1006/7/8.
- Various, *A Brief History of Ambient*, Virgin AMBT 1/7243 8 39041 2 9.

### III. Music in the Age of Electronic Reproduction
- A Guy Called Gerald, *Black Secret Technology*, Juice Box JBLP25.
- Akufen, *My Way*, Force Inc, FIM 060 CD.
- Bach, Johann Sebastian, *The Well-Tempered Clavier*, Book I, Glenn Gould, Sony Classical WS2K 52600.
- Basinski, William, *Shortwavemusic*, Raster-Noton VYR012 LP.
- Beastie Boys, *Paul's Boutique*, Capitol CDP 7 91743 2.
- Byrne, David and Brian Eno, *My Life in a Bush of Ghosts*, Sire SRK6093.
- Cabaret Voltaire, *Methodology, The Attic Tapes (1974–78)*, Mute 9211CD.
- Cage, John, *Williams Mix*, on Various, *OHM: Early Gurus of Electronic Music, 1948–1980*, Ellipsis Arts CD 3670.
- Collins, Nicolas, *It Was a Dark and Stormy Night*, Trace Elements TE-1019.
- Czukay, Holger and Rolf Dammers, *Canaxis*, Mute/Spoon SPOONCD15.
- Davis, Miles, *On The Corner*, Columbia CK 53579.
- DISC, *2xCD*, Vinyl Communications VC-134.
- Dockstader, Tod, *Quatermass*, Starkland ST 201.
- Faust, *The Faust Tapes*, Recommended RER F2CD.
- Kid 606, *Down with the Scene*, Ipecac IPC-7.
- Mathieu, Stephan, *frequencyLib*, Ritornell RIT23.
- Meek, Joe, *I Hear a New World*, Cherry Red RPM 502.
- Negativland, *These Guys Are From England and Who Gives a Shit*, Seeland 0021.
- Ostertag, Bob, *Like a Melody, No Bitterness*, Seeland 508.
- Oswald, John, *69 Plunderphonics 96*, Seeland 515.
- Oval, *Systemisch*, Thrill Jockey THRILL032.
- Parliament, *Mothership Connection*, Mercury 440 077 03202.
- People Like Us, *Recyclopaedia Britannica*, Mess Media MESS 001CD.
- Perry, Lee "Scratch"/The Upsetters, *Super Ape*, Mango 162-539 417.
- Public Enemy, *It Takes a Nation of Millions to Hold Us Back*, Def Jam 314527 358.
- Riley, Terry, *Music for The Gift*, Organ of Corti CORTI01.
- Subotnick, Morton, *Silver Apples of the Moon/The Wild Bull*, Wergo WER 2035.
- Stockhausen, Karlheinz, *Hymnen*, Stockhausen Verlag CD10.
- Tenney, James, *Selected Works, 1961–1969*, New World NW80570.
- Wall, John, *Fractuur*, Utterpsalm CD3.

### IV. The Open Work
- Berio, Luciano, *Circles/Sequenza I/Sequenza III/Sequenza V*, Wergo WER 6021.
- Brown, Earle, *Music for Piano(s), 1951–1995*, David Arden, New Albion NA082.
- Brown, Earle, *Chamber Music*, Matchless MRCD52.
- Braxton, Anthony, *Quartet (Coventry) 1985*, Leo CD LR 204/205.
- Braxton, Anthony, *Compositions No. 10 & No. 16 (+ 101)*, Guillermo Gregorio et al., hat[now]ART 108.
- Cage, John, *Music of Changes*, Joseph Kubera, Lovely Music LCD 2053.
- Cage, John, *Concert for Piano and Orchestra/Atlas Eclipticalis*, The Orchestra of the S.E.M. Ensemble, Peter Kotik, Wergo WER 6216.
- Cardew, Cornelius, *Treatise*, Jim Baker et al., hat[now]ART 2-122.
- Feldman, Morton, *The Ecstasy of the Moment*, The BartonWorkshop, Etcetera KTC 3003.
- Frith, Fred, *Stone, Brick, Glass, Wood, Wire (Graphic Scores 1986–1996)*, I Dischi di Angelica IDA 014.

- Haubenstock-Ramati, Roman, *Graphic Music*, Eberhard Blum et al., hat[now]ART 101.
- Morris, Lawrence "Butch," *Testament: A Conduction Collection*, New World NW 80478.
- Rosenfeld, Marina, *The Sheer Frost Orchestra: Drop, Hop, Drone, Scratch, Slide and A for Anything*, Charhizma CHAR 018.
- Sonic Youth, *Goodbye 20th Century*, SYR 4.
- Stockhausen, Karlheinz, *Klavierstücke Vol. II*, Bernhard Wambach, Koch 310 009 H1.
- Various, *New York School 3*, hat ART CD 6176.
- Zorn, John, *Cobra*, Tzadik TZ 7335.
- Zorn, John, *The Parachute Years: 1977–1980*, Tzadik TZ 7316-7.

## V. Experimental Musics
- Ashley, Robert, *Automatic Writing*, Lovely Music LCD 1002.
- Basinski, William, *The Disintegration Loops*, 2o62 0201.
- Behrman, David, *Wave Train*, Algha Margen ALGA 020.
- Behrman, David, *Leapday Night*, Lovely Music LCD 1042.
- Bryars, Gavin, *The Sinking of the Titanic*, Point Music 446 061.
- Bryars, Gavin/Christopher Hobbs/John Adams, *Ensemble Pieces*, Editions EG EGED22 LP.
- Cage, John, *Variations I, II, and III*, Mode 129.
- Cage, John, *Cartridge Music*, on *Music for Merce Cunningham*, Mode 24.
- Cardew, Cornelius and the Scratch Orchestra, *The Great Learning*, Organ of Corti CORTI 21.
- Dunn, David, *Angels & Insects*, OO Discs 49.
- Eno, Brian, *Discreet Music*, Editions EG EEGCD 23.
- Eno, Brian and Robert Fripp, *No Pussyfooting*, Editions EEG EEGCD2.
- Feldman, Morton, *Routine Investigations et al.*, Ensemble Recherche, Auvidis Montaigne MO 782018.
- Feldman, Morton, *String Quartet (II)*, Ives Ensemble, hat[now]ART 4-144/1&2.
- Farmer's Manual, *Explorers_We*, Or SQUISH04.
- Fujieda, Mamoru, *Patterns of Plants*, Tzadik TZ 7025.
- Lucier, Alvin, *I Am Sitting in a Room*, Lovely Music LCD 1013.
- Lucier, Alvin, *Music on a Long Thin Wire*, Lovely Music LCD 1011.
- Marclay, Christian, *Record Without a Cover*, Locus Solus.
- Mathieu, Stephan, *Wurmloch Variationen*, Ritornell RIT 16.
- Mumma, Gordon, *Live-Electronic Music*, Tzadik TZ 7074.
- Oliveros, Pauline, *Alien Bog/Beautiful Soop*, Pogus 21012 CD.
- Oval, *Ovalprocess*, Thrill Jockey THRILL 081.
- Random Industries, *Selected Random Works*, Ritornell RIT015.
- Riley, Terry, *You're Nogood/Poppy No Good*, Organ of Corti CORTI 5.
- Reich, Steve, *Early Works*, Nonesuch 9 79169.
- Rzewski, Fredric, *Main Drag: Chamber Works*, Alter Ego Ensemble, Stradivarius STR 33631.
- Sonic Youth, *Goodbye 20th Century*, SYR 4.
- Tudor, David, *Rainforest (Versions I and IV)*, Mode 64.
- Various, *Music from the ONCE Festival 1961–1966*, New World NW80567.
- Various, *Not Necessarily "English" Music: A Collection of Experimental Music from Great Britain, 1960–1977*, Electronic Music Foundation EMF036.
- Various, *Flux Tellus*, Tellus 24.

- Wolff, Christian, *Burdocks*, Tzadik TZ 7071.

## VI. Improvised Musics
- AMM, *AMMusic 1966*, Matchless ReR AMMCD.
- Bailey, Derek, *Aida*, Dexter's Cigar dex5.
- Bailey, Derek, *Guitar, Drums 'n' Bass*, Avant AVAN 060.
- Brötzmann, Peter, *Machine Gun*, FMP CD 24.
- Art Ensemble of Chicago, *Americans Swinging in Paris* (*Les Stances à Sophie/People in Sorrow*), EMI 5396672.
- Ayler, Albert, *Spiritual Unity*, ESP 1002.
- Brotherhood of Breath, *From Bremen to Bridgwater*, Cuneiform RUNE 182/183.
- Coleman, Ornette, *Change of the Century*, Atlantic 781341.
- Coleman, Ornette, *Free Jazz*, Atlantic 78137.
- Coltrane, John, *Ascension*, Impulse 314 543 413.
- Coltrane, John, *The Olatunji Concert*, Impulse 3145891202.
- Gayle, Charles, *Touchin' on Trane*, FMP CD 48.
- Harriott, Joe, *Free Form*, Polygram POLY 538184.
- Jackie-O Motherfucker, *Liberation*, Road Cone RoCo 031.
- Lewis, George, *Voyager*, Avant AVANT 014.
- M.I.M.E.O., *Music in Movement Electronic Orchestra*, Perdition Plastics PER 009.
- Mitchell, Roscoe, *Sound*, Delmark DE 408.
- Music Improvisation Company, *1968–1971*, Incus CD12.
- Musica Elettronica Viva, *Spacecraft/Unified Patchwork Theory*, Algha Marghen ALGA 038.
- No Neck Blues Band, *Letters from the Earth*, Sound@One S@1 26/27.
- Parker, Evan, *Monoceros*, Chronoscope CHR 2004.
- Parker, William, *O'Neal's Porch*, AUM Fidelity AUM022.
- Parker, William & the Little Huey Creative Orchestra, *Raincoat in the River*, Eremite MTE 036.
- Sonic Youth With Jim O'Rourke, *Invito Al Cielo*, SYR 3 CD.
- Spontaneous Music Ensemble, *Karyobin*, Chronoscope CPE 2001.
- Spring Heel Jack, *Live*, Thirsty Ear THI57130.2.
- Sun Ra, *The Heliocentric Worlds of Sun Ra, vols. 1 and 2*, ESP Disk ESP 1014/1017.
- Sun Ra, *The Magic City*, Evidence ECD 22069.
- Taylor, Cecil, *Unit Structures*, Blue Note B21Y-84237.
- Taylor, Cecil, *The Tree of Life*, FMP CD 98.
- Test, *Live/Test*, Eremite MTE-021.
- Vandermark, Ken, *Acoustic Machine*, Atavistic ALP128CD.
- Various, *Amplify 02: Balance*, Erstwhile ERST033-040.
- Various, *Improvised Music from Japan*, IMJ 10-CD.
- Various, *Jazz Actuel*, Charly 707.
- Various, *Wild Flowers: The New York Jazz Loft Sessions*, Knitting Factory Classics KCR-3037.

## VII. Minimalisms
- Aphex Twin, *Icct Hedral*, Warp WAP 063 CDP.
- Branca, Glenn, *The Ascension*, Acute ACT 002 CD.
- Brinkmann, Thomas, *Klick*, Max-Ernst MAXE 001CD.
- Brinkmann, Thomas, *X100*, Supposé LP.
- Budd, Harold, *Pavilion of Dreams*, Editions EG EEGCD30.

- Cale, John/Tony Conrad/Angus MacLise/La Monte Young/Marian Zazeela, *Inside the Dream Syndicate, Vol. 1: Day of Niagara*, Table of the Elements TOE-CD-74.
- Chatham, Rhys, *An Angel Moves to Fast to See*, Table of the Elements TOE-CD-57.
- Conrad, Tony, *Four Violins*, TOE-CD-33.
- Conrad, Tony and Faust, *Outside the Dream Syndicate*, Table of the Elements TOE-CD-03.
- DBX, *Losing Control*, Accelerate ACC102 LP.
- Dreyblatt, Arnold, *Animal Magnetism*, Tzadik TZ 7004.
- Farben, *Textstar*, Klang Elektronik KLANG CD 07.
- Flynt, Henry, *You are My Everlovin'/Celestial Power*, Recorded NAEM01.
- Fullman, Ellen, *Body Music*, Experimental Intermedia XI 109.
- Gibson, Jon, *Two Solo Pieces*, New Tone NT6756.
- Glass, Philip, *Music in Twelve Parts*, The Philip Glass Ensemble, Virgin 91311.
- Grubbs, David, *Banana Cabbage, Potato Lettuce, Onion Orange*, Table of the Elements, TOE-CD-30.
- Hood, Robert, *Minimal Nation*, Axis AX-007 2x12".
- Ikeda, Ryoji, *Matrix*, Touch TO 44.
- Kraftwerk, *Autobahn*, Kling Klang/EMI EMI46153.
- Licht, Alan, *Rabbi Sky*, Siltbreeze SILT076.
- Maurizio, *Maurizio*, Maurizio M-CD.
- M:I:5, *Maßstab* 1:5, Profan CD 3.
- Mills, Jeff, *Waveform Transmission Vol. 1*, Tresor 011 CD.
- The Necks, *Aether*, Recommended ReR NECKS2.
- Neu!, *Neu!* Astralwerks ASW 30780.
- Niblock, Phill, *YPGPN*, Experimental Intermedia XI 121.
- Mills, Jeff, *Purposemaker Compilation*, Purposemaker/Neuton NEUPM01.
- Moore, Anthony, *Pieces from the Cloudland Ballroom*, Blueprint BP 327 CD.
- Oliveros, Pauline, *Primordial Lift*, Table of the Elements TOE-CD-53.
- O'Rourke, Jim, *Happy Days*, Revenant 101.
- Palestine, Charlemagne, *Four Manifestations on Six Elements*, Barooni BAR 014.
- Papa M, "I Am Not Lonely With Cricket," on *Live from a Shark Cage*, Drag City DC170CD.
- Phuture, *Acid Tracks*, Trax TX142 12".
- Plastikman, *Consumed*, NovaMute NOMU65CD.
- Radigue, Eliane, *Adnos I-III*, Table of the Elements TOE-CD-55.
- Reich, Steve, *Works 1965–95*, Nonesuch 79451.
- Riley, Terry, *In C*, Columbia COL 94983.
- Riley, Terry, *Reed Streams*, Organ of Corti CORTI 02.
- Spacemen 3, *Dreamweapon*, Space Age ORBIT001 CD.
- Studio 1, *Studio Eins*, Studio 1 STU CD1.
- Suicide, *Suicide*, Mute/Blast First BFFP133CD.
- The Velvet Underground, *The Velvet Underground & Nico*, Polydor 31453 1250 2.
- U.N.K.L.E./Tortoise, "Djed (Bruise Blood Mix)," Thrill Jockey, THRILL 12.1 12".
- Villalobos, Ricardo, *Alcachofa*, Playhouse PLAYCD008.
- Young, La Monte, *The Well-Tuned Piano 81x25*, Gramavision 18-8701.
- Various, *Clicks & Cuts, Vols. I and II*, Mille Plateaux MP 79/98.
- Various, *Reich Remixed*, Nonesuch 79552.
- Various Arists, *Superlongevity 2*, Perlon PERL23CD.
- Various, *Basic Channel*, Basic Channel BCD 001.

## VIII. DJ Culture

- Burroughs, William S., *Break Through in Grey Room*, Sub Rosa SR008.
- Cage, John, *Imaginary Landscape #1*, on Various, *Early Modulations: Vintage Volts*, Caipirinha CAI2027.2.
- Cul de Sac, *Death of the Sun*, Strange Attractors SAAH011.
- DJ Disk, *Ancient Termites*, Bomb Hip-Hop BHH2009.
- DJ Spooky, *Songs of a Dead Dreamer*, Asphodel ASP0961.
- 4 Hero, *Parallel Universe*, Selector SEL3.
- Gang Starr, "DJ Premier in Deep Concentration," on Various, *Masters of the 1 & 2: History's Greatest DJs*, Priority PS 51169.
- Goldie, *Timeless*, FFRR 697-124 073.
- Grandmaster Flash, "The Adventures of Grandmaster Flash on the Wheels of Steel," on Various, *Masters of the 1 & 2: History's Greatest DJs*, Priority PS 51169.
- Grandmaster Flash, *The Official Adventures of Grandmaster Flash*, Strut STRUT 011CD.
- Ground Zero, *Ground Zero*, God Mountain GMCD-002.
- Institut für Feinmotorik, *Penetrans*, Staubgold STAUB 25 CD.
- Jeck, Philip, *Vinyl Coda I–III*, Intermedium, INTER 002.
- King Tubby, *King Tubby's Special 1973–1976*, Trojan CDTRD 409.
- Marclay, Christian, *Records 1981–1989*, Atavistic ALP 062.
- Marclay, Christian, *More Encores*, Recommended RER CM1.
- Marclay, Christian & Otomo Yoshihide, *Moving Parts*, Asphodel, ASPH 2001.
- Mixmaster Mike, *Anti-Theft Device* ASP0985.
- Pablo, Augustus, *King Tubby Meets the Rockers Uptown*, Shanachie 44019.
- Rosenfeld, Marina, *theforestthegardenthesea*, Charhizma CHAR003.
- Schaefer, Janek, *Skate/Rink*, AudiOH! AUDIOH 11.
- Tetreault, Martin, *Des pas et des mois*, Ambiances Magnétiques AM 017.
- Tone, Yasunao, *Yasunao Tone*, Asphodel ASPH 2011.
- Tortoise, *Millions Now Living Will Never Die*, Thrill Jockey THRILL 025.
- Various, *Macro Dub Infection Vols. 1 and 2*, Virgin AMBT 7 724384047528/GYR 6638.
- Various, *Metalheadz: Platinum* Breakz, FFRR 697 124 121.
- Various, *Monsters, Robots, and Bug Men: A User's Guide to the Rock Hinterland*, Virgin AMBT11 7243 8 4175 2 0.
- Various, *Retro Techno/Detroit Definitive*, Network, RETRO CD 1.
- Various, *Return of the DJ Volumes 1* and *2*, Bomb Hip-Hop BHH2002/3.
- Various, *Street Jams: Electric Funk, Vol. 1*, Rhino 70575.
- Various, *Techno! The New Dance Sound of Detroit*, Ten DIXCD75.
- Various, *The House That Trax Built*, Trax UK, TRX UK CD001.
- Various, *True People: The Detroit Techno Album*, React REACT CD 071.
- Various, *Turntable Solos*, Valve/Amoebic AMO-VA-01 CD.
- X-ecutioners, *Built from Scratch*, Loud/Columbia 086411.
- Yoshihide, Otomo, *Sound Factory*, Gentle Giant GG021 CD.

## IX. Electronic Music and Electronica

- Alva Noto, *Transform*, Mille Plateaux MP 102.
- Aphex Twin, *Classics*, R&S RS 95 035CD.
- Autechre, *Chiastic Slide*, Warp 49.
- Babbitt, Milton, *Ensembles for Synthesizer*, on *New Electronic Music from the Leaders of the Avant-Garde*, SONY (Japan) SICC78.

- Cascone, Kim, *Residualism*, Ritornell RITOR19.
- Fennesz, *Endless Summer*, Mego 035.
- Fenn O'Berg, *The Magic Sound of Fenn O'Berg*, Mego 031.
- Köner, Thomas, *Teimo/Permafrost*, Mille Plateaux MP CD 35.
- Kontakt der Jünglinge, *1*, Die Stadt DS 34.
- Kraftwerk, *Trans-Europe Express*, Capitol CDP 0777 7 46473 2 8.
- Matthews, Kaffe, *cd ebb + flow*, Annetteworks AWCD0005-6.
- Microstoria, *Init Ding*, Thrill Jockey THRILL031.
- More, Ikue, *Labyrinth*, Tzadik TZ 7068.
- Mouse on Mars, *Niun Niggung*, Thrill Jockey THRILL076.
- Oliveros, Pauline, *Electronic Works*, Paradigm PD04.
- Panasonic, *Kulma*, Mute/Blast First 9032.
- Parmegiani, Bernard, *De Natura Sonorum*, INA-GRM INA C 3001.
- Pole, *CD1*, Matador OLE 339.
- Radian, *Rec.Extern*, Thrill Jockey THRILL113.
- Roden, Steve, *Four Possible Landscapes*, Trente Oiseaux, TOC 005.
- Scanner, *Lauwarm Instrumentals*, Sulphur SULCD002.
- So, *So*, Thrill Jockey THRILL130.
- Squarepusher, *Feed Me Weird Things*, Rephlex CAT037CD.
- Stockhausen, Karlheinz, *Elektronische Music 1952–60*, Stockhausen Verlag CD 3.
- Varèse, Edgard, *Poème électronique*, on Various, *Electro Acoustic Music: Classics*, Neuma 450-74.
- Various, *Artificial Intelligence, Vols. I* and *II*, Warp CD6/CD023.
- Various, *Columbia-Princeton Electronic Music Center 1961–1973*, New World Records NW80521.
- Various, *Early Modulations: Vintage Volts*, Caipirinha CAI2027.2.
- Various, *Early Electronic Music: Cologne—WDR,* BVHaast CD9106.
- Various, *Microscopic Sound*, Caipirinha CAI2021.
- Various, *OHM: Early Gurus of Electronic Music, 1948–1980*, Ellipsis Arts CD 3670.
- Various, *Pioneers of Electronic Music: American Masters*, CRI CD 611.
- Vitiello, Stephen, *Bright and Dusty Things*, New Albion NA 115 CD.
- Wabi Sabi, *Wabi Sabi*, a-Musik a3.

# Selected Bibliography

I. **Music and Its Others: Noise, Sound, Silence**

Attali, Jaques. *Noise: The Political Economy of Music*. Trans. Brian Massumi. Minneapolis: University of Minnesota Press, 1985.

Bangs, Lester. "A Reasonable Guide to Horrible Noise." In *Psychotic Reactions and Carburetor Dung*, 301–304. New York: Vintage, 1988.

Burdick, Alan. "Now Hear This: Listening Back on a Century of Sound." *Harper's* (July 2001): 70–77.

Cage, John. *Silence: Lectures and Writings*. Hanover, NH: Wesleyan University/University Press of New England, 1961.

Cowell, Henry. *Essential Cowell: Selected Writings on Music*, ed. Dick Higgins. Kingston, NY: McPherson & Company, 2002.

Davies, Hugh. "The Sound World, Instruments, and Music of Luigi Russolo." *Resonance* 2, no. 2: http://www.l-m-c.org.uk.

Duguid, Brian. "A Prehistory of Industrial Music." ESTWeb: http://www.hyperreal.org/intersection/zines/est/articles.

England, Phil, "Acoustic Ecology: Making the Nature Scene." *The Wire* 226 (December 2002): 40–47.

Feldman, Morton. "Sound, Noise, Varèse, Boulez." In *Give My Regards to Eighth Street: Collected Writings of Morton Feldman*, ed, B.H. Friedman, 1–2. Cambridge, MA: Exact Change, 2000.

Gracyk, Theodore. "Pump up the Volume." In *Rhythm and Noise: An Aesthetics of Rock*, 99–124. Durham, NC: Duke University Press, 1996.

Hargus, Billy Bob and Eric Kauz. "Music as a Deadly Weapon." *Perfect Sound Forever* (November 1996/97): http://www.furious.com/perfect/weapon.html.

Hegarty, Paul. "Full With Noise: Theory and Japanese Noise Music." *CTheory* (November 8, 2001): http://www.ctheory.net/text_file.asp?pick = 314.

Hensley, Chad. "The Beauty of Noise: An Interview with Masami Akita of Merzbow." *EsoTerra* 8 (Winter 1999): http://www.esoterra.org/merzbow.htm.

Hinant, Guy-Marc, "TOHU BOHU: Considerations on the Nature of Noise in 78 Fragments." *Leonardo Music Journal* 13 (2003): 43–46.

Hodgkinson, Tim. "An Interview with Pierre Schaeffer." In *The Book of Music and Nature*, ed. David Rothenberg and Marta Ulvaeus, 34–44. Hanover, NH: Wesleyan University/University Press of New England, 2001.

Ilic, David. "Extreme Noise Terrors." *The Wire* (November 1994): http://www.thewire.co.uk/archive/essays/japanese_underground.html.

Kahn, Douglas. *Noise, Water, Meat*. Cambridge, MA: MIT Press, 1999.

Keiser, Garrett. "Sound and Fury: The Politics of Noise in a Loud Society." *Harper's* (March 2001): 39–48.

Kopf, Biba. "The Primer: Einstürzende Neubauten." *The Wire* 194 (April 2000): 38–44.

López, Francisco. "Schizophonia vs. l'Objet Sonore: Soundscapes and Artistic Freedom." *eContact* 1.4 (February 23, 1998): http://cec.concordia.ca/econtact/Ecology/Lopez.html.

Morgan, Robert P. "'A New Musical Reality': Futurism, Modernism, and 'The Art of Noises.'" *Modernism/Modernity* 1, no. 3 (1994): 129–51.

Palombini, Carlos. "Pierre Schaeffer (1910–1995) and Pierre Henri (1927– )." In *Music of the Twentieth-Century Avant-Garde: A Biocritical Sourcebook*, ed. Larry Sitsky, 432–45. Westport, Connecticut: Greenwood Press, 2002.

Pratella, Balilla. "Manifesto of Futurist Musicians." In *Futurist Manifestoes*, ed. Umbro Apollonio, 31–38. New York: Viking, 1973.

Radano, Ronald. "Interpreting Muzak: Speculations on Musical Experience in Everyday Life." *American Music* 7 (4) (1989): 448–60.

Reynolds, Simon. "Noise." In *Blissed Out: The Raptures of Rock*, 57–62. London: Serpent's Tail, 1990.

Russo, Marry and Daniel Warner. "Rough Music, Futurism, and Postpunk Industrial Noise Bands." *Discourse* 10 (Fall–Winter 1987–88): 55–76.

Russolo, Luigi. "The Art of Noises: Futurist Manifesto." In *The Art of Noises*, trans. Barclay Brown,23–30. New York: Pendragon Press, 1986.

Sanglid, Torben. *The Aesthetics of Noise*. Copenhagen: Datanom, 2002. http://www.datanom.com/noise/the_essay/

Schafer, R. Murray. *The Tuning of the World*. New York: Alfred A. Knopf, 1977. Reprinted as *The Soundscape: Our Sonic Environment and the Tuning of the World*. Rochester, VT: Destiny Books, 1994.

———. "Music, Non-Music, and the Soundscape." In *Companion to Contemporary Musical Thought*, Vol. I, ed. John Paynter et al., 34–45. London: Routledge, 1992.

Schwartz, Hillel. "Beyond Tone and Decibel: The History of Noise." *The Chronicle of Higher Education* (January 9, 1998): B8.

Sedgwick, John. "Cut Out That Racket." *The Atlantic Monthly*, 268, no. 5 (March 1991): 50–55.

Sinker, Mark. "Loud Bangs and Bestial Noises." *The Wire* 211 (September 2001): 44–49.

———. "Destroy All Music: The Futurists' Art of Noises." In *Undercurrents: The Hidden Wiring of Modern Music*, ed. Rob Young, 181–92. London: Continuum/The Wire, 2002.

Slouka, Mark. "Listening for Silence: Notes on the Aural Life." *Harper's* (April 1999): 63–68.

Sontag, Susan. "The Aesthetics of Silence." In *Styles of Radical Will*, 3–34. New York: Farrar, Straus and Giroux, 1969.

Strauss, Neil. "Crash Course: A Noise Music Primer." *Ear* (October 1998): 10–13.

Tone, Yasunao. "John Cage and Recording." *Leonardo Music Journal* 13 (2003): 11–15.

Twomey, Chris. "Developments from Industrial Music: Noise and Appropriation." In *Sound by Artists*, ed. Dan Lander and Micah Lexier, 267–81. Toronto/Banff: Art Metropole/Walter Phillips Gallery, 1990.

Vale, V. and Andrea Juno, eds. *Industrial Culture Handbook*. San Francisco: Re/Search, 1983.

Varèse, Edgard. "The Liberation of Sound." In *Contemporary Composers on Contemporary Music*, Expanded Edition, ed. Elliott Schwartz and Barney Childs, 196–208. New York: Da Capo, 1998.

Young, Rob. "Exotic Audio Research." *The Wire* 157 (March 1997).

## II. Modes of Listening

Ackerman, Diane. "Hearing." In *A Natural History of the Senses*, 173–225. New York: Random House, 1990.

Adorno, Theodor. "Types of Musical Conduct." In *Introduction to the Sociology of Music*, 1–20. New York: Seabury Press, 1976.

Barthes, Roland. "Listening." In *The Responsibility of Forms: Critical Essays on Music, Art, and Representation*, trans. Richard Howard, 245–60. New York: Hill and Wang, 1985.

Berendt, Joachim-Ernst. *The Third Ear: On Listening to the World*. New York: Henry Holt & Company Inc., 1992.

Bottum, J. "The Soundtracking of America." *Atlantic Monthly* 285, no. 3 (March 2000): 567–70.

Bull, Michael. *Sounding Out the City: Personal Stereos and the Management of Everyday Life*. New York: Berg, 2000.

Chambers, Iain. "A Miniature History of the Walkman." *New Formations* 11 (1990): 1–4. Reprinted as "The Aural Walk." In *Migrancy, Culture, Identity*, 49–53. London: Routledge, 1994.

Chion, Michel. "The Three Listening Modes." In *Audio/Vision: Sound on Screen*, 25–34. New York: Columbia University Press, 1994.

Cox, Christoph. "Abstract Concrete: Francisco López and the Ontology of Sound." *Cabinet* 2 (Spring 2001): 42–45.

Cutler, Chris. "Scale." *Unfiled: Music Under New Technology* (ReR/Recommended Sourcebook 0402): 59–64.

du Gay, Paul et al., eds. *Doing Cultural Studies: The Story of the Sony Walkman*. London: Sage, 1997.

Davis, Erik. "Acoustic Cyberspace." http://www.techgnosis.com/acoustic.html.

Eno, Brian. "Ambient Music." In *A Year With Swollen Appendices*. London: Faber and Faber, 1996.

———. "Aurora Musicalis." *Artforum* (Summer 1986): 76–79.

Freire, Sérgio. "Early Musical Impressions from Both Sides of the Loudspeaker." *Leonardo Music Journal* 13 (2003): 67–71.

Idhe, Don. *Listening and Voice: A Phenomenology of Sound*. Athens, Ohio: Ohio University Press, 1976.

Lanza, Joseph. *Elevator Music: A Surreal History of Muzak, Easy-Listening, and Other Moodsong*. New York: Picador, 1994.

Lester, Toby. "Secondhand Music." *The Atlantic Monthly* 279, no. 4 (April 1997): 42–47.

López, Francisco. "Blind Listening." In *The Book of Music and Nature*, ed. David Rothenberg and Marta Ulvaeus, 163–68. Hanover, NH: Wesleyan University/University Press of New England, 2001.

McLuhan, Marshall. "Visual and Acoustic Space." In *The Global Village: Transformations in World Life and Media in the 21st Century*. New York: Oxford University Press, 1989.

Miller, Paul D. "Chill: The New Ambient—Surround Sound." *Artforum* (January 1995): 60–62, 101.

Oliveros, Pauline. "Some Sound Observations" and "The Poetics of Environmental Sound." In *Software for People: Collected Writings 1963–80*, 17–28. Baltimore: Smith Publications, 1984.

———. "The Earth Worm Also Sings: A Composer's Practice of Deep Listening." *Leonardo Music Journal* 3 (1993): 35–38.

Prendergast, Mark. *The Ambient Century: from Mahler to Trance—The Evolution of Sound in the Electronic Age*. New York and London: Bloomsbury, 2000.

Reynolds, Simon. "Chill: The New Ambient—Muzak of the Fears." *Artforum* (January 1995): 60–62, 101.

Rösing, Helmut. "Listening Behaviour and Musical Preferences in the Age of 'Transmitted Music'." *Popular Music* 4 (1984): 119–49.

Rothenberg, David and Marta Ulvaeus. *The Book of Music and Nature*. Hanover, NH: Wesleyan University/University Press of New England, 2001.

Smalley, Dennis. "The Listening Imagination: Listening in the Electroacoustic Era." In *Companion to Contemporary Musical Thought*, Vol. I, ed. John Paynter et al., 514–554. London: Routledge, 1992.

Stockfelt, Ola. "Adequate Modes of Listening." In *Keeping Score: Music, Disciplinarity, Culture*, ed. David Schwarz et al., 129–46. Charlottesville, VA: University of Virginia Press, 1997.

Thompson, Emily. *The Soundscape of Modernity: Architectural Acoustics and the Culture of Listening in America, 1900–1933*. Cambridge: MIT Press, 2002.

Welsch, Wolfgang. "On the Way to an Auditive Culture." In *Undoing Aesthetics*, trans. Andrew Inkpin, 150–67. London: Sage, 1997.

Westerkamp, Hildegard. "Listening and Soundmaking: A Study of Music-as-Environment." In *Sound by Artists*, ed. Dan Lander and Micah Lexier, 227–34. Toronto/Banff: Art Metropole/Walter Phillips Gallery, 1990.

## III. Music in the Age of Electronic (Re)production

Adorno, Theodor. "The Curves of the Needle," "The Form of the Phonograph Record," and "Opera and the Long-Playing Record." In *Essays on Music*, ed. Richard Leppert, 277–87. Berkeley: University of California Press, 2002.

Beadle, Jeremy J. *Will Pop Eat Itself? Pop Music in the Soundbite Era*. London: Faber and Faber, 1993.

Chanan, Michael. *Repeated Takes: A Short History of Recording and its Effects on Music*. London: Verso, 1995.

Collins, Nicolas. "Exploded View: The Musical Instrument at Twilight." *Resonance* 3, no. 1: http://www.l-m-c.org.uk.

Corbett, John. "Brothers from Another Planet: The Space Madness of Lee 'Scratch' Perry, Sun Ra, and George Clinton." In *Extended Play: Sounding Off from John Cage to Dr. Funkenstein*, 724. Durham, NC: Duke University Press, 1994.

Cox, Christoph. "Sampling in Classical Music." *Pulse!* (June 2000): 50.

Cutler, Chris. "Necessity and Choice in Musical Forms." In *File Under Popular: Theoretical and Critical Writings on Music*, 22–38. New York: Autonomedia, 1993.

———. "Plunderphonics." In *Sounding Off: Music as Subversion/Resistance/Revolution*, ed. Ron Sakolsky and Fred Wei-han Ho, 67–85. New York: Autonomedia, 1996.

———. "Interview with Tod Dockstader." *Unfiled: Music Under New Technology* (ReR/Recommended Sourcebook 0402): 8–17.

Davies, Hugh. "A History of Recorded Sound." In *Poésie Sonore Internationale*, ed. Henri Chopin, 13–40. Paris: Jean-Michel Place Editeur, 1979.

———. "A History of Sampling." In *Unfiled: Music Under New Technology* (ReR/Recommended Sourcebook 0401): 5–12.

Davis, Erik. "Recording Angels: The Esoteric Origins of the Phonograph." In *Undercurrents: The Hidden Wiring of Modern Music*, ed. Rob Young, 15–24. London: Continuum/The Wire, 2002.

Dery, Mark. "Black to the Future: Interviews with Samuel R. Delany, Greg Tate, and Tricia Rose." In *Flame Wars: The Discourse of Cyberculture*. Durham: Duke University Press, 1995.

Durant, Alan. "A New Day for Music? Digital Technologies in Contemporary Music Making." In *Culture, Technology and Creativity in the Late Twentieth Century*, ed. Philip Hayward. London: John Libbey, 1991.

Eisenberg, Evan. *The Recording Angel: Explorations in Phonography*. New York: McGraw-Hill, 1987.

Eno, Brian. "The Studio as Compositional Tool." *Down Beat* 50, no. 7 (July 1983): 56–7, and 50, no. 8 (August 1983): 50–2.

Goodwin, Andrew. "Sample and Hold: Pop Music in the Digital Age of Reproduction." In *On Record: Rock, Pop, and the Written Word*, ed. Simon Frith and Andrew Goodwin, 258–73. New York: Pantheon, 1990.

Gould, Glenn. "The Prospects of Recording," "Music and Technology," and "The Grass is Always Greener in the Outtakes: An Experiment in Listening." In *The Glenn Gould Reader*, ed. Tim Page, 331-68. New York: Alfred A. Knopf, 1984.

Gracyk, Theodore. "I'll Be Your Mirror: Recording and Representing" and "Record Consciousness." In *Rhythm and Noise: An Aesthetics of Rock*, 37–98. Durham, NC: Duke University Press, 1996.

Grivel, Charles. "The Phonograph's Horned Mouth." In *Wireless Imagination: Sound, Radio, and the Avant-Garde*, ed. Douglas Kahn and Gregory Whitehead, 31–61. Cambridge, MA: MIT Press, 1992.

Hayles, N. Katherine. "Voices Out of Bodies, Bodies Out of Voices: Audiotape and the Production of Subjectivity." In *Sound States: Innovative Poetics and Acoustical Technologies*, ed. Adalaide Morris, 74–96. Chapel Hill: University of North Carolina Press, 1997.

Hitchcock, H. Wiley. ed. *The Phonograph and Our Musical Life*. New York: Institute for Studies in American Music, 1980.

Hosokawa, S. "The Walkman Effect." *Popular Music* 4 (1984): 165–80.

Hodgkinson, Tim. "Sampling, Power, and Real Collisions." *Resonance* 5, no. 1 (November 1996): http://www.l-m-c.org.uk/.

James, Robin, ed. *Cassette Mythos*. New York: Autonomedia, 1992.

Kevin, Kelly. "Where Music Will Be Coming From." *New York Times Magazine* (March 17, 2002).

Kittler, Friedrich. *Gramophone, Film, Typewriter*. Stanford: Stanford University Press, 1999.

Lange, Art. "*Musique Concrète*: The Primer." *The Wire* 174 (August 1998): 50–55.

Lee, Iara. "Interview with Teo Macero." *Perfect Sound Forever* (September 1997): http://www.furious.com/perfect/teomacero.html.

Levin, Thomas Y. "For the Record: Adorno on Music in the Age of Its Technological Reproducibility." *October* 55 (1990): 23–47.

Manning, Peter. "The Influence of Recording Technologies on the Early Development of Electroacoustic Music." *Leonardo Music Journal* 13 (2003): 5–10.

Morton, David. *Off the Record: The Technology and Culture of Sound Recording in America*. New Brunswick, NJ: Rutgers University Press, 2000.

Mowitt, Josh. "The Sound of Music in the Era of Its Electronic Reproducibility." In *Music and Society: The Politics of Composition, Performance, and Reception*, ed. Richard Leppert and Susan McClary, 173–97. Cambridge: Cambridge University Press, 1987.

Negativland et al. *Fair Use: The Story of the Letter U and the Number 2*. Concord, CA: Seeland, 1995.

Oswald, John. "Bettered by the Borrower: The Ethics of Musical Debt." *Whole Earth Review* (Winter 1987): 104–8.

———. "Creatigality." In *Sounding Off: Music as Subversion/Resistance/Revolution*, ed. Ron Sakolsky and Fred Wei-han Ho, 87–89. New York: Autonomedia, 1996.

———. "Plunderphonics, or Audio Piracy as a Compositional Prerogative." In Negativland et al. *Fair Use: The Story of the Letter U and the Number 2*. Concord, CA: Seeland, 1995.

Penman, Ian. "On the Mic: How Amplification Changed the Voice for Good." In *Undercurrents: The Hidden Wiring of Modern Music*, ed. Rob Young, 25–34. London: Continuum/The Wire, 2002.

Perkins, Stephen. "Plagiarism: An Interview with the Tape-Beatles." In *Sounding Off: Music as Subversion/Resistance/Revolution*, ed. Ron Sakolsky and Fred Wei-han Ho, 217–24. New York: Autonomedia, 1996.

Pouncey, Edwin. "Rock Concrète: Counterculture Plugs In To the Academy." In *Undercurrents: The Hidden Wiring of Modern Music*, ed. Rob Young, 153–62. London: Continuum/The Wire, 2002.

Reynolds, Simon. "Digital Psychedlia: Sampling and the Soundscape." In *Generation Ecstasy: Into the World of Techno and Rave Culture*, 40–55. Boston: Little, Brown, and Co., 1998.

Rose, Tricia. "Soul Sonic Forces: Technology, Orality, and Black Cultural Practice in Rap Music." In *Black Noise: Rap Music and Black Culture in Contemporary America*, 62–96. Hanover, NH: Wesleyan University/University Press of New England, 1994.

Sanjek, David. " 'Don't Have to DJ No More': Sampling and the 'Autonomous' Creator." In *The Construction of Authorship: Textual Appropriation in Law and Literature*, ed. Martha Woodmansee and Peter Jaszi, 343–60. Durham, NC: Duke University Press, 1994.

Schaefer, Janek. "AudiOh!: Appropriation, Accident, and Alteration." *Leonardo Music Journal* 11 (2001): 71–76.

Sherburne, Philip. "Splitting Bits, Closing Loops: Sound on Sound." *Leonardo Music Journal* 13 (2003): 79–81.

Stuart, Caleb. "Damaged Sound: Glitching and Skipping Compact Discs in the Audio of Yasunao Tone, Nicolas Collins and Oval." *Leonardo Music Journal* 13 (2003): 47–52.

Sousa, John Philip. "The Menace of Mechanical Music" (1906). Reprinted in *Computer Music Journal* 17:1 (Spring 1993): 14–18.

Sterne, Jonathan. *The Audible Past: Cultural Origins of Sound Reproduction*. Durham: Duke University Press, 2003.

Strauss, Neil ed. *Radiotext(e)*. New York: Semiotext(e), 1993.

Taylor, Timothy D. *Strange Sounds: Music, Technology & Culture*. New York: Routledge, 2001.

Théberge, Paul. *Any Sound You Can Imagine: Making Music/Consuming Technology*. Hanover, NH: Wesleyan University/University Press of New England, 1997.

Thornton, Sarah. "Authenticities from Record Hops to Raves (and the History of Disc Culture)." In *Club Cultures: Music, Media, and Subcultural Capital*, 26–86. Hanover, NH: Wesleyan University/University Press of New England, 1996.

Toop, David. "A Brief History of Sampling." *The Wire* 139 (September 1995).

## IV. The Open Work

Bailey, Derek. "The Composer." In *Improvisation: Its Nature and Practice in Music*, 59–81. New York: Da Capo, 1992.

Behrman, David. "What Indeterminate Notation Determines." *Perspectives of New Music* 3:2 (Spring 1964): 58–73.

Boulez, Pierre. "Alea." *Perspectives of New Music* 3:1 (Winter 1964): 42–53.

Brown, Earle. "Form in New Music." *Source* 1 (January 1967): 48–51.

———. "Notation and Performance of New Music." *Musical Quarterly* 72 no. 2 (1985): 180–201.

———. "Transformations and Developments of a Radical Aesthetic." *Current Musicology* 67/68 (Fall-Winter 1999): 39–57.

Cage, John. "Composition as Process, Part II: Indeterminacy." In *Silence: Lectures and Writings*, 35–40. Hanover, NH: Wesleyan University/University Press of New England, 1961.

Cardew, Cornelius. "Notation—Interpretation, etc." *Tempo* 58 (Summer 1961): 17–33.

———. "On the Role of the Instructions in the Interpretation of Indeterminate Music." In *Treatise Handbook*, xiv–xvi. London: Edition Peters, 1971.

Charles, Daniel. "Entr'acte: 'Formal' or 'Informal' Music." *Musical Quarterly* (January 1965): 144–65.

Childs, Barney. "Indeterminacy and Theory: Some Notes." *The Composer* (June 1969).

Cox, Christoph. "Classical 101: Graphic Scores." *Pulse!* (October 1999): 79.

Eco, Umberto. "Poetics of the Open Work." In *The Open Work*, trans. Anna Cancogni, 1–23. Cambridge, MA: Harvard University Press, 1989.

Feldman, Morton. "Predeterminate/Indeterminate." In *Give My Regards to Eighth Street: Collected Writings of Morton Feldman*, ed. B.H. Friedman, 33–40. Cambridge, MA: Exact Change, 2000.

Goldsmith, Kenneth. "Scored Improvisation." *Pulse!* (April 1999).

Hamilton, Andy. "The Music of Chance: Musical Dice Men From John Cage to John Zorn." In *Undercurrents: The Hidden Wiring of Modern Music*, ed. Rob Young, 209–21. London: Continuum/The Wire, 2002.

Haubenstock-Ramati, Roman. "Notation—Material—Form." *Perspectives of New Music* (Fall-Winter 1965): 96–101.

Heffley, Mike. *The Music of Anthony Braxton*. Westport, CT: Greenwood Press, 1996.

Lange, Art. Liner Notes to John Zorn *Cobra*. Hat Hut hat Art CD 60401/2.

Lock, Graham. *Forces in Motion: Anthony Braxton and the Meta-Reality of Creative Music, Interviews and Tour Notes, England 1985*. London: Quartet, 1988.

Lock, Graham, ed. *Mixtery: A Festschrift for Anthony Braxton*. London: Stride, 1995.

Nyman, Michael. "Indeterminacy 1960–70: Ichiyanagi, Ashley, Wolff, Cardew, Scratch Orchestra." In *Experimental Music: Cage and Beyond*, 93–118. New York: Schirmer, 1974.

Reynolds, Roger. "Indeterminacy: Some Considerations." *Perspectives of New Music* 4:1 (Fall/Winter 1965): 136–40.

———. "It(')s Time." *Electronic Music Review* 7 (July 1968).

Sutherland, Roger. "Graphics and Indeterminacy." In *unfiled: Music Under New Technology*, ReR/Recommended Sourcebook 0401 (1994): 80–93.

Whitehead, Kevin. "A Field Guide to *Cobra*." *Pulse!* (November 1994): 46-48, 112.

Zorn, John. "John Zorn." In *The Muse That Sings: Composers Speak About the Creative Process*, ed. Ann McCutchan. New York: Oxford University Press, 1999.

## V. Experimental Musics

Ashley, Robert. *Music With Roots in the Aether: Interviews with and Essays About Seven American Composers.* Köln: MusikTexte, 2000.

Ballantine, Christopher. "Towards an Aesthetic of Experimental Music." *Musical Quarterly* LXIII, no. 2 (April 1997): 224–46.

Bernstein, David W. "John Cage and the Aesthetic of Indifference." In *The New York School of Music and Visual Arts*, ed. Steven Johnson. New York: Routledge, 2002.

Cage, John, "Experimental Music," "Experimental Music: Doctrine," and "History of Experimental Music in the United States." In *Silence: Lectures and Writings*, 7–17, 67–75. Hanover, NH: Wesleyan University/University Press of New England, 1961.

———. *Themes & Variations.* Barrytown, NY: Station Hill, 1982.

———. "A Composer's Confessions." *Musicworks* 52 (Spring 1992): 6–15.

———. *Musicage: Cage Muses on Words, Art, Music*, ed. Joan Retallack. Hanover, NH: Wesleyan University Press/University Press of New England, 1996.

Cameron, Catherine M. *Dialectics in the Arts: The Rise of Experimentalism in American Music.* Westport, CT: Praeger, 1996.

Cardew, Cornelius, ed. *Scratch Music.* London: Latimer New Directions, 1972.

———. *Stockhausen Serves Imperialism and Other Articles.* London: Latimer, 1974.

Clark, Philip. "Morton Feldman: The Primer." *The Wire* 210 (August 2001): 40–47.

Cox, Christoph. "The Jerrybuilt Future: The Sonic Arts Union, ONCE Group and MEV's Live Electronics." In *Undercurrents: The Hidden Wiring of Modern Music*, ed. Rob Young, 35–44. London: Continuum/The Wire, 2002.

De Lio, Thomas, ed. *The Music of Morton Feldman.* Westport, CT: Greenwood Press, 1996.

Duckworth, William. *Talking Music: Conversations with John Cage, Philip Glass, Laurie Anderson and Five Generations of American Experimental Composers.* New York: Schirmer, 1995.

Dyson, Francis. "The Ear That Would Hear Sounds in Themselves: John Cage 1935–1965." In *Wireless Imagination: Sound, Radio, and the Avant-Garde*, ed. Douglas Kahn and Gregory Whitehead, 373–407. Cambridge, MA: MIT Press, 1992.

Eno, Brian. "Generating and Organizing Variety in the Arts." *Studio International* (Nov./Dec. 1976): 279–83.

———. Liner Notes to *Discreet Music.* Editions EG EEGCD 23.

Feldman, Morton. *Give My Regards to Eighth Street: Collected Writings of Morton Feldman*, ed. B. H. Friedman. Cambridge, MA: Exact Change, 2002.

Gagne, Cole. *Soundpieces 2: Interviews with American Composers.* Metuchen, NJ: Scarecrow Press, 1993.

Gagne, Cole and Tracy Caras. *Soundpieces: Interviews with American Composers.* Metuchen, NJ: Scarecrow Press, 1982.

Gena, Peter. "Freedom in Experimental Music: The New York Revolution." *Tri-Quarterly* 52 (1981): 223–43.

Gena, Peter and Jonathan Brent, ed. *A John Cage Reader.* New York: C.F. Peters, 1982.

Gray, Louise. "John Cage: The Primer." *The Wire* 161 (July 1997): 48–51.

Griffiths, Paul. "Gavin Bryars." In *New Sounds, New Personalities: British Composers of the 1980's in Conversation*, 148–59. London: Faber and Faber, 1985.

Gross, Jason. "Interview with Christian Wolff." *Perfect Sound Forever* (April 1998): http://www.furious.com/perfect/christianwolff.html.

Herwitz, Daniel. "The Security of the Obvious: On John Cage's Musical Radicalism." *Critical Inquiry* 14 (Summer, 1988).

Holmes, Thom. *Electronic and Experimental Music: Pioneers in Technology and Composition*, 2nd edition. New York: Routledge, 2002.

James, Richard S. "ONCE: Microcosm of the 1960s Musical and Multimedia Avant-Garde." *American Music* 5, no. 4 (Winter 1987): 359–90.

Kahn, Douglas. "The Latest: Fluxus and Music." In *In the Spirit of Fluxus*, ed. Elizabeth Armstrong and Joan Rothfuss, 101–21. Minneapolis: Walker Art Center, 1993.

Kostelanetz, Richard, ed. *John Cage: An Anthology*. New York: Da Capo, 1991.

Lewis, George E. "Experimental Music in Black and White: The AACM in New York, 1970–1985." *Current Musicology* 71–73 (Spring 2001–Spring 2002): 100–157.

López, Francisco. "Cagean Philosophy: A Devious Version of the Classical Procedural Paradigm." In *Sonic Process*, ed. Christine Van Assche, 111–15. Barcelona: Actar, 2003.

Lucier, Alvin. "Origins of a Form: Acoustical Exploration, Science and Incessancy." *Leonardo Music Journal* 8 (1998): 5-11.

———. *Reflections: Interviews, Scores, Writings*. Köln: MusikTexte, 1995.

Miller, Leta E. "ONCE and Again: The Evolution of a Legendary Festival." Liner notes to *Music from the ONCE Festival 1961–1966*, New World NW80567: http://www.newworldrecords.org/linernotes/80567.pdf.

Mumma, Gordon. "The ONCE Festival and How It Happened." *Arts in Society* 4, no. 2 (1967): 380–98.

Nicholls, David. *American Experimental Music, 1890–1940*. Cambridge: Cambridge University Press, 1990.

Nicholls, David, ed. *The Cambridge Companion to John Cage*. Cambridge: Cambridge University Press, 2002.

Nyman, Michael. "Cage/Cardew." *Tempo* (December 1973).

———. *Experimental Music: Cage and Beyond*. Cambridge: Cambridge University Press, 1999.

Oliveros, Pauline. *The Roots of the Moment: Collected Writings 1980–1996*. New York: Drogue, 1998.

———. *Software for People: Collected Writings 1963–1980*. Baltimore: Smith Publications, 1984.

Parsons, Michael. "The Scratch Orchestra and the Visual Arts." *Leonardo Music Journal* 11 (2001): 5–11.

———. "Systems in Art and Music." *Musical Times* 117 (October 1976).

Potter, Keith. "Just the Tip of the Iceberg: Some Aspects of the Music of Gavin Bryars." *Contact* (1981).

Pritchett, James. *The Music of John Cage*. Cambridge: Cambridge University Press, 1993.

Rockwell, John. "The American Experimental Tradition and Its Godfather (John Cage)." In *All American Music: Composition in the Late Twentieth Century*, 47–59. New York: Vintage, 1983.

Shultis, Christopher. *Silencing the Sounded Self: John Cage and the American Experimental Tradition*. Boston: Northeastern University Press, 1998.

Smith, Geoff and Nicola Walker Smith, eds. *New Voices: American Composers Talk about Their Music*. Portland, OR: Amadeus Press, 1995.

Sterne, Theresa. "Interview with David Behrman." *Perfect Sound Forever* (August 1997): http://www.furious.com/perfect/behrman.html.

Tamm, Eric. *Brian Eno: His Music and the Vertical Color of Sound*. Boston: Faber and Faber, 1989.

Taylor, Timothy D. "Moving in Decency: The Music and Radical Politics of Cornelius Cardew." *Music & Letters* 79 (November 1998): 555–76.

———. "A Music of One's Own: Pauline Oliveros." In *Global Pop: World Music, World Markets*, 99–112. New York: Routledge, 1997.

Tilbury, John. "Cornelius Cardew." *Contact* 26 (Spring 1983).

———. "The Experimental Years: A View from the Left." *Contact* 22 (Summer 1981).

Varela, Daniel. "Interview with Frederic Rzewski." *Perfect Sound Forever* (March 2003): http://www.furious.com/perfect/rzewski.html.

Wolff, Christian. *Writings and Conversations*. Köln: MusikTexte, 1999.

Zimmerman, Walter. *Desert Plants: Conversations with 23 American Musicians*. Vancouver, B.C.: A.R.C. Publications, 1976.


**VI. Improvised Musics**

Abrams, Muhal Richard and John Shenoy Jackson. "Association for the Advancement of Creative Musicians." *Black World* 23, no. 1 (November 1973): 72–74.

Ake, David. "Re-Masculating Jazz: Ornette Coleman, 'Lonely Woman,' and the New York Jazz Scene in the Late 1950s." *American Music* 16.1 (1998): 25–44.

Arias, Ricardo. "I Know It's Only Noise but I Like It: Scattered Notes on the Pleasures of Experimental Improvised Music." *Leonardo Music Journal* 12 (2002): 31–32.

Bailey, Derek. *Improvisation: Its Nature and Practice in Music*. New York: Da Capo, 1992.

Bangs, Lester. "Free Jazz/Punk Rock." *Monocular Times*: http://www.monoculartimes .co.uk/texts/songs/freejazzpunkrock_2.shtml.

Bartlett, Andrew W. "Cecil Taylor, Identity Energy and the Avant-Garde African-American Body." *Perspectives of New Music* 33 (1995): 274–93.

Baxter, Ed. "Davey Williams Interview." *LMC News* (December 1991): http://www.craig nutt.com/raudelunas/russell/fredlane/daveywilliams.html.

Burnett, Kelly. "Interview with La Donna Smith." *Perfect Sound Forever* (August 2003): http://www.furious.com/perfect/ladonnasmith.html.

Cardew, Cornelius. "Towards an Ethic of Improvisation." *Treatise Handbook*, xvii–xx. London: Edition Peters, 1971.

Childs, Barney and Christopher Hobbs, ed. "Forum: Improvisation." *Perspectives of New Music* 21 (1982–83): 26–91.

Christmann, Günter. "Free Improvisation." *Improvisor* 4 (1984): 35–38.

Corbett, John. "Ephemera Underscored: Writing Around Free Improvisation." In *Jazz Among the Discourses*, ed. Krin Gabbard, 217–40. Durham, NC: Duke University Press, 1994.

———. *Extended Play: Sounding Off from John Cage to Dr. Funkenstein*. Durham: Duke University Press, 1995.

Crispell, Marilyn. "Elements of Improvisation." In *Arcana: Musicians on Music*, ed. John Zorn, 190–92. New York: Granary Books, 2000.

Dean, Roger T. *New Structures in Jazz and Improvised Music Since 1960*. Philadelphia: Open University Press, 1992.

Durant, Alan. "Improvisation in the Political Economy of Music." In *Music and the Politics of Culture*, ed. Christopher Norris, 252–82. New York: St. Martin's Press, 1989.

Frith, Fred. "Tapped Teeth—Try Different Speeds: Notebook Extracts 1978–96." In *Arcana: Musicians on Music*, ed. John Zorn, 311–24. New York: Granary Books, 2000.

Gross, Jason. "Interview with Cecil Taylor." *Perfect Sound Forever* (January 2001): http://www.furious.com/perfect/ceciltaylor.html.

Hamilton, Andy. "The Aesthetics of Imperfection." *Philosophy* 65, no. 253 (July 1990): 323–40.

Hargus, Billy Bob. "The Real Godfathers of Punk." *Perfect Sound Forever* (July 1996): http://www.furious.com/perfect/jazzpunk.html.

Ekkehard, Jost. *Free Jazz*. New York: DaCapo, 1994.

Keenan, David. "Fire Music: The Primer." *The Wire* 208 (June 2001): 42–49.

Lange, Art. "The Art Ensemble of Chicago: The Primer." *The Wire* 198 (August 2000): 38–43.

Lewis, George E. "Improvised Music After 1950: Afrological and Eurological Perspectives." *Black Music Research Journal* 16 (1996): 91–122.

Lewis, George E. "Teaching Improvised Music: An Ethnographic Memoir." In *Arcana: Musicians on Music*, ed. John Zorn, 78–109. New York: Granary Books, 2000.

Litweiler, John. *The Freedom Principle: Jazz after 1958*. New York: DaCapo, 1990.

Mandel, Howard. *Future Jazz*. Oxford: Oxford University Press, 1999.

Morris, Lawrence "Butch." "Theory and Contradiction: Notes on Conduction." Liner notes to *Testament: The Conduction Collection*. New World NW 80478: http://www.newworldrecords.org/linernotes/80478.pdf.

Ochs, Larry. "Structured Improvisation." In *Arcana: Musicians on Music*, ed. John Zorn, 325–35. New York: Granary Books, 2000.

Otomo, Yoshidide, "Leaving the Jazz Cafe: A Personal View of Japanese Improvised Music in the 1970s." *Resonance* 4, no. 2: http://www.l-m-c.org.uk.

Pignon, Paul. "Far from Equilibrium." *unfiled: Music Under New Technology,* ReR/Recommended Sourcebook 0401 (1994): 37–42.

Prévost, Edwin. "The Arrival of a New Musical Aesthetic: Extracts from a Half-Buried Diary." *Leonardo Music Journal* 9 (1999): 63–67.

———. *No Sound is Innocent*. Matching Tye near Harlow: Copula, 1995.

Richards, Sam. *Sonic Harvest: Towards Musical Democracy*. Oxford: Amber Lane Press, 1992.

Rockwell, John. "Jazz, Group Improvisation, Race & Racism (The Art Ensemble of Chicago)" and "Free Jazz, Body Music & Symphonic Dreams (Ornette Coleman)." In *All-American Music: Composition in the Late Twentieth Century*, 164–75, 185–97. New York: Knopf, 1983.

Roe, Tom. "Generation Ecstasy: New York's Free Jazz Continuum." In *Undercurrents: The Hidden Wiring of Modern Music*, ed. Rob Young, 249–62. London: Continuum/The Wire, 2002.

Rosenfeld, Marina. "The Sheer Frost Orchestra: A Nail Polish Bottle, A Guitar String and the Birth of an Orchestra." *Leonardo Music Journal* 12 (2002): 59–60.

Rzewski, Frederic. "Little Bangs: A Nihilist Theory of Improvisation." *Current Musicology* 67/68 (Fall–Winter 1999): 377–86.

———. "Plan for Spacecraft." *Source* 3 (January 1968): 66–68.

Small, Christopher. "On Improvisation." In *Music of the Common Tongue: Survival and Celebration in Afro-American Music*, 281–310. Hanover: Wesleyan University Press/University Press of New England, 1998.

Smith, Leo. "Creative Music and the AACM" (excerpt from *Notes: 8 Pieces*). In *Keeping Time: Readings in Jazz History*, ed. Robert Walser, 315–323. New York: Oxford University Press, 1999.

Spellmann, A.B. "Cecil Taylor," and "Ornette Coleman." In *Black Music: Four Lives*, 1–150. New York: Schocken, 1966.

Sansom, Matthew. "Imaging Music: Abstract Expressionism and Free Improvisation." *Leonardo Music Journal* 11 (2001): 29–34.

Szwed, John F. *Space is the Place: The Life and Times of Sun Ra*. New York: Da Capo, 1998.

———. "Sun Ra: The Primer." *The Wire* 163 (September 1997): 46–49.

Toop, David. "Frames of Freedom: Improvisation, Otherness, and the Limits of Spontaneity." In *Undercurrents: The Hidden Wiring of Modern Music*, ed. Rob Young, 233–48. London: Continuum/The Wire, 2002.

Williams, Davey. "Toward a Philosophy of Improvisation." *Improvisor* 4 (1984): 32–34.

Wilner, Valerie. *As Serious as Your Life: The Story of the New Jazz*. Westport, CT: Lawrence Hill, 1980.

Witherden, Barry. "The Primer: Ornette Coleman." *The Wire* 181 (March 1999): 46–51.

**VII. Minimalisms**

Adams, John. "In Conversation with Jonathan Sheffer." *Perceptible Processes: Minimalism and the Baroque*, ed. Claudia Swan et al., 76–82. New York: Eos, 1997.

Berkowitz, Kenny. "Minimal Impact: The Sons of Minimalism." *Option* 77 (November/ December 1997): 49–55.

Bernard, Jonathan W. "The Minimalist Aesthetic in the Plastic Arts and In Music." *Perspectives of New Music* 31 (1993): 86–132.

Boon, Marcus. "The Eternal Drone: Good Vibrations, Ancient to the Future." In *Undercurrents: The Hidden Wiring of Modern Music*, ed. Rob Young. 59–70. London: Continuum/The Wire, 2002.

Cardew, Cornelius. "One Sound: La Monte Young." *Musical Times* (1966).

Chatham, Rhys. "Composer's Notebook: Toward a Musical Agenda for the Nineties." Kalvos & Damian's New Music Bazaar: http://kalvos.org/chatess1.html.

Conrad, Tony. "an EARful: *Four Violins* and *Early Minimalism*," "LYssophobia: on *Four Violins*," "MINor premise," "nAMIng," and "smsigyILIS." Liner notes to Tony Conrad, *Early Minimalism, Volume 1*. Table of the Elements TOE-33-CD.

———. "Inside the Dream Syndicate." *Film Culture* 41 (Summer 1966): 5–8.

Duckworth, William. *Talking Music: Conversations with John Cage, Philip Glass, Laurie Anderson and Five Generations of American Experimental Composers*. New York: Schirmer, 1995.

Duckworth, William and Richard Fleming, eds. *Sound and Light: La Monte Young and Marian Zazeela*. Bucknell Review XL, no. 1. Lewisburg, PA: Bucknell University Press, 1996.

Duguid, Brian. "Early Minimalism: The Primer." *The Wire* 206 (April 2001): 50–57.

Gagne, Cole. *Soundpieces 2: Interviews with American Composers*. Metuchen, NJ: Scarecrow, 1993.

Gann, Kyle. "A Forest from the Seeds of Minimalism: An Essay on Postminimal and Totalist Music." *Berliner Gesellschaft für Neue Musik* (1998): http://home.earthlink .net/~kgann/postminimalism.html.

———. "La Monte Young's The Well-Tuned Piano." *Perspectives of New Music* 31 (1993): 134–62.

———. "Minimal Music, Maximal Impact," *New Music Box* 31, vol. 3, no. 7 (November 2001): http://www.newmusicbox.org/page.nmbx?id = 31tp00.

Glass, Philip. *Music by Philip Glass*. New York: Harper and Row, 1987.

Hitchcock, H. Wiley. "Minimalism in Art and Music: Origins and Aesthetics." In *Classic Essays on Twentieth-Century Music,* ed. Richard Kostelanetz and Joseph Darby. New York: Schirmer, 1996.

Karolyi, Otto. "The Minimalists." In *Modern American Music: From Charles Ives to the Minimalists*, 101–19. London: Cygnus Arts, 1996.

Licht, Alan. "The History of La Monte Young's Theatre of Eternal Music." *Forced Exposure* 16 (1990): 60–69.

Licht, Alan. "Excavation of the Minimalists." *Pulse!* (May 1999).

Mellers, Wilfrid. "A Minimalist Definition." *Musical Times* (1984).

Mertens, Wim. *American Minimal Music.* Trans. J. Hautekier. London: Kahn and Averill, 1983.

Nyman, Michael. "Against Intellectual Complexity in Music." *October* 13 (1980): 81–89.

———. "La Monte Young: Lost in the Drone Zone." *Rolling Stone* (13 February 1975).

———. "Minimal Music, Determinacy and the New Tonality." In *Experimental Music: Cage and Beyond*, 139–71. Cambridge: Cambridge University Press, 1999.

O'Rourke, Jim. "Information Overload." *Pulse!* (May 1999).

Palmer, Robert. "A Father Figure for the Avant-Garde." *The Atlantic Monthly* 247, no. 5 (May 1981): 48–56.

Page, Tim. "Framing the River: A Minimalist Primer." *High Fidelity* (November 1981).

Pelinsky, Ramon. "Upon Hearing a Performance of *The Well-Tuned Piano*: An Interview with La Monte Young and Marian Zazeela." *Parachute* 19 (1980).

Polin, Claire. "Why Minimalism Now?" In *Music and the Politics of Culture*, ed. Christopher Norris, 226–39. New York: St. Martin's Press, 1989.

Potter. Keith. *Four Musical Minimalists.* Cambridge: Cambridge University Press, 2000.

Pouncey, Edwin. "La Monte Young on Record." *The Wire* 178 (December 1998): http://www.thewire.co.uk/archive/essays/la_monte_young.html.

Reich, Steve. *Writings on Music, 1965–2000.* Oxford: Oxford University Press, 2002.

Reinhard, Johnny. "A Conversation with La Monte Young and Marian Zazeela." *Ear* 7/5 (1982–83).

Rockwell, John. "The Orient, the Visual Arts & the Evolution of Minimalism (Philip Glass)." In *All-American Music: Composition in the Late Twentieth Century*, 109–22. New York: Knopf, 1983.

Schwarz, Robert K. *Minimalists.* London: Phaidon, 1996.

———. "Steve Reich: Music as a Gradual Process." *Perspectives of New Music* (1980–81): 374–92, and (1981–82): 226–86.

Sherburne, Philip. "MicroHouse: Rules of Reduction." *The Wire* 209 (July 2001): 18–25.

———. "Thumbnail Music: Six Artists Talk About Minimalism." *Urban Sounds* 2, no. 1 (2000/2001): http://www.urbansounds.com/us_current/thumbnail.

Smith, Geoff and Nicola Walker Smith, eds. *New Voices: American Composers Talk about Their Music.* Portland, OR: Amadeus Press, 1995.

Sterne, Theresa. "Interview with Terry Riley." *Perfect Sound Forever* (March 1997): http://www.furious.com/perfect/terryriley.html.

Strickland, Edward. *Minimalism: Origins.* Bloomington: Indiana University Press, 1993.

Strickland, Edward. *American Composers: Dialogues on Contemporary Music.* Bloomington: Indiana University Press, 1987–90.

Varela, Daniel. "Interview with Charlemagne Palestine." *Perfect Sound Forever* (June 2002): http://www.furious.com/perfect/charlemagnepalestine.html.

Warburton, Dan. "A Working Terminology for Minimal Music." *Intégral* 2 (1988).

Webber, Mark. "Dream Encounters: Interview with La Monte Young." *The Wire* 178 (December 1998): 34–45.

Young, La Monte. "Notes on The Well-Tuned Piano." Liner notes to *The Well-Tuned Piano 81x25*. Gramavision 18-8701.

Young, La Monte, and Marian Zazeela. *Selected Writings*. Munich: Friedrich, 1969.

Young, La Monte, and Morton Feldman."The Limits of Composition." *Resonance* 7, no 1 (December 1998).

## VIII. DJ Culture

Adorno, Theodor. "The Curves of the Needle," "The Form of the Phonograph Record," and "Opera and the Long-Playing Record." In *Essays on Music*, ed. Richard Leppert, 277–87. Berkeley: University of California Press, 2002.

Bruno, Franklin. "The DJs New Lexicon." *Da Capo Best Music Writing 2002*, ed. Jonathan Lethem and Paul Bresnick. Cambridge, Mass: Da Capo, 2002.

Burroughs, William S. "The Cut-Up Method of Brion Gysin." In *The Third Mind*, by William Burroughs and Brion Gysin. New York: Viking, 1978.

———. "The Invisible Generation." In *The Ticket that Exploded*, 205–17. New York: Grove, 1968.

Brewster, Bill and Frank Broughton. *Last Night a DJ Saved My Life: The History of the Disc Jockey*. New York: Grove, 2000.

Chopin, Henri. "William Burroughs." In *Poésie Sonore Internationale*. Paris: Jean-Michel Place Editeur, 1979.

Comer, M. Tye. "Culture Shock: The Rise of the DJ in America." *CMJ New Music Monthly* (February 1998).

Concannon, Kevin. "Cut and Paste: Collage and the Art of Sound." In *Sound by Artists*, ed. Dan Lander and Micah Lexier, 161–82. Toronto/Banff: Art Metropole/Walter Phillips Gallery, 1990.

Cox, Christoph. "Versions, Dubs, and Remixes: Realism and Rightness in Aesthetic Interpretation." In *Interpretation and Its Objects: Studies in the Philosophy of Michael Krausz*, 285–92. Amsterdam: Rodopi, 2003.

Davis, Erik. "Dub, Scratch, and the Black Star: Lee Perry on the Mix": http://www.tech gnosis.com/dub.html.

Diliberto, John. "Pierre Schaeffer and Pierre Henry: Pioneers in Sampling." *Electronic Musician* (December 1986): 54–59, 72.

Ehrlich, Luke. "X-Ray Music: The Volatile History of Dub." In *Reggae International*, ed. Stephen Davis and Peter Simon, 105–10. New York: R&B, 1982.

Eshun, Kodwo. *More Brilliant Than the Sun: Adventures in Sonic Fiction*. London: Quartet Books, 1998.

Eshun, Kodwo and Edward George. "Ghostlines: Migration, Morphology, Mutations." In *Sonic Process*, ed. Christine Van Assche, 101–8. Barcelona: Actar, 2003.

Géfin, Laszlo K. "Collage Theory, Reception, and the Cut-ups of William Burroughs." *Literature and the Other Arts: Perspectives on Contemporary Literature* 13 (1987).

Gelling, Randy. "Turntablism." *Perfect Sound Forever* (June 2000): http://www.furious .com/perfect/turntablism.html.

Gross, Jason. "Interview with Christian Marclay." *Perfect Sound Forever* (March 1998): http://www.furious.com/perfect/christianmarclay.html.

———. "Interview with Otomo Yoshidide." *Perfect Sound Forever* (May 1998): http://www.furious.com/perfect/otomo.html.

Gysin, Brion. *Back in No Time: The Brion Gysin Reader*, ed. Jason Weiss. Middletown, CT: Wesleyan University Press, 2001.

Hebdige, Dick. *Cut 'n' Mix: Culture, Identity and Carribean Music*. London: Routledge, 1987.

Katz, David. "Lee Perry: The Primer," *The Wire* 189 (November 1999): 42-49.

Kelley, Mike. "An Academic Cut-Up, in Easily Digestible Paragraph-Size Chunks; Or, The New King of Pop: Dr. Konstantin Raudive." *Grey Room* 11 (Spring 2003): 22–43.

Kahn, Douglas, "Christian Marclay's Early Years: An Interview." *Leonardo Music Journal* 13 (2003): 17–21.

Kun, Josh. "A Select History of Found Sound." *Option* 73 (March–April 1997): 64–8.

Lange, Art. "The Primer: Musique Concrète." *The Wire* 174 (August 1998): 50–55.

Levin, Thomas Y. "For the Record: Adorno on Music in the Age of Its Technological Reproducibility." *October* 55 (1990): 23–47.

———. "Indexicality Concrète: The Aesthetic Politics of Christian Marclay's Gramophonia." *Parkett* 56 (1999): 162–67.

Lydenberg, Robin. "Sound Identity Fading Out: William Burroughs' Tape Experiments." In *Wireless Imagination: Sound, Radio, and the Avant-Garde*, ed. Douglas Kahn and Gregory Whitehead, 409–37. Cambridge, MA: MIT Press, 1992.

Macaulay, Scott. "Interview with Christian Marclay." In *The Kitchen Turns Twenty: A Retrospective Anthology*, ed. Lee Morrissey, 65–69. New York: The Kitchen, 1992.

Martin, Kevin. "Scientist Meets the Ghost Captain: A Dub Genealogy." Liner notes to *Macro Dub Infection Vol. 1*, Virgin AMBT 7 724384047528.

Miller, Paul D. (DJ Spooky). "Cartridge Music: Of Palimpsests and Parataxis, or How to Make a Mix." *Parkett* 46 (1996): 183–88.

———. *Rhythm Science*. Cambridge, MA: MIT Press, 2004.

Moholy-Nagy, László. "New Form in Music: Potentialities of the Phonograph," "Production-Reproduction," and "New Potentialities of the Phonograph." In *Moholy-Nagy*, ed. Krisztina Passuth, 289–90, 291–92. New York: Thames and Hudson, 1985.

Poschardt, Ulf. *DJ Culture*. Trans. Shaun Whiteside. London: Quartet, 1998.

Potash, Chris, ed. *Reggae, Rasta, Revolution: Jamaican Music from Ska to Dub*. New York: Schirmer, 1997.

Reighley, Kurt. *Looking for the Perfect Beat: The Art and Culture of the DJ*. New York: MTV Books, 2000.

Reynolds, Simon. "In the Mix: DJ Culture and Remixology, 1993–97." In *Generation Ecstasy: Into the World of Techno and Rave Culture*, 270–81. Boston: Little, Brown, and Company, 1998.

Snead, James A. "Repetition as a Figure of Black Culture." In *Black Literature and Literary Theory*, ed. Henry Louis Gates, Jr., 59–79. New York: Methuen, 1984.

Shapiro, Peter. "Criminal Elements." *The Wire* 218 (April 2002): 46–51.

———. "Deck Wreckers: The Turntable as Instrument." In *Undercurrents: The Hidden Wiring of Modern Music*, ed. Rob Young, 163–76. London: Continuum/The Wire, 2002.

Shea, David. "One/Two." In *Arcana: Musicians on Music*, ed. John Zorn, 145–52. New York: Granary Books, 2000.

Smith, Oberlin. "Some Possible Forms of Phonograph." *The Electrical World* (September 8, 1888).

Stolzoff, Norman. "The Selector: The DJ as Artist and Performer." In *Wake the Town and Tell the People: Dancehall Culture in Jamaica*. Durham: Duke University Press, 2000.

Stuart, Caleb. "Yasunao Tone's Wounded and Skipping Compact Discs: From Improvi-sation and Indeterminate Composition to Glitching CDs." *Leonardo Electronic Almanac* 10, no. 9 (2002).

Toop, David. *Rap Attack 3: African Rap to Global Hip Hop.* London: Serpent's Tail, 1999.

White, Miles. "The Phonograph Turntable and Performance Practice in Hip Hop Music." *Ethnomusicology OnLine* 2 (1996): http://research.umbc.edu/eol/2/white/index .html.


## IX. Electronic Music and Electronica

Byrne, David. "Machines of Joy: I Have Seen the Future and It Is Squiggly." *Leonardo* 12 (2000): 7–10.

Cascone, Kim. "Laptop Music—Counterfeiting Aura in the Age of Infinite Reproduc-tion." *Parachute* 107 (2002): 52–58.

Chadabe, Joel. *Electric Sound: The Past and Promise of Electronic Music.* Upper Sad-dle River, NJ: Prentice Hall, 1997.

———. "Remarks on Computer Music Culture." *Computer Music Journal* 24, no. 4 (Winter 2000): 9–11.

Cott, Jonathan. *Stockhausen: Conversations with the Composer.* New York: Simon and Schuster, 1973.

Cranfield, Brady. "Producing Noise: Oval and the Politics of Digital Audio." *Parachute* 107 (2002): 42–51.

Diederichsen, Diedrich. "Digital Electronic Music: Between Pop and Pure Mediality, Paradoxical Strategies for a Refusal of Semantics." In *Sonic Process*, ed. Chris-tine Van Assche, 31–37. Barcelona: Actar, 2003.

Dockstader, Tod. "Inside-Out: Electronic Rock." *Electronic Music Review* (January 1968).

During, Elie. "Appropriations: Deaths of the Author in Electronic Music." In *Sonic Proc-ess*, ed. Christine Van Assche, 39–57. Barcelona: Actar, 2003.

Eimert, Herbert. "What is Electronic Music?" *Die Reihe* 1 (1958): 1–10.

Emmerson, Simon, ed. *Music, Electronic Media, and Culture.* London: Ashgate, 2000.

Ernst, David. *The Evolution of Electronic Music.* New York: Schirmer, 1997.

Gilbert, Jeremy and Ewan Pearson, *Discographies: Dance Music, Culture, and the Poli-tics of Sound.* London: Routledge, 1999.

Goldsmith, Kenneth. "It Was a Bug, Dave: The Dawn of Glitchwerks." *New York Press* (1999): http://www.wfmu.org/~kennyg/popular/articles/glitchwerks.html.

Griffiths, Paul. *A Guide to Electronic Music.* New York: Thames and Hudson, 1979.

Gudmundsdottir, Björk. "Björk Meets Karlheinz Stockhausen: Compose Yourself." *Dazed and Confused* 23 (August 1996): http://www.pip.dknet.dk/~pip971/bjork/ b_stock.html.

Hecker, Tim. "Sound and 'The Victorious Realm of Electricity'." *Parachute* 107 (2002): 60–67.

Holmes, Thom. *Electronic and Experimental Music: Pioneers in Technology and Com-position*, 2nd edition. New York: Routledge, 2002.

Loubet, Emmanuelle. "Laptop Performers, Compact Disc Designers, and No-Beat Techno Artists in Japan: Music from Nowhere." *Computer Music Journal* 24:4 (Winter 2000): 19–32.

Luening, Otto. "Some Random Remarks about Electronic Music." In *Contemporary Composers on Contemporary Music*, Expanded Edition, ed. Elliott Schwartz and Barney Childs, 251–60. New York: Da Capo, 1998.

Maconie, Robin, ed. *Stockhausen on Music: Lectures and Interviews*. London: Marion Boyers, 1989.

Manning, Peter. *Electronic and Computer Music*. Oxford: Oxford University Press, 1985.

Neill, Ben. "Pleasure Beats: Rhythm and the Aesthetics of Current Electronic Music." *Leonardo Music Journal* 12 (2002): 3–6.

Nelson, Peter and Nigel Osborne, eds. *Aesthetics of Live Electronic Music, Contemporary Music Review* 18, no. 3 (1999).

Ostertag, Bob. "Human Bodies, Computer Music." *Leonardo Music Journal* 12 (2002): 11–14.

———. "Why Computer Music Sucks," *Resonance* 5, no.1 (November 1996): http://www.l-m-c.org.uk/texts/ostertag.html.

Pousseur, Henri. "Calculation and Imagination in Electronic Music." *Electronic Music Review* (January 1968).

Reynolds, Simon. *Generation Ecstasy: Into the World of Techno and Rave Culture*. Boston: Little, Brown, and Co., 1998.

Roads, Curtis. *Microsound*. Cambridge, MA: MIT Press, 2001.

Russcol, Herbert. *The Liberation of Sound: An Introduction to Electronic Music*. Englewood Cliffs, NJ: Prentice Hall, 1972.

Shapiro, Peter, ed. *Modulations: Throbbing Words on Sound*. New York: Caipirinha/Distributed Art Publishers, Inc., 2000.

Sherburne, Philip. "Sound Art/Sound Bodies: Electronic Music's Anatomy Lessons." *Parachute* 107 (2002): 68–79.

Stockhausen, Karlheinz. "The Concept of Unity in Electronic Music." *Perspectives of New Music* (1962): 39–48.

———. "Electronic and Instrumental Music." *Die Reihe* 5 (1959): 59–67.

———. "Five Revolutions Since 1950." In *Contemporary Composers on Contemporary Music*, Expanded Edition, ed. Elliott Schwartz and Barney Childs, 379–83. New York: Da Capo, 1998.

Szepanski, Achim. "Digital Music and Media Theory." *Parachute* 107 (2002): 24–27.

Tagg, Philip. "From Refrain to Rave: The Decline of Figure and the Rise of Ground." *Popular Music* 13 (May 1994): 209–222.

Toop, David. *Ocean of Sound: Aether Talk, Ambient Sound, and Imaginary Worlds*. London: Serpent's Tail, 1985.

Witherden, Barry. "Karlheinz Stockhausen: The Primer." *The Wire* 154 (December 1996): 40–3.

Witts, Dick and Karlheinz Stockhausen. "Advice to Clever Children/Advice from Clever Children." *The Wire* 141 (November 1995): 33-35.

Young, Rob. "New Complexity Techno." *The Wire* 150 (August 1996): http://www.the wire.co.uk/archive/essays/techno.html.

———. "Worship the Glitch: Digital Music, Electronic Disturbance." In *Undercurrents: The Hidden Wiring of Modern Music*, ed. Rob Young, 45–55. London: Continuum/The Wire, 2002.

# Notes for Quotations

## I: Music and Its Others: Noise, Sound, Silence

1. Mel Gordon, "Songs from the Museum of the Future: Russian Sound Creation (1910–1930)," in *Wireless Imagination: Sound, Radio, and the Avant-Garde*, ed. Douglas Kahn and Gregory Whitehead (Cambridge: MIT, 1992), 197–98.
2. Aldous Huxley, *The Perennial Philosophy* (New York: Harper and Brothers, 1944), 218–19.
3. Lester Bangs, "A Reasonable Guide to Horrible Noise," *Village Voice* (September 30, 1981).
4. Christopher Small, *Music, Society, Education* (Hanover, NH: University Press of New England/Wesleyan University Press, 1996), 20–21.
5. John Zorn, liner notes to *Spillane* (Elektra/Nonesuch, 1987).
6. John Cage, "Experimental Music," in *Silence: Lectures and Writings by John Cage* (Hanover, NH: University Press of New England/Wesleyan University Press, 1961), 8.
7. Dan Warburton, "Radu Malfatti: Silent But Deadly," *The Wire* 211 (September 2001), 14.
8. Toru Takemitsu, *Confronting Silence: Selected Writings* (Berkeley: Fallen Leaf Press, 1995), 17.
9. Jacques Attali, *Noise: The Political Economy of Music*, trans. Brian Massumi (Minneapolis: University of Minnesota Press, 1985), 26–27.
10. Masami Akita, cited in David Keenan, "Consumed by Noise," *The Wire* 198 (August 2000), 26, 30, 29.

## II. Modes of Listening

1. Erik Satie as quoted by Fernand Léger in Alan M. Gillmor, *Erik Satie* (Boston: Twayne, 1988), 232.
2. Alvin Lucier, "Careful Listening is More Important than Making Sounds Happen," in *Reflexions: Interviews, Scores, Writings* (Köln: Edition MusikTexte, 1995), 430.
3. Toru Takemitsu, *Confronting Silence: Selected Writings* (Berkeley: Fallen Leaf Press, 1995), 84–85.
4. Otomo Yoshihide, "Listening," *JAMJAM DIARY* vol. 6, quoted in Yoshio Otani, "Improv's New Waves,"*Improvised Music from Japan Extra 2003* (2003), 7–8.
5. Roland Barthes, "Listening," in *The Responsibility of Forms: Critical Essays on Music, Art, and Representation*, trans. Richard Howard (New York: Hill and Wang, 1985), 245–60.
6. Quoted in Dan Warburton, "Radu Malfatti: Silent But Deadly," *The Wire* 211 (September 2001), 14.
7. Brian Eno and Anthony Korner, "Aurora Musicalis," *Artforum* 24:10 (Summer 1986), 77.
8. George Eliot, *Middlemarch* (New York: Bantam Books, 1985), 177–78.
9. Günter Müller, interviewed for *Balance Beams*, dir. Jonas Leddington (Erstwhile Records ERST 040). A portion of this passage is from the unpublished transcript.
10. Karlheinz Stockhausen, "Gold Dust" (text composition from *Aus den Sieben Tagen*).

## III. Music in the Age of Electronic (Re)production

1. Marshall McLuhan, cited in Julian Cowley, "The Limits of Language: Textual Apocalypse: Merz, Lettrism, Sound Poetry," in *Undercurrents: The Hidden Wiring of Modern Music*, ed. Rob Young (New York: Continuum, 2002), 200.

2. John Zorn, liner notes to *The Big Gundown: John Zorn Plays the Music of Ennio Morricone* (Elektra).

3. Friedrich Kittler, *Gramophone, Film, Typewriter,* trans. Geoffrey Winthrop-Young and Michael Wutz (Stanford: Stanford University Press, 1999), 23.

4. W.H. Preece, "The Microphone," *Nature* 18 (20 June 1878), quoted in John M. Picker, *Victorian Soundscapes* (Oxford: Oxford University Press, 2003), 3.

5. John Adams, "Conversation with Jonathan Sheffer," in *Perceptual Processes: Minimalism and the Baroque* (New York: Eos Music, Inc., 1997), 82.

6. Christopher Small, *Music, Society, Education* (Hanover, NH: University Press of New England/Wesleyan University Press, 1996), 174–5.

7. "Invisible Jukebox" with Ben Watson in *The Wire* 178 (December 1998), 23.

8. Cornelius Cardew, "Towards an Ethic of Improvisation," in *Treatis Handbook* (London: Peters, 1971), xx.

9. Quoted in Christoph Cox, "Jim O'Rourke: Studies in Frustration," *The Wire* 165 (November 1997), 39.

10. Lee "Scratch" Perry, cited in David Toop, *Ocean of Sound* (New York: Serpent's Tail, 1995), 113.

11. Tom Zé, liner notes to *Fabrication Defect* (Luaka Bop, 1998).

12. Sebastian Oschatz in "Gebrauchsmusik," an unpublished interview conducted by Andrew Deutsch in 2001.

## IV. The Open Work

1. Jacques Charpentier, quoted in Derek Bailey, *Improvisation: Its Nature and Practice in Music* (New York: Da Capo, 1992), 59.

2. John Cage, "Foreword," *A Year from Monday: New Lectures and Writings* (Middletown, CT: Wesleyan University Press, 1967), ix–x.

3. Morton Feldman, "Liner Notes," in *Give My Regards to Eighth Street: Collected Writings of Morton Feldman,* ed. B. H. Friedman (Cambridge, MA: Exact Change, 2000), 6.

4. Morton Feldman, "The Anxiety of Art," in *Give My Regards to Eighth Street: Collected Writings of Morton Feldman,* ed. B. H. Friedman (Cambridge, MA: Exact Change, 2000), 26.

5. Galen Wilson and David H. Cope, "An Interview with Pierre Boulez," *The Composer* 1:2 (September 1969), 82–3.

6. William S. Burroughs, in Daniel Odier, *The Job: Interviews with William S. Burroughs* (New York: Grove Press, 1974), 33.

7. Christian Wolff quoted on the web: http://ublib.buffalo.edu/libraries/units/music/exhibits/june/first.html.

8. Roman Haubenstock-Ramati, "Notation—Material—Form," *Perspectives of New Music* (Fall-Winter 1965), 97.

9. Anthony Braxton, *Tri-Axium Writings,* Vol. I (Hanover, NH: Frog's Peak Music, 1985), 366.

10. Iannis Xenakis, *Formalized Music: Thought and Mathematics in Composition* (Bloomington: Indiana University Press, 1971), 8–9.

11. Sebastian Oschatz in "Gebrauchsmusik," an unpublished interview conducted by Andrew Deutsch in 2001.

## V. Experimental Musics

1. John Cage, "Foreword," *M: Writings '67–'72* (Middletown, CT: Wesleyan University Press, 1973).

2. John Cage, "Experimental Music," in *Silence* (Hanover, NH: Wesleyan University Press, 1961), 7, 10, 12.

3. Morton Feldman, "Crippled Symmetry," in *Give My Regards to Eighth Street: Collected Writings of Morton Feldman,* ed. B.H. Friedman (Cambridge, MA: Exact Change, 2000), 142–43.

4. Cornelius Cardew, "Towards an Ethic of Improvisation," in *Treatise Handbook* (London: Peters, 1971), xviii.

5. Sachiko M, liner notes to *Improvised Music from Japan Presents Improvised Music from Japan* (IMJ 10-CD).

6. Bernhard Günter, *The Wire* 157 (March 1997).

7. Morton Feldman, quoted in Paul Griffiths, *Modern Music and After: Directions Since 1945* (Oxford: Oxford University Press, 1995), 305.

8. Pierre Lévy, "The Sound of Cyberculture," in *Cyberculture*, trans. Robert Bononno (Minneapolis: University of Minnesota Press, 2001), 116.

## VI. Improvised Musics

1. Ferruccio Busoni, "Sketch of a New Aesthetic of Music," in *Three Classics in the Aesthetics of Music* (New York: Dover, 1962), 84.

2. Eddie Prévost, "Improvisation," in *Cornelius Cardew Memorial Concert Programme*, 5–6.

3. Ferruccio Busoni, "Sketch of a New Aesthetic of Music."

4. Steve Lacy, *The Wire* 1 (Summer 1982), 6–7.

5. Derek Bailey, "Derek Bailey: Free Retirement Plan," in John Corbett, *Extended Play: Sounding Off From John Cage to Dr. Funkenstein* (Durham, NC: Duke University Press, 1994), 235.

6. Ben Watson, "Cyber Improv: Their Progress or Ours?" *Signal to Noise* 21 (Spring 2001), 8–9.

7. Graham Lock, *Forces in Motion: Anthony Braxton and the Meta-Reality of Creative Music* (London: Quartet, 1988), 240.

8. Anthony Davis, liner notes to *Episteme*, Gramavision GR 8101.

9. Elvin Jones, quoted in Arthur Taylor, *Notes and Tones: Musician-to-Musician Interviews* (New York: DaCapo, 1993), 228.

10. Quoted in John Rockwell, *All American Music: Composition in the Late Twentieth Century* (New York: Vintage, 1983), 166.

11. Keith Rowe, interview with Oren Ambarchi in *Balance Beams* DVD, dir. Jonas Leddington, Erstwhile Records ERST 040.

12. Kaffe Matthews, quoted in *Bruit Blanc 1: Mimeo 2000* (2001), 10.

## VII. Minimalisms

1. Tom Johnson, "La Monte Young, Steve Reich, Terry Riley, Philip Glass," originally published in *The Village Voice* (September 7, 1972), reprinted in *The Voice of New Music: New York City 1972–1982* (Eindhoven: Apollo Art About, 1989), 44–45.

2. Terry Riley, quoted in K. Robert Schwarz, *Minimalists* (London: Phaidon, 1996), 35.

3. John Cage, *Silence: Lectures and Writings by John Cage* (Hanover, NH: University Press of New England/Wesleyan University Press, 1961), 93.

4. Tom Johnson, "Explaining My Music: Keywords," liner notes to *The Chord Catalogue* (XI Records 123).

5. James A. Snead, "Repetition as a Figure of Black Culture," in *Black Literature and Literary Theory*, ed. Henry Louis Gates, Jr. (New York: Methuen, 1984), 69.

6. Deleuze and Guattari, *A Thousand Plateaus*, trans. Brian Massumi (Minneapolis: University of Minnesota Press, 1987), 267.

7. Quoted by Richard Cook in *The Wire* 188 (October 1999), 55.

## VIII. DJ Culture

1. John Philip Sousa, "The Menace of Mechanical Music," *Appleton's Magazine* (September 1906), reprinted in *Computer Music Journal*, Vol. 17, No. 1 (Spring 1993), 14–15.

2. Heinrich Burkhard, "*Anmerken zu den 'Lehrstücken' and zur Schallplattenmusik*" (1930), quoted in Thomas Y. Levin, "For the Record: Adorno on Music in the Age of Its Technological Reproducibility," *October* 55 (1990), 34.

3. Bill Brewster and Frank Broughton, *Last Night a DJ Saved My Life: The History of the Disc Jockey* (New York: Grove Press, 1999), 109.

4. Chrisian Marclay, http://www.clanjamfrie.demon.co.uk/marclay.html.

5. DJ Spooky, sound clip from battlesounds.com (recorded 8/95).

6. Brian Eno, "Gossip is Philosophy," *Wired* 3.05 (May, 1995), 207.

7. David Shea, "One/Two," in *Arcana: Musicians on Music*, ed. John Zorn (New York: Granary Books, 2000), 145.

8. John Zorn's liner notes to *The Carl Stalling Project* album.

9. Teo Macero, from "Interview: Teo Macero," *Modulations: A History of Electronic Music: Throbbing Words on Sound*, ed. Peter Shapiro (New York: Caipirinha, 2000), 54.

10. William S. Burroughs, *Nova Express*, excerpted in *Word Virus: The William S. Burroughs Reader*, ed. James Grauerholz and Ira Silverberg (New York: Grove Press, 1998), 240.

11. DJ Babu, Interview with Christo Macias, Palo Alto, CA, May 1996, quoted on www .turntablism.com.

## IX. Electronic Music and Electronica

1. Brian Eno, Liner notes to *Ohm: The Early Gurus of Electronic Music: 1948–1980* (Ellipsis Arts CD 3670), 9.

2. Brian Eno, "Strategies for Making Sense," interview with Paul Schütze, *The Wire* (September 1995).

3. Emannuelle Loubet, "Laptop Performers, Compact Disc Designers, and No-Beat Techno Artists in Japan: Music from Nowhere," *Computer Music Journal* 24:4 (Winter 2000), 29.

4. Simon Reynolds, *Generation Ecstasy: Into the World of Techno and Rave Culture* (Boston: Little, Brown, and Co., 1998), 10–11.

5. Philip Tagg, *Popular Music* 13, no. 2 (1994).

6. Marc Weidenbaum, "Popp Music: Oval, Microstoria, and the Man Behind their Curtains," *Pulse!* (December 1996).

7. Pauline Oliveros, in "Electronic Stategies with Pauline and Peer," an unpublished interview with Pauline Oliveros and Peer Bode conducted by Andrew Deutsch on March 3, 1999.

8. David Toop, liner notes to Rafael Toral, *Aeriola Frequency* (Perdition Plastics, 1998).

# Index

index • 451

index • **453**